THE
FAITH OF A MORALIST

SERIES I

THE THEOLOGICAL IMPLICATIONS OF MORALITY

MACMILLAN AND CO., Limited
LONDON · BOMBAY · CALCUTTA · MADRAS
MELBOURNE

THE MACMILLAN COMPANY
NEW YORK · BOSTON · CHICAGO
DALLAS · ATLANTA · SAN FRANCISCO

THE MACMILLAN COMPANY
OF CANADA, LIMITED
TORONTO

THE
FAITH OF A MORALIST

GIFFORD LECTURES DELIVERED IN THE
UNIVERSITY OF ST. ANDREWS, 1926–1928

BY

A. E. TAYLOR

Verus philosophus est amator Dei.—*Augustine*

SERIES I

THE THEOLOGICAL IMPLICATIONS OF MORALITY

Considerate la vostra semenza.—*Dante*

MACMILLAN AND CO., LIMITED
ST. MARTIN'S STREET, LONDON

1937

COPYRIGHT

First Edition 1930
Reprinted 1931, 1932
Reprinted with Series II, 1937

PRINTED IN GREAT BRITAIN
BY R. & R. CLARK, LIMITED, EDINBURGH

PREFACE

THESE volumes contain the Gifford Lectures given in the University of St. Andrews in the sessions of 1926–27 and 1927–28 substantially as they were delivered, though I have restored a number of sentences and short passages which had, for the sake of brevity, to be omitted in the actual delivery, and have, in several cases, printed as a single whole what had, in delivery, to be subdivided into two lectures. The unstudied, even occasionally conversational, style naturally employed in addressing an audience of recent colleagues and personal friends I have thought proper for retention in the published volumes; the material could not have been systematically recast in a severer literary form without an expenditure of time impossible to one still fully engaged in actual teaching work.

I trust that the title I have, with some misgivings, adopted will mislead no one. It is meant to indicate two things—that the attitude assumed on the great ultimate problems discussed avowedly involves a "venture of faith", and that, as I think, the venture should be found natural by anyone who comes to these problems with the special presuppositions of a moralist. I shall not, I hope, be thought capable of the impertinence of asking my readers to be interested in an intimate personal

Confessio Fidei; even if I had that vanity, I should also, I trust, have the sense to understand that the terms of Lord Gifford's bequest preclude a Gifford lecturer from using his position as an opportunity for propaganda on behalf of his own *Privatmeinungen*.

But for an Appendix, a Supplementary Note to one chapter of the first volume, and a number of footnotes, the text stands as it was originally written. This will explain why no notice has been taken of Dr. Whitehead's *Process and Reality* and other valuable works published since the end of 1927. It should be mentioned that, for the same reason, the criticisms passed in several places on views of the late Dr. McTaggart were necessarily written before the publication of the second volume of *The Nature of Existence*, and that allowance must be made for the fact.

I have done my best to indicate the writers to whom I am conscious of serious obligations by the references appended in my footnotes. But I should like to make a further special acknowledgement of the great debt I owe to four writers in particular—Dr. Whitehead, the late Baron von Hügel, Dr. Edwyn Bevan, and Professor C. C. J. Webb. To Professor Webb's work I should have owed even more than I do if I had not deferred making acquaintance with the volume of *Studies in the Relations of God and Man* until my own manuscript was out of my hands.

I am specially under an obligation to my friend and colleague Mr. A. C. A. Rainer, Shaw Fellow in the University of Edinburgh, for valuable help in proof-reading and the preparation of an Index of Proper

---

Names for each volume. I trust the analytical synopses prefixed to the volumes have made the addition of an index of subjects superfluous.

I take the opportunity to explain that while references to Kant's works in general are to the volume and page of Hartenstein's second edition, the *Critique of Pure Reason* is cited by the pages of the original edition (first or second as the case may be). Two abbreviations have been occasionally used, *E.R.E.* for *Encyclopaedia of Religion and Ethics*, and *E.M.L.* for *English Men of Letters Series*.

A. E. T.

EDINBURGH, *May* 1930

I take the opportunity afforded by this reprint of correcting a number of small errors of the Press, due to my own defects as a proof-reader, with many thanks to the friends who have helped me to discover them. I would also here recant, or qualify, the remark made about the late F. W. H. Myers on page 255. On re-examination I find I have exaggerated the rarity of the references to God in *Human Personality*, and I have been assured by those who have the best right to speak that their comparative fewness and their vagueness do not represent the writer's deepest personal convictions. I hasten to accept the correction and to express my regret for any misconception. With respect to a similar qualification of certain references to Dr. Gore see the Prefatory Note to Series II.

A. E. T.

May 1931

CONTENTS

THE RELATIONS BETWEEN ETHICS AND DIVINITY

ix

Illustration of this from the philosophy of Dr. McTaggart. The supposed absolute disjunction of fact and value a mistaken prejudice. It is true that very much which is actual is bad. This does not prove the hypothesis of the pessimist, but might suggest that the coincidence of fact and value is only accidental. Against such a view we may say (1) that it involves an unconscious false abstraction. What really has value is always the activity of a real individual. In a sense it is true that what we pronounce to have value is an universal, but it is an "embodied" universal, *in rebus*, not *post res*. And all judgements of value include a reference to *personal* activity. Illustrations from ethics and aesthetics. Discussion of the case of "truth-values". (2) The view that "ideals" have value but not existence is a consequence of an extreme logical "nominalism" which requires to be corrected by the Aristotelian doctrine of "analogous" predication. (3) In actual life, as it is lived by all of us, we find no separation between "facts" which are "given" and "valuations" which are "put on" the facts; the facts and their values are given together; both are found, neither invented. Or, rather, we have always "fact-in-valuation", never mere fact in isolation, nor mere valuation. Our "moral ideals" are not simply added by the mind to "the facts" *de suo*. We are no more justified in saying that our moral and religious life throws no light on the "actuality" than we should be in saying the same thing about the life-history of the species of organisms. It is more illuminating to know that the world is the *kind* of kinematical system in which the evolution of living species can take place than merely to know that it is a kinematical system. It may well be still more illuminating to know that the actual world is one in which artists, heroes, and saints have their place.

III. ETERNITY AND TEMPORALITY . . . .　67

The moral life a life of tension between the temporal and the eternal, only possible to a being which is neither abiding nor simply mutable, but both at once. What is characteristic of temporality is not the simple distinction of before and after, but the contrast of present with past and future. This contrast belongs not to merely physical nature but to the life of conscious conative creatures. The "dehumanised" mathematical time of classical kinematics is not *durée réelle*. Nature conceived as a mere kinematical system, has neither present, past, nor future. Hence Spinoza mistakenly calls the contemplation of such a system contemplation under the "form of eternity". It is really contemplation under a form of bare sequence. Temporality is the characteristic form of the study of that which has a history, *i.e.* of the object of the sciences of life

and mind. An *organism* has a true history because it is a
concrete individual using and feeding on an *environment*. Its
responses to this environment depend on its "particular go",
and its "particular go" is never independent of the route by
which it has reached its present state. In conscious life the
past is apparently never simply past and done with. On the
other hand, past habit is never unmodifiable. Hence in man the
possibility of the conquest of habit by intelligent foresight. In
a rational life habit is present everywhere, but everywhere
subordinated to foresight and plan. The plan, again, is not
clear from the outset, but only discloses itself progressively to
the agent himself. The past of *man* not a dead but a living
past. To be aware of our life as temporal is already to begin to
transcend the form of temporality. All human creation is an
attempt to experience the fruition of good in a *now* where
there is no consciousness of the no longer or not yet. Illustrations from intellectual and aesthetic enjoyment. Approximate
conformity of these experiences to the classical definition of
eternity by Boethius. They are only approximations because
the good enjoyed in them is not the *bonum consummatum*. If
the fruition of all secular good fails to attain this ideal we may
reasonably infer that the ultimate good of man is non-secular
and eternal, and that the *facts* of our moral being point to the
Christian conception of the transformation and completion of
nature by "grace". Now all secular good is defective, since it
cannot be enjoyed as a whole simultaneously, and one part can
only be enjoyed at the cost of surrendering others. But to acquiesce in this state of things and make it the rule to "live for
to-day" would be both immoral and irrational. Even the man
who lives for his "interest in this world" is morally far superior,
as Butler rightly held, to the man who lives for the "passion"
of the moment. Nor can it be an adequate account of the moral
end to say that it is "betterment", "leaving things a little better
than we found them". To say this would be to confess that
good is incapable of attainment and morality a forlorn adventure. But in so far as a good beyond which there is no better is
attained, life takes on the character of an eternity or abiding
now. The strictly ethical life is neither merely successive nor
wholly abiding. It is the life of advance from merely animal
acquiescence in succession towards the whole and simultaneous fruition of a complete good. Ascent in the scale is attended
by progressive "unification" of both good and virtue. Here
morality makes contact with religion. Our own character
answers to that of the good to which we aspire. The "soul" is
one or many according as the good to which it aspires is one or
many. The attainment of a fully unified personality depends
on finding our principal good in God, the concrete unity of all
good in its source. Impossibility of regarding the plurality of

goods as ultimate. The implication of morality is thus a double one. It points to the existence of God as the absolute and final plenitude of good, and to an eternal destiny for the moral person whose aim is the fruition of the good. Importance of "detachment" as an element in the moral life, equal importance of right use of "creaturely" good. Error of supposing that complete attainment would mean the cessation of life itself long ago exposed in principle by Aristotle.

The moral life, then, is one of endeavour towards an eternal good. So far as the endeavour is successful, we achieve a communicated eternity. The goal lies beyond the bounds of the historical, but the advance to it is historical and implies the reality of time, the characteristic form of the historical. Theories which regard time as an illusion falsify our conception, and, if acted on, spoil our practice, of morality. Time is the *stuff* out of which a personal moral life has to be made, and made by transcending time. The "natural" theology of a moralist is thus incompatible with (1) secularism, the identification of good with "worldly good", and with (2) all "theosophic" doctrines of the illusoriness of the moral struggle and the intrinsic divinity of the human soul, since they rest on the denial of any real difference of status between deity and humanity. In a moral world moral progress must be real. A moral theology must regard eternal life as something which has to be achieved and may be lost by sloth. The moral life is a real adventure which begins with "nature" and ends in "supernature". From the ethical point of view this consideration is fatal to all types of speculation about "reincarnation". Christianity strikes the truly ethical note by its doctrine of *final* salvation and reprobation, rightly understood. Progress from and through nature to supernature involves a right combination of "attachment" and "detachment", and it is just this which makes the moral life a difficult adventure. It is a hard task to cultivate the finite good so long as it is the "best" for me and yet to let it go when and because the better discloses itself. Illustration of this. Hence the speculative puzzle of Green's *Prolegomena* that all attempts to say what the moral ideal is appear to involve a "circle". We have no "clear and distinct idea" of the good; it discloses its character dimly and partially as we make advance towards it. We cannot describe the goal of the moral pilgrimage because we have never reached it, yet the reality of the pilgrimage involves the reality of the goal. The immediate and conscious aim of the good man may be for some definite and specific improvement in himself or his society, but the end really aimed at is a freedom from circumstance which involves the transcending of temporality. Again genuine moral effort is directed on the remaking not only of our "environment" but of ourselves as well, and of all the selves of our community. Unsatisfactoriness of Kant's formal doctrine on this point due to his forgetting that "practical reason" and moral personality are "in the making". My own "practical reason" therefore cannot be the ultimate source of the moral law. The moral law is discovered, not created, by *my* reason, and, for that reason, cannot be digested, in advance of experience, into a system of categorical formulae. Superiority of Aristotle's conception of "practical reason" to Kant's. The inevitable inference is that the reason which prescribes the moral law is one which is only gradually and partially communicated to us in proportion to our fidelity. Unless this were so, we could not feel unqualified "reverence" for it. Thus the ultimate moral legislator is the will of God. This means that we cannot distinguish in principle between the life of discharge of duty and the life of "faith". In all genuine moral life we "walk by faith".

Inadequacy of the treatment of evil in most works on ethics. (Plato and Kant are exceptions to the rule.) Moral badness is neither mere "atavistic" reversion to type nor mere disregard for reasonable rule. Our experience of personal guilt is *sui generis* and distinctively human. (1) It involves dissatisfaction with our self and self-condemnation, and differs in kind from any discontent with our surroundings. (2) It has a peculiar indelibility; guilt cannot be "worked off and paid for" by subsequent "making good" or by the infliction of a penalty, and this sense of the indelibility of guilt cannot be explained away as "morbid" or as the effect of non-ethical "theological" superstition. (3) The sense of guilt regularly accompanied by a demand for our own "punishment". Retribution essential to a genuinely ethical theory of punishment. Recognition of this in the Christian doctrine of "forgiveness of sins". The distinction between forgiveness and mere "condonation". (4) Significance of the universal association of guilt with "pollution". This is no mere accidental association. As civilisation advances particular acts may be removed from the category of the morally "dirty", but the sense of sin as polluting is intensified and becomes more inward. We come to demand the cleansing of the "thoughts of the heart", *i.e.* the remaking of the natural self from its centre. This is inconsistent with any ethics which

reduces morality to beneficent social activity. Fallaciousness
of the criticism which deprecates "purity" as a "negative"
virtue. Any morality has its negative side. Unsatisfactoriness
of an ethic of mere "efficiency". (5) What we feel to be outraged by sin or dishonour is not an impersonal law. The outrage is felt as personal treason against a person, yet not against
our own personality as it actually is, but against a real personal embodiment of our ideal of good, treason against a
"living God". Impossibility of accounting for this by regarding
God as an "imaginative personification" of the impersonal, like,
e.g., Britannia or "Humanity".

Moralists in general concern themselves almost wholly with
the analysis of the "good for man" and leave on one side the
problem of providing an adequate motive for the devoted pursuit of it, though the great practical need of life is just such a
motive. This is justifiable as a rule of method, but it makes
it impossible to regard such moral philosophies as entitled to
the position of directors of human action. We have to face
the question whether such adequate motivation can be found
apart from actual contact with a superhuman reality. Kant
tells us that early education is to train us to substitute reverence for duty for "inclination", but he never explains how,
on his theory of human nature, the lesson is to "get home".
Spinoza's attempt to explain how the transition from "bondage" to "freedom" is begun involves a formal self-contradic-
tion. And the course he actually recommends would be more
likely to lead to *acedia* than to "intellectual love of God".
What we really need is an ideal which is an efficient as well as
a final cause, and such an ideal is impossible if value and existence are really ultimately disjoined. Actual advance in good
must be a response to a movement initiated and sustained by
the eternal and divine. Morality itself then leads us up directly
to the "theological" problems of grace and nature, faith and
works. These problems are, in fact, simply one special form
of the more general problem of divine "transcendence". We
have to note that no pure "immanence" philosophy can take
morality with sufficient seriousness. Denial of divine "transcendence" leads to Pelagianism in theory and self-righteousness in practice, denial of divine "immanence" to antinomian-
ism. In moral practice you cannot rise above your present
level by "lifting yourself by your own hair", nor by the
strength of an ideal which is only "your own ideal". The
initiative in remaking of personality cannot come simply
from within the personality which is to be remade. In this
sense all genuine morality presupposes the supernatural as its

environment and nutriment. This does not mean that personality can be remade without genuine personal effort and hard work. But the hour of "vision" in which the inspiration for the work comes is one of a vision in which we look outward, away from ourselves. We do not find our route for the future from contemplation of the route of the past; the complete "ideal" is itself apprehended, however indistinctly. A natural theology which takes the moral life seriously should present three characteristics. It must regard God (1) not merely as Creator but as Redeemer and Sanctifier and (2) as the lover of men. This may be anthropomorphism, but it is unavoidable anthropomorphism. (3) It must regard the life of God as essentially an activity of self-communication, as is done in the orthodox doctrine of the Trinity. This makes it impossible to set "natural" and "historical" or "revealed" theology in sharp opposition, or to deny the reality of "revelation" on *a priori* philosophical grounds.

The problem of the destiny of the individual man is secondary and dependent; God, not immortality, is the primary interest of an ethical religion and theology. From this point of view, metaphysical arguments for the "natural immortality" of the human mind are of little value, besides being inconclusive. This is equally true of the alleged experimental proofs furnished by "spiritualism". Examination of McTaggart's objection to "moral" arguments for immortality. It can only be sustained if we accept the ultimate separation of value and fact, as McTaggart does, in principle, by excluding God from his metaphysics. Our problem is whether the moral nature of man indicates his destination for a future beyond the grave, and, if so, what light it throws on the quality of this future. In any case, we must not expect the light to be other than very dim. We may consider first (1) the argument from the *consensus* of mankind, (2) the appeal to the widespread *wish* for continuance. As to (1), the *consensus* seems in fact to be much more general than is often asserted, and thus to be at least a suggestive fact of human nature. As to (2), it may be urged that the existence of a wish is no proof that it will be gratified, and even that this particular wish is only a masked form of the instinct of self-preservation. But there are very grave difficulties in accepting this second statement; it seems insufficient to account for the *specific* beliefs of humanity about the "unseen world". The future, as contemplated by mankind in general, is not the kind of future we can suppose to be keenly desired. It may be said that we are dealing with a primitive impulse more deep-seated than conscious wish, but can we really think of "unconscious impulse" as capable of the effects the theory ascribes to it? The more old-fashioned "naturalistic" explanation of the facts by appeal to dream-experiences involves a similar difficulty. However such beliefs in the mere continuance of life beyond death originate, they are non-ethical. A genuine moral argument for immortality must be one to the effect that the destruction of human personalities would make the moral end unattainable. If *this* can be proved, the proof will be sufficient for those who believe in the absolute objectivity of moral obligation, though for no others. This is, in substance, the position of Kant.

We may fairly argue from the reality of a function to the reality of an environment in which it finds its use. The question at stake is whether the moral life presents us with functions which demand the "other world" as an environment, *i.e.* whether the "good" is such that it *cannot* be obtained "in this life". Is this world a home or a place of pilgrimage? This is not a merely speculative problem, since our rule of conduct is necessarily and profoundly affected by our answer. In the last resort the question is whether it is ever morally justifiable to sacrifice known "worldly good", except in the prospect of winning more good of the same kind. Mill, for example, regards such sacrifice as an unfortunate accident due to bad social conditions and never justified except by the prospect of creating a greater amount of "happiness". It is demanded as absolutely necessary in any moral scheme which aims at the "remaking" of personality, and no compensation "in the same kind" is contemplated. Is devotion to the temporal improvement of human society a sufficient justification of the moral imperatives? If not, the moralist, who is committed to holding that they are justifiable, must look to the "beyond" for the justification. Professor Laird's argument in favour of the "secularist" position summarised. Its vulnerable point is that it is only valid against one who says "Let us eat and drink for to-morrow we die", not against one who says "To-morrow will see the end of us all, therefore eating and not-eating are alike futile". Professor Laird himself holds that *all* "imperatives" are moral, that no imperative commands the impossible, and that the supreme imperative is to "make the best of yourself". He is bound to consider whether, without the "beyond", *this* imperative does not command the impossible. If it does not, the moral good must involve full mastery not only of our circumstances but of our "moods and passions", the completion of the making of our personality, and this involves transcendence of temporality and all finite loyalties. So the "well-being" we really desire for our successors is a better *personality*. The "paradox of humanitarianism" to which this leads. We cannot overvalue the temporal "good" of mankind, provided that

there is something we value still more, the "remaking" of
mankind. And that requires the surrender of every temporal
good "when the time comes". Yet, unless the moral imperative is self-stultifying, complete surrender must achieve the
"saving" of the moral self. This means that the moral good is
a personal life not expressible in terms of duration, and yet
intensely real, and not affected by death. Such a life involves
at once enrichment and "purgation", and there is no good
reason to think of the purgation as ended at death. Moral
superiority of the Christian conception of the "last things"
over oriental theories of "reincarnation". No reason to think
that spiritual "adventure" could be absent from the "life to
come". Bearing of this on the difficulties suggested in *Appearance and Reality*. The *possibility* of a "final reprobation" cannot be excluded from an ethical theory of the life to come.

If the moral life is marked by the tension between the temporal and the eternal, there must be an element of "other-
worldliness" in practical moral living, and we have to ask
what kind of other-worldliness is morally legitimate. The same
problem recurs in aesthetics. Here, too, by universal consent,
"earthiness" or "worldliness" is incompatible with the highest
achievement. The good man and the good artist must both
be "men of this world" and yet "unworldly". Illustration of
the combination from the work of Shakespeare (*Macbeth, The
Tempest, Antony and Cleopatra*). Life is equally spoiled by
concentration on a merely manageable "success" and by forgetting the duty of the moment in concentration on what lies
beyond all moments. The right rule is to make the very using
of temporal good itself an act of devotion to more abiding
good. The "flesh" is not simply to be suppressed in the interests
of the "spirit", but converted into its minister. The only way
to succeed in being a "good man" is to aim at being something
more. Not to do so leads to the degradation of morality into a
mere respectability, which is not likely to remain even respectable. It is fatal in principle to sever the life of the "divine
something in man" from the "work of *man*". Other-worldliness is either the death of all morality or the vital breath of
moral life, according as it is of the wrong or the right kind.
Ambiguity of the statement that all duties are "social". The
great "social" virtues themselves seem only to flourish best
when human society is not made the *supreme* object of loyalty.
Humanity is best served by those who do not make it their
"god". "Religious" and "secular" duties may be the same
duties, but it makes all the difference whether they are discharged in a "religious" or in a "secular" spirit. It is generally

true that the duties arising from an embodied loyalty will only be discharged to the height when they are "consecrated" by a supreme "unembodied" loyalty. The "other" world is to "this" world as "form" to "matter". "It is the death of idealism to transfer its ideals to the future" (Bosanquet). If this means that time and imperfection are illusions, it is merely false. A practical ideal *necessarily* involves reference to the future. But a sound ideal is a pattern which can persist with growing enrichment into a new and unfamiliar future. "The other world is only this world rightly understood". The truth or falsehood of the saying depends on what we mean by "understood". The process of acquiring moral personality, like that of learning to appreciate art, is one in which what begins by being the "other" and unfamiliar becomes increasingly dominant in the pattern of the "world" of our habitual interests, and what was at first familiar becomes strange, intrusive, and "other". The "real" world is hierarchised; the pattern of the whole is reproduced in the parts with varying degrees of distinctness. A subordinate pattern is not understood until it is discerned to be subordinate. Error of Professor Alexander on this point. Thus it is not true that the other world is this world understood, if you mean to imply that this world can be understood by taking as its dominant pattern one which can be detected by abstractive consideration of a restricted selection of characters, as is done, *e.g.*, when the saying is used as a sufficient disproof of the reality of miracles, grace, revelation, a future life. Practical bearing of this on the conduct of life. We only come to a right understanding of "this" world by incorporation of patterns originally felt to belong to the "other" and "unfamiliar". Understanding is not the same as the elimination of complexity. Every partial pattern has an "other" beyond it. Hence we only come near to grasping the pattern of the whole by looking for it in the rich concrete reality of spiritual life. This is the final justification of our refusal to accept an ultimate dualism of fact and value. Values are the dominant features of the pattern of the whole, and therefore must permeate and shape the course of actuality. Fragmentariness, dependence, and contingency are more characteristic of the "created" than error or sin. The moral growth of the individual as an example of the integration of partial patterns.

The allegation that the moral life is, from its very nature, one of aiming at the unattained and that with attainment morality itself would simply disappear. The "antinomy" of the moral life as stated, *e.g.*, by Bradley. "Morality is fighting against evil, but if evil were destroyed there would be nothing left to fight; hence morality is trying to annihilate itself." We cannot meet this allegation by saying that the moral life is a fighting not for victory but for the sake of the fight. Good is not made good by the fact that some men prefer evil. Men will not fight hard unless you convince them that they are contending for something worth fighting for. It is thus of the first importance to consider whether, after all, the fundamental aspiration of morality is self-destructive. This might be true if we could accept such an account of morality as H. Spencer's (as Bradley does not). Spencer's theory, in fact, contradicts itself, and is also based on a grave misreading of the facts of life. The sense of moral obligation does not in fact grow weaker as social life "evolves". It would be truer to say that the standard becomes more exacting and is more closely lived up to. Spencer's error seems to be due to the assumption that morality is simply putting right what is amiss and that there is only a limited amount of wrong social relation to be put right. Arbitrariness of these assumptions. It would be as reasonable to say that science is simply the correction of errors and that, since the number of errors to be corrected is finite, science will vanish from a "fully evolved" human life. (Cf. the thesis of Avenarius.) Spencer also confounds obligation itself with the awareness of it, and this with consciousness of disagreeable effort. Now morality is no more the mere righting of wrongs than science the mere correction of errors. Even in a society where there are no "abuses" there would remain the work of embodying the love of each for all in the detail of daily life. Bradley may, however, intend the criticism to be directed more specially against Kant, who makes the same sort of initial assumption as Spencer in a subtler form, by holding that it is of the essence of morality to be a struggle against "inclinations". If this is a sound position, a moral "rational theology" would have to reject the conception of a final "beatitude". Kant has forgotten that the final elimination of "inclination" would not really amount to the confusion of man with God. Fruition and aspiration may be blended, and such a life would be definitely man's and not God's. Green's view on this sounder than Kant's. There might well be progress in fruition in a life where there was no longer progress *towards* fruition. Life "in Heaven" would be life by "vision", but the vision might be capable of ever-growing enrichment. And those who see most might well have the "social service" of helping others to see. This would also leave room for endless spiritual adventure. To identify morality simply with the struggle against evil is like identifying art with the acquisition of technique. The main business of the social life is not simply to learn how to love rightly, but to love, and this may well persist in a state where we have no longer to unlearn unloving or

foolishly loving ways. Bosanquet's depreciation of morality as
the sphere of "claims and counter-claims" a mere caricature,
resting on the notion that finite individualities are necessarily
repellent of one another. This is really true of the shallow, not
the rich, personalities. In a heaven of beatitude, the moral
life would be transfigured but not transformed into something
non-moral. We need to employ the Aristotelian distinction between a "process" and an "activity". If we do so we shall see
that there is nothing irrational in anticipating a state in which
the process of forming character is over, while the activity
issuing from character remains. Such a view, no doubt, implies
that progress *in* good, though not progress towards good,
persists "in Heaven" and affords justification for the conception of our present state as one of "probation". It also implies
the presence of an irreducible element of succession and temporality in the life of all "creatures", an element which may
"decrease indefinitely" as we ascend higher in the scale of being.
Hence a knowledge which leaves no place for surprise seems
possible only to the Creator. Hence there would be room for
"practice" as well as "contemplation" even in Heaven.

I

INTRODUCTORY

O Wisdom, coming out of the mouth of the Highest, reaching from the beginning even unto the end, graciously and mightily ordering all things, come to us and teach us the way of understanding.—Antiphon of December 16th.

THOSE of us who are from time to time honoured by the invitation to lecture on Lord Gifford's foundation are placed under a definite restraint in the choice of our subject-matter by the fact that each of us is acting as temporary substitute for a permanent Professor of Natural Theology. We are instructed to deal, as such a Professor would be bound by ordinance to deal, exclusively with "natural" theology, and natural theology is a name with a well-known history and an established significance. The phrase was introduced into the vocabulary of educated men by Cicero's contemporary, the famous *littérateur* and antiquarian M. Terentius Varro,[1] for the express purpose of discriminating an account of God and divine things which makes the claim to be strictly true from two other accounts of the same matters which advance no such pretensions, the *mythical* and the *civil* theologies. Mythical theology meant acquaintance with the tales of gods and their doings told in, or implied by, current imaginative literature. Since the Periclean age, the current opinion in "enlightened" circles had been that these stories are the mere inventions of poets,[2] whose only aim is to entertain

---

[1] Augustine, *De civitat. Dei*, vi. 5.

[2] Cf. Euripides, *Heracles* 1346 ἀοιδῶν οἵδε δύστηνοι λόγοι, Isocrates, xi. 38 ἀλλὰ γὰρ οὐδέν σοι τῆς ἀληθείας ἐμέλησεν, ἀλλὰ ταῖς τῶν ποιητῶν βλασφημίαις ἐπ-

and amuse. Civil theology is knowledge of the various feasts and fasts of the State Calendar and the ritual appropriate to them, such as is imparted, for six months of the year, by Ovid's *Fasti*. The whole of this cultus, it was held, is the manufacture of legislators aiming at social utility and convenience. But *philosophic*, or *natural*, theology is a different thing. It is the doctrine of God and the divine seriously taught by scientific philosophers as an integral part of a reasoned theory of φύσις, *natura*, the reality of things. It thus makes a definite claim, well founded or not, to be genuine ἐπιστήμη, to give us truth, in the same sense in which geometry or arithmetic does so. The ground to be covered by such a doctrine of God had already been marked out with some precision by Plato in the tenth book of the *Laws*; it is the same ground to which, in the main, natural theology has confined itself ever since Plato's first erection of it into a scientific discipline.

It was Plato's conviction that there are three fundamental truths about God which cannot be denied, or even called in question, without poisoning moral life, personal and corporate, at its sources. They are these: (1) God, a perfectly good and wise supreme mind, exists and is the author of all "becoming", of all *we* call "nature"; (2) God controls all the events which make up nature for ends worthy of His perfect wisdom and goodness; (3) God exercises a moral government of mankind in accord with a law of sovereign and inflexible justice which ensures that each shall receive his deserts—a thesis from which the immortality of the human self follows as a corollary. From Plato's time to our own, the natural, rational, or philosophical, theologian has remained in principle true to this programme:

ηκολούθησας, οἳ δεινότερα μὲν πεποιηκότας καὶ πεπονθότας ἀποφαίνουσι τοὺς ἐκ τῶν ἀθανάτων γεγονότας ἢ τοὺς ἐκ τῶν ἀνθρώπων τῶν ἀνοσιωτάτων κτλ.

God, Providence, Judgement to come have been and are
his special themes; his confession of belief might be said
to be, *credo in unum Deum, vivum et remuneratorem*.[1]

Thus, to take one or two typical examples, we may
consider first the general scheme of the great classic
work of the golden age of Scholasticism on our subject,
the *Summa contra Gentiles* of St. Thomas.[2] We are told
there (*S.C.G.* i. 9) that the knowledge of God accessible
to the human mind independently of specific revelation
may be brought under three heads. We may consider
(1) what may be asserted of God in Himself, *quae Deo
secundum seipsum conveniunt*; (2) what may be asserted
about the procession of the creatures from God, *pro-
cessus creaturarum ab ipso*; (3) and about the ordination
of the creatures towards God as their end, *ordo creaturarum in ipsum sicut in finem*. The starting-point of the
whole inquiry will therefore be the demonstration of
the *existence* of God, *consideratio qua demonstratur
Deum esse*. In accord with this scheme, the first book
of the work is given to the consideration of the
existence and attributes of God, the second to God's
relation to the historical world of finite "creatures" as
its creator, the third to His fuller relation to the creatures as their "good", His providential government, His
eternal moral law, and His action as judge and as bestower
of grace. Only the last book falls outside this scheme,

---

[1] See the continuous exposition of this elementary theology in *Laws* x. 893 B 1-
907 D 1, and compare the brief statement, which we may fairly call Plato's
personal "confession of faith", *Ep.* vii. 335 A 2 πείθεσθαι δὲ ὄντως ἀεὶ χρὴ
τοῖς παλαιοῖς τε καὶ ἱεροῖς λόγοις, οἳ δὴ μηνύουσιν ἡμῖν ἀθάνατον ψυχὴν εἶναι δικα-
στάς τε ἴσχειν καὶ τίνειν τὰς μεγίστας τιμωρίας, ὅταν τις ἀπαλλαχθῇ τοῦ σώματος · διὸ
καὶ τὰ μεγάλα ἁμαρτήματα καὶ ἀδικήματα σμικρότερον εἶναι χρὴ νομίζειν κακὸν
πάσχειν ἢ δρᾶσαι.

[2] Thomas gives his reason for confining the argument to "natural" divinity at
S.C.G. i. 2. A Christian cannot appeal, in controversy with Mohammedans or
"Pagans", to the authority of a "scripture" acknowledged by both parties: unde
necesse est ad naturalem rationem recurrere, cui omnes assentire coguntur; quae
tamen in rebus divinis deficiens est.

since it is concerned with the "revealed" doctrines of
the Trinity, the Incarnation of the Word, the Sacraments, and the final state of the penitent and impenitent
—all matters in relation to which the function of human
reason is no longer positive demonstration, but the
mere dialectical dissolution of objections raised by "infidels" against the authoritative teaching of the Church.[1]

In the same way, the first half of Butler's *Analogy*,
which bears the sub-title *Natural Religion*, takes as its
topics in order, *The Future Life*, *The Government of
God by Rewards and Punishments*, the moral character
of this government, the conception of our present state
as one of probation, the moral freedom of man (ch. 6,
On the Opinion of Necessity); the *existence* of God being
treated as outside the argument on the ground that it
is not disputed by the Deists, against whom the whole
treatise is directed. So the famous *Boyle Lectures* of
Samuel Clarke[2] deal in order with the existence of God,
the attributes of God as Creator and Moral Governor
of the world, the certainty of a "state of rewards and
punishments", as truths assumed to be capable of formal demonstration, and then proceed to argue "dialec-
tically" for the necessity of a specific divine revelation
and to dismiss the objections urged against the claims
of Christianity in particular to be this revelation.

Kant's conception is, to all intents and purposes, the
same (*KdrV*[2] 659 ff.). With his usual quaintly pedantic

---

[1] *S.C.G.* iv., *Proemium*, Restat autem sermo habendus de his quae nobis
revelata sunt divinitus ut credenda, excedentia intellectum humanum. . . . Pro-
banda enim sunt huiusmodi auctoritate sacrae Scripturae, non autem ratione
naturali; sed tamen ostendendum est quod rationi naturali non sunt opposita, ut
ab impugnatione infidelium defendantur.

[2] The full title is "A Discourse concerning the *Being and Attributes of God*,
the *Obligations of Natural Religion* and the TRUTH AND CERTAINTY of the
Christian Revelation. In Answer to Mr. *Hobbs*, *Spinoza*, the *Author of the Oracles
of Reason*, and other Deniers of Natural and Revealed Religion. Being sixteen
Sermons Preached in the Cathedral-Church of St. *Paul*, in the years 1704, and
1705, at the Lecture founded by the Honourable *ROBERT BOYLE*, Esq.".

fondness for exhaustive formal classification, he begins
his criticism of speculative theology with the time-
honoured distinction between a purely rational and a
revealed knowledge of God. Rational theology is then
subdivided into two types, the *transcendental*, that of
the strict Deist, who admits only the existence of a *first*,
or *supreme*, or *necessary* being with a character wholly
unknown and unknowable, and the *natural*, that of the
Theist, who holds that some light on the character of
the Supreme Being can be derived by analogical reasoning from the known character of the human mind.
(Hume, we observe, would thus rank in Kant's classification as a Theist, since he admits at least a "remote"
analogy between the Supreme Being and the human
mind.) Strictly speaking, Kant goes on to say, such a
natural theology may take either of two very different
forms. "Natural theology concludes to the attributes
and existence of an author of the world from the structure, order and unity, found in this world, a world in
which we have to assume two kinds of causality with
their rules, Nature and Freedom. Hence natural theology ascends from this world to the supreme intelligence as the principle either of all natural or of all moral
order and perfection; we call it in the first case physico-
theology, in the second, *moral* theology. "But, he adds,
since we understand by the word *God* not an "eternal
blindly-working nature," but a supreme being "who is
to be thought of as the originator of things through his
intelligence and freedom", in rigid accuracy we ought
to deny that the mere Deist has any real belief in God,
though courtesy leads us to express ourselves more
gently by saying that the Deist believes only in a God,
the Theist in a *living* God. At bottom, then, natural
theology means for Kant the doctrine of God as free
intelligent creator and moral ruler of the Universe, and

we may note that on *his* classification the doctrine of Spinoza is a "true atheism".

It is, of course, no more true of ancient than of modern philosophers that they have spoken on these themes with a single voice. Of old, as to-day, the pure sceptic concluded that knowledge in such high matters is impossible to man; the Epicurean vigorously asseverated[1] that we can be sure of the existence of the gods, but still more vigorously that we can be sure that there is neither providence, moral government of mankind, nor life to come. But properly speaking an atheistic theology, or a theology of simple nescience, is still a theology, though it may be a poor one. Even to say that mankind is temporarily incompetent to decide the issues Plato had raised is to admit at least the competence of human intelligence to take cognisance of them. The court may find itself unable to reach a decision, but the questions have at least not been raised before the wrong tribunal. To get clean rid of theology we should need to maintain that its problems are not merely unanswerable by human intelligence, but are not even questions with an intelligible meaning, that they are mere strings of insignificant vocables with none of the characters of a genuine question beyond the rising pitch of the final syllable or the printed mark of interrogation after the concluding word.

It is, no doubt, conceivable that a man might take up this position; there seem even to be philosophers[2]

---

[1] Epicurus, *Ep.* iii. (Usener, *Epicurea*, § 123) θεοὶ μὲν γὰρ εἰσίν· ἐναργὴς γὰρ αὐτῶν ἐστιν ἡ γνῶσις; Κύριαι Δόξαι 1-2, τὸ μακάριον καὶ ἄφθαρτον οὔτε αὐτὸ πράγματα ἔχει οὔτε ἄλλῳ παρέχει, ὥστε οὔτε ὀργαῖς οὔτε χάρισι συνέχεται· ἐν ἀσθενεῖ γὰρ πᾶν τὸ τοιοῦτον. ὁ θάνατος οὐδὲν πρὸς ἡμᾶς· τὸ γὰρ διαλυθὲν ἀναισθητεῖ. τὸ δ' ἀναισθητοῦν οὐδὲν πρὸς ἡμᾶς.

[2] The sceptics, whose views are represented for us by Sextus Empiricus may serve as an example. Hobbes, again, seems to hold that "natural reason" requires us to make no theological assertion beyond that of the existence of an unknowable cause of the world.

who must be presumed to have adopted it if they are
to be supposed alive to all the consequences of their
principles, though such philosophers seem to be a small
minority. If I held the view myself, I should not, of
course, be attempting the delivery of a series of Gifford
Lectures, since it is the only theological position which
seems to be ruled out by the terms of Lord Gifford's
bequest. So long as the questions which give rise to
theologies are allowed to be genuine questions with an
intelligible sense, it is open to a lecturer on the foundation to treat them with complete freedom, provided only
the freedom is combined, as it always should be, with
sincerity, candour, and courtesy. He may contend that
human intelligence is debarred by its own inherent limitations from finding any answers to its own questions,
or again that in the present state of our information any
answer would be premature. Or he may find solutions
of some or all of the problems in an actual existing
theology or philosophy, or in a new philosophy or
theology of his own. He would be within his rights if
he saw fit to argue that the true answers to the questions
have been already given in the Catechism of Trent, the
Thirty-nine Articles, or the Westminister Confession,
that they are contained in the Christian, Jewish, or other
Scriptures, the Hermetic writings, the works of Mrs.
Mary Baker Eddy, or the *Philosophie positive* of Comte.
The only restriction on his freedom is the highly proper
one that when he finds the solution to a problem in the
dogmas of an existing theology or philosophy, he must
offer *reasons* for holding that the dogma in question
is true; he must not stifle examination of its truth by a
mere appeal to extra-rational authority. He may be
as orthodox, by any given standard of orthodoxy, as
he pleases; only he must not allege the orthodoxy of
his convictions as sufficient proof of their truth. He

may be as "unconventional" as he chooses, but he must
have something better to urge on behalf of his unconventional positions than the bare fact that they are
"heresies".

If the subject-matter of a course of Gifford Lectures
is thus limited by certain justifiable restrictions, none,
fortunately, are laid upon what it is the fashion to call,
by a metaphor from the national game of Scotland, the
speaker's "approach" to his subject. He may, if he
is a professional philosopher, directly attack the metaphysical problem of the nature of "ultimate reality,"
or the "epistemological" problem of the characteristics
of genuine knowledge and the conditions of its possibility. If his interests lie in either the exact or the
descriptive sciences, he may choose to discuss the
initial postulates, the special methods, and the present
achievements of his own study, and the worth of the
contribution it can make to a fully integrated and
co-ordinated reaction of the human person against the
total environment in which human life has to be lived.
If his concern has been more with the study of man
than with inanimate or infra-human nature, he may
speak to us, out of the fullness of his knowledge, and
beyond it, of our human past. He may seek, I know not
with what success, to throw light on the truth and worth
of religious convictions and practices by considering
them in their first beginnings, as part of the still crude and
inarticulate response of the nascent human intelligence
to its bewildering surroundings, and discussing their
social value as creating, supporting, or transforming the
corporate life of the family, the clan, the horde. Or he
may survey the customs and beliefs of men at a higher
stage of development; he may attempt to reconstruct
the thought of Israelites or Babylonians, Egyptians or
Iranians, Greeks or Romans, about man's unseen lords

and his dimly surmised destiny, may exhibit its significance for the culture of these peoples, and invite us to
consider what legacy from these old religions might
yet profitably be carried over into our own vision of the
world, and what we shall do well to reject as a *damnosa
haereditas* of error and folly. We might, again, be addressed by a poet, or other artist, anxious to discuss the
question what witness, if any, his own art bears to the
reality of the unseen things. The Gifford foundation
has already been fruitful in our Scottish Universities,
and not least in St. Andrews, in work by men of acknowledged eminence along most of the lines of which
I have spoken, and we must hope that it will continue
to bear like fruit in the future.

It is hardly necessary to state, before an audience in
the University where I so long and so recently had the
honour and happiness to teach, that I cannot undertake work of the kind I have been describing; you will
all know that I possess none of the qualifications. I
must not attempt even to attack the fundamental issues
of metaphysics and epistemology, and to offer you anything in the way of a novel conception of the nature of
reality or of knowledge. I am only too conscious that
any positions I have so far been able to reach by inquiry in these remote and difficult regions are provisional and tentative, and, I suspect, may not be too
self-consistent. I can well believe that others are more
fortunate, but, for my own part, the more I reflect on
the deliverances of philosophers with a system, even
those for whom I feel the highest reverence, the more
readily do the words rise to my lips, *mirabilis facta est
scientia tua ex me; confortata est, et non potero ad eam.*[1]
I cannot promise anyone who may care to attend these
lectures any new and startling information, or any

[1] Ps. cxxxviii. (Vulg.) 6.

particularly original fresh "orientation" in thought. What I propose to attempt is something less ambitious, though perhaps not without its use.

Since it has been my business in life for many years, and will remain so until my days for business are over, to introduce young people to the study of moral philosophy, it is most fitting that I should approach the questions which a Gifford lecturer is expected to consider from the side of ethics. There, if anywhere, I ought to be least out of my depth, or perhaps it would be more modest to say, sticking most strictly to my last. Such a treatment may be further recommended by a rather different consideration. No living theology has ever arisen from mere intellectual curiosity. The serious theologies have always come into being as the fruit of reflection upon lived and practised religions; hence the truth we all recognise in the saying that *pectus facit theologum*. And though a richly living religion is always something much more than a rule of conduct, it is never, for those whose religion it is, less than this. A religion we can accept means, among other things, a guide by the light of which we can face all the tragedy and all the comedy of life joyously and undismayed, without frivolity as without misgivings. The march of events in our own country and our own life-time has been suffi-cient to prove that the old combats which used to be waged between the professors and the assailants of our own religion, the Christian, over such problems as the discrepancies between Scripture and geology or as-tronomy, the date and authorship of the Pentateuch, the books of the prophets, or the Pastoral Epistles, were mere insignificant engagements between outposts. The infinitely serious issue for the whole future of European civilisation is that of the soundness of the Christian ideal of human character and the Christian rule of life.

If we can still maintain that in that rule and ideal we have something absolute and permanent, authoritative for Europeans of our own age no less than for Jewish and Hellenistic communities of the first century, or for our own ancestors of the thirteenth or seventeenth, it is certain that the Christian religion will survive uninjured any criticism it may yet have to encounter from biologists or anthropologists. If the finality of the Christian ideal of personal character and the Christian rule of conduct cannot be maintained, no temporary success of the apologist in rebutting this or that ill-considered " scientific" or "historical" criticism can alter the fact that the Christian faith, as a religion, is under sentence of death. And it is a chief symptom of the mental condition of our age that this precise issue is being pressed upon us with a wholesomely relentless insistence. As recently as the years of my own boyhood, the most prominent of the unfavourable critics of Christianity in our own country were usually the most anxious to declare that their quarrel was with bad science and false history, not with a bad ideal of life or a false rule of conduct. At the present moment the sons and daughters of the men of my own generation are expressly urged, by persons whose intelligence and conscientiousness are undisputed, to break with the whole moral tradition of Christianity, precisely on the ground of its inadequacy to furnish a rule of life for a society which, so it is assumed, has outgrown its past. The spirit of man, we are told on all sides, has "found new paths," and we must walk in them.

Indeed something more is at stake than the fate of a particular historical faith, however dear or august. Not Christianity only, but religion itself, is on its trial. It may quite well be that the future philosophical student of history will yet find the most significant and disquieting of all the social changes of the "Victorian age" to be the combination of universal state-enforced primary education with the transference of the work of the teacher to the hands of laymen under no effective ecclesiastical or theological control. The effect of this successful laicisation of education has inevitably been to raise the immediate practical question whether moral conduct, the direction of life, does not form a self-contained domain, and ethics a wholly autonomous science, neither requiring support or completion from religion, nor affording rational ground for religious convictions of any kind. The gravity of this practical issue can hardly be exaggerated. Something more momentous than even our national existence is at stake; the question is that of an ideal of life for the whole of future humanity. It is idle to hope, as some of our contemporaries perhaps are hoping, that the secularisation of education may at least leave religion in being as a graceful and desirable embellishment of life for the exceptionally sensitive and imaginative souls. It is of the very nature of a living religion to claim the supreme direction of effort and action. If the claim is disallowed, religion itself ceases to be real; if it is allowed, it is idle to dispute the right of religion to be made the foundation of education. A wrong answer to the question about the relations of morality and religion, once generally accepted, is certain, sooner or later, to be made the foundation of an educational policy, and adoption of a radically vicious educational policy means shipwreck for the spiritual future of mankind.

I propose, then, to discuss this question of the relations between morality and religion. I do not, of course, mean the subordinate historical question of the ways in which the actual ideal of character cherished, or the actual level of practice attained, by a given community

at a given date has been affected for good or bad by the
religious usages, traditions, and convictions of the community. Even had I the inclination to conduct an inquiry of the kind pursued in the mid-nineteenth century
in well-known works by such writers as Buckle and
Lecky, I have not the necessary minute erudition. The
question I would seek to answer, if I can, is definitely
not historical, but critical and philosophical. It is, in
fact, that which is raised, though inadequately, in
Kant's second *Critique*, and more simply presented by
Plato in the *Philebus*. What is the true character of
the "good for man"? Would successful prosecution of
all the varied activities possible to man, simply as one
temporal and mutable being among others, suffice to
constitute the "condition" which, in Plato's words,[1]
"will make any man's life happy"? Or have we to confess that, at the heart of all our moral effort, there is
always the aspiration towards a good which is strictly
speaking "eternal", outside the temporal order and incommensurable with anything falling within that order?
Is the world where we play a part for our three-score
years and ten what Wordsworth called it, to Shelley's
disgust, "the home of all of us," where we must "find
our happiness, or not at all," or is it, as others have
told us, a far country from which we have to make a
tedious pilgrimage to our genuine *patria*? In language
more fashionable to-day, have we as moral beings only
one "environment," a temporal, or two, a temporal and
an eternal? If the eternal exists, what light is thrown
on its character by our experience of the struggle to
attain to it? What kind of thing must it be, if it is
indeed the goal of all our human aspiration? As a
second question, if our true good is a "thing infinite

---

[1] *Philebus* 11 D 4 ὡς νῦν ἡμῶν ἑκάτερος ἕξιν ψυχῆς καὶ διαθέσιν ἀποφαίνειν τινὰ
ἐπιχειρήσει τὴν δυναμένην ἀνθρώποις πᾶσι τὸν βίον εὐδαίμονα παρέχειν.

and eternal," is it conceivable that it can be attained by a one-sided movement of endeavour on our part, or must we think of our own moral effort as a movement of response, elicited and sustained throughout by an antecedent outgoing movement from the side of the eternal? Is the reality of what Christian theologians call the grace of God a presupposition of the moral life itself? These are the questions to which we have in the first place to find an answer, when we undertake to discuss the relations between morality and religion and the bearing of specifically moral experiences on the issues of natural theology.

The attempt to answer these questions will naturally lead on to a further third question, that of the degree in which "autonomy" can rightly be ascribed to moral science in particular, or to science in general. If we should find that the basis of a sound rule of conduct and a true ideal of character have themselves to be sought in the eternal realities which religions claim to disclose, we shall be driven to reconsider the well-known grounds on which Kant proclaimed the "primacy of the practical reason", and to ask whether they do not prove something Kant would not have been willing to grant, the "primacy" not of ethics, but of divinity. We shall be face to face again with the claim made in the famous metaphor of St. Peter Damiani [1] that theology, the knowledge of God, is the rightful mistress; "philosophy" and "science", the whole body of our systematised knowledge of the creatures, only the handmaid. Manifestly, such a claim should neither be admitted nor rejected without careful scrutiny. Religion is, to put it bluntly, by no means an accommodating neigh-

[1] *De divina omnipotentia*, v. (Migne, *Patrolog. Lat.* cxlv. 603) "quae tamen artis humanae peritia, si quando tractandis sacris eloquiis adhibetur, non debet ius magisterii sibimet arroganter arripere, sed velut ancilla dominae quodam famulatus obsequio subservire."

bour: grant her a single inch, and she will promptly demand an ell, or rather, not an ell, but the whole compass of sea and land. She will have nothing at all, or else the supreme direction of all the activities of life. And we cannot well allow that claim without conceding a corresponding claim to primacy for theology, the organised body of our religious *knowledge*. To admit religion into life but exclude theology from science, fashionable as the compromise has been in recent times, would be like conceding the importance of the physician as a practical director, but dismissing physiologist and pathologist as impostors. Yet on the other side, theology is clearly not entitled to dictate to the student of morals, or of anything else, either his point of departure or his point of arrival in his investigation of the facts of life. Unless the investigation has been genuinely free from such interference, the witness of ethics, or any other study, to theology becomes worthless in the degree in which the evidence has undergone preliminary manipulation. We are thus compelled to deal in the last place with the double question: (*a*) What is the kind and degree of autonomy which may reasonably be claimed for any science? (*b*) under what limitations is it possible to claim some kind of primacy for theology?

The discussion of these questions ought not to demand any very minute or profound acquaintance with the technicalities of professional philosophy, or the special systems of individual philosophical thinkers. The issues to be faced are the same which confront any man who has become conscious of the duty of playing a man's part in the business of active living and the necessity, if he is to live in a way worthy of a man, of playing that part consistently and on intelligible principle. None but those who are content to drift through existence without any attempt to understand it can

ignore them or be indifferent to them. What they most
demand for their profitable discussion is not so much
information, or erudition, or even dialectical ingenuity,
as openness to the whole wide range of suggestion with
which all our active experiences are pregnant, combined
with the sound and balanced judgement we popularly
call common sense—the *esprit juste*, to speak with
Pascal, rather than the *esprit de finesse*.

In actual life these qualifications do not seem to
be more liberally distributed among metaphysicians,
psychologists, or constructors of theoretical systems of
ethics than among their neighbours. Hence, for our purpose the thought of great makers of literature who have
been also great readers of the human heart may be
much more important than the speculations of the professed metaphysician or psychologist. In particular, I
venture, at my own peril, to think that the popular
estimate of the authority attaching to the deliverances
of the psychologist by profession in matters of morals
and religion is grossly exaggerated, probably in consequence of an elementary fallacy of confusion. The
psychologist manufacturing, on the basis of his laboratory experiments, an artificial *schema* of the human
mind is too often confused with a very different person,
the reader of individual human character. Yet all of us
probably know able psychologists whose verdicts on
character or interpretations of motive we should never
dream of trusting in an affair of any practical moment,
and must certainly know many a man whose judgements of his fellows and insight into the possibilities of
life we should accept as highly authoritative, though we
are well aware that he knows nothing of the highly
abstract science of psychology, and would very possibly
be merely puzzled if he tried to study it. When we wish
to confirm or correct our reading of human life, it may

safely be said, we do not commonly think of turning in the first instance to the works of the metaphysician or psychologist, or, if we do, the metaphysician or psychologist whose view of life we trust is trusted because he is something more than a specialist in metaphysics or psychology. We all attach great weight to Shakespeare's interpretation of human life, or Dante's, or Pascal's, or Wordsworth's; even when we reject their testimony, we at least do not reject it lightly. I believe it would be safe to say that Plato is the only metaphysician to whose verdicts on things human we ascribe anything like this significance, and the reason is manifest. It is that Plato was so much more than the author of a philosophical theory; he was one of the world's supreme dramatists, with the great dramatist's insight into a vast range of human character and experience, an insight only possible to a nature itself quickly and richly responsive to a world of suggestion which narrower natures of the specialist type miss. If I am found in the sequel appealing to the testimony of "moralists", I trust it will be understood that by moralists I do not mean primarily men who have devoted themselves to the elaboration of ethical systems, the Aristotles, or even the Kants, but men who have lived richly and deeply and thought as well as lived, the Platos, Augustines, Dostoievskys, and their fellows.

Similarly the psychologist who can teach us anything of the realities of the moral or religious life is not the Professor who satisfies a mere intellectual curiosity by laboratory experiments, or the circulation of *questionnaires* about the dates and circumstances of other men's "conversions", or "mystical experiences". A man might spend a long life at that business without making himself or his readers a whit the wiser. So long as he looks on at the type of experience he is investigating simply from the outside, he can hope to contribute nothing to its interpretation. He is in the position of a congenitally blind or deaf man attempting to construct a theory of beauty, in nature or art, by "circularising" his seeing and hearing friends with questions about their favourite colour-schemes or combinations of tones. The psychological records really relevant for our purpose are first and foremost those of the men who have actually combined the experience of the saint, or the aspirant after sanctity, with the psychologist's gift of analysis, the Augustines and Pascals, and next those of the men who have had the experiences, even when they have been unable to analyse and criticise them, the Susos and the Bunyans. Mere analytical and critical acumen without a relevant experience behind it should count for nothing, since in this, as in all matters which have to do with the interpretation of personal life, we can only read the soul of another by the light of that which we know "at first hand" within ourselves. To put the point in a paradoxical way, when we try to interpret the life of another, we are in much the situation we should occupy if we had to light a candle to see the sun, and if the apparent luminosity of the seen sun were directly proportional to the brightness of our candle. *Wär' nicht das Auge sonnenhaft, Wie könnte es das Licht erblicken?* may perhaps—I am not confident on the point—be meaningless in the physical world, but is strictly true in the moral.

One final observation before I attack my problem directly. We are to be concerned in our discussion with "natural" theology, and the very name suggests to us, as it did not to its inventor,[1] a contrast with "revealed" religion and theologies claiming to be based on "revelation". For the purpose of exhibiting the point of the

---

[1] Cf. C. C. J. Webb, *Studies in the History of Natural Theology*, pp. 10 ff.

contrast, we may be provisionally content to understand by a "revelation" any kind of spontaneous self-dis-closure of a divine reality, as distinct from an attain-ment of knowledge about divine things reached purely by effort from our own human side. It is manifestly possible to hold more than one view of the relation of natural theology, as we have defined the phrase, in accordance with the precedent set by Varro, to a theology founded on revelation. One formally possible view, indeed, we may exclude at once, the view that a genuine natural theology and an equally genuine revela-tional theology might be in real contradiction. Such a contradiction would prove that either the natural theo-logy had not been reached by the right use of human intelligence, and so was not "natural" in the sense in which we are using that word, or the revelation on which the revealed theology was based no genuine self-disclosure on the part of the divine, and therefore no true revelation. But two possibilities still remain. We might conceive that a revelation, if there is such a thing, would leave the results won by the aid of "natural human reason" standing without modification, merely supplementing them by further knowledge not attainable by unassisted human effort; again, we might conceive that the effect of revelation would be not merely to supplement "natural" knowledge, but to transform it in such a way that all the truths of natural theology would acquire richer and deeper meaning when seen in the light of a true revelation.

Whether there is any subtle disloyalty to reason in-volved in such conceptions of the supplementation, or enrichment, of natural theology by revelation, and if there is not, in which of these alternative ways we ought to conceive the relation of the two theologies, will be topics for future consideration. At the outset I am concerned only to mention the simple fact that, as matter of history, natural theology has never been found an entirely adequate expression of the attitude of devout souls to their world. It may fairly be doubted whether any man has been able to live and die nobly solely in the strength furnished by a "natural" religion or theology. Even if we consider the cases of intensely religiously-minded philosophers who have been markedly out of sympathy with the institutional cults and traditions of their community—a Plato, for example, or a Spinoza—it is not difficult to see that the practical faith with which they have confronted the issues of life and death has regularly gone far beyond the limits of legitimate deduction from the professed principles of their philosophy. And in Christian societies natural theology has only been pursued with steady devotion by men who, in point of fact, were earnest believers in an historical self-disclosure of the divine, and active adherents of a positive institutional religion. It has been a factor in the great institutional and traditional religions of the world, not a rival to them. The attempt of the Deists of the eighteenth century to erect what they called the "religion of nature" into a rival of historical and institutional Christianity was, as we all know, a short-lived failure. Partly, the champions of the "religion of nature" were insincere; their alleged devotion to "natural" religion was often no more than an excuse for practical irreligion and worldly living. Partly the being proposed for worship in the "religion of nature" was found too thin and insubstantial an abstraction to evoke genuine adoration in a rational creature. Even when the "religion of nature" did not begin in irreligion, it speedily lapsed into it. To-day, I take it, few of us would quarrel with the title of one of Blake's *brochures*, *There is No Natural Religion*. Men who feel the need of religion as a guide, but cannot reconcile their intellectual convictions with unqualified acceptance of any of the institutional religions around them, fall back on some kind of tentative personal faith which has its roots in one of the great historical religions; from this they take what they can and leave the rest. Men who in the eighteenth century would have been among the more devotionally-minded Deists enroll themselves now as the advanced "Modernists" of Christianity or Judaism. They thus bear impressive witness to the truth that worship, like all the specifically human activities, morality, art, the pursuit of knowledge, and the rest, is a supra-individual activity, needing for its maintenance at a level of steady and vigorous efficiency all the support afforded by organised fellowship, definite institutions, and a great historical tradition.

It is a curious paradox, when one comes to reflect, that an age as alive as our own to the necessity for association, common interests, shared work, in the prosecution of science, and the value of a great inheritance of tradition for the production of living art, should tend to be suspiciously resentful of the suggestion that the same conscious fellowship in a great community of the living and the dead is equally important for the soul's religious life. We readily admit that the discovery of a great truth or the creation of a great poem, picture, or symphony, by a solitary, alone in a society which cares nothing for science or art and has no inheritance of tradition in either, would be something like a moral portent. Yet it is not uncommon to find estimable writers expressing themselves, with a touch of contempt and a curious disregard of the historical facts, as if there must be an actual opposition in principle between a living personal faith and an institutional religion, or as if the men of supreme insight and genius in religion were so many flowers blossoming alone in a desert, owing nothing to the educative influence of association for a common purpose with the like-minded among the living, and less than nothing, if that were possible, to the traditions which bind a living generation to the like-minded among the dead.

In sober fact things are not thus. Religion, like science, requires a communal background. What Royal Societies are to the one, Churches are to the other. Organised and accumulated tradition plays the same part in both as the conservator of sanity and protectress against the tragedy of merely futile effort. No one can deny that institutions, traditions, conventions, have their very real dangers in all departments of life, but in all they are indispensable. They are edged tools, if you like, but necessary tools. You cannot, to be sure, conserve sanity in thought, art, or living, without some risk of occasional cramping of genius. But without some organised protection of sanity the world would be filled not with men of genius, but with "cranks", faddists, and lunatics. The real enemies of spiritual life in all its manifestations are not conventions and traditions, but conventionalism and traditionalism, outward respect for the letter of traditions, or the form of institutions, which are no longer alive. This must be my excuse, if excuse is needed, for frankly approaching the study of the moral and religious life in no spirit of affected neutrality and aloofness, but from the point of view of one moulded by education in a definite moral and religious tradition, and actively partaking in the common worship of a definite historical community. There is no reason why such historical loyalties need make clear-sighted critical study impossible. If the difficulty were insurmountable, the effects would be felt far beyond the bounds of a study of religion. It should be possible,

and there is abundant evidence that it is possible, for
an intelligent man to be a loyal and whole-hearted
Scot, Englishman, or Frenchman without being
blinded to the defects of the national character or institutions. Where will is morally upright and intelligence alert, the loyal citizen, indeed, is more likely to
hit the mark with a criticism from within than the bene-
volent and intelligent foreigner, who must, to the end,
remain an "outsider" to so much. And it is even so
with the organised life of religious communities. You
must be an *insider* if you are to have full comprehension of their real weaknesses as well as of their strength.
In a world where the best of us carry about so much of
the *fomes peccati*, men are naturally not prone to carry
on the work of quiet criticism from within in public;
they prefer to descant on the mote in a brother's eye,
and to keep a decent silence about their troubles with
the beam in their own. Such merely polemical criticism
is seldom of much benefit to a man who honestly wants
to understand. What the faults of the Christian Church
are is probably better known to its devoted workers
than to the smart non-Christian journalist, and though
I have often listened, I trust in a spirit of willingness
to learn, to trenchant "exposures" of the errors and
sins of my own branch of that Church from representatives of other branches, I confess I have found the
quiet comments of loyal supporters from within more
enlightening. A "philosophy of religion", to be of
any value, must not come from the detached theorist
"holding no form of creed, but contemplating all"; it
must be the fruit of patient and candid self-criticism on
the part of men living the life they contemplate, each in
his own way, but each ready to learn, alike from the
others and from the outsider.

II

ACTUALITY AND VALUE

Io ti farò veder ogni valore.—DANTE.

ὡς ἀληθῶς τὸ ἀγαθὸν καὶ δέον συνδεῖν καὶ συνέχειν οὐδὲν οἴονται.—PLATO.

WE are now to attack the first of the questions we have proposed for examination. Does morality, if its claims are to be justified to the critical intelligence, involve any presuppositions which point beyond itself? Does it supply its own *raison d'être*? If not, does it receive its missing completion in the activities, however we define them, which are commonly called religious? To ask the question is to make the assumption that we are starting on our inquiry with some provisional definition, or at least description, both of morality and of religion. Such an initial statement may be highly tentative, as all "definitions in use" are bound to be. It will certainly need illumination, and probably need correction, as our discussion proceeds, since the distinctive characters of the merely ethical and the specifically religious attitudes towards life can only emerge gradually in the course of the argument. Thus any formula from which we may start must appear, in the first instance, more or less arbitrary; its true significance and its justification, like that of "real" definitions in general, can only be discovered from the use to which it is put. No harm will be done if we consciously follow the practice, so often adopted by Aristotle, of beginning with a current definition which needs immediate correction, if only it leads us directly to the raising of a problem relevant to our purpose. Accordingly, I propose to make such a start on the present occasion from a brief and trenchant saying of the late Professor Bosanquet which has the double merit of setting the contrast between mere morals and religion in high relief and of leading straight up to what is, in principle, the most formidable issue we shall be called on to encounter.

"In morality", says Bosanquet, "we know that the good purpose is real, in religion we believe that nothing else is real." [1] On the face of it, the sentence calls for a certain amount of interpretation. There is, for instance, apparently an intentional contrast, of which the precise character is left unexplained, between the "knowledge" said to be characteristic of morality and the "faith" distinctive of religion. On this we need not dwell, since we find on consulting the context of the sentence that morality also is held by the writer to depend on a kind of faith. It is plain, again, that neither "knowledge" nor "faith", as the words are being employed by Bosanquet, means *mere* intellectual assent to a proposition as true. No one would call a man virtuous on the strength of his mere speculative assent to the statements that lewdness and cruelty are bad, generosity to a successful rival, and fairness to a formidable antagonist good. Nor should we think a man religious simply because he believed it to be true that God exists and that God's kingdom will some day come, in the same way in which he believes that there is a President of the Argentine Republic, or that cancer will some day be suppressed by medical science. The knowledge and the belief spoken of must both be taken to mean a *scientia* or a *fides sapida*, a knowledge and a belief which affirm themselves in prac-

[1] "The Kingdom of God on Earth" (*Science and Philosophy*, p. 346).

tice by dominating and regulating the whole lives of those who are in earnest with them, a knowledge and a belief operative to "good works".

Once more, the second half of the statement might be criticised on grounds which appeal with special force to many of those whom we all recognise as most sincerely religious. To say that *nothing* but the "good purpose" is real at least *seems* inconsistent with any vivid sense of the tremendous actuality and vitality of sin, as well as of fruitless physical and moral pain, and it might be urged that the influence of the various religions on life and character has been, and is, purifying and elevating precisely in proportion to their insistence on the reality of these antagonists of the "good purpose" and the duty of consecrating life to a "holy war" against them. And manifestly a "holy war" is something very different from a sham fight. If there is "really" no enemy to be overcome, the injunction to put on the "whole armour of righteousness" must appear no more than a dull and impious jest. It would seem that any religion which affirms the *exclusive* reality of the "good purpose" must lead to some indifferentist or antinomian apotheosis of "things as they are". Such a religion, as we see in the cases of the merely lewd or cruel nature-worships of the ancient and modern East, may be potent for deadly moral and spiritual mischief; at its most harmless, as I think we see from the working of what is quaintly miscalled "Christian Science", it is powerless as an inspiration to active moral good. In short, we might be asked whether, on the proposed definition, we should not have to give the name religion to the un-ethical eroticism of a Persian Sufi and refuse it to the faith of a Paul or an Augustine.

This is a difficulty felt keenly by others than the merely unspeculative. It lies at the root of the lifelong

polemic of my honoured and lamented friend Dr. Rashdall against the traditional conception of divine in-
finitude, and largely explains the violent revolt of so
acute a thinker as Antonio Aliotta against Theism
itself.[1] To admit the existence of God, according to the
brilliant Italian philosopher, is equivalent to converting
the "good fight" into a mere parade manœuvre, since if
God is, the issue of the combat is already decided, and
hence history becomes a mere pageant. Thus Aliotta's
reason for renouncing the Theism with which he began
his career is precisely that Theism implies the very conviction with which Bosanquet at least *seems* to identify
religion. It is true, to be sure, that Bosanquet's real
meaning was probably not quite what some of his
critics have taken it to be. Whatever may be the case
with some of the recent Italian Absolutists, Bosanquet
cannot be supposed by those who knew him to have
intended to deny the actuality of evil, or to belittle the
significance of those experiences of struggle and conflict
which have led moralists and saints to speak so constantly in metaphors borrowed from the battlefield.[2]
Whether, in the end, his statement may be not so understood as to be true we may have to consider later on. At
present I am concerned only to maintain that, like the
saying of Parmenides about the impossibility of thinking
of "what is not", it is a dark and a hard saying, not to
be taken at its "face-value". If there is a sense in which
whatever falls outside the "good purpose" can be said
to be unreal, it must also be true that "what is unreal
is in a sense real", as Plato[3] maintained that, with all
respect for Parmenides, "what is not in some sense
also is".

---

[1] See Aliotta, *La guerra eterna* (ed. 1), pp. 156 ff.
[2] Though I think it true that, judged from a Christian standpoint, his "sense
of sin" is *inadequate*.
[3] *Sophistes*, 258 D 5 ff.

The value of Bosanquet's antithesis for my own purpose is independent of these obvious strictures. I quote it because it leads directly to a criticism which goes much deeper. By the use of the word *real* it raises the whole familiar problem of the relation between fact and value. Religion, it might be said, at any rate so far answers to the proposed definition that it certainly rests on the conviction that something is absolutely real, or, in plainer language, is "bed-rock *fact*". It may be hard to say just what that something is, but it is clear that *some* existential proposition or propositions must be at the foundation of every religious faith. Every such faith is a faith *in* someone or something, and so presupposes at least certain conviction that this someone or something *is*, and is a very active reality. And this is where a religion differs from a morality.[1] Morality, we are often told, has to do exclusively with values or ideals and is unconcerned with fact or reality. It deals entirely with what "ought to be" to the complete exclusion of what is. A moral conviction is a belief not in the actuality or reality of anything, but a belief in the *goodness* of certain things, or, if you prefer the alternative form of statement, in the *rightness* of certain kinds of conduct. What the moral conviction affirms is not a *Sein* but a *So-sein*, or perhaps we should even say, a *So-sein-sollen*. Hence it is never allowable to reason from the admitted goodness or rightness, the moral value, of any state of things, to its actuality, nor from its admitted badness to its unreality, any more than we may reason from "this is the only right thing to do" to "this is always done", or from "this is abominably wrong" to "this is never done". In a word, no ethical proposition is ever existential and no

---

[1] As Baron von Hügel was fond of observing, morality deals with an "Ought", religion with an "Is", and no amount of "Ought-ness" will make "Is-ness".

existential proposition ever ethical, and the one serious fault of Bosanquet's antithesis is its identification of morality with a knowledge of an existential proposition, "the good purpose is real". It may quite well be the case that whatever is is very bad indeed. Mephistopheles may be right in asserting that

alles was entsteht,
Ist werth—dass es zu Grunde geht,

and Kant may even have been justified in his uneasy suspicion that the history of the world has never recorded the performance of a single act of genuine moral value.

If this absolute and rigid divorce between fact and value can be maintained, it must follow at once that there can be no religious, and *a fortiori* no theological, implications of morality. It might still be the case that some or all of the propositions asserted by natural theologians are true and capable of being proved, or at least rendered probable, but knowledge of the moral nature of man will yield no grounds for believing in any of them, nor will any of them assert anything about the unseen which has significance for the personal moral and spiritual life of man. Natural theology, at best, will give us indications only of an "architect of the universe", not of a just judge of men, still less of an unseen friend and father. For, on the hypothesis, premisses drawn from ethics, being wholly non-existential, can never yield an existential conclusion, nor premisses drawn from the natural sciences, since none of them are assertions of value, any conclusion which asserts goodness or value. Hence, even if the philosopher finds himself able to assert any convictions about the being of God or the destiny of man, these convictions cannot be expected to dignify life by opening new vistas of spiritual values to be achieved. His natural theology will be at most Deism, in Kant's sense of the word, not Theism.

An illustration may be taken from the philosophy of the late Dr. McTaggart.[1] McTaggart was notoriously attached to one of the great traditional doctrines of Platonic natural theology, the dogma of the native immortality of the human soul, and much of his work is devoted to a gallant attempt to establish its truth. But he accepted, at the same time, the other, very un-Platonic, dogma of the irreducible antithesis between fact and value. Hence he contended that all "moral" arguments for man's immortality—all, that is, which are based on analysis of the "good for man" and the conditions of its attainability—are merely irrelevant. His own highly ingenious arguments are drawn entirely from metaphysics, metaphysics being considered simply as a body of true assertions of matter of fact about the structure of the existent. The practical consequences of this attitude are curious and instructive. The immortality which McTaggart's reasoning establishes, if we accept that reasoning as valid, and as the only valid ground for any conclusion on the matter, is virtually equivalent to a mere unending survival of numerically identical human persons, and the prospect opened up to us by the demonstration seems not to be of a kind likely to make any difference for the better in the quality of our interior life.[2]

Eternal life, conceived in the Christian sense, as a life in which human personality is transformed as it

---

[1] The remarks which follow were written long before the appearance of *The Nature of Existence*, vol. ii., and are necessarily based on two earlier books, *Studies in Hegelian Cosmology* and *Some Dogmas of Religion*. I do not see that the case is substantially altered by the publication of the posthumous second volume of *The Nature of Existence*.

[2] *Some Dogmas of Religion*, pp. 16 ff. I do not think the truth of the criticism affected by the fuller exposition of McTaggart's theory in *The Nature of Existence*, vol. ii.

gazes on the living and perfect good, into the likeness
of that which it beholds, immortality, conceived after
the fashion of Plato, as a life in which we are united
by a complete interpenetration of mind by mind, with
the best of our fellows, these are visions of a life which
is not merely "future", or "endless", but of ever ascending *quality*, a "new" or "changed" life; it is to such
transfigured life, not to an indefinite more and more
of an existence which men of high purpose have already weighed in the balance and found wanting, that
the "divine something" in man has always aspired.
McTaggart's purely non-ethical arguments, even if
we accept them as demonstrative, really hold out no
hope that *this* aspiration can ever be realised. Deathlessness *might* be no more than a condemnation to the
weary burden of mutability and temporality without
even the hope of release, to say nothing of escape into
worthier life. In his earlier work the one *definite* promise McTaggart holds out to us is no more than the
prospect of an infinite sum of pleasures, a prospect
which to many of us suggests boredom rather than
felicity, and if it is true, as is urged in his later writings,
that "nothing is too bad to exist", it would seem that,
after all, pure metaphysics cannot guarantee even the
Hedonist's sorry substitute for human good.

If there is none but an accidental conjunction between reality and value, the Is and the Ought, any conceivable theology must share this fate, since every theology will be a *mere* statement of fact, a theology for
the irreligious. Where there is nothing to adore, there is
no religion, and no man can adore a bald fact as such,
irrespective of its quality, any more than he can really
adore an ideal admitted to be a mere figment of his
own imagination. The possibility of genuine worship
and religion is absolutely bound up with a final coinci-

dence of existence and value in an object which is at once the most *real* of beings and the good "so good that none better can be conceived", at once the Alpha, the primary and absolute source of being, and the Omega, the ultimate goal of desire and endeavour. Only such an object can be adequate to the worship of a rational creature, for no other can rightly make the demand for the last and utter surrender which is worship in the spirit. Qualify the reality of the worshipper's *numen*, and his self-surrender becomes properly and necessarily hedged about by reservations and conditions; worship degenerates into an unhealthy admiration for the work of his own hands or his own brains. Take away the value, or set limits to it, and worse happens. We can at least admire or respect a mere ideal which we know to be our own creation, or at least we can admire or respect the exalted mood in which we created it, by contrast with the more common-place moods of every day. But in mere fact as fact what is there to respect? Mr. Russell, to be sure, once wrote a too-much-belauded essay on the *Worship of a Free Man* whose freedom is based on emancipation from the belief in any intrinsic connection between worth and fact. But I suspect that the title of the essay was only one of Mr. Russell's little ironies. In truth, his "free man" *worships* nothing, or, if anything, himself. He *despises* fact for its brutal stupidity and revenges himself on it by becoming the Narcissus of his own dreams.[1] The masters of the interior life would have told the writer that the one way to find yourself, no less than to find God, is to look *away* from yourself, and that "disdain" is a poison, not a food for the "free" soul.

Our very first step in our discussion, then, must be to show, if we can, that the supposed rigid disjunction

[1] Cf. B. Russell, *Philosophical Essays*, 66, 70.

of fact from value is, after all, a mere prejudice, too hastily conceived by philosophers who neglect the true business of "dialectic", repeated and thorough criticism of their own assumptions. It is worth while to remind ourselves how very modern this dogma is. We may trace it back, in the first instance, historically, to Kant's first *Critique*, where the purpose of the smashing assault on speculative theology, and, indeed, of the whole *Dialectic of Pure Reason*, is to divorce value completely from fact by denying that the "ideals" of speculative reason have any contact whatever with genuine knowledge.[1] Of course, in making this denial Kant is consciously rejecting the convictions which had been at the heart of the two great traditions which had dominated earlier philosophical thought, the Socratic doctrine that the ἀγαθὸν καὶ δέον, "the good and the ought", the supreme principle of valuation, is also the cement, so to say, by which the structure of the existent is held together, and the Christian doctrine that God, the source from which all creatures proceed, is also the good to which all aspire and in which all find their justi-fication. We all remember Kant's own dismay at the apparent success of his undertaking, and his strenuous efforts, after putting asunder what "God and nature" had joined, to bring the disconsolate halves together again by invoking reason "as practical" to undo the work of reason "as speculative". Perhaps some of us, however, are not careful enough to observe that this re-construction of a broken bridge is no "second thought", but is carefully prepared in the *KdrV*. itself; the *whole*

---

[1] I think we may take it as a result finally established by the work of Adickes and other scholars on the structure of the *KdrV*. that the *Dialectic*, as a whole, is the earliest and crudest section of the whole book. For the really fruitful ideas of the critical philosophy we must go elsewhere, to the ripest paragraphs of the *Analytic*. See the results of investigation as summed up in the *Commentary* of my colleague, Prof. N. Kemp Smith. The *Dialectic* is, in fact, vitiated throughout by the persistence of the Cartesian devotion to "clear and distinct ideas".

critical philosophy was never intended to be learned from the "transcendental Dialectic" alone and the interpretations of Kant based primarily on the *Dialectic* are all misinterpretations. If we are in error in denying the severance of fact and value, then we are, at least, erring in very good company and may take heart from the reflection.

Now what is the substance of the case we have to meet, when the problem is reduced to its simplest terms, and freed from all false dialectical subtleties? I will try to state it in my own words, but as fairly and forcibly as I can. It amounts, so far as I can see, to this. Plainly (*a*) we cannot argue straight away from the actuality of the actual to its goodness. The world is full of bad conduct, bad science, bad art. It is arguable—though I do not know how proof or disproof could be reached —that bad men and bad deeds are more common than good, and it is, at least, certain that very good deeds and very good men are both rare. We all understand how Mr. Pecksniff's mind worked when, as his biographer tells us, he said of anything very bad that it was "very natural". At any period we like to consider, there has been more bad art of every kind than good, more loose reasoning than accurate; great moral, scientific, artistic achievement is not common. If we consider the *cursus ordinarius* of nature, when all allowance has been made for sentimental exaggeration, it is undeniable that it is attended by a great deal of suffering and wretchedness, and much of this, we must agree, is decidedly very bad. The bad obviously is an actual feature in the products both of nature and of human art, no less than the good. Nor can we assume, with the light-hearted optimism of some of the eminent "Victorians", that the bad is regularly instrumental to a greater good, or that the normal trend or bias of nature and of human society is towards the steady minimising of the bad, possibly to its elimination. (We do not, indeed, see enough of the actual to be able to deny this as a possibility, but we see too much to be able to affirm it as a probability.) At most the advance of "evolutionary" science *may* perhaps have shown that it is probable that, in the region of the actual directly accessible to our own observation, there has been "progress" in the neutral sense of fairly steady development along continuous lines, but we cannot assume that the same thing has been true in regions of unexplored space and unrecorded past time inaccessible to our investigation, nor that the proposition will hold good of the unknown future. It might further be urged that much of the progress we can detect is only progress in this neutral sense of accelerated movement in the same direction. It has not been proved, and there is much to make us doubt, that it has equally been progress in the sense of advance towards the *better*. Our own experience of the life of Europe since the opening of the present century might, indeed, suggest an uneasy doubt whether the "advance of civilisation" may not have been progressive only in the sense in which a physician speaks of a patient's progress towards dissolution or a moralist of the "rake's" progress in debauchery.

Our verdicts, indeed, are inevitably passed on short views, whereas to pronounce on such a question with confidence, we should need to take the long view of spectators to whom the whole recorded history of man, or even the whole definitely ascertained physical history of our solar system, would be as yesterday by comparison with the vast immensity of pre-history. This is true; but we know enough to forbid any hasty inference from the actuality of a feature of the existent to its goodness. And it may be added that we are no less debarred from

arguing in the reverse way that what is not actual and
never will be actual cannot be good, and better than
anything which is, or will be, actual. The best in what
is actual has its recognisable defects; were there no
other, its very impermanency would be a defect. Even
when good only passes away to give place to better, we
must always think how much better still it would have
been if we could have had both goods—*e.g.*, the ardour of
youth and the wisdom of age—at once. The flower may
fall only to give place to the fruit, and we may perhaps
confess that, since we cannot have both, it is better to
have the fruit without the flower than the flower without
the fruit. Yet when autumn comes, we miss the flower.
The Callipolis of Socrates' dream never existed in
history, and there is no ground to suppose that it ever
will, but a man would have to be an extreme *Real-
politiker* if he took this as *proof* that its institutions and
life are inferior to those of London, Paris, Berlin, or
Chicago. We should understand, if we did not accept, the
view that all our "ideals" are no more than dreams, if
it were added that the dream is often nobler than waking life, where it is too frequently the ugly or sordid
dreams that "come true".

This, so far as I can see, is really the whole of the
case in support of the alleged rigid separation of fact
from value. It should, of course, be noted that the
most such arguments allow us to assert is that the conjunction of fact with value is "accidental", that there is
no inherent reason why what is actual should also be
good, or what is good also actual. Nothing in what has
been said compels us to go to the further length of pessimism, to hold that the good, from its very nature, must
be unreal, and the actual by an intrinsic necessity, evil
or imperfect. As I have said, I regard it as the most
important problem in the whole range of philosophy

to examine this alleged want of connection between reality, actuality, existence, or being, and goodness or value in a spirit of thorough criticism. I can do no more here than offer very imperfect and tentative hints towards such a truly critical examination, but I dare not do less. I cannot reconcile myself to the view that philosophy is a simple pastime for the curious, with the same attractiveness, and the same remoteness from all the vital interests of humanity, as the solution of a highly ingenious chess problem. If philosophy were really that and no more, I confess I should have small heart for the devotion of life to such "fooling". I am content, with Plato and Kant, to be so much of a "common fellow" as to feel that the serious questions for each of us are "What ought I to do?", "What may I hope for?", and that it is the duty of philosophy to find answers to them, if she can. If none can be found, so much the worse for philosophy, but her incompetence is not to be assumed lightly. I proceed, then, to offer some considerations which may fairly suggest that the connection between existence (or actuality) and value is not accidental (or extrinsic). Even if these considerations fall short of demonstration they may still have a real work as tentative "aggressions", and indicate the lines along which abler thinkers than myself may yet be able to reach a true solution of the problem.

(i.) It seems clear, to begin with, that most of the writers who insist on the radical separation of value from actuality are victims of an insidious fallacy of diction, a false abstraction due to convenient but ambiguous habits of speech. This particular point has been argued with admirable fullness and lucidity by Professor Sorley in his work *Moral Values and the Idea of God*,[1] but I may be allowed, in view of its

[1] *Op. cit.* pp. 139 ff.

importance, to dwell on it again. When we speak of virtue, art, science, health, as having *value*, it is never virtue, art, science, health, "in the abstract" to which we mean to refer, but always the actual virtuous conduct, artistic production, true thinking, healthy bodily functioning of persons conceived as existent, either in fact or *ex hypothesi*. The candid utterances, generous acts and impulses, the creation or appreciation of beauty, the comprehension of truth, the vigorous performance of the physical functions of life by existents—in fact by persons—are the real objects to which we are ascribing the possession of value; we are not predicating value of the logical "concepts", virtue, beauty, knowledge, or health. These, as the logician studies them, have been mentally isolated from all relation to the concrete individual existents in whose lives they appear, but it should be evident that in this process of abstraction they have been deprived of their specific value by being, legitimately enough for the logician's special purpose, cut loose from "existence". (In fact, the *concept* virtue, for example, has *no* specific ethical value; the value it has is merely that of being a "clear and distinct idea", and this value for classificatory purposes is common to it with the *concept* vice. So the health which has a value not shared by disease is not the "concept" health, but health exhibited in the functioning of existent organisms.)

No one could seriously maintain that there would be intelligible meaning in the statement that health has a value not shared by disease, if there were no actual living organisms. It is only a system which contains living organisms of which we can say that it is "better" if these are healthy and enjoy the exercise of their organic functions than if they are diseased and only perform the vital functions with pain. *Health is good* is only an abbreviated way of saying that it is good that *organisms* should live in a state of health, bad that they should live in a state of disease. *Pleasure is good* means nothing, or means that pleasure enjoyed by existents who can feel is good. So the knowledge we pronounce good means the active discovery and contemplation of truth by intelligent minds. And if it is suggested that not only knowledge but *truth* is good, I would reply thus. On the supposition that it is logically possible that there might have been a purely physical universe, containing no minds as constituents and contemplated *ab extra* by no transcendent mind from without, it would still be the case that some relations and interactions subsist between the constituents of such a universe and some do not, and if, as the common materialist holds, there was once a time in the past of the actual world when there were no minds, still there were certain events, and no others, which were then happening, and the common materialist believes it possible, in a general way, to say what those events were, *e.g.* to reconstruct in outline the story of the formation of our solar system. In a sense, then, if there could be, or ever has been, a world without minds or persons, there is a truth about that world. But this is not the "truth" of which we can intelligibly say that it has value.

What is really meant when truth is called a value is that *knowledge* of the true is good, the lack of that knowledge bad, the false conceit of it, acceptance of the false as true, worst of all. And by calling knowledge good, we do not mean that a particular pattern of black marks on a white surface, or a particular sequence of articulate noises, as such, is good. There would be no reason to ascribe any special value to a printed copy of Newton's *Principia* surviving in a world where there were not, and never would be, any minds to apprehend the meaning of the printed marks, or to the noises made by a gramophone repeating the propositions of the *Principia* on a mindless planet. If we could suppose the gramophone to be started on its work and all existent minds then to be annihilated, we should, I take it, not judge that it made any difference to the goodness or badness of such a state of things whether the event which annihilated the minds also affected the working of the gramophone or not. It would be as reasonable to ascribe "economic value" to a mass of precious metal supposed to be located somewhere on an uninhabited and wholly inaccessible planet.

We can, indeed, call one hypothetically assumed system in which mind is not actually present better than another, but I feel sure that when we speak in this way it is always with reference to the *future* of the two imagined systems. We judge that in which feeling and thought are expected to "emerge" and to get fair play better than that which either leaves no room for their appearance, or provides no chance of their adequate development. In a word—to condense my point into a formula—the knowledge we value as good is primarily always "knowledge in act", the life of an existent individual intelligence discovering or contemplating truth. It is only in a secondary sense that we go on to ascribe value also to knowledge in proximate or remote "potency to act", as when we speak of value in connection with knowledge a man has acquired but is not actually using, or even in connection with the contents of a library not actually accessible to the student. We say it is good that the library should still exist, because we trust that its stores will yet be utilised by someone, and will incite to fresh actual pursuit and enjoyment of knowledge. Hence the notoriously low value we set even on knowledge actually before the mind, when it is mere "erudition" which does not stimulate to further intellectual activity. To quote some pertinent words of Professor Eddington, "if we consider a world entirely devoid of consciousness . . . there is, so far as we know, no meaning whatever in discriminating between the worlds A and B. The mind is the referee who decides in favour of A against B. The actuality of the world is a spiritual value. The physical world at some point (or indeed throughout) impinges on the spiritual and derives its actuality solely from this contact."[1]

Now what is true in this case is equally true in the less obvious cases of the values we ascribe to great art and good moral practice. What we commend is not courage or temperance "in the abstract", an "universal" concept, but the characteristic life of a courageous or temperate man. What we condemn is not cruelty or adultery "in the abstract", but the characteristic acts and desires of cruel or adulterous men. Adultery "in the abstract" is *good* with the only goodness an "abstraction" can have; it is an admirable example of a "clear and distinct idea", and that is all there is to be said about it.

We may, indeed, say in a sense which is both true and important that in our moral judgements we are ascribing values to universals, and that the judgements would not be genuinely ethical unless this were so. But if the statement is not to prove a source of dangerous error, we must at once add that the "universal"

---

[1] A. S. Eddington in *Science, Religion and Reality*, p. 211. It may seem, at first, as though we have been confusing two theses: (*a*) value belongs only to the individual and existent; (*b*) value always involves reference to mind. The sentences quoted from Dr. Eddington indicate the intimate connection between the two apparently distinct theses. It is precisely because the two "physical worlds" A, B, of which the writer speaks, are purely constructions of the physicist and therefore consist of de-individualised "concepts" that existence and value are both meaningless when predicated of them. We shall have much more to say on this point in the sequel.

which has value—other than the merely logical value
of a "clear and distinct idea"—is always the universal
embodied *in rebus*, not the universal *post res* of the
nominalist logicians. "Mercy is good" does indeed
mean more than "this, that, and the other merciful acts
are good"; it means that these acts are good not incidentally, because, for example, they happen to have
been also pleasant or profitable, but because they are
merciful, and for no other reason. But the statement
does not mean that mercy is good, apart from its exercise in act. What is good is, in Aristotelian language,
the universal mercy as constituting the "form" of the
merciful man's acts, not as detached, for the purpose
of the logician, from its function as the form of those
acts, and "informing" the *intellectus possibilis* in the
logician. As the great schoolmen of the thirteenth
century were rightly careful not to make nonsense of
the doctrine of perception by confusing the "form of
lapideity" as it exists in the stone I see or touch with
the "form of lapideity" as it exists in the eye which
sees the stone, or the intellect which has "collected"
the concept of a stone from sense-experiences, so we
need, no less imperatively, to distinguish between the
mode of being of moral "universals" as they are the
"forms" of virtuous acts and their mode of being *per
abstractionem* in the thought of the student of ethics
contemplating the virtuous conduct of another party.
It is as "forms" of the good acts of virtuous agents,
and only as such, that they can be said to have specific
moral value, and as such forms they are not "abstracted" from their setting of concrete individuality.
The abstracting is done by the contemplating intellect
and affects only the universal *post rem*. (In short, the
primary meaning of *mercy is good* is that the mercy
shown by the merciful man is good, not that mercy as

contemplated by the "disinterested spectator" is good. If the act of contemplating and approving merciful- ness, performed by such a spectator, who is not himself at the time engaged in the exercise of mercy, is good, as it is, it is only good *because* showing mercy is good. The "disinterested spectator" *recognises* the already existing goodness of the act he rightly approves, he does not *bestow* the value on the act by his approving contemplation.)

The same thing appears to me no less true of all the values of art. What we really regard as so very good is beauty as constituting the characteristic form of the beautiful thing, beauty as *existing* in the poem, or symphony, or portrait, not beauty as a "concept", de- tached from the individual things of beauty in which it is embodied. Here, once more, those of our contem- poraries who are insistent in denying that "universals" exist, while they are equally sure that "value" belongs to the non-existent universal, seem to me mere victims of a vicious logical nominalism. A character in one of Mr. Lowes Dickinson's books suggests that it would make no difference to the *value* of a great picture if it were painted by an artist in a state of complete uncon- sciousness, and sunk, as soon as it had been painted, to the bottom of the sea.[1] It would be hard to find a better example of the double view that the universal, and only the universal, has value, but that it also has no actuality. And yet it is noticeable that the example does not succeed in that *complete* separation of value from actuality at which the speaker is manifestly aim- ing. What is spoken of here as beautiful is after all not "beauty in the abstract", but beauty as "informing" a particular picture. And we note too, that though the speaker is careful to exclude any reference to the

---

[1] G. Lowes Dickinson, *The Meaning of Good*, p. 110.

enjoyment of a possible *spectator* of the picture, he has not eliminated all reference to individual persons and their activities, as he should have done; he has kept the artist and his activity, though he reduces this to the minimum by imagining the activity to be unconscious.

Now why, we may ask, should the artist be brought into the illustration at all? For the purpose of the argument would not an arrangement of colours, or of light and shade, effected by unguided natural processes, have served as well, or better? Why, then, is a painter to be brought into the hypothesis, though an unconscious one, unless the writer secretly feels that the beauty we value as *good* must be the characteristic "form" of a personal activity, even though the activity is, inconsistently, imagined to be entirely "unconscious"? I seem to detect here an involuntary confession that the good beautiful thing must be a thing *made* by someone, a concession which might lead to some far-reaching consequences, if we went on to bring it into connection with the undeniable fact that a situation not brought about by any known human, or even animal activity, such as a sunset or a thunderstorm, may be exceedingly beautiful. I trust I shall not be misunderstood here. I am not for a moment defending what I regard as the wholly untenable view that truth, or beauty, or moral goodness is "subjective", in the sense that we can make propositions true, things beautiful, acts right, by thinking them so. I am not denying that there are truths which no man knows, truths which, it may be, no man ever will know, beauties which have no human spectator, heroisms and delicacies which no man's actual conduct has exhibited. I should be the first to admit that truth, beauty, goodness are not created but discovered by their spectators. My point is a different one and has a double edge. It is (1) that the truth, beauty, goodness to which we ascribe worth are in all cases "concreted", embodied in individuals of which they are the constitutive forms, and that our ascription of worth is only significant in view of this embodiment of the "universal" in the individual; (2) that in all such judgements of value the reference to *personal* activities is always more or less explicitly present.

This is clearest in the case of judgements about moral worth, where it is always explicit personal activity that is pronounced good or bad. Even Mr. Lowes Dickinson's Dennis has not suggested that the character or conduct of a man going through the business of life and performing "good works" in a state of complete somnambulism could intelligibly be said to have moral worth. He apparently allows that the somnambulist would have neither virtues nor vices, though he conceives that he might paint a beautiful picture, forgetting perhaps that it seems to be of the essence of all art to be *mimetic*, or representative of something. As for aesthetic values themselves, as I said, the introduction of the "unconscious" artist *seems* to imply that the same consideration holds good, though not so obviously. For it seems to be implied that we cannot properly call "natural objects" beautiful unless we think of them also as the works of a divine artist, or at least allow ourselves to imagine "nature" as an artist, though an "unconscious" one. In the case of truth, which is commonly classed along with beauty and moral goodness as a "value", reference to personal activity might seem to be absent, but this absence is only apparent. For (1), as I have said, what we really mean by calling truth a value is that the *knowledge* of truth is good, ignorance or error bad. If we are to speak of truth at all in a mindless universe, manifestly we cannot mean truth in what Aristotle calls the primary sense of the word, the sense in which we call *judgements* true. We must mean truth in that very vague sense in which the mediaeval logicians reckon truth, along with unity and goodness as one of the "transcendentals", when they lay it down that *quodlibet ens est unum, verum, bonum*. Even so, we have not really got away from the reference to mind, since, as St. Thomas explains[1] what is expressed in the statement that any *ens* is *verum* is *convenientia entis ad intellectum*, the intrinsic *knowability* of being. This is actually pre-supposed by the formula itself, when it treats *verum* as a predicate of *ens*. The formula, in fact, asserts just what the philosophers who detach value from existence are anxious to deny. "Values" not concreted in actuality would not be *entia*, and therefore, according to the Thomistic doctrine, would be entitled neither to be called *vera* nor to be called *bona*.

Also (2) it would be a paradox to say that all truths, because equally true, are equally valuable. By this I do not mean merely that a proposition may be true and yet be unimportant from its want of relevance to the special interests of a particular person. (Thus, for example, the statement of Mr. F.'s aunt in *Little Dorrit*, "there's milestones on the Dover road", was irrelevant to the immediate concerns of the hearers, though it might have been important enough to any one on the Dover road with a day's walk before him, who had to decide where he would break it for a meal.) Quite apart from this difference in accidental importance for particular individuals, there is an intrinsic difference between propositions, all equally true, in respect of their purely

---

[1] *De Veritate*, q. 1, art. 1, resp. "Convenientiam vero entis ad intellectum exprimit hoc nomen *verum*. Omnis autem cognitio perficitur per assimilationem cognoscentis ad rem cognitam. . . . Prima ergo comparatio entis ad intellectum est ut ens intellectui correspondeat: quae quidem correspondentia adaequatio rei et intellectus dicitur, et in hoc formaliter ratio veri perficitur."

theoretical significance. Some of them throw a flood of light on a wide range of the knowable, others do not. Every branch of knowledge has its illuminating truths and its merely curious truths; the value of the two is widely different, though they stand on the same footing in respect of being true. Reference to the highly personal activity of understanding is implicit in this inevitable distinction between knowledge which, apart from its so-called "practical" consequences, is valuable as highly illuminating and knowledge which has not this value. But if value always involves some kind of reference to the activities of persons, it cannot be true that value and existence (or actuality) are only accidentally conjoined. Indeed, it should be a truism to say that *ex vi termini* a value must be a good, and that, again *ex vi termini*, a good must be something that can be possessed and enjoyed by someone or something. In this respect it is with all values as with those of the economist; an article cannot intelligibly be said to be "worth" so much if there is no one *to* whom it is worth that price. Ice, for example, is valueless in the solitudes of Antarctica. St. Thomas (*loc. cit.*) may again be allowed to illustrate the point for us. He explains that *quodlibet ens est bonum* is meant to express the appropriateness of *entia* to appetition, as *quodlibet ens est verum* expresses their appropriateness to intellection. Hence both dicta convey a reference to mind, which unites in itself the *vis cognitiva* and the *vis appetitiva*. If there were no intelligence, nothing could have "truth-value", if there were no appetition, nothing could have value at all.[1]

---

[1] *Loc. cit.* "alio modo secundum convenientiam unius entis ad aliquid; et hoc quidem non potest esse nisi accipiatur aliquid quod *natum sit convenire cum omni ente*. Hoc autem est anima quae quodammodo est omnia, sicut dicitur in iii. *De anima*. In anima autem est vis cognitiva et appetitiva. Convenientiam ergo entis ad appetitum exprimit hoc nomen *bonum*."

(ii.) Again, consider some of the consequences which seem to follow immediately from the admission of either truths or the knowledge of them into the list of values. A truth, even a truth as yet undiscovered, is a proposition,[1] and it should have been quite evident, ever since Plato wrote the *Sophistes*, that to be significant at all, and therefore to be a proposition, an utterance must always be, directly or indirectly, an assertion about τὸ ὄν, what *is*. Everyone can see that this is so with singular propositions, and with "particular" propositions, which are equivalent to groups of singular propositions whose subjects are as yet unspecified. That "some men are mathematicians" is only significant because the statements that "*this* man (say Legendre) is a mathematician" and that "*that* man (say Gauss) is a mathematician" are also significant. And the subject of a singular proposition, being a "this", can never be simply non-existent; "this *nothing*" would be an unmeaning noise. (Hence the universal recognition that singular and particular propositions have always "existential import", with its necessary corollary that in strict logic a "subalternate" proposition can never be inferred simply from its *subalternans*.)

It is true that everyone who tries to treat logic seriously finds himself driven to deny that the universal proposition has direct existential import. But the consequence is that, if we consider closely, the "universal" reduces to something less than an actual proposition. It becomes what Russell and Whitehead call a "formal implication" not between propositions but between "propositional functions". That is, the true meaning of the statement "all men are mortal" can only be given

---

[1] At least this is the case with the truths contemplated by the philosophers who have most to say of truth as a "value". On the possibility of non-propositional truth and knowledge there will be some remarks to be made in our final lecture.

without excess or defect in the form "that x is a man implies that x is mortal". This again means, to state it more precisely, that "is mortal" is true of *any* subject of which "is a man" is true. To make a genuine proposition out of this blank form it is necessary that we should replace the symbol x, on both its appearances, by one and the same name or denoting phrase, indicating one individual *this*. Only when we have done so have we passed from asserting a relation between mere "propositional functions" to asserting a relation between *propositions*. And when we take this step, the propositions which figure in the (now "material") implication are seen at once to have existential import.

Thus, though we often utter the words that man is mortal, we never really mean no more nor less than we say. As Russell has remarked, we should not expect to find the decease of Man recorded in the *Deaths* columns of the *Times* or the *Morning Post*. On the other hand, we mean more than was supposed by Mill when he took the statement to be no more than the assertion of "is mortal" about each and every individual man who has actually lived in the past, is living now, or will live hereafter.[1] When I say that all men are mortal, I may not know that Botticelli is the name of a man and a Florentine; like the young gentlemen in *Punch*, I may believe that Botticelli is the name of a wine or a cheese. Yet I mean my assertion to cover the statement that *if* Botticelli is a man—which I hold not to be the case—Botticelli is also mortal. The subject of which something is asserted in the universal proposition is thus neither a definite collection of determined indi-

---

[1] *Logic*, bk. i. c. v. § 2: "When we say, all men are mortal, the meaning of the proposition is, that all beings which possess the one set of attributes possess also the other". Cf. bk. ii. c. iv. § 3: "A general truth is but an aggregate of particular truths; a comprehensive expression, by which an indefinite number of individual facts are affirmed or denied at once".

viduals, nor yet the "universal" or "concept" of which such individuals are "instances". It is *any* individual, known or unknown, of whom a certain statement is true, and what I assert is that a second statement also will be true of such an individual. If there should be *no* such individual, if, for example, there never should be any actual man, the statement (in this case, that all men are mortal) seems to me to lose its claim to be regarded as true. I see no way of successfully disputing the old dictum *nullius sunt nullae proprietates*.

The statement, often made by formal logicians, that *all* assertions are equally true of the "null-class" seems to me only a disguised way of making this admission. If you can assert a pair of contraries of the same subject, the distinction between truth and falsity loses its meaning so far as that subject is concerned; truth and falsehood cease to be *opposed* values, and so cease to be values at all. A genuine assertion with a *meaning* always makes a "claim", well-founded or not, to be true and not to be false. For that reason, I should say, it is impossible to make a genuine assertion about the merely non-exist-ent. If that is not "the expense of spirit in a waste of shame", what is? I confess I cannot enter into the state of mind of those agreeable and entertaining persons who suppose themselves to be recapturing the spirit of Plato's philosophy when they discuss propositions about the "round square" and other such impossible "object-ives". My own conviction is that Plato would have dismissed the topic with the single remark that, since there are no round squares, nothing can be significantly said about the "round square", and that human life is too short to be further curtailed by an expenditure of breath with no meaning behind it. Even the statement that there are no round squares is not, properly speak-ing, a statement *about* round squares, but rather a con-

fession that we have tried hard to make such a statement and found it impossible. We can make no statement which proves on analysis to be, in the terminology
of Frege, all "function" without any "argument".
Here again scholasticism puts the point excellently:
"Being is in a certain way affirmed about not-being,
in so far as not-being is apprehended by the intellect.
Hence the Philosopher says in the *Fourth* of the *Metaphysics* that the negation or privation of being is in one
sense called being; hence also Avicenna says, at the
beginning of his *Metaphysics*, that no enunciation can
be made except about what is. For that about which
the proposition is made must have been apprehended in
the intellect."[1]

At the cost of a seeming digression I should like here
to explain what I take to be the source of confusion
in the minds of those who think that the merely non-
existent can be the subject of a significant judgement
of value. It is the old and deadly error of supposing that
a word must be either simply *univocal* or merely *equivocal*, the same fatal error which Spinoza commits when
he assumes that either will and understanding, when they
are ascribed to God, mean precisely the same thing as
will and understanding in ourselves, or the double employment of the same words is as purely accidental as
the double use of the vocable *dog* for the friend of man
who guards our houses and a group of stars in the
nightly sky.[2] In exactly the same way, it is often assumed that "existence" or "actuality" must either
mean exactly what it does when we discuss the question whether the sea-serpent exists, or whether Prester
John actually existed, that is, occupation of a definite
region in the historical series of spatio-temporal events,

---

[1] St. Thomas, *De Veritat.* q. 1, art. 1, ad sept.
[2] *Ethica* i. 17 *Scholium.*

or mean nothing at all. Then, since "ideals" clearly
must not be said to exist in *this* sense, it is asserted that
"ideals" or "values" simply do not exist at all. Under
the baneful influences of an evil nominalistic tradition,
inherited from the senility of a scholasticism which had
lost its vigour, the great Aristotelian conception of the
"analogous" use of predicates has been allowed to fall
out of our modern thought, with disastrous consequences. It is simply not true that the alternatives,
univocal predication—equivocal predication, form a
complete disjunction. This is plain from the elementary
examples produced by Aristotle himself, when he
wants to illustrate the meaning of analogy. When I say
that a wise adviser and director is a physician of the
soul, I am manifestly not predicating "physician" of
such a man in the same sense in which I say of Mr.
Jones, or Mr. Smith, Fellows of the Royal College of
Surgeons, that they are able and experienced physicians. But it is equally plain that the use of the word
"physician" here is no mere historical accident of
language, as it is a mere historical accident that I call
a certain group of stars "the Dog", rather than "the
Cat" or "the Dodo". My soul is, indeed, not a body,
and it is not dieted with albuminoids or carbohydrates,
nor dosed with tonics or aperients. But there is a real
appositeness in the metaphor I use. But for an historical
accident I might call the group of stars a cat, a dodo,
a hyena, or anything you please, as appropriately as
I call them a dog; all that matters is that, whatever
word I use, it should be understood which group I
have in mind. But it is a *happy* and well-chosen metaphor I am using when I speak of a physician of souls,
or call the wise statesman who brings his country safely
through perils and disorders the "pilot who weathers
the storm". The one is not κυρίως, in the strict sense,

a medical man, nor the other a seaman, but it is true that the one stands to his "penitent" as the physician to his patient, the other to the nation as the pilot to the vessel and its company. Analogy in the strict sense, "analogy of proportionality", is a genuine feature in the structure of things. So again is analogy in the looser sense. As Aristotle observes, a surgical implement is not surgical in the precise sense in which an eminent operator is surgical, but again, it is no accident of language that we use the same epithet in both cases.

To take a less trivial illustration, the very word *life* itself, or, as Aristotle says in this connection, "existence", is not strictly univocal. When we say that what the best type of friend desires is neither entertainment nor advantage to be derived from his friend, but that friend's *existence*, that he prizes that friend's existence, even if he is henceforth to exist in conditions which preclude all possibility of further intercourse, what we mean, as Aristotle says, is that the good man finds a high intrinsic value in his friend's thinking and perceiving. Even the "Waring" whom we expect never to see again has not vanished, the world has not lost the value it gets for us from his presence in it as an alert and benign intelligence: "In Vishnu-land what avatar?" It would be another matter if our friend's mental activities of all kinds were irreparably annihilated. In a sense he might still be, but not in the sense in which our affections find their satisfaction in his being. Such being as he might still retain if he only continued to breathe, to be nourished and the like, in a state of complete "paralysis of the higher centres", would not be what we mean by the life of a *man*. In the case of a man, to be means to be alive, and to be alive in the special way in which "human beings"—the very phrase bears witness to the soundness of Aristotle's contention—are said to be alive. The hopelessly demented or paralysed are not what we mean by the very expressive slang phrase "live men". The man who only *is* in the sense in which a log or a stone is, if there is such a man, may fairly be said to "be no longer".[1]

If the existence, then, which we ascribe to the individual as a *proprium* is not an univocal word, is it merely a word which has an accidental plurality of unconnected senses, like *box*, or *dog*? Clearly it is something more than this. We can say of whatever is an individual and of nothing else, that it is actual, exists, or has existence, as the logicians recognise when they assert that the universal proposition differs from the singular or particular in not having "existential import". And if we ask what we mean by individual here, I can find no answer but that implied in the Aristotelian account of "primary substance", that the individual is that which can figure in propositions as subject, but never as predicate, or, to use Frege's terminology, that which is an argument of functions, but never itself a function of any argument. Clearly we have no right to assume without examination that only what we commonly call "fact", that which can be located and dated by reference to an interval in the spatio-temporal series, is thus individual. If we meditate the reasons which have led Professor Whitehead to make a sharp distinction between *events* and *objects* and to insist that location and date belong properly to events, to objects only secondarily, in virtue of their "ingredience" into events,[2] we might even be led to the very different view that *individuality* is precisely the feature in things which resists our attempts to locate and date it. It is at

---

[1] Cf. Aristot. *E.N.* 1170 a 32, τὸ δ ὅτι αἰσθανόμεθα ἢ νοοῦμεν, ὅτι ἐσμέν (τὸ γὰρ εἶναι ἦν αἰσθάνεσθαι ἢ νοεῖν).

[2] See *Concept of Nature*, c. vii. pp. 143 ff.

least clear that the assumption that the individual must always mean that which occupies a definite, *i.e.* a delimited, spatial and temporal interval has no real claim to be admitted as true without careful and searching criticism. It is conceivable that individuals may be of many types and that "existence", as asserted of them, may have as many shades of meaning as there are types of individual. This possibility forbids us to assume that the existent is simply that which can be located and dated, and consequently forbids us also to assert that "values" and "ideals", since they have admittedly no date or location, must merely be non-existent, not-actual, "what is not".

(iii.) These considerations, however, are only preliminary to the point on which I would rest the main weight of the case for refusing to admit the ultimate severance of value from existence. The point on which I would lay the chief stress is that any such severance falsifies the facts of real life, where existence and value appear always as distinguishable, but always as conjoined. The moral life is inevitably misconceived and its suggestions misread, if we start by thinking of the attitude of the man who is ordering his life as *Mensch mit Menschen* on the analogy of the attitude of a super-physicist or super-chemist to a laboratory problem. If we make this mistake of confusing the man who is seeking a rule of life to live by with that of a theorist speculating about the activities of the good life as lived by someone else, it is not unnatural to imagine such a theorist as first having the facts of life given, "thrown on the screen", "presented for his observation", and then bringing to them a scheme of valuation freely imposed by himself from the outside. Thus we come to think of the facts, or realities, as one thing, the valuation put on the facts by the "observer" as another independent thing, and so the question arises whether the valuation is not wholly personal to the observer, and so arbitrary, and devoid of all foundation in the facts, as we call them. But when we are addressing ourselves to the primary moral problem of living, facts and valuations do not present themselves in this neat antithetical fashion, as the given on one side, and the interpretation subjectively put on that given on the other. In life as we all, including the laboratory worker himself, live it, *all* is given, facts and valuations together, in an undivided whole. We find ourselves not passive spectators of a scene presented to our contemplation, but actors in the drama, taking our part in response to the suggestions of our environment, which is at least human, moral and social, as well as biological and physical. The living moral tradition of our community, the equally living tradition of the scientific, artistic, or religious group into which we have been initiated, are embodied schemes of valuation, but they are also as much facts and part of the given to which we have to make our response as the pressure of the atmosphere, or the gravitational "pull" of the earth. Our respect for our parents, our love for our friends, our loyalty to our country, our adoration of the divine, all are specific responses to specific features in an actual whole which is, in the first instance, given and not made. We are from the first creatures with a moral as well as a physical "environment", and the values of the moral life are themselves the constituents of the environment, not afterthoughts, or "psychic additions", of our own personal creation.

I may perhaps illustrate my meaning by a reference to the similar status of the so-called "secondary" qualities of sensible things, and again to what Professor Alexander and his admirers call "tertiary" characters. In spite of the utterances of a whole series of eminent philosophers, from Galileo and Descartes down to our own age, it ought to be patent that, whatever the ontological status of the greenness of the leaf and the redness of the rose-petals, they are no "psychic addition" made by the percipient subject to a given consisting simply of so-called primary qualities. The green colour of the grass, the crimson of the rose, are there in the world as it is given to us through the eye, no less than the shape of the blade or the petal. It is not my mind which, in knowing the grass or the rose, puts into it a green or a red which was not there; on the contrary, it is from an indefinitely rich and complex given that I come to single out these particular elements for separate contemplation. In this matter, once more, the greatest scholastics, I think, showed themselves better analysts of the facts than their successors of the more modern world. St. Thomas, for example, if I understand him rightly, as very possibly I do not, teaches a doctrine of perception which a thoroughgoing realist might accuse of containing the germ of the later heresy of representative perception. He holds to the Aristotelian formula that when I see, for example, a rose there is an actual presence of the "form" of the rose in my own sensibility, the *species sensibilis*. But he is very careful to avoid the mistake of supposing that the rose I see is the same thing as this "sensible species". The "species" plays a necessary part in the work of perception, but it is the *instrument* by which seeing is effected (the quo *videtur*), not the *object* seen (the quod *videtur*). What I see is the "form of the rose" embodied in the actual rose, not the "form of the rose" as present in my eye or my mind. This "form" *is* present there, or there would be no vision, but of the "form" as present in me I have no perception at all; I perceive, *through its instrumentality*, the corresponding

"form" as existing in the rose. The sensible species is
thus, in the *causal* order, a mediating link between me
and the rose; in *the order of perception and knowledge*
I apprehend the rose itself without awareness of any
intervening *tertium quid* whatever.[1] Now this may not
be a wholly satisfactory analysis. I own I am tempted to
say, with what a Thomist would probably regard as a
leaning to an *outré* realism, that there is really no evidence that anything *psychical* intervenes in the causal
order between the physiological processes in retina,
optic nerve, and cerebral centres, and the perception of
the rose. But at any rate the recognition that the "sensible species", if it is a psychical reality, is not itself
apprehended by sense, would have been enough to keep
the theory of knowledge off the false track on which it
has been sent for so many generations by the unhappy
influences of Descartes and Locke. We may at least say
that a sound theory must retain as a minimum of realism
the Thomist distinction between the *quod* and the *quo*
of perception.

The mistake of thinking otherwise would hardly have
been made if philosophers and men of science had
always drawn the important distinction, on which John
Grote used rightly to insist,[2] between the philosopher's
attitude to *his* given and that of the positive sciences to
theirs. The philosopher interested in analysing knowledge as a whole must inevitably take as his ultimate
antithesis that between the knower-agent, on the one
side, and the whole, as yet undifferentiated, continuum
of the known-and-interacted with, on the other. And
there can be no doubt on which side of the antithesis the
colour of the grass or the rose falls. It is not a knowing,

[1] Cf. *De Veritat.* q. 10, art. 8, ad sec. "in visione corporali aliquis intuetur
corpus, non ita quod inspiciat aliquam corporis similitudinem, quamvis per
aliquam corporis similitudinem inspiciat."
[2] *Exploratio Philosophica*, pt. i. c. I.

or an acting, but a fact known and reacted to, a feature in the continuum; not a response, but a percept which may provoke responses of different kinds, according as the percipient finds the colour pleasing or unpleasing, stimulating or depressing. It can only be mistaken for something else when we have first committed the blunder of confusing this most elementary antithesis of knower and known with the entirely different antithesis between the constituent of the known which I gradually learn to recognise as my own body and those constituents which I call foreign bodies. Then it becomes possible to argue, plausibly but fallaciously, that since the mechanical interactions between bodies can be understood without taking their differences in colour into account, and since, in the interests of exact science, we should like, if we can, to reduce all interactions between bodies, even in the case where one of them at least is alive and sentient, to the mechanical type, the colour which can be disregarded by "rational mechanics" is not really there, and must therefore be an "addition" made by the mind to the given. Or it is argued by philosophers of a different school, with equal disregard of concrete realities, that since we can, for various special purposes, break up the given into small fragments of simple and homogeneous quality, it was given in that form, and we get the really monstrous doctrine that the real or given consists primarily of detached *sensa* which knowledge somehow pieces together; the awkward problem then arises, with what justification the piecing together is done. If we would only look at the facts of life without this artificial distortion of perspective, we might see at once that what is given is neither a configuration devoid of sensible quality, nor a number of qualitatively definite disconnected *sensa*, but a single most imperfectly discriminated whole, in which shape,

colour, size, odour, sound, are all present from the outset, and that progress in knowledge means, not making
unauthorised additions to this whole, but becoming increasingly sensitive to distinctions within it.

In the same way the "presentation-continuum" itself
is not the whole of what, in the first instance, is given.
It is given itself as one with its setting, all of a piece
with elements which will be afterwards detached for
separate consideration as making up our specifically
human and social *milieu*. The mother's protecting care
is given in infancy along with and in the same sense as
the mother's features, or the bloom on her cheeks. And
to myself it seems clear, again, that the beauty of the
rose is no more read into, or added to, the fact of the
rose than its colour. Both are, in the first instance, *found*,
not brought, though, as the colour seems not to be found
except by creatures with eyes, so the beauty, too, is not
found by the man who has not the "inner eye" by which
beauty is discerned. At least the artists of the world
have commonly spoken and borne themselves as if it
would be the death of artistic endeavour to discover that
their work has been a process of inventing and not one
of finding.

Now all this seems to be no less true of our moral
"ideals". As I do not add either the tints or the beauty
of the rose or the sunset *de meo* to a rose or a sunset
"given" without beauty, or even without colour, but
find the colour or the beauty *in* the given, so I do not,
by an "act of valuation", make Jonathan's affection for
David or the self-devotion of Marcus Curtius, the humility of St. Francis, or the patient labour of Darwin
good; I find the goodness there in them. Presumably,
I should have had no moral "ideals" at all if I had not
begun in childhood by accepting "as a little child" the
moral tradition of my community with its witness to the

fact that qualities like these are "objectively" good, exactly as iron is hard and lead soft. And any tradition of living would soon cease to be a living tradition if men could be persuaded that it consists of "valuations" manufactured by themselves and imposed on the "real facts" of life from outside. A tradition thus degraded would lose all its power of inspiring to fresh endeavour and better action. The ideals of good which in actual history move men to great efforts only move so powerfully because they are *not* taken to be an addition imposed on the facts of life, but to be the very bones and marrow of life itself. Behind every living morality there is always the conviction that the foundation of its valuations is nothing less than the "rock of ages", the very bed-rock out of which the whole fabric of things is hewn. The mere suspicion, phrase it as we will, that "divinity gives itself no concern about men's matters", that "the universe is sublimely indifferent to our human distinctions of right and wrong", that "facts are thoroughly non-moral", when it comes to be entertained seriously, regularly issues in a lowering of the general standard of human seriousness about life. Serious living is no more compatible with the belief that the universe is indifferent to morality than serious and arduous pursuit of truth with the belief that truth is a human convention or superstition. In short, if one is thoroughly in earnest with the attempt to separate the given, the fact, from the superadded value, one will discover, on the one hand, that what one has left on one's hands as the bald fact has ceased to be fact at all by the transference of every item of definite content to the account of the added, and, on the other, that the "value" has lost all its value by its rigorous exclusion from the given. What confronts us in actual life is neither facts without value nor values attached to no facts, but fact revealing value, and dependent, for the wealth of its content, on its character as thus revelatory, and values which are realities and not arbitrary fancies, precisely because they are embedded in fact and give it its meaning. To divorce the two would be like trying to separate the sounds of a great symphony from its musical quality.

The point I am anxious to make, then, is one which would be generally admitted, so far as the mere epistemological problem is concerned. I do not believe that anyone who has seriously faced that problem will be disposed to deny that in our knowledge of the actual world it is quite impossible to make a hard-and-fast distinction between a kernel of reality or fact which is given as such once for all, and an interpretation, more or less doubtful, superadded by the apprehending mind. There is no specific datum of sense which can be isolated in this fashion, any more than it is possible, in the study of biological development, to mark off a primitive datum, as the given and original endowment of the organism, from the effects of interaction between this datum and its environment. Whatever we assign, in some specific investigation, to the organism as originally there, antecedently to a particular process of development through interaction, itself, on further examination, turns out to presuppose earlier processes of development by which it has come to be what it is. Everywhere in our biological science we are confronted by the distinction between developing organism and conditioning environment; but I suppose it is never possible, on either side, to accept any feature of a situation as simply given material for development, with no history of internal development of its own. So in the genetic study of the growth of our knowledge of the corporeal world around us. However far back you trace a man's cognitive relation to this world, you find

in it the two relatively opposed factors of passive reception of given data and active interpretation of the
data, but their apparent independency is only apparent.
We never reach any actual stage in the mental growth
of the individual man or the society so primitive that
we could say of it, "here all is passive reception of a
given with no element of disturbing interpretation",
any more than we can expect, at the other end of the
process, ever to achieve a "scientific understanding of
nature" in which everything should be interpretation,
and nothing uninterpreted given fact. There is no
reason to believe that even the simplest beginnings
of anything we could recognise as human cognition
present us with purely passive reception of the merely
given. Recognition, comparison, discrimination, where-
ever they show themselves, are already incipient
interpretation, and even the crudest human apprehension of the bodily world involves them all. We
may fairly doubt whether some such processes are not
characteristic of the perception of the lowest organisms
to which we can attribute any perceptiveness. If they
are not, then we have, at least, to say that so-called
"perception", in creatures to whom it is a purely passive
receptivity, must be so radically different from the
perception of man that the development of such organisms belongs, like the formation of the earth's crust, to
the prehistory, not to the history, of intelligence, and
that with the first dawn of human perception we have
a real discontinuity on the psychical side, a genuine
emergence of something wholly novel, which is only
very superficially masked by the mere temporal continuity of the sequence of physical and biological events.

What is thus generally allowed to be true of cognition is, I would contend, equally true of all the reactions of man against the wider world in which he

finds himself placed. Our moral "ideals" are not something added by the mind *de suo* to "facts" or "things-as-they-are". As all human perception is already intellectual interpretation, so all human practice is already reaction guided by the light of a tradition, however rudimentary, of the good, and all human art production inspired by recognition of beauty as a character of things. The conception of our ideals of good as simply derived from an earlier life of merely blind appetition, so that primarily "good" means only "what a man happens to be lusting after", is thoroughly unhistorical. So far as our personal memories carry us back in the reconstruction of individual experience, or our historical researches in the reconstruction of human experience at large, we never reach a stage at which appetition is more than *relatively* "blind", *i.e.* uncontrolled by a tradition of the good which presupposes intelligence. If we *could* get real evidence that in fact there was a time in the life of the individual or the community when the blindness was absolute, once more we should have to regard this time as belonging to individual or communal prehistory, and to recognise that there has been, with the dawn of *guided* appetition, in each of ourselves, or in humanity at large, a real, though masked, discontinuity. Purely blind appetition, if it exists at all, is qualitatively infra-human. The history of humanity, as T. H. Green rightly insisted, is a history of developing intelligence, not of the production of intelligence out of something else. The really given is a whole situation which includes ourselves, with our definite endowment of more or less coherent schemes of value, our hopes and fears, our choices and avoidances. The history of man is no tale of the superimposition of an edifice of "mental construction" on a basis of *mere* givenness; it is the story of the gradual

clarification and progressive definition of apprehensions, contacts with the "given", cognitive and practical
alike, which have been there all along in vague and
implicit form, in any life we can recognise as being
qualitatively of a piece with our own.

If this is so, it is merely arbitrary to assume that
while our physical structure and its history throw real
light on the general character of the system of realities
which includes human organisms among its constituents, our moral, aesthetic, religious being throws no light
whatever on the nature of this reality. We have every
right to hold that, however we conceive of the real, we
must not think of it in terms which could make the
actuality of this richly diversified life a mere unintelligible mystery. There must be at least as much to learn
about the inmost character of the real from the fact
that our actual spiritual life is controlled by such-and-
such definite conceptions of good and right, such-and-
such hopes and fears, as there is to learn from the fact
that the laws of motion are what they are, or that the
course of biological development on our planet has
followed the lines it has followed. It may be that this
is a grave understatement. Without prejudice to the
issues which are still ground of dispute between the
mechanist and the vitalist, we may, I take it, fairly say
that there is no likelihood that science will ever return
to the point of view of the best seventeenth-century
thinking, the point of view from which the one and
only thing of first-rate importance to be said about the
real is that it is a geometrical system. The development of evolutionary biology has at least had the result that we now recognise that it is more illuminative
to know that the real exhibits itself as a realm where
there is room for life and sentience than to know that
it forms a kinematical system. It is such a system,

but the important thing is that it is the *kind* of kinematical system in which living organisms can find a home. May it not well be even more important to know that it is a system in which moral, artistic, and religious aspiration can flourish and find adequate scope? On any theory the real must always remain very mysterious to our apprehension, but it *may* be that we come nearer to understanding its character when we know that it is the environment of organic life than when we merely know—if we do know it—that it is a closed energetic system, and nearest of all when we know that it is at once the stage and inspiration of the artist, the hero, and the saint. Our geometrical knowledge may be very much clearer and more articulate than our knowledge of life and sentience, and this again much clearer and better articulated than our knowledge of our own moral being, which is, as Shelley said, a "mystery, even to ourselves"; the knowledge we can have of God may be still more unclear and inarticulate. And yet it may well be that, for all its dimness, it is just this knowledge which brings us most directly into contact with the very heart of reality. Spinoza's ideal of a "theology" demonstrated, after the fashion of Euclid, as a consequence of self-evident premises may be the supreme vanity of vanities, and yet it may still be true that *perfecta scientia Deum scire*, that the knowledge of God is the most real knowledge we have.

III

ETERNITY AND TEMPORALITY

Τὸ μὲν γὰρ δὴ παράδειγμα πάντα αἰῶνά ἐστιν ὄν, ὁ δ᾽ αὖ διὰ τέλους τὸν ἅπαντα χρόνον γεγονώς τε καὶ ὢν καὶ ἐσόμενος.—PLATO.

> Heav'n
> Is a plain watch, and without figures winds
> All ages up.   VAUGHAN.

WE have decided, for reasons stated in our last lecture, that it is permissible to look to our personal experience of the life of aspiration after the good for indications of the true character of the actual. What is actual, we hold, must at least have such a character, the *So-sein* of the *Seiendes* must be such, that I can say, *What I ought to be, that I can be.* This, as we see at once, is what Kant meant by his famous saying that *I ought* implies *I can.* But Kant's formula is in one way defective. He is thinking, as he too often is throughout his ethical writings, rather of the single performance than of the *So-sein* which reveals itself in the performance. He means primarily What I ought, at this juncture, to *do,* that I can *do,* if I choose. Hence it is on *my own* nature as a morally responsible being that the principle, as Kant conceives it, throws a direct light; any consequences it may have for the understanding of the realm of the real as a whole are only reached, in the second *Critique,* "with windlasses and with assays of bias". But when we remember that on Kant's own theory, no less than in actual fact, deeds are only prized as having intrinsic and absolute worth so far as they can be taken

67

to be effects revelatory of a character or quality of the
doer who is their "free cause", we see that the ultimate
moral imperative is not "do this", but rather, "be this";
the tree must first be a good tree, if it is to bring forth
genuinely good fruit. Hence the second of the supreme
human problems is misstated in Kant's well-known
enumeration of them;[1] its true form is not, What acts
ought I to do, but What manner of man ought I to be?
Indeed, we might fairly say that Nietzsche has given
the perfect expression for the supreme "categorical imperative" in his injunction *Werde der du bist*, if only we
are careful to remember from the first that I do not, at
the outset, know *wer* or *was ich bin*; I am a riddle to
myself, and it is only through the process of the *Werden*
that I, slowly and painfully, gain some insight into my
Sein. Even in the artificially isolated "physical realm"
of natural science, what we study is never a *mere
Werden*, a mere succession of barely particular events
which just "happen"; we are dealing everywhere with
successions which exhibit pervasive "universal" characters, or patterns, events in which, in the terminology
of Whitehead[2], *objects*, that is "universals *in re*", are situated, "becomings" which, in the significant language
of Plato,[3] are γενέσεις εἰς οὐσίαν. Still less is any morally
significant act a mere event which happens. The
piquancy of the disparaging epigram that human life
is "one damned thing after another" is wholly due to
its glaring falsity as a description of any life but one
which would be morally worthless.

There is a famous passage in Plato's *Timaeus* in
which this point is made very strikingly. The Pythagorean Timaeus is there giving a pictorial account

---

[1] *KdrV.*[1] 805 (= *KdrV.*[2] 833).
[2] *Principles of Natural Knowledge*, pp. 82 ff.
[3] *Philebus*, 26 D 8.

of the "soul" which, as he teaches, animates the whole physical universe. God, he says, made it by mixing certain ingredients, as the master of a feast mingles the wine and the water for his guests, in the great mixing-bowl. The ultimate ingredients of the mixture are two, the *same*, "the being which is undivided and always self-same", and *the other*, "the being which becomes and is divisible in bodies" (*Tim.* 35 A 2). They are, in fact, just object and event, the eternal and the temporal. In the great world-soul, according to Timaeus, these ingredients are wrought into a perfectly stable compound. *Our* souls contain the same elements, but the brew is not of the same quality; we are made of the "seconds" and "thirds" (*ib.* 41 D). We may certainly take the meaning to be that in our case the resulting compound is always more or less unstable. In the world-soul, he means to say, eternity and temporality are together, in permanent interpenetration and equilibrium; in our human spiritual life there is a tension between them, more or less acute according to the quality of the individual life.

These remarks of Timaeus, divested of their trappings of imagery, may furnish a suitable text for some reflections on what, as I take it, is the most patent and universal characteristic of explicitly moral life wherever it is found. As morality becomes conscious of itself, it is discovered to be always a life of tension between the temporal and the eternal, only possible to a being who is neither simply eternal and abiding, nor simply mutable and temporal, but both at once. The task of living rightly and worthily is just the task of the progressive transmutation of a self which is at first all but wholly mutable, at the mercy of all the gusts of circumstance and impulse, into one which is relatively lifted above change and mutability. Or, we might say, as an

alternative formula, it is the task of the thorough transfiguration of our *interests*, the shifting of interest from
temporal to non-temporal good. It is this which gives
the moral life its characteristic colouring as one of
struggle and conflict never finally overcome. When the
conflict has not yet begun, or at any rate has not become
conscious struggle, there is as yet only the pre-moral,
or incipiently and unconscious moral, life of the natural
or animal man; if it finds completion in the entire transformation of the self and its interests from temporality
into the supra-temporal, the strictly ethical level of life
has been passed, and with it the *merely* human level.
Es strebt der Mensch, so lang er lebt, and we may add
that, *so lang er lebt*, man is always striving towards
something which he not merely has not reached, but of
which he only knows in the dimmest and vaguest way
what it is. The "Form of Good" may be "the master-
light of all our seeing", but if we are asked *what* it is,
though the better men we are, the less hopelessly vague
our answer may be expected to be, the best of us has
nothing like a "clear and distinct idea" of what he would
be at. Really to say what "the good" is, we should need
to be in fruition of it, and if we had the fruition, our life
would have become, in Aristotle's language,[1] no longer
that of man, but that of the "divine something" in man.
Or to speak more Christianly, to know what "glory"
is, we should need to be ourselves already "in glory".

"Now", says an apostolic writer, "we are sons of
God, and we know not what we shall be." The thought
finds an unexpected echo when our great master of
human experience, without any trace of theological
prepossession, wants to bring home to us the mingled
pathos and comedy of a distracted mind. "They say
the owl was a baker's daughter. Lord, we know what

[1] *N.E.* 1177 b, 27-28.

we are, but know not what we may be!" Its philosophical form is the thesis on which T. H. Green has so much
to say in the *Prolegomena to Ethics*,[1] that in all moral
progress to a better, the driving force is aspiration
after a best of which we can say little more, at any stage
of the process, than that it lies ahead of us on the same
line of advance along which the already achieved progress from the less to the more good has been made.
As usual, when we are trying not to rubricate knowledge already won, but to anticipate, poetry has here
the advantage over technical philosophy as a medium
of expression, for the reason that poetry can convey so
perfectly the sense of the tentativeness with which we
have to grope our way in the half-light which is, after
all, our "master-light".

> Shape nothing, lips; be lovely-dumb;
> It is the shut, the curfew sent
> From there where all surrenders come
> Which only makes you eloquent.

Or again:

> I know not what my secret is;
> I know but it is mine:
> I know to live for it were bliss,
> To die for it divine.

Yet the not uncommon experience is misread when,
as seems to be the case in Professor's Alexander's surrogate for theology,[2] it is interpreted simply as evidence
that the life of the mind is a stage on the way to the
evolution of something of which we can say nothing
whatever, except that it is, and must always remain,
the blankly inconceivable. The point of the experience
is precisely that though we could never say articulately
what the goal of the journey is without having reached
it, yet at every fresh step we are finding ourselves in a

[1] Green, *Prolegomena*, pp. 178 ff.
[2] Alexander, *Space, Time and Deity*, bk. iv. *passim.*

land which is no mere "strange country"; as the familiar
hymn puts it, we are getting "a day's march nearer
home", losing ourselves, quite literally, to find *ourselves*. It is not altogether true that manhood is *etwas
das überwunden werden muss*; it is rather true that it is
something which has to be *won*. So at least the moralist
who really believes in morality must hold; if science or
metaphysics profess to prove anything else, *he* can only
retort, "so much the worse for them". That is the moralist's special way of becoming "a fool for Christ's sake".

Let me devote the rest of this lecture to an attempt
to make my meaning clearer. And, first of all, let me
offer some remarks—at a later stage we may find it
necessary to return upon them—on the most tormenting of philosophical questions, the meaning of the
notions of time and eternity. I begin, as "better known
to ourselves", with Time, or, as I would rather say in
this connection, Temporality.

Temporality.—We must begin by an attempt to get our
minds clear on some important distinctions. Nothing I
have to say at this stage has any bearing on the puzzles
which may be raised about methods of *measuring* intervals of duration, or *locating* events temporally. It
is with duration and succession as features of human
moral life, not with the question of their measures or
magnitude, that I am now concerned. Again, what we
have to consider is not the mere fact of *successiveness*,
the relation of "earlier" and its converse "later", as we
find them in the course of physical events, but something very different, the distinction between *past, present*, and *future*. If we confine our attention to the
events of the physical order taken, by an artificial and
legitimate abstraction, apart from all reference to the
way in which they affect the emotional and conative
life of individual experients, we may fairly say that

though there are in "nature", as thus conceived, everywhere relations of before and after, there is neither
past, present, nor future. To introduce *these* distinctions
is to make explicit or concealed reference to the individual experient and his interior life of action and purpose, exactly as the same reference is introduced whenever we speak of "right" and "left", "before" and
"behind", "above" and "below". In a purely physical
world where there were no experients, there might be
earlier and later events, but no event would ever be
present, past, or future. Again, within the experience
of an individual experient, there may be a before
which is not properly to be called a past, and an
after which cannot rightly be called a future. I
must at least register my own conviction that the
purely "instantaneous" present, the "knife-edge", as
it has been called, is a product of theory, not an experienced actuality. The briefest and most simple and
uniform experiences we have "last", even if they only
last for a fraction of a second, and they are never merely
"static"; there is transition, and thus the before and
after, within them. For example, whenever we listen
to music, there is a before and after relating any two
immediately successive notes; [1] if there were not, or
if the relation were not actually constitutive of the
experience but merely "inferred" somehow "on the
basis of" the experience, we should have no apprehension of melody. But, equally certainly, we should
have no apprehension of it if we could not apprehend
the two notes and their successiveness, with its "sense"
as an ascending or descending interval, in a single
pulse of present experience. And I should say that

---

[1] And, for the matter of that, the individual single note, as heard, has always
its characteristic "protensity", as it has been called. We no more hear instant-
aneous sound than we see "mathematical points".

when we are listening to music in the proper mood, and with the right kind of appreciation, we appear to take in a considerable stretch of the successive as all alike there in one apprehended present, in spite of our definite awareness of elaborate relations of before and after between its constituents. If it were not so, I do not see how we could ever have come by awareness of a musical phrase—for example, any characteristic theme or *motiv* of Beethoven or Wagner—as a whole and a unit.[1] And more generally, though I cannot argue the point here, I should assert the *change* is actually "sensed", not, as some suppose, merely "inferred" from a succession of experiences all internally "static". It is, then, with the distinction of past from future and both from present, not with that of before from after, that we are now concerned. The point for us is not merely that events can be contrasted as earlier and later, but that they can be contrasted as "no longer" and "not yet".

Now *this* distinction is manifestly based directly on our own experience of ourselves as striving and active beings. The "future", the "not yet", is the direction taken by a conation in working itself out towards satisfaction (or towards being dropped, because it is persistently thwarted). The "not yet" is that towards which *I* am endeavouring, or reaching out. Its opposite, the "no longer", is that from which *I* am turning away. You might, indeed, conceivably try to get rid of the reference to action by distinguishing the two directions as those of anticipation and memory, prospect and retrospect respectively, if it were not that the very use of the familiar words *pro*spect, *retro*spect, brings back again the very reference on which I am dwelling. Strictly speaking, this antithesis only gets its full mean-

---

[1] The apprehension of a spoken syllable will, of course, illustrate the point equally well.

ing within the sphere of effort which is, at least, incipiently moral. In physical nature, as conceived by
the "classical" kinematics of the nineteenth century,
there is really neither past, present, nor future, no
emergence of the *not yet* into the *now*, nor fading of the
now into the *no-longer*. In dehumanising our experience to the "limit of opakeness", as we have to do if we
mean to think in terms of the classical kinematics, we
try to think away *these* distinctions and to retain only
a bare sequence of later or earlier, which is neither
within the present, nor yet *from* the past, *through* the
present, *to* the future. Bare sequence of this kind is not
succession as we actually apprehend it in the concrete
case, where the "passage of nature" regularly comes to
us as one factor in a striving and forward-reaching personal life. Just because such sequence as a science of
kinematics can contemplate is bare sequence, thus
artificially detached from its setting, it is never even
real sequence, and kinematics is a science of abstract
possibilities, not of actualities. The "flow of time"
contemplated in classical mechanics is not "real" time,
and its intervals are no *durée réelle*. In trying to conceive a world where simple successiveness is everything, we are inevitably driven to imagine a succession
which is not real succession and a temporality which
is not real time. We talk, indeed, of the "everlasting
hills", and of the "most ancient stars", but only by
an anthropomorphism which a strictly mechanical
science is bound to reject. What has no present, and
therefore also neither past nor future, cannot properly
be said to "last" either a short time or a long time, to
be recent or ancient. In a world where there was nothing but movement, or nothing but "matter" and movement, duration would have lost its meaning.

It is with the appearance of something which we can

call, by more than a "legal fiction", effort and purpose that the distinction between past, the direction of that from which effort is moving away, and future, the direction of that to which effort is tending, first becomes really significant, and, in becoming so, gives significance to the motion of the present, the "moment" which is not only "*a* now" but *now*. Time, we may say, as it actually is, is the characteristic form of the conative, forward-reaching life. So much, at least, we must all have learned from M. Bergson. This will enable us to understand why, though Spinoza, whose ideal for the sciences of the living organism and the living spirit was that they should all be reduced to the study of complicated kinematical configurations, could insist that it is vital to true thinking to contemplate its object "under a certain form of eternity", the tendency of an age which, like our own, has derived its ideal of science largely from the modern development of evolutionary biology, is rather to think it obvious that the "essence of true thinking" is to contemplate its object under a form of *time*, to write the object's life-history—exactly what Dr. Whitehead is trying to do by introducing the conception of "organism" into physics itself. Spinoza's thought is that so long as the durational form still affects our results, our thinking is missing its mark. Thinking which was thorough, through and through what thinking professes to be, would see the *facies totius universi* as something which has no history. The thought more familiar to our contemporaries is that really adequate knowledge, knowledge which is through and through all that knowledge ought to be, would see everything as something that *is having* a history, and a history which is never complete. We shall have to return to the point in the penultimate lecture of our course, and may then find that both conceptions sin by that commonest of all intellectual errors in philosophy, over-simplification. But for the present the point I want to make is simply this. What Spinoza calls "eternity" is precisely what might more truly be called the bare form of mere sequence, the contemplation of one kinematical pattern or another as the kaleidoscope of the universe turns in a "mathematical time" where there is neither present, past, nor future. He thinks he has eternalised a life-history by merely making it unhistorical. He reduces real action to a string of "configurations", and a mere configuration has no history, except by a misleading metaphor.

When we come to deal with the sciences of life and mind—I mean these sciences themselves, not the hypothetical kinematics into which they are sometimes sublimated by a crude metaphysics—we are dealing with processes which have a genuine form of temporality just because they disclose the activities of historical individuals, beings whose life is a *streben*, a reaching out from a past to a future. The route by which a mere configuration of points or of mass-particles has reached a given shape may be immaterial to the further succession of its shapes, the route by which an organism or a personality has become what it is is all-important, for the organism or person is charged with all its past and pregnant with all its future. Of it we may truthfully say, inverting a well-known line of Tennyson, that all it has seen is a part of it. This is why the organism, and still more the person, has a history in a sense in which a mere configuration has none. It may be, of course, and we shall yet have more to say on the point, that there is no actual reality which is a mere configuration of the kind contemplated in text-books of kinematics or dynamics. In that case we should have to say, and we should have the support of eminent living physicists in saying it, that Spinoza's ideal of knowledge is in principle unattainable, even in the sciences of the "inorganic"; physics and chemistry would be no less irreducible to complicated applications of rational mechanics than physiology and psychology. This is, in fact, precisely what Dr. Whitehead, for one, is saying very eloquently at the present moment. But *if* actual physical processes really are nothing more than changes of configuration in kinematical systems, or transactions between *kinetic* systems, then we should have to say that, in principle, when you know what the configuration, or the system of mass-particles, is "at any instant t_o", you know all that it has in itself to become; or, rather, the very motion of "becoming" is too deeply infected with historicity to be applicable to such a pattern. If it seems to us to "change", that is only because we have mistakenly treated it as having some unity and individuality of its own, whereas it is, in truth, only an arbitrarily selected piece of an indefinitely larger pattern. The more we widen our consideration to take in more of the pattern, the more does the appearance that it exhibits any change or development vanish.

The case is altered the moment we come to deal with the lowliest thing which displays a concrete individuality of its own. The simplest organism, recognisable as such, for example, differs from a mere configuration or a mere kinetic system by the fact that it has an *environment*, specifically distinguished from and opposed to itself, and lives upon this environment by "assimilating" material drawn from it, whereas the mere configuration or kinetic system has merely "surroundings", but no true "environment".[1] This duality

---

[1] And consequently Goethe's well-known thesis that "Natur hat weder Kern noch Schale" is *not* true of "organic nature".

in unity of organism and environment is fundamental for the understanding of transactions between them. A mere configuration, or a mere assemblage of mass-particles, as I say, has no "environment"; it is always itself a constituent part of a wider configuration or system, singled out for consideration in virtue of some "subjective" interest of our own, theoretical or practical. An organism is not, in like manner, a subjectively selected and artificially isolated constituent of its own environment. The antithesis between the two is significant for the organism itself, as well as for the student of it. A true organism, we might say, is always *Athanasius contra mundum*. It, as much as the student of it, has its "world" and stands over against that world, not, perhaps, necessarily in the cognitive opposition of knower to known, but at least in the practical opposition of user to used, feeder to thing fed on.[1]

Without this opposition, significant, as we are saying, in the highest degree for the organism itself, the organism would not have the sort of specific individuality it actually has; to use the terminology of a recent eminent occupant of this platform,[2] it would not be the special sort of "substantial unity" of its environment which, in fact, it is. Being the sort of "substantial unity of the environment" which it is, however completely its life may seem to be made up of responses to solicitations directly supplied by the environment, the responses are never completely determined by characters in the environment alone. How the creature will react to these solicitations depends also on the

[1] And, be it noted, the relation of organism to environment is not, like that of one kinematical system to another with which it interacts, a one-level relation; the transaction is not a mere "exchange". The organism "assimilates" what it receives from the environment; the environment receives excreta from the organism, but does not "assimilate" them.

[2] Dr. C. Lloyd Morgan. The reference here is to language used in Dr. Morgan's spoken Gifford Lectures. For the thought see *Life, Mind and Spirit*, lecture iii.

sort of creature *it* is, on *its* "particular go", and its "particular go" never seems to be quite independent of the route by which it has reached its present state, as that of a mere "energetic system" is held to be independent of the route by which it has come to its present condition. Certainly, the higher the creature ranks in the scale of evolutionary development, the more hopeless would it be to attempt to say how it will respond to the situation, on the strength of mere knowledge of its present condition. As we ascend in the scale, what the creature will do now is found to depend increasingly, in more ways than one, on what it may have done before. All that men of science have to teach us about the importance for a creature's life-history of the formation of routes of special permeability for the transmission of influence from the environment, or for initiated responses to such influence, or, at higher levels, about the importance of the formation of physiological routine and psychological habit, serves to illustrate the point. But it is also illustrated by the apparently antithetic facts which indicate that established routine and habit never become absolutely rigid. We observe apparently casual and unaccountable deviations from the most fixed established routine and habit in the lives of all lower organisms which we can subject to individual examination, as well as in our own, though in their case the interpretation of these deviations is necessarily tentative and ambiguous. (Indeed, I should be curious to know from competent observers whether even the "decapitated" frog of the laboratory is really quite as much of a piece of clockwork in its behaviour as it is made, for a legitimate purpose, to appear in the text-books which condense the results of countless individual observations into a summary formula. Are we not dealing, even here, with something like a "journalistic" exaggeration?) In our own case we can often see what the interpretation is.

We are not absolutely under the sway of the most thoroughly organised habit or the most constant of associations. At the lowest level of what we recognise as distinctively human conduct, the line of response which has not been usually followed in the past, the train of associations which has not been common, may sporadically reaffirm itself, as, to take a trivial example from my own experience, I occasionally find myself, for no discoverable reason, heading a letter with an address at which I have not resided for a quarter of a century. It does seem to be a fact of conscious human life, that, thanks to the pervasive omnipresence of memory, the past is real in our human "world" as it is not at lower levels. As F. H. Bradley says somewhere in one of his numerous scattered essays, the mere fact that a conscious response *has* once been made at some time seems of itself to be a possible cause of repetition. So much seems to be true not only of ourselves but of, at any rate, those higher animals who are at the nearest remove from us. With them, as with us, it is a mislead-ing metaphor to compare the establishment of habitual responses to the demands of the environment with the process by which the river digs out its own bed. Thus, to appeal to the example I have just given, I may perhaps make the mistake of dating a letter from the long-abandoned address twice at an interval of several years. During the interval I had perhaps never once made this mistake, though I had written and dated hundreds, or even thousands, of notes and letters. If the production of a habit, physical and mental, were really on all-fours with the formation of a river-bed, such complete disuse of the old reaction and repeated discharge of the new ought to have made the mistake impossible. The stream may depart from its formed channel because there is a present obstacle which blocks it; it will not diverge merely because there was once in the past a now long-removed obstacle at this particular place. With me, the mere fact that I used, twenty or twenty-five years ago, to date my letters from a particular address seems to be of itself a possible sufficient basis for doing the same thing now, unreasonably and in the teeth of a habit developed by the regular practice of years.

Further, as we all know, it is just this possibility which makes the conquest and control of habit by intelligent purpose and precept also possible. In the life of a reasonable man we find neither random spontaneity nor servitude to habit dominant. What we do find is a combination of habit and spontaneity, and a combination with a definite character. (Though we must not call this character a "law", if we mean by law anything for which we could supply a general "blank" formula.) We find habit everywhere, but habit subservient to foresight. What a man does at this present juncture, if and so far as he is a reasonable man, is primarily designed to meet the individual demand of this individual situation, and the demand of the situation must be taken to mean the call made on the agent in this situation by a coherent plan of purposive living. (Thus the "demand of the situation" will be different for different agents.) The character of the plan itself, as I have tried to indicate, is not known, even to the agent, fully and definitely from the outset; it reveals itself progressively as he meets and faces successive situations. An upright man has a certain "ideal" before him. His purpose is, in all situations—what they will be is largely unknown to him—to conform himself to the "holy" will of God, to promote the true good of his social group, to "keep his honour untarnished", or something of that kind. In spite of all that Kant has said about the clear and infallible guidance afforded by the categorical imperative of duty, no man knows in advance what particular line of conduct will, in some unrehearsed contingency, most surely conform to God's will or keep a man's honour bright. That is precisely what you can only discover, with any approach to certainty, when the contingency is upon you. Hence it is that, even of those with whom we are most intimate, we so often can say no more, if we are asked how we suppose they will act in some difficult position, than that we do not know what they will do, but are sure that their act, whatever it is, will be the act befitting a true Christian, or a high-minded man. We are sure that they will do nothing common, or mean, or unbefitting, and we are sure of no more. And when we say this, we do not mean to be uttering a triviality, or giving expression to the non-moral partiality which is ready to approve anything done by a friend because it is done by him. We mean that when the act in question has been done (and it may prove to be a complete surprise to us) we shall be able to see that it was the right and reasonable thing to do. Our judgement of approval is genuinely ethical and genuinely "synthetic".[1]

There is thus perpetual novelty, adjustment to the requirements of the moral ideal in a changing and unforeseeable environment, in all typically moral action, and, as I have said, even the precise character of the ideal itself only becomes partially and gradually clear

[1] Of course I am not denying the obvious fact that the lessons of the past all through play a part of fundamental importance in directing intelligence to the response demanded by the new situation. If the situation presented no recognisable analogy with anything in the agent's past history, intelligence would presumably be helpless to cope with it. But the lesson of the past is not one which can be got "by rote".

to us in the very act of meeting the demands it makes upon us. What demands it would make in a totally unfamiliar situation—as, for example, if I, with my special past history, should suddenly be called upon to exercise judicial functions on my own sole responsibility for some social group, I cannot even guess. But the point is that all that is ever handed over to the control of mere habit is the execution of the details of my act; the combination of the details, which is the important thing, is exactly what is always more or less novel and unique. If, for example, I have to write a letter of instructions to a subordinate about the way in which some practical task is to be executed, the mere formation of the marks on the paper is matter of habit, and the more completely so the better. The less I need give my attention to the spelling of the different words, or the grammar of the different sentences, the more fully can I concentrate my mind on the main problem of making my instructions reasonable and indicating them promptly, unambiguously, courteously and in the way likely to obtain hearty and willing co-operation from this particular subordinate. But the command over spelling and grammar which makes this concentration of attention on the main problem possible is itself dependent on memory, and so only itself possible in virtue of the fact that, in conscious human life, we are not at the mercy of mere "customary association", that standing source of irrelevancy. Everything depends on the principle that what has once been present may be present again, or perhaps it would be more exact to say, that what has once been operative may be operative again, apparently for no reason beyond the fact that it has once been operative and that it is relevant that it should be operative once more; recollection is not a mere function either of the recovery or of the frequency of experienced conjunction. To put the matter in a sentence, a human past may sometimes be a "dead" past; it is never safe to say of it, as we can perhaps say of the past of the lower animals, that it is dead and buried. This consideration has its important bearing on the quality of our moral life. Whether we like it or not, there are no more characteristic or common features of our human moral life than remorse and repentance. It may reasonably be doubted whether an "animal" is capable of either.

One might, indeed, possibly suggest that a well-behaved dog does exhibit something which looks like remorse, when it commits a fault for which it has usually been punished in the past. It is uneasy and shows its uneasiness; apparently, too, it has some kind of expectation of punishment. But I would take the opportunity to utter a humble protest against the over-hasty making of inferences about the mental life of animals in general from the behaviour of the few which we have not merely domesticated, but admitted to special intimacy with ourselves. It seems to me quite possible that the association of the house-dog, for example, with man may go a long way to humanise and moralise the dog and may make it something more than "only a dog". Before trusting confidently to conclusions about the capacities of animals based on the behaviour of our domestic friend I should like to be satisfied that the same behaviour is found, in some degree, in the dog in a state of nature, or the dog who has only associated with men markedly less moralised than ourselves. And even our most highly humanised dogs seem, at any rate, incapable of rising above the level of a rather crude remorse to anything like what we call, in the language of morality and religion, genuine repentance. Contrition —the first step to a true repentance—seems hardly to enter into their lives.[1] They may feel very uneasy until they have first been punished for an offence and then treated once more with the old friendliness. But when the offence has been "paid for", no dog seems to trouble himself about it. The mere fact of having offended does not seem to be felt as a man feels a past misdeed, a past stain on his honour, and often, ridiculously enough, a mere past piece of social *gaucherie*, as something which remains, after all "payment", a living and uneffaceable reality. "What I did is worked out and paid for" is a phrase we think characteristic of the attitude of the habitual criminal to his crimes; *pereunt et imputantur* is the language of morality; "my misdeeds prevail against me" is the cry of spiritual religion.

I might go on to illustrate my point further by dwelling on the way in which, in virtue of our possession of social tradition and history, the course of life of any one of us may be determined by a past which is neither, strictly speaking, his own, nor that of his own ancestors. Here we have a real difference between human and animal life, which remains real even if we take the most generous and least critical view of the facts which are sometimes alleged to prove the efficacy of so-called "racial memories" in the life of the animal. Our possession of recorded tradition, in the widest sense of that phrase,

---

[1] It is important not to confuse *contrition*, as Mill seems to do in his language about the "internal sanction" of morality, with regret or remorse. Regret may be felt for mere unfortunate circumstances. I may, for example, regret that I am not well enough off to do someone a social service which I should like to render, or that I have not the social influence which would procure him some advantage. It, to use Butler's distinction, concerns our "condition" rather than our conduct. Remorse, in our language, seems to mean exclusively dissatisfaction with one's own conduct, but it is a dissatisfaction which need have nothing to do with the moral quality of the conduct. Genuine contrition involves absolute and unqualified self-condemnation of one's conduct, and of one's personality, so far as expressed in that conduct, as *evil* or *sinful*. Hence its connection with the second stage of repentance—confession. The essence of confession is that it is recognition that an act which is absolutely to be condemned is my personal responsible act, and that, in condemning the act, I am condemning myself, so far as the act expressed myself, as guilty and evil without excuse.

makes it possible for us, as it is for none of the lower animals, to be guided in the shaping of our own present and future by almost any record from the past, even from a past that goes back into "geological time". It might be rash to say of any event known to have occurred in the earth's past that it is really over and done with, that it will never again be relevant to the shaping of the future. In the merely inanimate world, according at least to the conceptions of "orthodox" mechanics, the past seems to shape the future only in so far as it has not passed, but has persisted during the interval. In the merely animate world, the past which shapes a future seems to do so by the persistence of its contribution in the way of a series of effects through an interval. In the world of intelligent human action, the remembered past seems to be able to mould the future directly and immediately, striking, so to say, out of its own remote pastness, even though there has been no continuous persistence of itself or its effects through the interval. When remembered, it *lives* again in "ideal revival" in a more real sense than the makers of the old psychological terminology ever intended. In a purely physical world there would be no past, because there would be no present; in a world of mere perceptions, impulses, and instincts there would be only a dead past holding the present in the mortmain of habit; in the life of men, as intelligent and moral persons, and not at any lower level, we have a living past. The outward and visible sign of this is that man, at his lowest, has *traditions* where the animals seem to have only *instincts*.

I fear I have dwelt only too long on what must seem painfully obvious and familiar. But I have done so for a purpose. I would make it the more fully clear what is implied by saying that *time* is the characteristic form of the life of moral endeavour. It is plain, I hold, that apart from our personal experiences of endeavour and its gradual satisfaction, we should know nothing of past and future, though we might still be able to distinguish before and after. The past, let me say it once more, means that from which *we* are turning away, the future that to which *we* are turning. And I think, though to say this is to anticipate a little, if we were asked what a present, or "now", is, as it is actually lived and experienced, we should not be far wrong in saying that whatever we experience as *one* satisfaction of endeavour is experienced by us as *one* "now", as a present in which the before has not sunk into the past, and the after is not waiting beyond the threshold of the future.

But if the temporal is strictly and properly the form of the life of conscious appetition, it should follow that in being so much as aware of our life as temporal at all, we are already beginning to transcend the form of temporality. For what is it we are endeavouring to do in even the humblest and most rudimentary striving after a positive end? As the psychologist says, we are endeavouring to keep before consciousness, and, if we can, to intensify, an experience we find agreeable to ourselves. If there really is a still lower level of conation where the endeavour is only to banish from consciousness an experience found disagreeable,[1] we may, at least, fairly say that this level is passed by the human baby at a very early stage in its career, and does not concern us as students of morals. Now to endeavour even to keep an agreeable condition of bodily well-being, like that of the cat before the fire, steadily in consciousness, is already to be trying to transcend the merely temporal form of the experience. We want to

---

[1] But the truth rather seems to be, as is stated in Stout's *Manual of Psychology*^a, p. 113, that "appetition is primary and aversion derivative"; aversion arises "with regard to any situation incompatible with the desired end".

have the pleasant sense of warmth, to have it thoroughly, and to have it in a "now" where there may be a before and an after, but where we are not conscious of a no longer or a not yet. If we are aware of the not yet, that means that the thorough satisfaction of our endeavour has not been reached; if we are aware of a no longer, satisfaction is palling or fading. When satisfaction is at its height and fills our being, the sense of past and future is lost in a rapture which is all present, so long as it lasts.

At a higher level than that of mere animal enjoyment, such as we may get from basking before a good fire, or giving ourselves up to the delight of a hot bath, we know how curiously the consciousness of past and future falls away, when we are, for example, spending an evening of prolonged enjoyment in the company of wholly congenial friends. The past may be represented for us, if we stay to think of it at all, by whatever happened before the party began, the future—but when we are truly enjoying ourselves we do not anticipate it—by what will happen when the gathering is over. The enjoyment of the social evening has, of course, before and after within itself; the party may last two or three hours. But while it lasts and while our enjoyment of it is steady and at the full, the first half-hour is not envisaged as past, nor the third as future, while the second is going on. It is from timepieces, or from the information of others, who were not entering into our enjoyment, that we discover that this single "sensible present" had duration as well as order. If we were truly enjoying ourselves, the time passed, as we say, "like anything". I have heard that the late R. L. Nettleship was in the habit of dwelling on this familiar expression as indicating the real meaning of "eternity". The same thing appears to be true of the "aesthetic pleasures", and of the enjoyment of unimpeded intellectual activity. When our thought is moving readily and successfully, without being brought to a halt by any baffling obstacles, towards the solution of a problem which interests us and to which we are equal, the experience of advance from the statement of the problem to its solution is, of course, an experience of before and after, or it could not be a conscious advance, but it is a movement within a conscious present, from a before which has not faded into the past, to an after which is not felt as belonging to the future.

So again, if I may trust my own experience, which is not that of a *connoisseur* with any very special aptitude, but is, perhaps, all the more significant for our present purpose on that account, when our consciousness is really *filled*, as it can be, with the movement of a piece of music, so that the music is, for the time, our "universe". The "movement" is movement, and we apprehend it as such, but within limits which presumably vary with personal responsivity to the special "appeal" of music, the apprehension of a musical unit is sensibly simultaneous. It is not an attending first to one note or chord, then to the next, but an attentive awareness of the *form* of a whole phrase which is taken in as a whole, and felt as all *now* here. Everyone, I take it, apprehends a short and striking phrase of two or three notes or chords in this way, as a unit; most men can apprehend a larger phrase with a really marked form of its own, a "theme" from one of Beethoven's symphonies, for example, in the same way; a real musician, I suppose, would have the same apprehension of a whole "movement" as all present at once as a characteristic of his normal experience. It is, I imagine, experiences of this kind which Nietzsche had in mind when he said that *alle Lust will Ewigkeit*, and whatever the meaning of that verse may have been, it has always seemed to me that experiences of this kind—they are most common, I believe, in an intense form, when one is listening to music which really masters one, but they are found also in the enjoyment of drama and other forms of art[1]—it has always seemed to me that they give us the key to the famous and classic definition of eternity by Boethius, that it is *interminabilis vitae tota simul et perfecta possessio*, "whole, simultaneous, and complete fruition of a life without bounds".[2] What the definition excludes, as being proper to temporality, we note, is not the before and after, but the not yet and no longer which would mark an experience as *not* the "whole and complete" satisfaction of endeavour.

We all know the sort of criticism which has been directed against this language by Hobbes, and by numberless smaller men than Hobbes, the objection that the *"nunc stans* of the schoolmen"—Boethius uses no such words—is an unmeaning phrase. I should reply that the sort of experiences of which we have been speaking, *while they last*, conform exactly to the definition. When, for example, we are enjoying the music with heart and soul, in the first place we are engrossed by it; it is the *total* field of awareness, or, at least, of full awareness;[3] next we have a satisfaction of endeavour which not only fills the whole soul, but is also at once (*simul*) and complete (*perfecta*). And there is a further feature of the experience which corresponds to the clause *interminabilis vitae*. While

---

[1] Notably when we are following the movement of a powerfully wrought scene in a drama as actual spectators in the theatre.

[2] *De Consolatione Philosophiae*, v., pros. 6. Cf.

> " Then long Eternity shall greet our bliss
> With an *individual* kiss;
> And Joy shall *overtake us as a flood*."

[3] "I have no life, Constantia, now but thee,
Whilst, like the world-surrounding air, thy song
Flows on, and fills all things with melody."

the experience lasts, one really does seem to have been "translated" into a world of beautiful sound which is "without bounds"; one has a sense that one always has been, and always will be, floating on the tide of harmony. (I trust my language will not sound affected; it is the best I can find to render a not un-familiar experience faithfully.) There is, to be sure, illusion here, because, in the first place, we all have other interests than those which are satisfied by listening to music, so that we cannot get a *perfecta vitae possessio* in that way, and, in the next place, we are embodied intelligences, with nervous systems subject to fatigue and exhaustion; the flesh proves itself weak, even when the spirit continues ardently willing. But we can at least imagine the removal of these limita-tions. We can imagine a kind of life in which all our various aims and interests should be so completely unified by reference to a supreme and all-embrac-ing good that all action had the same character of completeness which is imperfectly illustrated by our enjoyment of a musical pattern; we can also imagine that nervous fatigue and its consequence, the necessity for the alternation between attention and remission of attention, were abolished. And in both cases, the method by which we succeed in imagining such a state of things is the legitimate, and often indispensable, one of "passing to the limit" of a series of which the law of formation is familiar and the initial terms known. If the limit were reached, experience as a whole would be a single enjoyment, at once completely centralised and steadily advancing; would it not thus have lost the elements of the no longer and the not yet? Would not "whole and complete life", really analogous to a "movement" in some great symphony, be the entrance into "the joy of the Lord", the real achievement of that complete and *simultaneous* fruition of a life without bounds of which Boethius spoke?[1] I think it would, and the further point I would make is that in the specific experience of the moral life we already have to do with endeavour which, from first to last, is directed upon the attainment of such a form of fruition, and yet, while it retains its specific character, can never finally reach its goal. If we are justified in treating our own existence and peculiar *So-sein* as moral beings as capable of throwing any light whatever on the character of the actual and real as a whole, we might then reasonably infer that we may argue, here as elsewhere, from the existence of a function to the reality of an environment in which the function can find adequate exercise. If the pursuit of temporal and secular good must inevitably fail to satisfy moral aspiration itself, we may fairly infer that there *is* a non-secular good to which moral endeavour is a growing response. In so far as such a good can be apprehended and enjoyed at all, temporality, with its antithesis of not yet and no longer, is itself progressively relegated to a secondary place in the life of enjoyment, time is actually swallowed up in eternity, the natural life in one which is, in the strict and proper sense of the word, supernatural, morality in religion. The conception of a realm of "grace" as transforming and completing the realm of "nature", so characteristic of Christianity, will then appear as suggested, and indeed necessitated, by the known facts of our moral being themselves.

Now, is secular good, obtainable under strictly temporal conditions, an object really adequate to

---

[1] I may be allowed to remind the reader of the great classic exposition of the thought in St. Augustine (*Confessions*, ix., x. 23-26, the scene at the window in Ostia).

evoke and to sustain this aspiration which gives the moral life its specific character as moral? In plain words, can a satisfactory morality be anything but what is sometimes called by way of disparagement an *other-worldly* morality? And if not, how precisely ought we to conceive the relation of the this-worldly to the other-worldly? In principle, I believe, the greatest moralists have always answered the first of these questions in one way. If there could be such a thing as a life of purely secular or temporal enjoyment, its special and characteristic feature as temporal would be precisely that its various goods or objects of aspiration *cannot* be had all together by anyone. They must be had one after another, on the condition that some are always not yet, and others no longer. This is the point of the familiar epigram already mentioned which describes a strictly worldly life as "one damned thing after another". (For reasons which will appear immediately, I make no apology for the vulgar, but really relevant epithet.) The delights of childhood, of youth, of mature manhood, of an honoured old age, are all good. Some of each class are among the best goods we know, but some must always be forfeited that others may be gained.

> All things are taken from us, and become
> Portions and parcels of the dreadful past;
>
> There's something comes to us in life,
> But more is taken quite away,

and utterances like these may not be the whole of the truth, but there is only too much bitter truth in them. We cannot have the ripe wisdom, assured judgement, and reflective serenity of maturity at its best without leaving behind the ardours and impetuosities and adventures of act which belong to youth, and these, again, you cannot have without losing much of the *naïf* wonder, the readiness to be delighted by little things, the divine thoughtlessness of childhood. All are good, yet none can be enjoyed except in the season of life appropriate to each, and the enjoyment is always tinged at once by regret for what has had to be given up and unsatisfied aspiration after what cannot yet be. One could not be happy, as the fable of Tithonus was devised to teach, in an immortality of elderliness, but one would be no less unsatisfied with an immortality of childhood, or youth, or mid-manhood. It would be as bad to be Peter Pan as it would be to be Tithonus, and even an unending prime would hardly be more desirable. To a deathless Olympian the sage might reasonably give the counsel of our own poet—

> The best is yet to be :
> Grow old along with me,

and, from the nature of the case, the counsel would be impossible to adopt.

We may say the same thing of the common, or social, good. In our generation it should be superfluous to insist that men as groups, or even humanity as a whole, always have to pay the price of temporal good won by the loss of temporal good. However much we gain in the way of good by what we call advance in civilisation, something which is also good has to be surrendered. Life is made more secure, but, in the course of becoming more secure, it loses its quality of adventure, and becomes tame and commonplace. Order is won, but at the cost of some real loss of individuality and initiative. International understanding and good feeling are promoted, but the "good European" has lost the passionate devotion to the *patria* which could inspire an

Athenian of the age of Pericles, or a Florentine of the age of Dante. Even those of us who, like myself, are keenly alive to the necessity and the duty of being "good Europeans" can hardly feel that the thought of Europe makes us, as the thought of England made Wordsworth's ideal warrior, "happy as a lover". Science "grows from more to more", and at each stage in the growth it becomes increasingly harder for the man who gives himself to the scientific life to be more than a specialist with a range of vision as lamentably contracted as the field of a powerful microscope. And so it is everywhere.

> We say that repose has fled
> For ever the course of the river of time,
> That cities will crowd to its edge
> In a blacker incessanter line,
> That the din will be more on its banks,
> Denser the trade on its stream,
> Flatter the plain where it flows,
> Fiercer the sun overhead.
> That never will those on its breast
> See an ennobling sight,
> Drink of the feeling of quiet again.

It is simply not the case that

> The old order changeth, giving place to new,
> And God fulfils Himself in many ways,

in the sense in which the words seem to have been understood when they were uttered. The new order does *not* simply take up into itself all that was good in the old and enrich it with further good, merely letting the bad slip away; it is won by the definite surrender of positive good, not by the mere elimination of defects, and the surrendered good is not reconquered. No doubt the vulgar epithet in the saying about life I have twice quoted is prompted by the sense that there is always this element of surrender clinging to every stage of

what we call progress. A more sentimental temperament reacts to the same situation by the development
of the *décadent* pessimism which tries to find the secret
of the goodness of the mutable in its very mutability—

> the very reason why
> I clasp them is because they die !

The logic here is, however, manifestly at fault. If the
summer's rose withers, so does the "stinking weed";
the worth of the perfume cannot really lie in that which
is common to it with the stench.

It might, of course, be said, that since all temporal
good is thus only "for a time", and it is not evident that
there is any good but that which is temporal, the reasonable attitude to life is that of the Epicurean; we should
live in the moment while it lasts, giving ourselves no
concern with what is beyond our immediate reach:
carpe diem, quam minimum credula postero. "Let us
enjoy the good things that are present, and let us
speedily use the creatures, like as in youth. Let us fill
ourselves with costly wines and ointments, and let no
flower of the spring pass us by." "Remove sorrow from
thy heart and put away evil from thy flesh, *for* childhood and youth are vanity."

> ὁ δαίμων, ὁ Διὸς παῖς . . .
> μισεῖ δ' ᾧ μὴ ταῦτα μέλει,
> κατὰ φάος νύκτας τε φίλας
> εὐαίωνα διαζῆν.[1]

But we only adopt such an attitude at the cost of a
breach with both morality and rationality, and since
men are, after all, moral and reasonable beings at heart,
"looking before and after", it is not surprising that the
Epicurean never is consistent. Lucretius may assert
in round words that, because we are merely ephemeral

---

[1] Euripides, *Bacchae*, 416 ff.

creatures, our concern is only with the moment, but he finds it necessary to preach on the text *nil igitur ad nos mors est* with a vehemence and at a length which shows that the sermon is delivered to himself as much as to Memmius. Horace never succeeds in disguising the fact that Lalage and the cask of Massic are the merest vain devices for concealing a "skeleton in the cupboard". A man, being a man, *must* "look before and after"; he cannot be really indifferent to the claims of the good that has to be left behind, or the lack of the good which is not yet to be had. Just in so far as he takes life seriously, his whole aim is to find and enjoy a good which is never left behind and never to be superseded. What his heart is set on is actually that simultaneous and complete fruition of a life without bounds of which Boethius speaks. As he grows more and more intelligent and moralises his life more and more completely, the nature of this underlying ethical purpose becomes increasingly apparent. As compared with the man who has no definite aim beyond getting the satisfaction of the moment, the man who has concern for what Butler calls his "interest in this world", even if that interest is taken to be limited to the securing of long life, health and comfort, has gone some way in the direction of overcoming the mere successiveness and temporality of incipient experience; the man who has learned to care for the well-being of a family or a house, still more the man who cares for the good of a wider, richer and more permanent community, or the man who cares first and foremost for the great so-called "impersonal" goods, art, science, morality, which can survive the extinction of a nation, an empire, a race, has proceeded further along the same road.

Yet it should be plain that even the last-named never really reaches the end of the road, if all he really achieves

can be adequately described in terms of mere successiveness and temporality. So long as there is wrong to be
put right, error and ugliness to be banished from life,
the individual or the community is still only on the
way to the possession of the heart's desire, and has not
yet entered on the enjoyment of the inheritance. The
best men often contrive to reconcile themselves to the
prospect of spending their life in the arduous effort to
make the pursuit of the unattained good a little less
difficult for their successors. It is enough for us, they
say, if those who are to come after us start on the pursuit at a point not quite so remote from the goal as
that where our own efforts began. But to make this
acquiescence seriously possible, it seems necessary to
forget that, in a human history dominated by the form
of successiveness, the result is still to leave every succeeding generation infinitely far from attainment.

The best type of Utilitarian, who makes his good in
practice of the removal of abuses, is a fine type of man, but
it is hard to think that human history as a whole could
have much value, or a human life much interest, if nothing
is ever achieved beyond the removal of abuses. If our
moral achievement always ends only in the attainment
of the slightly better, that of itself is proof that we never
attain the good. A good which is to give life all its value
cannot simply be a goal which lies ahead of us at every
step of our path and, in fact, recedes indefinitely as we
approach it. It must be something which is actually
being had in fruition through a present which does not
become past. And just in proportion as such abiding
fruition of good is a feature in our actual experience,
that experience is taking on a form which transcends
the moral, if by the moral we mean, as Kant, for example, did, the sphere where endeavour is always towards the simply future and unrealised, and the domi-

nant attitude is that of struggle. If human life, under the most favourable of circumstances, were a mere succession of increments of "betterment", it would be, in principle, a failure to achieve good; "meliorism" is only a foolish *alias* for pessimism.[1] If life is not a failure, then it cannot be an adequate account of the moral life to say that it is one of advance towards a future fruition which never becomes present. There must be another side to the facts. "A man's reach must exceed his grasp." Our experience must be something more than a progress in which the best we can say of every stage is only "not yet good, but rather better". There must be a sense in which we can be really in fruition, permanently established in a good beyond which there is no better. In the measure in which this can be truly said of any life, we may also say of that life that it is already shot through with the distinctive character of eternity and is an abiding *now*.

The distinctively ethical life, then, falls somewhere between these limits. It is not merely successive; if it were it would not even be a life of serious endeavour towards good. It is not simply a life of present and eternal fruition, from which succession and conflict have fallen away, for then it would be something more than ethical. In proportion to its moral worth, it is a life which is undergoing a steady elevation and transmutation from the mere successiveness of a simply animal existence to the whole and simultaneous fruition of all good which would be the eternity of the divine. As we rise in the moral scale, under the drawing of conceptions of good more and more adequate to sustain intelligent aspiration, living itself steadily takes on more and more a "form of eternity". For, in proportion to the level we have attained, each of our achieve-

[1] *Le meilleur est l'ennemi du bien*

ments becomes more and more the reaction of a personality at once richer and more unified to the solicitation of a good, itself presented as richer and more
thoroughly unified. As we rise in the moral scale, we
more and more cease to have many goods with rival
claims upon us, and come nearer to having one ever-
present good, just as—we have learned it long ago from
Socrates and Plato—we cease to exhibit a plurality of
virtues, or excellences, relatively independent of one
another, and come to display the "unity of virtue" in
every single act. He that is joined to the Lord is *one*
spirit.

Here we make a contact with the sphere of religion.
There is the closest correspondence between our character and the quality of the good to which we respond
in action. So long as we are moved to respond only to
goods which must be had one after another, our character itself must show a corresponding want of unity;
it must fall apart into phases and moods with no profound underlying unity. To the old Platonic question
whether the soul is one or many we can only reply, as
in effect Plato does, that it is as its desired good is. If
it has many goods, it is itself many, its personality is
loose-knit and incipient. It will only have a real, and
not a merely ideal, inner unity of personality when its
good is one and all-embracing, a real and living single
good which is the source of all goodness and leaves
nothing of the good outside itself. That is to say, unity
of personality and interest will only be attained, if at
all, by a soul which has come to find its principal good
in God. If God, the concrete unity of all good in its one
source, is not real, the complete unification of personality in ourselves, the very goal of all education of character and all moral effort, cannot be real either, and the
supreme purpose of the moral life will be a self-baffling

purpose. That "intrinsic goods", as they have been called, are an ultimate and irreducible plurality is just now something of a popular thesis with moralists, and there is great excuse for it as a salutary reaction against the view that all good is of some one kind.[1] But if the plurality is really ultimate, it should be an inevitable corollary that genuine moral personality is unattainable. Our growth, as we enrich our lives with more and more that is good, should be in the direction of multiplication and dissociation of the self. Such a view seems flatly at variance with the known facts of the moral life which fully bear out the familiar Socratic - Platonic contention that it is *bad* for character to exhibit the dexterity of the "quick-change *artiste*". It is only under the influence of the "pathetic fallacy" that we allow ourselves to think of the world as a stage "where every man must play a part"; to treat it as a stage where the best man is the man who has the widest repertory of different parts would be to invite practical shipwreck. In the world of life, to be "everything by turns and nothing long" is to be at the bottom, not at the top, of the ladder.

I conceive, in fact, that this doctrine of an ultimate irreducible plurality of goods would never have been maintained but for the prevalence of the logical error we have already had occasion to mention, the error of ignoring the reality of "analogical unity". Since it is clear that we can say of such very different things as bodily health, mental distinctions, self-forgetful virtue, that they are all good, it has been inferred, on one side, that the goodness we ascribe to them must be some one identical common quality, present alike in all of them, though in different degrees of "intensity", or with

[1] I am thinking, it will be seen, largely of the type of doctrine made popular by Prof. G. E. Moore's *Principia Ethica*.

some further specific *differentia* in each case, so that
the various goods form a plurality of irreducible, and
perhaps co-ordinate, species of a genus *good*. This assumption is easily shattered by criticism, and the critic
is thus prone to suppose that he has shown that *good*
has no unity *at all*, and must be a merely equivocal
term. Both positions rest on the uncriticised assumption
that predication must either be universal, as when I
call both rodents and ruminants mammals, or merely
equivocal, as when I call the domestic animal and the
constellation both by the name "dog". In the first case,
the rodents and the ruminants have in common not only
a name, but a group of characters which the name indicates. Both are, for example, vertebrates, red-blooded,
four-limbed. In the second, the household animal and
the constellation have nothing in common but the name,
and that they have even this in common is due to a
mere historical accident. Now, these alternatives are
not exhaustive, as we might all have learned from
Aristotle, if we had not been blinded by bad nominalistic traditions to the force of his doctrine of analogical
predication. Virtue and health are both called good, not
because they have a core of identical "common characters", further specially determined in each case, but
because virtue is *related* to one term x_1 in the same way
as health to a different term x_2. Virtue is the efficient
living of the social and intelligent life, just as health
is the efficient discharge of physiological function.
There need be no further correspondence in character
between social function and physiological function to
make the ascription of goodness in both cases highly
significant. In fact we see that the very qualities which
justify us in calling one thing good may equally provide the justification for calling a second bad, and,
again, may be wholly irrelevant to the goodness or

badness of a third. A good knife must be sharp, but a good poker blunt, a good mattress must be hard, a good pillow soft.

And yet the various goods of life are not simply a collection or aggregate; they form a hierarchy. What at one stage of mental and moral development seems complete satisfaction[1] of aspiration sinks, for the man who is living at a higher level, to the position of a mere pre-condition of getting satisfaction it cannot itself provide, or may become indifferent, or even a positive hindrance. At the highest attainable levels of human personal activity what we find in the moral heroes of our race is not diffusion of attention and endeavour over a vast multiplicity of radically incongruous objects of aspiration, but an intensely unified and concentrated endeavour towards a unified good. Ends not capable of finding their place in this unity have sunk to the level of mere pre-conditions, or of things which may, or perhaps must, be dispensed with, though at a lower and less human level any one of them may have been, in its time, a temporary substitute for the actual *summum bonum*. Mere dispersion is the characteristic moral condition of the amateur in living, as mere concentration on the partial is that of the fanatic. This is why I cannot but feel that, when all is said,

---

[1] May I take the opportunity of explaining that by using the notion of "satisfaction" I do not mean to suggest that everything which is actually desired by anyone is good, and good *because* he desires it. I know only too well that most of our desires are *vain* desires, desires for that which will *not* satisfy. When I speak of the good as the "satisfactory", I mean that it is that which contents men who are what they *ought* to be, and will content me when I am what I ought to be. (This is my reply to the old criticism of Professor G. E. Moore, who accused me (*Principia Ethica*, p. 160) of the "vulgar mistake" which he has taught us to call the "naturalistic fallacy". Unless Prof. Moore would regard it as "fallacy" to deny the unsupported allegation that there is no connection between "existence" and "value", I think I may confidently plead not guilty to the accusation, though I own I should have expressed myself more carefully if I had anticipated the misinterpretation. I am not anxious to defend a passage written thirty years ago, but the whole purpose of the argument of which Prof. Moore quotes a part was to *deny* that to enjoy and to approve are the same thing.)

the life of a man like Goethe, with its manifold but imperfectly co-ordinated and hierarchised responses to so many of the aspects of the total human environment, must be pronounced second-rate by comparison with the life of a man like Socrates. It is not only the specifically saintly man who can truly say of himself "*One* thing have I desired of the Lord".

It is clear that the implications of this tendency to unity and concentration of aim are double, according as we fix our attention on the character of the good aspired to, or on the aspiration itself. On the one hand, full achievement of the aspiration which lies behind all moral advance is only possible if there really is a good by the quest and attainment of which human endeavour will be finally unified and made single of aim. The moral quest will be self-defeating unless there is an object to sustain it which embodies in itself good complete and whole, so that in having it we are possessing that which absolutely satisfies the heart's desire and can never be taken from us. The possession must be possession of a "thing infinite and eternal", and this points to the actuality of God, the absolute and final good, as indispensably necessary if the whole moral effort of mankind is not to be doomed *ab initio* to frustration. On the other hand, if the effort is to reach its goal, the *possession* of the supreme good on our part must also be itself final; we must be able to look forward to having the infinite good, and to having it in perpetuity. But in such a fruition our own being would have been lifted above the level of successiveness; we should ourselves have passed from temporality to eternity, and the life we know as characteristic of morality, the life of effort, struggle, defeat and renewed endeavour, would have been transfigured into one of rest and enjoyment.

Thus morality itself seems to imply, as a condition of being something more than a mere crying for the moon, an eternal destiny for the human person, and so far as life becomes an endeavour to adjust the self to such a destiny, it would be ceasing to be merely ethical and taking on a specifically religious character. It would become our moral duty, and our highest moral duty, to aim at being something more than merely good neighbours and loyal citizens of the State.

This statement must, of course, not be misinterpreted. To say that a life which aims at nothing *more* than being a good moral life is itself morally defective is not to say that we can be content with less than this. I suppose there is no moralist of the first order who has not preached the supreme duty of cultivating a right detachment from the best and dearest of temporal goods. Even family affections, the "dear love of comrades", or selfless devotion to the cause of our class or our country, become snares, if we elevate family, friends, class, or country into goods to which all and every consideration must be sacrificed. From the point of view of religion this is to make them into "idols"; from the most strictly ethical point of view there are always things we must not do, even for the sake of wife and son, friend or country. I may lay down my life for my friend or my country; I shall not, if I am a truly virtuous man, think myself free to serve my friend by a perjury, or my country by an assassination. The mere admission that there are such limits to all temporal loyalties is a confession that no object of such loyalties is the supreme and final good. But this is not to say that these loyalties are not, in their place, imperative. There is no moral right to set a limit to loyalty to good, except on the ground that the limit is demanded by loyalty to better good. And thus the true detachment is not cultivated by simply turning our backs on secular good and temporal duties, but by service and fulfilment, always with the condition that we make the discharge of the duty and the enjoyment of the good instrumental to the attainment of the non-temporal highest good of all, that we serve and enjoy temporal good without losing our hearts to it. Half this lesson is well and wisely preached by T. H. Green, when he ends his *Introduction to Hume* [1] with the warning not to despise Hume's doctrine because of the secular character of the morality recommended by that philosopher, since "there is no other genuine enthusiasm of humanity" than one which has travelled the common highway of reason—the life of the good citizen and honest neighbour—and can never forget that it is still only "a further stage of the same journey". The other and equally indispensable side of the same truth is that the moral aim of humanity always is to be something more than a mere good citizen and honest neighbour, and that the man who has seen no glimpses of the way beyond is not likely even to get as far on the way as thorough good citizenship and honest neighbourliness. Indeed, the metaphor of the journey, as Green uses it, is not quite adequate, for the true business of man is not to pursue the temporal good first and the non-temporal afterwards, but, as Green would, no doubt, have agreed, to pursue both at once and all through his life, to be something more than citizen and neighbour in the act of being both, and to be both all the more efficiently that he is all the time aiming at the something more. It is just this impossibility of really making the right service of temporal good and the

---

[1] T. H. Green, *Works*, i. 371.

right detachment from it fall apart into two successive stages of a journey which, more than anything else, makes worthy moral living the hard thing it is, and, by making it hard, saves it from degenerating into a mere routine and gives it something of the character of perennial adventure.[1]

A few final words on a difficulty of fundamental principle. It may be said that life itself can only be thought of as a process of *never* completed "adjustment of organism to environment". If the adjustment were ever complete and no new readjustment ever demanded by variation of the environment, would not life cease automatically? Without the impulsion supplied by the pain or discomfort due to disturbance of adjustment, and the support of the effort towards better adjustment by attendant pleasure, what would there be to keep life, or at any rate conscious life, going? The thought is one which has been often expressed, but never better than by Hobbes in the

---

[1] I do not deny that there may be, for some persons, a vocation and a duty to renounce temporal good which it may equally be a duty for others to use. I am not denying, for example, that it may be right for some persons to give themselves to lifelong celibacy and poverty, though I am sure that such persons are a minority. What I do mean can be illustrated by a simple example. Suppose a man feels in early life a strong attraction to the life of a religious order, I should say that the attraction, however strong it is, is not of itself sufficient proof of "vocation". Before a man decides that it is his duty to follow it, he ought most earnestly to consider whether his action may not be a disguised shirking of moral obligations which no one is at liberty to disregard. If he has parents who are likely in their old age to need support and tendance which there is no one but himself to supply, he cannot ask himself too seriously whether *for him* the adoption of the so-called "religious life" may not be no more than the making void of the commandment to honour father and mother. This need not be so, of course; but there is always the danger of self-deception on the point. It is true that Christ calls on men "to leave father and mother", if need be, for His sake. But one needs to be quite clear that, in one's own case, the act really is done *for His sake*, not as a yielding to the tendency to do what demands the minimum of effort. The "conventual life", I should say, is all the more likely to be a man's real vocation if he does not find the prospect of it too attractive to "flesh and blood". Cf. the sober judgement of St. Thomas (*S.T.* ii.ª ii.ªᵉ q. 101, art. 4 ad 4ᵗᵘᵐ) that—contrary to the opinion of certain persons—to enter a monastery, leaving one's parents without proper support, is to "tempt God", *cum habens ex humano consilio quid ageret, periculo parentes exponeret sub spe divini auxilii*).

famous words in which he denies the very possibility
of a *summum bonum*. "Nor can a man any more live,
whose Desires are at an end, than he whose Senses
and Imagination are at a stand".[1] The obvious inference would be that the "eternity" of which we have
spoken is only another name for nothing. Everything
is "becoming"; nothing is "being"; things are always
in the making, nothing is ever finally made. What have
we to say to this highly popular way of thinking?

All I need say at the present point is that the reasoning rests on a grave *petitio principii* long ago exposed by
Aristotle in the *Nicomachean Ethics*.[2] Aristotle, it may
be remembered, has there to consider the bearing of a
similar theory on the question of the worth of pleasure. It was an argument of the anti-Hedonists in the
Platonic Academy that pleasure cannot be "the good",
because pleasures arise always and only in connection
with γενέσεις, processes of *transition*. We feel pleasure,
it was said, whenever the organism is in process of recovery from a preceding disturbance of its normal vital
equilibrium; when the equilibrium has been re-estab-
lished, the pleasure drops. We feel it, then, not when we
are, physically, "at our best", but only while we are
getting back towards our "best" from a condition in
which we are "not ourselves". This thesis was then
generalised into the statement that what we enjoy is
never *fruition*, but always *movement* towards a still
unreached fruition. When good is actually attained, full
enjoyment ceases. Though the argument was originally
meant only to prove that feelings of pleasure are not
"the good", it can obviously be used equally to support
the view that *life* itself, in any sense of the word in
which life has value and interest for us, is incompatible with full fruition, "man never is, but always to be,

[1] *Leviathan*, c. 11.   [2] *E.N.* 1158 a, 7 ff.

blest". Aristotle counters the argument, as you may recollect, by insisting on the radical difference between "becoming" (γένεσις), the process by which "adjustment to environment" is effected, and "activity" (ἐνέργεια), the exercise of a fully formed function, and actually maintains that, even in such cases as the enjoyment of appeasing felt hunger—the very cases which might seem to give the strongest support to the theory he is rejecting—the facts have been misread. Even in these cases, he urges, what directly occasions pleasure and is enjoyed is not the "recovery" from disturbance of the organic equilibrium, but the underlying discharge of function, which has not been inhibited or disturbed. He means that, for example, the "gusto" with which the hungry man relishes his meal is only indirectly dependent on previous "depletion". It is, strictly and directly, simply enjoyment of the normal vital functioning, which has persisted unimpaired all through, though masked by the superimposed special local inhibition of hunger.[1] Hence, on Aristotle's own theory, the connection between enjoyment and processes of transition to more satisfactory "adjustment" is incidental and indirect; such transitions are only attended by enjoyment because they involve the gradual removal of an inhibition. An activity, a vigorously discharged functioning, with no inhibition to be overcome, would be much more enjoyed. This is why Aristotle speaks of the life of God, a life liable to no inhibitions of function and never involving improved "adjustments", and thus including no experience of "transition", as the supreme example of enjoyment absolute and unbroken (χαίρει ἀεὶ μίαν καὶ ἁπλῆν ἡδονήν, he says, whereas our human pleasures are never pleasures unmixed[2]). As psychologists know, there is no theory of the conditions of pleasure-pain

---

[1] *E.N.* 1157 b, 35.   [2] *Ib.* 1154 b, 26.

which does not encounter grave difficulties,[1] but the
Aristotelian type of theory, which connects pleasure,
and enjoyment generally, with unimpeded functioning,
or activity (ἐνέργεια ἀνεμπόδιστος), seems, at any rate,
to be attended with fewer difficulties than any other,
and may prove to be absolutely right. (The only serious
difficulty I feel about it myself is that it is hard to say
what "unimpeded activity" we can suppose to account
for the intense enjoyment of "sweets" which seems to
be generally characteristic of palates not artificially
schooled. And, for anything I, who am a layman in
such matters, know, the *physiologists* may have discovered, or may yet discover, a complete answer to the
question.) If the Aristotelian theory of enjoyment should
be the true one, it would follow that enjoyment is not
bound up with "becoming";[2] Spinoza's assertion—
wholly inconsistent, by the way, with his own famous
doctrine of the intellectual love wherewith God loves
Himself—that we can enjoy nothing but becoming,
"*transition* to greater activity", will become simply
false.[3] The transcendence of the form of successiveness
involved in fruition of the good simple and eternal will
be also entrance upon the one experience which would
be, through and through, "pure delight". "They do
rest from their *labours* and their *works* follow them"
will be neither more nor less than the literal truth.

---

[1] See the discussion in Stout, *Analytic Psychology*, ii. pp. 268 ff.
[2] Cf. Stout, *Manual of Psychology*[4], p. 118.
[3] *Ethica*, iii. *ad fin.* Affectuum definitiones, 3. Si enim homo cum perfectione
ad quam transit nasceretur, eiusdem absque laetitiae affectu compos esset. (Cf.
iii. 11 *schol.* per laetitiam . . . intelligam passionem qua mens ad maiorem
perfectionem transit.) It might be urged that the definition is expressly given as
that of *laetitia* as a *passio*, and should not therefore be extended to cover the
"active" *laetitia* of iii. 58 and later propositions. But it should be observed that
in iii. 58 itself the *existence* of this "active" *laetitia* is inferred from iii. 53, and
that the proof of iii. 53 depends immediately on the definition in question.

SUPPLEMENTARY NOTE TO III

DR. McTAGGART'S DOCTRINE OF TIME

As has been already explained the references in the preceding pages to McTaggart's views were written before the publication of the posthumous part ii. of *The Nature of Existence*; (the essay of 1908, referred to in that volume (p. 23, n. 1) as expounding McTaggart's doctrine, much in its final stage, I had no doubt read at the time of its appearance, but not subsequently). It is therefore necessary to consider how far the comments of the text are affected by the full publication of McTaggart's view.

I admit at once that the position adopted throughout the post-humous volume is more in accord with what seem to me to be the implications of a sound religion and morality than that commonly favoured by idealists who pronounce time "unreal". For McTaggart holds strongly that, though time is itself "unreal", it is not a *mere* illusion. There is a real ordered series (the *C-series* as McTaggart calls it) of which the temporal order is a "mis-perception"; evil also is a reality. And McTaggart believes himself able to show further that the "*C*-series" has a sense corresponding to the temporal direction from past to future, and a "last term". This last term is a state of personal existence from which all evil, except the "sympathetic pain" arising from awareness of the evil which has preceded in "pre-final stages", has disappeared. (*Op. cit.* c. 65, p. 431.) Moreover, though this "final stage", when attained, is experienced as non-temporal, it inevitably appears from outside itself as something yet to be attained in the future, and as duration which has a beginning, but not an end. Hence, as against the usual versions of Spinozist and Hegelian doctrine, the Christian conceptions of the blessed hereafter are the truer; the Christian conception of Heaven is as nearly true as it is possible for any conception of the "final stage" on the part of persons who are not enjoying it to be, whereas the rival view—that the universe, in its "pre-final stages", is, and can be seen to be, perfectly good—is false, and makes ethics unmeaning. Christians, in fact, have been right all along, only that they are bad metaphysicians, and therefore cannot see why they are right. (*Op. cit.* c. 61, pp. 367-371.)

It will be seen that McTaggart thus concedes a great deal of what is contended for in the present volume. But there are important reserves which indicate that his position is by no means so "Christian" as he supposed it to be. Thus (*op. cit.* p. 432) we find the love of God specified, by the side of the pleasure of swimming, as a good which may exist in any of the "pre-final stages", but must disappear in the final; God can be loved everywhere *except* "in Heaven". (This is because, according to McTaggart, belief in the existence of God is an error, just as belief in the existence of water is an error. In the "final stage" there are no errors left. Consequently, in that stage, no one believes in the existence either of God or of water, and therefore no one can enjoy either swimming or loving God.) Since Christianity is not the only considerable religion which makes the *essentia* of the joy of Heaven to consist in the vision and love of God, McTaggart clearly overrates the support religion can give to his conceptions.

Now I think it not difficult to see that the divergence between McTaggart's anticipations for mankind and those of the greater ethical religions is determined in advance by his general attitude towards Time. On McTaggart's view, successiveness is itself an illusion, though an inevitable one. The illusion arises from "misperceiving" as successiveness what is really a logical relation of inclusion between the consequent terms of the "*C*-series" and their antecedents. (See *op. cit.* c. 60.) It follows that each of us is really an "eternal" being, in his own right, though it is only in the "final stage" that he becomes fully aware of his own eternity. There is no difference in reality, in this respect, between any one person and any other, and therefore, in McTaggart's scheme, there can be no God, no one who is *the* "eternal" being "who only has immortality". In the great ethical religions, on the other hand, the distinction between *the* one strictly eternal being and all others is fundamental, however we express it, and consequently it is fundamental that "passage" should be a real characteristic of the "creature". Successiveness, therefore, cannot be a mere "misperception" of a logical relation; it must be something inherently real in the constitution of the "creature", like "unactualised potentiality" in the philosophy of St. Thomas. This makes it desirable to re-examine McTaggart's final statement of his reasons for pronouncing Time "unreal". We need to do this carefully, all the more because McTaggart holds (p. 4) that whereas the positive results of the volume are only highly probable, the negative conclusions are demonstrated.[1]

---

[1] I think myself that this is an exaggerated confidence. Negative conclusions based on the incompatibility of a proposition with the principle of "Determining Correspondence" explained in vol. i. do not appear to me demonstrated, since—though I cannot argue the point here—I believe it can be shown that there can be no such relation as that described by McTaggart. The reasons alleged for regarding Time as "unreal" (*op. cit.* c. 33), however, are entirely independent of the theory of "Determining Correspondence", and thus might be demonstrative, even if that theory prove false or insignificant. Proof that there is no such relation would thus be fatal to McTaggart's reasons for holding that whatever is real is a self, or a part of a self, but would not affect his proofs that there is really no time.

McTaggart begins by distinguishing carefully between the distinctions *earlier-later* and *past-present-future*. A set of terms related only as earlier-later forms what he calls a *B*-series; terms related as *past-present-future* form an *A-series*. Time, if there is Time, requires the reality of both *A*- and *B*-series, and of the two the *A*-series (past, present, future) is the more important. On these points, as will have been seen, I am in full agreement with him. From these premises McTaggart develops a *reductio ad impossibile*. If there really is a temporal series, its generating relation cannot be simply *before-after*; it must be an *A*-series. An *A*-series is inherently self-contradictory and so impossible. The proof of the minor is sought in the ancient ἀπορίαι connected with the notion of *change*. This is the general character of the argument; we must now examine it rather more in detail.

As its author presents it, the argument consists of two stages: (1) There cannot be time without an *A*-series; a *B*-series by itself would not be sufficient to constitute Time. (2) And there cannot be an *A*-series. *Ergo.*

(1) is proved as follows. There could be no Time if nothing changed.[1] But if there is no past, present or future, nothing changes. The "earlier" and "later" events of a *B*-series always have been, are, and always will be, in precisely the same unchanging relations of priority and posteriority to one another. Each term in the series "from the dawn of time", as we say, to its close (if it has a close), occupies just one and the same position in the series. Change can mean only one thing, that a certain term in the *B*-series is differently determined by the terms of the *A*-series. *E.g.* the death of Queen Anne was once in the remote future, then in the near future, then in the present, then in the near past, and it is still becoming more and more remotely past. We conclude, then, that the *B*-series alone, if it exists, must be temporal, since its generating relation, before-after, is temporal, but it is not enough to constitute time, since it does not contain the sufficient conditions of change, which are to be found in the *A*-series.[2] This establishes our first proposition.[3]

(2) The second is established by considering what the generating relation of an *A*-series would have to be. In the first place, it must be a relation to some term which itself is not a member of the series, since, "the relations of the *A*-series (past, present, future) are

---

[1] McTaggart adds that, if anything changes, everything else changes with it, since the relations of every other thing to the changing thing are in some way modified by the change. But this further contention is irrelevant to the immediate argument.

[2] *Op. cit.* p. 13.

[3] In order to state the argument succinctly, I pass over here some five pages of polemic, directed merely against Mr. Russell.

changing relations", but the relation of a term of the series itself to other terms of it is unchanging. The A-series would thus be defined by the fact that each of its terms has, to an X which is not a term of the series, one, and only one, of the three relations of being past, being present, being future. All the terms of the A-series which have to X the relation of being present fall between all those which have to X the relation of being past, and all those which have to X the relation of being future. And it seems not easy to identify any term which fulfils the conditions thus required of X. But the still more fatal difficulty, the difficulty which forbids us to assume that there may be an X with which we are unacquainted, and which plays the required part, is that the characteristics of being past, being present, being future, are incompatible, and that *every* term of an A-series would have to possess them all. All of them are successively in the future, in the present, in the past. The only exceptions would be for the first and last terms of the series, if it is held that it has such terms. And even they would need to have at once two incompatible determinations. If there ever was a first event, or first moment of time, it was once present, and is past; if there can be a last, it is future, and will some day be present. To put it crudely, the present event is distinguished from past and future events by being at the present moment, but presentness is a characteristic of *every* moment. To try to distinguish *this* moment from any other by saying that it is the *present* "present moment" lands us at once in a "vicious infinite regress". An A-series is thus intrinsically impossible, and therefore temporality is an illusion.[1]

Now with some part of this criticism, as I have said, I should myself agree. I agree with McTaggart that Time cannot be reduced to a mere relation of before and after, the mere ghost of time. If our experience could be reduced to a "knife-edge", from which the relation *before-after* were merely absent, I agree that the very word "time" would be meaningless, because we should have no acquaintance with succession, and also, I should add, an experience of before and after in which the before did not fade into the past, nor the after "emerge" into presentness, would not be what we mean by "experienced" or "lived" time. There would indeed be successiveness within the content experienced, but not within the experiencer. We should be looking on at something we could call the "history" of the world around us, but *we* should have no history of our own. And I think I should further agree that McTaggart is right in saying that the determination of the terms of his A-series can only be effected by relation to an X which is not itself a member of the series. But with this my agreement ceases.

----

[1] *Op. cit.* pp. 19-22.

I think it possible to say what this all-important X is; it is the living, percipient, finite subject of experience. The *now* present, or "present" present, is whatever enters as a constituent into *my* act. I do not pronounce it actual because it is determined as present, but present because it is actual. It is the distinction between "act" and "potentiality" which must be taken as fundamental, and as the source of the temporality of our human experience.

What is more, if I were all "act", without any unrealised potentiality, I might observe a succession in things around me, but the succession would fall entirely within a "present". I could then say of myself, "Before Abraham was, I am". The secret of the puzzle which McTaggart goes on to develop is precisely that I do not merely *observe* the successiveness of events; my own being is immersed in successiveness. I am a γιγνόμενον, but a γιγνόμενον conscious that the end to which I aspire is γίγνεσθαι εἰς οὐσίαν. This, as I see the matter, is just the fundamental "surd" or "irrationality" involved in the existence of beings with a real history. That it cannot be "rationalised" away, that is, cannot be analysed into a complex of "clear and distinct ideas", is not, as McTaggart seems to suppose, a proof that successiveness is an illusion. On the contrary, it is *the* proof that the historical world of individuals is not a methodical fiction but a genuine fact. The contradiction McTaggart finds in the fact that what *was* present becomes past, and what *was* future present, would exist if the X by relation to which these distinctions are made were itself something all "act", without any "potentiality", but the X is myself, and I am not *actus purus*. All that McTaggart really proves is that if I were the suprahistorical God, there would be no past or future for me, because there would be none in me.

I conceive that it may be objected that the distinction between potentiality and act cannot be the foundation of the threefold distinction, past, present, future. It might serve to distinguish present from not-present, but how is it to distinguish past from future within the not-present, since the actual becomes potential, no less than the potential actual? May we not reply that this is never a complete account of the matter? The actual which is reduced to potentiality is not reduced to the same potentiality which was there before the actuality. We say that a very old man has fallen back into a "second childhood", but the "second" childhood is not an identical recurrence of the former. It is a "potentiality" with a difference. And the growing domination of physics by the "principle of Carnot" seems to show that, on a closer view, nothing in the history of the universe ever repeats itself identically. At most there are partial imperfect repetitions which may be treated as identical recurrences, relatively to some particular human purpose.

The traces of the past are really ineffaceable, and it is fully compatible with such indeterminacy as is requisite for morality that they should be so. Saul's past neither constrains him to disobey the heavenly vision, nor forces him to obey it. But whether he disobeys or obeys, in neither case will he be the same character he would have been if he had not been a party to the death of Stephen. The act may "make him a worse man", or a better; what in any case is false, is that "it will make no difference".

I should take objection to the whole conception of Time as we are familiar with it in our experience as being an "A-series" of momentary events which are successively present, as I should to the conception of change as some kind of "relation" between an event M and another event N, upon which McTaggart's whole chapter is founded. Change, I should say, is not a relation between one experienced event and another; the change *is* the event, and I hold that we have a direct and "irrationalisable" experience of change itself. We do not "experience M", then "experience N", and infer that there has been a change; "M changing into N" is a formula which is the first attempt at rationalising a refractory experience which is *sui generis*. (M persisting as M is itself one form of this experience.) "Becoming" is falsified by the attempt to rationalise it into a string of tiny atoms of "being"; it is *not* "being misperceived", and therefore the attempt to find the reality of it in a purely logical relation, made by McTaggart, is wrong in principle. That becoming is not being, and yet is not an illusion, any more than being is, is, in fact, the consideration which seems to me fatal to every form of "panlogism" in philosophy, and if the rejection of panlogism is what is meant by "irrationalism", I suppose I must be content to accept the name of irrationalist.

It may be said that, by this account, it follows that each of us has his own individual "personal" Time. I should admit this, and frankly concede that a "universal" Time is an impossibility, and a "common Time" a makeshift, devised for specific necessary purposes, like a common creed, or a common party programme. The "lived" Time of each of us is a "perspective" peculiar to himself; but the point I want to insist on here is that it is a perspective of a becoming, not of a stable being. That is to say, with Whitehead, and against McTaggart, I want to make a real distinction between the super-individual fact, "passage", or "becoming", and its "measure". McTaggart's arguments are formally directed to disproving the existence of the measure; what he really needs to do, if Time is to be made a "misperception" of a series generated by a purely logical relation, is to disprove the reality of "passage" itself. And that "passage" is real each of us is a living proof to himself, since he also "passes".

IV

FURTHER SPECIFICATION OF THE GOOD
NATURE AND SUPERNATURE

More! More! is the cry of a mistaken soul; less than all cannot satisfy Man.
                                                                 BLAKE.

WE have so far tried to find the inmost meaning of the
moral life of man by regarding it as an endeavour towards an eternal good made by a creature who, in so
far as he achieves the end of his endeavour, achieves
also a derivative, or communicated, eternity. The point
on which I propose now to lay stress is precisely the
communicated or derived character of the eternity thus
attainable by man. As I read the story of the "ascent"
of humanity, it is throughout a tale of the ways by
which a creature who, being a creature, starts at a level
of mere secularity or successiveness, advances towards
an "eternal state", in proportion to, and in consequence
of, the eternity of the contemplated good which all
along inspires all specifically human endeavour. In
other words, though the goal of human aspirations
would lie beyond the bounds of the historical, the advance to it is strictly *historical*, and the reality of the
advance implies the reality of *time*, the formal character
of the historical. Any metaphysical theory or theological speculation which reduces time, in the end, to
the status of an illusion must falsify our whole conception of the moral life, and, if seriously acted on, taint
our moral practice itself with insincerity and superfici-

ality. Any metaphysic and any religion for which the moral life provides inspiration must hold fast to two positions which it is difficult, but absolutely vital, to keep together in one "synoptic" view: (1) that time as we know it in our personal life—not the ghost of it we retain in our kinematics—is truly real, is, in fact, we might say, the very stuff *out of* which our life has to be made, though only the *stuff*; (2) that we only make a genuine human life out of this stuff in proportion as we transcend it, as a "more eminent" form is superinduced upon it. Temporality is there just to be overstepped.

> Man hath all that Nature hath, but *more*,
> And in that more lie all his hopes of good.

It will be seen, then, that on such a view there will be two antithetical false conceptions against both of which the natural religion and theology of a moralist will have to be in perpetual protest. One of these views is that which we may follow general usage in calling "naturalism", or "secularism", the theory which treats the form of temporality not merely as real, but as so deeply ingrained in all our experience that it is hopeless to dream of getting beyond it. From this point of view our whole conception of the moral life of man as a re-generation and re-making of the self in the likeness of a contemplated eternal good would have no meaning whatever. The only good for man would be a purely "creaturely", or temporal, or this-world good; what in his more exalted moments he takes to be his pilgrim-age to a land of promise would be only a roaming in a wilderness where he is destined to lay his bones. The generation of Israelites who fell in the desert would be the type of all the generations of men, with this difference, that there would be no Joshua nor Caleb in the host of adventurers who have gone out of the spiritual Egypt.

Of this type of view I have already said all that it seems in principle needful to say. I would only add now that its most plausible defenders seem usually to evade the surely imperative task of showing how it can be made to agree with the notorious facts of human moral inspiration. A recent eminent precursor of my own in the tenure of this lecture told us repeatedly that his own position was naturalistic "enthusiastically" and "to the core". But I observed that in the published volumes dedicated to the exposition of the position, though there was much patient and valuable discussion of the satisfactoriness of the scheme in biology and comparative psychology, the confrontation of it with the recorded moral and spiritual *history* of man was, to say nothing worse of it, perfunctory. And I note that, in the very last paragraphs of that work, the mere "ephemerality" of humanity is set over against the abidingness of God, apparently in fixed and final antithesis. "In our passing life we touch the fringe of immortality, when we acknowledge God as ultimate substance."[1] No doubt; but the question is whether nothing is permitted to me but a touching of the fringe. Can Moses not "enter into the cloud" and remain there? Is the promise *Io ti farò veder ogni valore*[2] kept to the ear and broken to the hope? Do we only touch the hem of the garment in our most favoured moments, or can we be grafted into the wine-stock and live with the life of the vine of eternity? *Sentimus experimurque nos aeternos esse*, "we perceive and know of a truth that *we* are eternal".[3] The words are those of Dr. Lloyd Morgan's favourite philosopher; are they only words with no substance? We may fairly expect the preachers

[1] C. Lloyd Morgan, *Life, Mind and Spirit*, p. 313.
[2] Dante, *Paradiso*, xxvi. 42.
[3] Spinoza, *Ethica*, v. 23, Scholium.

of naturalism to know and speak their minds on the issue.

The other type of view against which the serious moralist is, as it seems to me, equally bound to register his protest, needs more special consideration, because of the attraction it has always had for just those thinkers who have been most alive to the eternity of the good to which man aspires. It is the view which, in one way or another, contrives to reduce the temporal in the moral life to the position of an illusion by treating eternity as a character which inheres in man from the first, so to say, in his own right, not derivatively. This is the conception which appears in all those philosophies and religions which treat the human soul as a "fallen" divinity whose task is to recover its original place among the rest of the "gods". We find the religious expression of it, for example, in the well-known verses inscribed on tablets discovered in the graves of Orphic sectaries in Italy and Crete, where the soul of the deceased recites its celestial pedigree and claims, as of right, to take its place in the heavenly home to which it has found its way back,[1] and, again, in many of the gorgeous fragments of Pindar in which the same theme is elaborated. The appeal of the Pythagorean preaching of "transmigration"—in itself a mere naturalistic speculation about the kinship of man with lower animals— to souls really touched to fine moral issues, has also always been based on a further conflation of this inherently non-ethical belief with the Orphic conception of the fallen god who makes his way back to his first estate by slowly ascending the stages of the hierarchy of lives, from mollusc to man, and from humanity back again to divinity. In our own days we meet the same

---

[1] See the texts as given by O. Kern, *Orphicorum Fragmenta*, as fr. 32 (pp. 104-109).

idea among all the confusions and incoherencies of what calls itself theosophy, and, in more reasoned form, in the various metaphysical systems of those thinkers who, like Dr. McTaggart, resolve the universe into a vast collection of persons, all equally "unoriginate" and equally endowed with native eternity. Not all these various forms of belief openly and avowedly treat time as a mere illusion. But all, I venture to say, make an assumption which should lead in consistency to that position. They all abolish any real distinction of status between divinity and humanity. According to all of them, we, who suppose ourselves to be men, are really all along gods. There is no question of our becoming something which we are not "by nature"; our whole history is only the story of our coming back to a status which we had in the beginning, or even of the discovery that we have, and have always had, the status. Thus there is no real progress in the spiritual life of man; it is a mere climbing back up a ladder from the top of which we have fallen, or, perhaps, a waking from a mere dream of having fallen.[1]

One would be loth to speak hardly of any creed which has had at least the merit of fixing men's minds on the mark of a very high calling; yet I think it must be clear that all views of this kind, by making advance, at bottom, an illusion, must, if one is in earnest

---

[1] In the philosophical literature of the world this type of view finds its most perfect expression in the neo-Platonic version of the fall and descent of the soul as set forth by Plotinus. According to him, as his latest editor puts it (Plotinus, *Enneads*, iv. ed. Bréhier, p. 215), "our salvation is not to be achieved, it has been eternally achieved, since it is part of the order of things. Passion, suffering, sin, have never touched more than the lower part of the soul". Christianity, too, as traditionally presented, has its doctrine of the "fall". But then the "fall" is a *real* one which affects the soul to its centre and needs to be repaired by a *real* "work of grace". It is no service to the understanding either of Christianity or of Plotinus to obscure the point that neither sin nor grace, as conceived by Christians, has any place in a consistent neo-Platonism. In Plato himself there is no obscuring of the distinction between humanity and deity, and, perhaps for that reason, he contemplates a possibility of real "damnation" for the "wholly incurable".

with them, gravely impair the seriousness of our moral striving. The very reason why endeavour is so serious is that it is endeavour to become what we have *never* been, to rise above and out of our very selves. If we are really ourselves divine, and have been so from the first, it seems fairly obvious that we need not take the moral struggle so tremendously in earnest; we may surely trust nature to reassert herself in the long run, *expellas furca, tamen usque recurret*. Whether we run in the race with our might, like men contending for masteries, or saunter along the track, we may fairly count on reaching the goal sooner or later. At most all we can effect by taking life so hard is to get a little sooner where all of us are bound to get in the end, and it might be argued that since we are sure of reaching our destination, there is no need for hurry; we can all well afford to loiter, as we are all prone to do, among the flowery meadows on the way. Thus the doctrine of the native and original divinity of the soul, though it begins by an apparent complete break with naturalism, seems, when duly thought out, to lead to a naturalistic morality. It is perhaps signifi-cant that "theosophists" are notoriously hostile to the missionary effort to substitute practice of the Christian rule of life for rules based on puerile or lewd nature-worships, and, again, that Dr. McTaggart should once have come perilously near the suggestion that since we are all bound to reach "perfection" in the end, no matter what way we take through life, we may as well, in practice, take as our moral "criterion" pleasure, a thing we *can* miss.[1] This is as though one should say "all roads through the wilderness of the world end in the Celestial City. But the travel-ler is pressingly recommended to take the route by

[1] McTaggart, *Studies in Hegelian Cosmology*, p. 127.

rail[1] which leads through the populous and fascinating city of Vanity, and by no means to omit a long stay in its attractive neighbourhood."

If we are to be genuinely in earnest with a high ethical rule of living, it would seem to be indispensable that we should be convinced that there is something really at stake in moral effort, and that the something which may be won or lost is no less than the supreme good which makes life worth living. What we endanger by sloth must be something more than a quantity of interesting and agreeable incident; it must be the life of the soul itself. Eternal life itself must be something which conceivably may be missed, and, for that reason, the eternity to be achieved by right living must be something not inherent in humanity from the start, but something to be *won*, and therefore something communicated and derivative. Hence humanity and divinity cannot simply be equated by a theology which is to be true to the demands of ethics. The divinity accessible to man must be not *deity*, but *deiformity*, transfiguration into a character which is not ours by right of birth, but is won by an effort, and won as something communicated from another source, where it is truly underived and original. In plain language, we break with the presuppositions of the moral life equally whether we eliminate the natural or the supernatural from our conception of things. To think of the moral life adequately, we must think of it as an adventure which begins at one end with nature, and ends at the other with *supernature*. Whether, before it can reach this end, it must not itself be transformed into something which is more than mere morality, is an issue we shall have to face later on. For the present, I aim

---

[1] Cf. Hawthorne's story of the *Celestial Railroad*.

simply at making it a little clearer what I mean by the transition from nature to supernature, and removing some objections which may possibly be entertained to the very conception of a "supernatural".

I would first, however, interpose two remarks intended to call attention to the point that the objection I have taken to the types of theory I have classed together, as obliterating the distinction between divinity and humanity, is not captious or frivolous, but obvious and serious.

(1) Theories of this type seem to lead inevitably to the doctrine of successive reincarnations, in one of its numerous forms, since they are manifestly inconsistent with full acceptance of the apparent facts about the humble beginnings of our own personal existence in conception, birth and babyhood. So we find that not only the unphilosophical, but the metaphysicians themselves, when they commit themselves to a theory of this kind, regularly treat reincarnation either as an integral part of their doctrine, or as an almost certain inference from it. They constantly convert language like that of Wordsworth's great *Ode*, where our birth is called a "sleep and a forgetting"—language which the poet himself was careful to explain as imaginative symbolism [1]—into a record of supposed actual fact. That the facts are not actual cannot, we must admit, be demonstrated, but it is at least obvious that such a reading of the observed facts about growth and development, in the individual or the group, involves a reversal of what *looks* like the natural interpretation. What we seem to see, as we watch the growth of a child's mind and character, is a process in which an

[1] "I think it right", he says, "to protest against a conclusion, which has given pain to some good and pious persons, that I meant to inculcate such a belief. It is far too shadowy a notion to be recommended to faith, as more than an element in our instincts of immortality."

originally almost indefinitely plastic "raw material" of tendencies, dispositions, aptitudes, receives steady determination into personality and character with definite structure. We *seem*, at least, to be watching the actual making of a personality. And, again, there are only too many cases in which life seems to take a wrong turning. In this we *seem* to be watching the dissolution and degradation of a promising moral personality into the merely non-moral, under the influence of passion or sloth. The moral of *Richard Feverel*, "he will never be the man he might have been", does seem to be the moral of not a few actual lives. Indeed, which of us can be sure that it may not be the moral of his own?

On any type of pre-existence theory, this impression must be wholly mistaken. There is no authentic process of growing *into* personality, since what we have mistaken for the plastic material of a personality has, in fact, been itself already fully shaped by the supposed past.[1] And the same thing will be true of the history of human social groups. Society will not really be, as it appears to be, something which has grown up, by stages still in the main traceable, from indeterminate beginnings. Behind every such apparent beginning there will lie concealed the formative work of a presumably endless past; thus everything which could be called, in the now fashionable phrase, "emergent evolution" must be a pure illusion, from the point of view of what I might name the "Orphic" theory of personality. The indifference to history often shown by philosophers who favour metaphysical speculations of this type will be the natural consequence of their conviction

[1] It is not without significance that Dr. McTaggart, the author of the subtlest and most sustained argument for this type of theory in our own literature, was also an adherent of through-going "determinism". See *Some Dogmas of Religion*, c. 5.

of the complete unimportance of everything temporal.[1] But this indifference to the historical leads at once to a breach with the attitude of practical morality. It takes the tragic note wholly out of life.

It has often been objected to theories of pre-existence that they outrage our natural feelings by their implication that the *innocence* which is the great charm of infancy is a mere illusion. The "innocent" infant, we are asked to believe, has often really behind it, stamped on its soul, though in "invisible ink", the past of a rake, a harlot, a swindler, a murderer. Such a thought, it has been said, is an outrage on "a mother's feelings". This appeal to maternal feeling—I do not know why a *father's* feelings are usually left out of the count—may look like a piece of mere sentimentalism which should have no weight with the serious philosopher. But it is, perhaps, worth while to consider whether the argument may not be a popular and rhetorical way of making a real point. To me it seems that this is the case, and that the moralist has, at least, as vital an interest as the evolutionary biologist and the genetic psychologist in insisting on the reality of time, development and the historical "emergence" of the new from the old, the richer in content from the poorer, the definitely organised from the plastic.

---

[1] It must not be forgotten that I do not pretend that it is demonstrated by this reasoning that time and "emergence" are not illusions. I am only urging that the antecedent probability is very much against a theory which requires us to treat characters apparently so universal and significant as illusory. It is reasonable only to accept a metaphysic of this kind if we find ourselves driven to it by the most cogent logical necessity, and this, I venture to think, is not the case. I would add that strict logic appears to require that, with the abandonment of the admission of actual "indeterminateness" into the structure of the historical should be coupled the denial that there was ever a "first moment"; time must be a series in which there is no first term. It does not seem to me clear that an actual "infinity *a parte ante*" in which every stage is thus perfectly determinate is even conceivable, and on that ground I should regard the view that time is a series with a first term as, at least, the *opinio potior*. But I cannot argue the case here. (I may, perhaps, refer to Dr. C. D. Broad's article "Time" in *Encyclopaedia of Religion and Ethics*.)

As I have suggested in a note to the last paragraph, if we look at the arguments for pre-existence seriously we ought to see that they are all also arguments for a series of past existences which has *no* first member. If any human personality ever begins with a genuine infancy, there is no antecedent reason why what I suppose to have been the beginning of my own history as a person, some fifty odd years ago, should not have been what it seems to have been, a genuine first beginning. If it is impossible that I should have begun then, the same impossibility must attach to any earlier first beginning, however far back you locate it in an unrecorded past. We must assume, therefore, an ultimate plurality of persons who are one and all metaphysical "absolutes" and have never really grown to be anything at all. Dante's lovely description of the new-made soul, as it comes from the hands of the Creator,

> l' anima semplicetta che sa nulla,
> salvo che, mosa da lieto fattore,
> volentier torna a ciò che la trastulla,[1]

will describe nothing, for no soul has ever been an *anima semplicetta*; personality and character have had no real growth. And similarly the point will be taken out of Blake's reflection that "every harlot was a virgin once", since there will be just the same ground for adding that the virgin was also a harlot once. Now this means that we commit ourselves once for all to the fatalistic doctrine of the eternally fixed and unalterable "metaphysical" character, the doctrine of all others most fatal to genuine moral seriousness. There will be no such thing as real moral advance in goodness to be achieved or real moral degradation to be dreaded, since, on the theory, in whatever I do I am only show-

---

[1] *Purgatorio*, xvi. 88-91.

ing myself what I always have been and always must be. Our life will be not merely a stage-play, but a puppet-show. The prayer *cor mundum crea in me, Deus,* will be senseless, and in its place we shall have nothing better than the dreary confession—

> For a new soul let who so please pray;
> We are what life made us, and shall be;
> For you the jungle, and me the sea-spray,
> And south for you, and north for me.

It is a well-known doctrine of the great schoolmen that one of the inherent limitations of divine omnipotence is that "God cannot will that God should cease to be God", just because of God's intrinsic and underived eternity. But on the "Orphic" theory we may say much the same of every one of ourselves; Judas cannot will to cease to be Judas the traitor, nor Caiaphas to become anything but Caiaphas the hypocrite. Yet, unless Judas can will to become loyal or Caiaphas to become sincere, neither is truly a *moral* person, any more than either could be a moral person if he were fettered by an astrological horoscope to his "star". No one has employed the imaginative mythology of reincarnation with more splendid effect than Plato, but we have to observe that his moral earnestness forces him to break with the central thought of Orphicism just when he appears to be asserting its positions most unreservedly. The text on which the great myth of Er the Pamphylian, at the end of the *Republic*, is based is the saying[1] that "it is a momentous issue, far greater than men think it (μέγας ὁ ἀγών, οὐχ ὅσος δοκεῖ), whether we are to become good or bad", and the momentousness of the issue is expressed in the myth itself, when its main point is made to be that the "luck" (δαίμων) of our next life is one which we shall *choose*

[1] *Republic*, 608 B.

for ourselves, the wisdom of the choice, with the consequent felicity or misery of the life, depending on the
degree of singleness of mind with which we now pursue
wisdom and virtue.[1] Still more completely does the
moral break the bounds of the imaginative story when
the aged Plato, in the *Laws*, has to vindicate the reality
of the moral order against the belief in indifferent gods
who leave men's conduct unregulated. We are then
told simply that the "kingdom of nature" and the "kingdom of ends" are unified by the establishment throughout the universe of a single law of what we might call
spiritual gravitation. Souls, like liquids, "find their
level", though, unlike liquids, they find it by rising as
well as by sinking. A man tends to "gravitate" to the
company of his spiritual "likes". And this, of itself,
ensures that, through all conceivable successions of
lives and deaths each of us will always be in a "social
environment" of the like-minded, and so "will do and
have done to him what it is meet that such a one should
do or endure".[2] The genuine reality of moral ascent
and moral decline, which the pre-existence doctrine
taken seriously must tend to deny, could hardly be
asserted more impressively.

One might even add, if a momentary digression may
be pardoned, that traditional Christianity shows its

---

[1] *Ib.* 617 E οὐχ ὑμᾶς δαίμων λήξεται, ἀλλὰ ὑμεῖς δαίμονα αἱρήσεσθε.

[2] *Laws*, 904 C: "For as each of us desires and as he is in his soul, so and such,
to speak generally, he is coming to be. Thus all things that have a share in soul
change, and the source of the change they have in themselves, and as they change,
they are transported, in accord with the ordering and law of destiny. . . . 'This
is the doom of the gods in heaven', O boy, or lad, who deemest thyself overlooked
by gods, that as a man becomes worse he makes his way to the company of worse
souls, as he becomes better to the better, and thus, through life and all deaths, suffers
and does that which it is meet that the like-minded should suffer from their likes
and do to them. . . . In this judgement thou shalt never be passed over, though
thou be ever so small, and hide in the depths of earth, or exalt thyself and soar
to the sky: the penalty that is due thou must pay, while thou art still here among
us, or, after thy passage hence, in the house of Hades, or, it may be, by removal
to some region more desolate still."

moral superiority to theosophies of the Orphic type by precisely the very doctrine which is often made matter of reproach against it, its teaching on Heaven and Hell. Since these theosophies repose in the end on an un-ethical metaphysics, it is not surprising that they hold out the prospect of an unending alternation of temporary "heavens" with temporary "hells"; they all envisage the possibility that the Christ of this incarnation may be the Caiaphas of the next, and the Caiaphas of to-day the Christ of to-morrow. And why should this not be so,[1] if nothing is definitively won by moral victory or irretrievably lost by moral defeat? It seems to me that, in its substance—I say nothing now of disfiguring accidental accretions—the Christian doctrine of a *final* salvation and reprobation springs less from theological hardness of heart than from seriousness of moral conviction. It is the supreme assertion of the conviction that choice is real and that everything is staked on the quality of our choice. If happiness depends on character and character is genuinely made by our choices, we cannot refuse to contemplate the possibility that character, and with it happiness, may be lost beyond the power of recovery by sufficient persistence in choosing evil or sufficient indolence in choosing good. If we choose the worse long enough, or even neglect to practise choice of the good, we may conceivably end by making ourselves incapable of effective choice of the better, just as surely as by choosing good with sufficient persistence we may come to be incapable of choosing its contrary. One may legitimately *hope* that, by the mercy of God, no man will ever throw him-

---

[1] It may very well be so, even on Dr. McTaggart's version of the theory. For though he holds that we are all predestined to an ultimate Heaven of goodness and happiness, he also holds that, in the enormously long series of lives which precede this "ultimate stage", there may be any degree whatever of fluctuation both in happiness and in virtue (*Nature of Existence*, ii. pp. 473-7).

self away beyond all possibility of recovery. But only the morally indifferent would lightly deny that the thing may be done, and that I myself, if I am careless enough, may be the man to do it. Indeed, the more I allow myself to imagine that personality is something made once and for all, the more likely I shall be to draw the inference that I am, and must be, what "life" has made me, and so to desist from any real effort to become better than I now am.

Even if it were true that this cessation from effort does not mean, as in the moral life it does, that one does not remain long even at one's present level, the prospect of "staying where one is" would, I take it, be a fairly formidable "hell" to a thinking man fully alive to his actual moral and spiritual lack of order and comeliness. It may be an element in God's blessedness that He cannot so much as wish to be other than He is; our worth as persons, and consequently our happiness, is bound up with the aspiration to become what we actually are not, to be "divorced from the poor shallow thing which now" we are. We have to put on divinity, and the putting on is a process in which temporality, though increasingly subordinated, is never finally left behind. Our task as moral beings is to lead a "dying life"; to rest on our oars would mean a "living death", a very different thing.

(2) My second observation arises out of the first. Just because, in the moral life, conscious pursuit of a good definitely envisaged as supra-temporal grows out of, or emerges from, pursuit of a good which presents itself to the aspirant, in reflection on his aspirations, as temporal, progress in the moral life itself depends throughout, as has already been said, on a right combination of attachment with detachment. It is this which, more than anything else, makes a life of real

moral success exceedingly difficult. It is not difficult
to become wholly absorbed in the pursuit of some end
definitely limited and circumscribed by temporal and
secular conditions, and thus making a clear and definite appeal to imagination; to become, for example,
simply engrossed in the work of one's profession, in
cultivating the social graces, amenities, and affections
within the limit of one's family circle, or group of
friends, or in pursuing one's chosen "hobby". It is
a comparatively easy thing to map out a definite plan
of action and to say, "My aspirations shall be carefully
restrained within these limits and directed on what
is clearly capable of being compassed by reasonable
effort, within a reasonable time and with ordinary good
fortune. I will not run the risk of frustrating modest
and rational anticipations by indulging indefinite
desires and unclear aspirations after an infinite which
remains always in the clouds. My rule shall be carefully
to measure my coat according to my cloth, to demand
of life and of myself no more than they can be reasonably expected to accomplish, to know what I am equal
to, and to seek nothing beyond it." This is, in principle,
the counsel of Epicurus, and if "safety first" were
really a practicable rule of moral living, it would be the
right counsel. It means definite self-chosen attachment
to the known, familiar and finite; such detachment as
the Epicurean rule advises, or permits, is no more than
a "counsel of prudence". An Epicurean will try to be
cool in all his attachments, because reflection on human
experience has taught him that unforseeable adverse
fortune may at any moment deprive him of all he
cares most about, and time, in the end, must take all
things away. But his rule has no place for the spirit
of adventure which freely hazards the certain for the
always uncertain hope of a better to come. It is no part

of his wisdom of life to turn his back on the "unit", which may be had for the taking, for the chance of the "million" which it is always very doubtful whether he will win or miss. The call of the desert is inaudible to him, or if, by any chance, he ever catches it, his philosophy prompts the response, *quittez les longs espoirs et les vaines pensées.* Hence the secret fascination of the Epicurean creed and its preachers in literature, Horace and the rest of them, for all of us in our too frequent unworthier moods. Its appeal to the maxims of "safety first" and the "bird in the hand" comes home to us precisely *because* it is a proposal to make the great refusal *per viltà,* and there is so much *viltà* in all of us. We are uncomfortable in the presence of a Pascal, who insists on reminding us that *il faut parier,* and that the stake we must hazard in the game of life is ourselves. But a morality of unconditional obligation—and no other morality deserves the name—depends on frank recognition of the fact that its way of life cannot be anything but a "wager", with myself for the stake, in a game where I cannot see the cards before they are played.

There is, again, a kind of detachment which I conceive it is not unduly hard to practise, when the first plunge has been taken, the detachment which leads a man out into the Thebaid. Since none of the more palpable objects to which men attach themselves, family, wealth, power, knowledge, is an absolute and all-satisfying good, it is, at least, a simple and intelligible rule that one will turn one's back on them all, and treat what is, at most, second-best as though it were not good at all. It may, indeed, require iron resolution to lead the life of a Brand, but, at any rate, the man who braces himself to such a life has gained something very real by his simplification of the practical problem.

He escapes the most agonising difficulties of all, those which come of genuine perplexity. His rule, if only he can live up to it—and habituation can do much to remove the obstacles—is simple and unambiguous. The trouble is that the moral life itself is not a simple matter, and that over-simplification, whatever form it takes, leads to failure. The supremely hard task is that of bringing the "right measure" into life, effecting just the right adjustment of attachment with detachment. It is eminently hard to cultivate the particular and finite good heartily, because it is good and so long as it is the best for me, and yet to be able to let it go, in spite of its fully appreciated goodness, neither sullenly nor recklessly, but freely and gladly, when the better has disclosed itself and its call is imperative. No simple rule can be given for this,[1] and yet it is the secret of all high moral attainment.

Let me take a simple concrete example, to illustrate my meaning from a problem which most of us have to face in everyday living. Think of some of the things which are implied in the right ordering of what we call "romantic" sexual love. The problem is not at bottom, as it is sometimes made to appear in superficial works on ethics, no more than that of keeping an elementary physical appetite within safe and decent bounds. If it were only that, it would be without its most formidable moral difficulties. When, in the dawn of adolescence, the "young man's fancy lightly turns to thoughts of love", he must be a very poor kind of young man if, from the very first, the promptings of mere animal "passion" are not so overlaid with characteristically human affection and imagination that they are, for the most part, only in the background of consciousness.

---

[1] "Ah, what a dusty answer gets the soul,
   When hot for certainties in this our life."

Most of us, I suspect, are barely aware of them during the romance we call "love" and courtship; it is later on that we become fully awake to them. Still, of course, they are there, if only as undertones, and I should go further and say frankly that they ought to be there. The ends which they serve in any distinctively human life, even a prosaic and unimaginative one, are clearly *moral* ends, and include, at the least, the life of mutual trust and companionship in the joys and sorrows of earthly existence, the *consortium totius vitae*, and the bringing up of a new generation to be decent and useful members of the great fellowship of the living and the dead. These ends are not likely to be effectively attained where the primitive *physical* drawing of youth to maid, and maid to youth, is not adequately strong and real. That is not likely to be a wholly sound family life which has not begun with "passion", and though "passion" itself, felt for a *person*, is already physical desire in process of sublimation and translation into the super-physical, it demands the physical basis. When there is no call of the body to the body, there is no sufficient foundation for "true love". Now, the wrong, or at least inferior, kind of detachment is prompted by recognition of these facts and by the true reflection that the facts presuppose a physical condition and mental mood which, in the nature of things, cannot last. Physical charm and the ardours of physical desire belong to joyous youth and lusty prime; to any man the time must come, sooner or later, in the order of nature, when the grace and charm which stirred him have taken their place with the *neiges d'antan*, or when, even if they were less evanescent than they are, advancing years would compel him to confess of himself, "I take no pleasure in them". It is true and certain enough that

> beauty cannot keep her lustrous eyes,
> Nor young love pine at them beyond to-morrow.

Romantic passion may be the delight of a season; it cannot be of itself the business of a life. So it is easy to say, "Because this cannot satisfy beyond its season, it is clearly not the one abiding good, and a good which is not abiding is what I will have none of". But we can all see readily that the man who simply cuts romance and passion out of his life—except when he does so in strict duty at the summons of an imperative greater good, and even then he is paying a very real price for the greater good—is maiming his whole moral being. He is cutting himself loose from the whole circle of the experiences which do most to moralise the great majority of human beings, declining a high spiritual adventure. But a man may also maim his life by undue attachment. If no one will ever get all the moral wealth that may be got out of the life of family ties and responsibilities, unless he begins with the ardour and passion of the lover, it is true that no one will make the best, or anything like the best, of such a life who simply remains the youthful ardent lover all his life long. He will end by wearying himself and the object of his ardours; indeed, these ardours only minister to his moral being so long as they are spontaneous and unprompted. When the relation needs to be maintained by conscious effort, as it some day must be, if it is to last through the physical and mental changes of a lifetime, it may become a clog, instead of a support to the soul. "Some love too little, some too long."

Thus the problem life sets us is that of a steady progress in the conversion of passion ennobled by affection into affection intensified by its connection with passion, but the element of passion steadily tends to recede into the background of a mellow and golden past. It is good, in season, to have been the romantic lover, but it is only permanently good on condition that one reaches out to what is beyond, that the actual experience of ardent youth is made a stage on the way to the different experiences of a perfect middle age and later life. And the task of so living in the present while it lasts that one is helped, not hindered, in the advance to the future is so easily spoiled by the natural human reluctance to meet the new and untried that it demands unremitting vigilance and unrelaxing effort to escape the danger of moral sloth.

This is but one example of the problem which is raised by all the relations and situations of the personal moral life. To evade any of them is detrimental; to rest in any of them as final equally spoils them. All have to be used, as good in their measure, and all have to be transformed. It is because, with advancing years, we all tend to grow weary of the progressive transformation, and try to put off our harness, that middle age is attended, for all of us, with grave danger of moral stagnation. We all want to say to ourselves, "I have now come to the point when I may stand still; I want to be no better, no wiser, no more responsive to the call of moral adventure, than I am now. Henceforth let my life be a placid backwater." But to yield to the suggestion is moral death. Here is the special witness of the moral life to man's position in the universe as a creature whose being is rooted at once in time and in eternity.

This difficulty in finding the right adjustment of attachment to detachment is, of course, primarily a practical one. But, like most serious practical difficulties, it has a theoretical problem behind it. The

theoretical difficulty has found clear expression in the
sections of the *Prolegomena to Ethics*, in which T. H.
Green dwells on the apparent "vicious circle" involved
in every attempt to make definite and articulate statements about the character of the good for man, or moral
ideal. The same point is illustrated equally by another
great work on ethics of the same date and proceeding
from the same group of thinkers, F. H. Bradley's
Ethical Studies, where we find the relatively simple
ideal of faithful discharge of the "duties of our station",
on which we could fall back with confidence so long
as we were concerned merely with the refutation of
the deliberate pleasure-seeker, or of the fanatic for
a formulated code of "categorical maxims", proving
itself inadequate under more searching criticism.
Green's way of stating the difficulty has, for my
present purpose, the advantage of being the boldest,
and so making the point hardest to overlook. All
the moral progress of individual man, or of societies,
has found its inspiration in a "divine discontent",
a sense of a best which is beyond all the good that has
so far been achieved. It is the men who will be content
with nothing but the best whom we have to thank
for every serious advance which man and society
have actually made towards even a moderately
"better". If the merely "relatively better" were
enough to content us, it would not be apparent why
we should take even the first steps beyond the measure
of good already attained, for this is itself already a
"better" by comparison with something we have left
behind us. The moralist who is in earnest with life
is, necessarily and on principle, an *intransigeant*; he
means to aim not at the rather better, but at the
absolute best. And it is the tragedy of the moral life
that not only is the best never actually achieved at a

specific date and place, but that you cannot as much as make it really clear to yourself with any detail what the best is; you do not possess a "clear and distinct idea" of what you would be at.

From the point of view of the devotee of the "geometrical method", the life of unremitting moral endeavour, which we at least confess with shame we ought to be leading, however lamentably we fall short in our practice, is an unending aspiration after a *je ne sais quoi*, just as the life of the profound thinker or the great artist seems often, even to himself, to be one perpetual attempt to express the ineffable, or convey the incommunicable.[1] To the question, "But what is it all about, and just what is it you would have?" neither moralist artist, nor metaphysician has any definite answer to give. In the case of the moralist, in particular, any attempt to say precisely what it is he wants to do, or wants his society to be, leads straight either to the idle amusement of constructing a "New Jerusalem", or to the serious mischief of trying to force the "New Jerusalem" of one man's dream on the multitude who are quite unfit to inherit it. And we all know from experience that these Utopias of the *doctrinaires*, even at their best, have the fatal defect that the one thing they cannot guarantee is the one thing which matters; you may describe the walls of the city down to the smallest of the gems which glitter in them, or its police arrangements down to the size and material of the most insignificant button on the coat of the humblest official, but you cannot ensure that the inhabitants shall be "true Israelites" in whom there is no guile. Your Eden may be cunningly and

---

[1] Plato, *Ep.* vii. 341 C ῥητὸν γὰρ οὐδαμῶς ἐστιν ὡς ἄλλα μαθήματα, ἀλλ' ἐκ πολλῆς συνουσίας γιγνομένης περὶ τὸ πρᾶγμα αὐτὸ καὶ τοῦ συζῆν ἐξαίφνης, οἷον ἀπὸ πυρὸς πηδήσαντος ἐξαφθὲν φῶς, ἐν τῇ ψυχῇ γενόμενον αὐτὸ ἑαυτὸ ἤδη τρέφει κτλ.

strongly fenced, but no fence will keep out the old serpent. And yet, without the inspiration of the vision, you are certain to leave the old Babylon pretty much as you found it. There is no moral institution of all we inherit of which we can honestly say that, as we know it, it is worthy to be eternised because it gives us the best. However much we may appreciate its "spirit", the spirit comes to us always encumbered with a "letter" which it has not wholly informed, and we are incapable of saying in advance how this letter is to be permanently kept from becoming a *dead* letter. Moral traditions and institutions are always in process of transformation while they are alive, *because* they are alive; the attempt to provide them with an eternalised expression beyond which imagination is forbidden to travel would be, in principle, to kill them.

This is equally true of all attempts to imagine what attained perfection, or felicity, completed humanity, would be in an individual personality, as we may learn from consideration of the different pictures of the life of Heaven on which men have tried to feed their souls. I am not referring merely to the infinite dreariness and moral emptiness of the common "spiritist" revelations of our future, with the dreadful prospect they disclose of an eternity of aimless gossip and twaddle. In this kind the best, no less than the worst, are but shadows. Must we not, if we are quite candid, say even of Dante's Paradise, that though, for a moment while we are under the immediate spell of the poetry, it may seem to leave nothing to be desired, yet, when we reflect, if we take the imagery as more than symbolic of things the poet himself cannot really envisage, the spell is broken? We are in a world where the inhabitants seem to have nothing in particular to do, and where we feel that the intrusion

of the visitor from earth must have provided the beatified spirits with a welcome relief from monotony. It
is not surprising that Green should decide that there
is no way out of his "circle". What the best, which has
all along been the inspiration of moral effort, may be,
we commonly say, at any time, most inadequately
by pointing to the little better which has so far been
attained and saying that the best is that which has
inspired the achievement, and that advance to a better
state still means progress along the same road. What
the windings and turnings of the road may be, and
what new prospects each of these may disclose, we do
not know. We can only say that no advance will be
made by simply retracing our steps.[1]

Now, one sees at once what the mere "reformer",
with his insistence on immediate and visible practical
"results", is likely to say to such a declaration. His
objection, in fact, might be fairly summarised by the
mere grumble, "Toryism", in spite of the fact that
in practice Green was a zealous late nineteenth-century
Radical. If the critic designed to be more explanatory,
he would clearly have something not wholly unplausible to say for himself. What he might say, with fair
plausibility would, I conceive, be much this: "I fully
accept your statement that moral progress is not to be
made, in my personal life or in that of society, by
simply turning one's back on the route by which the
slow but real progress of the past has been achieved.
I agree with you that the spirit of all that is good in
existing practice and actual institutions ought to be
conserved. But the problem which confronts me is to
know how much, in our inheritance, is 'spirit' and how
much is 'letter'. Is a proposed modification of my personal rule of conduct, or of the social rule of the com-

_____
[1] Cf. *Prolegomena to Ethics*, pp. 183-4, 351, 404.

munity, which involves a marked and visible departure
from established convention, really a surrender of the
spirit of morality, or only revision of a letter which has
become obsolete? To adopt your own metaphor of the
journey, is one always really going back on one's
track whenever one seems to be doubling? The road
itself, you know, may wind, in spite of Bunyan's denial;
or, again, the traveller may have missed the obscure
right path some way back, and his one reasonable
course now may be to make for the road again across
difficult open country. Whether this is his case or not
could only be certainly discovered from careful study
of a good road-map, and, by your own confession,
even if Bunyan possessed such a map, you do not.
This being so, can you complain that your directions
seem to me a little like the bad and unsafe rule of
always following 'one's own nose'?" This, as I take it,
is the substance of Professor Hobhouse's grievance
against the whole social theory of Green's distinguished
continuator, Bosanquet, and there is an apparent good
sense about the complaint which finds an echo in the
hearts of many of us.[1]

Yet it is no less apparent that the "ordnance survey
map" of the road which mankind, or each of us, has
to take through human life is certainly not to be had.
It is not merely that the detailed Utopias which have
been imagined by one enthusiast after another are
all unsatisfactory, though I confess I have never
examined one of them which did not seem at least
as likely to prove a "hell on earth" as a "heaven
below". The root of the difficulty lies deeper. It is
vain to set yourself to picture a temporal "heaven on
earth", because earth is temporal and heaven is
eternal. Since the future is hidden from us, you can

---

[1] L. T. Hobhouse, *Philosophical Theory of the State*, pp. 80 ff.

never know that if you succeeded in setting up your
Utopia you might not find that you had surrendered
better for worse; you do not know the price which might
have to be paid for it. And, again, you do know at
least one thing about a temporal Utopia, that because
it is temporal, it could only be reached to be deserted
again. Once set up, it would cease to be a "better"
ahead. The attempt to depict an actual eternal felicity
is more hopeless still, because to know what it is one
would already have had to put off temporality and put
on eternity in one's self, and none of us has ever done
this. We cannot describe the goal of our pilgrimage
because we have never reached it. And yet we cannot
say, with Bunyan's Atheist, "there is no such place
on the map", and abandon the journey, because to do
so would be to cease to be serious with life, and that
we dare not do, so long as we remain moral. It is
moral aspiration which has humanised the human
animal, and we dare not believe that the humanisation
of man is an illusion, or a bad joke. The goal may be
out of sight, but a goal there must be, or

> There's nothing serious in mortality;
> All is but toys.

Green's problem of the apparent moral "circle", then,
seems to show us morality transcending itself and
passing into religion and worship in several ways,
some of which I will try to indicate briefly.

(1) As Green himself reminds us, the immediate
conscious demand of the man who is bent on bettering
himself, or his society, may be, for something quite
inconsiderable, the correction of a particular tendency
or habit in himself which prevents him from being in
some particular what he approves of being, the removal
of some little impediment to the successful prosecution

of a communal aim.[1] At our own level of moralisation, for example, the man who takes in hand to reform his life may be already conscious of nothing more than that it would be better for him to get up an hour earlier in the morning, to smoke one cigar a day less, or to pay his small bills a little more promptly as they come in; the man who wants to leave society "rather better than he found it", may start with nothing more "transcendental" than the desire to check some small waste in the spending of the local rates, to make some particular legal procedure a little less dilatory and expensive, or to secure for the community some hours more of sunlight in the year by the introduction of "summer time". But if you are in earnest with the spirit of "reform", though you may begin with the conscious intention of some one such definite minor correction, you do not stop there. The putting right of this or that defect does not prove to be a panacea for our human failure to make the best of life. The more you have succeeded in setting right, the more you find calling out for further treatment. Any earnest sense of the necessity for putting anything to rights can lead you, if you are logical and resist sloth, to the remaking of life as a whole. With each limitation surmounted, you become conscious of further limitations, still to be surmounted, of which you had never dreamed. Thus it is those who have made most, not those who have made least, progress in the moral conquest of themselves and their surroundings who are most keenly alive to human imperfection and finitude. The slave who, with some effort, has broken one link of his fetters is more gallingly aware of the chain that still binds him than the slave who has never dreamed that he may be free. Behind the whole process, and

[1] Cf. *Prolegomena to Ethics*, pp. 250-5, 265, 325-7.

giving it all its value, there is what an American might call the "urge", towards complete emancipation, but it is only as we steadily loosen one shackle after another that we discover that nothing less than complete freedom would satisfy the impulse which led us to break the first link. To become increasingly conscious of ourselves as finite and fettered is only the other side of becoming conscious of ourselves as made for, and destined to, freedom and self-mastery. But complete freedom and self-mastery lie beyond the horizon of temporality. So we end by making the discovery that what we began by mistaking for a mere attempt to adjust ourselves a little better to supposedly hard-and-fast conditions of our temporal environment is really the effort to transcend time and mortality altogether. The *larva* might fancy that its business on the leaf is merely to become a bigger and fatter *larva*; its true aim in feeding on the leaf, if it only knew it, is to turn into the *angelica farfalla*. You must become something more than "mere man", on pain of otherwise becoming something less.

(2) Next—and this is a point on which it is all-important to lay full stress—genuinely moral effort after a "better" is always double-edged. If the effort has "moral" quality, what moves us is never simply dissatisfaction with our *environment*, or, in Butler's phrase, our "condition"; there is always also dissatisfaction with *ourselves*, or, as Butler puts it, "our conduct", and the character of which that conduct is the expression. We will not merely that the course of things shall be different, but that we ourselves will be different. There is nothing "divine" about a discontent which is not also dissatisfaction with ourselves, in fact, self-condemnation. The eastern rhymester's longing to shatter the "frame of things" and make it anew, "nearer

to the heart's desire", has no moral quality, so long as
it does not put the heart itself at the very head of
the list of things to be shattered and remade. The making of a personality, like that of an omelette, requires
the breaking of eggs, and the first egg to be broken
is a man's own heart. Hence the superficiality of all
attempts to identify true moral progress with any mere
scheme of "social amelioration", or the moral ideal
with a well-constructed "social system". The builders
of the vulgar Utopias are all concerned only with
providing for the "heart's desire" of very imperfectly
moralised beings, the securing of felicity for men who
remain unenlightened and "unregenerate". The trouble
is that so long as one remains still the "natural man",
desiring as good only that which is good in part and
for a season, no satisfaction of such desires will yield
felicity. The merely "natural" man has only the choice,
at best, between satiety and disappointment. To
achieve felicity, one must first learn to set one's heart
on a good which can neither cloy nor be taken from
one, and no such good is discovered or desired without
a real travail of the soul. There is no genuine regeneration of society but one which is based throughout on
this transformation of personal aim and character.
Happiness, as Kant truly says,[1] would mean for each
of us that the course of the world should conform
completely to his "will and wish", but the conformity
is impossible so long as our "wills and wishes" remain
what they are, in many respects, even in the best of us,
sensual, foolish, peevish. We have to learn to care intensely for so much that, at first, had no attraction for
us, and to cease to care greatly about so much we all
begin by prizing highly.

Yet it is equally true that the activity from which

[1] *KdprV*. I. Th. ii. B. ii. *Hptstck*. (*Werke*, Hartenstein[2], V. p. 130).

all moral advance springs is directed outwards as well
as inwards. The progressive transformation by which
mankind are humanised and moralised is not only a
transformation of the self. The Stoic who limits himself
to the endeavour to "make a right use of his presenta-
tions" (ὀρθῶς χρῆσθαι ταῖς φαντασίαις), misses the mark
by one-sidedness as much as the mere "social reformer"
who dreams of regenerating the world without first
being regenerated himself. It is not only that the outward march of events has to be subdued to human
purposes by an increasing control of "nature" built on
patient study of "nature's" ways, and, again, that there
must be steady correction of hampering social habits
and conventions, if the "course of events" is to be
shaped into conformity with a sane human will. This
is true enough, but it is only half the truth. The other
half is that the genuinely moralised spirit is itself a
missionary spirit. What the good man wants to have
of the world, he equally wants his neighbour to have,
but, beyond this, what he wants to be, he wants his
neighbour to be also, and his neighbour's name is
Everyman. The moral aim is not merely that society
shall be rightly ordered in external matters and my own
will intelligent and virtuous, but that all men's wills
shall be as my own in these respects. The good man
could not find the best on which his heart is set in a
world where men's dealings with one another were
outwardly conformable to a right rule, and his own,
but his own only, further inspired by a genuine devotion to the rule for its own sake. If the best is really
to be achieved, we need to add that it must be in a world
where *all* men, not only "one strong man in a blatant
land", in Kant's formula, reverence duty in their hearts
as well as conform to it in their outward acts. It is not
enough that I should myself "reverence the moral law";

if the world is to be what it must be before the good
man can pronounce it what he would have it, *all* men
must bow in a common reverence. So it becomes no less
a part of the life "from duty" to set other men forward
on the way of desiring the truly supreme good than
it is to desire it myself with all my heart. It is quite
impossible to rest in the curious Kantian compromise
which tells me to promote in myself the spirit of reverence for duty, but to be content with assisting to promote my fellow-man's "happiness". Indeed, the compromise is incompatible with Kant's own final word
on "happiness", that happiness means a state in which
the rational will is actually realised in the course of
events.[1] So long as any man's will falls short of being wholly reasonable and humanised, the course of
events which realises the rational, *i.e.* good, will cannot
realise that man's will, so that I *cannot* propose to make
another "happy" without winning his will for goodness
and rationality. Kant might have learned something
on this matter from the saying of Epicurus, "If you
would make Pythocles happy, seek not to add to his
possessions, but to moderate his desires".[2] It is a badly
maimed account of the truly good will to say only, as
Kant sometimes does, that its object is that every man
should be made happy to the degree in which he is
deserving of happiness, and as a consequence of his deserving. So much might be secured in a world where
no man had any virtue and no man was happy, or even
in one where all men were very vicious and consequently very miserable. It is secured in Dante's horrible
picture of a Hell where the torments are ingeniously
graded according to the ill-deserts of the inhabitants.
But it would surely be a very doubtful morality which
could find a universe consisting of one vast Dantesque

---

[1] *Kdpr V. loc. cit.*   [2] Epic., Fr., 135 (Usener).

Hell "very good". (In fact, if a universe so constituted could be very good, one might say, in Dante's own words, *uopo non fosse partorir Maria.*) If Kant's formula were really the last word of morality, there seems to be no reason why a final shutting up of all creatures in condemnation, because all have been disobedient, should not be a perfectly satisfactory conclusion to history. It cannot be the supreme object of the good will that all of us should be "as happy as we deserve": it would be, at any rate, a less patently faulty formula to say that the good will wills that we should be made deserving of happiness and should attain the happiness we have been enabled to "merit". (I do not say that this statement is beyond criticism, but it is at least better than Kant's own.)

Even Kant's own statement seems to require that we should transcend the limitations of Kant's presentation of morality. Kant himself allows that a will which could effect the subordination of the whole course of history to a moral demand that the happiness of individuals shall be a consequence of their moral worth, and proportionate to that worth, cannot be the will of any finite creature. It must be a will backed by omnipotence, or, at least, a will which is supreme over the whole temporal order and wields every part as a wholly plastic instrument for a moral end. Thus it must be a living supreme divine will into conformity with which our own wills grow in proportion as we become what we ought to be.[1] And this consideration seems to lead us at once to grave dissatisfaction with Kant's own fundamental moral principle of *Autonomy* of the Will, as he himself states it. According to his own account, the reason why it is only reasonable and proper to pay unconditional reverence to the com-

[1] *KdprV.* I. Th. ii. B. ii. *Hptstck.* (*Werke*, Hartenstein[1], V. 131).

mands of the moral will is, in the last resort, that the
moral will is *my own* will, "as rational", so that in
obeying it I am obeying a law which I impose on
myself. I am to be wholly submissive because in
submitting I become my own master. It is true that
Kant guards himself, as I think some of his critics,
Neo-Thomist and otherwise, sometimes forget, by
an important *distinctio*. My will, according to him, is
legislative in the moral world, but it is not *sovereign*,
for the very reason that it is bound by its own commands.[1] The moral world of persons is a constitutional realm with a Parliament, and it may be—it was
Kant's opinion that it not only may be, but is—a
monarchy in which God is the constitutional monarch.
(In any case, Kant is clear on the point that *I* am
not monarch.) But this *distinctio* does not wholly
remove the difficulty it is intended to meet. What the
difficulty is we may see from consideration of another
Kantian thesis. When Kant is anxious to establish
the point that a morally good will cannot derive its
goodness from the character of the *results* it produces,
he rightly urges against all forms of utilitarianism,
that the good man's attitude in the presence of the
known moral law is one of unqualified reverence, and
that such reverence cannot be felt for any *product*
of our own action. We cannot, in fact, unless we are
idolaters, worship our own handiwork.

This should have prompted the further question
whether, without falling into the priggishness which
is a peculiarly detestable kind of idolatry, anyone
can worship *himself*. Now, if the good will is no more
than *my* will, or, to put it more precisely in the way in
which Kant puts it, if there is no more profound and
ultimate reason for my reverence for it than that it is

[1] *Grundlegung zur Metaphysik der Sitten*, ii. (*Werke*, iv. 282).

my own will, does not absolute reverence for the good will and its law of duty degenerate into self-worship? Are we not at least on the brink here of a paradox which is inevitable in any living morality, however simple? If the commands of the good will were *merely* the commands of some external power foreign to my-self, if my own will did not "go along" with them, in obeying, I should be no more than a slave. I might think obedience prudent, or expedient, but I could not obey with the joyous self-surrender of adoration. But, again, if these commands were only the commands of *my* will why should I reverence and adore? The power which sanctioned the command might surely at any time dispense with its own injunctions, on the principle *sit pro ratione voluntas*. The peculiar moral attitude seems only fully intelligible if we agree with Kant that the commands of morality are abso-lutely reasonable, but part company with him by immediately adding, as something more than an "open possibility", that they do not originate in a reason which is "my" nature, that they come from a supreme and absolute reason into likeness with which I have to grow, but which remains always beyond me. What "my" reason does, and does always only im-perfectly, is to *recognise*, not to *create*, the obligations it is my duty to fulfil. It is just because the reason which is the source of the moral law is not originally mine, nor that of any man or all men, that I can reverence it without reservations.

This is only another way of saying what Kant, and other "rationalist" philosophers too often forget, that man himself and man's reason are always things "in the making", never things finally made and once for all there. We do not come into the world rational: we have to achieve our rationality slowly and partially, with labour and difficulty. The moral law by which our conduct is to be judged is not, from our birth, written in indelible characters on the tables of the heart. It is gradually disclosed, as we gradually grow into humanity. Its primal seat, then, cannot be in a reason which is already ours by possession, but must be in that "reason" into conformity with which we are slowly growing. Only by some such conception do we escape the intolerable dualism of Kant's account of man's nature as compounded of a rationality which is already full-grown and perfect, and an animality which never grows into anything better at all. And only so do we find a place in our schemes of morality for some of the qualities which, when we are not under the domination of preconceived theory, we all recognise as the ripest fruits of spiritual growth.

(3) A moralist may be permitted to feel a special interest in this last-mentioned point and to leave it to the metaphysician to deal more fully with the formal difficulties inherent in an exaggerated dualism of "reason" and "inclination". What, we may ask, is the right moral attitude to the old problem of Job, the problem of the apparently wanton and pointless suffering and disaster life so often brings with it? It does not require very profound moral insight to understand that the practically sane attitude is neither that of stupefaction and moral paralysis, nor that of embittered "revolt". The spectacle of an eminent novelist shaking his fist at the "president of the immortals" because his heroine has come to the gallows is not morally edifying, and is, moreover, a little comical to anyone who remembers that, after all, it is not God, but the novelist himself, who "creates" the heroine and deliberately contrives her hanging. There is more to be said for the Stoic "resignation", which

takes refuge in a grim refusal to lower one's head under the "bludgeonings of chance", when the attitude is genuine, and not—as I suspect is more often the case—mere self-conscious theatrical "pose". But I think we all know of a better way, which is followed in practice by thousands of humble souls under burdens more grievous than those which send the sentimental-ists of literature to whining or cursing, according to temperament, and the literary Stoics to admiration of their own fortitude. It is possible to do better than to abstain from complaints or to cultivate pride; it is possible, and we all know of cases in which it is finely done, to make acceptance of the worst fortune has to bestow a means to the development of a sweetness, patience, and serene joyousness which are to be learned nowhere but in the school of sharp suffering.

> Count each affliction, whether light or grave,
> God's messenger sent down to thee; do thou
> With courtesy receive him; rise and bow;
> And, ere his shadow cross thy threshold, crave
> Permission first his heavenly feet to lave;
> Then lay before him all thou hast . . .
>   . . . Grief should be
> Like joy, majestic, equable, sedate;
> Confirming, cleansing, raising, making free;
> Strong to consume small troubles; to commend
> Great thoughts, grave thoughts, thoughts lasting to the end.[1]

There is the nobly ethical attitude to affliction, which does not merely safeguard moral good already won against degradation, as the Stoic resignation may do, but makes trouble itself the direct means to further enrichment. But this attitude is possible only on one condition: the affliction must be regarded as "God's messenger". One must really believe that "whom the

---

[1] Aubrey de Vere.

Lord loveth, He chasteneth". Is such an attitude possible in a life directed by the Kantian maxims? To my own thinking it is not. The point of the situation is that it is precisely the heavy afflictions which can be converted into the means to the greatest moral enrichment. And the sting of these afflictions lies just in their apparent wantonness, their seeming utter unreasonableness. If we come, in this life, to see any reasonableness in them, we do so only because they have already borne the fruit they can bear only on condition that they are first gladly accepted in all their apparent unreasonableness. Unless I mean by the "reason" I worship with unqualified reverence something more than the "reason I have now in possession", I own I do not see that we could admit this morally most fruitful attitude towards afflictions into a scheme of morality which is, *ex hypothesi*, to be a life "by the sole dictate of reason", and I note that I have found nothing in Kant's writings of any period to suggest that he himself dreamed of any attitude towards such visitations which goes beyond the "Stoic" retreat of the tortoise into its shell. Yet, if he did not, he was blind to the highest.

I should infer that here we have a concrete illustration of the way in which the moral life itself, at its best, points to something which, because it transcends the separation of "ought" from "is", must be called definitely religion and not morality, as the source and inspiration of what is best in morality itself, and that the connection between practical good living and belief in God is much more direct and vital than Kant was willing to allow. I cannot doubt that morality may *exist* without religion. An atheist who has been taught not to steal or lie or fornicate or the like is, probably, no more nor less likely, in average situations, to earn his living honestly, to speak the truth, and to live cleanly, than a believer in God. But if the atheist is logical and in earnest with his professed view of the world, and the believer equally so with his, I think I know which of the two is the more likely to make irreparable and "unmerited" grievous calamity a means to the purification and enrichment of personality.

(4) Again, we can see that the assumed identity between the right and the rational does not permit, as it should if the legislative moral reason were my own, in the sense of being an endowment which I have, and eternally have, in possession, of an inference which is absolutely vital to Kant's theory of the "categorical imperative" as a sufficient moral *criterion*. The injunctions of the good will, to which we must at all costs be loyal, cannot be digested, in advance of experience, into an articulated code of precepts sufficient to guide the upright man's steps, no matter how slippery the places where they have to be set. We are familiar enough in daily life with the truth that when we try to decide in theory what would be the dutiful course of action in a situation which has never confronted us in our practice, we most commonly find ourselves beset with considerations for and against every proposed course, considerations which we may balance endlessly against one another without coming to a conclusion. And yet we know that if we live in the dutiful spirit, when the responsibility of deciding rightly is thrown upon us, we can trust that it will bring with it the light necessary for the decision. The voice of enlightened conscience does not make itself audible until the duty of deciding is laid upon us. There could probably be no worse preparation for right action than careful anticipatory study of systems of casuistry; to know with a justified confidence that you can trust your "conscience" does not mean that you know in advance what the de-

liverances of "conscience" will be.[1] Similarly, I should
say, I may and do often feel a justified confidence that
my friend will acquit himself as a man should in some
situation of great "difficulty" and grave responsibility. But this need not mean, what only the muddle-
headed "determinist" takes it to mean, that I know
what my friend's decision will be before it has been
made. In many cases, especially when my friend is a
man of riper experience and higher moral wisdom
than myself, his decision may take me by complete
surprise.[2] He may do what I expected he would refuse
to do, or may take a line different from any of those
which presented themselves to me in anticipation. My
confidence is not that I know what he will do, but that
I know that whatever he does will be seen, *after* it has
been done, by myself or by others of more penetration,
to be the act of an upright and honourable man. (Just
so my confidence in a man's skill in chess, or his humour
in repartee, does not mean that I know by what move
he will counter his opponent, before the move is made,
or what he will say in reply to a challenge before he has
opened his mouth.)

There is nothing new in the particular point which
I am here urging. On the contrary, Kant's reliance on
the "imperative" as a *criterion* has always been felt
to be the very weakest point in his ethical doctrine. I
should actually be inclined to say that many of his
critics have fallen into the mistake of supposing that a
successful attack on the value of the "imperative" as a

---

[1] Mark Rutherford, *Clara Hopgood*, c. 5: "You are asking for a decision when
all the materials to make up a decision are not present. It is wrong to question
ourselves in cold blood as to what we should do in a great strait; for the emergency
brings the insight and the power necessary to deal with it. I often fear lest, if
such-and-such a trial were to befall me, I should miserably fail. So I should,
furnished as I now am, but not as I should be under stress of the trial." Yet this
position clearly needs some qualification, unless we are prepared to deny that
counsel is ever of practical use in a moral difficulty.

[2] On this point compare the moral of Browning's *Iván Ivánovitch.*

criterion of itself disproves its very different claim to be an adequate formulation of the supreme *principle* of right action, and that much of their criticism simply misses the mark in consequence of this elementary confusion. The point I want to make is rather different. Admitting that the "imperatives" of a moral code cannot in fact be used as a practical moral criterion, I would ask whether it is still not a direct consequence of the identification of the "morally legislative reason" with a reason I, and every man, have in possession that they ought to provide such a criterion, and whether therefore the manifest fact that they do not is not in itself a refutation of the "hypothesis" which demands the making of the false inference. The further comment I would make on the familiar facts is this, and it is the comment which naturally suggests itself to anyone who remembers Aristotle's admirable discussion of the relation between "practical goodness of intellect" and what Aristotle calls "goodness of character (ἠθικὴ ἀρετή, *virtus moralis*).[1] The facts must not be taken to mean merely that unless we keep the spirit of dutifulness alive by being daily dutiful in small matters, we are not very likely to have the strength to do our duty in the difficult situations when they arise ; that he who is careless in small things is likely to be careless, or worse, in great; though this is true enough. We must add that unless we live in the spirit of duty in the "small matters" of every day, we shall not be likely even to see what the path of duty is when the great responsibilities are laid upon us and we have to react to them. It is only as we become more and more personally moralised by faithful performance of already known duties that the full demand of duty upon us is progressively disclosed. We learn what the law of the moral life is by obeying

[1] *E.N.* 1144 a, 23 ff.

it; clear knowledge does not precede performance, but follows upon it. This, not the mere complexity of the conditions under which actual choices have to be made, is the chief ground of objection to Kant's singular contention that no honest man can ever be in doubt or perplexity about the path of duty.[1] I may be honest enough at the present moment in my desire to walk in the path of duty, but the price of past carelessness is too often inability to see which path is the path of duty.

Thus, again, we are pointed to the conclusion that the "reason" which, in the last resort, prescribes the law of duty is not ours in possession; it is a reason which is only communicated to us in part and gradually, and that in proportion to our faithfulness to the revelations already received. We do not make the law, we discover it and assent to it, and it is for that reason that no attitude to the source of the law is adequate, unless it has passed from mere respect into that unqualified reverence which we know as adoration and worship. And we cannot worship what is no richer in quality than our own self; we can only worship that which is already all, and more than all, we mean when we speak of ourselves as living, intelligent, moral, and personal. For that which we worship must be capable of continuing to sustain our worship, however much farther we may progress along the road which has already led us into such personal moral life as we enjoy. Thus viewed, the "supreme good" takes on the full character of a living, spiritual, and personal God, and the life of fulfilment of duty the character of a daily appropriation of the riches of God. The discharge of duty is seen to be the road to deiformity.

(5) This, again, means that we can make no hard-and-fast distinction of principle between the life of

---

[1] Kant, *Grundlegung zur Metaphysik der Sitten*, i. (*Werke*, iv. 251).

discharge of duty and the life of specifically religious faith. Faith is not a voluntary supplement, or append-age, to dutiful living, but its very breath of life. It would be misrepresenting the facts to think of the simple discharge of duty in the occupations of every day as a walking by sight, to be set in sharp contrast with the walking by faith characteristic of religion. To have a real and living faith means simply to be ready to stake yourself on what you know you cannot demonstrate, to be ready to stand by your conviction when all the appearances are against it. Now, it is not only in what are commonly called "religious" matters that this attitude is demanded of us, though, no doubt, it is there that its presence is most obvious, since it is so plain that a religion which means any-thing to a man's life means conviction of the truth of a view about the whole order of things which goes far beyond all that any man could propose to demon-strate. If we do not so readily discover the presence of the same element of faith in the unseen in the simple discharge of ordinary duty, the reason is probably that we are commonly contented with too low a stan-dard of the dutiful. We mistake for dutiful action action which is merely "according to duty", adopted for the reason that it is customary and conventional, and so "in the line of least resistance". But a morality reduced to acquiescence in the safe and customary, because it is the easier course, would be a morality from which all the life had evaporated. To perform even the simplest and most familiar act of duty in the dutiful spirit means to recognise it as the thing which is supremely worth while and would remain supremely worth while, were my whole existence at stake; of no act can it be demonstrated that it has this character of the supremely worth while. Of the heavier acceptances and surrenders of the moral life it is obviously true that in every one of them a man is risking the loss of his *anima*, and it is never demonstrable that the losing will end in a finding. The *appearances* are the other way, and that is why the acceptance, or surrender, needs a hero to make it. Even the call, for example, to what men call a "wider sphere of action" may, for all I know, or can prove, when I have to accept or decline it, be an invitation to expend my energy on a task to which I am not adequate, to the loss and deterioration of my personality. I may be taking myself where fatal trials and temptations await me, where the "contagion of the world's slow stain" will have more power upon me. The moral life, followed with a single mind, constantly calls us to put to the hazard not only health or comfort, but the soul itself. If we escape its perils, we escape in the strength of a faith which "appearances" cannot daunt.

It would be a total misconception to contrast the life of ethics as lived in the clear daylight with the life of religion as one of twilight, mystery, and danger. All these are to be found in the ethical life itself. There is the twilight; for, as we have seen, it is only gradually and in part that "conscience" provides light for our path; it enables us, at the best, to see where to plant our feet for the next step, but leaves the more distant scene in darkness. There is the mystery; for, in difficult cases, even the next step has so often to be taken with uncertain misgivings and the mental qualification, "God forgive me, if I am deciding wrong". There is the danger; since it may be the very foundations of our moral life which will be imperilled by a false step. If we allow ourselves to listen to the insidious suggestion that assent is only to be given to "clear and distinct ideas", we shall, of course, have to resign our-

selves to going through life without a religion; but
we shall equally have to go through life without action.
A worthy moral life, no less than the acceptance of
a religion, is an adventure by an uncertain light, and
the theses of Pragmatism contain at least this much
truth, that clearer insight has to be obtained by first
acting in the dim light we have, much as, in St.
Anselm's formula, belief in the verities of religion
precedes the understanding of them. The attitude of
practical piety is here only a further continuation and
completion of that which has been already adopted in
the simple resolution to live dutifully. That resolution
itself, formally no more than a determination to act
up to the standard of the best, so far as known, works
out in the end into the life which draws its continual
inspiration from contact with the living God, and is in
steady process of transfiguration into the likeness of
the source from which its stream is fed. The rule to
look "not to what I am, but to what I shall be", of itself expands into the rule of looking not to myself, but
to Him from whom what I shall be must come. *Werde
der du bist* is but an imperfect transcription of an
older maxim, ἕπου θεῷ.

V

MORAL EVIL AND SIN

Si dixerimus quoniam peccatum non habemus, ipsi nos seducimus.

I am myself indifferent honest, but yet I could accuse me of such things that it were better my mother had not borne me.—SHAKESPEARE.

IT is a commonplace to say that the most outstanding defect of ordinary philosophical treatises on ethics is their usually inadequate treatment of the problem of moral evil. Most writers on the subject seem to think they have done all that is to be expected of them when they have tried to tell us what the good for man is and what virtue, or the moral law, demands of us. What they set before us is either a theory of the good, or, it may be, a *Tugendlehre* or *Pflichtlehre*, and not much more. Even when the writer formally styles his exposition a "theory of good *and* evil", it is *good* of which he has most to say; evil usually comes off with a perfunctory consideration, and sometimes, as in Dr. G. E. Moore's influential *Principia Ethica*, is barely mentioned. So much is this the case that in many generally excellent moral treatises the very word *sin* never occurs, and the notion of sinfulness, or wickedness, is represented as a distinctively theological supplementation to, if not a theological distortion of, the plain facts of the moral life. It might not be going much too far to say that, of the major philosophers who have dealt expressly and at length with the moral life of man (independently of a theological tradition), there are only two, though they are two of the greatest, Plato and Kant, whose language reveals a keen and constant sense of human sinfulness. Certainly, one would look in vain for such a sense in the work of most of the best-known of these philosophers. It is not in Aristotle, nor in Descartes, nor in Spinoza, nor in Leibniz, nor in Hegel; least of all in the breezy and easy-tempered David Hume.[1] It is not even prominent in such vigorous champions of an "eternal and immutable" morality as Cudworth, Clarke and Price. The exceeding sinfulness of man is not one of their themes, and this is the more noteworthy that they are divines of a Church which teaches a dogma of "original sin", and professional preachers of a religion of redemption. They would, no doubt, if questioned, have given a formal assent to the proposition that actual human nature is "fallen through sin", but it is hard to believe that the assent would have been more than formal. I do not think I shall be seriously misrepresenting the habitual outlook of most moralists by saying that they take it very much as an obvious and regrettable incident of human life that we so often do what we ought not to do, but as nothing more than a regrettable incident. If they do not approach the spectacle of human wrongdoing in the spirit of such a maxim as "Better luck next time", or even, "There's no use in crying over spilt milk", at any rate they tend to the view that our misdeeds are just things to

---

[1] I do not forget Schopenhauer, but I think it would be true to say that his attention is given almost exclusively to "original" sin, to the exclusion of "actual", and that, with him, original sin itself receives a metaphysical interpretation which evacuates the meaning. When, for example, he quotes Calderon to the effect that

"el mayor pecado
Del hombre es haber nacido",

he forgets that Calderon was a Christian priest, to whom the words meant something very different from a thesis in metaphysics.

be put right and avoided for the future, and that there is something morbid in troubling ourselves greatly over them, when once we have done our best to "make good", by repairing the consequences of the past and reforming our habits. Amendment, attended perhaps with confession, virtually becomes, with them, the whole of penitence; the contrition which makes itself heard in the "penitential" Psalms seems almost unknown to "philosophical" ethics.

I would not suggest that this attitude to the problem is wholly without its historical justification. The traditional Christian dogma of original sin, its consequences and the mode of its transmission, as shaped in the West by St. Augustine, has always seemed to me, even in the moderated form in which it persists in the Thomist theology, manifestly the most vulnerable part of the whole Christian account of the relations of God and man, and to call more imperatively than any other part of the theological system for reconstruction in the light of philosophy and history. It would be ludicrous, if it were less sad, to see the Anglican communion at this moment fiercely engaged in polemics over eucharistic doctrines, where the differences are almost entirely about words, but apparently unconcerned by the fact that the language of its Baptismal office, if it means anything, seems to assert that millions of infants are condemned by a just judge to irretrievable exclusion from true felicity for a fault committed, as Pascal put it, by someone else thousands of years before their birth.[1] And yet, if we look more closely at the matter,

[1] The difficulty is not so apparent in St. Thomas, since he expressly teaches that the infant in *limbo* suffers only a *poena damni*, unattended by any *poena sensus*. But this does not seem to me to remove the root of the difficulty, which is, in fact, Augustine's division of evil into the two species of *malum culpae* and *malum poenae*. St. Thomas himself contrives, in his discussion of "vengeance", to bring all the "unmerited sufferings" of good men under the head of *poena* by arguing that they are "medicinal to the soul" (*S.T.* ii.ᵃ ii.ᵃᵉ q. 109,

there is something doubly strange about the current
ready acceptance of the fact of human misconduct.
From the speculative point of view there is a real problem here, a problem which has been set in the clearest
light by the Platonic Socrates. It surely is plain, as
Socrates is always contending in the dialogues,[1] that
though a man may, and often does, prefer the show or
the reputation of power, or riches, or beauty, or learning to the actual possession of them, there is just one
case in which no man prefers shadow to substance. No
one wants the show of happiness, good, felicity; we all
want the substance; we want to enjoy good, not to be
believed to enjoy it; to be happy, not to seem happy.
We have to reconcile this patent and undeniable fact
with the other equally undeniable fact that all of us,
in practice, so constantly take the shadow and let the
reality go. No one in his senses can suppose that we
act thus with our eyes open. There can be no real escape
from Socrates' conclusion that the wrongdoer acts from
"ignorance", in the sense in which Socrates used the
phrase; he mistakes for the highest good something
which is not the highest good, is misled by a deceptive
appearance of good. I confess that all the attempted
defences of the reality of "unreasonable action" impress me as mere sporting with words. If we look not to
words but to facts, it is incredible to me that evil should
ever be chosen just because it is recognised for what
it is. If I asked any man the reason why he preferred
A to *B*, I should think it a complete explanation to be
told "because I see that *A* is so much better than *B*",
even if I thought that "perception" an illusion. If I

---

art. 4 resp.), but unless we accept Augustine's forensic view of the implication
of unborn manhood in the sin of the first man, this is merely playing fast and loose
with the notion of *poena*. And if we did accept this Augustinian view, could we
logically object to his condemnation of infants wholesale to the "fire"?

[1] Cf. *Gorgias*, 466 E 1 ff.

received the answer "because I see *A* to be worse than *B*", I should certainly refuse to take my interlocutor seriously; I should suppose that he was "playing" with my question. There is a legend that Henry II. of England on his death-bed deliberately blasphemed God in order to ensure his own damnation. "Since thou", he is made to say, "hast taken from me the thing I most delight in, Le Mans, I will deprive thee of the thing in me thou hast most delight in, my soul." If any man, neither insane nor delirious, ever has behaved in this fashion, I can only say that, in fact, if not in words, he must have pronounced the revengeful frustration of God's purpose a good worth purchasing at the cost of his own ruin. He must have thought it would be truer happiness to look up out of the flames and see the Creator disappointed than to enjoy the delights of Paradise, but forgo wreaking his spite.

Yet the explanation that the choice of evil is due to ignorance or mistake only throws the difficulty back one stage. The problem of wrong choice, with this explanation, becomes a part of the more general problem of false judgement, or error, and this problem is itself a perplexing one. The real difficulty for the epistemologist is created, as Plato suggests in the *Theaetetus* and Descartes indicates more plainly in his *Fourth Meditation*, not by true judgement, but by error. Why do we ever judge falsely about anything? Descartes tries to answer the question, as you may remember, by saying "because we allow ourselves to make assertions when the evidence for them is inconclusive". But we may ask, as Spinoza said,[1] how it comes that we do this. If we perceived the insufficiency of the evidence, we could not give assured assent to the conclusion. We cannot make ourselves believe true what we see

---

[1] Spinoza, *Ep.* lix. (*V.V.L.*), to Tschirnhaus.

to be false, or believe proved what we see not to be proved. Why then does a creature, *ex hypothesi* endowed with "understanding", the power to discern the true from the false, not habitually discern that insufficient evidence *is* insufficient? Why, in particular, does the merely relatively and temporarily good ever impose itself on us as the absolute best? We all, to be sure, know how the evolutionist answers the question. He will tell us that the answer is that our own reason and judgement are themselves in course of development, things still in the making, not things made and completed. Judgement is untrustworthy and mistaken because it is, at every moment, making itself, and the method by which it makes itself is one of trial and learning from the consequences of error. We learn to think truly or to do right by thinking falsely or acting wrongly and having to "take the consequences", thus coming to readjust our ways of thinking, or acting, to the situation our error, or misconduct, has created. In both cases the process of correction is never fully completed, but in both it can be, and is, carried steadily further and further "without limit".

Whether this solution of the speculative problem of error is as satisfactory as it is simple is a question I must not raise here. For the present it is sufficient for my purpose to ask the more restricted question whether, as applied to the special case of *moral* error, it does anything like justice to the whole of the familiar facts of life. Does it really "save the appearances"? I think it is fairly clear that it does nothing of the kind. I cannot, indeed, undertake to offer demonstration on such a point; in matters of practice, as Aristotle should long ago have taught us, strict demonstration has no place. But I think it possible to show that any ethical doctrine which minimises the seriousness of human sinfulness

is incompatible with notorious facts of a moral psychology which any of us may verify in his own personal
experience, and that these facts cannot be disposed of
by treating them as illusion bred of antecedent theological prepossession. Our moral reaction to "wickedness" appears to me to be a genuinely ethical reaction,
and yet to bear witness to the impossibility of prevent-
ing the ethical habit of mind, once thoroughly awakened,
from developing spontaneously into a habit which
must be regarded as specifically religious. It is not, so
far as I can see, theology which has contaminated ethics
with the notion of *sin*; it is morality which has brought
the notion into theology.

The "naturalistic" interpretations of moral misdoing
may take more forms than one, and we may meet some
of them in philosophies based on metaphysical speculations which the consistently naturalistic thinker would
be careful to repudiate. Moral badness may be thought
of as no more than temporary or permanent failure to
keep up to the standard of adjustment of action to
situation already reached in our society, and, in the
main, in our personal conduct; as "atavistic" regression
to the ruder practice of a more "primitive" age. The
bad man may be regarded simply as a "barbarian"
among civilised surroundings, or an "animal" among
men. This is, in fact, the form in which the naturalistic
conception of sin most readily recommends itself to
the thoroughgoing evolutionist. But the same thought
may show itself in connection with a completely non-
evolutionist metaphysic, when sin is treated as nothing
more than a breach of a reasonable law. Thus Dr.
McTaggart, who regards the universe as a vast complex of persons all underived and ultimate, stands in
his metaphysic at the opposite pole from the evolutionist. From his point of view all "evolution" *seems*

to be, but really *is* not, and all judgements that anything
has "evolved", is "evolving" or will "evolve", are,
strictly speaking, false judgements. But McTaggart's
view of moral wrongdoing, pithily condensed by himself into the statement that it is good there should be
rules of conduct, good that we should have the spirit
to break them, and good that the birch should descend
on us when we do so,[1] is frankly naturalistic. It is
against every view of this easy-going type that I would
enter a protest in the name of a sound moral psychology. The point I am anxious to enforce is that, in
more ways than one, our human expression of wrong-
doing and guilt is so singularly unlike anything we can
detect in the pre-human world that we are bound to
treat it as something strictly *sui generis* and *human*,
not generically animal. If we could really succeed in
proving the existence of the same specific experience
in any of our humbler congeners, what we should have
shown would be, not that sin can be adequately described by the categories of "naturalism", but that
some of the creatures we have supposed to be "mere
animals" are more than we have taken them to be, that
the categories of naturalism will not even do all the
work moralists like T. H. Green have been willing to
concede.

There would be nothing necessarily paradoxical in
such a conclusion. We cannot be too careful to remember what "naturalists", good and bad, are too prone
to forget, that our notion of an "animal" is a highly
artificial one, constructed by starting with specifically
human experience, and leaving out of account the
features which strike us as most intimately human.
We have got at our conception of the animal's life by
trying to construct the whole of a comparative series

[1] *Studies in Hegelian Cosmology*, p. 174.

in which we really know only the first terms.[1] It is possible enough, proceeding in this way, to leave out too much. Any limit we construct in this way may be a merely "ideal limit" never to be met in actual fact. But if we commit the mistake of assuming that the ideal limit is actual fact, we clearly must not expect subsequently to be able to show the identity of actual human experiences with imagined experiences which are not even those of a real "animal". What it is like to be a non-human animal we do not know, and at best can only conjecture. The one thing we have no right to do is to mutilate the known facts of the only life with which we are directly and intimately acquainted on the strength of our conjectures about a life we can never experience.

Presuming, then, that "animals" really are very much what a naturalistic account assumes them to be, but being careful to remember that such an account may be inadequate, we may, I think, specify five familiar characteristics which distinguish our human experience of guilt and wrongdoing from anything which — at least on the naturalistic account of the matter—is to be found in the infra-human world.

(1) In the first place, it is characteristic of the human sense of guilt that it always involves condemnation of our own selves and our own doings, and is thus radically different from any discontent with our surroundings. As Butler says,[2] when he is contrasting self-condemnation with mere discontent, the one re-

---

[1] And this procedure may always involve error. To take a trivial example, I give you the first three terms of a series as 1, 3, 9, and ask you to say what the fourth and other terms, which I have not given, are. I am almost certain to be told that the fourth term is 27, the fifth 81, and so forth. But this may be a mere mistake; the fourth term may have been 25. I may have intended the series of which the "general term" is $1 + (n - 1) \cdot 2^{n-1}$, not that of which the "general term" is 3^{n-1}.

[2] *Dissertation of the Nature of Virtue* (ed. Gladstone, § 8).

gards our "conduct", the other our "condition". Butler
is here thinking of a case such as that of a man who
forfeits an expected inheritance through his own folly
or ill-behaviour, and of dissatisfaction which expresses
itself in an explicit judgement. He means that there is a
vast difference between the reflective judgements of the
man who finds himself disappointed by a senile freak
of the testator and the man who knows he has caused
himself to be disinherited for his idleness, profligacy, or
ingratitude. The one pronounces himself unfortunate,
the other, if he has any vestiges of a conscience, owns
himself deservedly punished. I take it Butler would
not have denied that the same kind of difference may
be found at a less articulate stage of mental development, at which no explicit judgement is formed either
on our conduct or on our condition. There may be some
analogy between the total mental reaction of a young
child who is disappointed of a holiday by the rain and
that of one who is deprived of the holiday as a punishment for quarrelling with his brothers and sisters, but
we all remember our own childhood well enough to
know that the reactions are not identical. If they were,
it would be unintelligible how, at a later stage, the
familiar explicit distinction between unmerited "hard
luck" and deserved unhappiness should ever have
been developed. We should not even remark it, as we
do, as a common feature of human nature, that men
so regularly try to awaken our pity for their mis-
fortunes by dwelling on the theme of their being due
"to no fault of their own".

The point is so obvious that I should think it needless to dwell on it but for the fact that so eminent a
philosopher as F. H. Bradley has, in one passage of
his best-known work, hinted that something at least
analogous to and continuous with moral self-condemna-

tion may already be found in germ in the sulky brooding of a beast of prey which has missed its "kill".[1] In
Bradley's mouth the words, I suppose, are not meant
to have a naturalistic significance. His meaning is
probably not that a man oppressed by the sense of
personal misdoing is no more than a sulky and disappointed brute, but rather that the brute may conceivably be something more than merely disappointed
and sulky. But it must not be forgotten that *if* the tiger
which has missed its spring is *only* disappointed and
sulky, there is a gulf which cannot be bridged between
the tiger's state of mind and that of the youngest child
who knows the specific "feel" of naughtiness. The
suggestion which Bradley's words at least *ought* to
imply is that the tiger is sulky and dissatisfied with
itself, not merely with the general state of things, however rudimentary its self-disapproval may be. I should
suppose that such a suggestion is one which will never
be capable either of definite proof or of certain disproof.
But if it is sound, it follows at once that a tiger is something very much more like a moral person than has
ever been supposed by those who have undertaken to
derive human morality from "animal" origins. The
attractiveness of the derivation for a certain type of
mind lies precisely in its apparent minimalisation of
the "nature" it requires us to accept as given fact;
its success would require us not to minimalise, but to
maximalise, "nature".

(2) A more striking difference between the moral
life of man and what appears to be the mental life of
animals is found when we consider the human attitude
to our own unsatisfactory past. Something has already
been said on this by way of anticipation, but we may
treat the matter at this stage a little more in detail.

[1] *Appearance and Reality*, p. 431 n.

Nothing is more characteristic of the human sense of guilt than its *indelibility*, its power of asserting itself with unabated poignancy in spite of all lapse of time and all changes in the self and its environment. It is only a man with the "mentality" of the animal who can reconcile himself to the comfortable view that what he has done amiss is "washed off" by punishment, or "made good" by subsequent better conduct, and so no longer any present concern of his life. From the point of view of secular society and its criminal law, it is no doubt true that the past is past, if the discipline of life has corrected a man's evil passions and habits, and the actual mischief he has done to individuals, or the community at large, has been compensated. So far we can understand the view that the criminal who has "purged" his offence and made restitution ought to be free from all reproach for his past. It is not for us to cast it in his teeth. But the point which, as it seems to me, all the moralists who treat the conduct of life as no more than a matter between the individual and "society" customarily overlook is that an offender who has been genuinely moralised by experience of the way of transgressors is never satisfied to take this view of *himself*. We may have lost the right to reproach him; he does not cease to reproach himself. He may know quite well that the "hurt" he has done to his victims has been abundantly compensated and that he has himself become a different man, and is no longer in danger of offending in the old way. But even if his past has been forgotten, or condoned by every one else, he does not himself forget or condone it. He is never secure, and does not seek to be secure, against the recurrence of the old self-condemnation in all the intensity of its bitterness. It is not likely that St. Paul's converts or fellow-apostles remembered

against him the part he had played in the death of
Stephen; from their point of view he had "made
good" many times over. But we see from his own
language that he had neither forgotten nor condoned.
Now the kind of experience which led St. Paul to
speak of himself, with the near prospect of crowning his apostolate by martyrdom before him, as the
greatest of sinners, seems to me to be one which we all
can detect in ourselves, sometimes in forms fantastic
enough. There are old misdoings, often they are such
as any kindly outside observer would dismiss as mere
trivialities, not infrequently they date from childhood
itself, which can haunt and torment us all through life.
The sting of them, often enough, does not seem to
lie in any social harm or distress they have occasioned,
nor yet in the apprehension that we are now tainted by
the particular moral defect they reveal. It is sometimes
the juvenile misdeeds which were not taken seriously
to heart by anyone at the time, caused no appreciable
hurt to anyone, and were prompted by cupidities and
tempers which have long since died out with the march
of time, that can wound most in the remembrance.
This goes a long way to explain why the best men
find that penitence and self-humiliation are no mere
occasional or temporary accompaniments of their experience, but a constant and ever-present feature in
the moral life.

I know, of course, that the numerous exponents of a
morality of "healthy-mindedness" would simply dismiss all such experiences as "morbid"—a convenient
way of burking serious thought by parrot-like repetition of a disparaging epithet—or account for them
all as due to an illegitimate influence of theological
"superstition" on our ethical outlook. Against the
charge of morbidity it should be enough to reply that,

if you allow yourself to dismiss any *universal* characteristic of life as "morbid", you lose the very basis for an intelligible distinction between health and disease. If we cannot take *quod semper, quod ubique, quod ab omnibus* as the standard of health and normality, what is to be our criterion of the normal and the morbid? If all men without exception are mad, how are we to draw the distinction between the sane man and insane? Whether the sense of the indelibility of *some* moral misdoing is in fact a universal feature of human experience can, of course, only be decided in one way. Each of us must ask himself whether there are not *some* episodes in his own past about which he himself feels it.

I do not mean to say that the feeling of which we are speaking is not, like other feelings, subject to strange aberrations. The memories which give me the keenest pang when they recur need not be memories of the worst acts I have committed. I may have forgotten, or may take credit to myself for, deeds which I should recognise to be the worst of my life, if my insight into good and evil were more penetrating. But these large possibilities of aberration no more prove the sense of personal guilt a "morbid" delusion than our sense of beauty is proved illusory by the indubitable facts that it is often powerfully affected by objects which, as we discover for ourselves, when our aesthetic perception has been refined and deepened, had little real beauty, and that from the dullness of our perceptions we often let exquisite beauty go unrecognised. The facts "are beyond dispute", but an intelligent man does not infer from them that beauty is an illusion, or that sensitiveness to it is not a real and very specific character of our human experience. In the same way, when a speaker says, as I have heard a distinguished scholar say, perhaps not wholly

in earnest, that he has no such sense of sin as books
tell of, and can only suppose that it is something of the
same kind as his own discomfort on the recollection of
a humiliating "social blunder", he is really bearing
witness against himself. He is testifying that he has
the feeling all the time, though it may, in his case, be
attached to the wrong objects, exactly as the man who
is thrown into transports of delight by the second-rate
in literature or music really has a sense of beauty,
though an untrained and ill-regulated sense.

Further, it should be evident that the attempt,
while admitting the actuality of the sense of guilt, to
explain it away as a consequence of the importation
of non-moral "theological" superstition into the ethical
domain, is a pure fallacy of *hysteron proteron*. This point
has been made so clearly and finally by Professor
Gilbert Murray[1] that I make no apology for openly
borrowing his example. If we examine the poetry of
Homer—and the same thing will be found true of any
literature which reveals much of human thought and
feeling—we shall note that there are some kinds of
conduct, even if they are few, which are regarded as
specially unpardonable and certain to provoke the
anger of the gods, the unseen guardians of the moral
law. To put poison on your arrows seems to be one of
these offences. The poisoned arrow appears to horrify
the Homeric Achaean much as "poison gas" horrified
us when it first made its appearance in the recent
War. According to *Odyssey a*, Odysseus was denied by
his friend when he requested a "deadly drug" for
this purpose: "he gave it not, for he felt an awe of the
gods who live for ever".[2] Now whence, as Murray asks,

---

[1] In his *Rise of the Greek Epic*.

[2] *Odyssey a*, 262:

ἀλλ' ὁ μὲν οὔ οἱ
δῶκεν, ἐπεί ῥα θεοὺς νεμεσίζετο αἰὲν ἐόντας.

has this conviction that the gods will not forgive the man who poisons his arrows come? Obviously not from observation of the experienced course of events. It can never have been the case that all users of poisoned arrows were remarked to come to mysterious and horrible ends, only to be accounted for as due to the anger of unseen beings. The order of thought, as Murray says, must have been that the poisoning of arrows is so hateful a practice that I should certainly take vengeance for it, were I a god; presumably, then, the real gods feel and act as I should do in their place. Therefore, I must never take this kind of advantage or have anything to do with others who take it. The crime is not believed unpardonable because it has first been believed that, as a fact, it is not pardoned. It is believed to be in fact never pardoned because it is first felt that it ought not to be pardoned.

The same thing is true about other offences which Homer treats as peculiarly unforgivable. They are all forms of what the Greeks of a later time called ὕβρις, taking full advantage of your superiority against the peculiarly helpless, orphans, beggars, strangers in the land, that is, those who have no visible human backer to do them right. (We see the same thing in the Old Testament in the special stress laid upon the duty of considerateness to orphan, widow, alien in the land.) In all these cases, it is plainly a strictly ethical sense of the enormity and indelibility of the guilt which has led to the belief, by no means directly suggested by observed facts, that it has its unseen avengers. And I would add that we cannot account for this antecedent moral conviction by any appeal to considerations of social utility. The facts in question, on the contrary, fairly *prove* that morality has its source elsewhere than in "usefulness". Poisoned arrows are eminently useful

to the group which has tribal enemies to resist and
can command a supply of an effective poison. It is
not ill-treatment of the widow or the defenceless alien,
but ill-treatment of a valuable member of the tribe
that should be the great offence, if moral codes were
no more than rules of social utility. Many of us, I
trust, to-day agree that the last war has revealed new
and unsuspected depths of turpitude in mankind,
against which we must be strenuously on our guard in
all time to come. But the reason for our unqualified
detestation of "scientific warfare" and all its devil's
paraphernalia of bombs and poisons is not regard for
social utility; it is our conviction that the whole thing
is a *disgrace* to human nature.

If we may fairly regard this sense of indelible guilt
as a genuine feature of distinctively human life, it
seems to me, as I have already hinted more briefly, to
reveal the presence in man of something we never
detect in the animals. Animals, it is often remarked,
and sometimes with a suggestion of envy, have no
sense of sin. I am not sure that the statement would be
admitted without fuller qualification by all observers.
There are those who profess that they can detect in
their dogs, after some breach of the customary discipline of the household, signs of a shame and uneasiness which might seem analogous with what we
men call consciousness of guilt. Thus I have known it
maintained that a dog which has transgressed in the
matter of cleanliness sometimes seems to be not merely
offended by the result, or apprehensive of punishment,
but actually ashamed of itself. The question of fact
would be hard to settle, and must be left to the determination of experts in animal psychology, of whom I
am not one. But I must repeat a remark which has been
already made and is, I think, of fundamental import-

ance. We are in grave danger of being misled if we
base our conceptions of an animal's psychology on the
conduct of just those animals which have been most
successfully made companions of man in his daily life,
our domesticated and civilised dogs. We have to
allow for the real possibility that the naturalistic
account of human conduct itself is wholly inadequate.
If it is, then man is something more than an animal,
and constant and familiar association with the life of
man may consequently have, in a lesser degree, made
the highly domesticated dog something more than an
"animal" too. If he has some *analogon* in his life to
what we know in ourselves as morality, the reason
may be that by association with man, who is a moral
person, he has become what he could never have become of himself. To understand the real limitations
of a purely animal life we should surely, as a matter
of method, start from consideration of animals which
have *not* been subjected to the possibly transfiguring
influence of association with man; our standard dog
should be "yellow dog Dingo". If we neglect this
caution we may obviously be led into a glaring *petitio
principii*. You must not argue that the behaviour of the
dog domesticated by man is sufficient proof that our
human morality is only a development from beginnings
all to be found in the infra-human animals, unless you
can first establish a merely naturalistic theory of the
genesis of human morality itself, and thus your argument from the behaviour of your dog presupposes the
very thesis it is meant to establish.

Still, even if we neglect the, as I think, necessary
caution which has just been given, we yet seem to
detect a real difference between human morality and
anything which the extremest believer in the *quasi*-
morality of the more highly domesticated animals can

fairly claim for them. Even if it is true that an animal
admitted to human fellowship does on occasion show
signs of feeling ashamed of itself, there seems no
sufficient reason to believe that there is any memory
of the shame which can be effective after the creature
has been duly punished and restored to favour again.
When that has happened, the animal's past seems, as
has been said already in a rather different context,
to be not only dead, but fairly buried. Now we, too,
speak of our "dead" past, but, as I have already said,
it is only the "criminal" who thinks of his past as
buried and done with when he has undergone his
appointed punishment. That he can thus feel at ease
with the past, which has been "paid for", is the very
thing which most certainly proves that he has not really
become a "new man". If he had become a "new man",
he would have to say, in the language of the familiar
hymn,

> Could my zeal no respite know,
> Could my tears for ever flow,
> All for sin could not atone.

The familiar human sense of guilt thus points directly
to that complication of the eternal and the temporal
which is characteristic of moral aspiration. To be
merely temporal would be to live wholly in the present
moment, to be, in the phrase I once heard wittily used
of a certain politician, "incapable of acquiring a past".
If our life were a mere pulse or episode in the "passage
of nature", the past, once past, would be left behind,
dead and done for. That is just what it is not and what
we must not aspire to make it. The man who is truly
aspiring to a better moral life is not aiming at "forgetting the past", painful as the memory of it may be.
If that were all his purpose, drink would probably
serve his end better than moral effort. It may be neces-

sary, at certain stages of his progress, that he should
be warned not to "brood" on the details of the past,
but simple unconsciousness of it is not the condition he
wishes to attain. Forgetting may be seasonable in its
time, but what we really aim at is a state in which we
can remember and yet feel no pang in the remembrance, because we see how all the evil has "worked
for good". Dante[1] has taken the point rightly when
he makes his ex-troubadour in Paradise recall his
disordered youth, not with shame and pain, but with
thanksgiving for the grace which has transmuted a
personality with such beginnings. Because we are
creatures with a passion for eternity, our characteristic moral endeavour is not to forget or cancel the
past, but to make it, with all that is worst in it, an
actual instrument to the achieving of a stable personality that will not pass. Whether our personal moral
effort, unaided by an antecedent free movement from
the side of the eternal to meet us, can achieve this task
is another question. It may be thought that the recurrent stings of guilt, odd as are the disguises they
sometimes assume, are just consequences of our secret
consciousness that the task of complete transmutation
cannot be achieved in our own unaided strength.

(3) A further peculiarity of the genuinely ethical
attitude towards sin seems to me to be that recognition
of our guilt is regularly attended by what we may call
a *demand* for punishment. In days now gone by, it
used to be a commonplace of the average sermon that
"sin *must* be punished", "God *must* execute justice on
the wrongdoer". Utterances of this kind are out of
fashion to-day, and I should certainly not care to re-

---

[1] *Paradiso*, ix. 103:

"Non però qui si pente, ma si ride,
Non de la colpa, ch' a mente non torna,
Ma del valor ch' ordinò e provide."

habilitate some of the ethical and theological tenets with
which it was customary to connect them. But I own they
appear to me to be prompted by a genuinely ethical feeling and to contain an important truth, though in a form
readily liable to unethical perversions. They have the
same value, and are open to the same misunderstandings
as the old doctrine, also now much out of fashion, of the
retributive character of punishment; a doctrine really
indispensable to sound ethics. We have to remark that
the notion of retribution, fundamental in this way of
thinking, has nothing to do, except accidentally, with
the gratification of revengeful passion; any psychological analysis based on the common confusion between retribution and revenge is a falsification of facts.
Revenge is essentially a *personal* gratification to be
enjoyed by a party who conceives himself to have been
in some way aggrieved or damaged. It follows, therefore, that if punishment is mere vengeance, its proper
measure is the material detriment, or the sentimental
grievance felt by the party who has been damaged or
affronted. If he feels no deep resentment, or is ready to
compromise his resentment for some material or sentimental offset, there can be no reason why the revenge
should be exacted. The detriment or affront is his own
personal affair, with which no one but himself is deeply
concerned. We have only to look at the way in which,
as society becomes more and more moralised, the
development of a satisfactory system of penal law depends on the withdrawal of the initiative in bringing
offences to punishment from the parties immediately
concerned and the lodging of it with bodies representative of the community at large, as well as on the substitution of a reasonable and "objective" for a personal
and arbitrary standard of penalties, to see that throughout the whole process retribution becomes more pro-

minent and more certain in proportion as the feature
of satisfaction for the desire of personal vengeance
sinks into the background. It would be a mistake to
suppose that the process is no more than one of sup-
pressing the excesses to which personal vengeance may
provoke an aggrieved party, though this is one side
of it.

It is true that when the initiative in the punishment
of homicide is taken out of the hands of the family of
the deceased it is no longer possible for the avenger
of blood to gratify his passion by torturing the culprit;
but it is equally true that the main motive for the change
of practice has, in fact, been not so much the desire to
avoid excessive severities as the desire to make it impossible for the shedder of blood to escape lightly by
compounding with the relatives of his victim. If we
look at the actual working of the system by which it is
left to private persons who feel themselves aggrieved
to bring offenders to justice, as we see it in operation
in historical societies, what most seriously outrages our
civilised sense of justice, I make bold to say, is not that
some offenders meet with excessive and inhuman treatment, but that most offenders escape so lightly. The prevalent mischief in the arrangement by which murder,
for example, goes unpunished, unless the relatives of
the murdered man initiate proceedings, is that most
murders are either disregarded or compounded for by
what we judge a wholly inadequate "blood-price". It
is even possible, with such a system, for the powerful
and violent to take the view that their crimes are "well
worth" the very moderate cost of patching them up.
Men in general are more indolent and covetous, and
less vindictive than they are supposed to be when
the transition from private to public initiative in the
prosecution of crimes is traced to a growing fear

of undue cruelty. We may fairly doubt whether, when all is said, the penalties for serious crimes are not, on the whole, severer as well as more certain in highly moralised than in more imperfectly moralised societies.[1]

Again, it would not be true to say that the change on which we are commenting leaves the connection between revenge and punishment unaffected, and merely substitutes the larger group of the community for the private person, or the smaller group of relatives, friends or associates, as the party exacting satisfaction for revengeful feeling. This is, no doubt, a small part of the truth. As we become increasingly humanised, we do learn to see more clearly how the interests of all are bound up together, and how the wrong which immediately falls on one member of the community more indirectly inflicts some injury on the others. But this is far from being the whole of the truth. It has to be added that the punishment of an offence by the agents of a

---

[1] Thus it comes as a shock to us when we first discover that, as recently as 1685 in our own country, perjuries like those of Oates, who deliberately for gain swore away the lives of innocent men, were legally only punishable as misdemeanours. We feel that they ought to have been capital felonies. It is absurd to pretend that suffering inflicted is made just punishment by the circumstances that the suffering is either (1) salutary to the sufferer, or (2) conducive to the general social welfare, or by both. It might be highly salutary to me to learn to bear the loss of eyesight, or to be reduced to extreme poverty, but it would be no "just penalty" if I were sentenced to lose my property, or my eyes, on that ground. And if I am sentenced to penal servitude for a crime, the sentence does not cease to be just because it is foreseen that my character will deteriorate Dartmoor. It is arguable that it would be socially beneficial to deepen the sense of responsibility in ambitious politicians by hanging ministers whose conduct of affairs is proved by the event to have been infatuated; it is quite another question whether the procedure would be just punishment. Justice is no more possible in a society which refuses to recognise retribution than chastity in one where

"man and woman,
Their common bondage burst, may freely borrow
From lawless love a solace for their sorrow".

It is arguable that in such a society there may be something better than either of these virtues, but not that it possesses *them*. To do Shelley justice, he never pretended to regard chastity as a virtue. Would that utilitarians had been as honest, or as clear-headed, about justice.

civilised society is, in principle, not a "revenge". We ourselves should be profoundly disturbed if homicides and forgers were not brought to justice, and we should not be disturbed merely because we thought our own chance of being murdered or cheated increased by the negligence of the authorities. Hume's moral theory is far from being the last word of ethics, but it has at least the merit of putting the "disinterested" character of moral judgements beyond dispute. But when the murderer and the forger are brought to justice, no section of a civilised society enjoys the pleasant feeling of gratified personal revenge. It is in the novels of Dickens, not in real life, that men get a thrill of personal satisfaction when Fagin is driven mad by the near prospect of the gallows, or Uriah Heep sent to solitary confinement. And I believe we should all agree to reject as immoral the view that if society felt so inclined it would be at liberty to compound with a criminal, as a man who has only his personal vindictiveness to gratify, and prefers making a profit to getting the gratification of vindictive feeling, may quite reasonably do. If this were our attitude to crime and criminals, I cannot help thinking there would be a much greater general readiness to "let the offender off" than serious men actually exhibit. We might have to reckon, on behalf of almost every criminal, with the regular defence that his crime can be argued to have been actually beneficial to the community, and that the benefit more than outweighs the indirect detriment caused by the encouragement that acquittal may give to future potential criminals. And in some cases, I believe, such a defence could be made good. It might be no more than the truth, in some cases of deliberate murder, that society had benefited much more by the removal of a bad and dangerous man than it stood to lose by the very

slight encouragement afforded to intending murderers
by an acquittal in this special case and on these special
grounds.

Yet I cannot think a sober moralist would contend
that the badness of a murdered man's character should
be a recognised ground for condoning murder.[1] The
reason given by Macaulay for condemning the illegal
punishment of so complete a scoundrel as Oates, that
illegal penalties inflicted on notorious villains are likely
to be made precedents for similar illegalities in the case
of less hardened offenders, though sound enough, does
not go to the root of the matter. The villain, villain as
he is, has his rights, and they must not be violated,
even though it were certain that the precedent would
not be abused. Morality is, indeed, society's great
weapon for self-protection, but it is something very
much more than a device for social self-protection; its
intrinsic character must not be confounded with this
obvious external effect.

What we all feel at bottom, I believe, is that the sentence of society, or of a court of law, inflicting punishment on an offender, if it is really a just sentence,
is only the repetition of one which the offender, if his
moral being remains sound at the centre, must already
have passed against himself. We recognise the justice
of a social penalty decreed upon us, when and if we
have already sat in judgement on ourselves. Similarly,
when pious men say that God "must" punish wrong-
doing, they are giving expression to a *demand* for punishment which they find in their own hearts. We may
understand the matter better in the light of our personal

---

[1] Thus society probably gains considerably when a professional blackmailer is
murdered by one of his victims. But I cannot believe that any one would seriously
desire to see it made a good legal defence against a charge of murder to prove
that the victim had lived by blackmail, even apart from the danger that such a
defence might often be pleaded in cases where it would be materially false.

feelings about our lapses from the standard of the best in things of which no society can possibly take cognis- ance. When, for example, we are convicted by our own conscience of disloyalty to a friend, even were it only a disloyalty of secret thought, it is intolerable to us that our friend should go on, in ignorance of the fault, treat- ing us with the same trust as though it had never been committed. We feel that we *must* make confession of it, and that we should be poor creatures if we congratu- lated ourselves on the absence of evidence of the fault and the certainty that it cannot come to our friend's knowledge, so long as we keep our own counsel. If we confess the fault and our friend treats it with careless condonation, our situation is made still worse. We feel that he is treating us as beings who are not fully human and accountable, creatures from whom nothing better than treachery was to be expected, and this puts an end to all possibility of all genuine human love and friend- ship. If we are capable of them, they ought to be ex- pected of us, and our lapses into treason *ought* to make a difference to our friend's attitude towards us. We may look forward to forgiveness, when we have earned it, or as freely given for the sake of some third party honoured and loved by both ourselves and the friend we have injured, but genuine forgiveness must, *of course*, involve, on the side of the forgiving party, the awareness that there has been something to forgive. We measure the moral nobility of the forgiveness by the magnitude of the fault to be forgiven. Forgiveness of injuries, prompted by love, is one thing; easy con- donation, really based on contempt, a very different thing. He to whom much is forgiven, the Gospel tells us, will love much; we cannot love much because some- thing has been lightly condoned to us. We appreciate a great forgiveness only because we credit the forgiver

with a true estimate of the gravity of the act he loves us
well enough to forgive.[1]

At the cost of a brief digression, I would remark here
that what we have just said needs to be kept carefully
in mind in estimating the ethical bearings of the Christian doctrine of the remission of sins. Two different objections are taken to the doctrine on professedly ethical
grounds, and both seem to me morally superficial. On
the one hand, it is urged that there is something morally
offensive in the doctrine that God's justice demands
any penalties for human wrongdoing, and that the remission of sins is only effected, as Christian theology
teaches, at an immense price, is purchased by the death
of the God-man. Justice, we are told, is unworthy of a
God; a God should simply "let us all off", and it should
cost him nothing to do it. On the other side, it is also
said that *any* remission is unworthy of a God. For
remission is "letting off", and it is always immoral
that anyone should be "let off" any part of the full consequences of his acts. Both criticisms, I believe, arise
from a confusion between forgiveness and condonation,
and one destroys the other. Mere light condonation,
such as that ascribed to God in the Persian scoffer's
quatrain about the potter who is a "good fellow", or by
the saying of the scientific man who informed us some
years ago that God "does not concern himself with our
peccadillos", is a wholly unethical attitude. A God who
"lets us off", because He does not care what such insects
do or do not do, would be a God who despised us, and
with whom we could have no vivifying relations. We
could not draw any real inspiration towards good from

---

[1] May this not explain why, as Macaulay says, so little gratitude was ever
called forth by the "cold magnanimity" of William III. to useful but treacherous
persons? The pardoned offenders felt that the pardoner despised them, and pardoned them because he despised them too completely to be moved by their
treacheries. Naturally, then, they felt little or no gratitude.

whatever relations we may have with a being who thinks
so little of us that he does not care what we may do.
Indeed such a being would be morally on a lower level
than ourselves, who may not care what we do as profoundly as we ought, but at any rate do care to some
extent. A "great first cause" of so unspiritual a kind
would plainly be no fit recipient of respect, to say nothing of adoration, from beings with a moral nature.
Still less would such a being be an unseen friend and
helper of man. For the paradox of Socrates in the
Gorgias[1] is no more than the truth. The offender who is
simply "let off" remains worse in himself, and so further
from true felicity, than the offender who is "brought to
book". It is good for us, and not bad, if the power which
rules the universe takes account of what we are in our
moral being; only on that condition can we expect that
experience of life will be a discipline into moral good.

It is often said—it is not for me to judge with how
much justice—that the Moslem confuses forgiveness
with mere condonation, a "letting-off" from a penalty
which is to be had for the simple ejaculation of an
astaghfiru 'llāh without any change of heart.[2] *If* this is
true, the Moslem must mean by divine forgiveness something quite alien to the spirit of genuine Christianity.
From the moralist's point of view it is a recommendation, not a defect, of the Christian conception that it
insists on the *justice* of God, which is but another name
for the fact that God is good, and, being good, cares for
the participation of His creatures in the absolute good
which He Himself possesses. It is because Christians
think of their God as "just in all His ways" that they
can also believe that His purpose with them is to make

---

[1] *Gorgias*, 472 e.
[2] Cf. Lane, *Modern Egyptians*, ch. xiii. (pp. 285-7 of edition published by
Gardner, 1895).

them a new creation, not simply to let them loose on a new environment. He makes them happy by first enabling them to "merit" their happiness. Because He is just, His forgiveness is no mere indifference, but a genuine moral forgiveness which means so much to Himself that it can remake the very self of the recipient, as, in a lesser degree, a man's self may be cleansed and remade by receiving a fellow-man's forgiveness for a grievous wrong, though never by being "let off" as a creature from whom nothing can be expected except that he should behave after his worthless kind.

The rival criticism is equally beside the mark. Careless condonation is rightly regarded as proof of moral indifference to justice. But we do not charge a man with injustice when he has been cruelly wronged, and yet, with full knowledge of the wrong that has been done, forgives because he loves. To be "let off" our disloyalties and infidelities because our friends expect no faith or loyalty and, at heart, do not much care whether faith and loyalty are shown, would be morally enervating and ruinous to any of us; to be forgiven by a friend with a finer sense of the loyalty of true friendship than our own may be morally regenerating to all but the "wholly incurable", if indeed there are incurables. Thus the Christian paradox that God is at once the supremely just and also the great forgiver of iniquities, so far from creating an ethical difficulty, is exactly what we should expect to find in a religion which has one of its roots in the ethical conviction of the absoluteness of moral "values". To boggle at it is proof that such religion as one has has not risen far above the level of naturalism.

(4) A further very striking and characteristic feature of our actual experience of the moral life, not always made sufficiently prominent in writing about ethics,

though abundantly witnessed to by the universal language of mankind, is our recognition of the peculiarly *polluting* quality of moral guilt. The vocabulary of all languages is full of expressions which prove how spontaneously men speak of whatever most offends their conscience in the same phraseology which they use about defilement by what is loathsome to sight, touch or smell. In all languages we find grave offences against the really living moral standard spoken of as things "filthy", "dirty", "stinking". The same feeling reveals itself in the numerous ritual practices of all ages which treat various forms of moral guilt, exactly like so many physical pollutions or infections, as things to be actually washed off by ablutions, or banished by fumigation, much as we fumigate, or destroy by fire, objects suspected of reeking with noxious germs. As Dr. Edwyn Bevan says, in his most suggestive essay on *Dirt*,[1] the philosophers in general have taken far too little account of the fact that this specific emotional reaction seems characteristic of humanity in all ages and at all levels of civilisation. They tend to treat the "moral sense" too exclusively as a sense of obligation, and the mental disquiet occasioned by wrongdoing as only an uneasy consciousness of violated or neglected obligation. They seem hardly even to have tried to fathom the significance of the standing association in popular language between "sin" and "uncleanness". "The man who is sorry for having done wrong does not only feel that he has violated an obligation; he feels unclean."

As Dr. Bevan goes on to say, this notion of the "dirty", whether in the physical realm or in the moral, suggests very interesting questions for the psychologist. In the realm of the senses, the "dirty" is often that which, because it is the vehicle of infection, is also

---

[1] E. Bevan, *Hellenism and Christianity*, pp. 152 ff.

dangerous. Yet it is certain that it is by no means always
the most noxious things which are regarded as peculiarly filthy or dirty.[1] As Dr. Bevan says, there is nothing
particularly noxious about human saliva as such; we
do not feel ourselves infected by its permanent presence
in our own mouths, and we are well aware that we do
not expose ourselves to any kind of infection by contact
with healthy saliva expelled from the mouth of another
person. Yet we should probably all think it a dirty
practice to wash ourselves in water in which another,
or we ourselves, had just cleansed the teeth; we do not
shrink to anything like the same extent from washing
ourselves in water in which we or others have cleansed
the hands, though the probability that the water contains noxious matter may be much greater in this case.
The point might have been made more apparent by
recalling the familiar fact that though a European has
no scruple about washing his face in the water in which
he has just washed his hands, and usually no serious
scruple about plunging his face in that in which he is
bathing his whole body, a scrupulous Indian Moslem
thinks it polluting to wash himself in water which has
been poured into a basin, because this involves allowing
the face to come in contact with that which has been
"defiled" by previous contact with the *sordes* of less
honourable parts. Similarly the least refined among us
would be pretty certainly withheld by an almost in-

---

[1] This state of things has its spiritual counterpart also. It is not always the
sins which are most destructive of our moral being which are commonly abhorred
as particularly "vile". Gross sexual offences, marked pettinesses, are commonly
felt as "viler" than the much more ruinous sins of spiritual pride and self-com-
placency. This has been remarked by von Hügel, and long before him by
St. Thomas (*S.T.* ii[a] ii[ae] q. 117, art. 2 ad 2[um] "non semper in actibus humanis
illud est gravius quod est turpius. Decor enim hominis est ex ratione; et ideo
turpiora sunt peccata carnalia, quibus caro dominatur rationi, quamvis peccata
spiritualia sint graviora, quia procedunt ex majori contemptu"). The same
consideration explains why in Dante's Hell Ulysses and Bertrand de Born are
placed lower down than Semiramis or Cleopatra, or Brunetto Latini. See *infra*.

vincible disgust from relieving severe thirst by drinking a liquid into which another, or even he himself, had spit; and in all societies, to spit on the skin or clothes of another is to offer him the most unpardonable, because the "dirtiest", of insults. Any ordinary Briton would rather a ruffian should strike him a severe blow than that he should spit in his face, though the first insult may be also a dangerous assault, while the second is normally harmless. And the same thing is true of moral "dirt". The "dirtiest" sins of civilised men are regularly sexual offences of various kinds, though the users of this language may be quite alive to the truth that aberrations commonly directly connected with unhappy physical constitution or condition—as these offences usually are—are far less ruinous to the moral life of the soul than the great "spiritual" sins—pride, cruelty, fraud, treachery. Cruelty is, as all moralists would admit, a more evil thing than any kind of mere perverted carnal appetite, and if we were angels, would presumably revolt us more. Yet in man, it seems clear, though calculating cruelty may awaken the severer reflective condemnation, it has to be excessive indeed before it arouses anything like the same *disgust*. What commonly revolts one in the character even of a Nero, as depicted in the Roman anti-Caesarean literary tradition, is not so much the stories of deliberate cruelty—which does not, in fact, seem to have been one of Nero's vices—as the anecdotes of a morbid and "unnatural" lust.

It would be interesting, with Dr. Bevan, to carry the attempt to analyse our repugnance to the morally "polluting" further, and to try to indicate its specific *differentia* more exactly, but that inquiry would take us too far away from our principal theme. For my own purpose I must be content to repeat one of Dr. Bevan's conclusions,[1] and to call attention to some inferences which seem to be justified. The physically "dirty" seems to be primarily *excrement* from our own bodies, and secondarily whatever we have come to associate in any way with the thought of such excrement. I would support this illuminating remark by adding that any calling, however honourable and beneficial, which brings its practitioner into regular contact with any of these *excreta* of the human body also seems to awaken in all of us a repugnance based on the feeling that the occupation is "dirty" work. Thus the physician is constantly compelled, for purposes of diagnosis, to examine specimens of the urine of his patients. We know that this work is an indispensable part of the routine of an ennobling and beneficent profession, that it involves no actual infection of the physician's person, and that there are many occupations, none of which revolt us, that bring the craftsman constantly into contact with matter much more noxious and much more directly unpleasant to our senses; but I believe we all have the secret feeling that this particular part of the physician's work is "disgusting" and "dirty". We should shrink from practising it ourselves, and it breeds a recognisable shrinking from the man who does practise it, a repugnance we only overcome by reflection and reasoning, or by a real effort to relegate our knowledge of the fact to the limbo of the unconscious.

Yet—and this is the point Dr. Bevan is specially anxious to make—the excretions which excite this violent disgust are only disgusting to us when they have been *expelled* from the organism. So long as they remain in it, they are not dirty. I do not regard my own body as dirty or disgusting, unless I am morbidly "cynical", by reason of the permanent presence

---

[1] *Op. cit.* p. 151.

within it of the very materials which, when once they have been expelled, are regarded as the vilest of "filth". There may be seen in this a striking illustration of that close association of thought exhibited by so much of the traditional vocabulary, between the holy and the unclean. The experience is seen in the attitude of all human beings who have an articulate moral tradition to that which has to do with the sexual side of life. It is at once "holy", as the source of the renewal and continuance of life itself, and yet is, in some mysterious way, "polluting". To quote Dr. Bevan, "It is the same act which in one moral context is the very type of impurity and in another context is the sacrament of love and life. It would seem as if some slight change in circumstances could transfer its character straight away from one end of the moral scale to the other. . . . Deep at the bottom of all our sense of uncleanness, of dirt, is the feeling, primitive, irresolvable, universal, of the sanctity of the body. Nothing in the material world can properly be dirty, except the body. We speak of a 'dirty road', but in an uninhabited world moist clay would be no more dirty than hard rock; it is the possibility of clay adhering to a foot which makes it mire." [1]

Now the same thing is true, *mutatis mutandis*, of the morally "dirty". At the root of our sense of moral foulness lies a "primitive and universal" feeling about the sanctity of the rational soul. Nothing can be morally dirty but an *anima rationalis*. I may illustrate, perhaps, from a distaste which I detect very readily in myself and suspect to be no personal idiosyncrasy. There is one part of any zoological garden which I find it almost intolerable to visit, that devoted to the monkeys, and what makes observation

[1] *Op. cit.* p. 153.

of monkeys so repugnant to me is, more than anything else, the preoccupation of the creatures with
the functions of sex. Yet I do not know that the preoccupation is really more patent in monkeys than it
is, for example, in our domestic dogs, whose corresponding behaviour gives me no conscious uneasiness.
What makes behaviour in a monkey disgusting to me
when the same behaviour does not disgust me in the
dog? So far as I can see, only the suggestion conveyed
by the monkey's general physique, but not by the
dog's, that the creature is half-human, that it has, as
the dog has not, a human soul to be smirched.

And this reflection leads, naturally, as I think,
to another. From a strictly naturalistic point of view
all repugnance to "dirt" is no more than a "subjective" illusion. Dirt is only what it has been called
by someone, "matter in the wrong place", and there
is no "objective" distinction between one corporeal
"substance" and another in respect of cleanness or
uncleanness. Matter which is in the "wrong" place has
only to be removed to its proper place—and all matter
has its proper place—and it ceases forthwith to be
"dirt", just as the "refuse" of an industry ceases to be
refuse, and is considered a valuable "by-product",
when it becomes the "raw material" of a second
industry. If the purely naturalistic conception of man
were an adequate one, then, we might expect that as
we learn more and more, as our scientific knowledge of
nature advances, to make some employment of every
kind of body, the notion of the "dirty" would be
gradually eliminated from our thinking. In a society
where science had called into existence a plentiful
supply of industries working on "refuse", we might
expect that the right place would be progressively
found for all forms of matter; there would no longer

be any "dirt", and in the end the very word "dirt" would disappear from language. We should learn to talk not of dirt, but of highly valuable "by-products" everywhere. Yet in actual fact the progress of science does not seem to have this result, of banishing the notion of "dirt" and the emotional reaction against it from men's lives. A cultivated Indian Moslem, Dr. Bevan says, thinks it an unspeakable pollution to bring into contact with the human mouth a tooth-brush made of bristles of one unclean creature, the pig, set in a bone of a second unclean creature, the dog. But a European does not feel himself "dirty" because he cleans his teeth with a brush made of these materials.[1] Yet, though the European has learned to think clean some things which the Indian Moslem regards as polluted, he has also learned to shrink from a great deal which does not offend Moslems as dirty. He is revolted, as Sir Richard Burton remarks that Moslems in general are not, by a "dirty" nose. I should suppose that we may take it as reasonably certain that, though our more "enlightened" posterity may come to live down disgust with some things we now regard as dirty, they will equally be astonished to read of our indiffer-ence to much they will have learned to think repulsive dirt; for example, the carbon-loaded atmosphere of our industrial cities.

We see the same thing in connection with the morally "dirty". As our code of moral values becomes more conscious and more coherent, and so, as we say, is pro-gressively "rationalised", we do not find that our sense of the "foulness" of sin is steadily giving place to an unemotional view of it as merely "unsuitable response", action in the wrong place. What actually happens is rather that our notion of the "polluting" is transferred

[1] *Op. cit.* p. 147.

to fresh types of action. It costs us some trouble to-day
to put ourselves back at the point of view of a hero in
Greek tragedy who regards himself as morally unspeakably polluted by a homicide which he has committed,
like Heracles, in a fit of madness, or even an "incestu-
ous" marriage, like that of Oedipus, contracted in
simple and unavoidable ignorance of the facts. The
situation of Heracles or Oedipus, of course, distresses
us intensely, but we cannot really "go along with"
their sense of their moral foulness. But we have also
developed a new sense of honour which would feel as
an uneffaceable stain deeds which the ancient world
left unreprobated, or even admired. To us, with our
tradition of the chivalrous, there are comparatively
few heroes of Greek epic story or Old Testament narrative who do not seem to have something of the "dirty
fellow" about them.[1] *Noblesse oblige* is a maxim with a
significance which is steadily being extended and is
very far from being exhausted by any interpretation
yet put upon it. And it is not merely that the range of
acts to which the principle is felt to apply is an ever
widening one. As the range of applicability widens, the
principle itself acquires a deeper inwardness at every
fresh stage in the process. It is not the overt act alone,
but the unworthy desire or thought, even the desire
which is regularly repressed before it can influence
action, the thought which arises only to be dismissed,
that our "honour" feels as a stain.

A fine sense of honour, no less than a genuine piety,
demands the "cleansing of the thoughts of the heart by
the infusion of a holy spirit", a remaking of the natural
self and its interests from their centre. Here we have,

---

[1] We all feel this about Achilles' treatment of Hector, and I own to something
of the same feeling in myself about David slinging his stones against a Philistine
who was expecting to be met honourably with lance and sword

as it seems to me, plain proof that the identification of the moral good with mere beneficent social activities is a superficial falsification of moral experience. If the whole of our aim as persons with moral aspirations were merely to act for the promotion of "social welfare", I can see no reason why our discontent with our own character should demand the purification of the inner man with all this intensity. So long as our unworthier thoughts and contemplations lead to no consequences in overt action, I cannot see why, on such an inter-pretation of morality, they should not be regarded as exempt from the judgement of conscience. Why should they not be smilingly dismissed with the reflection, *neque semper arcum Tendit Apollo*? Indeed, it might actually be pleaded that some indulgence in such thoughts and fancies is a *useful* practice for the man who is to do good, as providing a harmless discharge for tendencies which, if too vigorously repressed, are likely to take their revenge in explosive action. I myself have heard grossness in the conversation of our lighter hours de-fended, and I believe sincerely defended, by this plea of the need for a safety-valve. The gross in action, I have been told, are commonly reticent in speech, and the reticent in speech may be presumed to be secretly gross in act.

It might, of course, be replied to this last remark that even if we mean by morality no more than the promotion of social welfare, still we need to be care-ful about day-dreaming because our day-dreams are likely to come true in our conduct. I cannot think this of itself an adequate basis for regulation of the internal motions of imagination and desire. I should rather suppose that, if a day-dream is fantastic enough, one may safely disregard its possible influence on action, exactly as we may and do disregard dreams of the night. If I allowed myself to enjoy an "Alnaschar's dream" of unbounded wealth and sensual luxury, or to take pleasure in imagining myself a world-conqueror, my knowledge that I have not the remotest chance of becoming a multi-millionaire or a Napoleon would be quite enough to ensure that my imagination should remain a mere game of the mind with itself and should have no appreciable influence on my conduct towards my fellow-men. And yet, as it also seems to me, any serious morality is bound to treat the enjoyment of the dreams themselves, apart from any possible "consequences", as a fault calling for vigorous correction. And the reason is not far to see. "As a man thinketh in his heart, so *is* he", for the aspiration in which all moral goodness has its source is not a mere endeavour to *do*, but an aspiration to *be*. Or, if objection is taken to that distinction, I would at least say that the aspiration is not directed on any merely outward-issuing doing.

The right discharge of social function itself seems to be most regularly and most successfully attained when it arises from concern with the purification of the inner springs of our personal being. For that reason alone, I would urge, any moral theory which makes the notion of right conduct, the fulfilment of the precepts of a law of action, rather than the notion of good, the attainment of a personality of the highest absolute worth, primary would lead, if seriously acted on, to a lowering of the standard of outward-going action itself. Even if such a morality conceives its supreme law of action with the austerity of Kant, it leaves it at least a possibility that a man might say, truthfully and sincerely, "All this have I done from my youth up; I have been indeed a *profitable* servant"; there is no sufficient place left for the recognition that humility of spirit is the most exquisite flower of the moral life.

Even the Kantian morality, hard as it would be of achievement, would, I conceive, tend to make the habitually dutiful man into something of a high-minded Pharisee. If the criticism be thought too severe, I would only remark that the "stoical" tone of Kant's practical philosophy is matter of commonplace, and that the Stoics of literature are, almost without exception, Pharisees, unless, like Seneca, they have actual grave violations of their own precepts on their conscience. To be at once truly virtuous and truly humble is something beyond them.

At this point I think it may be in place to say a word in reply to a highly fashionable current criticism of the morality of true inwardness. It is common to represent such a morality as a life of preoccupation with mere negations. We hear Christian morality depreciated for its concern with purity of heart and will, on the ground that, as is alleged, it sets up "doing no particular harm" as its ideal. It is usual to make this a point of contact with the "superior" Greek conception of virtue, or goodness, as something positive, as efficiency in doing something definite. I presume that writers who are fond of the antithesis may fairly be taken to imply a preference for the man who has visible and palpable results of his mingling in the world's business to show, no matter with what stains of vice, or even downright crime, he comes out of the bustle, as against the man who has kept his ideal of personal being high, but cannot point to any very definite positive achievements. There is, perhaps, a touch of this temper about Hegel's well-known gibe at the schoolmaster who thinks himself a greater than Alexander, because, though he has taken no cities, he can keep his temper and has never murdered a friend in a tipsy brawl.[1] There is more than

---

[1] If it is his, I have not succeeded in verifying the reference.

a touch of it in the numerous writers who invite us to regard a coarse-grained political adventurer of genius like Caesar as one of the greatest in the kingdom of ends, on the strength of the real or alleged social benefits which have resulted from his pursuit of personal ambition, and still more in Nietzsche's fantastic glorification of Alcibiades, who effected nothing but the ruin of the society which allowed him to embark it on a grandiose criminal adventure.

I would not deny that this glorification of "efficiency" has elements of truth in it, when it appears merely as a reaction against the confusion of virtue with abstention from definite and recognisable ways of doing social harm. But I am sure that when it is taken as anything more than such a protest, it is morally mischievous. In the first place, it is a mere caricature to represent the ideal of inward purity as meaning only abstention from recognised wrong-doing. It is an endeavour to *be* something very real and positive indeed, and can only be taken to be a "negative ideal" though a double confusion. It is true that, for reasons which have already been pretty fully given, we cannot say in detail what the man who is aiming at becoming "as like as possible to God" is striving to be. This is not because he is striving to become something without positive character, but because the character he is seeking to acquire is too *rich* in positive content to admit of exhaustion by any formula, and because that content only discloses itself very gradually as the aspiration succeeds. Again, though it is true that such a life must have its negative aspect, since it is an unending "putting off of the old man", this correcting of the old self is not undertaken for its own sake, but as the indispensable means to a remaking: the "old man" is put off, not that we may be "unclothed", but that we may be "clothed upon", re-made in the image of the "new". To use a homely simile, you cannot take a bath without stripping yourself; but when a man comes home soiled with work and takes off his dirty working-clothes to step into the bath, his intention is not to remain naked, but to assume the clean raiment of family life and civilised intercourse. Seeing how much of the soil of the world we habitually contract in our daily life, I cannot believe that exhortations to care less than the little most of us do care about ceasing to do evil are likely to be very productive of doing good.

Further, those who have most to say in praise of the ideal of "positive efficiency" too often forget that the "positive" achievement of a life cannot be measured by a standard so crude as that of readily ascertainable specific results. Dr. Inge has truly said more than once that the most effective work in the way of "social amelioration" has usually been due to men who were all the while thinking primarily of something else. An example in point is the beneficent effect on art, literature, and social conditions in general directly traceable to the personality of St. Francis of Assisi, who all through his life troubled himself very little about any of the three. The same thing is equally true of the moral effects of any individual life of quiet goodness. It is not usually the persons who are most definitely preoccupied with this or that project of social reform as the great business of life, still less those who proclaim that their main interest is that of "making their neighbours better" in general, who actually most often send us away from contact with them better men than we were before. More commonly the best influence in our lives is that of quiet and unpretending persons who were quite unconscious of any intention to moralise us directly, and of whom we might find it hard to say just what special "good habit" or reform of our practice we owe to them, though we may feel certain that we "owe our souls" to them. The goodness of the tree, no doubt, is proved by the goodness of its fruit, but the fruit is not usually very precisely discerned by our imperfect vision. And Hegel's smart gibe misses the point. The schoolmaster who prefers himself to Alexander is, indeed, presumably a self-satisfied prig. If he were not a prig, the comparison would not be likely to suggest itself to him, or if it did, his verdict on himself would be less confident, did he remember, before passing it, as he should, that the real question is whether he would have mastered his temper better than Alexander in Alexander's position and with Alexander's temptations. But it still remains true that Alexander might have done much more for the world than he did, if he had known how to keep the strain of the savage in himself under better restraint, and so had not deprived himself of his wisest and most devoted counsellors. And it is not a preposterous view that, though in the eyes of the average man a schoolmaster may seem a little figure and a great conqueror an imposing one, there may be schoolmasters who are greater "in the kingdom of heaven" than Alexander or Napoleon. Plato would certainly have said that there are or may be; and if we desire the authority of a great name to support our considerations, Plato's name may count for as much as Hegel's. In fact, many at least of us would say that however much the world owes to Alexander, it owes much more to Plato, and Plato himself, when all is said, was a kind of pedagogue. Like Johnson, "he keepit a schule and ca'd it an Academy". The element of truth in Hegel's *mot* reduces to little more than this, that a schoolmaster who was really a greater man morally than Alexander would be very unlikely to be conscious of the fact. We must not introduce into

moral valuation that pernicious heresy of judgement
by grossly palpable results which has worked so much
havoc with education wherever it has prevailed.

(5) This rather desultory consideration of the implications of the sense of guilt may be brought to a close
with one further consideration. What is the *subiectum*
we feel to be defiled and polluted by contact with that
which awakens our sense of guilt, or wounds our sense
of honour? Assuredly nothing which we could plausibly
represent as primitive and elemental human nature;
the merely "natural" man, not yet caught up in the
advance of the moralising process, if such a creature
ever existed, must have known nothing of either sin
or honour; the sense of both is itself a product of the
moralising process. If a man could be serious with
the proposal to "return to nature" by expelling what
Nietzsche, with his unfortunate itch for journalistic
epigram, has taught a generation to call "moralic acid"
from his system, his first task would have to be to divest
himself once for all of shame, honour, and chivalry.
Modern advocates of *Herrenmoral* take a sentimental
pleasure in contemplating themselves as lions or eagles;
but the lion and eagle of their fancy have never existed
except in the bestiaries and romances. The real lion
and the real eagle are not the chivalrous beasts of fable
who disdain to harm a virgin or to taste carrion; they
are as much mere creatures of their appetites as the
wolf and the vulture.[1] Nor is it my own person as it
actually exists that is the object of this unqualified and
solicitous reverence. That, in many a case, already
bears the stain of so many disgraces that I might well

---

[1] So much at least was correctly understood by the "horned Siegfrieds" who
provoked Nietzsche's disgust by trying to act out his theories. No doubt, they
were young blackguards, but the humour of the situation is precisely that no one
could be a "superman" without being something of a blackguard, while the
inventor of the "superman" was at heart, after all, a "Christian gentleman".

feel that one more spot could not add much to its un-cleanness. What is defiled by sin and dishonour is the self I aspire yet to possess as my own, *quando che sia*. The poignant shame which goes with consciousness of guilt or dishonour gets its pungency from the con-trast with my ideal of what I, as a person, may be and am shaped to be, and this is why we all feel guilt and dishonour to be things much more intimate to ourselves than they would be if they were adequately described as mere infractions of an impersonal law. What is amiss with all of us is not merely that we have *done* this or that which we should not have done, or omitted this or that which "regulations" call on us to do, but that the very fountain of our moral personality is poisoned.

Whether Adam ever "fell" or not, *I* am a "fallen creature", and I know it. Our moral task is no mere business of canalising or embanking the course of a stream; it has to begin higher up with the purification of the bitter waters at their source. Hence, when we feel as we ought to feel about the evil in ourselves, we can-not help recognising that our position is not so much that of someone who has broken a wise and salutary regulation, as of one who has insulted or proved false to a person of supreme excellence, entitled to whole-hearted devotion. Similarly, even in lives in which the thought of sin as a personal offence against the living divine majesty is not operative, we all know that an adequate sense of the dishonour attaching to treason to a principle or a cause can only be awakened when one succeeds in "personifying" the cause or the prin-ciple. To make a man feel the shame of treason to the cause of his country as he ought to feel it, you must first make him accept a figure like that of Britannia as something very much more than a convenient abbreviatory symbol for "the system of social institutions and traditions in which I have been brought up"; if he is to care as he ought to care, he must somehow be got, in spite of himself, to feel that Britannia is a living person. Just so, if we are to think adequately of the shame of disloyalty to our best spiritual ideal, we have to learn to think of that ideal as already embodied in the living and personal God, and of falsehood as personal disloyalty and ingratitude to God. It is just because so many of our modern philosophical moralists are afraid to make the idea of God frankly central in their theories of conduct that their treatment of guilt is inadequate to the actual moral experiences of men with any depth of character.

It is easy to say that passionate loyalty can be and is awakened by the imaginative personification of Britannia, though no one really believes in the personification, and that, in the same way, the practical necessity of *imagining* moral guilt as an offence against a personal living God proves nothing as to the truth of such a conception. But the two cases are only imperfectly analogical. There may be no such actual person as Britannia, but we should remember that the loyalties symbolised and summed up for the patriotic Briton in the figure of Britannia are themselves, in the main, loyalties to persons. The symbolic figure represents the body of a man's attachments to a host of those whom he loves and respects, and has respected and loved from his childhood. Britannia means for him all his intensest and most deeply rooted loyalties to persons at once. If you could find a man without any of these personal devotions, a man to whom Britannia was *only* a "figure of speech" for a set of impersonal institutions of which he approved—the House of Commons, the Assizes, the Quarter Sessions, the Coroner's Inquest, and the like—I wonder how much power the figure would have to brace him for the great endurances and the great sacrifices. Not, I should suspect, very much.

Now the moral life, adequately conceived, is a life of unremitting endurances and sacrifices which go beyond anything that would be demanded by loyalty to our personal attachments to fellow-men, and may, at any moment, require the sacrifice of the most intimate of these attachments to a higher loyalty. Can this supreme loyalty be felt towards any object but one with which we stand in a *personal* relation more intimate than any that could come into competition with it? Can it be demanded, and, if demanded, is it likely to be displayed? To my own mind the answer is clear. The supreme endurances and surrenders can be made, but they can only be made by love, and who can really love a code or a system of institutions? Who could love the Categorical Imperative or the *Code Napoléon* or the perfected social organisation of a distant future? The more patent it is that it may be a good man's duty not to let love of friend, or mistress, or wife, or mother, be the paramount and final influence in all his choices, the more patent also, it seems to me, that this final motive must be found in another and a supreme love, and that such a love, like all loves, must have its real personal object. Thus once more I find myself forced back on the conclusion that, to be truly itself, the moral life must have as its last motive love to God, and so become transfigured into the life of religious faith and devotion. For the moralist, belief in the true and living God cannot be relegated to the position of an "extra", which we may perhaps be allowed on sufferance to add to our respect for duty or regard for the good of our fellow-men, if physicist, biologist, and anthropologist will be kind enough to raise no objection. Belief in the absolute reality of God, and love for the God in whom we be-lieve, are at the heart of living morality. The good of our fellow-men is unworthily thought of when we do not conceive that good as a life of knowledge of God and transformation by the knowledge into the likeness of God. And the love which arises from our belief is the one motive adequate to secure the full and whole-hearted discharge of the duties laid on us by our ideal.

If moralists are at times ready to compound with the naturalist on easier terms, the reason, I suspect, is that they have not always the courage of their convictions as moralists. They are not quite sure at heart whether the moral life is quite as much "hard fact" as the facts of which the natural sciences treat. If a man is seriously convinced that of all facts those of our own moral struggle are the most immediately sure and certain, that we have more intimate assurance of the reality of love and hate, virtue and vice, than of the reality of atoms or electrons, I do not believe he is in much danger of reducing Theism to the level of a meta-physical speculation or a "permitted" hypothesis.

VI

THE INITIATIVE OF THE ETERNAL

And why not grace? Why not God's grace, Hay? . . . We walk upon it, we breathe it; we live and die by it; it makes the nails and axles of the universe; and a puppy in pyjamas prefers self-conceit!—R. L. STEVENSON.

AMONG the writings accepted by antiquity as Platonic there is a curious fragment of a few pages called *Cleitophon* which raises a perturbing question. (Its authenticity has been generally denied throughout the last hundred years on grounds which, if not absolutely conclusive, are reasonably cogent.) The writer, whoever he may have been, urges that there is a formidable practical defect in the familiar Socratic doctrine of ethics. Socrates can succeed in convincing an auditor beyond all doubt of the supreme importance of having the right moral ideal and being in dead earnest with the business of "making the soul as good as possible". But when we go on to ask what are the steps to be taken in setting about this chief business of life, Socrates has nothing to tell us. He has convinced us, to speak in a metaphor, of the necessity of knowing the true route across the troubled and uncharted waters of life, but he cannot tell us how to set our vessel's course. In this respect, Cleitophon is made to say, even the slap-dash Thrasymachus has the advantage of Socrates. Whatever we may think of the goal Thrasymachus sets before us, at least he can give us definite directions for reaching it. It looks, then, as if Socrates has an unrivalled gift of awakening the "unconverted", but no message of guidance for the once awakened.[1]

As the fragment breaks off at this point, and has the appearance of never having been completed, we do not know how the writer meant to treat the difficulty he has raised. Conceivably his intention was to urge that the seemingly annihilating criticism is, after all, not valid, and it would not be difficult to suggest the line of argument he might have adopted for this purpose.[2] But his difficulty may be restated in a way which indicates the existence of a real standing limitation inherent in all moral theory, so long as it is content to remain *moral* theory and nothing more. It would not, indeed, be a sound criticism if it were taken to mean only that the moralist can give no such precise and specific instructions for living a good life as the boat-builder can furnish for the construction of a sea-worthy craft, or the physician for correcting a definite physical defect by regimen and diet. For it might be properly retorted that the physician, too, *can* give no precise directions for securing a lifetime of physical well-being, and that the moralist is not confined to mere generalities when the problem before him is that of getting the mastery of a specific evil propensity or habit. When his problem is narrowed down to the treatment of a particular fault, such as impatience of temper or undue cupidity for some particular carnal gratification, he, like the physician, can suggest useful special rules of hygiene. The serious difficulty is

[1] *Op. cit.* 410 B-C νομίσας σε τὸ μὲν προτρέπειν εἰς ἀρετῆς ἐπιμέλειαν κάλλιστ' ἀνθρώπων δύνασθαι, δυοῖν δὲ θάτερον, ἢ τοσοῦτον μόνον δύνασθαι, μακρότερον δὲ οὐδὲν . . . ταὐτὸν δὴ καί σοί τις ἐπενέγκοι τάχ' ἂν περὶ δικαιοσύνης, ὡς οὐ μᾶλλον ὄντι δικαιοσύνης ἐπιστήμονι, διότι καλῶς αὐτὴν ἐγκωμιάζεις· οὐ μὴν τό γε ἐμὸν οὕτως ἔχει· δυοῖν δὲ θάτερον, ἢ οὐκ εἰδέναι σε ἢ οὐκ ἐθέλειν αὐτῆς ἐμοὶ κοινωνεῖν. διὰ ταῦτα δὴ καὶ πρὸς Θρασύμαχον οἶμαι πορεύσομαι καὶ ἄλλοσε ὅποι δύναμαι.

[2] Cf. my *Plato, the Man and His Work*[3], Appendix, p. 537.

more fundamental. How are our desires for what, in our moments of insight, we can recognise intellectually to be the best to be made effectual enough to compete victoriously in practice with our strong concupiscences for things our understanding can clearly enough see to be not good, or, at any rate, not best? It may be true to say with Socrates that we all at heart desire good, or felicity, and nothing else; the trouble is that the desire is commonly a languid one, and yet has to become a "passion" if real progress in good is to be made. What is to supply the driving force which will fan languid and faint desire for the best into a flame? How are we to be made to care enough for the highest?

Mankind in general, and individual persons in particular, will not be regenerated unless moral aspiration becomes an overpowering passion; and how is such devotion to be secured? There may be a few men, like Socrates himself, in whom the intellectual discernment of a better seems directly able to arouse a passion for its attainment, but these are the exceptions among mankind, not the rule. It is the common experience of most of us that we assent pretty readily to the theses that ends to which the life of another man is consecrated are worthier than those we are pursuing ourselves, that we should be better men if we cared less for things we actually care a great deal about, and more for others in which our interest is actually lukewarm, or, again, if we could only get rid of what we know to be our special infirmities and vices. But our assent to these theses often provokes at best only a passing wish that we were men of different mould; it does not usually stimulate to devoted and unremitting labour at the task of the remaking of the self. For the work of life we need not only a vision of good, but adequate motivation to live by the vision. Mere philosophy tends to regard its business as confined to the delineation of the moral ideal, and to disclaim all pretension to the harder achievement of supplying the motive for devotion. In this sense, at least, ethics has always been what Bradley insisted it ought to be, a speculative, not a practical pursuit.

There can, of course, be no objection to the view that, for the convenience of the student, there should be this division of labour. There is no reason why the man who is trying to become a better man should be compelled also to work at the task of analysing the moral ideal which inspires him, or the man who is trying to analyse the good forced also to play the part of a preacher of righteousness, any more than a convalescent should study medicine, or a medical student convalesce. Each task is likely to be most effectually executed if the two are kept distinct. Thus we have no right to blame the moral philosopher if, on grounds of method, he confines himself to the attempt to tell us what, in principle, the best life for man is. To be sure, unless he is also seriously trying to live that life himself, his statements about its character are bound to be gravely defective. Yet he may have a special superior intellectual penetration, not shared by better but less reflective men, though some of these men may be actually living the best life more effectually than himself, just as we know that, though a man of a prosaic turn of mind will never be a good critic of poetry, the best critic is usually not a great poet, and the great poet often shows himself a mediocre critic. So far there is some real justification for the claim of Schopenhauer that he could depict sanctity without being himself a saint. But the very admission that the moral philosopher is not necessarily saint or hero in the same degree in which he is a good philosopher, while the men who are heroes and saints may have no articulate philosophy, involves the further admission that moral philosophy itself is not rightfully entitled to the position of supreme mistress and directress of human action. A φιλοσοφία which is to be what Socrates and Plato meant φιλοσοφία to be, the sovereign guide and support of life, must supply adequate motivation to the pursuit of the apprehended good as well as a sound conception of that good. The problem is whether this adequate motivation can be found anywhere in a life of response to solicitations to action which come solely from the human and infra-human environment, or whether it has not rather to be sought in actual contact with a strictly superhuman source.

This is an issue which seems to be forced upon us whenever we study the ethical deliverances of the greatest philosophers, not as youthful aspirants to qualify for the rank of doctors in spiritual medicine, but as patients seeking spiritual truth with a view to our own moral health. The doubt expressed by the writer of the fragment *Cleitophon*, whether the exhortations of a Socrates can really do more than make his hearers, like himself, eloquent preachers of the necessity of "care for the soul", whether they can actually contribute anything to the cure of the diseased moral personality,[1] is not to be stifled. Plato, for example, may convince us that only the man who makes "follow God" his rule will ever achieve true felicity. But suppose that a man—and this is the case with all of us for much of the time and with many of us all the time—does not care very much about "following God", how is he to be got to care? Diotima in the *Symposium* may be quite right when she teaches

---

[1] *Op. cit.* 409 B ἰατρικὴ πού τις λέγεται τέχνη·ταύτης δ' ἐστὶν διττὰ τὰ ἀποτελού-μενα, τὸ μὲν ἰατροὺς ἀεὶ πρὸς τοῖς οὖσιν ἑτέρους ἐξεργάζεσθαι, τὸ δὲ ὑγίειαν ... τῆς δὴ δικαιοσύνης ὡσαύτως τὸ μὲν δικαίους ἔστω ποιεῖν ... τὸ δ' ἕτερον, ὃ δύναται ποιεῖν ἡμῖν ἔργον ὁ δίκαιος, τί τοῦτό φαμεν ;

that the man who has once entered the right path by becoming awake to all that the beauty of one beautiful person means has only to "follow his nose" persistently enough, to find that his nose will lead him into the presence of the eternal Beauty. But to take even the first step on this road, you must first be already awakened from the deep sleep in which we all begin by being immersed, and what is it that effects the wakening? Aristotle's careful discussion of moral weakness (ἀκρασία) —the condition popularly described as knowing the good but doing the evil you know to be evil—raises the same question in a still acuter form. According to Aristotle, the man who yields to the suggestions of his worse nature is in a state analogous to that of a sleep-walker, or a man in his cups. He *talks* as though he knew the major premiss of the "syllogism of action", but his talk is mere babbling of words, with no more significance behind it than a drunken man's scraps of verse, or the apparently intelligent reply of a sleep-walker to a question.[1] When the man has recovered from his infatuation he will say the same things again, but with the difference that there will now be intelligent purpose behind his articulations, his words will really express his thought. And Aristotle goes on to suggest that there is a rhythm of spiritual waking and slumber in the moral life, exactly as there is a periodic rhythm of waking and sleeping in the bodily life.[2] We cannot help asking with some bitterness whether, when all is said, the exaltation of "practical intellect" really comes to no more than this singularly lame conclusion. Cannot a man be so effectually awakened that he will not often or lightly fall back into periodical sleep? Must we all be morally "in our cups" when the appointed hour comes round? If

---

[1] *E.N.* 1147 b 9 ff.
[2] *E.N.* 1147 b 6 (with Burnet's note *in loc.*).

we must, the analysis of the "best life for man" is much of a mockery; it is only a picture of a heaven which we may be sure none of us will reach. We find the same thing once more in Kant. Kant has set the life of "heteronomy", the life in which intelligence is only what Hume had maintained it ought to be, an ingenious minister to imperious lusts and cupidities, in the strongest contrast with the life of "autonomy", the life in which intelligence is pursuing an end which is its own, and is thus master in its own house. But what he never explains is how the man who is assumed to be, at the start, bound hand and foot in the chains of "inclination" is ever to get loose from them. It is to no purpose to urge that the chains will fall off of themselves if a man once cultivates the spirit of unqualified reverence for the law of duty. The whole problem is how a man who is absolutely under the domination of "inclination" ever comes to exhibit pure "reverence for duty", uncontaminated by all "inclination", in any the least and most trivial act of life.

Kant is admirably clear on the point that such reverence will never be produced by any demonstration, however successful, that the results of wrong-doing are unhappy, since no man can be made disinterested by an appeal to self-interest, and, for this reason, he, like Socrates in the *Republic*, proposes a revolutionary reform in the moral teaching of the nursery.[1] What he does not explain is how, if human nature in the as yet unmoralised child is what he takes it to be, the appeal to reverence for duty on which he would base the earliest moral instruction is ever to "get home". The famous Kantian mythus of the "ante-temporal" intelligible act of choice which fixes our status as sheep or goats once and for all[2] is no more than a confession that no

---

[1] *KdprV*. ii. Th. (*Werke*², v. 158 ff.).   [2] *Werke*², vi. 125.

explanation is forthcoming. At bottom Kant is merely reverting to the Augustinian nightmare of the *massa perditionis*, though he tries to "save the face" of his Deity by pretending that it is we who "reprobate" ourselves for all eternity.

Perhaps the difficulty is seen at its acutest in the ethics of Spinoza, as has been powerfully urged by a recent expositor, Mr. Guzzo.[1] As Spinoza conceives the moral problem, true virtue and true felicity, which are in the end the same thing, depend wholly on ability to base our conduct on "adequate" thought, a true conception of ourselves and our place in the cosmic system. But we all, without exception, have to begin life with highly inaccurate and inadequate conceptions, and to base our action on them; hence our unavoidable condition is initially that of "bondage" in which every man is a potential enemy and source of peril to every other, because all are rival competitors for the false goods which are competitive in character, and so only to be enjoyed by me on condition that I can exclude the rest of mankind from enjoyment. Now, if this is universally the "state of man by nature", how do we even begin to advance towards that true and adequate conception of human good which, as Spinoza agrees with T. H. Green in teaching, would disclose the truth that real good is not only non-competitive but can only be enjoyed by oneself in proportion as it is enjoyed by all? We might, as Mr. Guzzo says, conceive two possible alternative answers to the question. We might think that human regeneration begins in an intellectual enlightenment. Reflection might be supposed to convince my understanding of the inadequacy of my old notions of good and bad, and lead me to replace them by more rational conceptions. It is, one might suppose, a conse-

---

[1] Guzzo, *Il pensiero di Spinoza*, pp. 290 ff.

quence of this intellectual enlightenment that as the belief that the "competitive goods" are the worthiest objects of pursuit fades, attachment to them and lust after them will likewise fade, and thus there will be an end of the "passions" which made human life a chaos of mutual jealousies and aggressions. The cleansing of the "heart", in that case, would be an effect of an initial illumination of the intellect. But progress from bondage to freedom by *this* route is stopped completely by Spinoza's express declaration that our thought never can be adequate *until* we have emancipated ourselves from "passion",[1] the purification of emotion being thus called for as a pre-condition of the enlightenment.

Shall we say, then, that our deliverance is effected by the opposite route? That an elevated emotional mood, an *attachment* to something better than the "goods" coveted by the average sensual man, comes first and produces clarification of "practical" thinking as its effect? That it is noble emotion which purges the films from the vision of the "eye of the soul"? No doubt, we might point to examples from actual life where this process seems to be taking place under our observation, cases in which "passionate" devotion to a worthy person, or a worthy cause, seems to work a transformation of a man's whole outlook on life and estimate of its goods. But, again, Spinoza is debarred from accepting such an analysis of what happens in these cases by one of his own doctrines. So long as we have false and "inadequate" ideas, he holds, we are and must be at the mercy of "passion", the unworthy emotion and desire which are the inevitable outcome of false intellectual

---

[1] *Ethica*, iv. 14 "vera boni et mali cognitio, *quatenus vera*, nullum affectum coercere potest, *sed tantum quatenus ut affectus* consideratur". In other words, our emotions must be engaged on behalf of "true good" as a pre-condition of our recognition of it as such. See on this point Guzzo, *op. cit.* 146 ff.

presuppositions.[1] There are thus only two conceivable paths from bondage to freedom, and both seem to be barred. False thinking and unworthy action go together. So long as we think falsely we cannot act worthily, and therefore the regeneration cannot begin with the "passional" side of our nature. But equally it cannot begin with a "day of Damascus" in which the eye of the soul beholds a new and transcendent light, for it is our unworthy passions and the habits of action in which they have become embodied that *are* themselves the "scales" on the eyes of understanding.

In the sequel, it is true, Spinoza seems to fall back on one of the very ways to freedom which he has barred against himself. The practical rules laid down in the early proposition of *Ethics* v. are all rules for contemplating what befalls us as the inevitable result of a chain of causation which embraces the whole history of the universe, and where no link could be other than it is. Spinoza trusts to this speculative intellectual vision of all things as necessary to effect a practical moral regeneration for two reasons. When every event in an infinite series is thought of as playing its part in causing our joys and sorrows, it will be only a vanishingly small part of the effect we shall attribute to each particular member of the series, and this, it is held, will eliminate partial jealousies, rivalries, and hatreds, thus leading to settled contentment and general good will. Further, the same line of thinking will lead us, in the end, to regard God as the one real cause of everything which happens, and "no one can hate God", and thus we are led to "intellectual love of God" as our standing emotional habit.[2] But I think it may be replied that the line of reflection Spinoza recommends really leads to the conclusion that any specific

---

[1] *Ethica*, iv. 17 schol., v. 20 schol.   [2] *Ethica*, v. 18, 32.

person, act, or event must be as impotent and unimportant for good as for evil. The strictly "logical"
consequence of preoccupation with the thought that no
one agent or event plays any decisive part in effecting
our felicity or misery should be not a spirit of universal
cheerfulness or good will, but one of sullen, or apathetic,
indifference to all events and agents alike. And similarly, the identification of God with an indifferent and
non-ethical first source of good and evil alike ought
in consistency to lead to unconcern about God, and is
only too likely in practice, in the case of those whose
lot in the world is a hard one, to beget downright
hatred of God. Spinoza's recommendations are as
likely to lead to blasphemy as to piety, and in most
cases likeliest of all to lead to the dull apathy which
wiser men know as *acedia* and reckon among "deadly
sins". If Spinoza was led by them to the *amor intellec-
tualis Dei*, the manifest reason is to be found not in
his philosophy, but in his personality. Like more than
one other great philosopher, he clearly had a personal
religion which finds no adequate expression in his
professed metaphysic. The source of his actual piety
towards God and the happiness it brought him is not
to be found in the doctrine of *Deus-substantia* expounded in the *First Part* of the *Ethics*; we have to
look for it in deep impressions of early life based on
intimate membership of a Jewish family and a Jewish
community, familiar with utterances of psalmists
and prophets who most emphatically did not identify
Deus and *Natura*, but gave whole-hearted adoration
to the *Deus absconditus* who sits above the water-
spouts, "rage they never so horribly". There is something in Spinoza's Deity of the God of Abraham,
Isaac, and Jacob, as well as of the *Dieu des savants
et des philosophes*.

You see the point I am concerned to make. If a man is to be raised in his whole being above his present unsatisfactory level, it is not enough that he should be able to conceive of a self better than that he now possesses. The "ideal" must be able to draw him with an overpowering force; it must be an *efficient* as well as a final cause.[1] And it is only an efficient cause when the recognition of its goodness is accompanied by faith in its existence as the most assured of realities. The old Aristotelian principle that *ens in potentia* can only be "reduced to act" by that which is itself "in act", after all, holds good. The separation of existence and value uncritically acquiesced in by so many of our contemporary thinkers would be fatal to moral progress towards good in any man who should seriously believe in such a separation, where the important purposes of life are concerned. It is from its acknowledged and overpowering reality that the valuable draws its motive power. As Dr. Whitehead has recently said,[2] "There is no such thing as mere value. Value is the word I use for the intrinsic reality of an event."

We get here a hint of the true solution of the apparently desperate problem, how comes a man, being what at this moment he is and having just the worth he has, neither more nor less, at once to conceive the ideal of the better and to be drawn to it. If a man were really "what he now is", if his being were really a *being* and not rather a *becoming*, and a becoming open to the influence and pressure of the eternal Being which envelops all becomings, if in fact a man were a true Leibnizian "monad", self-developing and self-contained, the process would be wholly unintelligible.

[1] As Kant says, the "good will" must be a *will*, not a mere *wish*. The problem is how it is to become more than a fleeting wish.
[2] *Science and the Modern World*, p. 136.

It is actually intelligible only because the human "monad", in spite of Leibniz's denials, *has* "windows", and windows which are open to the Infinite. To be quite plain, in all moral advance the *ultimate* "efficient cause" must be the real eternal source of both becoming and value. The initiative in the process of "assimilation to God" must come from the side of the eternal; it must be God who first comes to meet us, and who, all through the moral life itself, "works in us", in a sense which is more than metaphorical. Our moral endeavours must be genuinely ours, but they must be responses to intimate actual contacts in which a real God moves outward to meet His creatures, and by the contact at once sustains and inspires the appropriate response on the creature's part.

But to say as much as this is to say that the every-day moral life of simple discharge of recognised duty transcends the artificial limits we set to it, for our intellectual convenience, when we discriminate between morality and religion. Such a life itself is, after all, from first to last, a life inspired by "faith". The notion that whereas religion makes the demand for faith in the beyond and dimly descried, morality does not, but is a matter of walking in the full daylight, can only arise when we mistakenly think of moral virtue as being nothing more than the routine practice of a set of duties which are perfectly familiar to us all, from our inheritance of social rules and traditions. The life of genuine morality is always something indefinitely more than this. It involves a progress which is not merely improvement in the performance of tasks we have always known to be incumbent on us, or the cor-rection of faults which we have seen, or could have seen, at any moment to be faults. In truth, with every step taken towards a life of more habitual loyalty to known duty, or correction of known faults, we also discern new and unexpected duties with claims on our loyalty, and unsuspected faults calling for correction. Every self-surrender not only receives its reward in the enrichment of the personality we had set on the hazard; it also points the way to undreamed-of greater surrenders. Consequently, the common saying of the old poets, that the uphill road to the dwelling of virtue is steep at first, but becomes easier at each successive step, is a dangerous half-truth; the gradient is really growing steeper all the time. Years of self-discipline may make it easier for a man to practise duties he once shirked or ignored, or to avoid vicious courses which were once alluring, but they also bring their own fresh demands with them, and compliance with the new demands "costs" more than compliance with the old. The way of life does not merely begin as a *via crucis*, it remains a *via crucis* all through. The attempt to walk that road simply in my own strength is as likely to be fatal to my moral being if I make it late as if I make it early. Morality itself, when taken in earnest, thus leads direct to the same problems about "grace" and "nature", "faith" and "works", with which we are familiar in the history of Christianity, the religion which stands supreme above all others in its "inwardness" and takes the thought of regeneration of the self from its centre with unqualified seriousness.

At the risk of a short digression from our immediate topic, it may be worth while to point out that this problem of divine initiative equally arises outside the strictly practical domain of the moral and religious conduct of life. It even meets us, in a more external form, in the course of reflection on nature and natural causality. We may readily illustrate the point from the natural theology of Aristotle, the least "inward" of all philosophers of the first order of greatness. Of all great metaphysicians Aristotle is perhaps the one of whom we can most safely say that his vision in metaphysics is in least danger of being distorted by excessive pre-occupation with the problems of the moral life. No one can reasonably suspect him of being unduly in-clined by personal temperament to over-ethicise his metaphysic, since he is curiously devoid of the moral inspiration so manifest in Plato and Kant, and, with a good deal of detriment to logical consistency, in Spinoza. So far as the *Nicomachean Ethics* go, indeed, their doctrine is excellent enough. Aristotle has a high standard of personal behaviour, and is anxious that it should be faithfully lived up to; his practical counsel on the formation of good habits and the avoidance of bad is admirable in its common sense. A society trained as he would have it trained would be eminently law-abiding, orderly, and decent. Yet his treatment of "practice" has always been felt to be wholly devoid of "inwardness". His morality is a highly "this-world" affair of setting up a manifestly sensible rule of be-haviour and observing the rule carefully. Only in one matter does he get perceptibly beyond this very "external" conception of the moral life—in the matter of the analysis of the personal affections on which the worthiest human friendship is based. The sense of sin, so conspicuous in Platonic and Christian ethics, is conspicuously wanting in him, and he seems to have no idea of any moral life which aims at more than the punctual discharge of the social obligations which must be enforced, if a community is to be free from serious disorders. It is not from him that we learn of the moral life as a pilgrimage from bondage to freedom, or an escape from the intolerable burden of an unworthy selfhood. We can hardly say that he feels, as Plato,

Spinoza, or Kant felt, that there is any grievous burden or bondage to escape from. The *Hang zum Bösen* in the human heart is not a reality to him. And the reason is not far to seek. Aristotle's interest in human life itself is at best secondary. What he really cares intensely for is the scientific contemplation of the natural world; he values morality chiefly as a means to something other than itself. A well-ordered πόλις, fair-dealing neighbours, and a good personal character are but prerequisites indispensable if the "fine flower" of the community are to have the security, quiet, and leisure they require, in order to devote themselves to cosmology and astronomy. You cannot give your heart to the prosecution of such studies if you are all the while set on the enjoyment of sensual pleasures, or the accumulation of wealth, if you are at the mercy of ill-educated neighbours, or if your city is incessantly contending with enemies from without, or distracted by the factions of the malcontents within. But the supreme business of life is to be neither saint nor hero; it is to be something like a President or Fellow of a Royal Society.[1]

Yet the problem we might imagine evaded by this relegation of the life of moral inwardness to a wholly secondary position breaks out even in the theology of Aristotle. The one and only purpose for which his philosophy requires God is a strictly naturalistic one. God is there, not to supply moral initiative by the drawings of "grace", nor even to provide an ideal of perfected personality, to which we might aspire in our own strength. Aristotle, as you know, thinks it actually absurd to ascribe moral personality to his God. God is wanted simply to provide initiative and support for a

---

[1] Cf. *E.N.* 1178 b 3 τῷ δὲ θεωροῦντι οὐδένος τῶν τοιούτων (sc. τῶν ἐκτὸς ἀγαθῶν) πρός γε τὴν ἐνέργειαν χρεία . . . ᾗ δ' ἄνθρωπός ἐστιν καὶ πλείοσι συξῇ, αἱρεῖται τὰ κατὰ τὴν ἀρετὴν πράττειν.

physical movement, the supposed eternal and uniform
diurnal revolution of the outermost "heaven". One
could not well go much further in the reduction of God
to a mere "unknown x", necessary to complete a system
of sidereal mechanics, and so having the same *status*
as the problematical "cause of gravity" mentioned in
the *Scholium Generale* at the end of Newton's *Principia*.
Yet Aristotle, if we are to take him at his word, goes
rather further. His God is to be only the "First Mover",
the postulated solution of a real or supposed problem
in dynamics. But the movement he initiates and supports apparently involves no outgoing activity on
his own part. We are told that he moves the "first
heaven" in the same way in which the object of concupiscence or love moves love or concupiscence.[1]
The point of the comparison is that, in both cases,
the whole process falls wholly within the being who is
"moved". To repeat an illustration I have used elsewhere, the Princess of Tripoli, in a sense, "moved"
Jauffré Rudel, by supplying the initiative for his
famous voyage. Yet it may well have been the case
that the Princess was not so much as aware of the
existence of her lover. And, since Aristotle insists that
the life of God is one unbroken contemplation of a
single object, himself, to the exclusion of all others, it
would seem to follow that God does not even know of
that existence of the "heaven" which he "moves".[2]

As a fact of history, this was the interpretation put
on the doctrine by the soundest Aristotelian expositor
of antiquity, Alexander of Aphrodisias. Alexander was
careful to explain that God, in Aristotle's system, is
only the τελική αἰτία, the "final" cause, of the diurnal

[1] *Metaphys.*, 1072 a 26 ff.
[2] It would be unjustifiable to interpret Aristotle in the light of the later scholastic doctrine that God, *cognoscendo se, et alia cognoscit. That* presupposes the
Trinity.

revolution; the universe finds its satisfaction, exercises its function, in executing this uniform unending revolution, and this is the only way in which there is any connection between the world and God. That one does not need to be biassed by specifically Christian sentiment to find this doctrine of a merely self-absorbed Deity intolerable is shown by the zeal with which it is denounced, for example, by the learned Neo-Platonic scholar Simplicius. Simplicius is no Christian—in fact he was one of the sturdy pagans who migrated to Persia from antipathy to Christianity when the schools of Athens were closed by Justinian—but he is a Platonist, and as such determined to find nothing in Aristotle incompatible with the definitely ethical and theistic philosophy of Plato. Accordingly, he sets himself to argue more ingeniously than successfully for an interpretation by which God shall be less completely cut off from contact with the world.[1] If Simplicius cannot break with Aristotle in his exaltation of the "theoretical life, he is bound, as a Neo-Platonist, to give his supreme principle, as an essential consequence of its inward activity of self-concentration, a further outgoing activity, in virtue of which it παράγει, produces, creates, the world. Thus the attempt to adjust Aristotle with Plato leads directly up to the recognition of what is now called divine "transcendence" and the problem of the relation of this transcendence to the divine "immanence". This problem may occupy us further in the sequel, but for the present I would be content merely to note that no philosophy of pure "immanence" can take the moral life seriously. The special problem of the ultimate source of initiative towards the morally better, which is familiar in theology as the problem of "grace", is

---

[1] See the polemic on this point in his commentary on the *Physics* (Diels, pp. 1360-1363).

but the particular form assumed by the more general problem of "transcendence" when raised with special reference to human personal activities. The metaphysical denial of divine transcendence carries with it self-righteousness in morality, as well as Pelagianism in theological speculation. (It is only just to add that exclusive insistence on transcendence has its dangers too; it leads to "supralapsarian" theology and an antinomian "going as you please" in morality. Such is the price we have to pay for over-simplification of our problems.)

I must be content, then, at the risk of being thought, as Socrates anticipates in the *Phaedo* that he may be thought in a similar case, "*naïf* and rather simple",[1] to insist on one point. A man cannot receive the power to rise above his present moral level from his own inherent strength, because the process is one of rising above himself, and, in the moral as in the physical world, you cannot lift yourself by the hair of your own head. Nothing can rise in virtue of its inherent gravity. And, again, you cannot borrow strength from an ideal which is only an ideal, a value without actuality. If the ideal indeed draws you upward, and unless it does so it is not *your* ideal, it does this because it is not divorced from reality, but is more real than anything else you know. It is what we too often call the "actual", that which we are here and now, that is relatively unreal. It is relatively unreal because our life is a becoming, and therefore the so-called actual is always slipping away into the no longer actual. To-day's actuality is to-morrow's "dead past". The "ideal" is above becoming, and escapes this fate. We cannot say of it that the ideal of to-day gives place to the different ideal of to-morrow by becoming to-morrow's mere actuality. As we make

[1] *Phaedo*, 100 D 3 τοῦτο δὲ ἁπλῶς καὶ ἀτέχνως καὶ ἴσως εὐήθως ἔχω παρ' ἐμαυτῷ.

moral progress, we do not reach and pass the ideal of to-day, and say good-bye to it. What happens is that we discover to-morrow that to-day's ideal "had more in it" than we had supposed. Life is not a succession of excursions, each with a destination which is reached and left behind; it is a single journey towards a goal which, in what we see of life, or should see if its duration could be indefinitely prolonged, is never finally reached. The task of putting off temporality can no more be finished at a given date than the evaluation of a "surd" can ever be completed by writing down the last significant digit of the unending "decimal".

A great deal of otherwise admirable ethical literature seems to me to commit a fundamental error by conceiving of the moral life too simply, as a giving *expression*, through outward speech and action, to our inward personality. The real task is not merely that; it is rather the task of the reshaping and transfiguration of the inward personality itself, and the initiative to *such* an undertaking manifestly cannot come simply from within the personality which is to be remade. It must come in the end from contact with an ἀρχὴ κινήσεως which lies outside and around what is, at any given time, internal to the self, and the whole problem is how to live on this source in such a way that it is steadily drawn more and more into the self and yet never brought completely within it. When St. Paul writes to his converts that the life he is now living is "not I, but Christ alive in me", he is using the language of exalted religious adoration, but a not dissimilar statement, pitched in a lower key, would be in principle true of the life of any man who is seriously trying, in however humble a fashion, to be a "better man". Morality itself, taken in earnest, thus involves the "supernatural", in the proper sense of that word, as its environment and daily nutriment. A morality without an ultimate source of initiative in the eternal would amount to a prolonged attempt to breathe *in vacuo*, or to feed one's body on its own fat. We all know what would happen to an animal if it always "hibernated", or if it had to inhale endlessly air which had already passed through its lungs; yet, except in the New Testament and in Plato, the indispensability of τροφή from without for the moral life seems never to have found adequate recognition.

To say this is not in any way to deny the equal in-dispensability of personal effort and persistence for all moral and spiritual progress. Not only may "tasks in hours of insight willed" be fulfilled in hours of "dry-ness" and gloom, but we may add that they never will be fulfilled in any other and easier fashion. The re-fashioning of personality will no more take place in a man without sheer hard work and endurance on his own part than a great work of art will ever be thrown off without effort in an hour of indolence. *In sudore vultus tui comedes panem.* But the question is about the hours of insight themselves, and the inspiration which is re-ceived in them. And with regard to them the truth seems to be that vision, in the moral as in the physical world, presupposes a real object of vision. The revela-tion of physical beauty begins not with a discovery of the beauty of the visual organ, but with perception of the loveliness of the colours and lines of things seen. In like manner discernment of "moral" beauty begins with the contemplation of an object which *gives* itself to the inward eye. In moral and physical vision alike, we have first to look *away* from ourselves. If we are to grow into the likeness of the thing we contemplate, this can only be because the thing we contemplate is *not*, in the first instance, the thing we are; it is not *in rerum natura* at all.

Here, in fact, we have a characteristic of the moral life which removes it definitely from the domain of "nature", even as understood by a thinker like Dr. Whitehead, who is thoroughly in earnest with the conception of nature as an unresting "becoming". It is true that such a conception as this breaks once for all with that uncritical materialism which confuses the "real" with the contents of a "cross-section" of space[1] "at the moment t"; it brings us back to the Leibnizian view of nature as a system in which every constituent is weighted by the whole "past" and pregnant with the whole "future", and so delivers us from confusion of the infinite riches of the real with the poverty-stricken abstraction "nature at a given instant". But even the Leibnizian has to admit that, though every "monad" may be big with the future, we can only read the future of the system by the light of its past; the way in which its members have become what they are is our only clue to what they will yet become. In moral experience it is different. We do not first decipher from the past the route towards the better future, and then take the path so deciphered. It is very often *après coup*, after we have already taken the decisive movement for the better, that we discern by later reflection the continuity of the path we have traversed. In a moral interpretation of history it is actually by the consideration of the future that we discover the true significance of the past. It is not nature but super-nature that can say "what I do thou knowest not now, but thou shalt know hereafter".

I do not, of course, forget that, in the study of the natural sciences themselves, the true significance of the stages by which an organ or structure has been developed can only be comprehended properly when we first know the function the developed organ or structure is

[1] Or, rather, of the spatial-temporal continuum.

to discharge, and that this lies in the future relatively
to the process of development. But relatively to us who
are fashioning the natural sciences, the function is not
in the future. For us the functioning organ must be
already there and functioning, if we are to read its pre-
history by its own light. But in all moral appreciation
the *ex hypothesi* unattained ideal of the best is always
actually apprehended, in however vague a fashion. *Der
Mensch ist etwas, das überwunden werden muss.* Perhaps; but we have not to wait until the problematical
"superman" appears before we can pronounce on the
question whether Nietzsche's *Weg zum Übermenschen*
is the road to heaven or to hell.

If the considerations so far urged are sound, we may
proceed to formulate some important conclusions concerning the type of doctrine about God which ought to
characterise any "natural" theology which takes the
moral being of man into account as part, and the most
important part, of what it regards as the φύσις, *natura*,
or given reality which is not to be paltered with or
explained away.

(1) Since the moral life, rightly conceived, is no mere
readjustment of outward reactions of a self, given once
and for all, to its environment, but a reconstruction
of the whole personality round a new centre, an ethical
religion is inevitably, in the jargon made popular by
William James, a religion for the "twice-born". *Thou
must be born again* is the central proposition of all
genuine morality, and it is therefore indispensable to
an ethical theology that it should conceive its God not
only as the Maker who has brought man, like the rest
of the creatures, into temporal actuality, but as the
source and sustainer of the aspirations by which man is
made a *new* creature and puts off his first merely self-
contained and temporally confined selfhood. God, that

is, to use language technical in the thought of Christianity, must be conceived not only as Creator, but also as Redeemer and Sanctifier. From the ethical point of view, acquirement of our heritage of true personality demands something much more than the correction of bad habits and the formation of good; it demands the transformation of what is best in its own kind into something which is good in a higher kind, and it is here that most of us come so lamentably short in our practice.

To illustrate the point more fully by an example, let us consider any morally valuable institution, such as permanent human marriage. So long as we see nothing in the *consortium totius vitae* but an excellent social arrangement for the rearing of successive generations of the physically and mentally sound, and the maintenance of social quiet and order by the canalisation of a dangerous source of jealousies and rivalries, we are thinking what is true enough, but still we are not thinking worthily of human marriage. It is the fact that, as Milton says, it is the source of our best natural affections, and that by it

> adulterous lust was driv'n from men
> Among the bestial herds to raunge; [1]

but this is less than half of the truth. The Greek formula that the end of matrimony is παιδοποιία γνησίων τέκνων, the perpetuation of the civic life, in fact, even when the words are made to mean the utmost that can be fairly read into them, does not exhaust all the significance of the conception of Roman lawyers that *matrimonium* is *consortium totius vitae*. The end conceived as a partnership in the whole of life, a complete sharing of all interests such that every joy and every

---

[1] *P.L.* iv. 753.

sorrow is the joy or the sorrow of *two*, is something which immeasurably transcends the mere association of man and woman in the work of bringing a new generation of public-spirited citizens into the world and preparing them for maturity. It already involves a genuine enriching transformation of personality, and one which, if we will be honest with ourselves, most of us must, to our shame, confess ourselves to attain only very imperfectly and with grievous lapses. It is hard, terribly hard, not to have some interests which are not thus completely shared, some joys and sorrows, hopes and fears which remain incommunicable, even in the most successful of family lives. And so long as there is this hard core of unshared experiences, the ideal of the *Institutes* remains something not wholly realised or even in process of steady realisation, however true it may be that the failure to realise it may be traceable to no voluntary fault of the parties concerned. The interest from which a man's wife, or a woman's husband, is shut out, remains as an obstacle to the ethical transfiguration of personality from the form of *I* to that of *We*.

But, further, so long as we think of the life which is to be "shared" only as one of secular and temporal joys and sorrows, we are not yet thinking of it as it is in its full ethical significance; our conception is still only very imperfectly moralised and humanised. The complete transfiguration of the animal into the human is only effected when the shared life is itself a life of common aspiration after the supreme moral good. In such a life it is not enough that there should be nothing which would commonly be recognised as a clash of incompatible interests, or that either party should feel pleasure and pain in the pleasure and pain of the other. Every incident and every act of the rightly shared life would be one in which either party was assistant and co-operant with the endeavour of the other towards the putting on of a personality purified from the last taint of native egotism and secured against mutability, a ministrant to the other of a spiritual sacrament.

We do not, except in a distressingly inadequate fashion, find ourselves attaining such an ideal; if we did, it would not be the fact, as it so often is, that the least animal and most human of our personal affections prove, to the noble mind, the sources of the most dangerous temptations to be false, for the sake of a loved person, to the demands of the ideal for the supreme surrenders. It would not be a duty demanded of the dutifully minded man that he must be prepared, if the call comes, to *forsake* parents and wife and children, since when personality had become what it ought to be and is always striving to be, the parent, or wife, or child would not feel the surrender to be a forsaking. It would be impossible any longer to say

> I could not love thee, dear, so much
> Loved I not honour more,

since the two loves contrasted by the poet would be too completely one to be opposed, even in thought. Only where such an ideal had become matter of fact would it be possible, from the ethical point of view, to pronounce the most intimate and devoted of human attachments an unqualified good. And the ideal simply cannot become matter of fact in our natural life.

The reason is not merely that our moral will is infirm and suffers constantly recurring lapses, true as this is. Even if we could always presuppose a maximum of good will, the conditions under which we have to gain insight into another's personality set limits to

the insight so gained. For those who love to be thus
entirely at one, it would be needed that each should
read the other's personality to its depths with the
knowledge of direct and infallible vision, and in the
life we are conversant with there is no such *scientia
visionis* of one another, nor even of ourselves. There
is always something hidden from us in those who have
stood longest most near to ourselves; there are things
hidden from us in our very selves. Thus it is only the
bare truth that realisation of the moral ideal in the
simplest relations of human life is a thing impossible,
if it has to be achieved purely by our own strength,
and in the light of our own insight; as divines have
said, every marriage—and we might add every other
personal relation of life—is an adventure which is only
kept from ending in disaster by the perpetual influence
of transforming and sanctifying grace. So long as any
human relation rests for its support on a basis of un-
transformed "nature", it must inevitably be numbered
among the things of which we must expect, sooner or
later, to have to say, "I have no more pleasure in them".

(2) Now if this is so, the God of a Theism which is
definitely ethical cannot be thought of as related to
man, and the system of creatures generally, simply as
Creator or a "great First Cause". If natural religion
be taken, as it was taken in the eighteenth century, to
mean no more than recognition of such a "First Cause",
it becomes a mere hypothesis for cosmology and loses
all moral significance. In doing so it loses its right to
the name "religion", and all that remains to be said
of it has been said in five words in the title of one of
Blake's tracts, *There is no natural religion*. On this
point enough has been said already in connection with
our comments on the theology of Aristotle. But it is
equally true that the God of a true ethical Theism

cannot be thought of adequately as no more than an embodied, or personalised, moral end, as the "great example" whom we are to follow—a representation common in philosophies of a Platonising type. It is, indeed, already much that God should be thought of in this way; we are already delivered from the depreciation of moral values inevitably prompted by a merely cosmological theology into which God enters, as with Aristotle, as a non-ethical being. We have an inspiring rule and an end set before us which we cannot simply reach and leave behind, when we are commanded to "follow God", to grow, as nearly as may be, into the likeness of that which the "father and maker of all" eternally is. But with all its moral elevation the conception fails us when we ask how this work of becoming like God is to be set about.

The first step towards the "conversion" of the soul from the world to God, as we learn from the Platonic Socrates, is that knowledge of self which is also the knowledge of our own ignorance of true good. How do we pass from the discovery that we are in this miserable and shameful ignorance of the one thing it is incumbent on us to know to apprehension of the scale of true good? How do we get even so far beyond our initial complete ignorance as to be able to say that a good soul is immeasurably better than a good body, and a good body than abundance of possessions? We know how the Augustinian doctrine, which is Christian as well as Platonic, answers the question. It does so by its conception, traceable back to the New Testament, that God Himself is the *lumen intellectus*, a view which has been, in substance, that of all the classical British moral philosophers from Cudworth to Green, and seems, in fact, to be, in principle, the only solution of the difficulty. We know our true good, which is no other than

God Himself, by obscure, but none the less real and impressive, personal contacts with God. Without this real contact with the eternal, the process of winning a true personality could not be begun. Any such view further implies that because God is the *lumen intellectus*, He is also the inspirer of endeavour in all of us, since each of us, as Socrates, Plato, and Aristotle agree in teaching, always endeavours after what appears to him his *good*. An ethical Theism has then to conceive God as the "efficient", as well as the "exemplary" cause of the whole moral life. From its humblest beginnings that life is, at every step, one of transformation into the likeness of that which we contemplate.

(3) This may seem an obvious point, but it carries far-reaching applications. If God is not only the goal, but the author and sustainer of moral effort, the whole moral endeavour of man must be a response to what we can only call a movement from the other side. It is, indeed, our own because it is the response of such moral personality as we already possess, but none the less it is a *response* to a divine initiative. In that language of human social relations on which we have to fall back whenever we try to speak of these matters, we love God because God first loved us. The "good shepherd" does not leave his strayed sheep to find its own way back; he goes out into the darkness and dangers of the wilderness to find it. When we use such language, we know, of course, that we are speaking "anthropomorphically", and that all "anthropomorphic" utterances about the divine are imperfect and attended with danger. But the attempt to expel anthropomorphism from our language about God is attended with worse dangers. Indeed, since we, who have fashioned language, are men, the only language we can use or understand is necessarily anthropomorphic, no matter what its

reference may be. We can see nothing outside ourselves, except through a human medium. Even when we talk of "inanimate nature" we never really succeed in getting quite rid of "anthropomorphism".

This was patent enough in the ordinary old-fashioned textbooks with their free employment of such words as "force", "constraint", "cause"; it is only half-hidden even in the phraseology of the thoroughgoing "positivists" of science who have demanded that physics shall be denuded of the last rags of a terminology which goes beyond the extreme abstractness of pure kinematics. No one has yet succeeded, and no one ever will succeed, in banishing the notions of change and process even from a natural science reduced to pure kinematics. And change is as completely an anthropomorphic conception as "force". If there is any living philosopher of whom we could say that the elimination of the anthropomorphic is a passion with him we must say it of Professor Alexander. Yet when Professor Alexander finds himself called on to assign a reason for the unceasing "emergence" of novel and, according to him, always brighter and better orders of existents, he finds the reason in what he calls the "restlessness" of space-time, thus simply transferring to his ultimates Locke's doctrine of the "greatest present uneasiness" as the standing incentive to action. If this notion of "restlessness" as the source of progressive efforts after betterment is not anthropomorphic, or rather, perhaps, theriomorphic, one would be glad to know what is.[1]

It ought to be obvious that we cannot speak at all of the superhuman or the infrahuman except in terms which derive all their significance, in the first instance, from that with which alone we are immediately familiar

[1] S. Alexander, *Space, Time and Deity*, ii. 345 ff.

from its presence in our own experience of living and striving—the strictly human. We cannot make our science or our theology really non-anthropomorphic, even if we would. Our choice is between speaking of the divine in terms of what is richest and most fully human in our own lives, or in terms of what is poorest and least human. And there should be no difficulty in making the choice, if once we are in earnest, as any genuine recognition of the moral life of man as a manifestation of the real compels us to be, with the notion of the divine as an efficient cause, and, in the end, *the* "first" efficient cause, of human moral advance. We *must* think of the divine on the analogy of all that is richest and most human, not only in our actual character, but in the better we aspire to be. The danger incurred when we represent God, for example, as standing to us in the relation of a noble human lover to the object of his love is not that we are attributing too much to God—it is the "natural" sciences in which *that* kind of risk is real —but that we are attributing too little. For so much of what we call love, when we speak "after the manner of men," is unworthy of the name.

Sometimes we mean by the word little more than a mere *amor concupiscentiae*, a carnal passion in which we care for the object only as an instrument of our own enjoyment and as nothing more.[1] When we mean more, as, thank God, most of us usually do, we still do not always discriminate very clearly between a "love" which is still mainly infrahuman and is concerned chiefly with "taking" and the love which is primarily anxious to "give". There are presumably few human

[1] Cf.

> "He will hold thee, when his passion shall have spent its novel force,
> Something better than his dog, a little dearer than his horse."

Even this, however, is something. There are men who "love" a woman, or a fellow-man, much as an epicure "loves" truffles or claret.

relations in which the two are not inextricably bound up together. We talk, for example, of Lear's feeling for his daughters, as Lear himself does, as a "love" of peculiar intensity. But Lear's vehement fury of recoil at the first manifestations of coldness and ingratitude on the other side shows that, if he is to be called a passionate lover at all, his passion is overwhelmingly of the kind which is much more eager to take than to give. He calls himself, indeed, a father whose kind old heart "gave all", but the words are profoundly untrue. He gave, what after all cost him little, kingdoms, because he wanted to take what he cared more about, caresses and *câlineries*. Brought face to face, in the case of Cordelia, with the love which really gives all, he confuses it with want of "natural affection". At heart, Lear is as much one of "nature's takers" as Goneril or Regan, though the thing he lusts to take is less sordid.

Again, even when we are alive to the distinction between the taker's love and the giver's love, we continually confuse the love which aims at giving what is best with that which is content to give the second-rate or third-rate. We do not distinguish, as we ought, between a seeing love and a blind. By a loving father we mean, only too often, more precisely one whose only desire is to give his children what they like rather than what is good for them. In especial, we are apt to be blind to the reality of a love which demands high performance and lays hard tasks on its recipient, for the sake of the strength and beauty of personal character which are not to be had on easier terms. We confuse love with weakness, and this confusion is the source of a great deal of the current literary revolt against the idea of God.

It is held either that all love must be weak indulgence, and that the conception of God as loving us is therefore an unworthy one, or, on the other side, that the undeniable hardness of the tasks life sets to the best men is proof that the author of life is profoundly unloving, and so morally inferior to ourselves. The source of all this confusion is the assumption that, if we speak of God's love for men, we are not to interpret such language in the light of the strongest and wisest human love, but in that of weak and unwise love. That error arises not from too much anthropomorphism, but from too little, from readiness to think of God in terms of something lower than our highest human standard of excellence. An ethical theology is necessarily anthropomorphic, in the sense that it interprets God and God's ways by the analogy of all that is most nobly human, and always with the further caution that as a completely humanised man would be all we can picture to ourselves of what is admirable in man and something more, which we cannot yet picture because we ourselves are so far from being wholly humanised, so God is all that perfect human excellence would be and abundantly more. Thus the simple statement that God, whose initiative is the source of all our advance in good, loves man as a father loves his children is inaccurate only because it ascribes too little to God. It falls short because no actual human father loves his children with a love which is wholly bent on giving, wholly wise and wholly unspoiled by facile sentimentality.

(4) The main point on which I would wish to be clear, however, is that to think ethically of God means to break finally with the bad "deistic" tradition which finds its clearest expression in the Aristotelian theology. The God of a truly moral Theism cannot be a purely self-centred being, "making eyes at Himself", to borrow a phrase from Bradley, like some Narcissus. His fundamental activity must involve expansion. And when we would think of His action upon the world, we can only

think of it as a life in which He gives Himself freely and generously to His creatures that they may be able to give themselves to Him. As Timaeus says in Plato[1] the very reason why there is a world of creatures at all is that the All-good is wholly free from φθόνος, the "dog-in-the-manger" spirit which seeks to engross felicity to itself, and therefore makes the creatures for His goodness to flow out upon. He cannot be wholly blessed, except in blessing.

I may, perhaps, be reminded at this point that, on a *prima facie* view, the tradition of Christian orthodoxy would seem to be at variance with the spirit of what has just been said. It is notorious that Christian theologians have all but unanimously agreed in rejecting the view, characteristic of Neo-Platonism, that the world of creatures emanates, or emerges, from the Creator by some sort of "natural necessity"; creation, they have taught, is a freely willed act of God. He might conceivably have willed to create no world at all, or to create one different in every detail from that which is actual. Not a few eminent Christian philosophers and theologians have gone still further. They have denied that the divine choice to create the actual world is due to its superior goodness when compared with other possible worlds, and some of them apparently have even denied that there is any reason whatever for the choice, thus apparently making both the existence of a world of creatures and its specific character the outcome of something like a divine "whim". Against all such language I would venture, with due modesty, to suggest that both the rival doctrines of a necessitated creation and of a capricious creation rest, in the end, on confusion of thought. It is important to an ethical Theism to insist that there is no necessity external and

---

[1] *Tim.* 29 E I, ἀγαθὸς ἦν, ἀγαθῷ δὲ οὐδεὶς περὶ οὐδενὸς οὐδέποτε ἐγγίγνεται φθόνος.

superior to the Creator; He neither creates because He is constrained to create, nor gives the created world the structure it actually has because that structure is dictated by antecedent conditions. He is the foundation and absolute *prius* of all actuality and all possibility, and He is all, and more than all, we understand by an intelligent and righteous will. To safeguard such a Theism it is needful that we should clearly repudiate the suggestion, which haunts all philosophies of the Neo-Platonic type, that the Creator "has" to create, and to create the world we know, so to say, "willy-nilly", and this cannot be better done than by saying that creation is an act of free and intelligent choice.

But when we go on to add that, therefore, "God might have willed to create no world at all, or might have willed to create an entirely different world", we are, it seems to me, at least on the verge of a dangerous fallacy of ambiguity. We may mean only to give a piquant expression to the thought that the world is and is what it is because God is and is what He is. But we may also mean, and theologians seem sometimes actually to have meant, that God might be the God He is and yet that His creative will might be absent from His being, or might be other than it is. And if we mean this, then, I should say, we are introducing into the divine being itself the element of contingency, or, what comes to the same thing, we are making a distinction, and a *real* distinction, between God and God's will. That is, we are reintroducing the distinction between the possible and the actual into that which we also recognise as the foundation of both possibility and actuality, and so allowing ourselves to forget that God's will *is* God, that *Deus est suum velle*. When once we understand that this distinction can have no place within the being of God, it seems to make no real differ-

ence whether we say that God produces the creatures
by an act of free will, or, with Spinoza,[1] that He produces them "by the law of *his own* nature", since in
God, who is the absolute *prius*, there can be no distinction between *Deus* and *deitas*, such as there is in
us, who are always *in fieri*, between the man and the
humanity he is ever "putting on", but has never fully
put on. In us it is true that there is a distinction between *natura* and *voluntas*, for the simple reason that
we have to become true persons with a reasonable will
by a gradual and difficult process; in God, who does
not become but is, the distinction seems to have no
place. My objection to Spinoza's formula would be
based not on what it asserts but on what it denies. It
asserts, truly as it seems to me, that God acts "by the
law of his own nature", but falsely sets such action in
God in opposition to "free action", as though the complete identity of *voluntas* and *natura* were not itself the
very ideal of perfect freedom.[2]

Whatever may be thought of these remarks, it seems
at least plain that anxiety to banish the last vestiges of
egoistic self-concentration from the idea of God must
have been at work all through the formative period of
Christian doctrine in leading up to the final elaboration of the great theological dogma of the Trinity. Why,
we may reasonably ask, was the Church so profoundly

---

[1] *Ethica*, i. 16 *ex necessitate divinae naturae infinita infinitis modis (hoc est omnia quae sub intellectum infinitum cadere possunt) sequi debent;* i. 17 *Deus ex solis suae naturae legibus, et a nemine coactus agit.* But I regard it as mere con-fusion to say that "all that can be known by an infinite intellect is actual", and, as Spinoza adds at i. 33, that "things could not have been produced by God in any order other than that in which they have been produced".

[2] On the other hand, I find myself in full agreement with the conclusion of St. Thomas (*Quaest. disp. de potentia* q. 3, art. 15), that things have proceeded from God *per arbitrium voluntatis*, and with the reason he gives for the conclusion, but dissatisfied with the rejection of the alternative *per necessitatem naturae*, unless it is understood that "nature" is here taken to be something other than "the nature of God". I desire more emphasis to be laid on what St. Thomas himself asserts, that *voluntas* and *natura, prout in Deo sunt*, are *secundum rem idem*.

dissatisfied with what looks, at first sight, the simple and intelligible doctrine of an "economic Trinity", a trinity of "parts" sustained by God as successively the Creator, the Redeemer, and the Sanctifier? Why were the thinkers who gave orthodox Christianity its pattern driven, we might say in spite of themselves, to make the distinctions of "persons" something more than a distinction of simple temporal *rôles*, to make it "essential" and eternal? And what did they mean by introducing the supreme difficulty involved in the culminating assertion that, in spite of this essential and eternal distinction, there is a perfect *circumincession* of the three "persons", such that each eternally contains and is contained in each? Was it from mere caprice that the apparently simple and intelligible was persistently rejected for the admittedly mysterious and paradoxical? The typical eighteenth-century answer to the question is that of Gibbon,[1] that contradiction and nonsense have an inherent attractiveness of their own for an ambitious "priesthood" bent on enslaving the human mind; the consecration of gibberish is the supreme triumph of a caste set on domination. Such an explanation can only satisfy an age which thinks so unhistorically as to mistake the makers of a great theological tradition for designing and clear-sighted hypocrites not themselves imposed on by their own decisions, and nothing can be clearer than the historical fact that if the Christian divines who drew up the standard formula were indeed canonising gibberish, they at least believed ardently themselves in their own gibberish.

[1] *Decline and Fall*, c. xxi. "an eager spirit of curiosity urged them to explore the secrets of the abyss; and the pride of the professors, and of their disciples, was satisfied with the science of words . . . the Christians proved a numerous and disciplined society; and the jurisdiction of their laws and magistrates was strictly exercised over the minds of the faithful . . . the authority of a theologian was determined by his ecclesiastical rank", etc., etc.

The real source of their most paradoxical definitions seems to me to have been mainly ethical. It was felt that the doctrine of an "economic" Trinity does not make *giving* as fully and inwardly characteristic of the divine life as it requires to be made. With such a doctrine, the giving and self-emptying may, no doubt, be real, but it remains something external, an incident arising from the relation of the Creator to a creation which has somehow "gone off the lines". Room is left for the thought that if there had been no "fall", if the creature had not "gone wrong", there is no inherent reason why the divine activity should have been one of utter and complete self-bestowal, and thus the possibility is left open of regarding that activity, even in its relation to the creatures we know with all their faults and defects, as not penetrating the inmost depths of the divine life. The god of such a theology may, after all, have a core of self-centredness; he may be, like a magnified Stoic sage who, when all is said, at bottom "keeps himself to himself", in spite of his apparent preoccupation with the "common" good, always at heart frigid and unsympathetic, because the thing of highest worth in the scale of goods is just that in himself which he never shares.

This, I take it, is the reason which would not let Christian divines rest until they had declared that the "personal" distinctions are eternal, internal, and essential to the divine being itself. The thought was not merely that, as was generally assumed, creation had only happened some few thousand years before their own time, and that *some* activity must be found for the divine which has no beginning. There was, further, a consideration which would still remain, even if the world of creatures were held to be without beginning. The divine, infinite, and eternal can only communicate to the created and finite so much of itself as the creature can receive without ceasing to be a creature. Hence if the world of finite creatures is the only object on which the divine activity of giving can be exercised, the riches of the divine nature must remain as good as uncommunicated; in its foundations the divine life must be egoistic. To love with the love that gives must be only a surface characteristic of the life of God. And since such isolated selfhood is un-ethical, there is no room for the ethical in the inmost life of God, when it is conceived thus. To make room for the ethical we have to think of the divine, even apart from its relation to the creatures, as having a life in which there is, within the Godhead itself, an object adequate to the complete and absolute reception of an activity of giving which extends to the whole fullness of the divine nature, so that there is nothing which is not imparted and nothing which is not re-ceived. Because the mutual love in which each party bestows himself freely and completely and is freely and completely received is ethically the supreme spiritual activity, the life of God is thought of as involving an internal distinction as well as an internal unity, in order that the whole activity of the divine life may be one of perfect and unlimited self-bestowal.

> *Est totus in Nato Pater,*
> *in Patre totus Filius;*
> *Natoque plenus et Patri*
> *inest utrique Spiritus.*[1]

The motives which led to the foundation of the doc-trine of *circumincession*, called by Gibbon the "darkest corner of the whole theological abyss",[2] cease to be so perplexing if we regard them as arising in the attempt

---

[1] *Paris Breviary*, Office Hymn for *Lauds* of Trinity Sunday.
[2] *Decline and Fall*, c. xxi. n. 59.

to say what God must be if we are to take the moral relations of persons as the least hopelessly inadequate clue to the inmost character of the real.

(5) These observations, however, are by the way. A point of more immediate moment is that, in the recognition that a moral Theism must take account of the initiative of the divine, and so reckon seriously with grace, free movement outward on the divine side, as the ultimate source of human moral endeavour itself, we are implicitly abandoning the deep-seated prejudice that there is any real opposition in principle between "philosophical" or "natural", and "historical" or "revealed" theology, or between a philosophical and an institutional religion. If it is true that our most inchoate visions of an ideal good are themselves the issue of actual imperfect contacts with a divine reality, then the supposed opposition becomes only a distinction, and, I would add, a distinction which it is a mistake to make too rigid. All our moral vision of good may be truly said to be due, in the end, to reve-lation, self-communication on the part of the divine reality, and it will become impossible to deny that the value of what is revealed regularly depends on the capacity of the recipient to whom the disclosure is made. *Quidquid recipitur recipitur ad modum reci-pientis*. And clearly, again, no metaphysician has the right to pretend to determine *a priori* beforehand what form the contacts with the divine from which living inspiration to good arises must take. That we must be content to learn from the event. Since they are all contacts *in caligine*, we should be prepared to find that their occasions are often such as might have been thought unlikely and surprising; it is of the nature of the case that they should, for example, occur in the lives of the "babes and sucklings" and should

appear mere foolishness to the worldly-wise. It is no derogation from the genuinely supernatural character of these self-disclosures of God to men to say that the "rationalistic" attempt to judge of them otherwise than by the effects, where they are accepted, on a man's life, is of a piece with the similar less often advanced pretence to say what *must* be the quarter in which "original genius" of any kind should be looked for, or in what strange and unexpected ways it may disclose its presence.

The true distinction will not be between a certain type of religious life or theological belief which is complete in itself and justifiable by "human reason", and another which is wholly non-rational or super-rational and has simply to be accepted on authority of some kind. The true distinction will be rather between that in the divine which is generally disclosed to men with a very commonplace level of moral insight and practice and that which is only directly disclosed to special recipients, why selected we cannot always say, and justifies itself, in the end, by its practical effect in the inward reconstitution of the lives of those who accept the disclosure in good faith. There is no philosophical justification for confining the channels by which the divine may disclose itself, or the persons to whom the disclosure may be made, within limits marked out antecedently by a human theorist.

We may not, for instance, assume that whereas the vision of the divine in Hebrew prophecy must have come simply by "revelation", the insight of the Hellenic moralists must everywhere have a less exalted source; or, again, that though a man cannot afford to lose the religious guidance and support of the lessons of great poets and philosophers, he can afford to dispense, and it will make for his spiritual progress to dispense, with membership of a society of worshippers with a definite tradition of doctrine and worship. We may not assume at this stage of our discussion that the highest attainments in the spiritual life can only be mediated through membership of some specific community and participation in its distinctive rites, but neither have we any right to deny the truth of this assumption on general and *a priori* grounds. It may be that in every religion, as it actually exists in the life of the community which lives by it, there are apprehensions involving real and direct contacts with the divine, and that thus, in the end, every religion contains its basis of "revealed" truth. Yet it does not follow that the quality of all the revelations is the same, nor even that among the revelations of the divine to be found in the history of mankind there may not be some one which corrects and integrates the partial lights of the rest, while not itself calling for correction by any "higher synthesis". In that case there will be, as Christians claim that there is, an historical religion which is, in principle, final and absolute, and not a mere best among many good, or a best as yet accessible. But these are problems which will concern us further in the sequel.

So it may perfectly well be that direct access to the divine has been provided for men in countless ways. Perhaps the "one true light" may at times be caught in the "tavern", though the poet from whom the sentiment comes[1] has generally been regarded as a light-hearted mocker by those who know him at first-hand. And no doubt it is better to catch a distant glimpse of the light in the tavern than to miss it altogether in the temple. Yet it may also be that though many who worship in the

---

[1] For the original verses see Whinfield's text of Omar Khayyám, quatrain 262. ("To speak in secret with Thee in taverns is better than to offer prayer without Thee in the *mihráb*. 'Tis in Thy will, O Thou, beginning and end at once of Thy creatures, to burn me, and in Thy will to cherish me.")

temple are blind to the light, he who refuses to cross its threshold will never enjoy the fullest illuminations. That the Highest should communicate spiritual life to us through the institutions of a particular society with their physical instruments may be strange, but no stranger than that poetical and musical genius of the first order should make its appearance in the seemingly untoward circumstances among which it often displays itself. Could we have been told at the beginning of the last century that the world was on the eve of receiving the gift of a supreme poet with a direct vision of beauty which would inspire and support the poetic literature of a hundred years and still remain unexhausted, probably the last place where we should have been predisposed to look for the man who was to make us see beauty again would have been the quarter from which John Keats actually emerged. We might not have been clear about the fact even in 1821, when the poet's own short life had come to an end; we know now, because we see the facts in the light of the influence he has exercised, and thus know, for example, how all that is best in Tennyson comes out of Keats.

So it is with the institutions of a living religion. What they are we can only judge by the quality of the life they bring into the world. Antecedently we might be disposed to say, for example, that the ritual breaking and pouring and sharing of bread and wine would be very unlikely to mediate, to those who participate in it with simple and humble hearts, a quality of life they could win in no other fashion. But whether it is so or no cannot be decided by consideration of antecedent probabilities; the appeal has to be made to the effects revealed in the lives of the worshippers. We cannot come to the philosophic study of religion or of theology, the theory of the life of which religion is the practice, with too open minds. It would be very unsafe to infer that what claims to be a special self-disclosure of the divine must be what it claims to be, *because* it is surprising. But it would probably be a good rule to say that God does "move in a mysterious way", and that the most unlikely thing of all would be that a true religion should contain *no* surprises. But this, again, is a thought we shall need to develop further.

VII

THE DESTINY OF THE INDIVIDUAL

Ψυχῆς πείρατα οὐκ ἂν ἐξεύροιο πᾶσαν ἐπιπορευόμενος ὁδόν.—HERACLITUS.

Videmus nunc per speculum in aenigmate.

THE question we are now to consider has only too often been treated as the central and supreme issue in all religion. There is a type of mind—it is exemplified in men like F. W. H. Myers, or, at a much higher intellectual level, Dr. McTaggart—which apparently feels no imperious necessity to worship, but is anxiously beset by the old question, "If a man die, shall he live again?" Such minds have no difficulty in acquiescing in a world without God, but are deeply revolted by the suggestion that their own personality may not be able to survive the shock of bodily dissolution. With them proof of the immortality of the soul, drawn either from general metaphysical postulates or from alleged empirical evidence of the continued activity of the dead, tends to replace the whole of theology. In the many hundred pages of Myers' *Human Personality* there are, so far as I recollect, not many references to the existence of God. Dr. McTaggart has even professed to produce proof that theistic belief is almost certainly false, and quite certainly superfluous.[1]

I suppose I need hardly remind you that this attitude of mind is diametrically opposed to that characteristic of the Christian religion, and almost as completely

[1] *Some Dogmas of Religion*, cc. vi.-viii.; *Nature of Existence*, ii. c. 43.

opposed to the great Platonic tradition in metaphysics. In both Christianity and Platonism, it is the thought of God as at once the source of being and the goal of moral endeavour, the A and Ω, that is central; the high prospects both hold out to the individual man who "perseveres to the end", or, as the *Phaedrus* has it, chooses the "philosopher's" life thrice in succession,[1] are, in the end, based on their conception of the God into whose likeness it is man's vocation to grow; with both it is *deiformity*, not mere endless continuance, which is held out to man as the prize of his calling. If I have delayed discussion of human immortality so long, my reason is that I find myself wholly at one with the Christian and Platonic tradition on this issue. Apart from an adequate doctrine of God, it is, as I believe, impossible to find any secure foundation for a doctrine of human immortality, or any ground for thinking the prospect of such immortality attractive. When we consider human personality as we are actually acquainted with it in ourselves, apart from convictions about the vocation of man based on the identification of the *summum bonum* with the living and eternal God, we are treating personality, after all, in a purely naturalistic fashion, and, as far as I can see, a merely naturalistic perseverance in existence, even if it could be made probable, might well be, like the deathlessness of a Struldbrug, the supreme curse. On that point I may be allowed to refer once for all to the imaginative development of the theme in the *intermezzo* intercalated between the eighth and ninth chapters of Jean Paul Richter's *Siebenkäs*, so admirably rendered by Carlyle.[2]

Thus I do not propose to concern myself here with either of two very familiar types of argument for human

---

[1] *Phaedrus*, 249 A.
[2] At the end of the 1830 *Essay* on Jean Paul Friedrich Richter.

immortality, the metaphysical argument from the alleged character of the soul as a simple substance, or a primitive fountain of internally originated motion, and what we may, without prejudice, call the empirical argument from the real or alleged facts of necromancy. For neither line of argument, be its cogency what it may, has any real connection with the subject of all our reflections, the light thrown on man's nature and status, and consequently on his destiny, by study of his specific-ally moral being. As to the metaphysical argument, it is enough to say, what would probably be conceded by almost all careful metaphysicians, that, even if we grant, as we could hardly do without a great deal of prelimin-ary discussion, that the soul is a simple substance, or a primitive fount of movement, it does not necessarily follow that it is imperishable. All that necessarily follows is that if the soul vanishes from the sum total of the actual, its disappearance must be strictly instant-aneous; it must perish, if it perishes at all, by annihi-lation or inanition, not by dissolution. This is, in fact, all that Leibniz, for example, ventures to assert of his spiritual simple atoms or monads. When we further seek to complete the argument by proving that annihilation may be excluded from the range of possibilities, either we have to fall back, as Leibniz does, on the appeal to the known goodness of God, or we fall into the material-istic fallacy of arguing that the self is a bit of "mind-stuff" and that the annihilation of "stuff" is inconceiv-able. Reasoning of this kind may have seemed plausible in days when the conservation of mass could be taken as a first principle too axiomatic to call for discussion; in our own time, when distinguished physicists are declaring that the doctrine of conservation of mass is only a deduction from the conservation of energy— itself no necessity of thought—and is only true under

restrictions,[1] and distinguished astronomers can propose to employ the notion of a progressive annihilation
of mass as a key to the life-history of the stars,[2] we
clearly cannot repose much confidence in the extension
to "mind-stuff" of an apparently antiquated physical
prepossession. Even if we could, it is plain that survival
as a "bare monad", or a bit of "mind-stuff", or a mere
initiator of movements, is not a destiny which can inspire a man with hope or stir him to noble living. The
hope of immortality has been morally inspiring only
when immortality has been understood to mean persistence after physical dissolution of the moral and intellectual character which has been slowly built up in the
course of this present life through struggle and sacrifice,
and the prospect of building further on the same foundations elsewhere. What we want is to "see of the travail of our souls and be satisfied", and this is just what
no *mere* doctrine of the "natural immortality" of the
soul can ensure. Even Leibniz ends by resting his hopes
not on anything he believes himself to have proved
about the nature of a simple monad, but on the undemonstrated conviction that a good God will not allow
monads which have attained the status of moral and
intelligent persons to fall back to the level of "mere"
monads.[3]

The same considerations apply equally to those
alleged facts of necromancy on which the "spiritists" of
all ages are accustomed to rely. It must be doubtful
whether, in any case, when we have excluded everything which can be most probably accounted for by
conscious or unconscious fraud, or by obscure, and as

[1] Eddington, *Space, Time and Gravitation*, pp. 141-2; *Nature of Physical World*, 50, 59.
[2] J. H. Jeans in *Evolution in the Light of Modern Knowledge*, p. 14; *Universe Around Us*, 182-90.
[3] See Leibniz, *New System*, 5, 8; *Principles of Nature and Grace*, 14, 15.

yet ill-understood, communication between embodied minds, very much of the supposed facts is left. If anything is left, I still must agree with critics like Bradley that there is always a plurality of alternative hypotheses open to us. To prove, if it can be proved, that I am in communication with an intelligence other than that of an incarnate human person, is by no means to prove that I am communing with the "mighty dead". The traditional view of the Church that all such communications, if genuine, come from "the devil" may perhaps be over-hasty, but is certainly incapable of refutation, if the name "devil" is used widely enough to cover possible low-grade personalities which are merely silly or mischievous, as well as those which are actually morally wicked. And even if we could exclude, as we cannot, the possibility that all genuine communications from "the other side" come either from freakish imps or from wicked beings laying cunning plots for our moral ruin, the prospects held out to us by spiritists are not of a kind to rejoice a true man. Myers may be right, though it is hard not to doubt his complete satisfaction on the point,[1] when he says that mediumistic communications show no trace of actual moral depravity; but one has only to read the journals which profess to record these messages to be satisfied that, at all events, they display a distressingly low level of intelligence. They are mostly a medley of sentimental gush and twaddling sermonising. If their authors are, as it is often alleged that they are, the great moral and intellectual heroes of our past, it would seem that the brightest prospect the unseen world has to offer is that of a gradual declension of mankind into an undying

---

[1] F. H. Bradley expressed himself to me, at the time of publication of Myers' book, as highly indignant at the omission from the long discussion of "possession" of any reference to its commonest form, "diabolic possession".

society of trivial sentimental bores. Some of us might prefer Dante's Hell, where the damned at least retain something of human dignity. One would rather be Farinata on his couch of fire than Shakespeare complacently dictating drivel. Fortunately my subject relieves me from any necessity of prosecuting this argument further. What we are now concerned with is the light thrown on man's destiny by his moral being, and we may fairly say at the outset that if our moral being indicates anything about our inmost nature and its destiny, we may be confident that that destiny is not to persist either as "bare monads", or as talkers of wordy twaddle of which we should have been ashamed even when "the eternal substance" of our souls was half subdued to its prison in the "sinful flesh".

The limits we have thus prescribed to ourselves, then, demand that we confine our attention strictly to an examination of what is known as the "moral" argument for immortality. And here we find ourselves confronted at the outset by the assertion of a formidable body of contemporary students of philosophy that a "moral" argument must be worthless, from the very nature of the case. It will be instructive to consider the reasons given for this contention by so eminent a philosopher as Dr. McTaggart. Since McTaggart was in fact eager to establish a doctrine of immortality, and made immortality a leading feature in his interpretation of the world, we may be sure that rejection of the "moral" argument does not, in his case, arise from any secret bias against the conclusion it has been used to prove. He would presumably have been glad to reinforce a belief which he ardently cherished by any legitimate argument in its favour. If *he* denies the validity of the "moral proof", the denial must be based on sincere conviction of its worthlessness, and such a conviction on the part of an exceptionally subtle and acute dialectician is reasonably felt to constitute at least a strong antecedent presumption against the line of reasoning so condemned, and must therefore be faced seriously.

Dr. McTaggart has explained fully what he means by a moral argument and why he thinks all moral arguments about human destiny worthless.[1] By a moral argument he says he means an argument by which we infer that some state of things must be real on the ground that it is highly desirable that it should be real. Thus the moral argument for immortality is taken to be to the following effect: "It is so good that we should be immortal that it must be true that we are immortal"; or, "The extinction of human personality at death is so great an evil that we cannot conceive it to occur". McTaggart's comment is, briefly, that so much that would be good is unreal, and so much that is bad is real, that we have no right to say that anything whatever is so bad that it cannot be real, or so good that it must be real.[2] In a world where there is so much evil as there undeniably is in the actual world, nothing is "too bad to be true". Now, undeniably this looks, at first sight, a telling, perhaps an overwhelmingly convincing criticism, though we may note that it is not specially novel, since it is merely the moral of Voltaire's *Candide* compressed into an epigram. But on reflection I believe we shall find that the reasoning of Voltaire and McTaggart is very far from being as convincing as it looks. It is to be observed that McTaggart's

---

[1] *Some Dogmas of Religion*, pp. 53 ff.

[2] It is only fair to say that McTaggart only denies our right to assume as a premiss the proposition that "reality is not hopelessly evil". He holds that it can be demonstrated, or at least proved sufficiently, that the good in the universe is enormously preponderant over the evil. But we must first prove human immortality, among other things, before we can advance to this conclusion. This, however, is enough to invalidate all "moral" arguments for immortality itself.

quarrel is not with the expressed premiss of the reasoning. He at least takes no exception to the statement that it would be very good that human persons should be immortal and very bad that they should not. What he objects to is not the explicit premiss of fact, but the implied premiss of principle, that what is supremely good *must* also be fact. For my own part I should have thought that the proposition thus allowed to pass without examination is itself questionable, unless it is safeguarded by a good many restrictions. I do not feel at all sure that unending existence might not be a very bad thing. Huxley, we remember, once wrote that he found the thought of hell less depressing than that of annihilation. But I believe that if we asked ourselves the question whether we should prefer for one whom we loved and respected endless existence in the ice of Dante's *Giudecca*, or in the sufferings of cancer, or in a state of idiocy, to cessation of all being, there can be no doubt what our answer would be. We should welcome, or at least accept, the cessation of our friend's existence as a "blessed relief" from cruel suffering; we would rather think that a teacher whose character and intellect we had reverenced was now nothing at all than that he was still surviving as a "driveller and a show".[1] A great thinker, now himself deceased, once remarked to me that his first words on hearing of the death of his mother, a lady of brilliant parts whose mind had been enfeebled in her last years, were "Thank God!"

It is surely still more certain that most of us would prefer that a beloved son or sister should be clean cut off out of the land of the living than that he or she should continue to live and to enjoy a life of degraded

---

[1] Or undergoing the doom Dante inflicts on the man who had taught him *come l'uom s'etterna.*

"animalism", or sordid dishonesty. A decent man, with no real belief in any future life, would probably much rather see a much-loved daughter "in her grave", as our proverbial phrase is, than see her flaunting it as the most famous and flattered harlot of London, or New York, or Paris. It may be replied that *in a man's own case*, when it comes to the point, experience shows that the love of life is so strong that he will usually consent to live even with deep dishonour, if he cannot live with honour. And I own that I have no confidence that sudden "fear of the dark" might not make a recreant of me in this matter. But for the purposes of our present argument, what we are concerned with is not the *strength* of unreasoned cravings and instincts, but the character of a reflective judgement of good, and for that very reason, it is our judgement on cases other than our own, where the mere instinct of self-preservation does not come into the account, that I take to be decisive. It is plain, I think, from these cases that we do not seriously judge immortality to be good at all, unless we have some guarantee of its quality. And if Huxley had said that he would rather think of, say, an infant son or daughter who had died unbaptized as burning with the *massa perditionis*, than as having ceased to be, frankly I should refuse to believe him.

Next, as to McTaggart's argument that in a world where there is so much evil we have no right to say that anything whatever is "too bad to be true". To my mind, this argument is vitiated by a transparent fallacy, introduced by the words "so much". It is assumed that we know how bad the various evils to which the argument appeals, are. In other words, it is assumed that we already know their final upshot. But this is never the case, unless, indeed, we admit "faith", as McTaggart does not, as a source of know-

ledge. To take an obvious example. Few things in
the actual world would be judged more manifestly and
gravely bad than acute, prolonged, and sordid suffering,
wholly undeserved and productive, so far as can be
seen, of nothing good for the sufferer or for anyone else.
But since we do not "see to the end" in any case, we
cannot assert *as a fact of experience* that the upshot
of the worst the world has to show in this kind may
not be, as on the Christian theory it will be, the production of an overwhelming good, for the virtuous
sufferer and for others, which perhaps could not have
been produced in any other way. It is at least *possible*
that the world's worst victims may yet live to smile
at the worst that has befallen them, or even to feel
that they would not on any account have been without
it. Even within the limits of our own vision of life, it
often enough happens that a man comes in the end to
give thanks for what had seemed his most intolerable
afflictions as the best things his life has brought him.
And so I should reply to McTaggart that until we
know whether what we see of a man's life, between
cradle and grave, is all there is to see, we are not in
a position to say how bad the things the argument
pronounces very bad are. None of them are incompatible with the belief, which was, in fact, McTaggart's
own, that reality is overwhelmingly good. But *if*
what we see of man's life is all there is to see, that is,
if there is nothing beyond the grave, then, and only
then, I confess, it becomes undeniable that history is
a scene where dubious good is achieved at the cost
of intolerable evil. I submit, then, that we are not
entitled to argue from the actuality of evils which,
for anything we *know*, may flower in overwhelming
good to the possibility that the actual is so constituted that evil cannot be overcome by good, and that

McTaggart's attack on the "moral argument" is therefore unsound in principle. It only seems conclusive to him because he has *ab initio* excluded God from his metaphysical scheme.[1]

In fact what lies at the bottom of McTaggart's distrust is simply the unexamined assumption that value and fact are two wholly disconnected realms.[2] If it were so, obviously no proposition about value or goodness, however true, could be a relevant premiss in any argument, demonstrative or probable, which concludes to fact. We have already tried to satisfy ourselves that this divorce of value from actuality is itself a mere product of unreflecting prejudice and that the very point of all genuine religion is that it expressly asserts, as morality tacitly implies, the conjunction of the two. To have a religion, or at least to have an ethical religion, means to believe seriously that though many things may be too bad to be true, nothing is too good to be true. If we sometimes think otherwise, it is because the things we pronounce too good to be true are not really as good as we take them to be. Thus a man offers us some panacea for the body politic and promises that, by adopting it, we shall attain the New Jerusalem within a generation. We may *say* that such promises are "too good to be true", but it does not take much reflection to see that they are really not good enough. It would not be good, in the actual state of our civilisation, that society should be deprived of the incentives to industry,

---

[1] It might be said that McTaggart virtually admits what is here contended for, when, in the passage referred to, he confines his objection to the introduction of a premiss affirming the goodness of "reality" in the initial stage of the argument. I should reply that it is my conviction that unless the proposition is admitted in the initial stage, it will not be possible to establish it at all. I cannot believe that the reasoning of the second volume of the *Nature of Existence* would have appeared probative to its author had he not all along subconsciously made the very "venture of faith" which he wishes to discredit.

[2] And the assumption is one which McTaggart's own philosophy is a continuous attempt to disprove.

patience, self-denial, and brotherly help which are
provided by the inevitable imperfections of our social
system. A moralist, if he could be offered the opportunity of, *e.g.*, abolishing all bodily disease at a stroke,
might reasonably hesitate to avail himself of it. He
might feel the gravest doubt whether radiant physical
health for the whole community, not accompanied by
a miraculous moral rebirth, would not tend to lower
its moral status, by depriving it of graces of character
far more exalted in the scale of goods than physical
well-being.

And, after all, to say that nothing is too good to be
true is only to show as much faith in the divine nature
as good men habitually show in human nature. It may
be doubted whether there are not some things too bad
to be credible of any man, even of the worst, but no one
who has within him the faith in human nature without which life would not be worth living would admit
that there are deeds which are, in the strict sense of
the words, too good to be achieved, calls of duty too
arduous ever to be obeyed. At the most, a man who
has the faith in the possibilities of his kind necessary to
save him from an immoral cynicism would only say
of the great moral responsibilities that compliance with
duty is hard and is only achieved by the few heroic
souls, and by them only when they do not confide
solely in their own strength. Also it is a recurrent
and a joyful surprise to find that when the occasions
for the supreme heroisms arise, so many whom most
observers would have judged as mere "average" men,
or something worse, rise to the occasion. We as a
nation are not likely soon to forget the revelations
of unsuspected capacity for heroism in the ordinary
person which came to us during the War of 1914–1918,
and I cannot doubt that every nation engaged in

that struggle on either side has much the same story to tell. Naturally the disclosure was a double-edged one. We also learned with shame and distress that very horrible and bestial things could be done by men who normally conduct themselves in more ordinary situations without gross criminality.[1] We learned, too, that the temptation to shirk burdens and dangers, or even to make one's private market out of the public necessity, could prove too powerful for the integrity of some whom we should have thought above suspicion. Probably we all learned to be at least a little more uncomfortable about our own moral standing. Yet, on the whole, the revelation of good was more impressive than the disclosure of evil. The worst misdeeds established against offenders were all of a type with which we had been made acquainted by the lives of our "criminal classes". More men fell low than perhaps we had expected, but I doubt if any fell lower than we already knew men could fall; multitudes rose higher than we had dared to hope they had it in them to rise. To doubt whether something may not be too good to be true is really to doubt whether the things which are possible with men may not be impossible with God.

We may, then, dismiss this initial objection to the principle implied in the "moral" argument for human immortality. The real question we have to consider is whether the moral being of man in fact *is* such that it affords indications, or at any rate a presumption, that he is destined to survive the shock men call death, and, if so, what further light ethics can throw on the quality

---

[1] I am not thinking so much of bad conduct on the part of our opponents—though I am perfectly convinced by the evidence for *some* of this—as of bad conduct on our own side, such as the now admitted circulation, for purposes of propaganda, of discreditable stories against the enemy which were apparently not believed by the persons responsible for their circulation.

of human life beyond the grave. We must be prepared to find that any light we can discover reveals very little and leaves natural curiosity far from satisfied. It may illumine no more than the next few steps of the road to be trodden through life. Yet this would be indirectly a considerable gain for theory as well as for practice. If there should be a real further "revelation", or self-disclosure of the divine, among the religious faiths of mankind, agreement or discrepancy with what we can learn from ethics may well be the touchstone by which we can safely·distinguish the genuine light of revelation from specious but misleading counterfeits.

To what, then, speaking generally and roughly, does the moral evidence for human survival of death amount? There are two preliminary considerations on which it seems desirable to make some remarks. If we take the expression "moral argument" in the widest sense, it may fairly be held to cover two familiar lines of thought on which the defenders of the hope of immortality have laid weight, the argument from the *consensus gentium* and also the direct appeal to the real or alleged universality of the wish for continuance as evidence of its own fulfilment. Neither line of argument can be regarded as manifestly conclusive, yet we may fairly doubt whether either deserves the unqualified rejection both often receive from philosophers in our own day.

(1) First, then, as to the argument from the presumed *wish* for immortality to its reality. It is interesting to note how powerfully this reasoning often appeals to minds we might have supposed to be impervious to the rather different type of argument from *consensus*. The case of Shelley affords an apt illustration. No one could well be less inclined to accept a widespread belief on the ground that it is widespread and therefore, presumably, natural than Shelley. Those who knew him

intimately have recorded that it was a favourite saying with him that "everyone's saying a thing is true
does not make it true", and, apart from this testimony,
his works bear abundant witness to a deeply rooted
suspiciousness of all widely received traditions which
amounted to something like a positive disease. From
the moralist's special point of view—and it was a point
of view from which the poet himself always professed to
desire to be appreciated—it is Shelley's most obvious
intellectual defect that he never seems to have been able
to understand the value of a moral tradition, supported
by the practice of generations of civilised men and the
approval of the most eminent reflective thinkers, as witness to its own fundamental soundness. The very fact
that a practice or a belief had been a permanent factor
in shaping the civilised society of Western Europe actually seems to have operated with him as a reason for
suspecting its validity. Theoretically, indeed, he maintained only that a belief may be false, or a custom baneful, in spite of its apparently universal acceptance; but
in practice, when he came to deal with specific beliefs
or customs, he habitually tended to assume that what
all men accept must be false or pernicious just *because*
everyone accepts it.

A typical example of this eccentricity is his notorious
and singular craze, revealed no less by his private correspondence than by his poems, for the glorification of
incest. The reasons which have led civilised societies to
condemn the practice so vehemently and unequivocally,
or at least some of these reasons, are so obvious and so
weighty that one can hardly suppose them to have been
ignored by Shelley or any other man not an imbecile.
In this matter there seems to be no ground whatever for
the poet's challenge to the universal tradition of civilised Europe, beyond a prejudice against it based on its

very universality. From a mind so constituted we might have expected a similar acrimonious rejection of the hope of immortality, just on the plea that so widely diffused a hope must be one of the illusions of the "tribe". Yet we find Shelley, in fact, in the notes to *Hellas*, manifestly cherishing the hope in the very act of declaring it to have no foundation beyond a wish. "Let it be not supposed", he says, "that I mean to dogmatise upon a subject concerning which all men are equally ignorant. That there is a true solution of the riddle, and that in our present state that solution is not attainable by us, are propositions which may be regarded as equally certain : meanwhile as it is the province of the poet to attach himself to those ideas which exalt and ennoble humanity, let him be permitted to have conjectured the condition of that futurity to which we are all impelled by an inextinguishable thirst for immortality. Until better arguments can be produced than sophisms which disgrace the cause, this desire itself must remain the strongest and the only presumption that eternity is the inheritance of every thinking being." Even apart from the light thrown on such a passage by recorded utterances of the poet in conversation, which cannot all be ascribed to the invention of his associates, it is manifest that the words are written in good faith by one who himself shares in the desire of which he speaks as a universal and inextinguishable thirst, and that when the desire is said to be the "strongest" presumption of its own fulfilment—a remark logically superfluous when it is also declared to be the only such presumption— there is no ironical *arrière-pensée*. The poet seriously means to say that this "only presumption" really is a strong one.

Now it might plausibly be urged on the other side that the poet's statement of the alleged facts is an exaggeration. Appeal might be made to the apparent acquiescence of millions of the human race in religions which are said to contemplate the extinction of human personality as the crown of felicity, to the notorious absence of all reference to the hope of the world to come from all but the very latest parts of the Old Testament scriptures, and other similar facts, in support of the view that what Shelley represents as a deep-seated aspiration of universal humanity only exists, to any marked degree, within the limits of a special civilisation —our own—which owes its moral tradition to the specific influences of Greek philosophy and Christian theology. And it might further be contended, even more forcibly to-day than a century ago, that the "desire" is not universal even within this particular civilisation itself. We must all know among our own personal acquaintance, intelligent and virtuous persons who appear to be quite indifferent to the prospect of a life to come, and possibly some who even seem to regard any such prospect with actual repugnance.[1]

I own that personally I am not as deeply impressed as some moralists seem to be, by this alleged counter-evidence. The evidence supposed to be afforded by the wide prevalence of a religion like Buddhism, for example, may well strike the layman in these studies as at least ambiguous. The experts seem at any rate to be far from certain as to the real meaning of the Founder's teaching, and it is significant that, in its development into a widespread religion, Buddhism has no more been able than Judaism to retain an attitude of negation or mere agnosticism towards human destiny after death. Similarly, we may set against arguments drawn from the theoretical attitude of the agnostics of our own civilisation a fair counter-argument founded on the

---

[1] Cf. McTaggart, *Some Dogmas of Religion*, p. 57.

curious inability of these very agnostics to be fully consistent with themselves. No one, I take it, has ever denied that Spinoza's metaphysic expressly excludes the admission of any sort of persistence of the individual person after the physical dissolution of his body. Yet it is quite impossible to read the famous series of propositions in the *Vth Part* of the *Ethics* which deal with the "eternity of the mind", without perceiving that the writer of these propositions has a personal faith which is his supreme inspiration in life and is quite unjustified by his professed philosophy.[1] Spinoza's "way of life" is based on the conviction that the wise and virtuous "mind" has a prerogative of "eternity", not shared by any other "finite mode"; if Spinoza's metaphysic is sound, no "mode" can be eternal except in a sense in which all are eternal alike. No one, again, will credit Renan with anything but a strict agnosticism in theory; yet it is impossible, I should conceive, to mistake the tone of the dedication of the *Vie de Jésus* to the author's dead sister for that of empty decorative rhetoric.

Thus, when all legitimate deductions have been made, I confess that the "inextinguishable thirst" for immortality of which Shelley speaks does, to my mind, remain a very impressive fact. It is impressive specially for two reasons: (*a*) it seems to be felt as acutely by men who have drunk deep of a long inheritance of science and philosophy as by men who have never learned to think or question, and is therefore emphatically not one of those aspirations which are automatically destroyed by mere progress in intellectual development; (*b*) and, again, even those who profess themselves, no doubt with sincerity, to be most emancipated from reverence for the traditions of a human past never seem able, in

---

[1] Cf. C. D. Broad, *Five Types of Ethical Theory*, pp. 15-16, and T. Whittaker, *Transcendence in Spinoza* in MIND, N.S. 151.

their moments of high emotion, when they have forgotten the demands of an official *credo*, and are most
near to saying what they really in their hearts believe,
to escape the use of language which either means nothing or means that this aspiration is alive in the speaker.
On the whole, then, I think we must accept it as fact
that the aspiration towards the "unseen" future is *allge-
mein-menschlich*, and "natural", in the sense in which
abhorrence of cannibalism or incest is natural. Individual
exceptions, or even exceptions extending to the whole
of special minor social groups, prove no more in the
first case than they prove in the other two—viz., that
there are abnormal individuals, and that special conditions may lead to the prevalence of an abnormality
over a whole restricted social group.

Still, even when so much is granted, we must expect
to be met by the objection that a wish may be universal
in the fullest sense in which we can call any characteristic of human life universal, and yet may be doomed
to mere disappointment. That everyone wishes for a
certain thing is no proof that anyone will ever get it.
A man might, as Aristotle remarks, wish never to die
at all, and, as I suppose every priest knows, all of us
in certain moods fiercely resent the necessity of dying
as an "infamy of our nature". Yet most of us, like
Aristotle, are agreed to regard this craving as a wish
for the merely impossible.

There is, indeed, a counter-assertion of which too
much, perhaps, has been made. It has been urged that
a *universal* wish must be regarded as the expression of a
"natural instinct", and that it is not "nature's" way
to provide creatures with instincts which are destined
to have no fulfilment. Stated thus baldly, the reasoning does not appear very impressive. Without going
into the very difficult questions of the proper definition

of "instinct" and the worth of "instinct" as explanatory hypotheses in biology and psychology—topics on which much that is impressive was said in this place by my eminent precursor, Dr. Lloyd Morgan[1]—we may certainly retort, with truth, that the "instincts" of which the argument speaks are very often not fulfilled in the most obvious sense of the word fulfilment. Thus the attraction of male and female animal to one another is "instinctive" in the sense of the argument now under consideration, and the fulfilment of the "instinctive" craving would be said to be found in the propagation of a new generation of the species. But the "instinct" itself, as felt by the pairing male and female, is not an instinct to procreate, but an instinct to *mate*, and when it gives rise to a conscious wish, the wish is not primarily a wish for the offspring but a wish for the partner. We see this clearly enough in our own human life. There are those who unite because they are lovers, and those who unite because they want sons or daughters; in most cases, perhaps, the two motives are conjoined, but commonly with a predominance of the one or the other. But the most ardent lovers are not usually those who are most desirous of progeny, nor the persons in whom the passion for paternity or maternity is consciously strongest the typical lovers of "romance". (It has been said of Burns, and, I conceive, with truth, that he had an exceptionally strong and sincere passion for paternity. But though the orators of our Burns clubs might resent the remark, it is equally true that Burns had no passion for "love", and that we cannot understand either his life or his poetry unless we recognise that fact.) In literature, we note, the great lovers are mostly sterile; the typical fathers and mothers are of quite a different spiritual

[1] See *Life, Mind and Spirit*, lect. **v**.

pattern from the Lancelots and Tristrams and Helens and Didos. And in life itself, it is a source of tragedy when the man or woman with the temperament of the lifelong lover discovers that maternity or paternity is the supreme passion of the "other party". The now too notorious "Oedipus-complex" may probably be no more than a singularly ugly piece of pseudo-scientific mythology, but its inverse is a familiar fact of life. We need no myth to explain why fathers are often secretly jealous of their sons, or mothers of their daughters.

Thus it is readily intelligible why a sceptic should seek to disable the argument from the supposed "instinct" for immortality by the retort that the "inextinguishable thirst" is really no more than an expression of the primitive "instinct of self-preservation", and that it gets all the fulfilment it ever need get in the part this "instinct" plays in securing and prolonging our life here in the body. The real question, as I think, is untouched by these superficial logo-machies. We have to ask whether it is clear that the widespread belief in the world to come could so much as be causally accounted for on these lines as the product of a wish or "instinct" of any kind whatsoever. And this brings me to a more general consideration of the *consensus gentium* and its presumable foundation. If the "naturalistic" "explanation" of the *consensus* breaks down even as an account of its origin, *a fortiori* it can do nothing to discredit its value.

(2) Now there are certain features about this widespread belief, testified to by the general prevalence among mankind of theories about the land of the dead and practices intended to facilitate the reception of the dying in that region, or to secure their position there, which it seems hard to reconcile with any form of the "naturalistic" theory of the sources of these

beliefs and practices. I speak, of course, as a layman in these matters, and mean to be referring only to certain outstanding features of what appears to be historically the belief and practice of the human race in the earliest stage of its existence as yet known to us with any certainty. But I believe it may fairly be said, without much danger of contradiction from those who know, that, in the view of the world which we loosely call "primitive", because we find it already widely diffused among peoples whose civilisation is the least developed known to us, and because we cannot say at present what views, if any, may have preceded it, the survival of the mysterious thing called the soul is universally taken as a matter of course, and it is also taken as a matter of course that this continued existence is a continuance of the same kind of life we know on our side of death. The chief remains a chief, the hunter a hunter, the common man a common man, the slave, where slavery has found a footing, a slave "yonder", as he was "here". Future existence is not, as we who have inherited the traditions of philosophy and Christianity are prone to assume that it must be, *better* existence, or existence "at a higher level"; still less is the world to come a scene in which the "wrongs" of this world are "put right". At most existence in that world is the old familiar kind of existence with some obstacles and disappointments removed; the hunter roams through "happy hunting-grounds", where the game is more plentiful and the hunter's aim more regularly successful.

Often enough the whole colouring of the picture is a gloomy one, as in Homer and the most ancient parts of the Old Testament, where the condition which awaits the dead is a mere joyless shadowy prolongation of their occupations here, and to "go down to the pit" is the inevitable worst which comes to us all in our time. It may be urged, with a great deal of force, that these Homeric and Hebraic conceptions reproduce the ideas of an age in which belief is fading, and that the Greek ghost, as we can still see from Attic tragedy, and presumably the Israelite ghost too, had once been thought of as a much more real being. But so far as our evidence goes, it is much clearer that these ghosts were thought of as formidable to the survivors than that they were ever supposed to have themselves an enjoyable or enviable lot. And when we further consider what kind of life men must have led, in the distant prehistoric times, when they were mainly engrossed in a grim struggle for bare existence against a hostile, or at least a "stepmotherly", nature, I find it very hard to believe that the *wish* for the prolongation can have been an adequate cause of the general belief in the fact.

It might, no doubt, be replied that the word "wish" is out of place; we are not dealing with a conscious wish, but with a primary impulse more fundamental and persistent than any wish, the native fierce resistance of the living body to its own dissolution, in virtue of which a drowning or choking man will still make a furious physical fight for life, even though it may have been deliberate preference of death to life which brought him into the water or the gas-poisoned atmosphere. Yet I own to a still unremoved difficulty in understanding how a supposedly unconscious organic impulse could of itself—as the explanation implies—give occasion to a widely diffused conscious aspiration which, in its turn, coloured, and still colours, men's whole attitude to their world, in view of the conditions which must have made life anything but enjoyable to the great majority of men in the earliest age of the conflict with a niggardly

"Nature". Indeed, it might be *à propos* to reflect that, according at least to one version of the curious "psychology of the unconscious" now fashionable, the supreme "unconscious impulse" of every organism is precisely to get rid of its own existence as *this* organism; all are "unconsciously" trying to die in every act of their lives. It seems to me, then, that "naturalistic" theories are manifestly inadequate as causal explanations of the apparent universality with which men who have not acquired an artificial scepticism accept the "spirit-world" as fact, and that the inadequacy cannot be removed by attempts to get behind conscious wish to an unconscious original *libido* which each theorist is free to interpret just as he pleases.

Though I am perhaps diverging from our special topic in adding the remark, I seem to myself to detect the same inadequacy in the more old-fashioned naturalistic theories which lay no special stress on wish or *libido*. It looks at first plausible, for example, to find the origin of our belief that the dead are not wholly lost to us simply in our dreams about them; the man I saw and spoke with "in dream" last night, clearly still is something and somewhere. What such a theory leaves unexplained is why mankind should feel the concern they do feel in their waking life for the denizens of the dream-world and for their own destiny when they come to inhabit that world themselves. In general, it cannot have taken long to discover that the stone, or arrow, with which I was wounded in last night's dream leaves me uninjured to-day, that the possessions into which I came then vanished at my waking, that my living friend has not made the promise uttered by his "double" in my dream, and the like. Why, then, should my dreams about the *dead* long retain an importance and significance which has already been lost by my dreams about the living? Why do I go on practising rites based on the conviction that I really see and hear my dead father in my dreams, so long after I have lost the belief that I really see my living contemporaries when I dream about them?

Again, I dream that my dead father complains to me of being cold and hungry. But do I not equally dream that I feed him and warm him at my fire? Why does not the dream-feeding discharge my obligations in relation to the dream-hunger? Why must I make a visit with an offering of food to my father's tomb when I awake from my dream? I confess there seems to me to be a problem here for which the "naturalist" neither provides, nor attempts to provide, any solution. Thus it seems to me that the way in which personal continuance is apparently taken for granted as something obvious in what is called the "primitive" view of life and the world is a singularly impressive fact, not by any means adequately accounted for by any of the "naturalistic" explanations. So far the appeal to the *consensus gentium* does seem to have more significance than it is at present fashionable to admit.

But the main point on which I am concerned to lay stress is that, be their origin what it may, these beliefs in a continued existence much of the same kind as that we now lead on earth, perhaps without some of our present "disagreeables", are wholly different in quality from definitely *ethical* convictions. Their sources are not specifically ethical, and the kind of immortality they hold out to us is non-moral. It is neither a source of moral inspiration nor an implication of the objectivity of right and wrong. If we were asked to believe in a life to come simply on the alleged ground that we should all very much like to have a perfect and unending "good time", it would be pertinent to make two points in reply. (1) We can easily wish for what we know, or think we know, to be entirely impossible. The elderly can easily wish, and literature is full of eloquent expressions of the wish, like the famous chorus of Euripides' *Heracles*,[1] that they could have their flaming youth over again, or perhaps even that they could combine all the freshness of its ardours with the insight which has come to age through experience. Yet all of us, except the few who base wild aspirations on experiments done with extracts of monkey-glands, are probably convinced that rejuvenescence in late life is fully as impossible as Nicodemus thought it, and we are, I suppose, convinced, without any exceptions whatever, that at any rate the combination of the ardour of youth with the wisdom of age is impossible, since the ardour depends for its specific quality on the fact that the young adventurer is breaking new paths, sailing an uncharted sea, where experience is not at hand to prescribe his course. It is just this sense of dangerous adventure into the unknown and unexperienced which gives our youth its peculiar charm; the youth *plus* age of some of our dreams would be only the not very delectable "youth" of Meredith's Adrian Harley.

(2) Again, it might be said, though we may all have these wishes at times, it is very doubtful whether a wise man or a good man would really choose to have them gratified. In the wise and good such yearnings are likely at most to be arrested in their incipient stage as mere "velleities"; they will not rise to the level of serious and steady *voluntas*. When we reach a certain level of moral ripeness, we can see that the gratification would not really be a good thing for us; hence such moods cease to represent our genuine self, just as the

---

[1] Euripides, *H.F.* 655 εἰ δὲ θεοῖς ἦν ξύνεσις | καὶ σοφία κατ' ἄνδρας, | δίδυμον ἂν ἥβαν ἔφερον | φανερὸν χαρακτῆρ' ἀρετᾶς | ὅσοισιν μέτα, κτλ.

dreams in which we occasionally find ourselves back in childhood, with the hope and fears of childhood, cease to represent it. Wishes which are specifically un-ethical cannot figure as the basis of a "moral" argu-ment for anything, since they cease to be even real wishes in proportion as we put on morality. If there is an ethical justification for anticipations of a future beyond death, it cannot be founded on the mere con-sideration that all or many of us more or less passion-ately wish for such a future. A *moral* argument for immortality should take the form of an argument that the destruction of our human personalities must stultify the whole moral life by making its supreme end un-attainable. If this conviction can be justified, it clearly affords anyone who believes that the moral life is identical with the truly human life the best of reasons for holding that there is a destiny of the moral person beyond what we can now see. But the argument has, of course, no weight for anyone who denies that the life of morality is the fullest expression of our distinc-tive character as human, and therefore cannot pro-fess to be a *demonstration* valid for everyone who will accept the general laws of logic and the merely "non-moral" facts of existence, though it may rightly be treated as decisive by all believers in the absoluteness of the demands of the moral law. From their point of view, the argument will be, succinctly formulated, that since the moral law can rightfully command us to live as aspirants to eternity, eternity must really be our destination. This, if it can indeed be made out, is, I must hold, an absolutely valid ground for those who believe in unconditional moral obligation to believe also in a coresponding attainable moral goal.

It is, you will observe, in substance the contention on which Kant relies when he introduces into the *Critique of*

Practical Reason as a postulate presupposed in morality that very belief in the immortal "soul" which he had done his best to prove indemonstrable in the *Critique of Pure Reason*. It is, in fact, a legitimate inference from the reality of a function to the reality of the environment where the function will find its use.

The real problem to be faced is not whether reasoning of this kind from the reality of function to the reality of the environment in which it can function is valid. To raise doubts on that point would be fatal to the admission of enough rationality into the cause of things to make science itself possible. The real question is rather whether in fact examination of the moral life reveals the reality of any such functions. The issue is raised with the utmost clarity by the proposition of St. Thomas [1] that "the final felicity of man is not to be obtained in this present life". *If* this is true, then, always on the fundamental presupposition of the moralist that there is no absolute disjunction of "fact" from "value", the conclusion is obvious; the true destiny of man is not to be found "in this present life" either.

But it may be asserted, in direct opposition to St. Thomas, that human felicity *can* be obtained in this life—in fact that it can be obtained nowhere else, since it proves on analysis to consist altogether in the exercise of activities correlated with the experienced temporal environment of the human organism, and in nothing else. Here it is, I should say, that we find ourselves face to face with the supreme practical issue. Is "highest human good" conceivable simply in terms of the activities we exercise, and the environment with which we are familiar in this our temporal and embodied life, or is the moral end one which defies complete resolution into the successful prosecution of any or all of these "secular"

[1] *S.C.G.* iii. 48.

activities, much as a "surd" defies complete expression
in the form of a terminated or recurrent decimal fraction? Is the world about us what Wordsworth called it
in the verse which moved Shelley's disgust, the "home
of all of us", where "we find our happiness, or not at
all", or is it what it has been called by so many, a place
of exile, an Egypt where there may be "flesh-pots",
but where we have no free citizenship? Is it our great
business to "make ourselves at home" in it, or to escape
from it, even though the road should lead out through
a barren and dry land where no water is? Both views
cannot be equally true, and neither is, on the face of it,
visibly so false that a man must be a fool to acquiesce
in it. And since we have to live somehow, we cannot in
action adopt a "non-committal" course of simple agnosticism. We must act on the one assumption or on the
other; *il faut parier*. Our attitude on the question of
man's destiny not only may, but must, in the end be
determined by the choice we make between the view
of the world familiar to us from the literature of Platonism and that represented on the whole and with qualifications by Aristotle, and without any qualification at
all by the persuasive voices of the *mondains* and secu-
larists of all ages.

Manifestly our whole practical rule of life will be
different according to the choice we make.   If the
Platonic and Christian view is true, it must follow "as
the night the day" that we dare not lose our hearts to
any temporal good. The rule of detachment will be
the obvious supreme rule of successful living; the moral
task of man will be to learn so to use and prize temporal
good as to make it a ladder of ascent to a good which
is more than "for a season", *ita per temporalia transire
ut non amittamus aeterna*. If the numerous moralists who
take the other side are right, the moral business of man

will be wholly to secure the temporal goods, the only goods there are, in the life of "practice". There will be plenty of room for care and delicate discrimination in preferring the higher of these goods to the lower, but there will be no justification for any sacrifice of temporal good to "some better thing" which, on the theory, must be an illusion. In *this* morality, at its best, there will be no room for the injunction, "love not the world, nor the things of the world".

I cannot think, as Dr. McTaggart appears to have done, that this difference is merely one of ethical speculative theory; it must, as it seems to me, directly affect the most momentous practical choices we are called on to make in the conduct of our lives. From a strictly "this-world" point of view, for example, the whole purpose which dominated a life like that of St. Francis must be pronounced to be fantastic. It might be admitted that incidentally, very much against the intention of St. Francis himself, the Franciscan movement, with its varied repercussions on economics, art, letters, and politics, was in fact productive of a vast amount of what a discerning secularistic moralist would recognise to be true good, but in principle this will merely illustrate the familiar proposition that good, and even an overplus of good, may arise from what is itself not good, or even actually evil. In principle, Francis will be in exactly the same position as Caesar or Alexander, on the supposition that Caesar and Alexander were men whose actual aims were perverse and largely evil, though they were so situated that in serving their perverse personal aims they inevitably benefited humanity. From the anti-secularistic point of view it is at least conceivable that this verdict should be exactly reversed and that we ought rather to say that while incidentally, owing to personal limitations, Francis may have drawn the distinction between the temporal and the eternal too crudely, and thus rejected as illusion much which is true eternal good, in principle he was right. It may be the evil, not the good, in the Franciscan movement which will prove to be the merely incidental and unintended.

To put the point more generally, though on any interpretation of life which is not merely flippant, morality will demand a good deal of genuine sacrifice, the sacrifice of real and definite temporal good will, to the secularist, never be justified except where there is at least a reasonable hope of securing a definite secular better.[1] If there is good which is better than anything secular, this restriction will lose its justification, and it may be a plain duty, for some men at least, and possibly for all men, to sacrifice definite secular good for something different in kind and only dimly apprehended, with the certainty that the sacrifice will never be compensated by any gain in the same kind. It is this apparently *unreasonable* choice that St. Paul calls the "foolishness" of this world; the question is whether St. Paul was right in saying that this foolishness of the world is wisdom with God.

Let us try to state the problem in the form most favourable for the secularist; we do not, I hope, want to gain an easy victory over a "man of straw" of our own manufacture. Under the head of secular good, then, I mean now to include everything which can be really attained and enjoyed in human life on the assumption that human life means no more than existence as a member of the human species, under the conditions imposed on us by place and time, as part

---

[1] And this is just the view taken, *e.g.*, by Mill in his *Utilitarianism*: "The only self-renunciation which it [the utilitarian morality] applauds is devotion to the happiness, or to some of the means of happiness, of others" (12th ed. p. 24).

of the "complex event we call nature". Thus I mean the phrase, in the present context, to cover not only physical health, longevity, comfort, and fertility, but the minimising of all the ills which attend disharmony with our physical environment and friction with other members of our social world, as well as the satisfaction of our interests in natural knowledge and sensible beauty. The ideal proposed for valuation shall be that of the progressive establishment of a human society on earth in which want, disease, physical pain and mental deficiency are, if not abolished, at least reduced to a minimum, offences against the social order obviated by a sound tradition of human good will and solidarity, and art and natural science made the delight and business of everyone. It may fairly be said that such a conception of a secularist ideal, if it sins at all, sins rather by generosity than by niggardliness. The question I wish to propound is this—allowing our secularist's ideal thus to include everything which has been recognised as good by a high-minded Utilitarianism like that of Mill, or an aesthetic Utopianism like that of William Morris, is the perpetuation of such a social life of humanity through the largest vista of successive generations a wholly satisfactory final aim for moral aspiration? Or do we all feel that, if the Utopia became fact, we should not, after all, have attained the best, that there would be missing something elusive and impossible to define precisely, and that something *the* thing without which everything else loses its value? May it not be that all along, if we make humanitarianism, however generous, our supreme rule of life, we are living only for a second-best?

I state the problem in this way in order to make it quite clear that there is one cheap and common line of adverse criticism which merely misses the point. The demand for a "felicity beyond this life" has too often been represented as having its roots in a vulgar personal selfishness. Hegel, according to Heine's story, talked with contempt of the man who expects a *Trinkgeld* beyond the grave for not having beaten his mother, and I observe that in the most recent study of Ethics which has come into my hands, Professor Laird's excellent *Study in Moral Theory*, the same conception is made prominent as one of the alleged bases of the moral argument for immortality, which the author is anxious to deprecate.[1] I confess that this demand that "virtue" shall receive a "reward" does not seem to come legitimately into the argument, and I should gravely doubt whether it has ever been the real inspiration of the hope of immortality in any mind of the first order. There may be some persons who seriously reason in the way derided by Bradley, "if I am not to be paid hereafter for living virtuously, virtue will involve genuine self-denial, and morality will turn out not to be the same thing as prudent self-seeking".[2] But I do not believe that such reasoning is common. Even those who speak most often of "reward" probably do their own thought an injustice by the language in which they express it. And I might remark in passing that, when this language is employed, it is most often not used by a man about himself. It is much more common to say of another that he has "passed to his reward" than it is to speak of myself as expecting my reward, and the fact should not be insignificant to a really acute psychologist.

But be those who clamour for their personal *Trink-*

---

[1] *Op. cit.* p. 312, with its pleasantries about "medals" bestowed for doing our duty.

[2] *Appearance and Reality*, p. 508.

geld many or few, it is not thus that Plato and Kant
and other great moralists who have championed the
cause of hope have spoken. Their thought has not been
that morality and decency are a disagreeable task
only to be made tolerable by high pay, but that the
good which the virtuous man seeks is of a kind not
expressible in the currency of secularism. It is not
that he demands the "Union rate of wages" for his
good performances and abstentions from mischief, but
that the social utility of his life has been all along
a by-product achieved in the process of aiming at
something different, something which is merely illusory,
if the secularist estimate of human nature and its
destiny is the correct one. No one denies that there are
real sacrifices to be made; the question is whether they
are all, in the end, sacrifices to idols.

Nowhere does this come out more plainly than in
the familiar New Testament language about sacrifice.
Emerson once caricatured the current hopes of heaven
by representing the believer as saying to the sinners
of this age, "You sin now, we are going to sin hereafter". But this is, of course, caricature, and conscious
caricature. The hope of "sinning hereafter", if it is a
hope entertained by anyone, is at least not the hope
of what a Christian or a Platonist means by heaven.
We are told in the New Testament that we must be
prepared to cut off the right hand or put out the right
eye, if they "offend" us, since it is good for us to enter
into life with one hand or one eye rather than to perish
with two. It is not suggested that the hand we have
cut off, or the eye we have put out, grows again
miraculously as we enter the gates of life. For the
man whose conception of good is exhausted by the
kind of good that may have to be sacrificed, there is
no promise of any kind of "compensation" such as he

could appreciate. The whole point of the language is that the sacrifice *is* sacrifice of a good and that it is irrevocable. The cutting off of the right hand may, for example, in a given instance symbolise the sort of choice which haunted the imagination of T. H. Green, the deliberate abandonment of a promising literary or artistic career for one of useful but dull drudgery as a sanitary engineer, or a civil servant. A man who makes the hard choice *may* enter into a life from which he would have been debarred if he had evaded the choice, but it is not suggested that he will hereafter be, "in eternity", all the more an artist or a scholar. Or, again, the call of duty may come between a man and the supreme personal love of his life. He may "make his soul" by following this call of duty, but it is the modern sentimental novelist, not Christ, who tells him that he will some day be repaid by being once more the Romeo to his old Juliet "in eternity".

Indeed, it is constantly urged further, with some in-consistency, against the Platonist or Christian who takes his convictions seriously that he pushes the demand for sacrifices to a fantastic extreme. The humanitarian of the type of Mill admits that, as the world goes, in its present very imperfect condition, the best men must be willing to make considerable sacrifice of genuine good; they may often, as Mill phrases it, have to do without happiness. But there is a restriction which Mill is careful to mention. The sacrifice is only justifiable at the bar of reason when there is the prospect that a surplus of good of *the kind thus sacrificed* will be secured for someone else, and if we assume, as humanitarians like Mill regularly do, that all the great outstanding evils of life are due to bad physical and social conditions, and therefore removable, as science indicates improved

methods of grappling with hindrances of both kinds,
and the gradual perfection of our social system diminishes the competition of "classes", it fairly follows that
the demand for the making of such sacrifices will be
diminished beyond all assignable limits. As we approach
the ideal humanitarian state, the sacrifice of "my own
happiness" to anything else will steadily tend to disappear from human experience; the way of virtue
will come, in the end, to be for everyone the flowery
path.

Now this view of the place of self-denial and sacrifice
in life is wholly different from that of the Platonist,
to say nothing of the Christian. Both conceive the
supreme good, or felicity, of man in a way which makes
it incommensurable with the enjoyments the humanitarian calls collectively "happiness", since both look
upon the task of right living as a remaking of character round a new centre. It is not a man's circumstances, according to this view, but his personality
which must be unmade and remade if felicity is to be
obtained. He must grow into a personality which has
its centre not in the competitive finite selfhood with
which we all begin, but in the infinite and eternal.
Every stage in the process is a dying out of the natural
man into the spiritual man, and in all of us the natural
man "dies hard". Hence the "war in the members"
is no temporary incident in the moral history of man,
but its fundamental and persistent character. The
demand for "costing" sacrifice can never be eliminated
by the application of physical science to the abolition
of disease and want, or by the introduction of an
improved set of social institutions. Amelioration of
this kind, at the most, will provide men and women
with better opportunities of making the most of their
humanity—if they choose to do so, and do not grow

weary of their choice. The "naughting" of one merely natural concupiscent self is not, in the end, undertaken for the purpose of providing gratifications for the concupiscence of some other such selves, but because it is the only way into true life for all selves. In principle, even if Utopia could be realised to-morrow, the "naughting" of the natural man would still remain imperative. However delightful our temporal environment might be in Utopia, it would still be the "work of a man" not to lose his heart to it, to use it and pass through it without setting up his rest. And here, again, there would be no convenient compromising and calculating and striking of a balance.

After all, on the premisses of secularistic humanitarianism, the desires of the natural man are to be accepted without qualification as right and to be gratified, when they do not seriously clash with the similar desires of other specimens of the natural man; hence for many or most of us life is, on the whole, a business which only calls for real sacrifice and self-denial at intervals and as the exception. The opposite view, be it right or wrong, is that we have the "old man", who must be "put off", with us all the time, and our business with him is not merely to see that he makes no one else unduly uncomfortable by his methods of enjoying himself, but to see that the sentence of death is duly executed upon him. The end, in fact, is to "follow God"; the things which humanitarianism regards as supreme ends-in-themselves are, at best, subordinate incidents in the attainment of an end which humanitarianism leaves out of account. *This* end is not pleasing yourself without prejudice to the equal claim of your neighbour to please himself; it is wholly different from any kind of self-pleasing. Hence, entirely apart from any question of interfer-

ence with one's neighbour, the moral life, so conceived, is a life in which denial of self is demanded at
all times and in all situations, if we are to become what
we aspire to be. And hence, again, the Christian
demand for a purity of the secret places of the heart,
which means much more than abstinence from the
gratification of desires it would be socially harmful to
satisfy, and the violent metaphor by which such a life
can be called one of "concrucifixion" with Christ.

We do not conceive of such a life rightly if we think
of it as inspired by the purpose of pleasing the natural
self of any man; it is the life of one who means what
Nietzsche merely said, *der Mensch ist etwas, das
überwunden werden muss.* The thought which in fact
inspires it is the conviction that each of us only becomes
human in the full moral sense of the word, in so far as
he forgets about pleasing himself or pleasing other
men, in his determination to serve God. This is all
through life a hard task, and one in which we all fail
shamefully, for two reasons, that we all begin with an
imperious passion for gratifying ourselves, getting "what
we want" as the supreme end of ends, and also that
we may miss the mark of "pleasing God" and putting
on a true moral personality in either of two contrasted
ways, the way of Epicurus or the way of Stylites.
The task is to use our inheritance of environment and
natural endowment in such a way as to attain true
spiritual manhood; we fail in this task alike whether
we make lower good a principal end or refuse to make
it an instrument towards something better. We do not
need the psycho-analyst to tell us that it is the same
libido of the natural self that displays itself alike in the
abandonment of the victim of unrestrained passion
and in the self-torture of the "pillar-saint". The kinship of lust and cruelty is an old and familiar fact with

obvious implications. If I certainly cannot make sure
of pleasing God by doing what I like, it is also hopeless to propose to please Him by making it a rule to
do what I loathe. I am more likely to gratify only an
evil pride which is as incompatible as any "carnality"
with the single eye and the pure heart.

All this, however, is by the way. The main question
for us at the moment is whether we really are unavoidably driven, when we consult the witness of conscience,
to admit that the ideal of good which has inspired our
historical moral achievements proves on examination to
be something not included in good as good can be legitimately conceived by the humanitarian. Is devotion to
the temporal welfare of human society the sufficient justification of the imperatives of morality? If it is not,
then, unless we admit—and the admission would be
fatal to all moral philosophy—that moral imperatives
cannot and need not be justified at all, and so have no
genuine obligatoriness about them, we must be prepared to admit that there is good rational ground for
anticipating a destination of human persons which is
ignored when such persons are thought of as merely
transient; morality will thus bear a real witness of
its own to the presence of the seeds of immortality
in us.

You see, no doubt, what is the objection a Platonist
or Christian philosopher has to face. We may expect
to be told that sufficient justification is provided for all
the imperatives of an earnest and elevated morality
if we take as our supreme good the retention and
further development of all the inheritance the human
race has won in its slow and painful struggle out of the
savagery with which certified history begins. We can
set ourselves to play the part of men in the transmission of science, and art, and sound social morality

to our successors, and the slow improvement at once of the traditions we have received in all these matters, and of man's physical estate. None of us will accomplish much, and no single age will accomplish much, for the execution of this task, but we have a reasonable prospect that the work may be continued through an enormous number of generations, and imagination has no right to set any limits to the cumulative result.

It may, indeed, be said that we have no certainty that our efforts may not be neutralised by some stupendous unforeseen cosmic convulsion of nature, or, still more probably, by a wanton self-destruction of humanity in national or class conflicts. But the reply to this suggestion is obvious; if the past history of mankind affords no grounds for induction to the future, we are wholly in the dark about the probability of this dismal end to history, and need not distress ourselves unduly with mere bad dreams: if the past does justify induction, it is at least a probable contention that mankind will prove equal, in the future as in the past, to recovery from their worst set-backs. And if it is argued that, at any rate, our planet must sooner or later become unfitted to support life, and that human moral civilisation and all its products must therefore be some day as though they had never been at all, we may even be told that this prophecy itself is based on physical theories which have never been *proved* to be true, and so may turn out to be mistaken, and that, in any case, the good achieved has been great and real good while it lasted. As Professor Laird[1] ingeniously pleads, the argument of those who say "since to-morrow we shall die, there is no worth in anything beneath the glimpses of the moon; so let us eat and drink and be merry" refutes itself. For even they

[1] *Study in Moral Theory*, p. 311.

assume that our perishability leaves untouched one judgement about "value", the judgement that while we *are* here it is better to eat, drink, and be merry than to fast, go thirsty, and be miserable. But why should any judgement of worth be affected if this one retains its validity? On these lines it is argued by many, most recently and persuasively by Professor Laird, that the absoluteness and rationality of moral obligation affords no ground whatever for the "great hope" of the Platonist and the Christian.

But now, is the case quite as simple as Professor Laird, for one, takes it to be? The ingenious flanking argument just cited from him strikes me, at least, as more ingenious than solid. What if the unnamed opponents to whom it is addressed had the full courage of their convictions? If indeed they draw from their premises the conclusion Professor Laird expects them to draw, the usual conclusion of the unthinking man, I own they stand convicted of glaring inconsistency. But suppose they say—and it is what I have myself only too often been tempted to say when depressed by the apparently formidable presumptions of our impermanence—"since to-morrow we die, and there will, sooner or later, be a morrow when all the persons, nay, all the sentient beings we can conceivably affect in any way by anything we do, will be dead, it really does not matter a jot whether to-day we or anyone else eat and drink, or go hungry and thirsty: there *are* no values at all, and good is a mere illusion". I shall, no doubt, eat to-day when I feel the pinch of hunger, even though I know I am appointed to be hanged to-morrow and believe that this will be the last of me. But in so eating, in so much as breathing, I am only providing one more object-lesson in the fundamental unreasonableness of all human behaviour.

As I say, I admit that in moments when the thought

of the apparently inevitable final frustration of all human endeavour has weighed heavily on me, it has never occurred to me personally to draw the conclusion "let us eat and drink and be merry", but rather to say "nothing has any value, and the one rational state of mind is sheer indifference", and this conclusion would paralyse not only all morally good action, but all consciously purposive action whatsoever. Nor do I think I am exceptional in feeling thus. I suspect Huxley meant the same thing when he said that he would prefer life in hell to annihilation. Dr. Bevan[1] expresses the same thought by his saying that he can endure to see life tragic, but cannot endure to see it trivial.

How would Professor Laird meet this more logical employment of the argument he wishes to dispose of? I presume by a mere assertion that he himself perceives that, even if we were all certain of extinction to-morrow, it would still be better to eat our meals to-day. He would be of the mind of the condemned murderers, who, if the newspapers can be trusted—though it is surely questionable whether they can—usually "make a hearty breakfast" immediately before being hanged. But would he go the length of the felon of the anecdote, who asked to have an umbrella held over him on the way to the gallows, because "it was a drizzly morning, and he was apt to take cold"? If it really "all comes to the same thing in the end" whatever we do, as we must anticipate if there is in reality no sort of connection between fact and value, then, I confess, to set assertion against assertion, I do not see why it is more reasonable to be hanged on a full stomach than on an empty. Once more I want

---

[1] *Hellenism and Christianity*, p. 173. Cf. the complaint of Arnold that

"Each day brings its petty dust
Our soon-choked souls to fill,
And we forget because we must
And not because we will."

to protest against the dogmatic assumption that there
is a divorce between the two.

I am not in the least perturbed when Professor Laird
goes on, as he does, to insist that the world of the actual
is visibly full of things which are valueless or downright
bad. To pronounce anything valueless, I should need
to know the whole of its contribution to the scheme of
things. This is true even of specifically moral evil. I
may say of Judas, or of Nero, that they were bad men
and did bad acts, but before I could go on to say that
a world which contains Judas and Nero is less valuable
than an alternative world which would not include
them, I should have to know, as I assuredly do not
know, that the total effect, including the moral effect,
of the presence of Nero and Judas in the scheme of
things has not been a good which would have been
missing without them. The world might contain as much
evil as you please, provided that all this evil serves as
opportunity for a sufficient overplus of good, and yet
be not only the "best of possible worlds"—that need not
be saying much for it—but unspeakably glorious and
good. Until you are in a position to *prove* that there is
actual evil which is not turned to "glorious gain"—and
no one can prove this—you cannot appeal to the admitted presence in things of evil which, to us while we
are immersed in it, seems intolerable, as any proof that
"the good" is not the ultimate *raison d'être* of all things.

Indeed I think Professor Laird may fairly be cited
as evidence against himself. Unlike some of the moralists who would make human good a merely terrene and
temporary affair, Professor Laird is very much in earnest indeed with the problem of the right conduct of
human life, and as uncompromising as Kant himself
on the absolute and unconditional character of moral
obligation. He nobly refuses even to hear of the possible

clash of a man's "moral" duty as a man and citizen with
alleged extra-moral obligations of art or science.   As
he says,[1] an artistic or scientific imperative, if it is really
imperative at all, is itself a moral imperative. The man
who is a conscientious and industrious historian, or
physicist, or painter, but a bad husband or bad friend,
is simply doing what we all do, discharging one part of
his moral duty and neglecting another. In fact, though
Professor Laird does not put the point in this way, Kant
was simply right when he assigned the primacy to the
"practical reason" on the ground that *all* interest is
practical. And, again, Professor Laird fully agrees with
the common verdict that nothing can be a duty unless
the performance of it is possible. All imperatives are
moral, and no imperative commands the impossible.
And, finally, all moral imperatives are included under the
supreme formula that it is a man's absolute and unconditional duty to make the best of himself.[2] I cannot well
suspect Professor Laird of writing the sentence with
the suppressed ironical qualification that, though we do
well not to say so, the man will always be "making the
best of a bad job". On these premisses it seems to me
clear that *if* the "best" at which the moral struggle aims
all through really is a best which cannot be achieved in
a temporal environment, the supreme moral imperative
is not justified, as Professor Laird himself rightly insists
that all imperatives ought to be, unless the temporal environment of man is not his only or his ultimate environment. It is a true, if a homely saying, that you cannot
make a silk purse of a sow's ear, and ought not to waste
energy and ingenuity on the attempt.

---

[1] *A Study in Moral Theory*, p. 58.
[2] *Op. cit.* p. 56, "The ultimate moral question for any of us is the best use of
the whole of our resources, capacities, and opportunities"; p. 201, "It is self-evident
that anyone ought to do the best he is able to do, and that, if any given action
is not the best he can do, then it cannot be his duty to do it".

Thus, after considering the attempts which have been made, with more or less subtlety, to stop discussion *in limine*, I find myself at last brought face to face with the central issue : assuming ourselves to be satisfied of the genuine authoritativeness of the imperative which commands us to make the best of ourselves, are we obeying it by devotion to the attainment and extension of distinctively secular good, even if we rate the possibilities of such attainment and extension as high as they have ever been rated by the most optimistic humanitarians? For more than one reason, it seems to me, we must say *NO*, and must therefore conclude that secular good is not the adequate object of the moral quest, which yet must have its adequate object, if it is to be justified as rational.

(1) An obvious feature of all moral aspiration is that, however it conceives the good on which it is directed, it at least always conceives it as something which is a secure and abiding possession, inseparable from our very personality, something, as Aristotle said, which is οἰκεῖον καὶ δυσαφαίρετον, "our very own, not lightly to be taken away". A man who is at the mercy of his circumstances is morally, so far, a slave, not a free man, and one thing at least which a sound morality ought to achieve for us is to make us free. And to be free we must be masters not only of our fortunes, but of our moods and passions, in other words, of all that is mutable and temporal within us as well as without us. Short of this we have no security that our character and personality may not be wrecked at any time by the unforeseeable calamities the course of events may bring with it, or the unforeseeable changes our own individual being may suffer. To attain the good at all a man must be master of his fate and himself. And if man is a merely temporal being, and nothing more, he can be master of neither.

The old Epicureans were often ridiculed by their rivals
for their assertion that their ideal "sage" would be
thoroughly happy, even if he were being roasted alive.
Even in the "bull of Phalaris", he must be able to say
"how delightsome this is", "how I am enjoying myself".[1]
But, as Dr. Bevan reminds us,[2] the bull of Phalaris is,
after all, not an impossible contingency, and we might
add that there are lingering and torturing afflictions,
fully comparable with the "bull", which are only too
often actual, and a morality is defective if it cannot
teach serenity and cheerfulness even in these extreme
cases. The true paradox is not so much that the "sage"
should be undismayed by the prospect of the "bull",
but that he should be so, if his "good" is no more than
what Epicurus declared it to be, "a healthy condition
of the flesh and a confident expectation of its continuance".[3] Contingencies much less unusual than consign-
ment to the bull of Phalaris are enough to make both
constituents of *that* good impossible.

To put the point quite generally, we should do no
injustice to a purely secular interpretation of the good
if we said that the secular moral ideal is to "have a good
time", taking care, of course, not to identify a "good
time" with the satisfaction of our grosser cupidities.
The sting of the phrase lies in the introduction of the
"time" into the matter. No man is really free so long as
he is dependent on having a good time, since he can

[1] Cicero, *Tusculans*, ii. 7. 17 sed Epicuro homini aspero et duro non est hoc
satis, in Phalaridis tauro si erit, dicet: quam suave est, quam hoc non curo.
Seneca, *Epist. Moral.* 66. 18 Epicurus quoque ait sapientem, si in Phalaridis tauro
peruratur, exclamaturum: dulce est et ad me nihil pertinet. (For further references of the same kind in Cicero, Seneca, Lactantius, see Usener, *Epicurea*, pp.
338-339.)
[2] *Hellenism and Christianity*, pp. 170-1.
[3] Metrodorus, Fr. 5 (Koerte) ἀγαθὸν ψυχῆς τί ἄλλο ἢ τὸ σαρκὸς εὐσταθὲς κατάστημα καὶ τὸ περὶ ταύτης πιστὸν ἔλπισμα; Epicurus Fr. 68 (Usener) τὸ γὰρ εὐσταθὲς
σαρκὸς κατάστημα καὶ τὸ περὶ ταύτης ἔλπισμα τὴν ἀκροτάτην χαρὰν καὶ βεβαιότητα
ἔχει τοῖς ἐπιλογίζεσθαι δυναμένοις.

guarantee neither the continuance of the environment on which he relies for such a good, nor that of the inner moods of soul in which he will find contentment in it. The elementary requirement that our morality shall make us independent of change and circumstance should be enough to prevent confusion of the good at which a "virtuous" man, as such, is aiming, whether he knows it or not, with any combination of goods which are, from their very nature, *temporanea*, πρόσκαιρα.

There are two ways in which we might try to turn the edge of this reflection, neither, as it seems to me, satisfactory. One might conceivably urge that permanency through an interval of time, though something quite different from eternity, is all we need demand of the good, and that where moralists and philosophers have demanded more, it has been from mental confusion. And permanency, it may be said, unlike eternity, can be secured under favourable conditions. It is, after all, possible to anticipate with a considerable probability a lifelong fruition of the good things you personally care for, just as you can, by prudent investment, make it "as good as certain" that you will have a lifelong income sufficient for your wants. And if you take care to form the right kind of habits, you can also anticipate, again with high probability, that the kind of life which satisfies you now will continue to satisfy you. What is more, a whole generation may have the same sort of confidence that the general structure of their "civilisation" will not only "last their time", but be perpetuated to, and improved by, succeeding generations. A general collapse of the foundations of Western European civilisation, for example, is a contingency so remote that its bare logical possibility need not give us any uneasiness.

No doubt there is something in these consolations,

so long as we do not examine them too narrowly. But I cannot believe they will stand really close scrutiny. Even the assurance that "Western civilisation" will last our time and our children's time is hardly likely to rank as even an approximate certainty with us, who have seen the great war of 1914–18 and the years of danger and insecurity which have followed and are following. And if there had been no "great war", still the humanitarian cannot really "make quick-coming death a little thing". It is not merely that we know that each of us will soon have to die himself; the sting of our mortality is that the same fate equally awaits the children on whom the humanitarian tells us we should set all our hopes, and their children after them. If all things human are utterly perishable, the moral would seem to be the uncheering one:

> Reck little, then, I counsel you
> What any son of man can do;
> Because a log of wood will last
> While many a life of man goes past,
> And all is over in short space.

Or, in graver language, "as soon as thou scatterest them, they are even as a sleep, and fade away suddenly like the grass. . . . We bring our years to an end as a tale that is told."

The thought is hardly one which can reasonably evoke a high estimate of any good which the passing generations can achieve in their brief passage across the stage, or any very thorough endeavour after it. If our life is no more than the strutting of a player through his part in a short scene, sheer quietism would seem to be the attitude towards it indicated by reason and reflection. One might add that, from the point of view of secularistic humanitarianism itself, the best of temporal good seems to be most certainly attained by those who have set their hearts on something different. When I am told that, if you must set your heart on the future at all, you should set it on your children,[1] I cannot but repeat that all human experience seems to show that devotion to children or wife, party or country, is only regularly fruitful of the good it desires when the devotion is kept on the hither side of idolatry. It sounds a hard saying when we are told in the Gospel that the man who would enter life must be prepared to forsake parents and wife and children and lands, but we all recognise the truth of a similar thought, pitched in a lower key,

> I could not love thee, dear, so much,
> Loved I not honour more.

The rule of all wise and profitable love of everything that passes is to love without losing one's heart. He who wishes for the true good of wife or child or country must love them dearly, but there will be something he loves more; if there is not, his love will carry in it the seeds of a curse for the very beings he loves most. To make a god of one's child is to spoil the child of your idolatry; to make "my country, right or wrong," the principle of your action is to do what lies in you to turn your country into one which is not worth loving. And to be devoted exclusively to the good of the "next age", like those who set their hearts on "Socialism in our lifetime", or the "evangelisation of the world in the next generation", is pretty certainly not the best way to provide the "next age" with either the worthiest of social systems or the soundest of gospels. The true secret of life is to love these things well, but to love something else better. And we have only to think of the various names we give to that something else the love of which keeps all our loves for particular things sane and sweet, to see that, whether we call it "God", or "beauty", or "the right",

---

[1] Bosanquet, *Science and Philosophy*, p. 334.

or "honour", by all these different names we mean something which is "not of this world", but stands above and untouched by the temporality and mutability it transfigures.

Once more, the same moral may be pointed in a rather different way. When a man sets his heart, to the best of his power, on the good of the successive generations of mankind, what is the "good" he desires for them? It, no doubt, includes such good things as greater average longevity, a higher standard of physical health, better economic conditions, a more general diffusion of the love of knowledge and beauty, and the like. But, besides these identifiable particular "goods", does not the "good" always include something more, something we could not define or describe, but still felt to be of greater importance than all the particular "goods"? We desire, rationally enough, that the coming generations should be healthier than our own, should know more truth, should find the world fuller of things of beauty, and should not have to wrestle, as we have, with the presence of disease, dirt, penury, and ignorance. But we desire even more that the men and women of the future should be *better* men and women than ourselves, or, at least, if we do not actually desire this ardently, we censure ourselves for our moral lukewarmness. And this means, among other things, that they should be *more* devoted than we are ourselves to the promotion of good for generations which will still be for them future and unborn. We desire that our descendants should have the same difficulties to grapple with as ourselves, or even worse difficulties, but should face them with a higher self-devotion, rather than that they should enjoy all the other goods which have just been enumerated a hundred-fold, but fall behind ourselves in the spirit of sacrifice. We do not, unless in consciously unmoral moods, desire for them, any more than for ourselves, increase of good things in possession at the cost of an inferior moral personality; it is not our ideal for them that they should "fleet the time carelessly", like the heroes of socialistic Utopias.

This simple consideration that we do not want our children, or our children's children, "to fleet the time carelessly" leads at once to a dilemma, if we think of man as capable only of temporal and secular goods which can be particularised. If what we really prize as the thing to be won by our own unselfishness is some kind of temporal Utopia, it seems rational to agree with one of the speakers in Mr. Lowes Dickinson's dialogue,[1] that we should set ourselves to fashion the Utopia for our contemporaries and our children, who do exist and in whom we can take a personal interest, not to sacrifice their best chances of good for the benefit of a remote posterity which may conceivably never exist at all, and in which we can take no sort of personal concern. It seems preposterous, if all human good is temporal, to demand that every one of a countless succession of generations should sacrifice the enjoyment of it in order that it may be possible for beings belonging to a problematic and indefinitely distant future. But if we act on this advice, plainly, we must at least go on to draw the hazardous inference that moral goodness itself is no part of the "good for man", but a mere means to non-moral good.[2] For the generation for which the Utopia is created will be simply entering on an inheritance which it is merely to enjoy in possession; it has no *work* to do, and moral goodness is wholly concerned with the doing of the work by the pre-millenarian generations. The happiness of the favoured generation is, in fact,

[1] G. Lowes Dickinson, *Meaning of Good*, pp. 111 ff.
[2] Cf. *op. cit.* p. 136.

bought at the price of the destruction of moral personality, and, from the moralist's point of view, the world,
or a thousand worlds, is not well won at the cost of
human souls.

On the other hand, if the moral goodness *we* value,
genuine moral personality, is what we specially desire
to see produced abundantly in those who are to succeed
us on the stage of history, we cannot find our aspirations
realised in the life of a society where there is no call
for risk, adventure, and sacrifice. If personality of the
quality we prize is to subsist under temporal conditions
at all, there must be the stimulus to its development in the
form of sufferings to be relieved, dangers to be faced,
wrongs to be redressed, ignorance and ugliness to be
overcome. It is certain enough that, in any imaginable
generation,

> Pity would be no more,
> If we did not make somebody poor,
> And mercy no more would be,
> If all were as happy as we.

And thus the humanitarian, unless he is willing to
sacrifice personality to possessions, would seem to be
compelled to introduce into his Utopia with his left
hand the very conditions he is trying to exclude with
his right. His rule would seem to be, in a very singular
sense, not to let his right hand know what his left hand
does. At least, like Penelope, he would spend the
night busily undoing the results of the day's work.
The moral life would become a hopeless task of creating
wrongs that they might be put right.

I state what may be called the fundamental paradox of humanitarianism thus crudely and baldly of set
purpose, because the very baldness of the statement
sets the paradoxicality of the position in bold relief.
Its point is that you cannot overvalue the highest tem-

poral good, nor promote it for humanity too ardently, so long as you care more yourself, and labour as far as is in you that mankind shall care more, for something else. You may have it all in possession without detriment to your moral being, so long as you hold it with a loose hand, and do not close the fingers on it. Every iota of it will go, in its due time, from you and from every son of man down to the last-born, and any part of it may go at any moment, and one must be ready to let it go without reluctancy. For the business of man as a moral being is, after all, a simple one; it is the "making of his soul", a making impossible except at the cost of the steady unmaking of the "private self", whose real defect is precisely that its centre lies in some possession which must not be surrendered. What makes our "finite selfhood" the contradiction so many moralists have called it is not that no self or subject is identical *numero* with another, that there are *many* selves, but that each clings to some possession which it dares not let go for fear of losing the very core of personality.[1] Yet, as we may all learn from experience of such surrenders as we actually make, it is just in letting go the cherished possession, when the call comes, that we learn the real strength and richness of the personality which can let so much go and yet survive, because it is not tethered. What we should really learn from these experiences is that there is that in our personality which is not fettered to any temporal good and can emerge enriched, not impoverished, from the surrender of them all. The good on which personality feeds, and severed from which it would die of inanition, is something which is not any nor all of the describable and imaginable goods circumscribed by place and time.

[1] This is what Goethe personifies as Frau Sorge in the closing scenes of *Faust*.

One side of this thought, the conviction that the world is what Keats called it, a valley of soul-making, and that the soul is made by surrenders, has been expounded, with a power I can only contemplate with admiring envy, in Professor Bosanquet's well-known lectures on the *Value and Destiny of the Individual*. But Bosanquet seems to me to have ignored the other half of the same thought. When all is said, he holds out as the ultimate goal to be reached by the supreme surrender what seems to be merely the resolution of moral personality into nothing. True personality, it would appear, is made only to be lost in the very act. This, I am convinced, is a misreading of the facts to be interpreted. The natural interpretation would rather be that as the self which is enriched by partial surrenders remains *my* self, though its centre is increasingly displaced from my exclusive possessions, so the self to be won by the supreme surrender of all that is temporal is still *my* self, though its centre has become the one and abiding eternal. Heaven, to put it pictorially, is not a realm of selves, each clinging pertinaciously to some secret possession which it will share with no other, but Heaven is a realm of selves for all that, selves whose whole life is one of the supreme adventure, losing themselves in God, but with the result that in the very plunge out of self they find, not nothing, but themselves, and themselves with a richer content.

Need I say much about that other way of dealing with the problem created by the transience of all temporal good illustrated, for example, by Mr. Bertrand Russell's only too famous essay on *The Free Man's Worship*?[1] It is, in a sense, a desperate way of trying to escape from temporality. We are to

[1] B. Russell, *Philosophical Essays*, pp. 59 ff.

recognise to the full the unsatisfactoriness of the temporal, and at the same time to lift ourselves above it by a quietistic scorn for a reality which is as much inferior to ourselves in worth as it is superior in brute force. The "free man" is to be Prometheus on his rock—a Prometheus after the fashion of Shelley rather than of Aeschylus — despising the "omnipotent matter" which Mr. Russell sets in the place of Zeus. To some of Mr. Russell's readers, I know, this attitude of contempt for the stupid "omnipotence" which produces intelligence, beauty, and goodness only to crush them, has seemed sublime; at the risk of being dismissed in such quarters as a *Durchschnittsmensch*, I must own that the pose strikes me as rather one of solemn conscious futility. If the case of man were really thus, "silence after grievous things" would be more becoming than any rhetoric, even Mr. Russell's, or, if words there must be, one phrase of Johnson's would be sufficient, "a man knows it must be; it will do no good to whine".

But I should like to make the further comment that the state of soul described in Mr. Russell's essay seems to leave no real place for either freedom or worship. Freedom is excluded by the fact that the standing attitude of our latest Prometheus to his Zeus, "omnipotent matter", is one of scorn and conscious superiority, "proud defiance". Now scorn and inner freedom simply will not keep house together, as Shelley was aware when he made *his* Prometheus expressly disclaim any feeling of contempt for his tormentor.[1] He who scorns, in fact, suffers from a double unfreedom. He must be conscious of the obtrusive and unwelcome presence of the object of his contempt, and thus he cannot get away from what

[1] *Prometheus Unbound*, i. 1. 53.

Spinoza, with more insight, reckons as one of the "passive affects" which inhibit and make unfree.[1] And this is not all: to feel scorn, a man must also be concomitantly conscious of himself and of his own superiority, and this is to be more or less of a bitter "prig". To be free you must get rid of *all* preoccupation with yourself, and for that very reason a "superior person" never is really free.

Again, the scorner, with his consciousness of his own superiority, cannot really know what it is to "worship". Worship is for the *sancti et humiles corde*, and one only knows it when one's mind is filled by an object which leaves no room for consciousness of one's self by the side of it. This, by the way, is also why Kant's attitude to the moral law and its source never really rises into worship. To be conscious of the moral law as an unconditional imperative is, as Kant himself knew, to be conscious of yourself as inhibited by it. To use the fashionable jargon of to-day, an "inferiority-complex" is attended by a painful awareness of the self as depressed and thwarted. Worship is possible only when one can forget one's self and one's own inferiority; it is this which gives it its character of free and joyous *abandon*. All worship is at heart an incipient *iubilus*.

But the main comment I would make on the whole attitude is that morally it is condemned by the simple consideration that it is bound to hinder the production of good works. As Spinoza reminds us,[2] *Laetari* and *bene agere* go together; a view of the world which makes simple-minded joyousness impossible cannot be the view required for men whose lives are to be fruitful in good works, and therefore, *if* our moral life discloses anything whatever about the framework of

---

[1] *Ethica*, iv. 46 Corr. 1, Schol.   [2] *Ethica*, iv. 73 Schol.

reality in which it is set, such a view cannot be the truth. If the real world indeed meets the moralist's demand on it, it must be a world to be met neither with scorn nor with resignation, but accepted and welcomed with single-hearted joyfulness.

If the inmost secret of the moral life is that it is a life of "making the best" of ourselves, of achieving, out of the crude and conflicting stresses and tensions with which we start, a genuine personality which is free and its own master, and if the price which has to be paid for every advance towards such freedom is surrender, then, as it seems to me, we can think of such a life as not condemned in principle to futility only on one condition. The condition is that we anticipate the completion of the process as found in the winning of a personality absolutely above circumstance and mutability by a supreme surrender of the whole realm of merely temporal values, as dying out of time into a real eternity. What such an eternal life would be like is, of course, more than we can imagine, since all our imaginations are borrowed from the temporal. What we imagine we imagine as a tissue of "events", though some of the events may be "slow-moving". Still, imaginable or not, and the human imagination is no criterion of the real—that dying out of the temporal into the eternal which writers like Suso spoke of as "passing away into the high godhead" must be real, and must be no mere negation, but the final affirmation of the moral self, if morality itself is to be, in the end, more than a futility. What is put off in such an achievement of the moral end must be not personality or individuality, but that inner division of the soul against itself which makes the tragedy of life and leaves us here mere imperfect fragments of persons.

In the traditional language of Christianity, it is the life of the "flesh" which must be surrendered if eternal life, the life of the "spirit", is to be won. And this opposition the "flesh", as we see from St. Paul's description of its characteristic "works", includes a great deal more than we commonly mean by "carnality". To live to the flesh is to make our supreme good of anything which is no more than the gratification of incidental passions and desires, followed merely because I happen, for my own particular, to feel them strongly, though they are incapable of justification by the standard of absolute good. It is to take "I want it" as a last and sufficient legitimation of any pursuit. In this sense of the word, a life directed to the prosecution of science or art, or to the enjoyment of the social relations of the family, or the friendly circle, may itself be one of living to the flesh, if I follow science as no more than a means of satisfying curiosity, or art as a mere profession, or a mere hobby, or am interested in the members of my family or circle of friends merely because they happen to be there, and to be mine. To die to the life of the flesh need not mean that I am not to find my vocation in life in the pursuit of science, or in the filling of my place in a family and social group. To "spiritualise" such a life is so to live it as to achieve for myself, and to help others in achieving, a moral personality, proof against all shocks and all disappointments. Any life so lived ceases to have as its inspiring motive a lesser and circumscribed loyalty which may be a hindrance to the supreme loyalty to the best, and becomes itself an expression of the supreme loyalty. Yet, at the same time, all loyalties but the supreme loyalty *may* become clogs upon us, and all are therefore conditioned. Even if no actual conflict arises, they are all loyalties to objects which endure only for a time, and the good man whom morality contemplates must not be left without any-thing to live for, if one and all of these objects should be taken from him. Like Mary, he must choose as his object of supreme loyalty a good part which cannot be taken away. In that sense we might accept the poetic phrase

> Ich hab' mein Sach auf Nichts gestellt;
> Drum ist's so wohl mir in der Welt

as our motto.

I know well enough, of course, that few or none of us actually live up to this moral ideal. It is pitiful to think what a little thing will make shipwreck of the life of any of us by taking away some minor good to which we cling over-passionately. Yet if we are morally reflective creatures, we have at least the grace to be heartily ashamed of ourselves when the failure of one of these temporal attachments tears up our life by the roots. And my argument is concerned not with our sorry practice, but with what we know our practice ought to be. Hence I feel bound to hold that the plain fact that there is no loyalty to the best of temporal goods which it may not become a duty to subordinate to the supreme loyalty to Good itself is ground for the conviction that we have a good, and consequently a destiny which is not expressible at all in terms of duration, and yet must be attainable, if it be true that the moral life itself is no dream or illusion, but the most insistent of realities.

If this is so, there are important consequences to be drawn, and I would indicate some of them very briefly. It will follow that our possession of a moral being gives us a right to a reasonable hope that the attainment of a truly free personality, in which we rise above contingency and uncertainty, because we have learned the lesson of surrender, really lies before us. This will, of course, involve the hope and conviction that the crown of moral attainment remains secure, even against the shock of that general dissolution of our bodily organism which we call death. Free personality is manifestly not to be completely won while we are in the body, "servile to all the skiey influences"; while the "displacement of a grain of sand in the urethra" can stultify a man's highest intelligence and purpose, he is obviously very much in chains, and if the moral order is a reality, we cannot believe that he wins his freedom only in the moment of ceasing to be anything at all. But this rational moral hope is strictly limited by its character and foundation. It is a hope that we shall win our way into a true free moral personality as our final and inalienable good, and we can say no more than this. What it is to enter on the fruition of eternal life we cannot so much as imagine: *trasumanar significar per verba Non si poria.* At the most we can only say that such a life would have always and in perfection the quality we experience now, rarely and imperfectly, when we have made one of those surrenders which we find it so hard to make, and have made it heartily and with a will.

Perhaps an illustration may be taken from an experience which must have come to many during the war of 1914–1918. There are probably among my audience some who, as young men rejoicing in their youth and all its promise of a full and varied life, then made, from sheer loyalty to a higher good, the surrender of hazarding all they prized most to play a man's part in their country's struggle, and made it with the full sense of the preciousness of all they were setting on the hazard, and yet gladly and ungrudgingly. I take it that if any man can recall, as perhaps it is hardly possible he should, what the quality of his life was when he was making the choice, he knows by analogy what is the abiding character of eternal life, as a life in which, to use the traditional language of noble livers, the soul is "oned" with the Most High, or, to fall back on words which perhaps come home more directly to modern men at large, in which one has ceased to be one of the world's takers and become finally a giver, and so, in fact, has found the good part which nothing can take away, because one has no longer anything which is a mere private possession to be shared with no one, but lives wholly by bestowing.

I cannot myself see anything self-contradictory in the conception of a community of many members each of whom has his own special individuality as a recipient of the infinitely varied and manifold graces of the Bestower of all good, and yet keeps back nothing, but is a channel through which all he has received flows out freely on all his fellows. Such, I take it, would be the "life of gods and godlike men", in which the "flesh", the world's grabber, is once and for all dead, and there is no life but that of spirit.

If this is what an eternal life satisfying the aspirations in which morality has its source would be, it follows that ethical considerations can do nothing to confirm anticipations not covered by such a conception, and may actually negative imaginations which prove to be inconsistent with it. In any conception of our destiny which appeals to morality as its sanction, or one of its sanctions, there will inevitably be the touch of austerity which is as characteristic of sound morality as of serious art. I confess that not a few of our current imaginative forecasts of "immortality" seem to me to be tainted with moral superficiality. They do no sufficient justice to what experience reveals to us all in varying measures, the indispensability of detachment and surrender as the one pathway into ascending life. We are all too prone to forget that the road to life is, from first to last, a "purgative" way. I know that so rare and delicate a thinker as the late Mr. Clutton-Brock[1] has declared that what most of us need is not so much purgation as enrichment. But I cannot help thinking that this sharp contrast between the two is a misleading antithesis which its author would have found it hard to defend as it stands. Certainly, enrichment is the obvious need of us all; our moral life is dreadfully poverty-stricken; it is our curse that our loves are so few and so feeble. But, so far as I can see, it is regularly by purgation and simplification that enrichment has to be won. Our loves are deepened and enlarged in the same proportion in which our hungry cupidities are suppressed. We love too little and too feebly because we lust—I use the word in its wide old acceptation—so passionately and for so much. Our problem is to learn to live by our loves and not by our cupidities; the second must be surrendered that the first may flourish. We shall never be truly rich until we have learned the lesson that *unum est necessarium.*

And I see no reason in the nature of things to suppose that the surrender of the bodily life with all its accidents, which each of us has to make at death, need be the end of the process. It would be more natural, to my mind, to think that even the vanishing of the so-called "bodily" lusts with the body itself leaves a hard purgation still in front of most of us. There are such things as unwise personal attachments, involving no element of physical "appetite", to unworthy objects, undue and disordinate

---

[1] See a passage in the composite volume *Immortality: an Essay in Discovery* (London, 1917), pp. 234-6.

devotions to supra-personal objects short of the highest, rooted prejudices and false judgements, and I cannot see why removal from the body should, of itself, purge us of these defects. A Nelson, in the life beyond the grave, would, I take it, have to unlearn an exclusive idolatry of England and an irrational animosity against "the French", an Aristotle to overcome a one-sided superiority to simple and unlettered loving souls, before either could enter fully into life, and in both cases the lesson involves a great purification and simplification.

Hence there seems to me to be a profound truth, un-affected by the secondary errors grafted upon it by the demand for detailed imagining of the unimaginable, in the central thought of the doctrine of Purgatory, a doctrine which I believe to be really held, in one form or another, by the thoughtful even in communities which nominally repudiate it.[1] I cannot conceive that most of us, with our narrow range of understanding and sympathies, our senseless antipathies and indifferences, and our conventional moral outlook, could ever be fitted by the mere fact of escape from the physical limitations of the body to enter at once into the eternal life of the simply loving souls. I should think it more probable—always with deference to wiser judgements —that death leaves us, as it finds us, still far too much takers and too little givers, and that the process of purgation, begun in this life in all who have made any progress in good, needs, for all but the very few, to be continued and intensified, and that, for most of us, this means severe discipline. It may be well to have got rid of the crude imagination of "Purgatory-fire" as a "torment", and still better to have lost the belief that

---

[1] Thus the Articles of the Anglican Church repudiate "the Romish doctrine of Purgatory", whatever that may be; but Anglicans who think at all, regularly, as I should say, believe in *a* Purgatory, whether they call it by that name or not.

one can purchase remission of the torment by cash payment into an ecclesiastical treasury, but the main thought that the hardest part of the work of putting off temporality may, for most of us, lie on the further side of the physical change called death seems to me eminently sound. It is a true philosophical instinct which has regularly led great Christian theologians to look for our final consummation not only beyond the dissolution of the body, but beyond the great closing of history at the "Day of Doom". The popular theology of our own country, which finds expression in hymns, according to which the "faithful dead" enter "into immediate rest", has done only too much to deprive the doctrine of immortality of moral seriousness, but it is not the theology of the great divines of any section of the Church.

Still more frivolous, to my own mind, are the attempts made, independently of theology, to construct a doctrine of human immortality apart from a profoundly ethical conception of God, and from the conviction that the true basis of a wise and good man's hopes for himself must be found in aspiration after unification of the human will with the divine. I have spoken sufficiently already of the moral triviality and tediousness of most of the alleged revelations of "spiritualism" about the eternity of boredom which awaits us all. The same criticism seems to me applicable to all attempts to base our highest hopes on the so-called "oriental" lore of transmigration and reincarnation. There is no particular reason for entertaining these speculations as more than doubtful fancies, unless they can be shown to be involved by our conviction that the moral end must be capable of achievement, and from the moralist's point of view they would seem to make the very possibility of achievement questionable. If we

think of the supposed series of births as actually unending, it is clear that the moral end, if we have divined
its character rightly, is never attained. The doctrine,
so taken, converts eternity into the mere repetition of
temporality and thus holds out as a boon what the
morally aspiring man most wants to escape, bondage
to the round of circumstance. In this respect, indeed,
the old Orphicism has the advantage of some of its
modern substitutes; it did, apparently, contemplate, as
the prize of those who have trodden the way of purgation to the end, escape from the "weary wheel". Origen
is alleged, truly or falsely, to have flirted with the fancy
that, in a coming age, Christ and Caiaphas may change
places; in our own days F. W. H. Myers could gravely
give the preference to Buddhism over Christianity in
one respect, on the ground that the former teaches, or
is said to teach, that the Buddha had "often been in
hell for his sins".[1] But clearly the ethical implication
of such fancies is highly dubious. They mean that free
spiritual personality is only achieved to be lost again;
our completest moral victories are only passing incidents in a campaign which ends in nothing. A sane
moralist may or may not be a believer in the dogmatic
theology of Christianity; in either case he can hardly
be blind to the ethical superiority of the religion which
teaches that, "Christ being risen from the dead, dieth
no more; death"—the supreme external manifestation
of temporality—"hath no more dominion over him".

On the other side, if the "wheel" is ever to be escaped,
there seems to be no reason why the episode in our
moral ascent which is terminated at death should
necessarily be repeated. There may be many stages,
and hard stages, still before us in our journey, but
why should we assume that one march has to be accom-

[1] *Human Personality*, ii. 289.

plished twice? One would more naturally suppose,
though all supposals are uncertain, that no day's
march repeats itself, just as within the life we know
there is no recurrence of childhood, or adolescence,
or the prime of manhood. I own that it is surprising
to me to find a philosopher of the distinction of Dr.
McTaggart favouring speculations of this type, on the
ground that they provide opportunity for the making
of a diversity of experiments in living. They give us,
he says, the prospect of being Galahad in one life and
Tristram in another.[1] Now I do not know in what order
Dr. McTaggart would propose to take these two lives,
but, for my own part, I cannot conceive that it would
be anything but an apostacy and a return to the flesh-
pots of Egypt for one who had been Galahad to lead
the life of Tristram, and though Tristram might come,
after long and bitter purgation in the fires of adversity,
to be something like Galahad, it could only be when he
had thoroughly learned the lesson that it is not good
to be Tristram. The kind of immortality contemplated
is radically unethical; it is not an advance towards
the achieving of a free personality, and therefore leaves
no room for that giving and hazarding all that a man
has by which free personality is won. Dr. McTaggart's
immortals, in fact, may put on in succession the masks
of Galahad and Tristram, and, for all I know, of
Mordred too, but all through these are only "impersonations"; there is no growing personality behind them.
And hence Dr. McTaggart is strictly consistent in refusing to allow any weight to "moral" arguments for
such an immortality, for the future he anticipates is,
after all, a non-moral one. It may be a future of unending duration, but, against Dr. McTaggart's own intention, it does not seem to have the quality of eternity

[1] *Some Dogmas of Religion*, p. 138.

about it. I should expect such a cycle of adventures to leave men, as it finds them, "quick-change artists".

It is true, as I know, that Dr. McTaggart proposes to be certain on metaphysical grounds, most fully explained in the second volume of *The Nature of Existence*, that the succession of impersonations must culminate in a "timeless" perfection for each of us. But I am far from understanding clearly what "perfection" can mean in such a context. Whatever it means, it seems to be deprived of genuine moral significance by the consideration that, according to the system, it is something fated to happen to us, not something to be won by personal effort. Apparently we have it thrust upon us, whether we will or no, as Malvolio's greatness was thrust on him.[1]

It seems to me important, again, to realise that if the only sort of continuation of life into the unseen for which we can hope to find justification in the analysis of the moral good is the completion of the process of putting off the temporal to put on the eternal, it follows that we do not know how much which, at our present stage in the pilgrimage, appears as though the very roots of our personality were twined about it may not have to be let go before the eternal is really put on, in the full measure possible to men. To speak imaginatively, we may reasonably anticipate that the law of dying into life holds good for Heaven itself, as well as for Earth and Purgatory. Like T. H. Green,[2] I see no difficulty in conceiving of a society where there is no longer wrong to be put right in the relations of the members to one another, nor evil to be burnt away out of the individual desire and will. But even in such a community there need not cease to be differences of

---

[1] Cf. the utterances on this point in *Studies in Hegelian Cosmology*, c. iv.
[2] *Prolegomena to Ethics*, pp. 195, 328.

insight between the members, and, arguing by analogy from what we see of the life of personality, the deepest insight would be the reward of the completest self-abandonment, the most adventurous loss of self in the "divine dark" of the Godhead. There, no doubt, the dark would have its own special quality; it would not arise, as so often with us now, from the resistance of obstinately self-centred will to the rays of the spiritual sun, from coldness of heart, but from the very unapproachableness of the light itself. That dark would be a "deep, but *dazzling* darkness". And one would return from every adventure of the spirit simply enriched with a fuller insight, and a more vivid life, not, as we too often do from our present imperfectly pure adventures, maimed and numbed. And, again, the return would make us more and more complete givers and bestowers of all we had won by the adventure on every member of the society. But the rule would still be, there as here, that it is only he who will lose himself beyond rescue who finds himself to eternal life. The difference between the eternal life of face-to-face vision and the life of time, where we see only *per speculum in aenigmate*, would lie in the completeness of the abandonment of self and the consequent enrichment without compensatory loss with which the soul returns from the adventures.

While the self is still bound up in temporality, the self-abandonment is never quite complete, and by consequence the adventure always entails some element of loss amidst all its profit; there is always love which, because it has not been wholly converted from mere lusting into love, has to be starved. In eternity, all loves would be wholly subordinated to the supreme and irresistible love of God; all would be ventured and, for that very reason, all would be found to be completed and satisfied. But *how* they would find this completion is just what cannot be known by anticipation; that is the "transhumanisation" of humanity of which Dante[1] says that it cannot be expressed *per verba*, and it is because any imagined Paradise, like Dante's own, is an attempted description of the undescribable, a would-be "evaluation" of the everlasting "surd", that all such imaginings leave us with some sense of hollowness. Even Dante's must, at moments, have suggested to most of us the disquieting reflection that it has an unfortunate resemblance with a glorified firework night at the Crystal Palace, or a gaudy celebration of the Vespers of Our Lady. In principle, the note of austerity characteristic of all true morality is not silenced by the hope of Heaven. We cannot say of any of the relations to which we cling most fondly how much they might need to be transfigured to find their completion in eternity.

This is the answer to the kind of sceptical puzzles with which play is made in *Appearance and Reality*.[2] Bradley asks, for example, whether two men who had buried their quarrel in a woman's grave would be friends in the resurrection, or whether all of us would be content to sit down among the angels without recovering our dogs. The question only has serious point for those who sympathise with what Bradley calls modern Christendom's "repeal of the austere sentence" of the Gospel.[3] I venture to think that if modern Christians really abolish the "sentence" in question, that "in the resurrection they neither marry nor are given in marriage", they are so far false both to their professed Christianity and to the fundamentals of a sound ethics. How all the loves which go to the making of moral personality are to be completed in a society where the

[1] *Paradiso*, i. 70.   [2] *Op. cit.* p. 509.   [3] *Loc. cit.*

love of God is supreme, we have no means of saying; Bradley's difficulty arises from the assumption that, if completed at all, they must be completed in some way of which we, who are still distracted by conflicting loves, can form a clear picture. And this is false in principle and is the very error of the Sadducees, who erred "not knowing the scriptures nor the *power* of God". Though this particular difficulty, I should have supposed, does sometimes find its solution even on earth. Even here, at our best, we do find doors of escape from "all the little emptiness" of merely competitive loves, so far as we learn to set our hearts more on giving than on taking. Eternal life in fruition would be a life which is all giving without taking, and therefore also all receiving; we think falsely of it if we import into it any relation not consonant with this principle.

It would not be honest to leave this subject without some reference to a further matter upon which clear thinking is much needed—the old problem of the fate of the "finally impenitent". If we are to think ethically of human destiny, we must be prepared to face the possibility that there may be those who obstinately shut the windows of the soul against all influences from the divine, until they have made themselves impervious to them. A man may conceivably so harden himself against good that he ends by becoming incapable of it, or by sheer protracted sloth he may lose the power to make the surrender by which we die into true personality. At least we have, as moralists, no right to say that such a thing is intrinsically inconceivable. If it is conceivable, then it is conceivable that a man may finally and irretrievably miss the very end to which his being is ordained. There may be a definitive "second death" which is a death not into eternity, but into complete and hopeless temporality. We may, indeed, hope

that none of us will ever actually incur this fate, that
the long-suffering and bountifulness of the Giver of all
good will, in the end, break down the wilfulness and
sluggishness of the least responsive among us. But I
do not see how we can be confident that it is so, and I
am sure that if anything can frustrate attainment of
our final good, it is the besotted fancy that this good
is bound to come to us, unstriven for, in the course of
things, whether we choose or not, and that we may
therefore neglect the arduous business of the "making
of the soul". No dictum can be morally shallower than
the often-repeated current assertion that "Hell" is only
a nightmare begotten of superstitious fear of bad and
vindictive gods.

Historically this is *obviously* untrue; it is clear, from
considerations already dwelt on in an earlier lecture,
that the belief that sinners are punished in Hell, like
the belief that they are exposed to special "judgements"
in this present life, is no induction from a misunderstood experience, but the expression, in crude forms,
of a real *a priori* ethical conviction. Men argue that
there *is* a Hell because they are convinced, on moral
grounds, that there *ought* to be one, if eternal justice is
not to be mocked. It is the faith that there is a moral
order in the world, and that it is founded on justice, that
is the parent of belief in retribution beyond the grave.
What is felt to be morally intolerable is that by the mere
fact of dying betimes the impenitent wrong-doer should
triumphantly escape the operation of a law of universal
justice. As Plato puts it, in his admonition to the young
man who is led to the denial of God's moral government of the world by the spectacle of apparently successful lifelong transgression, "You shall assuredly never
be passed over by God's judgement, not though you
make yourself never so small, and hide in the bowels

of the earth, or exalt yourself to heaven: you must pay the penalty due, either while you are still with us, or after your departure hence, in the house of Hades, or, it may be, by removal to some still more desolate region".[1] Belief in a penal and retributory Hell, as contrasted with the older and non-ethical conception of a shadowy continuation of this present existence in a ghost-world, arises directly from the moralisation of men's outlook on the future, though it may take ages of deepening moral reflection before the misdeeds which are held to receive their deserts hereafter come to be identified wholly with what men with a lofty ethical rule of life recognise as moral guilt, in distinction from ceremonial and ritual shortcomings. And in principle, as we can readily see, the rose-coloured anticipations of an easy-going unethical Universalism are as illogical as unethical.

If there is a supreme good for man which yet is not to be attained without personal effort, it must follow that the man who refuses, or persistently neglects, to make the effort towards that good imperils his felicity. He is trying to live in an environment for which *he* is not designed, and to which he cannot adapt himself without ceasing to be truly man. "Heaven" is, of all others, the society in which such a man would be most utterly "in the wrong place"; he would there be the proverbial "fish out of the water", and consequently miserable. It is idle to fancy that God, if He liked, could make the criminal, or the sensualist, or the trifler, happy by translating him to Heaven. To quote Plato once more, the supreme law needed to ensure moral order in the world is a very simple one; it is that men, like liquids, "find their level"; they are drawn, as by a sort of moral gravitation, into the company of the like-

---

[1] *Laws*, 905 A.

minded, and so they "do and have done to them what it befits them to do and to endure".[1] There we have the reality of which the various pictures of the fires of Hell are so many imaginative symbols, and in a morally ordered world it could be no otherwise. It is in mercy, not in wrath, that the way of the transgressor is made hard. There is a *bottom* of truth in a modern poet's paradox that God's mercy

> I do think it well,
> Is flashed back from the brazen gates of Hell,[2]

and in the better-known words of a greater poet, that the maker of the dreadful realm was

> La divina potestate,
> La somma sapienza e il primo amore.[3]

Once more we must remember that we are not to take our symbols for facts. We do not *know* that any man actually has sinned, or will sin, himself into complete death to the supreme good, and it is not surprising that Christian theologians, with no desire to be unorthodox, have sometimes reminded us that the united Christian Church has never formally condemned the doctrine of universal restoration, achieved through grim experience of the way of the transgressor, taught by some of the most eminent among the early Fathers. And, again, we do not know what the ultimate consequences of complete absorption in mere temporality would be. It is tempting to suppose that the culmination of such a process would be such a forfeiting of personality that the consciousness of the man who has wholly lost *lo ben dell' intelletto* would resemble that of Leibniz's "mere monad", or, as I think Baron von Hügel has said somewhere, would be like mere aware-

---

[1] *Laws*, 904 B-E.   [2] Francis Thompson, *The Child-woman.*
[3] Dante, *Inferno*, iii. 5-6.

ness of what Bergson calls "clock-time". Thus, by refusing to deepen his personality, a man would end by losing even what personality he has; "from him that hath not" there would literally be taken away "even that he hath". And we could not imagine that such a process would be anything but grievous in the extreme to the man who, by his own fault, brought it upon himself, just as any one of us would be profoundly unhappy if he found himself steadily declining into physical and mental imbecility, with the knowledge that he had brought his fate on himself by his own vices.

All this is speculation about the unknown, and, as one of our divines sensibly says, it is not very profitable to speculate about a future which must receive us and may prove to be singularly unlike anything we had conjectured. But it should be plain that a genuinely ethical faith can have nothing to do with theories devised simply to get rid of the principle that the way of transgressors, in a reasonably ordered universe, is necessarily hard, and that if eternal life is a thing that has to be won, there is always the grim possibility that it may be lost. A creed constructed to reassure the careless can hardly be a morally sound creed. We need to contemplate the possibility of Hell not, as superficial caricaturists represent, in order to have the pleasure of consigning our enemies, or our neighbours, to it, but to warn ourselves against the risks we run by disloyalty to the best. I venture to think that this may be a sound ethical reason for dissatisfaction with the rather fashionable conception of a "conditional" immortality, which does not pertain to man as man, but may be achieved by a select few. To say nothing of the danger of spiritual pride involved, as the history of Gnosticism in its manifold forms shows, in any such distinction, all such theories seem to me to ignore that deep division of the soul, as we find it, against itself which testifies to man's double environment—temporal and eternal. They conceive man as primarily a being with a strictly natural environment and destiny. This seems to me in conflict with our moral experience; the division of the soul against itself, its inability ever to be wholly content with natural good, are not, so far as I can see, peculiarities of a few, but are written large on the inner life of us all. And in principle Aristotle[1] appears to me to be right when he denies that some members of a γένος can be perishable and others imperishable. A bad-living man, after all, or a carelessly living man, is not a "mere animal", and it is not reasonable to anticipate for him a mere animal's destiny.

The difficulty becomes acute when we remember that we have to take into account not two classes of men only, but three. There are those who seem never to have been awakened out of mere worldliness, those who have been wakened by the call of the eternal and have followed it, and there are also those who have heard the call and refused to follow, or have followed for a time and turned back. To me, as to von Hügel,[2] it seems clear that the troublous problem is that of the destiny of this third class, the "apostates", who make the "great refusal".

I have indeed owned already to a doubt about the very existence of men who not only *seem*, but *are*, wholly unawakened. It is not clear to me that there are any merely "animal" men, who have *never* felt, however obscurely, the solicitation of a more than temporal good. But *if* there are such men, it would be conceivable that their destiny should be as limited as the good to which they respond. Their destination

[1] *Met.* 1058 b 26.   [2] *Essays and Addresses* (First Series), pp. 195 ff.

might conceivably be that suggested by von Hügel, unending enjoyment of a purely temporal good in a *Limbo* which is technically, indeed, "Hell", but is, in fact, a more satisfactory habitat than Europe, even in the pre-war days.

But there is no doubt whatever about the existence of men who are "spiritually awake" and yet false to the good to which they are awake. James Boswell may serve as a tragic historical example of the class, and it is well with any of us whose conscience does not misgive him that he may be in the same group. What I find clearly incompatible with an ethical faith is the easy belief that the destiny of the "awakened" man who obstinately persists in disobedience to the heavenly vision can possibly be the same as that of the man, if there is one, whose "vegetable" slumber has never been disturbed at all. Good nature is surely at variance with ethics when it suggests that the man who chooses known evil, and persists in his choice, remains on the moral level of the "human animal" who makes no genuine choices. What the "second death" may be, I trust none of us may ever find out, but in a morally ordered world it must surely be a terrible possibility.

The world does not become unethical because it contains potentialities of tragedy; there is the possibility of the tragic in all ethical situations. It would become an unethical world if it were so constituted as to make human choice merely frivolous; μέγας ὁ ἀγών, οὐχ ὅσος δοκεῖ, τὸ χρηστὸν ἢ κακὸν γενέσθαι.

Hence there seems to me to be something seriously unethical in the view that we stand to win eternal life if we make our choice rightly, but to lose only temporal good if we persist in choosing wrongly. There is something, to my mind, unsuited to the moral dignity of man in the thought that the end of the man hardened

in wrong is the "end of a dog"; it is worthier of humanity that there should be no escape from the law that,
for good or bad, we gravitate to our likes and "do and
have done to us what is befitting". We are here in our
life somewhere on a ladder, where there are as many
rungs below us as above. Happily, we know that he
who has descended very far and very often may begin
to climb again, and may even outstrip some who had
long been above him, but that every descent will be
followed by a reascent seems to me to be what we may
possibly hope, but have no sure ground for affirming.

As Glaucon said long ago to Socrates,[1] there are
always the disquieting examples which seem to show
that even exceeding wickedness does not tend of itself
to impair intense intellectual vitality. Stupidity and
animality are not the special characteristics of the
"incurables", the greatly bad men who are the curse
of humanity. It is perhaps not clear that even the
sturdiest theistic optimism absolutely requires us to
expect the complete elimination from the world of the
spirit
    der stets das Böse will, und stets das Gute schafft.

Even if this should be an implication of the ethical
view of the world, at least it does not carry with it the
further implication that we can escape the full consequences of our persistent evil-doing by simply "paying the debt of nature". A living divine was recently
reported, correctly or not, to have declared that "if
there are really diabolical men, no doubt, their destiny
is perdition, but I should hope that such men are very
few". I should like myself to hope that there are none
such, but there is just one man, of the many whom I
have known, about whom I feel it is salutary not to be
over-sanguine, myself.

[1] *Republic*, 610 D 5.

VIII

OTHER-WORLDLINESS

As Birds robb'd of their native wood,
  Although their Diet may be fine,
Yet neither sing, nor like their food,
  But with the thought of home do pine;

So do I mourn and hang my head,
  And though thou dost me fullness give,
Yet look I for far better bread,
  Because by this man cannot live.
                                    VAUGHAN.

Exeamus igitur ad eum extra castra.

THROUGHOUT our past argument we have repeatedly
spoken of the contrast between the eternal and the
secular, or temporal, as something familiar and fundamental in the common experiences of the moral life.
We have thus assumed that there is an element of the
"other-worldly" present throughout in the common
everyday life of the simple good neighbour and honest
citizen, that it is a duty for all of us to practice other-
worldliness, and not to live as though "this" world
were the only world there is. It may be well to pause
here and ask ourselves to what practical rule of conduct
such an assumption commits us, and whether that rule
indeed has the sanction of the morality by which we all
live. What is the true relation of the "other" world to
the whole system in which we find ourselves bound up
by the fact that we are members of a great animal
"kingdom", existing in a definite space-time region of

the universe, and members, moreover, of a historical society of humanity, living and deceased. We cannot but remember that while this thought of the dual citizenship of man, as at once a "child of nature" and a being who is something more than "natural", has inspired the practical teaching of the greatest of philosophical moralists from Plato to Kant, it is also fashionable among reputable philosophers to decry this so-called "dualism" as a fatal error, and to find in it the central flaw of Platonism, the "excrescence" on Kant's doctrine which had to be cut away by the surgery of Fichte and Hegel before the critical philosophy could bear its true fruits.[1] There are not two worlds, it is often said, but only one; that "other world is just this world rightly understood": it is the death of all morality to direct our aims or set our hopes on a *saeculum venturum*, just as Bosanquet has said that it is the death of idealism to project its ideals into the *future*.

The same radical conflict of standpoints meets us in the estimation of poetry, and the arts generally. We are told, to be sure, of the "consecration and the poet's dream", and of the "light that never was on sea or land" as the aspiration of all high artistic endeavour; to say that a poet, or a painter, however admirable his work may be in other respects, is "of the earth earthy", is felt as denying his claim to rank among the greatest, even by critics wholly free from prepossessions in favour of any specifically theological interpretation of the world, just as the most unqualified opponents of

[1] "If Aristotle is limited and thwarted in his idealism by the want of formulae more elastic than those proper to number and magnitude, he less frequently lapses into the false dualism of soul and body, mind and matter, ideas and things, which made Plato, against his principles, a mystic, and which has clung like a body of death to Platonising philosophy ever since" (T. H. Green, *Works*, iii. 47). "The conception of a Ruler of the world, apparently external to the spirit of man, and of a future life, continued in Kant's philosophy as survivals, though they are, in my judgement, quite unessential to it" (Bosanquet, *Science and Philosophy*, p. 349).

any intrusion of theology into the field of ethics commonly regard it as an imputation on a man's moral theory or practice to call either "worldly". Yet, on the other side, a modern poet whom most of us would be inclined to call the reverse of a "worldling" or "worldly-wise" person, could make it his boast that

> Earth of the earth is hidden by my clay.

And it is the commonest of disparagements to say of poets and artists that they lose themselves in a world of dreams, or that their work has no contact with the coarse, brutal, fetid, but living world of common flesh and blood.

The curious fact, disclosed by this universal linguistic usage, is that, in the conduct of the life of business and social relations, we plainly agree that it is a duty to be, in some intelligible sense, a "man of the world", and yet a grave defect to be "worldly". The good man ought, if the phrase may be allowed, to be an unworldly man of the world. And, as if to warn us that we are not dealing with some mere confusion of thought, due to the imperfect emancipation of morality from the foreign control of a "moribund" theology, we find just the same seemingly paradoxical combination of qualities demanded, in the name of art, from poets, painters or musicians. They also, if they are to rank with the immortals, are to be men of this world without being worldly-minded. It is just where men believe themselves to find both qualities in perfect balance, for example in Shakespeare, or it may be in Goethe, that they confess the presence of supreme genius. It is made a claim for Shakespeare that his thought moves in the world of the actual, not in a beautiful but fanciful kingdom of dreams; *he* at least is no "ineffectual angel". But it would be felt at once to be an absurd charac-

terisation of him to call him, what we all agree to call
his brilliant contemporary Bacon, "worldly-minded".
We are commanded by our own religion, in language
familiar to us all, to be *in* the world and yet out of it.

Shakespeare was no divine, nor, so far as it is possible
to discern his personality behind his work, does he
seem likely to have felt the specifically religious aspiration to a supernatural "holiness"; yet it would be hard
to find a better phrase by which to describe the character of his ripest work. *Macbeth*, or even *The Tempest*,
deals with a life which is "of this world", the life of men
and women of flesh and blood, not that of angels or
devils, nor yet of elves or fairies. Macbeth may have
his traffic with demons; yet he is no "devil incarnate",
but a man, with a man's temptations and crimes, and
also with a man's qualities of heroism and resolution.
Ferdinand and Miranda meet and love in an enchanted
island, but they are "sublunary lovers", after all. Their
life is to be lived out in the world of common realities, and it is to be the "practical life" of marriage, the
family and mundane affairs at large. "Pictures in
their eyes to get" will most certainly not be all *their* propagation,[1] and their maturity, as the poet is careful to
let us know, has before it the very business-like task of
adjusting the affairs of two communities on a sound
basis. Milan has been thrust from Milan that his heirs
may become rulers of Naples. Even Prospero, who had

---

[1] Donne, *The Extasie*:

> "So to' entergraft our hands, as yet
>   Was all the meanes to make us one,
> And pictures in our eyes to get
>   Was all our propagation."

Contrast the tone of Prospero's warning (*Tempest* iv. 1, 51):

> "Look, thou be true; do not give dalliance
> Too much the rein: the strongest oaths are straw
> To the fire i' the blood: be more abstemious,
> Or else, good night your vow!"

once neglected his duties as duke to bury himself in his library of books of magic, has learned a more practical wisdom by the event. His island is a temporary place of refuge, not a home, and the great object to which his wizardry has been made instrumental is to effect his return to the world which "is the home of all of us".

Yet, for all this, worldliness is the last charge we should be likely to make against *Macbeth* or *The Tempest*. Shakespeare can, of course, be worldly enough when he pleases. Falstaff and Prince Hal, for example, think and speak, from first to last, "like men of this world", and it is just their fundamental earthiness which makes the second repellent and the first, at his brightest, a creature to whom no one could lose his heart. But it is not in such characters that we see Shakespeare's measure of humanity, nor, I would add, to them that we must believe their creator's heart to be given. Macbeth sinks into a hell of murderous frustrated ambition against which a man like Falstaff is secured by his very carnality; yet, even in his ruin, it is Macbeth, not Falstaff, who ennobles our conception of humanity by the revelation of what a man can be, for good or evil. The Beatrices and Rosalinds of Shakespeare's earlier days are, at bottom, "good girls" enough; the Cleopatra of his maturity is an incarnate corruption; yet, with all the corruption, Cleopatra has the touch of a quality which the earlier sympathetic heroines do not reveal. She has, as no Rosalind nor Portia of them all had, "immortal longings", windows of the soul open on Heaven and on Hell, and the difference makes her not less, but more, a revelation of the universal woman in all women. The presence of something which is not "of this world" in her makes her the more overpoweringly real. If there are good and evil characters in Shakespeare's gallery

of whom we could say with some measure of justice
that they are dreams rather than solid realities, we
must say this of just the more ordinary good and bad
figures of his less fully mature work.

By the side of Othello, Henry Vth is unreal, Brutus
is unreal; all the earlier women are dreams and fan-
tasies by the side of Lady Macbeth or Cleopatra. It
is just where the figures, for good or evil, impress us
with the sense of being something more than earthly
that we feel the poet's grip on the realities of our
"moral being" firmest. Othello and Macbeth are not,
like so many characters in Shakespeare's earlier work,
merely playing their parts in a pleasant interlude, nor,
like even Henry Vth, walking in a pageant in honour
of England. They are fighting for their lives in a
battle where the stakes are Heaven and Hell, and it is
because the battle is so grim and the stakes so fearful
that we feel that the fight is being waged, not in fairy-
land, but in the real waking world of our common life.
And if anyone should fancy that *The Tempest*, at any
rate, is only a dream of an enchanted island, he must
be curiously blind to the truth that, there too, the same
battle is being waged, however fantastic the weapons,
for the souls of a criminal king and his more criminal
counsellors.

> You are three men of sin, whom Destiny—
> That hath to instrument this lower world
> And what is in't—the never-surfeited sea
> Hath caused to belch you up; and on this island
> Where man doth not inhabit, you 'mongst men
> Being most unfit to live . . .
>   . . . whose wraths to guard you from—
> Which here, in this most desolate isle, else falls
> Upon your heads—is nothing but heart-sorrow
> And a clear life ensuing.

The words are spoken by Ariel in the disguise of a

Harpy, but they fix us at the heart of real life. The
element of the fantastical is in their setting, not in
their sense. Similarly we misread the famous words of
Prospero, that

> We are such stuff
> As dreams are made on, and our little life
> Is rounded with a sleep,

if we hear nothing more than an echo of the Horatian
pulvis et umbra sumus. They would be both trivial and
misplaced if we did not understand that there is an
infinite seriousness behind the seeming futility of the
parts man plays in the brief puppet-show. It is the tension between the sense of this underlying earnest and
the apparent vanity of life that explains the speaker's
reference to the "beating mind" from which his words
come.

We are not to be surprised, then, if the same problem of a life which has to be lived out in "this world",
with all its apparent tangle of accident and restricted
incidental issue, and yet is directed on an end which
redeems life from tedium and frivolity, precisely because this world cannot exhaust it, reappears, in principle, in the most measured and sober rule of practice
a moralist can devise. We shall expect to find that life
may be marred in practice in either of two ways. It
is marred if we lose ourselves in concentration on
a mere manageable success which we, or our children,
can see with our own eyes; if we mistake the proverb
of the bird in the hand for the last word of moral wisdom. It is marred in another way, if we lose our sense
of the imperatively necessary "here and now", the
duty of the moment, in preoccupation with what lies
beyond every now and every here. We need to learn
the double lesson that there is no more certain way
of being unfaithful in much than to be careless of

being faithful in little—for there are, indeed, no mere "littles" in the moral world—and no more certain way of being unfaithful in little than to be satisfied with aiming at little. In fact, we need to reconsider and state more correctly a familiar formula which has already been used in a context where it was accurate enough for the immediate purpose. The true rule of life, we said, was to combine detachment with attachment, to use and love all goods but the highest without losing our hearts to them, that when the call to let them go comes to us we may be able to obey without breaking our hearts. But, if we would speak with a nicer accuracy, we must rather say that the rule is not simply to make the best use of the lower and temporal goods, while they last, and then to let them go with a will; it is to use them in such fashion that the very using is itself an act of devotion to the higher and more abiding. It is not enough that whole-hearted possession should be *followed*, in due time, by equally whole-hearted surrender; there is a more excellent way which unites possession and surrender in the same act.

This is the most difficult of achievements for us, who, even in what is called the autumn of our lives, are mostly mere beginners in the pilgrimage from the seen to the eternal, but it is a task which we must essay, unless our lives are to end in moral failure. Unless we have at least a beginning with the lesson, the division of the self against itself is not even on the way to be healed. We are still at the mercy of the before and after, still "in our sins". We have found, it may be, an answer to the two first of R. Hillel's pithy questions, "If I am not for myself who is for me, and if I am only for myself, where is the good of me?" The third still confronts us, unsolved and insistent—"And if not now, when?"

Let me illustrate what I mean by a concrete example which I have used elsewhere.[1] "A man discharges the duty of a husband and a parent in a secular spirit, if he has no aim beyond giving his wife a 'happy time of it' and bringing up his children to enjoy a lucrative, honourable or comfortable existence from youth to old age". I interrupt the self-quotation to add that a man would still be discharging *these* offices in a secular spirit if, Indian fashion, he had it in mind, later on, when the work has been done, to retire to the forests, and there give his old age to retired meditation. The more excellent way—one says it with shame, as one reflects on the failure in one's own practice—is that indicated in the sequel of the quotation, to which I return: "Marriage and parenthood become charged with a sacramental spirit, and the discharge of their obligations a *Christian* duty, when the 'principal intention' of parents is to set forward a family in the way to know and love God, and to be spiritual temples for His indwelling". Where such an end is attained, and so far as it is attained, the "flesh" is not merely "suppressed" in the interest of the "spirit", it is made the minister of the spirit, as "necessity", in Plato's *Timaeus*, is made the Creator's "workman",[2] perfectly subdued to His purpose in the ordering of the world. Where it is not achieved there is a double failure. A man, for instance, cannot set his son forward on the way to know and love God, except by bringing him up to some definite honourable and useful life of service to a specific community; but, again, he cannot bring him up to render the service adequately if

---

[1] *Essays Catholic and Critical*, p. 81.

[2] ὑπηρέτης. Cf. Plato, *Tim.* 46 c 7 ταῦτ᾽ οὖν πάντα ἔστιν τῶν συναιτίων οἷς θεὸς ὑπηρετοῦσιν χρῆται τὴν τοῦ ἀρίστου κατὰ τὸ δυνατὸν ἰδέαν ἀποτελῶν, 68 E 4 χρώμενος μὲν ταῖς περὶ ταῦτα αἰτίαις ὑπηρετούσαις, τὸ δὲ εὖ τεκταινόμενος ἐν πᾶσιν τοῖς γιγνομένοις αὐτός.

he himself looks, and teaches his son to look, to no end beyond that definite service to that specific community.

If, for example, a man wants his son to give of his best to Scotland as a public servant, it is not enough that he should educate the son to be a public servant; he must be even more concerned that the lad should be a good Scotsman than that he should be a good civil servant. And if he would have the boy a good Scotsman, he must make it a still more vital concern that he shall become a true man. And a true man's ultimate loyalty cannot even be to "humanity". There are services which I must not render, even to "the well-being of humanity". If I may indulge once more in self-quotation,[1] "it may be argued that for the good of the human race I ought to be prepared to sacrifice the very independence of my native land, but for no advantage to the whole body of mankind may I insult justice by knowingly giving sentence or verdict against the innocent".

In a word, just as the only way to be a thoroughly good professional man is to aim at being something more than a professional man—for example, at being a good citizen—and the only way to be a thoroughly good citizen is to aim at being, at any rate, a "good European", or something of the kind, so the only way to be a good man or a good "citizen of the world" is again to aim at being something more. I believe no moral theory can ignore this without identifying morality with mere conventional respectability, and so stultifying itself. For we may take it as certain that a moral code which enjoins respectability as the supreme obligation will not long ensure that its followers shall remain even respectable. As T. H. Green[2] says of

---

[1] *Essays Catholic and Critical*, p. 61.
[2] *Works*, i. 371 (*Introduction to Hume*, II.).

Hume, it is because he derationalises respectability that "he can find . . . no room for the higher morality. . . . An 'ideal' theory of ethics tampers with its only sure foundation when it depreciates respectability." Green goes on to say, in impressive words, that "there is no other 'enthusiasm of humanity' than one which has travelled the common highway of reason, the life of the good neighbour and honest citizen, and can never forget that it is still only on a further stage of the same journey".

But it is obviously implied in such a statement that the goal of the "journey", though it may not disclose itself to the traveller's conscious vision until many stages of the way have been achieved, from the first lay beyond anything which can be adequately described as "citizenship" or "neighbourliness", and therefore beyond the horizon of the "temporal" world. Thus, in spite of a certain tendency to minimise the "supernatural" factor in the moral life, a tendency which leads him from time to time to depreciate the significance of moral crises and "conversions", and, on occasion, to caricature Platonism, Green bears witness, one might almost say *malgré lui*,[1] to the impossibility of getting the note of "other-worldliness" out of a genuine practical morality.

At the same time, it is equally clear that there is no way of effectively "having our citizenship in heaven" except the way of discharging the specific duties of this place and this time *as* duties which have an ultimate source of obligatoriness lying beyond the now and here, thus making God, in the scholastic phrase, our "principal intention"[2] in the discharge of those homely duties.

---

[1] Or, more truly one might say, *malgré la tradition hegélienne*, to which Green, happily, was not completely subdued.

[2] Not necessarily our conscious intention. "The supernatural should not be directly identified and measured by the amount of its conscious, explicit refer-

You cannot do justice to the demands of morality itself if you follow the lead of Aristotle by bisecting human life into a "service of the divine" to be achieved by "speculation", and a lower "practical life" of service to the human community. This is, in effect, to have one aim for the working-days of the week and another for Sundays, to be the honest citizen and good neighbour on common days, the "thinker" or man of science on high-days and festivals. In practice such a sundering of the life of the "divine something in man" from the "life of man" is bound to degrade both. If our duties as men and citizens are regarded as something secondary and inferior, it will not be long before they come to be discharged in a perfunctory fashion, as tasks to be got over and out of the way that we may escape with all speed to the higher work of the study and the laboratory; we shall be too anxious to be good physicists, or chemists, or metaphysicians to be more than very second-rate men. Again, by being thus cut off from the "work of *man*" the speculative life itself becomes impoverished and loses its seriousness. The resulting degradation may show itself in a great variety of ways. In some lives it appears as engrossment in so-called "religious" duties to the neglect of the simple humanities of life. Then we get the man, for example, who identifies the "spiritual life" with absorption in ceremonial "devotions", or solitary meditation, at the cost of forgetting to be a good husband, or father, or neighbour. Or we may consider the type whose prosecution of the "speculative life" takes the form of preoccupation with a science which has become dehumanised, the man who pursues knowledge as a mere gratification

for his curiosity, or even devotes himself to the discovery of new curses for humanity — "poison-gases"
and the like—for discovery's sake.

In principle, the source of the degradation is the
same in all these cases: the devotee of a life of the "divine
element in man", supposed to be severed from the
"work of man", naturally becomes a specialist in something at the cost of failing to "make a *man* of himself".
It is a little strange that Green, of all men, should have
reproached Plato with a "false dualism which has clung
like a body of death to Platonising philosophy ever
since",[1] without reflecting that *this* "dualism" is specifically Aristotelian. Its source is, in fact, the fatal error
of dividing life into a higher sphere of "speculation"
and a lower realm of "practice", which, as it is supposed,
can be kept distinct, and it is against just this fatal
severance of "active good living" from the "higher
spiritual life" that Plato is setting his face when he
insists that neither the "philosopher" nor the "king"
can be what he should be until the two parts are united
in the same person.[2]

There is, then, a sense in which "other-worldliness"
would really be the death of all morality. Morality
withers at once if we are serious with that bisection of
life into one part devoted to the "secular", and another
given to the "eternal", which is made verbally by anyone who draws a sharp distinction between "secular"
and "eternal" interests, or "secular" and "religious"
duties. But there is also a sense in which "other-worldliness" is the very breath of the moral life. If we understood by a "religious" duty a duty which can be discharged otherwise than by making the right response

[1] *Works*, iii. p. 47.

[2] Cf. *Rep.* 497 A 3 οὐδέ γε, εἶπον, τὰ μέγιστα (*sc.* διαπράξεται ὁ φιλόσοφος), μὴ
τυχὼν πολιτείας προσηκούσης· ἐν γὰρ προσεχούσῃ αὐτός τε μᾶλλον αὐξήσεται καὶ μετὰ
τῶν ἰδίων τὰ κοινὰ σώσει.

here and now in a temporal situation, we should have
to say that morality recognises no such duties; all duties
are acts which it is incumbent to perform in some *now*.
But, in another sense, morality recognises no "secular"
duties; all its tasks are "religious", in the sense that, to
be adequately discharged, they have to be undertaken
in a religious spirit, a spirit of loyalty to something
which may demand the renunciation, and always does
demand the subordination, of every loyalty to concrete
temporal individuals and communities. How deeply
rooted genuine morality is in such a loyalty to the
"other" world we see most clearly, if we consider the
glaring and fatal objection to "humanitarianism", that
is, to the theory which finds the justification of moral
imperatives simply in the representation of them as
the claims of a human society, of the present or the
future, on the loyalty of its individual members. Perhaps, in view of the unfortunate popularity of a false
humanitarianism in current moral speculation, and the
grave danger that speculative error of this kind may
infect practice, a brief digression may be permissible at
this point.

(1) All duties, so we are told by a host of fashionable writers, are *social* duties. And the theory has been
sometimes preached, even by those who should know
better, to the length of denying that prayer, meditation,
participation in the public worship of God, sacramental
or other, are duties at all, on the ground that we cannot
specify the human persons with reference to whom, or
the precise ways in which, these activities are socially
beneficial. This is obviously hardly a fair deduction
from the premises of humanitarianism itself. For it
might well be that a man's whole discharge of his
functions as citizen and neighbour is made much more
thorough and single-minded by his hours of private

or public devotion, though we cannot specify any particular person, or group of persons, particularly benefited, or any particular performance which is the direct outcome of this devotion. Indeed—and this is a consideration to be remembered in estimating the social value of the technically "religious" life of the "monk" —the practice of the whole community may be affected in the same way for the better by the presence within it of individuals or groups whose whole activity is given to such devotion.[1]

But there is a criticism which it is not so easy for the humanitarian to dispose of, and this criticism may take several forms. We may ask, for instance, whether it is really true, as some writers are fond of asserting, that a Robinson Crusoe—at any rate an "atheistic" Crusoe— convinced that his restoration to human society is out of the question, ceases to be under any moral obligations; or whether it is true that, if the human race knew itself to be menaced by inevitable destruction in some cosmic cataclysm to-morrow, there would be no moral objection to general abandonment to-day to a frenzy of license. The behaviour of whole populations in times of pestilence or civil war, when a general dissolution of society is apprehended to be at hand, as well as the conduct of castaways, or the disturbing facts which not uncommonly come out at inquests on persons who have joined in a "death pact", seems to show that there is some ground for believing that many men do *de facto* draw the conclusion, "since we must die to-morrow, we cannot be blamed for giving the rein to our lusts to-

---

[1] Cf. Bradley, *Ethical Studies*[2], p. 337: "However secluded the religious life, it may be practical indirectly *if* through the unity of the spiritual body it can be taken as vicarious" (a correction of his own earlier attack on the *religieux*). For a rather reckless development of the view to which objection is taken in the text cp. the essay of Bosanquet, *The Kingdom of God on Earth*, already referred to (*Science and Philosophy*, pp. 333-51).

day". But the question still remains whether to act in this way is not to degrade our personality? If it is, *why* may I not spend my last moments in degrading my personality? We must not say, "because the effects on humanity will be so evil", since *ex hypothesi*, there are not going to be any effects. If our Robinson Crusoe may not "make a beast of himself" on his island— assuming him to be reasonably certain, as he might be, that he will never live to escape from it—this must be because to "make a beast of himself" is something more than an offence against a community from which he has been finally sundered.

Or we may take a different illustration which does not require the introduction of so exceptional a case as that of the solitary. Wanton cruelty is admittedly one of the vilest things we know; any man would be turned out of the most tolerant society of decent men if he were known to be in the habit of getting entertainment from the tormenting of a cat, or even of ants and flies. But *why* is such conduct reasonably held to be unpardonable? Surely not merely on the ground that because, though otherwise innocent, it may easily lead to the habit of practising cruelty towards human beings, or may be taken as an indication that the offender would certainly practice such cruelty if he had the chance. The fact is, at least, doubtful. Persons in southern Europe who show themselves callous to the sufferings of the animals, on the plea that they are not "Christians", and that we may therefore treat them as we please, do not seem to be more indifferent than Northerners to the sufferings of their fellow-men, and we all know the odious type of person whose sensibility to the sufferings of animals is only surpassed by his indifference to those of his own kind. We are familiar with the kind of man who writes indignant letters to the newspapers about the brutality of stamping out hydrophobia at the expense of a temporary muzzling order, or the selfishness of those who object to the intrusion of his dog into a railway compartment. Nor yet can we say that the exceeding vileness of the cruelty is measured by the suffering inflicted on the victim. It must be highly doubtful, for example, whether a fly or an ant is really capable of feeling much in the way of suffering. So far as we can tell, the "corporal sufferance" of the beetle on which we tread is *not* comparable with an ordinary human toothache. Yet the strongest conviction that this is so does not affect our abhorrence of the human being who amuses himself by treading on the beetle or pulling the wings off the fly.[1]

So far as I can see, the real ground of our judgement is not that the creature suffers so much; indeed, I own that personally I should feel some touch of the same repugnance for a man who wantonly defaced the lilies of the field, which presumably do not suffer at all, and I believe I could show this feeling to be justified. But, be that as it may, I feel sure that it is the cruel *man*, rather than the suffering he causes, who is the direct object of our loathing. If there is any foundation for this judgement, it follows that our condemnation of cruelty itself, the very vice specially abhorrent to the humanitarian, has its roots in a supreme loyalty which

---

[1] Cf. J. Laird, *A Study in Moral Theory*, p. 302. As will be seen, I agree entirely with Prof. Laird in his thesis that "it is not simply the evil effects of cruelty upon humanity that makes the torturer what he is". It will also be seen why I am not satisfied with his own explanation that the "sufferings of the victims who are not men" are the "chief condemnation" of the torturer. In many cases our tendency is to exaggerate these sufferings by imagining what we suppose we should feel if, retaining our own acute sensibility, we were subjected to analogous treatment. We think of the fly deprived of its wing suffering what *we* should suffer if our arm were torn from us, exactly as, in Adam Smith's familiar illustration, we judge of the cheerfulness of the condition of a lunatic who is completely self-satisfied, by imagining what we suppose we should feel, could we *per impossibile* be at once the lunatic and the sane spectator.

is not loyalty to the fellowship of human persons, nor even to the fellowship of sentient creatures.

(2) It is the same with all the virtues which ennoble human life. They are all to be found at their best only where human society is not made the *principal* end and the *supreme* object of loyalty. As has been already said, the noblest national life is impossible where nationality is taken as the ultimate principle of allegiance and *salus rei publicae suprema lex* as the great commandment. So a world-wide federation of mankind would prove morally disappointing and, in fact, would hardly be likely to subsist long, unless it were recognised that there are some prices too heavy to be paid even for the continued existence of federated humanity. Mankind itself is best served by those who feel the duty of serving it to be one they owe to something more august and worthy to be loved than humanity, just as, to use the words of one of our most penetrating critics, "the advance of civilisation is, in truth, a sort of by-product of Christianity—not its chief aim; but we can appeal to history to support us that this progress is most stable and genuine when it is a by-product of a lofty and unworldly idealism".[1] (A considered study of the social, economic, literary, and artistic debt of Europe to St. Francis, or of England to men like Wesley, or the Tractarian leaders, would furnish an interesting commentary.)

The point we are concerned to make, then, is that "other - worldliness" does not mean the neglect of obvious duties of the temporal world in which we are living, for the sake of some wholly different set of obligations. It means the discharge of the duties of the situation as the man who is unworldly sees them, in a spirit of loyalty to a kingdom which is not of this world.

[1] Inge, *Personal Life and the Life of Devotion*, p. 84.

We may say, if we please, that, at bottom, "religious" and "secular" duties are the same, but that they may be discharged in a secular or in a religious spirit. Even what are properly called more specifically the "duties of religion" have their secular side, their value in holding the actual community of the living together in a bond of good fellowship. For example, a man who, from intellectual conscientiousness, cuts himself off from the public worship of his society may, in a particular case, have no alternative, if he is to be an honest man, yet his efficiency as good neighbour and citizen will, none the less, often be really impaired.[1] The Oxford latitudinarian tutor of a (probably apocryphal) story, who urged an agnostic undergraduate to communicate with others at the altar, on the ground that "it keeps the College together, like dinner in Hall", was uttering a sentiment which I take to be no less repugnant to Agnostics than to Anglicans. Yet the remark, so far as it goes, is undeniably true. What really shocks a finer nature is not that the statement is untrue, but that it bases an obligation which, if real, ought to have a more august source, on merely secular principles. It treats an act which, to be adequately justified, must be justified by a relation between man and God as though its *raison d'etre* could be furnished by a mere social relation between members of the same college.

We put the same thought from a different point of view when we say, in the fashion of George Herbert, that any so-called secular duty becomes "work for God" when it is done in the spirit of service to Him, and thus acquires a new "sanctification":

---

[1] I remember years ago hearing F. H. Bradley make the point in a conversation on the "ethics of conformity" by asking the question whether an "agnostic" lord of the Manor would not have a duty to attend Church regularly, if the parson were an admirable man whose moral influence for good in the parish would be seriously impaired by the "squire's" non-attendance on his ministrations.

Who sweeps a room as for Thy laws
Makes that and the action fine.

And the principal matter is that "secular" duties
themselves are only then most efficiently performed
when they receive this sanctification. If a room is to
be well swept, an empire well governed, or any other
piece of service to be discharged as well as it can
be, the work must be done by someone who does not
regard the sweeping, or the governing, as its one be-
all and end-all, just as to make any human relation
yield its worthiest fruit, it must not be treated as an all-
sufficient end in itself.[1]

Speaking generally, we may say that we shall not
detect the indispensability of "other-worldliness" in a
sound morality if we look exclusively for evidence
to the moments of tension and crisis, when there is
a direct clash between the embodied loyalties of the
family, the nation, the brotherhood of nations, and an
unembodied loyalty to something which lies beyond
them all. These crises are, after all, exceptional occasions; in the average life of the simple good man they
never present themselves recognisably. He may never
be faced with the clear and sharp alternative of disobeying God to obey man, or disobeying man to obey
God; at any rate, such sharply defined alternatives are
not habitually characteristic of the ordinary dutiful
life. But the other characteristic of the moral life of
which we have been speaking—viz. that the duties
arising from our embodied loyalties are only discharged
to the height when they receive a final consecration
from a loyalty which has no embodiment—is omnipresent and all-pervasive. To serve men with one's

[1] Cf. St. Thomas, *S.T.* ii[a] ii[ae] q. 123, art. 7 resp. dicendum quod duplex est
finis, scilicet proximus et ultimus . . . sic ergo dicendum quod fortis sicut proxi-
mum finem intendit ut similitudinem sui habitus exprimat in actu . . . finis
autem remotus est beatitudo vel Deus.

might, one must do the service "not as to men, but as to the Lord". A morality in which there is not this pervasive and ever-present note of the "other-worldly", I would urge, has already lost that which makes all the difference between a living morality and an ossified conventionalism. It has lost that possibility of adventure which is the soul of morality and science.

Thus, ethically considered, the relation between, "this" world and the "other" is not that the "other" is something wholly foreign which is to follow upon "this" world. The "other" is with us already, seizing on "this" and transforming it, and, by that very fact, providing the element of adventure without which "this" life would sink into a monotonous routine. Eternity is not a time to come after time is over; it is rather, to use the imagery of Heraclitus, the ever-present fire to which time is the fuel. Or we may put the situation in Peripatetic phraseology, if we say that "this" world is to the "other" as matter to form. The moral problem is the problem of educing from, or superinducing on, the familiar stuff of our daily secular life a form or pattern which endows it with the quality of completeness and finality.

Possibly I may make my precise point more clearly by considering the significance of two well-known deliverances which have won a considerable amount of acceptance, the sayings that "it is the death of idealism to project its ideals into the future", and that "the other world is simply this world rightly understood". The first of these sayings, perhaps, bears more directly on the practical business of the right direction of conduct, the second on the speculative question of the philosophical implications of loyal acceptance of the ethical standard. But the spirit of both is the same, and it will clarify our thoughts to ask how far we can accept either.

(1) "It is the death of idealism to transfer its ideals to the future." The words are Professor Bosanquet's, but my object is not to discuss the particular question of the sense in which their author meant them to be understood. There is obviously a sense—though I do not suppose it to be what Bosanquet intended—in which the statement is wholly true. It would be the death of all practical idealism to lose itself in a day-dream of a good and beautiful world, thought of as not here now, but bound, in the nature of things, to arrive in a "good time coming". The business of morality is not to find an escape from the triviality, sordidness, or cruelty of the actual present by dreaming idly of a Utopia; it is to make the present better by reshaping it in the image of the ideal. Or perhaps even that statement is misleading, since we do not and cannot enjoy a clear and well-defined picture of our ideal as embodied in concrete institutions. At best we see two or three steps ahead of us; we know certainly of this or that which is amiss and demands to be righted now and here, and we know the spirit in which the adventure of righting it ought to be undertaken. Contemplation of imaginary Utopias, unless it is undertaken half in play, and more with a view to illustrating the spirit of social goodness than as a programme of actual reform, is probably, in the main, mischievous. It means, according to personal temperament, either cessation from actual strenuous effort to "set the crooked straight", or the frustration of effort by the attempt, characteristic of the *doctrinaire* in all ages, to "canalise" life once and for all. An "ideal" of practical value cannot be a vision of the future, pure and simple, because it must be an inspiration and a call to daily and hourly action now.

And, again, there is a different sense in which the statement would be merely and very dangerously false. The meaning may be—on the lips of some of those who use this language, I suspect that it is—that time, and, along with time, imperfection and evil and the moral struggle are mere illusions. It is a pure mistake to suppose that there is really anything which calls to be put right here and now, for *here* and *now* are themselves illusions. If we could only see things from the "point of view of the Absolute", we should see that what is is already a finished and flawless whole; everything is not only "the best possible under the conditions", but wholly and perfectly good.

Plainly this kind of metaphysical optimism, if we could seriously make it the spirit of our lives, would be the ruin of all practical effort; it would leave us with no rational justification for doing anything in particular, rather than anything else. And, no less plainly, the theory involves a hopeless logical contradiction which makes it as false speculatively as it is pernicious in practice. It asserts the existence of both evil and succession in its very attempt to deny them. For it declares that everyone, except its own adherents at moments when they are under its own sway, is suffering from an "illusion" due to a partial, and therefore falsified, outlook on the world. And it exhorts us to replace this partial view by one taken from "the standpoint of the whole". Thus it says at once that there is no evil and that there is at least the one and all-inclusive evil that we—or most of us—mistakenly believe in the existence of evils; it says that there is in truth no futurity, and also that we should, *for the future*, believe that futurity is an illusion. Reduced to its simplest terms, it in fact maintains that *time* is a word with no significance, an "unmeaning noise". And with this metaphysical view morality too, must become an illusion; for morality is *making* the best of ourselves, our endowments and opportunities, bringing what *ought* to be into actual existence—that or nothing.

If, then, it is false to think of an "ideal" simply as something which is not as yet, but some day will be, it is equally false to think of it as having no reference to futurity. The better is not simply what is yet to be, but it *is* something which is not yet actual, and for that very reason it impresses on us the obligation to act with the intention that it shall be brought about. When all is said, the moral life really is a γένεσις εἰς οὐσίαν, a growth into moral maturity, and its claims on us are bound up with the recognition that "becoming" has its place in reality, no less than "being". Growth is not mere succession or transience, nor even mere transience according to some regular pattern of transition; it is rather the achievement of an identity of pattern which steadily makes itself, within a succession where there was at first random variation.

So far, at least, the nineteenth century evolutionary formulae are clearly sound; as anything grows, it acquires an increasing power of maintaining its own *esse* by increasing skill in self-adaptation to changes in its surroundings. It may begin by being changed almost out of recognition in response to modification without. It only becomes *mature* in the degree to which it learns to meet such modifications by responses which leave it more and more recognisably the same. A thing which had "perfectly adapted" itself would neither remain obstructive and irresponsive against suggestions from without, like a lump of granite, nor take a new impress from every change of circumstance, with the ductibility of an ideally plastic sheet of wax. It would be infinitely rich in artifices of response to the variations in its surroundings, and yet, under all the variety of its responses, it would keep the pattern which was definitely its own, as a profoundly civilised human society proves its high civilisation by ability to reproduce its typical institutions without impairment under transplantation to unfamiliar climates. An Englishman or a Scot, it is said, will remain an Englishman or a Scot, if you translate him to the North Pole or the Equator. He carries his pattern with him wherever he goes. This is sometimes regarded as a mark of "insularity"; to me it seems rather a presumption of high civilisation. *Plus ça change, plus c'est la même chose* should be exactly true of the "perfectly evolved" type; the types which "go under" are those which either do not know how to change, or do not know how to be *la même chose* under the variations.

(2) And this, in principle, decides our verdict on the second saying, that the "other" world is "the world rightly understood". The saying may be true or false, according to the sense put on the word "understood". We have probably all heard the *mot* which defines a violin solo as the "dragging of the tail of a dead horse across the intestines of a dead cat", and perhaps other sayings which dispose of intimate human relationships in the same fashion. Nor do I doubt that there really is a type of man to whom a definition like this would appeal as a correct account of what music "really is"; what is more than this in the significance of music to the music-lover, such a man would say, is simply unreal, a pleasing illusion, perhaps, but still an illusion which is dissipated by being "understood". Philosophers of the now, as I hope, diminishing school who maintain that all nature's apparent wealth of colour, sound, and scent is somehow merely super-

added by "the mind" to a "reality" which is only a
complicated kinematical dance of particles seem committed by their metaphysics to a view of the kind. But
we should hardly claim for the serious champion of
such a view that he had much "understanding" of
the music. In fact, our homely vernacular comment on
his utterance would probably be couched in the words,
"the man who can say that simply does not understand what music is". To him the "world" in which
the man who does "understand" music habitually lives
would be simply an "other" world, to which he possesses
no key; it is because that world is so wholly "other",
that he calls it illusion. From the musical man's point
of view, it is his own "world" of beautiful melodic
or contra-puntal pattern which is "this" world and
the reality; the dead horse and the dead cat belong
to what is, to him, an "other" world of the merely
irrelevant and "unreal".

The philosopher, with both views before him, has
the task of integrating them. From his point of view,
neither the melody with its qualitative wealth, nor
the dead horse and dead cat, can be dismissed as
simply unreal, or belonging to a "world" of illusion.
In the one world of the real, as he sees it, there are both
the melody and the dead brutes. But they are not
connected by a mere "togetherness", and do not stand
on the same level. The hairs of the dead horse and the
guts of the dead cat, as constituents of the violinist's
bow and violin, have a real character which they have
not outside that setting, simply as so much dead hair or
gut. Further, bow and violin in use are themselves
simply *instruments* for the creation of the heard
music. What the "Philistine" calls the reality is only
the *matter*, the melody itself is the *form* of the whole
reality, and the dominant feature in it. The man who

discovered how to make the remains of the dead horse and dead cat minister to the musician was not super-imposing an illusion on reality; he was revealing to his fellows rich characters of the real world to which they had formerly been deaf, by teaching them *how* dead gut and dead hair enter into the pattern of the real, *how* these "objects" are "ingredient into events".

The long line of discoverers who have gradually fashioned our instruments of music, and the long line of composers and executants who have made them increasingly instrumental to the expression of beautiful patterns, have disclosed to us a world which is startlingly "other" by contrast with all the reality accessible to those who came before them, but the disclosure has been all along a disclosure of the riches contained in the complex pattern of the real world, not a "psychic addition" of steadily accumulating unreality. Only in that sense can the "other" world of music be fairly said to be "this" world of horse-hair and catgut "rightly understood"; and that is not the sense in which those who accuse Platonism, or Christianity, of a false other-worldliness commonly wish the saying to be interpreted. Like all discoverers and inventors, by teaching us what can be done with certain things the musicians have taught us to know what the things "really" are. In a recent bad novel, a materialistic professor was credited with the statement that he himself *was* "four buckets of water and a bagful of salts". But, of course, a living body, even when it is not the body of a distinguished scientific professor, is *not* pailfuls of water and a few salts; it is a living human body. And a violin is *not* so many feet of catgut stretched on a board; what it *is* you learn by hearing a great violinist play great music on it.

We might say, then, that what happens to us as

we learn to appreciate the beautiful, in music or any
other art, is that just those features of the rich and complex pattern of reality which were, to begin with, to us
an "other" world, dimly descried and dream-like, become increasingly relevant and dominantly real; what
was our given "reality" becomes increasingly subordinate and unreal. It is not too much to say that, as
we advance in appreciation, substance and shadow
exchange parts. And this is also exactly what happens in the process of moral development, as immediate
and appetitive goods and circumscribed loyalties give
place to the more remote and intellectual goods and
the larger loyalties. As in the one case, so in the
other, there must always have been the capacity for
appreciation, or the transition could never have been
effected. But whereas we begin, in both cases, with
the dominance of the immediate and obvious, and the
appeal of the more remote and ultimate, when it is
consciously felt, comes to us as an irruption or invasion from the strange and dim, breaking in on the
familiar and firmly grasped, so also, in both cases, the
suggesting "environment" to which we are growing
more sensitively responsive steadily takes on more and
more the character of a "world" in which we habitually live, and are "at home", while the once familiar
becomes an "other" from which we are increasingly
estranged. Thus it is with the cultivation of a true
"public spirit". At first it is with difficulty and on
special occasions that we are conscious of a loyalty to
something beyond our own narrow circle of relatives
and friends; the learning of citizenship is a process by
which we come habitually to take the whole body of
our fellow-citizens as the community which is to be
the standard object of reference in our conduct.

This may seem only a very small advance in moral-

isation, but it is not so small as it looks. How many
of ourselves, for example, in recent years of warfare,
showed that we had not yet learned even to think of
our country as our moral "world", by the contrast
between our readiness to fight to the last man "in the
good cause", so long as the person to be conscripted
was our neighbour, or our neighbour's only son, but
changed our note at once, as the thing "came home
to us", when it looked certain that, unless the struggle
was abandoned, we ourselves, or our own sons, would
have to be called up? It is easy to repeat the language
of devotion to an object which has rightful precedence
over our domestic ties, but far from easy to breathe
an habitual moral atmosphere in which this devotion
is always present and dominant. Yet, as we learn to
breathe that atmosphere, we are steadily coming to
"be at home" with that which once was to us the
"uncanny" and "wholly other", and to find "uncanny"
just what was once the everyday and familiar. But
patriotism is not an illusion or dream superimposed
on a "real" moral world of narrow family attachments;
family affection and patriotism belong, after all, to the
same "world". In learning to let our private family interests be subject to national public spirit, once more
we are discovering, not inventing, a pattern which is
"really" there, embedded in our "real" human nature.

Thus far, then, it seems to me that the saying "the
other world is this world rightly understood" is true.
The whole complex pattern of the one world in which
we live and have our being is made up of the most
varied strands. And it is not simply a pattern with
many and various strands; it is a pattern whose constitutive elements are themselves patterns, reproducing, in varying degrees of fullness and distinctness, the
characteristic pattern of the whole; and this is why we

can speak of the pattern of the whole as *all*-pervasive, though more clearly discernible in some of the sub-patterns than in others. This is the underlying conception characteristic of all those philosophies, such, for example as that of Plotinus in the ancient, or Leibniz in the modern world, which have made it a capital point that the real world is a hierarchised, or many-levelled, whole. How great a future such a type of philosophy has before itself is suggested by the vigour and originality with which it has been restated, almost at the present moment, by Dr. Whitehead[1] as absolutely necessary for the deliverance of Physics from the confusions of nineteenth-century material-ism, and, again, by the emphasis laid on the concept of "emergence" in the predominantly biological thought of Professor Alexander and Dr. Lloyd Morgan.

It is not my business now, even if it were within my capacity, to criticise these thinkers or to develop their suggestions further. What is to my immediate purpose is just this. The pattern of the one world embraces the whole of our own life and all that sustains it. It is not therefore to be learned only from the physical and the physiological sciences, nor even from the whole body of the sciences, since all of them, at the best, deal only with artificially constructed abstracts from the complex wealth of life, and that real world in which life is set. What is before us to be deciphered is nothing less than the whole of life; to make out its underlying pattern we must take into the account morality, art, religion, as living things. Manifestly, we cannot expect that the pattern of patterns which embraces them all should be discerned by ourselves except in dim and tentative fashion, and even this must remain impos-sible if we persist in taking so much of the pattern as

[1] Whitehead, *Science and the Modern World*, cc. ix.-xi.

is disclosed by the analysis of its more elementary features—those, for example, which are disclosed by a study of sub-patterns common to all merely physical, or even to all merely biological, structures—for the whole.

The "dominant" characters of the pattern should only be recognisable for what they really are when we set ourselves to study it in the light of the richest sub-patterns of all, those of the highest structures known to us, living and *intelligent* creatures; even then our insight must be expected to be very imperfect. The "synthetic philosophy" of Spencer, now fallen "on evil days, and evil tongues", should at least have the credit of having rightly discovered what the true problem of the philosopher is—the detection of a pattern of the whole which repeats itself in, and dominates, the patterns of its parts. The mistake of this philosophy was that it attempted to find this dominant pattern expressed fully and unambiguously in the simplest and poorest of all sub-patterns, those which are disclosed by consideration of merely physical structures. Hence its initial blunder of *defining* "evolution", taken as the key to the whole pattern, in terms of the "integration" and "disintegration" of "matter" and "motion".

Against all such attempts to find the dominant pattern of the real world in the most rudimentary abstractions, I would urge that, as our example of the violin suggests, we only succeed in "understanding" the more rudimentary pattern by recognising it as a subordinate element in the richer and more "concrete". When we say of the man who takes the scraping of the tail of the dead horse across the guts of the dead cat to be the "reality" that he only thinks this because he has no "understanding" of the music, what we mean is that, as we also habitually say, he does not "appreciate "the music, does not know how to "value" it. Our very use of the words *understanding* and *appreciation* as equivalents in such sentences is itself tantamount to denial of the alleged separation between a realm of facts, or actualities, or realities and another realm of values. To understand any partial pattern is the same thing as to appreciate it, to recognise it for what it is, a subordinate arrangement *instrumental* to a richer pattern.

Mere analysis of the violin and the bow into *their* simpler physical components would contribute nothing to this understanding. The "Philistine" in musical matters might successfully analyse the movements of the laws of the bow and the answering vibrations of the strings into a marvellously complicated dance of atoms or electrons. But however far he carried his analysis he would be no nearer "understanding" what happens when great music is greatly rendered at the end of his task than he had been at the beginning. Understanding only comes in when that which the "Philistine" takes to be the whole "pattern of the event" is seen to be only a subordinate and instrumental factor in a richer pattern whose dominant characters are just those which the "Philistine" has *ab initio* excluded from consideration; or, in other words, when the event is considered, to use Platonic language, as one in which ἀνάγκη is the ὑπηρέτης of νοῦς; or yet again, to speak with Aristotle, when the event is contemplated in the light of the *end* which gives it its characteristic *form*.[1]

A hierarchised world like the world of reality, is

---

[1] This is, in fact, the point of the famous chapter of the *Phaedo* (98 B-99 D) so much admired by Leibniz, in which Socrates explains the ground of his dissatisfaction with the doctrine of Anaxagoras. The use of the distinction between νοῦς and ἀνάγκη to make the same point comes, of course, from the *Timaeus* (47 E ff.).

necessarily a teleological world, and for that reason "materialism", in the proper philosophical sense of the term, the substitution of *analysis* into subcomponents for *integration* by reference to a dominating principle as the ideal of explanation, is strictly incompatible with real belief in any genuine "emergence".[1] This is the rock of offence on which, as it seems to me, even so subtly worked out a materialism as that of Professor Alexander, must, in the end, be shipwrecked. Since every event we can observe, from the displacement of a grain of sand to the taking of an heroic resolution like that of the three hundred at Thermopylae, or the planning of a symphony or a cathedral, or the moral transformation of Saul the persecutor into an apostle of the Gentiles, is something which has its own here and now, Professor Alexander exhibits space-time to us as the one reality of which everything is "made". The apostle of the Gentiles, for example, actually *is*, in reality, a complicated space-time pattern and, on the

---

[1] This incompatibility, as I venture to think, *saute aux yeux* all through Dr. Lloyd Morgan's volume on *Emergent Evolution*. Dr. Lloyd Morgan constructs his metaphysical scheme on the basis of two initial postulates: (*a*) Spinoza's doctrine of the independent but exactly correspondent divine "attributes"; (*b*) the reality of the "evolution" of the genuinely novel. But the reason, and the only reason, why Spinoza has to insist on (*a*) is that *he* disbelieves (*b*). If (*b*) is true, there is no reason at all why the "antecedents" of an event which is a "mode" of *cogitatio* must be looked for exclusively among other modes of the one "attribute"; on the other hand, if (*a*) is true, there has never been, and could never have been, any genuine "emergence". It is the second alternative which Spinoza adopts. Nothing can be clearer than that his view is that, *e.g.*, every movement of a living organism is completely explicable without remainder by the laws of kinematics; "adequate knowledge" of such a movement would mean the deduction of it from the attribute of *extensio*, in other words, its complete reduction to a kinematical problem.

This is logical and heroic, though wholly incredible. Dr. Morgan wants to equivocate at pleasure, to "save his face" with the high-and-dry metaphysician by calling in the authority of Spinoza, and with the biologists by zeal for evolution. This is human and pardonable, but neither heroic nor logical. Either kinematics is the one and only key to everything, or it is not; you cannot possibly have it both ways. If Spinoza's philosophy is true, the world is not "hierarchised", and there is no real "evolution"; if there is real "evolution", the world is "hierarchised", and Spinoza's philosophy is false, and cannot be saved as a compliment to his personal moral excellence. *Utrum vultis, Quirites?*

premisses of this philosophy, is nothing else, however much Professor Alexander may protest that he
is also a new pattern "emerging" from his "day of
Damascus".

In truth, the most poverty-stricken of events is infinitely more than a combination of *heres* and *nows*.
To be a space-time pattern is the most rudimentary
and general character of the most diverse events, not
the full truth about any one of them. It is precisely
because another contemporary philosopher, Dr. Whitehead, sees this so clearly that he finds himself driven
first to introduce into his own analysis of the simplest
facts something over and above the events, viz. the
"objects" which are "ingredient" in them, and then,
in his description of those objects, to construct a whole
hierarchy of "abstractions".

Now this very different rendering of the facts, which
involves recognition of the "eternal", and ultimately
of God, as an implication of all that happens seems
clearly much sounder than Professor Alexander's.
By constructing his world out of mere events without
"objects" ingredient in them, Professor Alexander involves himself in the difficulty that he has to identify
actual processes with the mere fact that *something*
is happening, without being in a position to say *what*
it is that happens. The cruder and more old-fashioned
corporealistic materialism, which did try to deal with
this question, by saying that *what* happens is displacement of permanently self-identical little bits of
stuff, may have given a very unsatisfactory solution
of the problem, but it had at least the merit of seeing
that there is a question to be answered where Professor
Alexander is content to be wilfully blind. It rightly
recoiled from the monstrosity of identifying *all* quality
with the material structure of the *ex hypothesi* quality-

less, even though, by a blunder, it reduced the list of qualities ascribed to its real world to an inadequate *minimum*.

Dr. Whitehead's theory enables him to do better; he is in a position to find a place in his real world for the infinite variety of characteristic quality with which actual life confronts us. Both he and Professor Alexander are in justifiable revolt against the bisection of this world of qualities into a real and an illusory part. But where the one saves the whole of the experienced physical fact for the real world, the other, whether he knows it or not, empties the real world of all possible content. This is the price which a philosophy has to pay when it begins by assuming that the complete explanation of a fact can be given by assigning its ἀρχαὶ ὡς ὕλη, or, in other words, that we know all about a thing when we can say "what it is made of".

What I am trying to urge, then, is this. The statement that the "other" world is "this" world rightly understood is false and mischievous, if you take it to mean that "this" world can be rightly understood by taking as its dominant pattern some pattern which you have detected by abstractive consideration of a certain restricted selection of characters. But this seems to be meant in fact by most of the philosophers who lay stress on the *dictum*. They have commonly a polemical purpose at the back of their minds; some type of event is to be excluded *a priori* from actuality and relegated to the level of "illusion", on the plea that it will not fit the known pattern of "this" world. The characters to be eliminated in this "high *priori*" way are not the same in all cases. The saying may be used as a plea for dismissing to limbo miracle, or revelation, or divine providence, or prayer, or the anticipation of a future beyond death, or almost anything you please. And, in some at least of these cases, the effect of the exclusion must be, in the long run, to make a considerable difference to the regulation of conduct. If, for example, it is baseless superstition to expect the help of God's grace in the task of living rightly, or to believe that human beings have a future beyond the grave, we should surely do right in regulating our lives on the assumption that these beliefs and expectations are illusory, and wrong in acting as though they may be something more. If they are something more, they ought to be effective in the regulation of our conduct.

Prudence is, perhaps, too often rated lower than it deserves to be by modern moralists, from the singular prejudice that it must be purely selfish in its operation, though we all know that there is such a thing as prudent regard for the interests of our children, and that a man may come short in his conduct as a father from imprudence, no less than from want of affection. But even those moralists who most degrade the meaning of prudence have not usually gone so far as to deny that it would be a moral fault in a man to neglect insuring his life when he has the opportunity, or to build his house in a region subject to dangerous earthquakes, without taking the probabilities of an earthquake into consideration. In the same way, even as a matter of prudence in the less worthy sense of the word, a man's practical decisions may be reasonably affected by his estimate of their probable effect on his own destiny—unless one is prepared, as I am not, any more than Butler[1] was, to hold that it is no culpable

---

[1] *Dissertation of the Nature of Virtue*: "It deserves to be considered, whether men are more at liberty, in point of morals, to make themselves miserable without reason, than to make other persons so. . . . It should seem that a close concern about our own interest or happiness, and a reasonable endeavour to secure and promote it, which is, I think, very much the meaning of the word prudence, in our language; it should seem that this is virtue, and the contrary behaviour faulty and blameable." Butler thus agrees with St. Thomas ($S.T.$ ii.^{a}ii.^{ae} q.4, art 4 resp.),

thing to make one's self miserable without a cause. Still more obviously may it rightly make a serious difference to the way in which a conscientious man will train his children what he expects *their* ultimate destiny to be, and to his view of the good to be promoted for mankind what he anticipates as the outcome of all human action.

When it is said, then, that the "other" world is "this" world rightly understood, I would urge that the statement should only be accepted as true with the important proviso that we can only come to a *right* understanding of "this" world as we advance in incorporating into our conception of it character after character which was originally felt as unfamiliar and belonging to a "beyond". In particular, we shall certainly be led astray if we assume that we already understand the true pattern of "this" world, when we have considered simply the patterns which present themselves in an isolated study of characteristics common to all kinematical systems, or even to all biological organisms. That which we leave out in all such specialisation — for instance, the "imponderables" which make all the difference to the moral and religious life of mankind—is no less constituent of "this" world than what we retain. To understand "this" world rightly, in any full sense, we should need to be omniscient, not merely in the sense of being acquainted with all the "facts", but in the further sense of seeing them all in their right proportions, and thus apprehending correctly the relations of dominance and subordination between them. We properly isolate different features of the whole reality for specialist study, but we should

that prudentia non solum habet rationem virtutis quam habent aliae virtutes intellectuales, sed etiam habet rationem virtutis quam habent virtutes morales, quibus etiam connumeratur.

never allow ourselves to forget that this is a process of artificial isolation, and that, in the full actual situation from which our selection has been made, the dominant factors in the pattern may conceivably be precisely those which the selection, made relative to special purposes of our own, has quite properly left out of the account.

When Laplace, if the famous anecdote be true, told Napoleon that he had omitted all mention of God from the *Mécanique céleste*, on the ground that he "had no need" of the theistic hypothesis, he may have intended a sarcasm, but he said no more than the truth. For the *analysis* of the movements of the planets, it is plainly superfluous and irrelevant to make any reference to a *Creator*, just as it would be irrelevant to introduce a theistic reference into a proof of the Pythagorean theorem. But the silence of Laplace in the one case, like the silence of Euclid in the other, affords not the faintest presumption against the theist's belief that the domination of the whole world-pattern by God is the most significant and pervasive fact in "this" world of actual life.

More generally, when we speak of understanding the world rightly, it is imperatively necessary that we should not be led astray by the Cartesian identification of "understanding rightly" with the reduction of complexity to a few simple types of relation between elements which seem, but only seem, to be self-luminous. The history of science during the last three centuries is itself the sufficient proof that this demand for "clear and distinct ideas" as the sole test of understanding has only one possible issue, the reduction of reality to a kinematical pattern, and the purely kinematical world of mere changes of configuration is the most unreal of unrealities, because it has been deliberately invented on the principle of emptying the world in which we live, and to which we have to respond, of everything which proves its reality by confronting us with an unsolved problem. It is true that, as the philosophical physicists are themselves hastening to inform us, this ideal can never be actually attained in practice. Closer examination reveals that the fundamental assumptions of a kinematical construction never are in fact the absolutely simple and obvious things they were meant to be; the apparent transparency of the deductions is only procured by the device of putting the opaque and "arbitrary" into the initial postulates.

Descartes, for example, proposed to reduce all physical and biological science to kinematics, because to his mind the postulates of an Euclidean geometry of configurations appeared matter of course, "evident by the natural light", and Leibniz cherished the same ideal. Both were condemned to failure in physics as a consequence of the impossibility of admitting into their schemes anything so "arbitrary" and devoid of "evidence by the natural light" as the concept of mass, and the gravitation-formula. Physics could not so much as get on its legs without that initial stiff dose of "arbitrary" brute fact, for which no reason could be assigned. In a sense, the more advanced of the advocates of "relativity" may be said to have realised the Cartesian programme, of the geometricising of physics, which had seemed to be ruined once for all by Newton, since they replace the whole apparatus of "forces" familiar to us in the classical Newtonian mechanics by varying "curvatures" in space-time, and thus do away with the time-honoured distinction between bodies moving "under the action of no forces" and bodies whose movements are deflected or constrained by external "forces".[1] But, as Mr. Meyerson has observed,[2] the programme is only realised by substituting for Descartes' simple and uniform "extension" a space-time continuum as complex and apparently arbitrary as the whole Newtonian scheme of "forces".

If we ever could succeed in eliminating the element of mystery and apparent arbitrariness from our accounts of the real world, we should feel that, in doing so, we had emptied it of its reality and were left with a mere product of our own imagination.[3] The real world is precisely the world in which there are no absolutely closed sub-systems or spheres; every region in it is open to influences from every other. It is the

---

[1] Hence, from the point of view in question, gravitation is the great "irrationality" of the scheme. The Newtonian *Laws of Motion*, it is assumed, are evident by the "natural light"; it is not thinkable that they should not be universally valid. This comes out with exceptional lucidity in Clerk Maxwell's treatment of these laws (*Matter and Motion*, c. iii.). The "first law" is pronounced (art. 41) to be a proposition the denial of which "is in contradiction to the only system of consistent doctrine about space and time which the human mind has been able to form", and it is clear from the reasoning by which this conclusion is reached that Maxwell really means by this that the law is "evident on inspection", that a denial of it must be not merely false, but meaningless. Even of the "third law" it is expressly said (art. 58) that denial of it is not "contrary to experience", and that "Newton's proof" of it is no "appeal to experience and observation, but a deduction of the third law of motion from the first" (in spite of the fact that Newton himself does appeal to facts of common experience—the horse pulling on the rope, etc.—to establish the proposition). The gravitation formula, on the other hand, from the time of Newton onwards, has always been admitted to have no semblance of self-evidence or rational necessity. It has to be accepted as a "brute fact" which might, for all we can see, equally well have been otherwise, and this is why Newton himself, in the well-known *Scholium Generale* at the end of the *Principia*, assumes that there must be a *cause* of gravity, though he is unable to say anything about the character of that cause. He clearly means that the truth of the laws of motion is "evident by the natural light", and so no reason need be given for their validity; this is not the case with the gravitation-formula, and therefore we must demand a reason for its truth.

[2] É. Meyerson, *La Déduction relativiste*, c. 10 (*l'explication globale*), 11 (*la matière*), 23 (*l'évolution de la raison*) especially pp. 314-16.

[3] Cf. Meyerson, *op. cit.* p. 204: "si le géométrique est moins rationnel et plus réel que l'algébrique pur, il est plus rationnel et moins réel que le physique. . . . Et l'ensemble de ces considérations tend certainement à nous confirmer dans cette opinion que c'est bien, en fin de compte, le non-déductible . . . qui apparaît comme constituant l'essence du réel"; p. 205, "la science est réaliste; mais nous savons cependant que d'explication en explication, *elle ne peut aboutir qu'à l'acosmique, à la destruction* de la réalité". (Italics mine.)

pattern of the whole which repeats itself, more or less distinctly, in the pattern of every part, and by consequence, no analysis of any selected part will sufficiently reveal this pattern of the whole. Leibniz may have been wrong in making this an objection to atomism as a physical hypothesis, but he was clearly right in urging against metaphysical atomism the difficulty that it implies the false consequence that the whole pattern of reality could be discovered by sufficiently minute analysis of a single given constituent of the real, *e.g.* the "world-line" of a single atom.[1]

If the views just indicated are sound, every partial system will have a reality beyond it which, because "non-deducible" from any analysis of the system in question, will be, relatively to that system, "another" world. There will be features in the pattern of the whole which could not be discovered by concentration on the analysis of any of the partial patterns, or all of them, and this means—since every part is conditioned by the character of the whole—that such an analysis will always be imperfect, even as an account of the pattern of the part itself. In our scientific theory, as in our moral life, advance will regularly depend on the absorption into our "world" of what had been initially marked off as belonging to the "other", and consequent transformation of what was originally taken as *our* "world".

Thus, not to recur to the already mentioned example of the device by which exponents of "relativity" have

---

[1] *Primae Veritates* (*Opuscules et Fragments*, ed. Couturat; p. 522), "*Non datur atomus*, imo nullum est corpus tam exiguum, quin sit actu subdivisum. Eo ipso dum patitur ab aliis omnibus totius universi, et effectum aliquem ab omnibus recipit, qui in corpore variationem efficere debet, imo etiam omnes impressiones praeteritas servavit, et futuras praecontinet. Et si quis dicet effectum illum contineri in motibus atomo impressis, . . . huic responderi potest, non tantum debere effectus resultare in atomo ex omnibus universi impressionibus, sed etiam vicissim ex atomo colligi totius universi statum, et ex effectu causam."

transformed the notion of a "geometrical world" by incorporating in that world elements of heterogeneity regarded as foreign to it in the classical rational mechanics, we can see at the present moment that one of the outstanding scientific tasks of the coming generation will pretty certainly be to break down the old isolation of physics and chemistry from biology and physiology, and that the synthesis will not be effected by the reduction of living organisms to the level of kinematical, or even kinetic, configurations, but by the introduction into physics and chemistry of concepts already disclosed in the study of the life-patterns of organisms.[1] It is only in this way that the more "abstract" sciences can hope to lose their present character as analyses of complexes which are products of an artificial isolation, and become, what they aim at being, adequate analyses of the rich actual complex in the midst of which our life is set, accounts of the real world, not of an imaginary "ideal" substitute for that world, which has no being except in the imagination of the laboratory student.[2]

But even when physical and biological science have been successfully integrated, there must remain a final, and still more difficult, integration. Artistic making, moral action, religious adoration, do not belong to a world, or worlds, of their own; they too, no less than movement, chemical combination, growth, reproduction, and death, belong to the one actual world in which all life is lived, and their specific patterns disclose features of its pattern. It will hold

---

[1] I am thinking here more particularly of the demand of Dr. Whitehead that the concept of "organism" shall be introduced into physics (*Science and the Modern World*, 150, 190 *al.*), and of Professor Eddington's very frank recognition of "indetermination" in nature.

[2] We shall have more to say on this "historicising" of the natural sciences in the penultimate lecture of our second series.

good here also that every real physical, or physiological, process is a moment in the full life of a real
world not made up of *merely* physical, or physiological,
processes; its full actual character will thus only be
understood when we see it as one subordinate strand
in this ampler tissue. And, again, we may expect it
to be true that the resulting account of any actual
process of the kind will be schematic and misleading
in proportion as, for specialist purposes, we have
denuded the actual "happening" of its contents.[1] It
is to the richest and fullest patterns of all that we must
look for the least inadequate glimpses permitted to us
of the pattern of the whole. We should not be safe in
taking either ethics or physiology alone as the key to
a "clear and distinct" comprehension of ὄντα ᾗ ὄντα,
but we shall be less widely astray if we use physiology
as our key to the real than if we relied on kinematics,
and nearer the truth in interpreting the world by the
light of the moral life of responsible and intelligent
creatures than we should be if, with some of our contemporaries, we took our highest "categories" from
physiology. The whole pattern must, no doubt, always
remain incomprehensible to us, but the richer partial
patterns at least indicate to us what are relatively the
dominant features. This is the final justification of the
refusal we long ago made to admit any ultimate dualism of a realm of actuality and a distinct and separate
realm of value. "Values", we meant, are simply the
dominant features in the pattern of reality.

On such a view there can, of course, be no ultimate
distinction between "two worlds". If the accusation

---

[1] Dr. Whitehead's remark (*Science and the Modern World*, p. 116) that "the
electron blindly runs either within or without the body; but it runs within the
body in accordance with its character within the body; that is to say, in accordance
with the general plan of the body, and this plan includes the mental state", is an
apt illustration of the principle we are concerned to maintain.

of "other-worldliness" is meant as a protest against "metaphysical dualism", it hits no man so hard as it does the "naturalist" of that half-hearted type which lacks the courage—or "face"—to deny the legitimacy of judgements of value *in toto*, but attempts to make its peace with morality, art, and religion by relegating "value" to some kingdom of the ideal, supposed to be situated outside the boundaries of the actual. In our view, the so-called "values" must be the most potent of all the "forces" or influences which shape the course of actuality. We indeed only discover their shaping influence when we study the richest of all the partial patterns which are open to our inspection, the life-patterns of the artist, the hero, or the saint. We may be convinced that they also dominate the course of historical development at the sub-human level, the history of the "inorganic" and the merely "organic". But that, if a fact, is a fact not disclosed by inspection of these realms themselves, and this, presumably, is what Hegel really meant when he spoke of the "lapse into immediacy" characteristic of "nature",—the historical but sub-human.

While we are as we are, conviction on this point must remain a matter of "faith", not of "sight", even though the faith may be a firm assurance of the reality of the things which are not seen. If we could *see* by our own direct inspection that the "values" which are fundamental for the spiritual life of man are also the dominant characters in the whole pattern of reality, we should be in present fruition of that "beatific vision" of God, *per essentiam suam* which Christian theologians agree in regarding as reserved for the pilgrim who has reached his home in eternity. What is popularly called the "other" world would once and for all have absorbed for us what we are accustomed to call "this" world.

But, as it is, we are not yet *in patria*; in art, science, morality, religion alike, we are, at best, only on the way thither. The "other" world is being taken gradually up, and is transforming our vision of "this" world, but the transformation is not complete. There are always fresh horizons beyond us, and unsolved enigmas, spots of deepest shade and obscurity, within our temporary horizon.

The tension between *this* world of the familiar and *that* world of the baffling and "unseen" is not peculiar to the experiences of the strenuous noble liver, or the aspirant after the vision of the "Holy"; it is no less characteristic of the experience of the votary of science. Dr. Whitehead is putting his finger on it when he remarks that it is distinctive of the science of to-day by contrast with that of ages which had carried investigation less deep, that no one can say what apparently hopeless nonsense may turn out to be the great scientific truth of to-morrow.[1] It may be, and has been, held that this tension is not only real, but inherent in the very nature of things; that there would no longer be knowledge in a world where nothing was unknown, nor a moral life where evil had ceased to be, and that thus knowledge and goodness would both disappear in the very act of winning a final victory over their opposites. In that case, we should have to pronounce the inspirations to which we owe both what of knowledge and what of genuine virtue we have won in our historical advance to be illusions. There could be no "celestial city", and there would equally be no "Solomon's house". On the suggested conception of human life as an unending battle in which victory is never won, I propose to say something in our next lecture. For the

---

[1] *Science and the Modern World*, p. 166, "Heaven knows what seeming non-sense may not to-morrow be demonstrated truth".

present, I must be content to have offered some defence
of the thesis that the concepts of the "other world",
and of the transformation of *this* "given" world into
the likeness of the "other" as the grand concern of the
moral life, are at the root of all sane thinking about
the regulation of conduct.

It is important to observe that the thought expressed
by this contrast between the "this-worldly", natural,
or secular, and the "other-worldly", into which it is our
task to transform the given and familiar, is even more
fundamental to a metaphysic of morals than the concept of *sin*. As we have seen, the sense of sin committed bears forcible and unmistakable testimony to
the real being of the God against whom sin is done.
But I think we may say that conclusive testimony to
God would be yielded by our moral experience, even
if it included no consciousness of committed sin. Sin
does more than anything else to estrange man from
God, but it cannot be said to be the only, or the primary, source of the consciousness of separateness. Our
moral struggle and progress are not merely an attempt
to put right what has gone wrong, any more than
the struggle of the intellect towards truth is a mere
attempt to correct past errors.[1] Ignorance is a more
ultimate fact in our lives than error. Even if all our
judgements had been true without exception, so far
as they went, we should still, in virtue of the very
fact that our life is a becoming and a growth, have
work enough, and hard work enough, for the intellect
to accomplish in the way of extending our mental
horizons, integrating truth already discovered with
truth in process of disclosure. If it were feasible, as

---

[1] As it would be on the theory that all science is a partial recovery of knowledge possessed in perfection by the first man, prior to his "Fall", or that, as
Roger Bacon held (*Opus Maius*, ii. 9) "eisdem personis data est philosophiae pleni-
tudo quibus et lex Dei, scilicet sanctis patriarchis et prophetis a principio mundi."

Descartes fancied it feasible, to acquire a kind of artificial infallibility,[1] it would still be true that the work of extending the system of true judgements to cover the whole range of the knowable would be a slow one, sufficient to task the intelligence of an indefinite number of generations.

And similarly with the practical task of the regulation of conduct, the very fact that our minds grow would entail the consequence that, even in a world where every act was conscientiously regulated, men would have to advance from the execution of regulation by reference to a tiny "circle" to regulation by reference to ever-extending "circles". If as children we were never wilful or naughty, we should still need to learn, as we passed from the nursery to the school, and from the school to the world at large, how to practise towards more comprehensive systems the same loyalty which had moulded our conduct when its effective environment was the little family group, and the lesson would need time for its mastery. Here also there would be ignorance to be overcome, even if sin were eliminated. Apart from the estrangement brought about by actual misdoing, there would still be in our experience a contrast between our familiar special "world", or setting, and an, as yet, mysterious and disturbing "other". In virtue of the fact that we have always, ultimately, the whole of what is for the setting of all our acts, our ethics would still require a note of "otherworldliness"; it would still be our task in life to learn to transfer loyalties from a "here" to a "yonder" and to make that "other" our home. And this task is one which would never be completed in any life of which time or succession remained the dominant formal char-

---

[1] *Meditatio* iv. "possum tamen attenta et saepius iterata meditatione efficere ut . . habitum quemdam non errandi acquiram."

acter. For it is just in so far as we are creatures of time and space that the problem arises. It would cease to exist only if every when and every here could become *our* now and here; then, and only then, would the antithesis of "this" and that "other" have lost all its significance. It is in this fact that each of us, when all is said, occupies some regions of the space-time continuum, but not others, that we seem to discern most obviously the difference between ourselves as creaturely and our Creator.

It is true, no doubt, that we may widen the range of what I may call our "effective occupation" of space-time. It is not bounded by the surface of our bodies, or the dates of our birth and death. There is a real sense in which I may be said to occupy all regions of space and time which my understanding can contemplate, or my will affect, but there are, for each of us, some regions of space-time which our knowledge and our will never pierce; which are, for us, only the unknown outer darkness. It is true that effects, even from that outer darkness, register themselves in my body, and that my body in turn "mirrors" itself in effects even upon the unknown. Yet this does not make me, in the full sense, truly all-pervasive. It may be that the effects of my moving a finger here at this present moment are felt through all space and all time. But we must also remember that from any point in the space-time continuum to any other there are always alternative routes. The route from the region which contains the movement of my finger to some other might be quite different, and yet the region reached the same. In other words, it is not rigidly true, as the vulgar determinism assumes it to be, that the "physical state of the universe" a hundred years, or a hundred seconds, hence *cannot* be the same if I do not now move my finger as if I do. This would be true if I were in the strict sense all-pervasive, in no sense confined within some limited region, however vast. But if I were so unconfined I should not be *a* being, I should be *the* Being, not a creature, but the Creator who upholds all things by his power.

To put the point in still another way, the very sense of an "other" lying beyond my horizon is testimony to my utter *dependency*; the consideration that from any region of the continuum to any other there are alternative routes means that, in every act and process which enters into the being of the finite, there is an ineradicable element of real *contingency*, or indetermination. It explains why, for example, in any possible physical theory, the complete system of the laws of motion must contain something which is not the formulation of a logical principle and therefore appears *arbitrary*. Now this constitutes an important point of contact between science, morality, and religion. For religion also, as von Hügel has said,[1] the sense of our own contingency and dependence is even more fundamental than the sense of sin. We can at least conceive that there might be a man who was sinless but still simply man, as we can conceive that there might be a man who had never asserted a false judgement. But even a sinless man would not be God. There would be no chasm between him and God brought about by wrong-doing, but there would still be the unbridgeable gulf between the dependent and the wholly independent. Only a being who had no *locus* in the continuum, and to whom, for that reason, the whole continuum would be equally present, could be independent and free from all contingency, and such a being would not be a "creature".

---

[1] *Essays and Addresses* (First Series), p. 43.

The thought has been rightly seized by traditional Christian orthodoxy. According to the traditional story, Adam before his transgression was a sinless man, not in the sense in which a brute without intelligence and responsibility is sinless, but in the sense that his intelligence was clouded by no error, his will perverted by no evil appetition; his judgement was sound and his volition right. He was what Dante, through the mouth of Virgil, professes himself to have become once more, after his ascent through the terraces of Purgatory.[1] But for all that, Adam, before the "fall", was not divine, he was man *simpliciter*, a creature of contingency, and so liable to fall from good, not permanently established in it. Those who win through the world to eternal life, indeed, are said by the same theology to be finally and permanently established in good. Yet even they still remain "creatures", though beatified creatures. For their final establishment, as they are well aware, is not a conquest of their own right hand. It is given them, and they receive it gratefully as a free gift. This is why humility persists and is the very vital air of their Paradise. The most exalted simply creaturely figure of Dante's Heaven is also the lowliest, *umile ed alta più che creatura*.[2]

It is manifest that the actual growth of any human individual into genuine moral personality will itself provide numerous illustrations of that integration of partial patterns, and domination of the pattern of the part by that of the whole, of which we have been speaking. In our childhood the proverb that "to-morrow is

---

[1] *Purgatorio*, xxvii. 140,

> "libero, dritto e sano è tuo arbitrio,
> e fallo fora non fare a suo senno."

[2] *Paradiso*, xxxii. 2.

a new day" has a degree of truth which it should not retain beyond childhood. The single day, the lesser divisions of the day, have their own interests and their several patterns, and if we go far back enough, these patterns will be found to have little inner connection with one another beyond one which is unconscious and supplied by the mere fact that they are all dominated by the periodicity of the general rhythm of the organism. As we grow older, we learn by degrees to have a conscious pattern or plan which connects the action-patterns for the whole day, the whole week, and so forth, into a whole larger pattern, and connects them by establishing a subordination among them. As our personality develops, the periodic rhythm of waking and sleep, work and rest, does not cease, but it does become increasingly dominated and regulated by far-reaching purposes which fill our whole life.

We need not be perpetually reflecting on such a life-purpose; indeed, it depends for vigorous and successful prosecution on the thoroughness with which it is so stamped upon our behaviour that we cease to have to attend specially to the work of regulation. Regulation by a pattern of purpose repeating itself with the necessary adjustments in its various partial sub-patterns becomes a matter of habit. But, of course, the domination is all the more really present the less we need to attend consciously to the dominant pattern. To develop a genuine moral personality is to pass from a condition in which there is little more to connect the partial patterns than the periodicity of organic rhythm to one in which this periodicity itself becomes instrumentally subservient to "dominant" pattern. Thus, in an intensely rich personal life, we have not simply, for example, the rhythm of alternate movement and repose, or work and play; the specific character of the repose or the play is that it is the *kind* of resting or playing which is congruent with the ever more and more clearly "emergent" pattern of the unique personal life.

Even our dreams, I should say, come in this way to take on the impress of our waking life in various subtle ways; they become less of a riot and begin to exhibit traces of organisation. Our imagination is still at play in our hours of sleep, but the play becomes more and more definitely the play appropriate to a being with a distinctive personal character. We are organising a personality strong enough to persist in the face of the marked organic difference between the waking and the sleeping condition.[1] There seems no sufficient ground for denying that this process of organisation may be carried beyond assignable limits. When we have liberated our scientific thought, as we should do, from the "determinist" superstition which treats actual concrete "becoming" as a secondary consequence of mere displacements of stuff, and have come to understand that the real and primary fact is this concrete "becoming", which is lived through, but never analysed in reflection, except in respect of a few of its more obvious characters, we shall, I think, see that here too we have an example of the parallelism of greater and lesser rhythms.

Sleeping may be the "image of death" in this sense too, that the life-pattern which can persist undestroyed through the alternation of waking and sleeping may also be able to persist, modified but unshattered, through the vaster change we call the death of the organism. The Greeks may have been guided by a sounder

[1] Perhaps *Socrates* asleep really *is* "the same person" as Socrates awake, in a sense in which the statement could not be made, without qualification, of me. That is because he has "lived in φιλοσοφία" (*Phaedo*, 69 C-D), as I, to my shame, have not.

analogy than we commonly suppose, when they found a symbol of the soul in the butterfly emerging from the cocoon. An entomologist friend has declared to me his own conviction that inspection of the cocoon at a sufficiently early stage reveals no manifest persistence of anatomical structure; the caterpillar appears, for the time being, reduced to a mere featureless pulp. Yet in the end the moth or butterfly emerges with a definite structure somehow reconstituted out of this apparently structureless "mess", and the *imago* of each species emerges with its own specific structure. This may, perhaps, be what befalls the human person after its apparent loss of all traces of individual structure at the dissolution of the visible corporeal frame. What has been taken for a pleasing poetical fancy may be the actual fact, as nearly as fact is expressible in language.

And, similarly, it may be that another thought, familiar to readers of Spinoza, is truer than many of them have supposed. It may well be that, in proportion to our success in organising our character into a personality capable of resisting transformation by revolutions in "circumstance", the "carry-over", so to speak, at death may be more or less complete. The supreme physical shock, which may all but completely unmake the loosely knit or wrongly knit character, may leave the well-developed and finely knit "personality" comparatively unaffected. So that it would be no more than the truth that the man who has made the fullest use of the opportunities for the development of a genuine human personality has the mind in which "the greatest part is eternal". To some of us, the shifty and chameleon-like, and again the merely blockish, who hardly grow at all intellectually or morally, the death of the body may well mean entrance into a realm which is overpoweringly unfamiliar, and where we cannot "be ourselves"; to others it may be escape to a sphere where we find ourselves truly "at home" at last. Then it would be the simple fact to say of such a one,

> Not with lost toil thou labourest through the night!
> Thou mak'st the heaven thou hop'st indeed thy home.[1]

The same dark may well be to the idle servant an "outer darkness where there is weeping and gnashing of teeth", but to the good and faithful servant the "night more lovely-fair than any dawn" which "unites lover and beloved".[2]

---

[1] M. Arnold, *East London*.

[2] S. Juan de la Cruz. The words are from the fifth stanza of the Canción prefixed to the famous work on the *Dark Night of the Soul*:

> "¡Oh noche que guiaste,
> Oh noche amable más que el alborada,
> Oh noche que juntaste
> Amado con amada,
> Amada en el Amado trasformada!"

IX

THE GOAL OF THE MORAL LIFE

All casuall joy doth loud and plainly say,
Only by comming, that it can away.
Only in Heaven joyes strength is never spent;
And accidentall things are permanent:

.   .   .   .   .

This kinde of joy doth every day admit
Degrees of growth, but none of losing it.

DONNE.

I HAVE kept to the end the discussion of a difficulty which has been stated by no one with more force and directness than by Bradley in one of the chapters of *Appearance and Reality*, where the moral and religious life itself comes under the sentence of being, after all, only the appearance, though an exalted appearance, and not the reality. So far, we have been urging, as I fear with monotonous persistence, that the familiar conception of this life as a pilgrimage from the temporal to the eternal is wholly true, and that the reality of the pilgrimage is itself evidence of the reality of a goal which is plainly not to be reached, if life under terrestrial conditions and limitations is the only life we have. But it may be retorted that the argument is of the kind called by the Greek logicians λόγοι ἀντιστρέφοντες; it "cuts both ways", and makes as much against our conclusion as for it. For if the pilgrimage were ever to reach its goal, moral goodness, it may be said, would itself disappear. We are moral beings only because, and so long as, there is a goal beyond us which

386

we have not reached. If we had reached it, there would be nothing left to inspire effort and prompt to progress, and characteristically moral life would come to an end. Morality *is* progress, says Kant, and many another champion of "life in a world to come", and without survival of death that progress can never be completed. Morality *is* progress, replies Bradley, or, at least, so you tell me. Then *with* endless survival it must become endless progress, and therefore must remain everlastingly uncompleted.[1] As an *argumentum ad hominem*—or perhaps more precisely *ad clerum*—we are further reminded that in the Christian Heaven there is no progress, but only fruition; you are at home, and your journeys are over and done with. Hence if, like Kant, you base a hope of immortality on the alleged need of endless life, if there is to be endless progress, you have broken with the teachings of Christianity.[2]

The conclusion meant to be drawn is that, in any case, the task we set before ourselves in our moral life is one which, from its nature, cannot be achieved, and that the whole of that life is thus based on a salutary illusion. (Religion is dealt with less drastically than morality, but only, I think, because Bradley tended habitually to underestimate the closeness of the connection between morality and religion, to the point

---

[1] *Appearance and Reality*, p. 508: " 'But without endless progress, how reach perfection?' And *with* endless progress (if that means anything) I answer, how reach it? Surely perfection and finitude are in principle not compatible. If you are to be perfect, then you, as such, must be resolved and cease; and endless progress sounds merely like an attempt indefinitely to put off perfection." I presume that the criticism is directed particularly against Kant's position in *KdpV*. I, Th. ii. bk. ii. *Hpst*. iv. (*Werke*, Hartenstein[2], v. 128 ff.).

[2] *Appearance and Reality*, p. 500. "If progress is to be more than relative, and is something beyond a mere partial phenomenon, then the religion professed most commonly among us has been abandoned. You cannot be a Christian if you maintain that progress is final and ultimate and the last truth about things. And I urge this consideration, of course not as an argument from my mouth, but as a way of bringing home perhaps to some persons their inconsistency."

of almost making the second simply a ἕξις θεωρητική. If it is true, as it seems to be, that theology has a double foundation, in Ontology and in Ethics, Bradley's theology seems to suffer no less gravely from disregard of the ethical foundation than Kant's from neglect of the ontological.) One may add that, as Bradley is clearly aware, the Christian doctrine, which he has invoked to stop the mouth of the Kantian believer in endless progress, must be an illusion too, for it tells us that we *are* to be perfect, as its own supreme practical injunction, and such perfection is certainly not capable of being attained in this moral life, where we are all, more or less, always at the mercy of the unknown and incalculable, and must in the end be defeated by the inevitable falling of the night.

Is there any way for us out of this unwelcome dilemma? It seems to me that there is a way which has long ago been indicated for us by the great philosophers. But the difficulty ought to be fairly faced, if we are not to admit in the end that in taking our life as *moral* beings as a clue to reality we have been simply losing ourselves in a maze from which there is no exit. If, indeed, we could be content to adopt any of the views which make an absolutely sharp distinction between religion and morality—for example, the view that morality is wholly a matter of attaining a "terrestrial felicity" with which religion, as concerned with a strictly "supernatural good", has no concern—there would be no problem for our discussion. We could then, if we pleased, simply concede all that Bradley asserts; we could say that the pursuit of ethical "perfection" is, as he maintains, the pursuit of an impossibility, but that this does not affect conceptions of our future in a land of supernatural blessedness. Heaven, we might say, is not to be won by morality, and it is strictly in keeping with this to hold that moral action is no feature of the life of the denizens of a heavenly Paradise. They have left morality behind them on entering into their reward; to be moral is to be still engaged in "work", but in Heaven there is no more work to be done; one rests from one's labours. But to adopt that position, or any similar position, would be to acquiesce in the very severance of "nature" and "grace" against which the whole of what has gone before has been a protest. For us, at least, that way out is stopped.

The difficulty we must face, then, when reduced to its simplest terms, is this. To live morally is to live to make the good real. But this very statement implies that there is good which is not real and has to be made so. If once we succeeded in making good wholly real and reality wholly good, there would be nothing left for us to live for, as moral beings. The supreme command of all morality is thus a command to make morality itself superfluous. But to aim at the supersession of morality is to be radically immoral, since to be truly moral means to be moral for morality's own sake, to lead the moral life because of its own worth. Or, still more bluntly, morality is unremitting war against evil, but where there is no evil there can be no war against evil. The good man, therefore, must will at once that evil shall exist, that it may be overcome, and also that it shall be overcome, that is that it shall not exist. Thus his whole life is a hopeless attempt to will two incompatibles at once.

Now an irrationalist, like Professor Aliotta,[1] may

---

[1] For the views of Aliotta see his vigorously written manifesto, *La guerra eterna e il dramma dell' esistenza* (Naples, N.D., but apparently published about 1918. I regret that I have not seen the later and revised form of this interesting little book). Professor Aliotta in effect accepts Bradley's thesis and turns it against every form of monistic belief in metaphysics. *Because* there cannot be good where

hold such a view without being much disturbed by it,
since he appears to take the view that the whole worth
of life depends on the fact that it is an "eternal war",
where the issue of the campaign is never decided. It is
the fight, not the victory, which gives life its value in
his eyes. (Mr. Chesterton has somewhere said virtually the same thing—how he reconciles it with his
professed theological views I do not know—when he
declared that in life there is no such thing as taking
care to be "on the winning side", because "you fight to
find out which is the winning side".[1]) But such a view
should hardly commend itself to any but a very boy-
ishly minded philosopher. When you come to think
it out, it means that a thing only becomes good, and
so worth fighting about, because someone makes it a
bone of contention. The good would not really be good
unless there were a party who think otherwise and are
ready to fight in the quarrel. This is certainly not in
accord with the principles on which reflective men
commonly base their conduct. To get men to fight at
all, if you are dealing with men who are more than
overgrown schoolboys, you have to begin by persuad-
ing them that they have a good cause. Men and nations
have often waged arduous wars for causes which the

---

there is not also evil, as there cannot be sunlight without shadow, it is inferred, the
real world must be the battle-ground for an unending internecine conflict between
rival "reals"; the *mundus intelligibilis* is, in fact, a sort of magnified and never-
ending *Caporetto*. Theism is rejected explicitly on the ground that, if God is, the
issue of the conflict between good and evil is *not* doubtful; the moral struggle,
therefore, we are told becomes only a *sham* fight: "Che io mi affatichi o mi
abbandoni, è del tutto indifferente: così il mio lavoro, come la mia ignavia
rientran egualmente nell' ordine providenziale; e Dio troverà sempre modo
(o meglio l' ha già trovato) di accommodare le cose. Il risultato finale del
dramma sarà sempre lo stesso: l' eterna divina commedia che si chiude col
trionfo definitivo del bene" (*op. cit.* 135). This emphatic insistence on a "moral"
argument for atheism is the more impressive that it represents a complete *volte-
face* on the part of the brilliant Italian author, who had, in 1914, concluded the
English edition of his work, *The Idealistic Reaction against Science*, with an
"epistemological proof" of the existence of God (*op. cit.* 463 ff.).
[1] *What's Wrong with the World?* p. 12.

"disinterested spectator" has to pronounce thoroughly bad, but surely no people ever put forth its energies steadily and vigorously, at the cost of heavy sacrifices, in a war for a cause recognised by itself to be a bad one. Thus, in the last world-war, our opponents were anxious to justify their attack on Belgium by the plea —quite a good one, if it could have been made out— that the Belgians had in some way violated their own neutrality, and we may feel sure that the argument was not invented simply to make an impression on "neutrals"; those who devised it were, at bottom, trying to convince themselves. To quarrel about nothing is universally recognised as no behaviour for rational and civilised men. They may "find matter in a straw", but only when they can get themselves to believe that it is the straw which "shows how the wind blows". It is not the straw itself, but "honour" that is at stake, and honour is not nothing.

No one seriously behaves as though he believed that a good thing is made good by becoming the argument of a quarrel; men quarrel because they think that they are being wrongfully kept out of the good thing, or that their enjoyment of it is menaced. The only way to dispute this would be to adopt the extreme irration-alist view that life is never really regulated by con-scious purpose, but wholly by unconscious *libido*. But a moralist who accepts this position, even if his theory of conduct is a thorough-going "immoralism", stulti-fies himself. All moral rules, even the rule of ruth-less cultivation of the "will to power" and contempt for the "conventions of the herd", are imperatives, addressed to conscious intelligences. It would be waste of breath to formulate them, if we seriously believed that purposes and intentions are not, in the end, the real directive agencies which mould a man's life. Nietzsche's commands are as "categorical" as Kant's.[1]

If we stop short of this excess of irrationalism, which, in fact, would render us unfit to give or receive argument, it must clearly be a really serious question, affecting our whole estimate of the worth of ethics as a source of suggestion for metaphysics, whether the aspirations fundamental to moral action are self-destructive. If they are, we have merely been misguided in supposing that our experience of moral obligation throws any light on human nature or human destiny.

---

[1] It may perhaps be said that these considerations hardly meet the main point of an argument like Aliotta's. Granted that there must be a real good to fight for before men can be expected to fight, does it not take the reality out of the *struggle* to believe that God is on the side of right, and right certain to win? Is not this belief tantamount to a doctrine of absolute predestination, and does not belief in predestination paralyse effort?

We may say (1) All experience shows that in fact even belief in absolute predestination, the so-called *fatum Muhammedanum* of which Kant speaks, does *not* paralyse human effort. The belief that the "Lord of hosts is with us", and that our cause *must* therefore win, has always been found in fact to give men heart for a stubborn contest, as no other belief does.

(2) The popular conception that the predestinationist does not believe in the reality of human "free will"—and it is this conception which underlies Aliotta's argument—seems to be a mere mistake. We can see clearly enough that this was not the case, *e.g.*, with St. Augustine, who was at once the originator of Christian doctrines of predestination, and the most vigorous of assertors of the reality and importance of human will. It is said also to be the case with Mohammedans, though here I can only speak at second-hand. Cf. Otto, *The Idea of the Holy* (E. tr.), pp. 92-3: "In many typical Mohammedan narratives . . . men are *able* to devise and decide and reject; but, however they choose or act, Allah's eternal will is accomplished to the very day and hour that was ordained. The purport of this is precisely, *not* that God and God alone is an active cause, but rather that the activity of the creature, be it never so vigorous and free, is overborne and determined absolutely by the eternal operative purpose." "This is a predestination which presupposes free will just as its foil."

(3) The interest of a fight does not cease for me because I feel sure of the issue. I still have a real concern in being among "those that triumph", or, it may be, among those who perish with their honour unstained. In the final assault on Thermopylae, Leonidas must have "known" who would "win" the pass, and he may conceivably have been equally convinced that the Hellenes would, in the end, come out of the war as victors. Neither assurance removed his interest in fighting a good fight.

It will, I hope, be understood that I am not here expressing any views of my own about predestination. I am only concerned to maintain that even the most absolute predestination is not incompatible with human "free will", and that belief in it neither has, nor logically need have, the consequences supposed by Prof. Aliotta.

In spite of a well-known mot of Bentham, it is plainly absurd to speak of an obligation to supersede obligation. To say that there "ought to be no *ought*" is only another way of saying that there really *is* no *ought*; if there is not, any conclusions based on the conviction that moral obligation is the most illuminating fact of human nature will be merely worthless.

We need, therefore, to discuss carefully the question whether the goal presupposed in moral endeavour really is such that the reaching of it would destroy *moral* personality itself. For my own part, I cannot but think that the contention rests on a fallacy of ambiguity. I grant at once that Bradley's criticism is justifiable, if it is taken as aimed at certain specific ethical theories. It is, I apprehend, wholly just as a criticism of a doctrine like that of Herbert Spencer, and there are indications in the relevant chapters of *Appearance and Reality* that the writer has Spencer very much in his mind. (I am thinking of the repeated allusions to a certain "New Jerusalem".) According to Spencer, we must remember, obligation is always an indication of some unremoved misadaptation of our agent to his "environment", and will consequently disappear in the Spencerian "New Jerusalem", where the agent is perfectly adapted to an environment apparently assumed to be absolutely stable, and is therefore no longer, "evolving", but completely "evolved".[1] This particular conception had already been submitted by Bradley to an annihilating criticism in *Ethical Studies*,[2] where it had been urged that (1) the assumption of the absolute stability of the "environment" to which the "evolving" moral community is taken to be "adapting" itself is glaringly at variance with all we know, or have reason to believe, about our historical situation as deni-

---

[1] *Principles of Ethics*, i. 127 ff.   [2] *Ethical Studies*², p. 91 n.

zens of this planet; and (2) that, if complete adaptation could ever be reached, there is no reason to believe that it would be permanent; indeed, on Spencer's own arbitrary postulate of the "instability of the homogeneous", one would have to infer that a really complete adaptation must be momentary.

If the concluding divisions of Spencer's *Principles of Ethics* had been published when *Ethical Studies* was written, it may be said that polemic on *this* point would have been superfluous. For we find there that it was Spencer's own belief that complete adaptation by evolution is only attained to be immediately lost again; evolution does not, after all, lead to the establishment of a permanent "moving equilibrium", but begins to undo its own work as soon as the "moving equilibrium" has been reached. It is more to my purpose to remark that Spencer's account of the character of the process during the half of the cycle in which it is advancing in the direction of a momentary "moving equilibrium" seems to be based on a curious misreading of the facts. It is *obviously* not true that as a community advances in moral civilisation its members lose the sense of their reciprocal moral obligations to one another. It would be much nearer the truth to say that what we call "social conscience", the acuteness with which the ordinary good man—good that is, according to the conventional standard of his society—realises these obligations, becomes intensified. And it is not hard to see why this should be so. The less highly developed a society in moral civilisation, the more elementary the rights and claims of which its members are conscious, the narrower also are the limits of the body to which loyalty is habitually paid, and the less clearly does the average member understand the ways in which his own action affects other members of the community. To learn this lesson, we do not need to go back to prehistoric ages, or to compare the working morality of European civilisation with that of contemporary barbarism. We have only to compare our own conceptions of our "social obligations" with those of very excellent men of a hundred years earlier to see that there has been a marked intensification of the sense of obligation between 1825 and 1925.

We may remind ourselves, for example, of the change in the general opinion about the obligation of providing all citizens with the opportunites of education, or of making dwellings sanitary and comely, or of paying a "living wage", to see how great the difference is. Or more simply still, we might contrast the purposes for which we think it imperative that an income-tax should be levied with the views which must have prevailed at the much more recent date at which Gladstone could promise the total abolition of the tax in the event of the return of his party to power. I think that it would, further, be fair to say that, during the last hundred years, we have not merely come to have a more exacting standard of social obligation; we have also come to feel more acutely about our own personal defections from that standard. The "whole law", as we now conceive it, embraces a great deal more than our great-grandfathers supposed, and we are at least as sensitive as they, and probably more so, to the moral urgency of fulfilling the law. As the generations succeed one another, men who wish to have a conscience void of offence find that task more, not less, difficult.

I can only account for Spencer's apparent blindness to such plain facts by supposing him to have reasoned somewhat as follows. Society is engaged in steadily "adapting itself", that is, in putting right what is wrong. Hence in each successive generation of a morally progressive society there is less left to be still put right than there was in the generation before it, and therefore less need for painful and strenuous effort. Further, the *habit* of putting right the wrong grows stronger with practice through the generations.[1] Therefore the conscious sense of effort to be made and duty to be done must be steadily growing fainter. Thus we may look for a climax when there will be no wrongs left to be righted, and the now superfluous sense of obligation will die out.[2]

If this fairly represents Spencer's line of thought, one may make the remark that several dubious assumptions seem to be presupposed. It is taken for granted that a "perfectly evolved condition", in which there is no evil left to be got rid of, can be reached in a finite, though perhaps a very long, time, or, in other words, that the amount of wrong to be righted before a society is "fully evolved" is a fixed finite *quantum*. The "absolute difference" between the amount of evil now present in a society evolving towards "moving equili-

---

[1] I do not suggest that this reasoning is wholly sound, but it would be in keeping with Spencer's own unqualified belief in the "heritability of acquired characteristics".

[2] It is instructive to observe that the writer of the article "State of the Dead" (Christian) in the *Encyclopaedia of Religion and Ethics* describes the final state of the lost in Hell precisely as Spencer describes that of the "perfectly evolved society". "The faculty which, in the case of the finally impenitent, has been wholly and irremediably abused is that of free will, and therefore, whatever else eternal loss may involve, it must involve the loss of this. . . . The lost, deprived of all power of volition and choice, will sink to the rank of necessary agents. . . , Thus they can sin no more, and will perform the will of God unerringly, which will surely be for their good. Moreover, their enjoyment of natural goods, though impaired, will not be destroyed. In fact it even seems possible to regard their condition as one of relative happiness of a purely natural kind." I am not sure how far this anticipation is coherent, since it seems to assert in one breath that the "lost" both are, and are not, genuinely human beings, but there is exactly the same difficulty about Spencer's description of the life of his "millennial" age. There, also, the "fully evolved" men and women have no real choice; their will is always determined *ad unum* by a natural necessity, and Spencer regards this condition as one not only of "relative" but of supreme happiness. The only difference is that the (Anglo-Catholic) writer of the article makes the condition he regards as "damnation", but Spencer as the highest felicity, perpetual. So much for Spencer's courteous standing insinuation that the "orthodox" clergy are "devil-worshippers". But, like most "agnostic" critics, Spencer had probably never troubled to study the religion he satirised.

brium" and zero steadily diminishes as the evolution goes on, and presumably the rate of diminution is also steadily accelerated. No sufficient account is taken of the possibility that the very same progress which introduces superior adaptation in some special respects may bring with it new, and possibly more serious, departure from adaptation in others, though one would have thought this consideration could hardly be missed by a writer who lived through the "industrialisation of England", even without the rival theories of Spencer's antagonist Henry George to call attention to it.

It *seems* to be assumed, again, that moral action consists merely in putting wrongs right, and that if there should ever come a time when there are no more wrongs to be corrected, "practice" will have "done its do". This is a point to which I shall have to recur; for the moment, I would only observe that the assumption seems about as reasonable as it would be to say that the sole task of science is to refute "vulgar errours", and that, if they were all once thoroughly refuted, nothing would be left for science to do, so that in a "fully evolved" society the sense of truth would share the fate of the sense of obligation. Avenarius, if I understand him rightly, actually professed to believe something of this kind. As far as I can fathom the main argument of his chief work, his thesis is that the intellectual evolution of a society will be complete when every "stimulus" evokes a response composed exclusively of expressions of "pure" experience. But response to stimulus only has *significance*, or *meaning*, so long as it contains an element which is not "pure" experience, but *interpretation* of the "experienced". In the final stage, the stimuli contained in the "environment" will evoke "responses" from the members of the "perfectly evolved" society, and some, no doubt, of these responses will be vocal, reactions of the organs of articulation. But they will have no *meaning*, will *signify* nothing beyond themselves. They will be knocked out of us by events, exactly as a roar or a squeak may be produced from a toy lion or toy bird by pinching it in the right place.

This seems to me an inevitable consequence of Spencer's premisses, though it never occurred to Spencer to draw the conclusion. Avenarius, if I understand him, did draw it, and it is just the reckless clear-sightedness with which he drew it which gives the *Kritik der reinen Erfahrung* its great value. The book is a final *reductio ad absurdum* of the attempt to treat intelligence as the product of the adaptation of a relatively plastic organism to a fixed environment.[1]

Finally, there is in what I take to have been Spencer's thought a gross double confusion of the *fact* of obligation with the *sense* of being obliged, and of this sense with the consciousness of a disagreeable *effort*, as though awareness that "I ought to do this" were always attended by the thought "but I would much rather not". The first of the confusions should be impossible to anyone who refuses to subscribe to the wholly immoral doctrine that a man escapes his obligations by systematically ignoring them; that a husband, for example, has no obligation of fidelity to a wife whom he has married without any thought of being faithful, and has habitually neglected for other women. The second only seems plausible through an error of mal-observation. We are, no doubt, most powerfully *impressed* by the "sense of duty" when there are great sacrifices to be made, when the act to be done is almost

[1] Of course, it is very possible that I have misapprehended the main thesis of a work so difficult and diffuse as the *Kritik der reinen Erfahrung*. But this is what seems to me to be the conclusion to which the argument inevitably leads.

too hard for human flesh and blood; but in the case of the more usual daily obligations of good citizenship and neighbourliness we are at once aware that the good offices are *incumbent* on us, not works of supererogation, and also that it is pleasant to discharge them. A man may feel the imperativeness of duty with uncommon intensity when the duty is painful or difficult, as he may feel the strength of a personal affection most keenly when he is suffering bereavement. But though, in this sense, "we never know how we loved our friend until we have lost him", this is no proof that we do not love our living friend, or that we are not aware that we love him.[1] In the same way, even if it were true that every step in moral progress leaves us with so many fewer and less formidable temptations to encounter, it would not follow that, as we "go on to be perfect", either our obligations or our sense of them must decrease. If a "fully evolved" society is to mean a society which is fully moralised, such a community would not be one where no one had a sense of obligation; it would be a society in which every member was more thoroughly alive than in any other to the full range of his obligations, and more careful to fulfil them.

But, of course, moral progress no more means the mere putting right of wrongs than intellectual or artistic progress means the simple correction of old errors. The correction of errors is only a subsidiary task for the intellect. Its primary business, which would still remain in illimitable fertility, if there were no more

---

[1] And, similarly, it has been observed that a virtuous man never *feels* the sacredness of an accepted moral maxim so acutely as on those exceptional occasions when he, rightly or wrongly believes that it is a *duty* to depart from it. In ordinary life we tell the truth as a matter of course, without reflecting on the sacredness of truth or the immorality of lying. A good man, convinced that, in his present situation, he ought to keep back the truth, or to equivocate, is likely to be very exceptionally conscious of the sacredness of the general obligation to veracity and candour.

"false opinions" to be corrected, is the exploration of ever new regions of truth. If an artist could overcome all the difficulties created for him by the intractability of the materials through which he has to express himself and by his own limitations and bad mannerisms, if he became a "perfect master" of his instruments and his own moods, there would still be the endless work before him of giving actual embodiment to his vision of beauty. And, in the same way, the moral life would not disappear even from a world in which there were no wrongs left to be righted. Even a society in which no member had anything more to correct in himself, and where "thou shalt love thy neighbour as thyself" were the universally accepted rule of social duty, would still have something to do; it would have the whole work of embodying the love of each for all in the detail of life. It is this, not the mere abolition of abuses, or the elimination of unfavourable circumstances from the environment, which is the paramount business of the moral life.

The description of that life as a phase in "evolution", which is destined to disappear, when and if evolution becomes complete, is thus based on confusion of thought. But it has also to be added that the attempt to represent the "completely adapted" society as a possible product of natural "evolution" is itself inherently absurd. "Evolution" itself is, in its very nature, a becoming, not a being, and it is a double becoming. The "environment" is something which becomes, no less than the "organism", though its rate of becoming may be slower. Evolutionary adaptations are adaptations to a changing, not to a fixed, environment—unless, indeed, you mean by the "environment", as Spencer did not, the intimate presence of the living and abiding God to and in all His creatures. And though the planetary environment, which is all that Spencer takes into account, may usually change very slowly, this need not always be the case. It may be that there are no sudden catastrophic changes on the large scale in the developing organism, but we have to reckon with their possibility as features of the planetary environment. We are not, after all, *assured* against cataclysms which permit of no adaptation, and, even apart from such cataclysms, we have every reason to expect that the society which Spencer calls "fully evolved", because it has adapted itself to a relatively stable environment, must inevitably degenerate again, as changing terrestrial conditions make the maintenance of a high level of civilisation increasingly difficult. A high morality "evolved" after millenniums of struggle would only be won to be lost again in succeeding millenniums. If we may trust the physicists with their "principle of Carnot", the "cave man", or something of the same kind as the "cave man", lies ahead of us, as well as behind us—unless, indeed, the perfectly evolved society should escape an old age of decay by perishing in its prime, either by a "bolt from the blue" or by *felo de se*. Mankind, as their moral life unfolds, are seeking a house eternal and abiding, and it is evident that such a house, if it is to be found at all, must be found in some other world than one where succession and temporality are dominant.[1]

Probably, however, it is Kant rather than Spencer whom Bradley's argument has most particularly in mind. As against Kant, the argument takes the form that the Kantian philosophy enjoins moral faith in

---

[1] Evolution, as conceived by Spencer, is, after all, no genuine *historical* process. The fact is shown by his complete disregard of the "principle of Carnot", which forbids us to regard "becoming" as reversible. On this extraordinary oversight see the pertinent criticisms of James Ward, *Naturalism and Agnosticism* [1], i. 192-195.

immortality on the ground that the particular good morality consists in seeking is one which we can never obtain in a limited time. Morality is the progressive acquisition of self-mastery, complete domination of irrational impulse and inclination by the rational will. But what makes the essential difference between God and man is that irrational inclination and impulse are ineliminable from humanity. We cannot become beings with purely rational wills; all we can do is to make will more and more preponderant over inclination, without ever getting rid of inclination altogether. If we are to achieve anything of moment in this conflict, we must have an endless time for the work, so that we may "approximate without limit" to an ideal we never actually reach. Against such an argument it is pertinent to object that a goal to which you can only make unending approximation is, *ex hypothesi*, never attained. On Kant's own showing, the man who makes the exercise of the morally good will his aim in life—and no other man is morally "good" —is, at best, the Achilles of Zeno, attempting the impossible task of coming up with the tortoise. Assuming that Zeno's analysis of the problem is correct, we can only say that Achilles shows himself no mathematician by consenting to the race. He should have known that he was trying to do what, from the nature of the case, is not to be done. The sooner he gives up his impossible pursuit, the more rational we shall think him, as we should have thought Hobbes less irrational in his determination to "square the circle" if he had not spent so many decades over the problem. Indeed, we do Achilles an injustice by this suggested comparison, for the tortoise has at least only a finite handicap, and this Achilles steadily reduces, though he never wipes it out. But God, with no "lower nature" at all, is presumably as infinitely

ahead of the Kantian good man after untold millions
of years of respect for duty as at their beginning. One
is reminded of Pindar's μὴ ματεύσῃ θεὸς γενέσθαι.[1]

Here, again, I confess I find Bradley's comment just.
Kant has the merit of seeing far deeper into the real
nature of the moral problem than Spencer and the
evolutionary moralists in general. The evolutionists as
a body seem to me to take a hopelessly "external" view
of morality. They appear to regard it as a mere matter
of devising an ideally frictionless social machine, which
may be counted on to minimise the risks society runs
from collision with its physical environment, and perhaps actually to abolish the evils arising from competition between its members. If they can be cheerily
optimistic about the coming of a "perfectly evolved"
morality, it is only because they set morality no more
difficult task. Kant is resolute to demand more from his
good man; he will not be satisfied with anything less
than the cleansing of the thoughts of the heart, the
inner purification of all the sources of will, and he sees
clearly that this is not feasible for mankind in general
without a discipline extending far beyond the limits of
our earthly existence. If we are to be schooled into perfect obedience by the things we suffer, it seems plain
that, for most of us, the schooling we get in our three-
score years and ten is only a small part of the training
we need. We leave this life before we have well learned
even our alphabet. But the central difficulty still remains. According to Kant himself, the lesson is always
learning, never learned. Hence it is in point to raise the
objection that if morality means learning a lesson a
man never masters, it should seem that if he once did
master it he would cease to be a moral being, since to
be moral means to be engaged in learning the lesson.

[1] *Ol.* v. 24.

Thus the duty of a member of the "kingdom of ends" would appear to be to do his utmost to abolish the kingdom of ends itself, and this hardly seems reasonable.

Yet, on reflection, it appears that Kant is really making the same assumption as Spencer, in a subtler way. He, too, is assuming that there would be no moral life to be lived where there was no longer wrong to be put right. His one advantage over Spencer is that he conceives of the process of putting the wrong right in a more inward fashion. The wrong to be righted is no mere misfit of the organism to its environment, but a wrong relation between reason, the higher, and inclination, the lower, element within the moral personality. The unruly motions of the flesh must be brought into subjection to the motions of the spirit. But if the flesh should ever be so completely subdued that it no longer lusted against the spirit, man, as a moral being, would, on Kant's theory of the moral life, have ceased to be. The person in whom the good will was now finally established would no longer be a man, but a god, and this complete transformation of humanity into deity Kant rightly pronounces impossible, thereby, may we not say, revealing that at heart he has retained much more of the old metaphysic, with its distinction between being absolute and in its plenitude, and being contingent and restricted by limitation, than the professions of the *Critique of Pure Reason* would justify. But the point for us is that, however right he may be in holding that the conversion of the creature into the Creator would be an absurdity, in his determination to avoid that absurdity he makes the moral life a battle which never ends in victory, and that all thinkers who do this lay themselves open to Bradley's criticism that such an identification reduces morality itself to the position of an illusion which, for moral reasons, we must be tender of exposing. It is only a secondary further consequence that any testimony the moral life may appear to yield in favour of our immortality must be pronounced worthless. If Achilles can never catch the tortoise, his chances are not improved by giving him a race-course of indefinite length.

Is it, then, really true that it is of the *essentia* of the moral life that it should be a struggle with evil, whether in the form of an environment which is a misfit, or in the more insidious form of "inclinations" which persist in remaining imperfectly subdued?[1] Would the interests which sustain the life of "practice" simply disappear if moral and physical *evil* were really overcome? The question is an important one, since, if we answer it in the spirit of Kant, we shall have to say that a *moral* "rational theology" must definitely reject any doctrine like that taught by Christianity about the final state of the saved; there can be no "Heaven" where those who have come through the struggle "reign with Christ": there may, conceivably, still be an adventure which never finishes, but it is an adventure like the quest of El Dorado, or the philosopher's stone, and such a prospect, I fear, grows less attractive the more steadily it is regarded.

I venture to think that Kant, at any rate, would have come to a different conclusion, if he had not falsified the problem by an over-simplification arising from his distrust of ontology. In his anxiety to build his philosophical theology on ethics and nothing but ethics, he

---

[1] Kant's assumption that there must be such an element of "inclination" in every "creature"—its presence being just what distinguishes the "creature" from the Creator—is a relic of the "Augustinian" doctrine that all "creatures" exhibit the composition of "form" with "matter". He does not consider the rival Thomistic view, which founds "creatureliness" on the distinction between *essentia* and *esse*, the "what" and the "that", and consequently recognises the actual, or possible, existence of creatures (the angels) in whom "form" is uncompounded with "matter". If the Thomistic view is tenable—I do not say that it is, or that it is not —the moral life, as conceived by Kant, would not be possible to an angel.

has misread the lessons of ethics itself. If we look more closely at the problem, I believe we shall see that the elimination of evil and its source in unruly inclination would still leave the ultimate distinction between God and man untouched, and consequently could not affect the essential characteristic of the moral life, that it is a life of *aspiration*. There is a possibility which combines attainment and aspiration, and would thus leave room, within a society of just men made perfect, for a very real and intense moral life. In fact, in our familiar experience of the moral life, as we now have to live it as a life of warfare, we do not see it in its truest character; we see it, as Socrates says in the *Republic*[1] we now see the soul, incrusted with all sorts of accretions which disguise its true lineaments; to discern them, these accretions must be purged away. With the passage from struggle to triumph, morality would no doubt undergo a transfiguration, but it would be a transfiguration and not a transformation.

This, I may remind you, was definitely the conviction of Green, who expressly says, in opposition to the view that the moral life can be simply equated with a life devoted to "reforms", that "the character of the moral reformer is not merely a means to the perfect life, but a phase of the same spiritual principle as must govern that life. But whereas we cannot but suppose that, if the perfect life of mankind were attained, the spiritual principle must have passed out of the phase in which it can appear as a reforming zeal . . . we cannot suppose that, while human life remains human life, it can, even in its most perfect form, be superior to the call for self-abandonment before an ideal of holiness. There is no contradiction in the supposition of a human life purged of vices and with no wrongs left to be set

[1] Plato, *Republic*, 611 C-D.

right. . . . In such a life the question of the reformer,
What ought to be done in the way of overt action
that is not being done? would no longer be significant.
But so long as it is the life of *men*, *i.e.* of beings who
are born and grow and die . . . in whom virtue is not
born ready-made but has to be formed (however unfailing the process may come to be) through habit and
education in conflict with opposing tendencies; so long
the contrast must remain for the human soul between
itself and the infinite spirit."[1]

Green, as his language shows, is thinking here of life
within the limits in which we are acquainted with it,
and is apparently willing to concede, for purposes of
argument, that "complete adaptation to environment"
might be permanently attained in such a life. His point
is that though the attainment would do away with the
special vocation of the "reformer", or "social worker",
it would not, as Spencer supposed, abolish morality and
obligation. There would still be something to be lived
for, the completer assimilation of the activities of the
human spirit to those of the divine, the practice of
adoration, humility and the reception of the grace of
God. If you choose, by arbitrary definition, to restrict
the name *morality* to the life of struggling to "put the
crooked straight", you would have to say, indeed, that
morality had been transcended, but it would only have
been transcended by transfiguration into a life continuous with itself and inspired by the same ideal of
"imitating God" which has been operative from the
first in producing the most elementary of social and
moral "reforms".

Now this, provided only that we substitute, as I
think we fairly may, for Green's more specific mention
of birth and death a more general reference to becom-

---

[1] *Prolegomena to Ethics*, sect. 302 (p. 328).

ing or succession as that which distinguishes the life of
the creature from the life of the Creator, seems to me to
be the truth of the matter. The interest which sustains
the good man in what he knows now as the conflict with
evil of every kind need not be exhausted by the mere
removal of evil; the termination of the battle in a decisive victory need not put an end to the activity to
which the victory has been due, though it would make
a significant difference to the form that activity would
assume. To use the language of the devout imagination,
the winning of heaven would not leave the pilgrim
arrived at the end of his journey with nothing further
to do. In heaven itself, though there would be no longer
progress *towards* fruition, there might well be progress
in fruition. Life "there" would be, as life "here" is not,
living by vision, as contrasted with living by faith and
hope; but might not the vision itself be capable of ever-
increasing enrichment?

To put the same thought from rather a different
point of view, I do not see why "social service" might
not be as characteristic of heaven as of earth, though
it would have a rather different quality "there". On
earth we have in the main to serve our neighbour by
removing the sources of temptation and the other
obstacles to the good life put in his way by untoward
circumstances, or by the undisciplined cupidities and
resentments within his own soul. Each of us has to set
others forward, and to be set forward by them, in the
way of purification from inordinate devotion to lower
good and intensification of devotion to the highest. In
the heavenly city, as conceived, for example, by Christianity, there would be no further call for this particular service, since it is a community of persons who are
all in love with the highest good. But even in such a
heaven, we have heard, one star differs from another

in glory. Even in a society where every member was in actual enjoyment of the "beatific vision", it would still remain the fact that some see more of the infinite wealth of the vision than others, but each receives according to the measure of his capacity. We could thus understand that those whose vision is most penetrating might well have a heavenly "social service" to discharge in helping their fellows to see, and might find a deep significance in the speculations of "Dionysius" and his mediaeval followers about the part played by the higher orders of angelic intelligences in "illuminating" those beneath them. When all "see God" face to face, some may yet see more than others, and may be supposed to help those others to see more than they would if left to themselves. A friend whose vision is keener than my own may not only render me valuable help in scaling a mountain-top; when the summit has been reached, his aid may actually enable me to discern the prospect more perfectly than I should have done if I had stood on the peak alone.

There is also another side to the same thought. To many imaginations, I believe, there is something repellent, or at least profoundly depressing, in the current representations of Heaven. It is made to appear as a region where there is no room for the *adventure* which is the very salt of life, the abode of a monotonous self-sameness of boredom. It is not every temperament that expresses itself in the words

> There remaineth a rest for the people of God,
> And I have had troubles enough, for one![1]

But the conception of Heaven as adventureless is really unjustified. There is no sufficient reason why the disappearance of wrong, within or without ourselves

---

[1] R. Browning, *Old Pictures in Florence.*

to be put right should put an end to adventure and novelty. Even in a life where there was direct vision of God, we can readily understand that no vision could ever be complete, just because the object of vision is infinitely rich; there would always be the aspiration to see further, prompted by the splendour of the vision already granted, and we may readily conceive, with von Hügel,[1] of this aspiration as only to be satisfied by bold adventure in self-forgetfulness. It would be the spirits who plunge most venturesomely into the "divine dark", not knowing what it may have to disclose, who would most completely make themselves, returning from the plunge into the Godhead with clearer and deeper perceptions, for the nourishment of their own being and that of their less venturesome companions.

Thus a life in which the struggle with evil to be put right was a thing of the far-away past might also exhibit its continuity with the "militant" life of earth, by retaining the characteristic notes of social service, of self-forgetfulness, and of the winning of self by the adventurous staking of self. Even in Heaven life would have its astonishing and joyful surprises for everyone. The "finite God" of some modern speculations might, no doubt, come to bore us badly, because, since he is finite, we must expect, sooner or later, to have nothing more to find in him or receive from him, but this creation of dualistic metaphysics is not the God of the saints, nor of any considerable religion. One might recall, in this context, words of John Bunyan, no less appropriate that they were primarily written to a rather different purpose: "Christ Jesus has bags of mercy that were never yet broken up or unsealed. Hence it is said he has goodness laid up; things reserved

---

[1] *Essays and Addresses* (First Series), p. 218 ff.

in heaven for him. And if he breaks up one of these bags, who can tell what he can do? Hence his love is said to be such as passes knowledge and that his riches are unsearchable. He has nobody knows what for nobody knows who."[1]

I take it, then, that we need no more suppose there would be any loss of continuity with present conditions in a moral life carried on into a realm from which evil had disappeared than there would be in the pursuit of fresh knowledge by a society whose "vulgar errours" had all been corrected, or the pursuit of art by artists who had attained full mastery over their medium of expression. We have no actual experience of such a state of things, but we can, at least, see that the follower of science who had no longer misconceptions and mistakes to be got rid of, or the artist who had no longer to wrestle with the refractoriness of his materials, the defects of his implements, and the unskilfulness of his own right hand, would still have a boundless field of the unexplored and the unexplained in which to find ample employment for his energies. We do not, in fact, find that the musician or painter who appears to have nothing more to learn about the management of his violin bow or his brush is driven to abandon his art because he has acquired mastery of this kind. He goes on to *use* his mastery, and there is no reason in the nature of the thing why he should not go on to use it indefinitely, for the production of beauty which is perennially new and increasingly *more* beautiful. To think otherwise is to make the mistake of confusing mastery of technique with the whole of art. The same thing is equally true of the business of the moral life.

---

[1] Bunyan, *The Jerusalem Sinner Saved*. Bunyan's immediate purpose is to reassure a sinner who is tempted to despair by the blackness of his record of past transgressions, but the thought lends itself equally well to our present argument.

The moral life does not consist merely, or chiefly, in *getting* into right relations with our fellows or our Maker. In our earthly house we have constantly to be doing that, but it is only the preliminary to the real business, the προοίμιον αὐτοῦ τοῦ νόμου ὃν δεῖ μαθεῖν; the real business is not to establish these relations, but to live in them.

To illustrate the point in the simplest possible way, we may say that we have, for example, to learn to love our parents, our friends, our fellow-men generally. At first our loves are too often languid, and even when they are not languid they are "inordinate", not under the direction of clear-sighted wisdom. But even on earth we have something to do beyond merely un-learning unloving, or unwisely loving, ways. As we learn to love rightly, we have to exercise the love we have learned by giving it actual embodiment in the detail of our lives. And so, if we found ourselves in a world where every one of us had unlearned unloving-ness and foolish loving, one part of the moral business of our life on earth would, no doubt, be done with. We should no longer have the old aversions, or indiffer-ences, or wrongly directed affections to unlearn. But the *main* business of the social life, the putting of wise and right love into act, would remain; we should find occupation enough in *showing* our love, and this would be an occupation continuous with what is morally of highest importance and value in our present life.

This may seem a painfully obvious remark, but I make it for the purpose of entering a protest against what appears to me a gross caricature of the moral life, which is only too fashionable in certain philosophical quarters, and can unfortunately shelter itself behind the authority of at least one recent *clarum et venerabile nomen*. You will doubtless remember how Bosanquet

was given to characterising "morality" as a realm of
" claims and conflicting counter-claims", and using the
description as the basis of a subtle depreciation of the
specifically moral attitude towards life. In fact, religion,
as conceived by Bosanquet, consists precisely in "transcending" this ethical system of claims and counter-
claims, in soaring above morality into something different and better, and, obviously enough, such a view
of the practical life plays straight into the hands of
Bosanquet's favourite metaphysical doctrine that individual human personality is a mere illusion.[1] No one
would desire to speak of Bosanquet except with the
deepest respect, and yet I must protest—*ich kann
nicht anders*—that his habitual description of the moral
life in such language seems to me a misrepresentation
as grotesque as dangerous. (Dangerous because, with
men of less fine moral fibre than Bosanquet himself, it
is apt to engender the delusion that it is "spiritual" to
be a-moral, if not actually immoral, in fact, that one can
be at once "in grace" and leading a careless, or even
an actually bad, moral life. And it is a short and easy
step from this theoretical delusion to practical ill-living.)
    I must ask, then, whether, for example, the life of
family affections, or of intimate reciprocal friendship, is
something "super-moral" or not. Has a man who does
not know what it is to be a good father, or son, or husband or friend, really lived the "moral" life? Has any
man done so if he has merely respected the precisely
definable "rights" of his fellow-citizens, without having

----

[1] For Bosanquet's use of such language see, for example, *Value and Destiny
of the Individual*, lecture v. *passim*. I am, of course, aware that it may be said
that the same type of view is equally to be found in Bradley, though not, I think,
quite so consistently adhered to, or so clearly formulated. But I feel bound to
protest against it, wherever found, as leading, if taken seriously, to a confusion
of spiritual religion with an easy "Nature-pantheism" which is at variance with
the real intentions of both philosophers at their best. Green is nobly free from *this*
defect.

lived the "shared life" with any of them; or does not
the very suggestion arise from a dangerous confusion
of the ethical with the merely juristic point of view? I
should myself say that it is just the relations such a man
has been unfortunate enough to miss—in many cases,
of course, it may really be his misfortune rather than
his fault—which are the finest flower and the most
perfect expression human history has to show of the
ethical spirit. It is not without very good reason that
Aristotle's account of the life of "practice" culminates
in the description of the φιλία of the good man. In
this relation, when obligations cease to be capable of
formulation as definite "claims" and "counter-claims",
a man is not rising *out of* the realm of morality
into something higher; he is finding himself, for the
first time, *in* a region where the ethical spirit gets unhampered expression.

Or can it be—as I can scarcely believe—that those
who·use language like Bosanquet's really believe that
the best family life, and the noblest types of friendship,
really fall within the system of "claims and counter-
claims"? This I should call a mere distortion of the
facts. It is just because there is no room in these relations
for insistence on claims and counter-claims that they
have been the great instruments by which man has
been historically moralised. In a business partnership
it may be possible to delimit the respective claims and
obligations of the parties, and, in view of our human
frailty, it is important to do so, though no man would be
the best of partners, even in business, if he did not recognise, as conscientious men of business habitually do,
that, even here, the spirit of partnership calls for mutual
confidences and services which cannot be strictly delimited, nor set out in the letter of any bond. But in the
realm of marriage, or in a friendship "based on good-

ness", the relation itself would be merely destroyed by any attempt to reduce it to the rendering of specific reciprocal services. A marriage which has the quality of an ethical marriage is always at the least what the Roman lawyers called it, a *consortium totius vitae*,[1] and a friendship which is a matter of the *quid pro quo* is what Aristotle calls it, only an imitation of the genuine thing.

So far from morality being the sphere of "claims and counter-claims", it is only when you begin to rise out of that region that *any* social relation, even that of mere "neighbours", begins to acquire a genuinely ethical character, and in the most truly moralised intimate relations, which do most to make personal character, one has left the region of "claims and counter-claims" altogether. What you give, or should give, to your wife, or children, or to your chosen friend, is nothing less than yourself, whole and without reserve, and you receive, or should receive, the like. If in practice we all come badly short of this ideal, that is not because the ideal is "super-moral", but because, in actual fact, we are all only very imperfectly moralised. It is intolerable that metaphysicians with a spite against personality, "the noblest gain of Christian thought",[2] should foist on us a caricature of true moral personality as a device for reconciling us to their substitution of an impersonal Absolute for God.

What we are now saying is not inconsistent with our former insistence on the relativity of all loyalties except

---

[1] This is the real and insuperable *ethical* objection—independent, by the way, of any theology—to the substitution of any kind of *union libre* for marriage. The terminability of the "free union" is only a consequence of its inner moral vice, that it is an attempt to give something less than the whole self, to keep back "part of the price". A relation which *must* be a moral failure, unless it is based on full and free self-surrender, is undertaken "with a mental reservation". Marriage only succeeds in being what it can be at its best because both parties enter into it knowing that there can be no "backing out".

[2] Martineau, *Types of Ethical Theory*, ed. 2, p. xxviii.

the highest. There is a loyalty which each of us must put even before loyalty to the wife of his bosom or the children of his loins, but it is not a loyalty to some supposed inaccessible and impenetrable kernel of his own individuality, and it is a supreme loyalty which is equally recognised by the other party, if the relation between the two human persons is what it ought to be. The fullest recognition that there is such a highest loyalty to someone or something other than this or that human person, or group of persons, does not involve that conception of human personalities as, in the last resort, merely mutually exclusive and repellent which apparently accounts for Bosanquet's depreciation of the moral and his hostility to finite individuality. It is emphatically not true that we must either hold that personality is mere "appearance" or regard the real world as composed of mutually repellent atoms. In truth, the richer your individuality is the more personality you have, the more you have to share with others, and the more urgently you feel the necessity of giving and receiving. It is the shallow, not the deeply and richly human, personalities which are gardens shut up and fountains sealed. No doubt a bountiful nature *may* be driven back on itself by the world's refusal of its gifts, or indifference to them, but it is not the richest in gifts to bestow who are the most easily repulsed. And the due recognition of the higher loyalty is not the same thing as a niggardliness in bestowing. The hero of the song who "loves honour more" is not really offering a gift of less value to his beloved than the idolater who forgets "honour". He is not loving the less because he loves in a fashion more worthy of a man.

Thus I think we may dismiss the conception of the sphere of morality as one of collision between "claims and counter-claims" as a misunderstanding. We may, no doubt, say that where the fulfilment of all loyalties has been ordered by the principle of degree and subordination, so that there remains no conflict of lower with higher, we have got beyond anything that can be significantly called *mere* morality, but we have only done so by learning to be wholly true to the spirit present in all morality. Our moral life, to repeat a distinction already made, may have been transfigured, but it has not been transformed; the victory and the struggle are connected by a continuity of interest, and there is no real ground for the fancy that victory would somehow eliminate finite moral personality. There is nothing unintelligible in the conception of a society of "perfected" persons, where all would be faithful mirrors, each from his own perspective, and, so to say, with his own curvature, of the infinite light and love of their common source, each having his own special contribution to make to the love and joy of all, each bestowing as well as receiving. Thus, in such a life to come as would be life in which man, as a moral being, had found his permanent home, *morality*, as we know it, could not rightly be said to be transcended; what would be transcended is the limit now set to the expression in act of the moral spirit, partly by our dependence on circumstance and physical environment, partly by the fact that all of us are only so imperfectly moralised in the intimate recesses of our souls. There would be no more progress *towards* goodness of environment or character, but there might be abundant progress *in* good, onward movement in the manifestation of the principle of the good life in ever more varied and richer forms.

I take it we might illustrate this distinction between progress *to* and progress *in* from the history of the arts.

Do there not seem to be periods in the life of a man or a people when there is no more to learn about methods of expression, though the periods are not empty or barren, but employed in the actual embodiment of what has been learned in a succession of "masterpieces"? Shakespeare's highest mastery in the tragic art, for example, is shown not in one such masterpiece, but in several—*Macbeth, Othello, King Lear*. We can say of his earlier work that it reveals him advancing, or progressing, towards finding himself as a supreme tragic artist. *Hamlet* has been specially remarked as showing great progress, in this sense, by comparison with *Julius Caesar*, and I believe it will generally be admitted that *Macbeth, Othello, Lear*, all of them show progress by comparison with *Hamlet*. But it does not follow that any one of the supreme three can be said to show progress from any other. It is at least an intelligible statement to say that all are *equally*, though each in its own special way, revelations of achieved mastery.

In fact, the very distinction we seem to be feeling after has long ago been expressly drawn for us by Aristotle. It is just his distinction between a γένεσις, a process of becoming, or development, by which some capacity comes to its full growth, and the ἐνέργεια, or activity by which the capacity, once developed to maturity, exhibits itself as a feature in the world-pattern. In life as we know it morality exhibits both γένεσις and ἐνέργεια inextricably. We are all along—it is to be hoped—growing into morality, *becoming* better men and women, and, at the same time, so far as our character acquires fixity of pattern and organisation, that fixity reveals itself in activities issuing from it. But there is nothing in itself irrational in hoping for a stage in our existence in which finality may have been actually reached, so far as development of personal character is concerned, and yet endless room left for the embodiment of the character so won in varied action. With the disappearance of growth, or becoming, of character we should not have lost our unique personality; we should have at last come into complete possession of it.

If we study the way in which character visibly makes itself under our eyes, we do indeed find that the process is marked by the disappearance of eccentricities and fluctuations; the more completely the individuals who share a common great tradition appropriate all that tradition has to yield, and make it into the stuff of their own personality, the more clearly do a common set of principles stand out as regulative of their life-pattern. Yet the persons do not lose their peculiar individuality. The "prentice work" of two great poets of the same age and language may be much the same kind of thing, and it may be hard, or impossible, to discriminate the manner of the one from that of the other. It is precisely in the work of their maturity that they may show themselves inspired alike by the same traditions and ideals, figures of the same age and the same "movement", while each is yet unmistakably himself and not the other. There might easily have been several men of the same time and the same sort of endowments, any of whom might have been the author of *Love's Labour's Lost*, or the *Two Gentlemen of Verona*; it is conceivable, though less likely, that there might even have been two men at the time of Shakespeare, either of whom might have written *Romeo and Juliet*; it would be much harder to believe that there could have been two contemporaries, either of whom might have given us *Othello* or *Antony and Cleopatra*.

It is the same with goodness. Two great figures of the moral or religious life, belonging to the same era, and subjected to the same general "influence of the age", let us say, by way of example, a Dominic and a Francis, or, if you prefer it, a Mill and a Ruskin, may both be eminently good, but each with his own special way of being good. Francis and Dominic are both definitely thirteenth-century figures, Mill and Ruskin both "Victorian", but the type expresses itself differently in Francis and in Dominic, in Mill and in Ruskin. This much by way of comment on the view that, in a Paradise where all men were sinless, there could be none of the variety, multiformity, and individuality which give zest to life. It seems to me nearer the truth to say that it is just the limitations on "genius" of every kind, deriving from the general character of men's "ages", "centuries", "surroundings", which are the obstacles to complete individuality. In Paradise I should expect individuality to reach its *maximal* expression, if Justinian there is no longer *semper Augustus*,[1] nor Bonaventura a cardinal, nor Cacciaguida a soldier, but one and all are *Menschen mit Menschen*.

There are certain implications of this view which I could wish to set out explicitly before I bring this first half of my programme to its close, always, I trust, with due submission to better judgements.

(1) It is clear that if we have conceived rightly of the kind of final destination of man which would be a real attaining of the moral ideal, the completest transfiguration of "this" world into the "other" of which we can reasonably conceive would not wholly abolish the successiveness of human experience. Even a heavenly life, such as we have tried to imagine, would still be a forward-looking life. The "glorified" would, indeed, no longer be looking forward to a future in which they had

[1] Dante, *Paradiso*, vi. 10:

"Cesare *fui* e *son* Giustiniano."

still further to put off the old man with the passions and the lusts, or in which they would still be waiting for the "beatific vision", and so far, it is true, that faith and hope might be said, if not to have ceased, at any rate to be no longer the dominant notes in life. But there would still remain an undertone of something analogous to those virtues, since the blessed would always have new discoveries awaiting them, more to learn than they had already found out of the unspeakable riches of the wisdom of God, and these inexhaustible surprises would be won, as deeper insight is won here, by humility, trust and self-surrender, by letting self go, following an apparently paradoxical inspiration. Heaven—if a heaven indeed there is—we may safely say, must be a land of delightful surprises, not a country of Lotus-eaters where it is always afternoon. And in the same way, if we are to think morally of Heaven, we should, I suggest, think of it as a land where charity *grows*, where each citizen learns to glow more and more with an understanding love, not only of the common King, but of his fellow-citizens. In this respect, again, there would be one lesson mastered before the portals of Heaven would open to admit us. We should have learned to love every neighbour who crosses our path, to hate nothing that God has made, to be indifferent to none of the mirrors of His light. But even where there is no ill-will or indifference to interfere with love, it is still possible for love to grow as understanding grows.

We can see both growths illustrated often enough in the conditions of our earthly life. As to understanding, in a sense anyone who is aware of the meaning of the equation $x^2 + y^2 = k$, or $xy = k$, and knows how to plot out a graph of the functions, may be said to "understand perfectly" what a circle, or an equilateral hyperbola, is; there is no error infecting his thought, and no further discovery he may make about properties of these curves will lead to any revision of the equations. But the greatest mathematician does not know all the fascinating properties which may be discovered from the equations. It is conceivable that, after so many centuries of geometrical study, the most elegant and attractive of the discoveries still await some geometer of the distant future. And as to love, a brother and sister may love one another with all their hearts in the nursery, and they may also love with all their hearts after the joys and sorrows of a long life; but if one has grown in the right way, one has more "heart" to love with at sixty than one had at ten, because one has so much more insight. There may have been full and complete sympathy at the earlier age, yet there has been progress *in* loving, though not progress, in the supposed case, *from* half-hearted or intermittent love to steady and whole-hearted love. The progress *in* loving has been from a blind to a seeing love.

(2) If our general principles are defensible, we clearly may have to reconsider the worth of a once familiar conception which is now very much out of general favour, the conception of our earthly life as one of *probation*. I know that this thought, the theme of countless sermons in the days of my own youth, is unpalatable to two quite different sets of thinkers, the spiritualists and theosophists, who seem to have no place in their scheme of things for the eternal, and those "absolute Idealists" who rightly perceive that, on their metaphysical theory, time itself must be an illusion. The first party will hear nothing of final beatitude at all, but only of an unending series of promotions in a *cursus honorum*, or even of endless alternations of promotion and disgrace; thus they lay themselves open to all those hostile criticisms of "endless progress" with

which we have just been dealing. The second would
have us believe that, if we only knew it, we are already
at the end of our road and "in Heaven", though, for
some mysterious reason, we are unaware of the fact.
But so long as there are such moods within us as indifference and mutual ill-will, this is *manifestly* not the
case. If our life is really a journey, it should be clear
both that there is a home to be reached, and that we
have not yet reached it—indeed, that most of us presumably have a great deal of the worst of the journey
still before us.

But if this is so, it is true, again, that the great business of our life here must be to find the right road and
to walk in it. As I have said, we do not yet love all the
creatures of God, nor even all our human neighbours,
and those we do love we too often love "inordinately",
not in the right way or the right measure. There is a
lesson which has to be learned not only by those who
value wealth, or reputation, or power, but by those, for
example, who love their own puppy-dog better than
their fellow-man. Now, it is at least conceivable that
the crisis we call death, in which the mind partner in
the mind-body relation is dissociated indefinitely from
its fellow, may put the gravest of obstacles in the way
of our mastering this lesson. If we have not begun to
learn it here, it may be that our subsequent experiences
will not be such as to enable us to repair the neglect. (I
do not assert that this is so, but I say that we have no
assurance that it is not so.) The true nature and extent
of the crisis is more than we, who have yet to pass
through it, know; but when we reflect on the far-reaching effects of lesser organic crises on our moral being,
analogy suggests that the moral consequences of
physical death may be still more serious. Hence I cannot think the present-day fashion of minimising the

spiritual significance of death altogether wholesome or becoming a

> Being breathing thoughtful breath,
> A traveller between life and death.

To be sure, when we remember how often Christianity has been degraded in practice from being the life of the love of God and His creatures to being a purely prudential attempt to secure the individual against *post mortem* suffering, we inevitably feel some sympathy with some of the motives which account for the fashion;[1] but it is mere folly to treat our mortality and uncertain tenure of bodily life as of no moral significance, forgetting that there may well be lessons which must be learned, if we are ever to attain true felicity, and must be begun here in the body, or not at all. On this point a sober moralist must surely feel dissatisfaction with the attitude expressed when death is compared with "going from one room to another", and find much more wisdom in the old-fashioned evangelical insistence on the text that "*now* is the accepted time, and *now* the day of salvation". None of us *know* that if we wait for to-morrow, to-morrow may not be too late. There is at any rate one very real "hell" to which a man may consign himself, the hell of ever-renewed and ever-baffled endeavour, and a man can never know that he may not send himself thither by present negligence. Even if he escapes that doom, in a morally ordered world, we must believe, neglect to tread the steps of the moral ascent at the suitable time can only be made good by an ascent gravely more tedious and more painful. The present would be a better age than it is if we all lived more in

---

[1] It is painful to note the frequency with which the suggestion that the main concern of life is to insure myself against future torture recurs in the hymnology of the Wesleys, or how the same preoccupation seems to haunt Newman in his *Apologia*, though, no doubt, the *main* motives in both cases were of a nobler kind.

the habitual temper of men who remember that they
have an account to give.

(3) In trying to develop the thought of a beatitude
which includes progress *in* attainment, though not progress *to* attainment, we have not finally succeeded in
overcoming the antithesis between time, the successive
and fleeting, and eternity, the complete and non-suc-
cessive. It has been implied that succession would still
be a feature in the life of a creature, though a feature
steadily decreasing in importance, even in a Paradise
of light and love. This was a prominent doctrine of the
late Baron von Hügel;[1] how far it would be admitted
by the official exponents of the theology of his church,
or any other, I do not know, but I feel convinced that in
substance, at any rate, it is sound. I may remind you
that a distinction which seems to be much the same in
principle is made by two great philosophies, each in its
own way. The Neo-Platonists, who ascribe *eternity*
both to the being and to the operations of Intelligence
(νοῦς), and to the being, though not to the operations
of souls (ψυχαί), make it a capital point that even
"eternity" may not properly be predicated of the supreme
source of all being. The One, or God, is actually προ-
αιώνιον, *prae-eternal*.[2] St. Thomas naturally follows the
language of Scripture in asserting "eternity" of God,
but he is careful to insist that this eternity, in the strict
and proper sense of the term, is intrinsic to God. Angels
and the beatified in Heaven possess only a "participated eternity", and possess it as a gift from God,
which lifts them above their own level. The intrinsic
"measure" of the life of spirits, considered apart from

---

[1] I would refer here to the full exposition of the Baron's views in his study,
Eternal Life (1912), also to the second essay in *Essays and Addresses*, second
series.
[2] See, for a formal exposition of the Neo-Platonist doctrine, Proclus, *Institutio
Theologica*, props. 48-55.

this supernatural gift, is neither eternity nor time, but *aevum*, which is spoken of as something intermediate between the two. The difference is explained thus. Eternity is, in the famous phrase of Boethius, "occupation whole and altogether of a life without bounds," *interminabilis vitae tota simul et perfecta possessio,*[1] and thus can have no element of successiveness, no before or after, connected with it. Time is purely successive; what is simply temporal has becoming, not being; its *esse in transmutatione consistit. Aevum* is itself "all at once", and so far is like eternity, but it permits of having a before and after "conjoined" with it.[2] Hence St. Thomas says of the angels that they have an *esse substantiale* which is intransmutable, but is conjoined with transmutability *secundum electionem* (since, according to the well-known traditional account, they were subjected to a test, with the result that some of them chose to rebel, others to adhere to good), and conjoined similarly with transmutability of *attention* and, in some sense, of *location* (since angels can descend and reascend).

I do not know whether experts in Thomist philosophy would accept an interpretation that suggests itself, and would make this account of *aevum* exactly what our own argument needs for its purpose. The distinction between former and later which Thomas excludes altogether from eternity should, in strictness, I take it, be interpreted not as the distinction between antecedent and sequent, but as that of past and future. How the world is apprehended by God none of us would venture to say, but we cannot conceive that it is not apprehended as an ordered scheme exhibiting what is fundamental to the moral life, the one-sided and

---

[1] Boethius, *De Consolat.* v. pros. 6.
[2] *S.Th.* I^a q. x. art. 5. See further I^a q. x. art. 4, 6.

inversible relation of real causal dependence. In that sense, I take it, there must be a *prius* and *posterius* in the world as apprehended by God. But there is no *prius* or *posterius* in God, or in God's *apprehension* of the world. The whole process, *prius* and *posterius* alike, would fall for God, who never becomes, but is, within a single present, just as in our own experience apprehension of the present is never awareness of an object in which there are no relations of before and after, but always apprehension of a *present* object which embraces a before that has not yet faded into the "past", and an after that has not to emerge from the "future". We all know that it is to some extent a matter of native endowment how extensive a slice of "what is there" we can apprehend as being all at once with all its interrelations, including those of before and after; we know also, I think, that with care and practice one can learn to take in bigger "slices" in this way. We can and do cultivate the power of thus taking in at a single glance more and more of the detail of a situation to which we have to make practical response, or to appreciate the bearing of a proposition in the sciences, without that conscious advance of attention from each step in the argument to the next which we found necessary when we were beginners.

The same thing is seen in the case of appreciation of aesthetic form. There is, I understand, some doubt about the genuineness of the letter in which Mozart is supposed to speak of his ability to hear his own compositions "all at once" by an interior audition, and of the incommunicable rapture of the experience. Yet I imagine it is not really doubtful that the great artist in every kind must really possess some such power of envisaging as a *totum simul*, however imperfectly, what he can only convey to us by means of a detail which he has to elaborate, and we to "follow", in the form of long-drawn-out successiveness. Not to speak of the vision of the artist himself, which is, after all, the artist's secret, if we consider only our own imperfect appreciation and enjoyment of the artist's work when it is already there for us, it seems to me that as we learn to appreciate better, the work we appreciate and enjoy steadily sheds its successiveness. There was first a stage in which single stanzas of the poem, single scenes, or even speeches, of the drama, single phrases of the melody, were all that could fill our minds at one time; appreciation of the whole as a unity with structure had to be won with difficulty and the aid of conscious recollection and reflection. This is afterwards succeeded by a stage at which the impression is made by an inter-related whole, and our judgement of appreciation passed primarily on the whole as such, with a conscious immediacy.

To take an illustration which I purposely make childishly simple. I suppose we all know the sort of person who reads a great work of fiction in the mood appropriate to a railway detective story, for the sake of its surprises, and would have his enjoyment spoiled by any chance remark disclosing the turn the story will take. I had once myself a friend of this type; it was impossible to discuss or describe in his company any work of fiction he had not read, because, as he used to say, "I might some day want to read the book myself, and I shall get no pleasure from it if I know before-hand what is coming". In men of this kind, whose enjoyment depends almost wholly on being perpetually taken by surprise, I suppose we might say the appreciation of narrative and dramatic art is at its lowest. To one who wants to appreciate the art of the story, or the play, the element of mere surprise is a hindrance; it is an advantage to him to know beforehand what the incidents to be treated are, that he may be free to concentrate his attention on the structure of the whole. And, similarly, the great artists are those who depend least for their effects on the administering of *pure* surprises. What shocks are there in the *Iliad*, or, again, in *Tom Jones*? Could either of these works be rightly appreciated by anyone hearing the narrative for the first time? Fielding, I know, does contrive to keep up a mystery, though a fairly transparent one, through the story. But how much does it contribute to the real merits of his tale, or which of us would find his appreciation of the book affected if the author had taken the reader into his confidence from the start? It cannot even be said that Fielding has at least availed himself, for artistic effect, of the uncertainty whether his hero will eventually be rewarded with the hand of his mistress. Anyone aware of the literary tradition to which the book belongs knows from the outset that the pair are meant to make a match of it. For the matter of that, most of us, I believe, would not in the least mind if they did not. What we really care for is that the end of the story, be it what it may, shall be of a piece with what has gone before.

These remarks may seem below the dignity of our theme, but I think they are really in point. They indicate the possibility of a knowledge of the successive which would involve no uncertainty, and no element of pure surprise, and yet would apprehend the successive in its order as successive. That is, the successiveness would be *wholly* in the things known; it would not be a successiveness in the knower, or his knowing. If we conceive such an apprehension to embrace the whole of that which happens, it would be knowledge of the whole course of temporality by a knower to whom Boethius' definition of eternity would be strictly applicable, a knower possessed of "unbounded life" wholly and all at once. Such apprehension would realise Spinoza's ideal of "knowledge under a form of eternity", but it would not get this quality of eternity, as Spinoza imagined it must, by denuding the known of its temporal form. It would be the knower, not the history he knows, who would have eternity as his proper "form".

Now such knowing as this, so far as I can see, would be quite impossible, in its perfection, for man, or any creature. It would be, as I have said, knowledge from which the last vestige of uncertainty, and capacity for being surprised, had vanished. This does not mean, as Spinoza took it to mean, that such "divine" knowledge would apprehend all events as *necessary*. Since the world of creatures actually is a world of becoming, contingency and partial indetermination, if God apprehended it otherwise, God would be Himself the victim of illusion; this so-called knowledge would not be knowledge. A being in possession of all knowledge must, of course, know the incomplete as incomplete, open alternatives as open alternatives. But the point is that, though there might be contingency enough in what such a knower knows, there would be no contingency in the knower himself. He would, for example, know that at this moment of my life there are alternatives between which I can choose; but, since he sees all at once, he would also know that I am in the act of choosing one of the alternatives by my choice, and which I am choosing. He would not be taken by surprise when I choose.

So, in a sufficiently familiar situation, I myself know, when I make a choice, that I really am choosing, not finding out that choice has been precluded by my circumstances or my "past", and yet I am not taken by surprise by my own choice. Such complete freedom from uncertainty would seem, from the nature of the thing, impossible to a creature. For every creature is not merely set in a background of the uncertain; he also has the uncertain within himself. He is a dependent being who is not his own *raison d'être*, and he cannot sound the whole mystery of the being upon whom he is, in the last resort, dependent. There is more in God than any creature will ever find out. At most a creature can only be assured that nothing still remaining to be found out will belie what has been disclosed.

This, I suggest, is what is really meant by the "participated eternity" enjoyed by creatures in Paradise, in virtue of their direct vision of God. With them "vision" has replaced "faith"; they "behold God *per essentiam suam*"; what they behold is truth, pure and unalloyed, and obscured by no metaphor or irrelevant symbolism, exactly as mathematical truth may be to the mathematician truth without confusion, metaphor or alloy, but they never see all there is to be seen of the *essentia* of God. There is always more to be seen, as there is always more mathematical truth to be discovered. Thus, for any creature, however exalted in goodness and wisdom, there are always possible surprises in store, though in a world from which evil had disappeared the surprises would always be "joyful". But for a being who can be surprised, even if the surprise takes the form of delight "beyond expectation", futurity must remain as an uneliminated feature of experience.

Hence I think von Hügel on the right lines in regarding the life of creatures as one in which successiveness and futurity never wholly vanish, though they may become of decreasing importance "beyond all assignable limit". The tension of anticipation of the unknown would be less pronounced in the higher ranks of a Dantesque empyrean than in the lower, but it would still be there, as the witness to the unbridgeable gulf between the independent and the wholly dependent, Creator and creature. And I find it hard to believe that St. Thomas can have thought otherwise, especially when I note that the eternity in which the beatified participate is made to depend on their vision of God. This "participated" eternity would thus seem to be actually *God's* eternity, as contemplated by the beatified. In virtue of the principle that we become like what we behold, a soul in actual vision of God is assured that it cannot forfeit that vision, for he who *sees* the good can desire nothing else. But there is always also the awareness that there is more to be seen than the soul has yet taken in, and thus the mind's attitude does not cease to be forward-reaching. Complete ἐνέργεια ἀκινησίας, activity, which is rest and nothing but rest, is reserved for the Creator alone. But to say this is not to say that the struggle with the bad is ineradicable from creaturely life.

(4) We must, however, be very careful how we identify the best life, in Aristotelian fashion, with *vita contemplativa*. There are qualifications which must not be forgotten. In such a heaven as we are trying to imagine, the conflict of right with wrong, truth with error, has no place, and thus the "practical life", as understood by Kant and others who simply identify it with this struggle, would be no more. But if we may conceive of a "blessed" life as providing opportunities for progress in vision, to be achieved by intellectual adventure, and to bear fruit in the illumination of others besides the adventurer, then clearly the spirit of the "practical life" continues at this higher level.

Contemplation of the vision is the inspiration of the adventures, and their fruit is neither the righting of wrongs nor the amendment of errors, but enriched contemplation. Yet the adventures themselves are "practice", and the ultimate goal of action is not to pass out of being, but to be made wholly fruitful in contemplative rest. Such a goal is in keeping with the spirit of morality, as the mere disappearance of "action" is not. We make war, as Aristotle said, that we may have peace, and we discharge business that we may have leisure. But peace and well-spent leisure are not the same as sloth and inaction. It would be a false psychology that should treat "contemplation" as passive, in the sense of being inert. To contemplate aright we must, indeed, be wholly *receptive* towards suggestions from without; we must lay the whole self open to the object contemplated, lose the self in it. But to be thus receptive takes all the energy with which a man is endowed. Contemplation and laziness will not keep house together; and we should merely misunderstand the great masters of the mystic way if we supposed their traditional language about "passive contemplation" to mean that our highest felicity is a state comparable with the lazy enjoyment of a hot bath. Rightly understood, the life of fruition of the vision is not the supersession, but the fulfilment, of the life of dutiful practice of the modest virtues of the family, the city and the nation. What is superseded is only the conflict with adverse elements in the self and its environment, and that is only superseded because it has been brought, by God's grace, to a victorious issue.

The very mention of God's grace reminds me that I am touching on matters more properly reserved for the second part of our programme, in which we are to consider the relations between such a natural theology as is directly suggested by reflections on the implications of ethics and the theologies of the historical religions. So long as we are within the bounds of the purely ethical, it may be said, the moral conflict must be thought of as one in which man fights for himself and must win any success he does win by his own unaided efforts. But according to any religion which is not a mere "Pharisaism", no one achieves "eternal life" by his own effort; it is the "gift of God". How, then, can we speak of it, as we have just spoken, as the supersession of the moral struggle by a *moral* victory? I must not now anticipate the course of the reflections with which we shall be occupied later. So I will only add that the paradox, if it is a paradox, is inherent in the *Christian* religion itself. The fruits of the tree of life, and the hidden manna, are expressly spoken of as *gifts*, but they are gifts said to be reserved for victors. "I *have* overcome the world", said One; but it is said in order that each of us also may overcome. We are still the *ecclesia militans*, and *our* victory is still to be won.

INDEX OF PROPER NAMES

END OF VOL. I

THE

FAITH OF A MORALIST

SERIES II

NATURAL THEOLOGY AND THE POSITIVE RELIGIONS

MACMILLAN AND CO., Limited
LONDON · BOMBAY · CALCUTTA · MADRAS
MELBOURNE

THE MACMILLAN COMPANY
NEW YORK · BOSTON · CHICAGO
DALLAS · ATLANTA · SAN FRANCISCO

THE MACMILLAN COMPANY
OF CANADA, LIMITED
TORONTO

THE
FAITH OF A MORALIST

GIFFORD LECTURES DELIVERED IN THE
UNIVERSITY OF ST. ANDREWS, 1926–1928

BY

A. E. TAYLOR

SERIES II

NATURAL THEOLOGY AND THE POSITIVE RELIGIONS

Not where the wheeling systems darken,
And our benumbed conceiving soars!—
The drift of pinions, would we harken,
Beats at our own clay-shuttered doors.
FRANCIS THOMPSON.

MACMILLAN AND CO., LIMITED
ST. MARTIN'S STREET, LONDON
1937

PRINTED IN GREAT BRITAIN
BY R. & R. CLARK, LIMITED, EDINBURGH

PREFATORY NOTE

I HAVE nothing to add here to what has already been said in the Preface to the first volume of these Lectures, further than to request the reader's particular indulgence for such oversights of the Press as he may discover in the last third of the text, which has unavoidably been "corrected" in great haste and at a distance from books. I have done my best to detect and remove errors, but it is only too possible that I have not been wholly successful.

A. E. TAYLOR

GOATHLAND, *August* 1930

Dr. Gore has called my attention to what I regretfully admit to be a double injustice to himself—though an unintentional injustice—on pp. 113 and 142. It is apparently implied in what is said there that Dr. Gore would "exclude from active participation in the devotional life of the Christian community" all who are not prepared to pledge themselves to the historical fact of the 'Virgin Birth'. I ought to have remembered that in other writings than the book from which I was quoting, Dr. Gore had expressly explained that he proposes only to exclude such persons from the ministry of the Church. And I ought also to have known that Dr. Gore has equally expressly defined his attitude on the matters referred to in the footnote on the same page.   I should therefore have raised the point there dealt with but without mentioning Dr. Gore's name.   In the reprint I have made what changes I can in this sense in the wording of the footnote and of the reference on p. 113.   I trust that this sincere expression of my deep regrets will be accepted.

A. E. T.

EDINBURGH, *June* 1931

CONTENTS

NATURAL THEOLOGY AND THE POSITIVE RELIGIONS

We have so far discovered three great "supernatural" implications of the moral life, God, grace, and eternal life. These
may be called the central "themes" of the great historical
world-religions; an historical religion which should present
them all adequately and preserve the right balance between
them would be the "absolute" religion for mankind. In actual
fact, no historical religion presents these themes in their pure
metaphysical abstractness; each has what we may call its contingent side. It claims (1) to trace its origin back to a definite
historical founder: (2) to bring men a message which could not
have been discovered by demonstration or probable argumentation, but to be "revealed" through an historical founder: (3) to
present this message in the name and with the authority of
God, the source of all truths, and to possess an authoritative
tradition of the right interpretation of the message: (4) and to
prescribe a common rule of life and worship for the community.

"Natural" religion and theology themselves have been the
products of the meditation of thinkers brought up as members
of societies with such specific religious traditions, and have
never flourished except in a soil and atmosphere of historical
religion. This can be illustrated by considering the case of influential teachers who have been personally in revolt against
the prevailing tradition, *e.g.* Plato, Spinoza, George Fox. We
have, then, to ask what is the right attitude for the individual
man who accepts our general position to adopt towards positive
institutional religions? Are the "historical" and contingent
elements in them related to their permanent content as "husk"
to "kernel", or rather as the skin of the living animal to its
flesh? Ought a religiously minded philosopher to cultivate an
attitude of detachment from the positive religious life of the
community, as was often held in the nineteenth century?
"Anti-clericalism" has its historical explanation, but the ex-

vii

planation is not an adequate justification of religious individualism, nor is the "Church" the only, or the most presently dangerous, claimant to excessive authority. Piety, like any other
activity of life, is not likely to flourish vigorously in the individual unless it is sustained by a corresponding organised
activity on the part of the community. "Saints" presuppose a
community which cares for sanctity, as artists a society which
cares for art. Yet it may be asked how we can be justified in
finding any "authority" in religious matters for the individual
but that of his own reason and "common sense".

On the other side all reference to the community involves
the acknowledgement of some authority which is not the individual's reason and yet has a right to his allegiance. This
may be illustrated by considerations taken from the fields of
scholarship, science, art, morals. Even the man who effects a
"Copernican revolution" is revolutionary only in respect of
this or that principle; the whole body of his convictions is not
a merely personal construction. It would be a paradox if
religion and theology were the one sphere of human life in
which authority had no place. But there is the difficulty that
elsewhere the authority recognised is admittedly human and
therefore limited in its range and relative, whereas the authority
appealed to in the great religions is asserted to be that of God
and consequently to be absolute and to be unlimited. An honest
thinker, it may be argued, cannot recognise this kind of authority, and hence must practise complete detachment from the
life of an historical "church".

There is a real and difficult problem here which must not be
met by a crude over-simplification. We are not entitled to
assume that authority in religion can only be secondary and
subordinate, since it is conceivable, until the opposite has been
proved, that there have been special critical contacts between
the divine and the human, of special significance for the
spiritual life of mankind, in fact, "revelations" through historical persons. If this is so, that which is communicated to the
recipient will come to him with the character of an immediate
given disclosure from the side of God, and his message will be
believed in by others primarily as something which has the
absolute authority of God behind it, not because it is supposed
rational evidence of its truth may or might be produced. There
will be a real justification for distinguishing between religious
truths which can be discovered by the "natural light" and
those only known on the strength of a specific "revelation".
The acceptance of such a view makes the practice of an historical religion hard for the thinking man, since it raises the
difficult problem of distinguishing the substance of the
"revelation" from its accidents. But the power and value of a
purely non-historical religion may be immeasurably inferior.

CONTENTS

CONTENTS ix

PAGE

II. REASON AND REVELATION 43

Each of the historical world-religions professes to be in possession of truth about the unseen order which could not be discovered by reflection on the features common to human experience but originates in a specific self-disclosure from the side of the unseen, and is therefore, in some sense, final, not provisional. Is it disloyalty to intelligence to concede that there is a sense in which religious truth is unprogressive? If it is, no historical religion can be universal, the only universal religion will be "religion within the limits of mere reason". There is a practical side to this issue. Each great historical religion has actually claimed to be *the* universal world-religion; hence their mutual exclusiveness. God cannot have spoken with equal finality through Moses, through Jesus, and through Mohammed, for their witness does not agree.

Against the claim of any historical religion to be the universal religion it may be argued (1) that a specific revelation is antecedently very improbable, if not impossible. Its content is either false or superfluous: (2) that no self-disclosure of God can be final, since, to be intelligible at all, it must be adapted to the peculiar "mentality" of the man through whom and the society to which it is made, and the "mental" outfit of men varies indefinitely with time and place: (3) that, in fact, the element of permanent value in all the religions has proved to be their insistence on a high moral standard which is much the same for worthy professors of them all: (4) that every such religion has included as part of its "revelation" assertions about nature and human history which are irrelevant to the spiritual life, and, in some cases, can be shown to be false. But one may reply that as to (4) it is a stricture on the incidental errors of theologians and no more. As to (3) the argument forgets that the highly virtuous outsider has regularly got his moral inspiration in the first instance from the social traditions of the believing community. Kant's "categorical imperative", for example, only yields moral direction which would satisfy Kant when it is applied by a person who has first absorbed the general moral tradition of European Protestant Christianity, as Kant himself had done. And it could not be replied that the morality characteristic of a world-religion and its other contents are "conjoined, not connected". These religions have been the most potent forces in producing moral reform, though none has ever aimed at moral reform as its chief objective. All are concerned primarily with God; the moral change follows as the effect of a new disclosure about God. Their moral effects depend on the relations with God into which they bring their adherents. In this respect religion presents an analogy with science and art; they, too, have a moral effect on those who are devoted to them, but an indirect effect. They "do us good", but not by directly, in the first instance, improving our discharge of our duties to our families and neighbours. So religion has a much more powerful influence on the discharge of social duties and yet is primarily worship, something quite different from a moral rule of life.

As to (2), it is true that any truth must be a truth for its own particular time and place, and this holds of the truths of natural science as much as of those of theology. So a great work of art, or a great philosophy, is always instinct with the spirit of its "age", and has to be understood "historically". But the question is whether because every truth must be a truth for *its* time, no truth can be a truth for *all* time. We cannot decide the issue by appealing to the propositions of pure mathematics as the type of "eternal verity". For even in mathematics there are limits to the possibility of stereotyped "symbolism". And again, mathematics at best only amounts to the construction of a formal abstract type of pattern inadequate to describe the simplest piece of concrete fact.

A more fruitful analogy is offered if we consider the works of art and imagination which are found to have permanent significance. Their "universal appeal" seems to be due to the depth with which they are rooted in the special life of the society from which they spring (*e.g. Hamlet*). The same thing is true of systems of scientific or philosophical thought, and there is no reason why it should not be true of a "revelation". Even the recipient, however, can only put the content received into words in an inadequate fashion, and he has again to communicate it to others in the language *they* understand best. Hence there is always for the theologian the problem of distinguishing the permanent substance of the "revelation" from its imperfect expression. Also, it is only tentatively that we discover what is the substance, by experience of the spiritual life of the community. This may be illustrated by consideration of the question, *e.g.*, of the value of prayer, and the objections urged against it by Kant and others.

As to (1) the objection might equally be raised against all that we call "genius". Genius has the same "intrusive" character as revelation, and a "materialistic" age is commonly sceptical about both, exactly as it is sceptical about the objectivity of the world of sensible qualities. In the life of the "genius" also we have the startling and sudden self-disclosure of realities not equally disclosed to all men and at all times, which may be called "natural revelation". The world at large only learns to apprehend the reality disclosed to the man of genius by beginning with an "act of faith", and it is reasonable to anticipate that the same thing will be true of the self-disclosure of God. In neither case does this mean that the reality disclosed is created by the recipient, nor yet that it could have been reached, without him, by the "unaided" natural light. The "surprises of Shakespeare" are an illustration of this. It is quite rational to hold that there is this revelational element in all the world-religions and yet to hold that some one of them may be the "final" revelation of God in any sense in which we can speak of a "final" revelation. The visible sign of the finality of a religion would be its success as a universal missionary religion (*e.g.* whether it could produce British, French, Indian, Chinese followers who could make it "native" to themselves).

The difficulty of distinguishing between a permanent "deposit of faith" and the always progressive theological formulation of it. This cannot be overcome by identifying "religion" with mere emotion, nor by the distinction between believing a statement and believing *in* a person. I cannot believe *in* a man without believing some statement about him, or share in another's faith without having some intellectual conviction in common with him. A complete divorce between religion and "dogmatic" theology is as impossible as a complete dissociation of the "physicist's world" from the "real" world of everyday life. In physics a theory which involves consequences to which our senses give the lie is thoroughly discredited. So a theological doctrine is discredited if its truth would require that the religious life of the soul should be fostered by conditions which in fact thwart it, or checked by conditions which in fact further it. Refutation of this kind, when obtainable, is final. And the attempt to dispense with intellectual formulations of faith is as real a danger to religious life as the premature stereotyping of formulae. It is not well done to leave all doors indiscriminately open.

What has been said so far would leave it an open possibility that the *contents* of a "revelation" should all be truths of a strictly super-temporal order disclosed through historical persons and on historical occasions. But among the *credenda* propounded for belief by the great positive religions there are, in every case, some which are assertions about historical facts, past or future, and this is especially the case with Christianity. The historical religions treat these assertions about historical fact as essential, and it might be said that this, rather than the concept of revelation, is the *crux* for the philosophic mind. How can a statement about historical fact have the value of "saving truth"? Can convictions about alleged "events" have any real bearing on the spiritual life? The difficulty is increased by the considerations (1) that every great religion has, at one time or another, been forced to modify its list of such *credenda*.

(2) that many of the events propounded for belief are "miraculous" and without parallel in the ordinary course of nature, and may thus be said to be incompatible with the intelligible unity of the world. It is thus tempting to look for the fuller spiritualisation of religion by frank elimination of the historical from the contents of its creeds. But is such an attitude really justifiable? If it is, it should follow that the spiritual value, *e.g.*, of Christianity would persist undiminished if the theories of the *Christ-myth* speculations became the universally accepted tradition of mankind. But this seems incredible. The cultivation of the specifically Christian life would be destroyed by the reduction of the story of Christ to myth or allegory; a mythical Christ would no longer be evidence to the character of God. In a lesser degree other religions would suffer in the same way from the discrediting of their historical *credenda*. We might, in fact, fairly anticipate that the religion which grapples most successfully with the practical task of the reorganisation of life with God as its centre would be the religion which brings God most intimately down into the historical story of the creatures. The exceptional prominence of the historical in its *credenda* may be a proof of strength rather than a source of weakness. The completest "revelation" conceivable would be an actual temporal life, subject as such to the contingency characteristic of the temporal, which should be also, in all its detail, the complete and adequate vehicle of the eternal. That such a life has been lived in actual fact is the conviction which gives Christianity its distinctive character. Acceptance of the conviction as true demands a specific act of "faith", and cannot be fully justified by appeal to empirical evidences, a consideration too often forgotten in popular apologetics. It has to be admitted that the impartial historian must regard very few facts of the life of Christ as known with certainty, and that the Gospel narratives must not be treated as beyond the range of critical scrutiny, and again that the Gospel contains no formulated complete rule of life for all times and places. Appeal to the records at best avails to show that it is *possible* to interpret the narrative of Christ's life in a way consistent with the claims made by Christianity for his person. And it seems clear that the first historians did not base their faith either on detailed acquaintance with their Lord's biography or reflection on the excellence of his moral teaching, but on the direct impression of contact with a "numinous" personality. What facts they knew they saw in the light of Pentecost. There is, indeed, a real appeal to history by which a religion may be judged, the raising of the question whether its founder has brought a new spiritual quality into human life. The historian who is to try this issue must himself have the gift of genuine spiritual vision. His verdict will thus always involve a personal factor, as, in

fact, all serious historical appreciation always does. It cannot
be given on the strength of mere erudition and critical acumen.
In the case of Christianity the verdict on the attempt to retain
the specifically Christian spiritual life while reducing the
person of Christ to a symbol is not really in doubt. Such attempts are as old as the dawn of Christian speculative theology.
The struggle with Docetism and Gnosticism was already beginning before the latest New Testament documents were
composed. Though, in some ways, the Church suffered in the
conflict, it is historically undeniable that the victory of the
heretics would have killed its spiritual life. At bottom the
attempt to divest religion of attachments to historical persons
and events is an attempt to manufacture the supreme reality out
of mere "universals", or to make an "is" out of a mere "ought",
and ends by degrading religion into theosophy. The presence
of statements about historical facts among the *credenda* of the
great religions is thus no mere accident. But it is not possible
to say with finality just how much in the tradition is historical
fact. Consensus as to the historical character of the central fact
is compatible with wide divergence in the estimation of details.
On the other side it is dangerous to dismiss such a *credendum*
summarily on the ground that it has no "spiritual value", and
is therefore irrelevant to religion. The *presumption* is that the
proposition asserted was asserted because it was taken to have
such a value, and my personal inability to discover the value is
not sufficient proof that it no longer exists. Private judgement
needs here to be tempered by docile humility. It may be urged
that the authority of the spiritually-minded should not be
taken into account in these matters on the ground that
spirituality and sound historical judgement are not *in pari
materia*. This would be conclusive but for one consideration,
viz., that the point on which the appeal is made is not a point
of naked fact. But it remains true that the rights of spiritual
intuition are narrowly circumscribed. There is also an equal
need for humility and docility on the part of the representatives
of an official tradition.

A special difficulty is created by the "miraculous" character
of some of the historical facts included in the *credenda* of the
positive religions. Apart from the old *a priori* rejection of such
events as impossible, they are attacked either on the ground
that increasing acquaintance with natural science leads one to
believe that such events do not happen, or on the ground
that anthropology can account for the belief in them without
admitting its truth. Why should we desert in one case the
anthropological explanation we accept in all other similar

cases? This is really the most powerful of the current arguments against "miracles", though it probably exaggerates the degree of resemblance between the "miracles" asserted by the great religions and the tales of folk-lore. The question for us is whether the conception of the relation of the world to God implied by "miracle" is unphilosophical. It is important to distinguish clearly between the notions of the supernatural and of the miraculous. There can be no religion without belief in the supernatural, but there may well be religion without belief in the miraculous. It may be held that the "supernatural", just because it is present everywhere, must not be looked for in any special unusual or startling events, and that the tendency to look for it in that quarter is a "survival" from primitive superstition. Yet the belief in the great miracles of, *e.g.*, Christianity did not arise in a society with the supposed "mentality" of the primitive savage, unaware of the existence of a "routine of nature". What the belief really illustrates is the persistent tendency of minds to which that conception is familiar to expect that the unexpected will attend the doings of men through whom God discloses himself, as a "sign". The persistence of the tendency is no proof of its soundness, but does suggest the question whether it is merely mistaken. We might conceive of an eternal purpose either as quietly pervading the whole course of history or as also revealing itself specially by "intrusions", and antecedently neither conception seems more reasonable than the other. Such analogies as are afforded by the relations between novelty and routine in a well-lived life or a work of art cut both ways. The saint or hero or genius is neither an "eccentric" nor a creature of routine. We can "count on" him, and yet he does surprise us by his "originality", though, after the event, we find the "surprise" eminently rational. The success of such theories as that of "emergent evolution" seems to show that something very much like "miracle", an element of the abrupt and discontinuous, meets us in all fields and cannot be "rationalised" away, since the historical and individual cannot be analysed completely into universals. And in human life the reality of what are called "miracles" of genius or of grace is indisputable. Refusal to allow the occurrence of anything analogous in the course of "nature" seems to be due to mere prejudice. The historical is really one, not divided into two water-tight compartments, the physical and the mental. This does not mean that reality is irrational but merely that we never succeed in completely rationalising it; the rationality of the whole is a "postulate of the practical reason", and it is never a final argument against the reality of a fact to say that it cannot be harmonised with the "laws of nature" as at present known. Nor is the reality of miracle disposed of by the true contention

that the vast majority of "miraculous" narratives are untrustworthy. We may say in general of "nature-miracles": (1) that
to call an event a miracle means that it is at once startling, a
"portent" and also a "sign", a special disclosure of the divine
purpose; (2) that the event belongs to the *sensible* order. An
event might be startling without being a "sign", or might be
a "sign" without being startling, but such events would not be
called miracles. Hence there are two distinguishable questions
about an alleged miraculous event—(1) Did it occur? (2) Has
it the religious value of a "sign"? (*e.g.* it would be possible to
hold that Christ rose from the dead and yet to deny that this
event has any significance). "Historical evidence" only goes to
establish (1), and leaves (2) untouched. The event can only be
recognised as a "sign" by an act of faith. This suggests that
"miraculous" is a relative term, like "probable", and that
what is "miraculous" relatively to one "standard of reference"
may not be so relatively to another. This view would be incompatible with the traditional distinction between events produced "immediately" by God and those produced "through
second causes", but this distinction itself is difficult to sustain.
A miracle, then, would be an event recognised as having a
"numinous" character. That this character is often wrongly
ascribed is no sufficient reason for holding that the description
is always incorrect. Right recognition of the "numinous" may
be as hard as right recognition of beauty. The conception of
the miraculous is only in place in a *rationalist* philosophy. In
an irrationalism like Hume's, where anything is possible and
nothing is significant, the problem does not really arise. A
theist and a non-theist will necessarily differ about the kind of
"singularity" which may be expected in the course of events,
and this makes it reasonable that they should estimate the
"evidence" for an alleged miracle differently.

Somewhere, in every great positive religion, appeal is made
to an authority which claims to be that of God and therefore
absolute. What comes to us with this authority, it is claimed,
must be accepted, whether it commends itself to our judgement
or not, with a *foi du charbonnier*. But it is also maintained that
to recognise any such absolute authority is treason to reason.
It is held that there ought to be no initial acceptance by faith
of that which is unexamined; that there is no more absolute
and divine authority than the individual human reason and
conscience. Yet it is clear that individualism of this kind must
logically be fatal to the claim of any religion to be universal or
supremely directive of life. Historically, religious movements
which guide and deepen spiritual life seem to be regularly

accompanied by revival of insistence on authority of some kind. All attempts to locate authority in a definite seat seem to fail, and yet it seems also impossible to conceive of an adequate religion without an element of mystery and a consequent note of authority. The presence of mystery is, in fact, a direct consequence of the individuality of the real. The function of intelligence is always to transubstantiate immediate apprehension into recognition, and this function can never be completely achieved. Authority is the assertion of the reality of an experience which contains more than the individual experient can analyse out for himself. This may be illustrated analogically by the authoritativeness of sense-perception for our knowledge of physical reality. If there are undeniable facts received on the testimony of sense which will not square with our intellectual constructions, it is always these constructions which have to give way, and sense-perception thus has a position analogous to that claimed by the theologian for his authority. The appeal to authority thus means that the object of religion is not constructed or postulated by the intellect but found as given in a context which contains something more than mere thinking. It should be noted that in neither case can we demonstrate that "givenness" is not an illusion, and in neither can we come upon any primitive experience which consists purely of the "given" without any element of intellectual interpretation. The simplest attempt to say what is given already involves interpretation. This is why the "infallibility of sense" does not guarantee the inerrancy of any single "judgement of sense". There is a sense in which sense is authoritative, or even "infallible", and yet no record of observation is beyond criticism. Similarly in respect of human knowledge of God, if it is to be genuine knowledge and not mere personal opinion, there must be authoritative control of my convictions by a reality not "constructed" but "given", and impressive contacts with such a reality, not being indispensable to the mere maintenance of the organism, are not given to all of us. This is why we cannot find our authority in the "common sense" of the average man, any more than we can make the musical perceptions of the average man an authority. In all these cases the individual experience at once invites and defies intellectual analysis. The rightful demand of the intellect for freedom to think and for protection against the vagaries of pure subjectivity are only to be harmonised by the cultivation at once of docility and adventurousness. The docility must not be confined to one section of the community and the adventurousness to another. Official custodians of truth who lose the spirit of docility proportionately forfeit their claim to authority. And it is imperative to recognise that rightful authority is not the same thing as inerrancy, and that the permanence of truth is compatible with the obsolescence of the formulae in which we seek to convey it. True docility on the part of the official representatives of theology would have as a consequence a salutary advance on the part of philosophical thinkers from religiosity to religion and an increased respect for the dogmatic formulae of the great religions. It would be increasingly understood that in no field where there is a genuine "given" for the intellect to work on can the fruit of the protracted elaboration of this "given" be neglected.

Is it a valid objection to this distinction between authoritativeness and infallibility to urge that it may hold good when the authority appealed to is that of accumulated human thought or experience, but not in theology, where the authority appealed to is divine? When we remember (1) that the self-communication of the divine is always conditioned by the creatureliness of the recipient and (2) that nature and supernature have the same source, the objection seems to lose its force. The real worth of an authority which is not tantamount to formal infallibility may be well illustrated by considering the authority of conscience. Conscience is not infallible; yet its authority constitutes a strict obligation.

VI. INSTITUTIONALISM . . . . . .

The history of any of the great religions will illustrate the universality both of the tendency of religions to create an elaborate system of institutional and ceremonial worships and of the opposition that tendency awakens. We find everywhere both the drift towards conventionalising the expressions of the religious life and the rebellion against this tendency as "unspiritual". ("Ritual" not to be confused with pomp. The antithesis is not so much between splendour and simplicity as between convention and spontaneity.) The tendency to conventionalism and the tension against it are equally to be found in connection with other characteristic human activities. Every social activity tends to create its ritual, and the ritual tends to provoke a reaction against itself. Neither the tendency to ritual nor that away from it is wholly good or wholly bad. Every social activity, if it is to be preserved from debasement, needs to find worthy outward expression, and if it is to be kept alive, needs to have its occasions of special prominence, and it is here that "ritual" has its justification; the most adequate "ritual" is always in danger of becoming merely external; hence the necessity for a perpetual tension against it. The antithesis is the same which we meet everywhere between the devotees of significant form and the enthusiasts for a vitality which bursts all bounds. The absolute rejection of "ritual" would mean complete quietism, and a complete quietism would be fatal to vitality itself. We may illustrate from a consideration of the results of neglect of the "ritual", *e.g.*, of family or national life. Some "ritual" is demanded for the simple reasons that men are forgetful creatures, and the extemporised expression is always liable to be inadequate. These considerations apply to the activity of the community in worship, and here the tension is naturally felt at its keenest. Ritual form seems to be specially necessary for the activities in which the community is to be most completely lifted above the level of worldly transactions, and yet the very intimacy of the relation of the worshipper to God makes him resentful of confinement to special occasions and modes of approach. Hence the modern tendency to imagine a sharp contrast between a "prophetic" and a "priestly" type of religion, and to regard the latter as unspiritual. On a lower level, the opposition to institutionalism may be prompted by worldliness and indifferentism, or again by the view that the whole value of religion lies in its perceptible results in the promotion of good morals. But it is a bad mistake to value religion solely as instrumental to morality. To degrade worship into a mere means to moral reforms is like degrading art into a mere vehicle of instruction. Both religion and art owe most of their moralising and reforming influence to the fact that they aim primarily at something else. And religion is degraded again when it is regarded as merely a private transaction between the individual and God. The object experienced, which gives the experience its significance, is not private. Hence it is no valid objection against the forms of an institutional religion that many of them have no direct connection with moral improvement, and again it is unreasonable to demand that the community's forms of worship shall always be those sensibly beneficial to myself in particular. Neither religion nor art is the speciality of a small *intelligentsia*, and to overcome our personal repugnance to that which appeals to cruder minds is a reasonable exercise in humility. Nor is it really true that even the most artificial "institutional" worships exclude the spontaneous lifting up of the heart. Still the attainment of the right balance in devotion between freedom and prescribed form is always a "costing" thing, and it might be well if communities, and even individual congregations, took more care to avoid becoming slaves to a single "use".

VII. SACRAMENTALISM   289

A special difficulty is often felt about the sacramentalism characteristic of historical religion. A sacrament is a ritual act which besides being a ritual act is held to be a channel of grace, an *efficacious* sign or "instrumental cause" through which the Creator acts on the created spirit. It is said that belief in such sacraments is irrational, a survival of "materialistic magic". This language, however, obscures the real issue. Some acts which originated in savage "magic" may perhaps have been continued into the sacramentalism of the historic religions, but they owe their place there as sacraments to their having received a significance which takes them out of the category of the magical (*e.g.* circumcision in Judaism, the Lord's Supper in Christianity). The act is regarded as sacramental because it is believed to be of divine appointment and to have specific consequences attached to it in virtue of this appointment. It does not produce the effect, as a magical act does, automatically. Magic is, like its descendant natural science, a strictly "this-world" affair; a sacrament is an occasion of activity coming from the "other-world". The problem is whether it is irrational to hold that specific bodily things and acts may become by divine appointment the usual vehicles of a specific contact between the divine and the human spirit. The prejudice on this point is only one form of the more genuine prejudice of a false spirituality against the body. In fact it is the general rule that the physical is everywhere instrumental to the spiritual. If we take the word sacrament in a wider sense to mean any physical occasion which normally ministers to the soul's life, there are natural sacraments and the physical world is pervaded by them. (A man's thinking and conduct are normally influenced for the better if he is properly fed, gets proper sleep, air, and exercise.) Here, as in the sacraments of religion, the dependence of the effect on the instrument is usual, not universal, and the benefit presupposes the co-operation of the right disposition in the recipient. The possibility of a "nature-miracle" does not justify negligence of the regular "means". Again specific intellectual, artistic, moral achievements are normally dependent on the awakening of interest by features of the physical environment. Normally genius gets its opportunity from occasions furnished by specific surroundings. We might thus expect that if there is a still higher level of spiritual life concerned with conscious relation to the eternal, the body and its occasions would have an analogous place to fill at that level. It is true that in the cases we have considered the instrumentality of the bodily is part of the *cursus ordinarius* of nature, and does not depend on a special historic divine appointment, but this difference cannot be regarded as ultimate by a theist. Or it might be said that if the bestowal of grace is a supernatural transaction between Creator and created, there should be no instrumentality at all. Logically, perhaps, this view is tenable, but it would be as fatal to belief in the "ministry of the word" as to belief in sacraments. The true question, however, is not

how God must act but how He does act. Hostility to sacramentalism largely arises from the inability to think historically
characteristic of philosophies which regard mathematics as
the one type of true knowledge. The true question, then, is
whether if there is a quality of life which is specifically religious, life with that quality is normally exhibited at its
highest in connection with definite practice of sacramental acts
or in detachment from them. The appeal requires to be made
to the history of whole communities if it is to receive a definite
answer, and attention should not even be confined to the history of a single great religion. Thus it is desirable to compare
the spiritual effects of a highly sacramental religion like
Christianity with those of a non-sacramental religion like
Mohammedanism, and the comparison should be a double
one, of the saints of one religion with those of the other and
also of the average sinners of both. The effects to be considered, again, should be those which are fruits of the
specifically religious life.

VIII. The Ultimate Tension 320

The source of the apparent incompatibility of so many of
the leading characteristics of the great positive religions with
a rationalistic metaphysic seems to lie in a rooted prejudice of
the metaphysical mind against ascribing reality and significance to the historical. The positive religions ascribe so much
more reality to the temporal than is conceded by many metaphysicians. (The same prejudice has shown itself in Christian
theology in the traditional doctrine of the divine impassivity.)
It is significant that there seems good reason to hold that it has
been the permeation of Western European thought by a positive religion which has taught us to think historically in a way
not possible to the ancient world. (*Cf.* the objection of Celsus
that the Christians "believe in a myth which does not admit an
allegorical explanation.") Our own outlook in physical science
itself is historical in a sense in which that of the Greek philosophers was not. What the influence of Christianity brought
into the world was an adequate sense of the significance of
individuality, and the present trend in the philosophy of the
sciences towards an "historicising" of the physical sciences is
itself an effect of this. Hence it would be a strange paradox to
hold that in religion and theology reversion from a historical
to a "geometrical" way of thinking could be an advance. The
distinction between "historical" and "geometrical" illustrated
by reference to the contrast between Time as described in the
Timaeus of Plato and the *durée réelle* of Bergson, or the
space-time of later thinkers. The important point is that *real*
duration is "local" time, and that every different type of con-

tinuant in the cosmic "becoming" has its own characteristic intrinsic *tempo*, and its own "biography". For the philosophy of History this means that the conviction that history is a drama with a meaning and an author does not furnish us with any means of anticipating the actual movement of events on the strength of a formula, or of saying in advance where we may expect the incidents which unveil the purpose of the drama. Contingency requires to be recognised as more intimately ingrained in the historical than philosophers have been willing to admit. The attempt to reach the deepest truth about the world, after the fashion of Spinoza, by contemplating the historical "under a form of eternity", *i.e.* as not really historical, is necessarily illusory, a mere deindividualising of a reality which is through and through individual. Spinoza himself should have been led logically to the conclusion that the "attributes of God" are totally unknown to us. In the actual world we never come upon anything which has no more individuality than consists merely in being located here and now in a framework of reference; we do come upon endless degrees of wealth of individual character. The richer the individuality, the less are its adventures prescribed for it by relation with individuals of an inferior type. Completed individuality, such as could only be found in the *ens realissimum* would mean that the intrinsic character of the individual is the sole determinant of its life. What we see in "historical" individuals is neither such stabilised "being", nor mere "becoming", but "becoming" tending to the establishment and maintenance of stable activity of self-expression. The bearing of this on (*a*) the practice of an institutional religion, (*b*) the difficulties connected with the conception of divine immobility and impassivity.

Final words on the degree of autonomy which may rightly be claimed for the sciences in general and for ethics in particular. This autonomy is real and genuine, in the sense that every science is entitled to pursue its own problems by its own methods without dictation from either metaphysics or theology as to the results it shall arrive at. But the principle itself also incidentally justifies theology in refusing to be made into a mere instrument of ethics. And it is a consequence of the unity of life and experience that the bearings of the conclusions of any science on morality and religion are relevant to the truth of those conclusions. "Autonomy" must not be confused with a supposed right to dictate. Nor must it be forgotten that knowledge is more extensive than science, and life than both.

I

THE PROBLEM STATED

Καὶ ἔχομεν βεβαιότερον τὸν προφητικὸν λόγον, ᾧ καλῶς ποιεῖτε προσέχοντες.—
2 Pet. i. 19.

IN the first series of these lectures we have been concerned to argue that whole-hearted acceptance of the
postulates of the moral life itself involves an outlook on
the world and on man's place in it which is more than
merely moralistic. The good man who thinks out to
the end the implications of his loyalty to the moral
good, we urged, will find that he is pledged to something more than simple recognition of an ideal of conduct as entitled to his unqualified respect. He is committed, we held, to a belief in the final coincidence of
the "ought" and the "is", in virtue of their common
source in a transcendent living and personal Good—
one, complete, eternal—the only belief which rightfully
deserves to be called belief in God. He is also committed
to the recognition that whatever is, other than God
Himself, is a creature of God, having the token of its
creatureliness stamped upon it by its temporality and
"passage"; that for a reasonable creature, such as man,
the fundamental concern of life is a reorganisation of
personality, only possible as a response to an initial
movement manwards on the part of the Eternal itself,
by which reorganisation the creature comes to seek and
find its own intimate felicity not in the temporal, but
in the abiding; that the very imperativeness of this

quest makes it only reasonable to anticipate ultimate attainment in a life no longer condemned to failure by its inherent successiveness. In a word, we tried to show that the moral life of man, rightly studied, bears impressive testimony to three great strictly *supernatural* or *other-world* realities—God, grace, eternal life. An attitude to life and the world dominated by these recognitions is clearly entitled to be called definitely religious, since it is they which are the mainsprings of what we know in history as the great positive religions of mankind, and can be seen to be so with increasing clearness in the proportion in which each of these religions has proved able to control the type not of some one minor social group, with special local, racial, or other characteristics, but of humanity at large.

God, grace, eternal life, we may say, are the three interconnected themes from which all the great religions have been built up, much as a whole series of musicians, from Nicolai to Mendelssohn, have left us their different versions of the melody known, I believe, as the *deutsche Gloria*. Or, to express the same thought in a different terminology, they might be called the "arguments" of which the great positive religions are "functions", or the "determinables" of which these religions are "determinants". One religion may, indeed, give special prominence to one of these "themes" or "arguments" at the cost of others, with consequent loss to itself in wealth of contents. Thus, I take it, it would not be wholly unjust to say that in Mohammedanism—I speak as a mere outsider and always subject to the correction of those who know from within—the themes of "grace", as something distinct from a mere condonation of offences, and "eternal life", as other than mere unending continuance of a life of strictly temporal quality, are very much in the background. In some modern

versions of Christianity,[1] and, again, I should suppose
—speaking again as a very ill-informed outsider—in
Buddhism, it is God, the most fundamental theme of
all, that is relatively obscured. To preserve the right
balance between all three is no easy matter, and the
faith which can do this effectively may fairly be said to
have made out its superior claim to be the "absolute"
or final religion for man. But all three, I should say,
are to be discerned in any religion which has proved on
the large scale its power to govern the hearts and minds
of humanity. The mere absence of any is, as it seems to
me, just what makes the difference between a religion
and a, possibly splendid, speculation. Spinozism, for
example—I mean the convictions to which Spinoza is
strictly entitled if his professed premises are true and
his conclusions validly inferred from them—remains a
speculative metaphysic and nothing more, just because
there is no room in the scheme for "grace", the outgoing movement of God towards man. "Theosophy" and
"spiritualism", again, are speculations, and at bottom
I think we must say irreligious speculations, because
both make God really superfluous and know nothing
of a genuine sense of "creatureliness".

If we turn from our three great themes to the actual
religions in which they have been embodied, we are at
once struck by the fact that the three great "determinables" are never found actually operative as dominating human life in their pure metaphysical abstractness.
They actually dominate only as further specified in all
sorts of ways by particular "determinants". Every religion which has ever achieved anything of moment
towards lifting men above mere worldliness has been

---

[1] I am thinking of the kind of religion which von Hügel had in view in his
warnings against undue "Christo-centricism". F. H. Bradley once remarked to
me years ago, in the same spirit, that "the modern Christian really worships
Jesus Christ, not the Father".

more than a metaphysic of God, grace, and eternal life. All have their *philosophical* side, but all have also another side, which we may call the *contingent*, or, in a sufficiently wide sense, the *historical*. For one thing, unlike tribal cults and nature-religions, all claim not to have sprung up no one knows how or when, but to trace their origins back to definite historical "founders" —Our Lord, Moses, Mohammed son of Abdullah, Zoroaster, Gautama, Orpheus.[1] Each insists on at least one fact of the historical order as vital to itself, the alleged fact that its characteristic teaching, rule of life, or worship, goes back to a founder who was a genuine man among men. In each, again, this founder is held to have brought men a message of some kind not attainable, independently of his personality, by any process of demonstration, or weighing of probable arguments. The founder is always believed to have spoken with immediate knowledge of matters which the rest of mankind could never have known except as mediated by his direct apprehension. Each of these religions thus claims to be a *revelation*, a disclosing, through an historical personage, of some truth of the supra-historical order which we should not have learned but for that specific disclosure. In almost all cases the founder is held to have received the disclosure which constitutes his message, or mission, immediately from God. Buddhism, indeed, standing as it does on the border-line between a religion and a metaphysic, may be said to be an exception, but it is an exception of the kind which is said to "prove the rule". Even in the Buddha's case, his message to men, though not supposed apparently to come from God—of whom Buddhism origin-

---

[1] I would add that the "historicity" of the founder seems to be a *genuine* historical fact in all the cases mentioned except the last, and that even "Orpheus" is quite likely to be no real exception. The name probably does conceal some actual "prophet" of whose personal history we know nothing.

ally apparently knew nothing—retains the significant appellation of the "great *illumination*". That is, I presume, it is regarded as a *sudden immediate* disclosure of truth, following on, but not inferred from, the intensely concentrated meditation said in the legend to have prepared the way for its reception. In some form or other, immediate revelation, to and through a particular historical person, seems regularly to appear as the asserted origin of all the great religions which in any way lift man above mere "nature". It is surely significant that it should be only the nature-religions that do not claim to have begun with a *revelation*, an *intrusion* of the "other" and supra-historical into the ordinary historical routine of "becoming".

A further direct consequence of this abruptness and intrusiveness of origin is that in all the great positive religions there is a sheer *authoritarian* element. For the followers of any of them, there are things of the first importance to be believed, or to be done, which must, in the first instance at least, be accepted, not because their reasonableness is self-evidently or demonstrably established, nor yet because these things have been believed or done through an immemorial past, and so are a part of the "customs of our ancestors", but because they have been asserted or commanded by an infallible voice from the "other" world. Normally, the voice is, in the last resort, that of God, the eternal source of all truths, directly disclosing truth to the founder—Moses, or Zoroaster, or Mohammed,[1] or, as in the case of Christianity, speaking more directly still

---

[1] I do not forget here that, to be precise, the Mohammedan tradition is that the Prophet's revelations were brought to him through the medium of the angel Gabriel, but this is a matter of detail which does not seriously affect the statement of the text. It might be urged that, according to the general view of scholars, *written* "scripture" is a relatively late thing in Hebrew religion, unknown to the earlier prophets. But my point is that Judaism only became a world-religion when it had come to appeal to a *written* "Law of Moses" as its basis.

through the mouth of a person who is actually God as well as man. Usually, again, the authoritative revelation is not confined to a single short message; it has an extended compass and is embodied in *scriptures*, sacred writings of considerable magnitude, and these have consequently an authority derived from their transcendent source. An extreme example is the well-known doctrine of Mohammedan theologians that the actual vocables of the Koran are uncreated and eternal.[1] The Christian scriptures have rarely, if ever, been exalted by theologians to quite this position; yet the Vatican Council was only declaring what was, until less than a century ago, the general conviction of Christians, and is still the conviction of great numbers of Christians, when it laid down that the Holy Spirit is the *author* of the whole of the canonical writings of the two Testaments, that is, that every statement in them is made on His authority and with His guarantee of its truth.[2]

Commonly, again, perhaps universally, a religion which claims to possess an authoritative Scripture claims also to enjoy a more or less ample authoritative tradition, supplying the key to the interpretation of this Scripture, and to have, by consequence, a permanent authority, vested in its officials, to determine controversies, speculative and practical, as they arise. The bitter disputes about tradition which have marked the internal history of more than one of the great religions have rarely been disputes about the existence or non-existence of such an authoritative tradition. The rejectors of the prevalent tradition have regularly challenged it in the name of some older and purer tradition of which they have claimed to be the restorers. Thus

---

[1] See the article "Qur'an" in *Encyclopaedia of Religion and Ethics*, x. 538 ff.

[2] "Spiritu Sancto inspirante conscripti (*sc.* libri canonici) *Deum habent auctorem.*" See the explanation of the formula (by E. L. van Becelaere) in art. "Inspiration" (Roman Catholic doctrine), *E.R.E.* vii. 350 ff.

the original Protestant reformers of the sixteenth century, in general, professed not to be rejecting tradition
in principle, but to be restoring the genuine apostolic
tradition which had been corrupted in the course of the
dark and middle ages of "Papistry", just as, it was held,
the first Christians had rescued the truer tradition of the
meaning of the Old Testament from the perversions of
the "Scribes and Pharisees".

Finally, the great organised positive religions have
always been expressions of the convictions and aspirations of whole societies, and have inevitably exhibited
themselves as features of the social life of communities
with a common core of belief and a common worship
and rule of life. They have therefore regularly found
embodiment in institutions and institutional churches.
So, if we try to construct a *type* of positive world-religion from consideration of the various actual religions
which a reasonable classification would recognise as
falling under the type, we may, I think, fairly say
that historical origin, revelational character, authority,
tradition, institutionalism, are all features of the type.

The point, then, to which I would call attention is a
twofold one. In the first place, there never has been
an actual religion, with real power over men's hearts,
which has had no content beyond that of such a natural,
or philosophical, theology as we have been hitherto considering. There has never been a society of men with a
living religion whose religion has made no appeal to the
contingent, known of no historical founder, no revelation, no tradition, claimed no authority, or embodied
itself in no institutions. Every great religion which has
done much for the spiritual regeneration of mankind
has done the work just in proportion as it has made God,
grace, eternal life, realities to its followers, but none
has ever made them real except through and in depend-

ence on the contingent, insistence on historical persons
and happenings, specific revelations, authoritative traditions, venerated institutions. Men have never been regenerated by a faith like that of Rousseau's Savoyard
Vicar, never been trained for eternity by the cult of
Robespierre's *Être suprême*. Moreover, "natural" religion and theology themselves have regularly made
their appearance as products of the meditation of men
brought up as members of a community with a specific
religious tradition of its own; and, further, the quality of
the philosophic theology and devotion of the thinkers
who have been historically important in this field is
found on examination to be deeply coloured by the
positive religious tradition of the society in which such
a thinker has been brought up, even when he happens
to be personally in marked rebellion against that tradition. There seems to be little ground to believe that
philosophical theology itself would flourish, except in a
soil and atmosphere saturated with historical religion.

Thus in Plato we have—in the tenth book of the
Laws—a resolute attempt to *demonstrate* the main
tenets of a philosophical or natural theology, the existence of God, the moral government of the world, the
eternal abidingness of the issues of human conduct,
independently of any appeal to history, revelation, or
authority; but if we seek to discover the source of these
passionately held convictions, we surely must go back
to the influence of the example of the life and death of
Socrates, and the *Apology* of itself makes it abundantly
clear that the personal faith which inspired the life of
Socrates had been fed by the revelational religion of the
Orphics.[1] Spinoza is perhaps the most striking case

---

[1] I may be allowed, since the point is important, to quote my own words in
another place. "The specific allusions of [*Apol.*] 41 A to Hesiod, Musaeus, Orpheus
and the Orphic judges of the dead . . . make it clear that Socrates' convictions
are not meant as simply inferences from 'natural theology'; we have to see in

among modern thinkers of a man who makes the impression of having a purely natural or philosophical religion of his own, wholly unindebted to the doctrine or practice of an historical religious community, as its author, in fact, lived an outcast from the Synagogue, without either receiving or seeking admission into the Church. If we could look anywhere for religion wholly independent of history, revelation, authority, institutions, it is hard to see where we might look with better prospect of success than in Spinoza's *Ethics*. Yet, when we come to the one specifically religious element in Spinoza's great book, the element which was manifestly more precious than any other to the philosopher himself, the doctrine of that "intellectual love" of man for God which is one with God's "infinite" and eternal love for Himself, and, for that reason, is man's only way of escape from slavery to paltry vanities and passions into freedom, we see at once that the whole conception of this way of salvation is at variance with the naturalistic foundations of Spinoza's metaphysic and psychology. If "God" is only an honorific name for nature, conceived as a simple, everlastingly self-same, "conservative system"; if love is "delight accompanied by an idea of the cause of the same", and delight the "transition from a less to a greater perfection"—all assertions formally made in the *Ethics*[1]—

---

them the influence of the Orphic religion, though the *Euthyphro* and the second book of the *Republic* show that Socrates thought very poorly of the ordinary run of 'professing' Orphics in his own time" (*Plato, the Man and His Work*, p. 167).

[1] *Ethica* i. def. 6, props. 14, 29, 33; ii. 44; iii. affectuum definitiones 2, 6. The drift of the whole is that there can be no *amor* where there is no *laetitia*, no *laetitia* where there is no *transitio* to a higher level of "perfection". But God, or nature, the one really existing substance, is once and for all completely perfect and experiences no *transitio*. We cannot even say of Spinoza's *substantia, plus ça change, plus c'est la même chose*, since, in fact, *ça ne change point*. Indeed, in rigour it is inconsistent with Spinoza's nominalism about "universals" to admit that "Peter or Paul", or anything else, can really become more or less "perfect". In strictness all *amor* should be the effect of an illusion which adequate thinking dissipates.

to say that "God loves himself with an infinite intellectual love", and that man can enter into that love, is to utter a meaningless contradiction in set terms. Clearly we must look for the true source of the very doctrine which has won for Spinoza the reverence of so many fine natures, distracted by the warfare of creeds and confessions, outside the four corners of his own system. The God who thus loves Himself is not really the "substance" of the *First Part* of the *Ethics*; He is the "Blessed One" of the devout Jewish home in which the philosopher had been brought up.[1]

We may fairly apply to the philosophical theologian who fancies that he has cut his religion and theology loose from all attachments to the historical and contingent what von Hügel has excellently said of the type of Christian who, like George Fox,[2] sets himself in violent opposition to all that is recognisably authoritarian or traditional in Christianity. The individualist is anxious to acknowledge no source of his inspiration except a strictly personal and incommunicable "inner light"; yet, since he is, after all, a man born of woman, not a solitary of nature like the fabled phoenix, he invariably reveals his own dependence on tradition and the community in the very act of defiance, as Fox did, when he announced as his own particular illumination doctrine actually to be found in set words in the Fourth Gospel, the most authoritarian and sacramentarian of the New Testament documents. Or as Descartes did, in a different sphere, when he reproduced Proclus' doctrine of causation as a thing "immediately evident by the natural light".[3] An impressive example on the

[1] Kant's "moral theology", again, is all through really moulded by the evangelical Pietism against which Kant himself is in such violent revolt, as is manifest to the reader of *Religion innerhalb der Grenzen der blossen Vernunft*.
[2] *Essays and Addresses*, first series, pp. 92, 293.
[3] *Med*. iii. lumine naturali manifestum est tantundem ad minimum esse debere in causa efficiente et totali, quantum in eiusdem causae effectu, etc. The *causa*

other side, illustrative of the way in which a "natural religion", deliberately cut loose and kept loose from attachments in the historical community's tradition of belief and worship, soon degenerates into a naturalism with nothing religious about it, is afforded by the history of English Deism in the eighteenth century, with its rapid descent from a genuine, if thin and sentimental, devoutness into coarse and commonplace worldliness.[1]

Reflection on these familiar facts seems to force on the thoughtful mind the question, What is the right attitude for one who agrees with the main conclusions we have so far reached to adopt towards positive institutional religion? Is the quintessence of true piety to be looked for in a purely philosophic religion, wholly detached from all the revelational, historical, authoritarian, institutional elements of the existing faiths of mankind? Is all this "contingent" factor in those faiths no more than an accidental husk of disfiguring accretions, of which we may expect to see "true" religion divest itself more and more to its own great advantage, as its spiritual and abiding significance is more clearly understood?[2] Or may it possibly be that these elements of the contingent and particular are not irrelevant

---

efficiens is simply the παρακτικὸν ἄλλου of Proclus, and the principle assumed is equivalent to *Inst. Theol.* 7 πᾶν τὸ παρακτικὸν ἄλλου κρεῖττόν ἐστι τῆς τοῦ παραγομένου φύσεως. The distinction of *formaliter, obiective, eminenter,* on which Descartes' subsequent reasoning turns, is just Proclus' distinction of καθ' ὕπαρξιν, κατὰ μέθεξιν, καθ' αἰτίαν.

[1] Contrast the temper of Shaftesbury, for example, or, for the matter of that, of Locke's *Reasonableness of Christianity*, with that of Collins or Toland (if, that is, the historians of philosophy, on whom I am here dependent, have not misrepresented the latter two).

[2] Cf. the tone of Pope's *Universal Prayer*, or, to take an example from a different quarter, of the quatrain numbered 34 in Whinfield's text of Omar Khayyám. (I quote Whinfield's version of the lines.)

> "Pagodas" [the text says bluntly "idol-houses"], "just as mosques,
>   are homes of prayer,
> 'Tis prayer that church-bells chime into the air,
> Yea, Church and Ka'ba, Rosary and Cross
> Are all but divers tongues of world-wide prayer."

trappings, but themselves an integral and indispensable factor in a living religion? Possibly the very metaphor of the "husk" should serve to remind us that
though the husk is not the kernel, the kernel will certainly not ripen without any protective husk, and still
less can an animal thrive without its skin. When we
dream of a "true" religion without creed, church, or
institutions, we may be making the same mistake as
those physicists of the last century who supposed themselves to be getting down to the "reality behind appearances" by converting the physical world into a vast
apparatus of differential equations. This is the issue
to which I propose to devote the remainder of our
inquiry.

It has, indeed, been suggested to me that in even
raising the question I am travelling outside the bounds
set to the treatment of my subject by Lord Gifford's
directions. I cannot see that the suggestion is justified.
Certainly, Lord Gifford's expressed intentions would
make it improper to convert these lectures into a simple
apologetic for the specific *credenda* or *facienda* of a particular historical religion, a thing I have no desire to do.
But I do not see how the instruction that the subject
of religion is to be treated "from the point of view of
natural reason" can in any way preclude us from raising the question whether natural reason does, or does
not, demand from those who would be loyal to it an
attitude of hostility to, or at least detachment from, the
organised life of the religious community. Whether it is
irrational to believe in the possibility or the fact of a
"revelation", to profess a creed, to join in the *cultus* of
a specific community, are questions of vital concern for
the whole future of religion among mankind, questions
which the very necessity of ordering our own personal
life on some definite plan forces upon each of us, and

natural reason may fairly be presumed to have something to say in the matter. We cannot, even if we
would, debar the intellect from asking the question
whether "philosophic theology" is to be regarded as
one theology among others, competing with the rest for
the exclusive allegiance of mankind, or rather as an
element all-pervasive in every faith worthy of respect,
but incapable of constituting by itself the whole of a
reasonable man's faith. We might as well deny the
right of the intellect to raise the question whether the
truth about the natural world can be reached by exclusive reliance on *a priori* rational mechanics or not.
It would, no doubt, be a violation of Lord Gifford's
instructions to make consideration of this broad issue
of the relations between Faith and Reason into a
polemic in favour of the distinctive *credenda* or practices
of a particular historical religion, such as Christianity or
Judaism, and against those of others, and a still worse
violation of them to conduct the polemic by appeal to
any extra-rational authority. I must not, for example,
tell you that you are to believe or do this or that, *because* Scripture, or the General Councils or the Pope,
has commanded so. But I see no ground for objection
to discussing the question whether it is or is not reasonable to recognise the claims of an authority of some
kind in matters of faith and practice, and on what
grounds or within what limits such recognition of
authority is reasonable, if at all. There can surely be
no impropriety in illustrating a discussion of so general
an issue by reference to beliefs and practices in which
all of us were probably brought up, with which we are
familiar, and which most of us, in some degree, presumably continue to share, or at any rate to respect.

I know, of course, that there is a certain weight of
accumulated prejudice to be encountered by one who,

speaking in the name of philosophy, ventures to suggest that there are reasonable grounds for doubting the satisfactoriness of a "religion within the limits of mere reason". All through the last century, there was in the best minds a certain ingrained prejudice in favour of the view ascribed by Bishop Burnet to Algernon Sidney, that "religion ought to be a sort of divine philosophy in the mind",[1] without scriptures, creeds, or visible institutions, and that whatever in the historical religions is more than this can at most be tolerated for a time on the score of human weakness. The philosopher was commonly expected to prove his own exemption from such weakness by sitting in solitary majesty

> Like God, holding no form of creed,
> But contemplating all,

and consequently to withdraw himself from all active participation in the specifically religious life of his society.

Oddly enough, this distrust of historical attachments was often markedly characteristic of philosophers of the very school who made it their boast that they had learned from Hegel to think historically. I well remember the warmth with which the eminent Professor Josiah Royce explained to me that he held it a point of conscience, as a metaphysician, never to set foot in a church; yet Royce regarded himself as anything but an enemy to Christianity. An equally distinguished philosopher, well known in St. Andrews, Professor Bosanquet, exhibited the same prejudice no less unambiguously. He has laid it down in express words, in an essay reprinted very recently (1929) in the collected volume of his

---

[1] *History of My Own Times* (Oxford, 1833), ii. 351: "He seemed to be a Christian, but in a particular form of his own; he thought it was to be like a divine philosophy in the mind; but he was against all public worship, and everything that looked like a church."

scattered papers called *Science and Philosophy*,[1] that the whole historical element in the religions of the world is "mere accident", and belongs to the "childhood of humanity", that revelation is a word which is only harmless if it means "nothing in the world but our own common sense and reason", and that "authority", whether of Church or of Scripture, is a "very mischievous doctrine", because books and men cannot have any rightful authority—"except by convincing our own minds".[2] Religion, it should seem, is a purely individualistic affair, and the Church, the Synagogue, or whatever other name man has given to the religious community, is only to be tolerated on the understanding that it is reduced to the *status* of an ethical society. Strangely enough, Bosanquet seems to have fancied that in saying these things he was reproducing for a perverse generation the thought of St. Paul!

Now, one understands quite well the historical *causes* of this attitude of ultra-individualism. No one, with the history of Europe before his eyes, can dispute the

---

[1] See the essay, "The Kingdom of God on Earth", in *Science and Philosophy*, p. 333 ff.

[2] To be "convinced" that the circle cannot be "squared", one needs to be satisfied that it has been proved that neither π nor π^2 can be the root of an algebraical equation with rational coefficients. To understand the proof one needs a fair acquaintance with a considerable amount of mathematics. It cannot "convince the mind" of a man whose mathematical knowledge, like that of most circle-squarers, is confined to the "four rules" of arithmetic. Does it follow that the *consensus* of mathematicians should have no weight with the mathematically uneducated circle-squarers? One has only to read the contemptuous anonymous refutations of Darwin, or the "higher criticism", with which the correspondence columns of our evening papers abound, to see that their authors have no conception of the kind of evidence which is relevant in biological or historical study, and are therefore incapable of being "convinced". Are we to say that their contempt is justified? Would Bosanquet himself have claimed the authority attaching to an expert pronouncement in some science with which he was personally unacquainted? I should say myself that it is an important mark of the educated man that he can judge soundly when he must be content with authority, precisely because *he* is not in a position to be "convinced by the evidence". It is deplorable to find a really eminent philosopher holding out so much encouragement to the self-confident ignorance which denies that there is justification for a statement merely because it is not itself capable of seeing the justification.

enormous spiritual evil which has been done by illegitimate insistence on the principle of authority, though it
would be only fair to observe that priests and preachers
have not been the only offenders in this kind. Possibly
the State may have done as much harm to mankind as
the Church by claims to an unlimited authority, though
Bosanquet, all through his life, seems to have been in
theory as favourable to the absolutism of the political
Leviathan as hostile to the absolutism of the ecclesiastical *civitas Dei*, as anxious to maintain that the citizen
has *no* rights against the State as to deny that the
Church has *any* rights against its individual members.[1]
We have also known something of the effects of the
same authoritarian temper in ecclesiastics in retard-
ing the progress of medicine, and even of theoretical
natural science, though fortunately not with the same
addition to the sum of human misery. But one might
suggest that there is, after all, a real difference between
psychological explanation and rational justification.
Memories of the fires of Smithfield, the "horrors of the
Spanish Inquisition", the fanatical opposition of misguided pietists of a later date to the introduction of
anaesthetics into medicine, even of the rather farcical
"persecution" of Galileo and the foolish squabbles
about Darwin and Bishop Colenso, may explain a religious individualism like Bosanquet's; they certainly
do not justify it.

In our lifetime the serious dangers to reasonable

---

[1] Cf. the trenchant language of Prof. Hobhouse about the Hegelian theory of
the State as expounded by Bosanquet. "This theory is commonly spoken of as
idealism, but it is in point of fact a much more subtle and dangerous enemy to
the ideal than any brute denial of idealism emanating from a one-sided science "
(*Metaphysical Theory of the State*, p. 18); "this theory . . . by which, in the judgement of so many able men, the state assumes in the modern world a position which
earlier ages might have given to the church or to the Deity Himself" (*ib.* p. 25).
(Prof. Hobhouse, indeed, in my opinion, errs by going to the opposite extreme of
assuming that there is an antecedent probability that *any* "rebel" is in the right
against the institutional State.)

personal liberty of speech and action have not in the
main came from that much-abused body "the clergy";
at the present moment one might rather be tempted to
accuse "the cloth" of over-eagerness to divest themselves of all vestiges of a claim to authority. There is
point in the complaint I have read somewhere that
the first question the modern working "parson" asks
himself about everything is not "Is this true?" but "Can
I induce Mr. Jones to look at the matter in this light?"
I cannot help suspecting that the anti-clericalism of
many philosophers, which makes them so prone to see
an "obscurantist", and possibly a concealed Torque-
mada, in anyone who ventures to hint that authority
has its place in religion, and that the historical may
be of some importance, is little more than a belated
survival of the diatribes of eighteenth-century free-
thinkers against "priestcraft", and as much out of
relation to the realities of life as the diatribes of the
same century, which our Hegelians do not repeat,
against the "barbarism" of Shakespearian drama and
Gothic architecture.[1] We have long enough taken a
complacent pride in our possession of the historical
mind; I fear there is still too much of the "old Adam"
of the deistic "enlightenment" persisting unsubdued in
too many of us.

It may be a suitable preparation for the balanced
consideration of our problem to start from a penetrating observation made by von Hügel.[2] We all
remember the famous epilogue of the three rings in

---

[1] "I would observe that in this charge of Lysicles there is something right and
something wrong. It seems right to assert, as he doth, that the real belief of
natural religion will lead a man to approve of revealed; but it is as wrong to
assert that Inquisitions, tyranny, and ruin must follow from thence. Your free-
thinkers, without offence be it said, seem to mistake their talent. They imagine
strongly, but reason weakly; mighty at exaggeration, and jejune in argument!
Can no method be found to relieve them from the terror of that fierce and bloody
animal an English parson?"—Berkeley, *Alciphron*, v.

[2] *Essays and Addresses* (second series), pp. 122-3.

Lessing's *Nathan der Weise*, and the complaint there suggested, that it should be so impossible to find a man content to be just a man, without further qualification as Moslem, Jew, or Christian.[1] Manifestly the complaint carries its own answer with it. A man who is a religious man without having any religion in particular is hard to come by for the same reason that it would be hard to find a man who is a good citizen, but a citizen of no city in particular, or a man who is a human being without being European, Asiatic, Negro, American Indian, or anything more specific than just a member of the genus *homo sapiens*. The curious thing is that, except in this one matter of religion, we are all so familiar with the principle that the determinable is only to be found specified by determinants ($\dot{\epsilon}\nu$ $\tau o\hat{\iota}\varsigma$ $\epsilon\check{\iota}\delta\epsilon\sigma\iota\nu$ $\tau o\hat{\iota}\varsigma$ $a\dot{\iota}\sigma\theta\eta\tau o\hat{\iota}\varsigma$ $\tau\dot{a}$ $\nu o\eta\tau\dot{a}$ $\dot{\epsilon}\sigma\tau\iota$), and yet so obstinately prone to make an exception for this one case. We have long ago learned that it is no way to promote the spirit of devotion, to the public good of mankind, to make ourselves, like Aristippus, "aliens wherever we go",[2] that the man who sits loose to the duties of family life cannot be trusted to be a dutiful citizen, or the man who is "agin the government", wherever he happens to find himself, to be a self-sacrificing servant of the brotherhood of man. We fully understand the point, whether or not we admit the justice, of Swinburne's charge against Byron, that he fancied himself to be writing like a good European when he was only writing like a villainously bad Englishman. It is only of religion we tend to think as a spirit living most vigorously when denuded of the last vestige of a body.

I say this partly, though not wholly, simply to remind

---

[1] *Nathan*, iii. 7.

[2] Xenophon, *Memorab.* ii. i. 13 $o\dot{v}\delta'$ $\epsilon\dot{\iota}\varsigma$ $\pi o\lambda\iota\tau\epsilon\dot{\iota}a\nu$ $\dot{\epsilon}\mu a\upsilon\tau\dot{o}\nu$ $\kappa a\tau a\kappa\lambda\epsilon\dot{\iota}\omega$, $\dot{a}\lambda\lambda\dot{a}$ $\xi\dot{\epsilon}\nu o\varsigma$ $\pi a\nu\tau a\chi o\hat{v}$ $\epsilon\dot{\iota}\mu\iota$.

you that piety, like art, or science, or any other activity of life, is an affair of the community, as well as
of the individual. None, I imagine, is likely to deny
that intense spiritual vitality of any kind can hardly
flourish in individuals unless it is nourished by a corresponding activity on the part of the community at
large. No one counts on a succession of great scientific
men in a society grossly indifferent to science and preoccupied with war or money-getting, nor a succession
of great painters or composers in a community whose
interest in painting and music are not well-developed
and widely diffused.[1] The society which produces great
artists need not, indeed, be one in which all men, or even
most men, are themselves artists. Much nonsense has
been talked about the supposed passion of the "average
Athenian" for art from simple neglect of this consideration. There were plenty of "Philistines" at Athens—
they furnish Aristophanes with such figures as Dicaeo-
polis, Strepsiades, Trygaeus—just as in our "nation of
shopkeepers" there are plenty of persons who could
not keep shop for a month without having to put up
their shutters. But though every Athenian was not a
Phidias or Polyclitus, a succession of men like Phidias
and Polyclitus could not have existed at Athens unless
a large number of Athenians had been enough interested in their art to feel proud of it and to desire that it
should be encouraged. But for this the artists would
have starved for want of support, or gone elsewhere. So
it will presumably be conceded that a succession of
saints is only reasonably probable in a society which,
at least, appreciates and admires sanctity; sanctity,

[1] A striking example is furnished by the history of philosophy. We are all
accustomed to talk loosely of Athens as the very home of philosophy, and yet, as
Professor Burnet has more than once remarked, there are only two philosophers
of real eminence in the whole history of Athens, Socrates and his immediate
disciple, Plato. The reason is that philosophy never was one of the "communal
interests" of Athenian society.

like everything human, must meet with some measure of sympathetic response if it is to be kept alive. But where is the relevance of this consideration, which may be readily admitted, to the notion of *authority*? Greatly religious persons, when they are not the rarest of exceptions, may presuppose a religious community. How does this justify us in holding that there can be any *authority* in religion for the individual except that of his own "common sense and reason"?

I must not anticipate here the detailed discussion of the notion of authority in religion, which I am reserving for special treatment later. But I would at once make some remarks on a matter of general principle. Reference to the community at once carries with it acknowledgement of authority *of some kind* which is independent of the "common sense and reason" of the individual, and may yet properly claim a right on his allegiance and submission. Nowhere, when we are dealing with a supra-individual manifestation of rational and spiritual life, can the personal judgement of the individual be taken as the single and sufficient rule for his direction. It is constantly a problem—often a difficult, sometimes a well-nigh insoluble, problem—to decide when "private judgement" is entitled to take the lead, and when it is a positive duty to subject it to an authority external to the individual. Anyone who has tried to work at an historical or philological subject knows perfectly well that it is his business to form opinions for himself about the true sequence of events related in conflicting ways, the genuineness of a document, the soundness of a "reading"; he knows also that though he may sometimes be right in preferring his personal judgement to any consensus on the other side, he would often go wrong in doing so. There are cases in which a judicious man would think it no more than right to leave some disputed point undecided in deference to the "weight of authorities", or to retain an MS. reading in his text of an author, though he knows that his own personal judgement all the time is that the disputed point is not really an open question, or the MS. reading not really defensible. Indeed, I believe we might say that in this field authority has so much weight that a man will at times do right to defer to it when his own individual opinion is not merely wavering, but definitely made up in a different sense. There is, for example, an amount of authority which would make it impossible for a scholar of any modesty to make a change in the reading in a classical text, even though his own definite private conviction were that the *textus receptus* is "not Greek", or "not Latin", as the case may be. The consensus of great scholars who are at issue with the individual judgement of the particular editor may be such that it is the decided probability that his strong personal conviction is mistaken after all. There are few qualities more valuable to the scholar than the *flair* which tells him instinctively when he should adhere to his own judgement in the face of formidable agreement against him, and when even a strong personal judgement should give way to opposing "authority". It is chiefly because this *flair* is so difficult to acquire, and presupposes such delicacy of perception, that truly great scholars are as few as they are, and that mere industry, or mere brilliance, does not give a man a place among them.

The same considerations apply to "authority" in the various sciences still more obviously. The field of the sciences is so vast that no man can be personally completely at home in more than a tiny region of it. The schoolmen were therefore right in the main when they laid down the rule that the "artist", that is, the specialist, must be believed in his own speciality, and right for two reasons. For one thing, the man who will admit the actuality of no facts which he has not ascertained by his own personal observation or experimentation, and the validity of no methods which he cannot personally follow with comprehension, is plainly likely more often to be wrong than to be right; the appeal to our *own* "common sense and reason", if the phrase means, as it should, what a given person can see for himself to be rational, is notoriously the favourite controversial weapon, not of men of science conducting a scientific argument, but of the uninformed, and obstinate "faddists", the "flat-earth men, anti-gravitationists", fundamentalists, and their likes.[1] I clearly must not deny that a proposition in the *Principia* is rationally demonstrated on the ground that I, who have perhaps never given an hour's study to the elements of geometry in my life, cannot see for myself the compelling force of the proof, and that, even among the "educated", it is only a small minority who profess to be able to see it. Moreover, in the sciences, as in the practical affairs of life, so much depends on the soundness of *immediate* judgements, and for this no general criterion can be laid down. Only the specialist, habitually familiar with

---

[1] For a beautiful illustration of the point compare Whewell's crushing refutation of the circle-squarer James Smith recorded in De Morgan's *Budget of Paradoxes* (ed. 2, ii. 24). The refutation consists in a single sentence, "In the whole course of the proof, though the word cycle [? circle] occurs, there is no property of the circle employed". To anyone who understands the elements of mathematical reasoning this is final, but it made no impression on Mr. Smith's "common sense and reason". It is not uncommon to find it urged, even by men who are good reasoners in some quite different sphere, as a fatal objection to analysis of a work like the Pentateuch into its component parts, that no one can produce the alleged earlier documents, there is no extant copy of "D" or "JE". An argument of this kind which, if valid, would prove that there has *never* been any such thing as a "composite document" of which the separate components have perished, is frequently treated as a triumphant appeal to "common sense" against the vagaries of pedantic scholars. If, however, by "common sense and reason" Bosanquet meant, as he presumably did, something *not* peculiar to the individual, his remark is the emptiest of truisms, and only means that "authority" cannot establish what can be shown to be false. No one, I take it, disputes that.

the careful observation of facts and the weighing of evidence *of a specific kind,* is really competent to say with any confidence what the precise bearing of a well-established but complicated set of observations, or the probative force of an intricate piece of scientific reasoning, really is. The specialist's judgement on such a question is a *reasonable* judgement, an interpretation of data by intelligence, though it would often be impossible for him to exhibit the whole of his "reasons" for his decision in a form which would carry conviction to the acutest logician not at home in this particular province of scientific work.[1] It is thus intelligence itself we respect when we properly defer to a weighty "consensus" of the experts in a case where our own personal "reason and common sense", left to themselves, might leave us in suspense, or even lead us to decide in a contrary sense.

It is also clear that, in the application of science to practice, we should often be doing grievous wrong if we did not *act* on such respect for authority. Thus a medical man who should insist on always following his own personal judgement exclusively in diagnosis, or in treatment, against that of colleagues or the profession at large, would often do serious harm to his patients, and I conceive that in some cases, where death had ensued, he might properly be severely censured by the coroner. There are times when the physician would be justified in taking the risk of such complete defiance of authority, as there are times when the individual

---

[1] Cf. Burnet, *Greek Philosophy, Pt. I.,* i. p. 1: "A man who tries to spend his life in sympathy with the ancient philosophers will sometimes find a direct conviction forcing itself upon him, the grounds of which can only be represented very imperfectly by a number of references in a foot-note. Unless the enumeration of passages is complete—and it never can be complete—and unless each passage tells in exactly the same way . . . the so-called proofs will not produce the same effect on any two minds. That is the sense in which philological inquiry, like every other inquiry, requires an act of faith."

scientific man does right to stand alone in rejecting an unanimously supported established theory, but it requires the nicest judgement to know when this is right and when one would be merely perverse in taking such a line, and it is always blameable to take it without a grave sense of responsibility.

The same problem meets us in questions of art or moral conduct. As Dr. Edwyn Bevan observes, in an admirable essay dealing with this very question of authority,[1] a man would often be justified in saying, "Though I cannot myself see that this painting is admirable, though, in fact, I neither like nor admire it, I know it is highly admired by others whose taste in such matters is entitled to respect, and I suspect therefore that my dislike, or my inability to admire, is due to some personal defect in myself", and a man charged with the duty of recommending the purchase of pictures for a public collection would be acting improperly if his recommendations were not influenced by this kind of deference to authority. So in difficult questions of moral conduct, it is manifest that personal inability to see the reasonableness or unreasonableness of a certain course of action may often be due to want of fine ethical discrimination, or to inability to keep all the relevant features of an unfamiliar or complicated situation clearly before the mind. This is the reason why all but the criminally rash, when they have to make a decision in such cases, are careful to allow great weight to the accepted ethical traditions of a society with which they are in general moral sympathy, and, again, to the counsels of persons for whose uprightness and clearness of moral insight they have what they believe to be a well-founded respect. It is also the reason why in dealing with situations of an unfamiliar kind—as

[1] *Christianity and Hellenism*, p. 245 ff.

when a retired student has to deal with a problem of
investments—we do wisely not to torment ourselves
with scruples which are in all probability fantastic and
due to our own unfamiliarity with the kind of details
in question. If I, for example had to act as trustee for
a minor, I should do well to act on the principle that
an investment recommended to me as morally above
suspicion by a business man whom I know to be both
at home with such matters and personally honest is
above reproach. In practice, I believe, we all recognise
that it may often be no less than a bounden duty to
follow a moral judgement which is not our own, but
comes to us primarily on the authority of the community, or an individual "spiritual adviser", even
though the adviser may not have been able to formulate the grounds for his counsel in a way which compels assent, or even to formulate them at all. For my
own part, I confess that there are some persons whose
mere declaration, "I feel sure you will be acting
wrongly if you do that, though I cannot prove the
point", would, in some matters, be decisive, and I do
not suppose that I stand in the least alone.

The same thing is true about issues of public
morality. A modest man, for example, would not, as I
think, lightly refuse services demanded by the government in war-time on the ground of his inability to
convince himself personally of the justice of the national cause. He would, at least, take into account the
presumption that a cause seriously regarded as just by
the bulk of the responsible members of the nation, and
by a reasonably honest ministry, probably is just, and
that his difficulty in seeing the point for himself arises
from his inevitable ignorance of many of the relevant
facts, or his inability to keep the facts as a whole, and
in their due proportions, before his mind. This pre-

sumption, of course, would not hold if he antecedently believed the bulk of his community to be morally corrupt, or the ministry to be a set of knaves, and it is, in any case, one which consideration *might* destroy, but a man of modesty would, at least, recognise its existence and allow very fully for it. He might be prepared to be a "conscientious objector", if he felt the call of duty imperative, *after* due consideration, but not *before* consideration; he would not fall into the strange mistake of supposing that loyalty to "conscience" can take only one form—that of *dissent* from the "general conscience" of the community.[1]

The same considerations probably explain the hostility of most highly conscientious men to casuistical discussion of moral situations which are merely theoretical. They have a deep, and I should say a generally reasonable, distrust of their own verdicts of right and wrong in unfamiliar and complex situations, where there is no clear social tradition with recognised authority, and a decision, if reached at all, must be reached by the individual wholly for himself. It is because casuistry, if used as a direct guide to action, threatens to make right and wrong a purely individualistic affair that it is widely felt to be destructive of the genuine spirit of morality. (At bottom, it is this same distrust which explains Hegel's exaltation of *Sittlichkeit* at the expense of *Moralität*.)

Perhaps I am unnecessarily labouring a point which should be obvious when we consider the history of the formation of our convictions. It is surely beyond ques-

---

[1] It may be true that, as the "born dissenter "is fond of saying,

> "He's a slave, who dares not be
> In the right with two or three";

but (*a*) Is there any special virtue in being in the *wrong* with a small minority? (*b*) and Is the mere fact that I am in a small minority sufficient presumption that I am "in the right"?

tion that everywhere, alike in science, in art, in matters
of conduct, the bulk of any man's convictions are never
reached in a way independent of *some* authority external to the individual. In all these matters we begin
as *learners*, taking our beliefs on the authority of a
scientific, artistic, or moral tradition, which we have
done nothing to create, and have, in the first instance,
simply to receive and assimilate.[1] As we advance in
discernment of the principles underlying the tradition,
the case is altered. We learn, though we learn only if
we begin with the docility which submits to learn before
it attempts to teach, to see for ourselves the justification of much that we took at first on trust. It is but a
further step in the same process by which we discover
the defects in the tradition of the "elders". No man
can criticise or reform a great tradition effectively,
except from within; the traditions of the "authorities"
are only remoulded by those who have first proved
them in use. And, again, the convictions even of the
outstanding "rebels" against tradition, the eminently
"original" thinkers, artists, men of action, for the most
part and in most matters remain convictions which
they have not originated for themselves, but taken over
from the community of their fellows. Even the man
who effects a "Copernican revolution" in some department of thought or life is a revolutionary only in respect
of this or that principle; the *body* of his convictions is

---

[1] This seems to me the truth which Professor Wm. James and others misrepresent when they talk about our "passional nature" as the source of our beliefs.
The average man believes that God exists, that one must tell the truth, that the
earth is round, all for much the same reason, that he has been taught all these
things in early life. He could not give any very convincing reasons for any of
these beliefs, but, because he has been *taught* to hold them when his mind was
most plastic, he looks on the atheist and the earth-flattener alike as uttering
absurdities. He is impatient with both for their "unreasonableness"; his "passional nature", if it is the source of his theism, ought also to be called the source
of his geography. His *reason* for impatience with the atheist is that he regards
him as denying what is "plain" to common sense and reason.

not a purely individualistic construction, as subsequent generations regularly discover in due course.[1]

It would thus be at least singular if the pure individualism of regard for nothing but what approves itself to my own personal judgement, so impossible in every other department of human thought and life, could be the one right rule in religion. Life and the human spirit are, after all, one in all their manifestations, and for that reason we may fairly expect to find that tradition and authority have their place in religion and theology, no less than in science, art, and practice. It would be really paradoxical, were it the fact, that there should be just one realm where a man is justified in refusing to acknowledge any truth but that which he has reached by his own personal efforts, or, indeed, where profitable intellectual ability is possible, except on the basis of antecedent receptivity. In principle this should be a sufficient reply to the extreme zealots of individualism who treat the very recognition of any kind of authority in matters of religion as a merely "mischievous" disloyalty to reason.

No doubt there is an important further *special* problem arising from the special nature of the authority which has been claimed in matters of religion for Scriptures and Churches. It may be said that in all other matters the authority for which deference is claimed is admittedly that of the body of acknowledged experts in the field in question; it is therefore never

---

[1] Copernicus himself may serve as an example. In essentials his doctrine was a *revival* of the tradition of the heliocentric astronomers of antiquity, Aristarchus and Seleucus. He took from them both the fruitful part of their ideas, the ascription of the "annual" and "diurnal" motions to the earth, and the unfruitful and erroneous conception of the sun as "at rest" in the centre of an outermost "sphere" with the stars all equidistant at the outer surface. What was *personal* and specifically "Copernican" in this hypothesis was its weakest feature, the superfluous "third motion" intended to explain the parallelism of the earth's axis to itself, and this is just the one feature of the "Copernican hypothesis" which had to be most promptly suppressed.

supposed to be absolute, and it is always allowed to
be confined to some particular realm of knowledge
or practice. But the authority claimed for Scriptures
or Churches professes to be that of God, and consequently to be final and to extend to all questions whatsoever. When we respect human authority, it is thus to
"reason" itself, as embodied in the accumulated tradition of the community, that our respect is paid, and
therefore the respect is always qualified; our regard for
the gathered wisdom achieved in the living tradition in
no way precludes us from revision and purification of
the tradition in the light of growing knowledge. But in
every historical religion we meet with the notion of a
depositum fidei which claims to be final truth, permitting of no revision. Again, since authority in the non-
religious sense is always understood to be restricted
in its sphere, the claim advanced for the "consensus
of experts" is limited by the principle *ne sutor ultra
crepidam*, the "artist" is only to be believed "in his own
art". There is never in theory, whatever may be the
case in practice, any question of a right of the moralist
to prescribe, in virtue of his authority as a moralist,
what we shall receive as true in physics or physiology,
or of the physicist or physiologist to prescribe what we
shall believe about right and wrong, or of the historian
to dictate to either moralist, physiologist, or physicist.
But experience has abundantly proved that the theologian, who claims to speak with the authority of God,
the source of all truth, will recognise no limitations on
the scope of his competence. At any moment he may
demand, in the name of God, that propositions shall
be regarded as true in natural science, or in history,
which the specialist in those spheres, who adheres
loyally to his own canons and methods, is bound to
pronounce doubtful, or actually false, or the rejection

as false of propositions which the specialist in history or the sciences is bound to accept as true. What Newman said of the Christian Church might be said to be historically borne out by the procedure of every religion professing to be based upon a revelation. "It claims to know its own limits, and to decide what it can determine absolutely and what it cannot. It claims, moreover, to have a hold upon statements not directly religious, so far as this, to determine whether they indirectly relate to religion, and according to its own definitive judgement, to pronounce whether or not, in a particular case, they are consistent with revealed truth . . . and to allow them, or condemn and forbid them, accordingly. It claims to impose silence at will on any matters, or controversies of doctrine, which on its own *ipse dixit* it pronounces to be dangerous, or inexpedient, or inopportune. . . . And, lastly, it claims to have the right of inflicting spiritual punishment, of cutting off from the ordinary channels of the divine life, and of simply excommunicating, those who refuse to submit themselves to its formal declarations."[1]

It is true that not all organised religious communities make such frequent use of this authority as that to which Newman belonged when he wrote these words, or possess the same formidable machinery for exerting it, but it is also true that if most of them refrain from making much use of this tremendous authority, and are careful not to remind us very often of its existence, the claim to possess it is still there, in the background, it may be, but ready to assert itself whenever it is felt to be challenged. Hence it may be said that the claim to authority *of this kind* inevitably creates a problem which can never arise in connection with the narrowly established claim of the "expert" to authority within

[1] *Apologia*, pt. vii.

the limits of his own competence, the problem of the legitimacy of "faith" as an independent source of knowledge. Here, it may be urged, we find real justification for such language as that of Bosanquet about the purely "mischievous" character of the claims of Churches and Scriptures to authority. What the honest philosophical thinker must not admit, we shall be told, is authority in this absolute sense, and with this unrestricted range, and his quarrel with all the positive religions is that all of them, some more and some less explicitly, lay claim to this kind of authority. And, in the last resort, it is precisely because they are all *historical* that they cannot avoid making the claim. The appeal to the final and imprescriptible authority of God cannot consistently be absent from a religion which professes to have originated in a direct revelation from God. Consequently in rejecting absolute authority, a philosophic, or natural, theology must inevitably reject the claim of any religious community to possess such an historical revelation. We can understand, therefore, why a metaphysician like Professor Royce should have thought it a duty to refuse the sanction of his presence to the worship of an historical Church.

The problem is undeniably a very grave one and will call for careful special discussion in a later lecture of our course. For the present I would content myself with a few preliminary remarks intended to urge the point that it is a real problem and to plead against any attempt, from the side either of "churchman" or of metaphysician, to get rid of it by a facile solution. It is easy to dismiss the whole question *ab initio* in either of two ways. There is the way of the pure Fideist, which is to invalidate all opposition to the extreme authoritarian position by rhetoric about the uncertainty of science and the deficiencies of human reason. Absolute and blind dependence on authority may be justified by a metaphysic of complete scepticism. We are, to put it bluntly, to take the Pope's word, or the word of the Wesleyan Conference, or that of our favourite biblical commentary, or our favourite preacher, for everything, *because* there is never adequate rational ground for believing anyone's word about anything, and where everything is so utterly uncertain, the Pope's word—or that of any other of the "authorities" just mentioned—is in no worse case than the word of another. This, I hardly need say, is not the position of sober theologians of the Pope's, or any other, persuasion, nor do I suppose it likely to commend itself to many of my hearers. Yet some such theory has had its defenders, and not all of them are intellectually negligible. I suppose we might say that Tertullian and Pascal, in certain moods, come near it, and we all remember the line taken by Montaigne in his *Apology for Sebundus*,[1] and by Philo in Hume's *Dialogues concerning Natural Religion*, who, at least, pretends—though one may reasonably doubt his entire sincerity—that his universal scepticism is adopted as the surest way to Christianity.[2] Even in our own days Lord Balfour has been, in my own opinion most unjustly, represented by hostile critics as arguing that in a world where everything is entirely uncertain we may as well

---

[1] "Voulez-vous un homme sain, le voulez-vous reglé, et en ferme et seure posture? affublez-le de tenebres d'oysivité et de pesanteur: il nous faut abestir, pour nous assagir; et nous esblouir, pour nous guider" (*Essais*, ii. 12). This is presumably the source of Pascal's famous *cela vous abêtira et vous fera croire*.

[2] Hume, *Philosophical Works* (Green and Grose), ii. 467: "A person, seasoned with a just sense of the imperfections of natural reason, will fly to revealed truth with the greatest avidity: while the haughty Dogmatist, persuaded that he can erect a complete system of Theology by the mere help of philosophy, disdains any further aid, and rejects this adventitious instructor. To be a philosophical Sceptic is, in a man of letters, the first and most essential step towards being a sound, believing Christian."

acquiesce in what is put forward on authority by the established Church of our country as in anything else.

My only concern, at this moment, with this extreme Fideism is to remark that, impossible as it is for men who mean to think seriously, it reaches its conclusion by the exaggeration of what is, after all, true. It is true, and no one knows this better than the men of science themselves, that the actual achievements of science, great as they are, are much more modest than they are supposed to be by the "man in the street" and the literary representatives of his point of view. There are no specific scientific laws or theorems, not tautological, which are not provisional, and, in theory at least, subject to modifications of unknown extent, as the recent overhauling from within of the "classical" Newtonian scheme has forcibly reminded us. It is true, again, that, as Dr. Whitehead puts it, the whole body of philosophical principles of natural science, which not a hundred years ago seemed so sure and certain, has now gone into the melting-pot. (You may remember that in our first series I quoted Dr. Whitehead's epigrammatic statement, that what seems to-day the sheerest nonsense may be the accepted scientific truth of tomorrow.[1]) It is true, again, that the whole theory of inductive method, without which a rational natural science cannot advance a single step, seems to have been riddled through and through by the destructive criticism of the scientific workers themselves. No one to-day seems able to give any tolerable answer to the

---

[1] *Science and the Modern World*, pp. 24, 80, 166. Since this lecture was delivered, Professor Eddington has told us much more to the same effect, in sparklingly epigrammatic language, in *The Nature of the Physical World*: "The law of gravitation is—a put-up job" (p. 143); Sir W. Bragg "was not overstating the case when he said that we [the physicists] use the classical theory on Mondays, Wednesdays, and Fridays, and the quantum theory on Tuesdays, Thursdays, and Saturdays" (p. 194).

two questions which Mill disposed of so jauntily in his famous *Logic*, what exactly are the methods the experimental worker follows in eliciting his scientific theories from his elaborately established records of data, and what guarantee has he that the postulates about the structure of nature which those methods presuppose may not be radically false. The writers of the textbooks of logic, for the most part propound a version of the matter which is openly inadequate, even where it is not manifestly untrue; the working men of science go on their way without asking themselves whether their methods have a rational justification or not, exactly as the Fideist in religion acquiesces passively in the declarations of *his* authority.[1] And I understand that it it also true that, in many cases, our accepted special hypotheses are under the disadvantage of being inconsistent with some part of the very facts they are devised to explain. Men who ought to know tell us, for instance, that in the theory of light at the present moment, there seem to be only two options, to explain the facts by a theory of undulation or by a theory of emission, and that there is one group of facts which obstinately refuses to be explained by the former, a second which cannot be explained by the latter.[2]

---

[1] Whitehead, *Science and the Modern World*, p. 35: "The theory of Induction is the despair of philosophy—and yet all our activities are based upon it". Mill comes face to face with the central difficulty once (*Logic*, bk. iii. c. 3, § 3) when he asks "Why is a single instance, in some cases, sufficient for a complete induction, while in others myriads of concurring instances, without a single exception known or presumed, go such a very little way towards establishing a universal proposition?" That is the problem Mill ought to solve, but he finds no more to say than that the man who can solve it "knows more of the philosophy of logic than the wisest of the ancients". As Dr. Broad remarks (The *Philosophy of Francis Bacon*, p. 67), Mill "closed the door of the cupboard" on the skeleton and tactfully "turned the conversation into more cheerful channels".

[2] Whitehead, *Science and the Modern World*, p. 264: "To-day there is one large group of phenomena which can be explained only on the wave theory, and another large group which can be explained only on the corpuscular theory. Scientists have to leave it at that, and wait for the future . . ." Cf. Eddington, *Nature of the Physical World*, p. 201: "We can scarcely describe such an entity [as light]

Amid all these difficulties, one thing seems to be clear. Scientific theories only retain unqualified convincing force so long as we keep them strictly *abstract*;[1] so long, that is, as the theory aims at being no more than a logical exposition of the consequences entailed by a set of initial assumptions, artificially made precise and simple. As soon as we bring a theory into connection with the "unfaked" facts of the real world, the peculiar certainty so often claimed for science as a way of knowing begins to vanish. Science, in fact, may give us our best examples of clear and transparent connection between the various consequences of a set of assumed principles, but scientific theories, if taken to be propositions asserted about the "actual facts", are very far from being our best examples of certainty. Our existence would be far from happy, if we could not be much more sure of the truth of the propositions which matter most for the conduct of life than we can be about our scientific and philosophical theories. He would be an unfortunate man who had no more certainty of the loyalty of his friend or the fidelity of his wife than he is warranted in feeling about his metaphysical speculations, or his theories in chemistry. So much, by way of a general caution, against oversimplification of our problem by the assumption that, in a conflict between "science" and "authority", should

---

as a wave or as a particle: perhaps as a compromise we had better call it a 'wavicle' ".

   [1] Cf. Whitehead, *Science and the Modern World*, p. 36: "If we confine ourselves to certain types of facts, abstracted from the complete circumstances in which they occur, the materialistic assumption expresses these facts to perfection. But when we pass beyond the abstraction . . . the scheme at once breaks down. The narrow efficiency of the scheme was the very cause of its methodological success." Eddington, *Nature of the Physical World*, p. 53: "To think of a man without his duration is just as abstract as to think of a man without his inside. Abstractions are useful, and a man without his inside (that is to say, a *surface*) is a well-known geometrical conception. But we ought to realise what is an abstraction and what is not." And on the whole subject see the third lecture in J. Ward, *Naturalism and Agnosticism*, vol. i.

such a conflict arise, we may safely assume *a priori* that authority is a mere impostor, because "science" is the one source of assured truth and is infallible. It is the perception that this claim for "science", that it is co-extensive with knowledge, will not really stand examination which is the grain of truth contained in the wild diatribes of the Fideist.

The rival over-simplification is that of the "rationalist" of the type who understands by the "rational" that of which I have been personally convinced by arguments, or which I at least believe to be capable of being established by arguments, decisive for those who are in a position to follow them. When it is denied from this point of view that there can be any real conflict between "authority" and reason, since authority has no rightful claim upon the intellect, we must be careful to draw some necessary distinctions, if we would appreciate the force of the "rationalist's" contention. It is not, of course, seriously meant that any proposition which is, as a matter of fact, asserted by me "on authority" must be false. It may quite well be a true proposition, but, if it is true, either there are, or there will some day be, or, at the very least, there *might* be, adequate *grounds* on which it may be justified, independently of the authority on the strength of which I am, in point of fact, advancing it. So long as this justification is not forthcoming, the authority of the person, or the body of persons, making the assertion must not be alleged as a "motive of credibility". (Thus a statement contained in one of the books of the Bible may be true—as the extremest "rationalist", if he is sane, will allow that hundreds of such statements are—even though there may happen to be no means of proving its truth—as, *e.g.*, we have no means of *proving* that the name of King David's father was Jesse, though no one doubts that it was so;[1] but the mere fact that the work in which such a statement appears is a canonical Christian "scripture" must not be put forward as *proof* that the statement is true, any more than the occurrence of a statement in the works of Aristotle may be regarded as proof of its truth.)

If we take this to be the last word that can be said on the question, authority is obviously relegated to a purely subordinate place in religion. A clear-cut rationalism of this kind can, of course, afford to recognise the practical *usefulness*, or even the practical *necessity*, of some kind of *administrative* authority, prescribing what may be said or done publicly in the name and with the sanction of a given society. Administrative, or executive, authority is indeed the only protection of any society against the merest anarchy of individual caprice, and does not go beyond the limits of the kind of practical regulation which is exercised by a University, or an Education Department, when it has to decide what works may be used as text-books. But there is an end of all pretence that authority, as such, has any place in the determination of what is true. A

---

[1] An interesting parallel may be adduced from so severely "rational" a discipline as pure mathematics. Some of Fermat's most fascinating propositions in the Theory of Numbers were enunciated without proof, and were still unproved, as one sees by Legendre's treatment of them, at the opening of the nineteenth century. For all that a non-mathematician like myself knows, some of these theorems may still be undemonstrated. But it would not be *irrational* to believe them true, on the ground that Fermat may have had demonstrations of some of them, which he never published, or that, even if he had not, such demonstrations may yet be discovered, since it is not probable that a Fermat should have enunciated false propositions in the Theory of Numbers. Thus Fermat enunciated the proposition that the sum of the nth powers of two integers is never itself an nth power of an integer, if n be greater than 2. The proposition is given as a truth in the relevant section of Peano's *Formulaire Mathématique*, but, in vol. 4, with the observation that, though it can now be demonstrated for values of n up to 100, "la demonstration complète est encore inconnue." (This remark no longer appears in the subsequent edition (vol. 5) of the *Formulaire*). It is implied, of course, that we may hope that the "complete demonstration" will not always be "unknown"; this is what differentiates the case of such a theorem from that of a truth accepted "on the authority of revelation", according to the traditional view of the matter.

University, or an Education Department, would not merely be within its rights, it would be doing no more than its plain duty, in refusing to prescribe as a text-book some work in which views were freely advanced at variance with the general body of "expert" opinion. It would, I conceive, have been unjustifiable to pre-scribe the *Origin of Species* as an "authoritative" educa-tional text-book at a time when Darwin's central theory was a novelty still awaiting the judgement of biologists and naturalists at large. But no one imagines that the truth of a theory is in any way affected by the fact that the "educational authority" has not yet seen fit to enjoin the teaching of it. Statements are not true be-cause they are to be found in the standard text-books; they are found there—if the "authorities" have made their selection wisely—because there is ground for be-lieving them to be true. Thus in matters of science there would seem to be no place for any real conflict between "reason" and authority. The issue between the scientific "paradoxist" and his opponents is, or ought to be, simply, on whose side "reason" lies.

It is naturally tempting to extend this view of the functions of authority as secondary and purely admin-istrative to the field of religion and theology, and all the more tempting that history has striking examples to show of the mischief or futility of attempts to hold up the advance of knowledge by appeal to an authority asserted to be divine, and therefore infallible. Yet it should be clear, apart from all that we have said about the fallibility of science itself, that we are not really entitled to deal with the problem in quite this summary fashion. It is at least *conceivable*, until the opposite has been proved, that there may be, and actually have been, special critical contacts between the divine and the human, charged with a peculiar significance for the spiritual life of mankind. Since such contacts, if real, would be directly due to the outgoing activity of the divine and transcendent, to us they would inevitably wear the appearance of sudden and inexplicable "irruptions" into the familiar course of human life. We could not say theoretically when they may be expected, nor devise any kind of formula connecting them with "antecedent circumstances". We could, at best, recognise their significance after the event, and note their occurrence as significant, and, from our point of view, wholly contingent matter of historical fact. "The spirit bloweth whither it listeth, and thou canst not say whence it cometh, nor whither it goeth." Such a sudden intrusive contact, originating on the side of the transcendent, would be exactly what has always been meant by a specific historical "revelation"; its occurrence is no more to be ruled out of the scheme of things on purely *a priori* grounds than the similarly apparently sudden and inexplicable appearance of genius of the highest order in thought or in art. Whether this is or is not God's way of communicating religious insight to man, we could determine only by consideration of the history of the spiritual growth of our race, not from principles of metaphysics. If it is, then revelation through definite historical persons is as much a fact as the disclosure of the meaning and resources of art through specific persons and in specific environments. Thus, for example, the old cavil that it is unreasonable to ascribe to the great succession of the Hebrew prophets a spiritual enlightenment significant for all time and strictly *sui generis*, mediated to the rest of mankind through this channel and no other, will lose its apparent force; the fact, if it is a fact, will be really analogous with the fact that it happened, once and only once, at a particular juncture in Attic history, that there arose a philosophical genius of the first order, Socrates, and that he exercised a dominant intellectual and moral influence on the life of a second genius of the same order, Plato; or, again, that there should have been a Beethoven just once in history, and that Beethoven should have lived just where and when he did, and have done and suffered just what he actually did and had done to him.

If these things are facts, it is also clear that the experiences of the recipient of such an enlightenment will be for himself unmediated, direct disclosures from the "wholly other" and supernatural, not reached by inference and reflection, but *seen*, as in everyday life the wealth and riot of colour is *seen*, not inferred. It will be a distinctive feature of them that the "seer" has an overwhelming sense of their *givenness*, comparable with our familiar sense that, when the neo-Kantian from Marburg has said all he has to say, the sensible world remains something we do not construct, but find given to us. The seer will be unable to give any grounds for this conviction of his except that it comes to him from God, *haec dicit Dominus, factum est verbum Domini ad me*, and his message will be believed and received by others, to whom such a direct vision has not been granted, on the strength of their conviction that it had this origin, and that the authority behind it is the authority of God. Thus, in the fact of the reality of special direct spiritual insight enjoyed by specific historical persons, if it is a fact, we should find reasonable ground for belief in divine authority as a basis for convictions in matters of religion.

In that case, such authority really would be different in kind from the secondary authority we ascribe to "experts" of all types in their own speciality. All that we mean by such secondary authority is that the expert presumably has good reasons for his conclusions, which could be convincingly presented to any second person with sufficient special training to estimate them correctly, though not to the untrained "layman". But the *givenness* of the religious revelation means that the recipient *cannot* present compelling evidence of this kind to a second person, as he might if he were dealing with inferences of his own, any more than I can produce such evidence for the veracity of the "revelations" of my senses. If I, not being myself the recipient of the revelation, believe in its content, I am not simply accepting "for the time" a belief which I expect to find, in process of time, converted into a demonstrated conclusion, simply seeing with another man's eyes until I have learned to see with my own. To see the same thing with my own eyes, I should need to receive the same revelation a second time in my own person; unless, or until, this happens I am believing on the word of another something for which I can have only his word. And this, of itself, means that no historical religion can be sublimated without remainder into a philosophy, however true or exalted, without destroying its peculiar character. If revelation is a fact, there must be an historical element in a true religion which cannot be eliminated, and there will be a genuine justification for the theologians who have distinguished between those truths about God and the eternal order which are cognisable by the "unaided light of natural reason", and others, vitally significant for the spiritual life, which are not so cognisable, however hard it may be to draw the dividing line with precision.

It is plain, no doubt, that acceptance of the view that a complete religion involves this element of the historical, revelational, and authoritative makes the practice of such a religion hard for the thinking man. It confronts him at once with the difficult problem of distinguishing, in the revelation he accepts, between the divine content and the accidental and temporary form due to the personal temperament and situation of the immediate recipient, of judging how much of the always largely traditionary, "sacred story" is inseparable from the reality of the revelation, and how much is legendary accretion, of saying where the legitimate assertion of authority passes into the abuse of it. It is much easier to have a religion, like that of Plotinus or Kant, with no historical attachments, than it is to believe *ex animo* in any version of historical Christianity. In a critical age, like our own, the "option" for Christianity, or any other historical religion, must bring a perpetual tension into one's intellectual life from which acquiescence in a "religion within the limits of mere reason" would leave us free. But it would be unsafe to assume that in matters of religion, or in any others, the option which makes things easiest must be the wisest. "How the world is managed, and why it was created", says a great living scholar, "I cannot tell; but it is no feather-bed for the repose of sluggards".[1] We could get rid of the tension equally readily by blind acquiescence in tradition and authority, or by a cheap and easy rejection of both. But it may well be that the sort of religion with which either simplification would leave us would be immeasurably inferior in strength and renewing power to that we may have if we are willing to pay its price. It may be, as von Hügel held it is, that the *cost-ingness* of a faith which will sacrifice neither history nor metaphysics, the torment of mind, if you like to call it so, by which such a faith is won, or held fast, is itself evidence of its worth.

---

[1] A. E. Housman, *Manilius I.* p. xxxii. Cf. Ward, *Naturalism and Agnosticism*[1], i. 108: "Dangerous as teleological arguments in general may be, we may at least safely say the world was not designed to make science easy".

II

REASON AND REVELATION

If my puffed life be out, give leave to tine
My shameless snuff at that bright lamp of thine:
Oh what's thy light the less for lighting mine?
F. QUARLES.

IT is characteristic, as we have said, of all the great religions which have claimed to be universal, that is, to have a right to the allegiance of mankind, irrespective of distinctions of race, nationality, local history, on the ground of their intrinsic truth, that each of them professes to rest, in the last resort, on a *revelation*. Each claims to be in the possession of truths of moment about the unseen which have not been, and could not have been, found out by any process of reflection upon the common features of all human experience, but contain an element derived from an immediate self-disclosure, an irruption of the unseen order itself into the visible and familiar, an element which is accepted as *given*, not discovered by man's own activity. It is a consequence of this givenness of the central content of the revelation that it also regularly claims, at least in respect of what is essential to it, to be, in some sense, *final*. The disclosure, because coming spontaneously from the side of the divine itself, is not subject, like the results of scientific inquiry, to unlimited revision and restatement. There is something in it which is not *provisional*, but once for all, and yet cannot be, and never will be, established like the so-called "immutable" laws of

43

pure science. Hence the unending difficulties in which the divines of the various universal religions have found themselves involved when they begin to discriminate between the elements in their own teaching, as formulated at a given time, which really belong to this unchanging "deposit" or "core", and those which are only part of its accidental setting, and admit of legitimate accommodation to the changing intellectual "environment" of successive generations. Hence also the question, inevitable for any really critical age, whether it is in principle legitimate to admit the possibility of *any* "deposit" with this unchanging character. Is it disloyalty to intelligence itself to concede that there is some sense in which "religious truth" is *un*-progressive? If it is, it must also be an equal disloyalty to believe seriously in such self-disclosures of the divine as we have contemplated, and there will really be an unbridgeable gulf between the theology possible to a thinking man and that of any of the historical universal religions. There will, in fact, be *de iure* only one universal religion and theology, one confined rigidly "within the limits of pure reason", and we ought to anticipate, and do all we can to forward, the arrival of a day when all the historical religions shall have purged themselves of what is specific to each, and are indistinguishably merged in such a pure natural religion, just as there are those who would have us work for a future in which national loyalties will have lost themselves in a common attachment to a "commonweal of mankind".

The problem thus has its very practical side. Just as it is a practical question for each of us whether we serve mankind best by sitting loose to ties of nation and race, or by setting ourselves to be good Britons, or Frenchmen, or Germans, so it is a practical question whether we serve God best by owning no allegiance to a particular faith or Church, or by doing our best to be good Christians, or good Jews, as the case may be. It is true, to be sure, that the parallelism between the two situations is not complete. For no man, as I take it, seriously supposes that the universal brotherhood of man, if it is to be achieved, will be achieved by the expansion of the British Empire, or the French or American Republic, over the whole globe. But the good Christian, or good Jew, in proportion as he deserves the name, does look for the ultimate achievement of unity in religion, if it is ever to be attained, by the conversion of mankind to Christianity or to Judaism. Religions which claim to be universal claim also, in virtue of the element of finality in them, to be permanent, in a way in which states do not : there is a real exclusiveness about them, and it is inevitable that there should be. A brotherhood of all mankind would be consistent with the retention of separate local loyalties, so long as these latter were kept subordinate and secondary. In a "federated" religion for mankind, Christianity, Islam, and the rest of the universal religions would simply have lost their being. The "missionary" spirit is inseparable from all of them, because none can regard itself as a mere temporary precursor of the world-religion yet to come, without abandoning its pretension to be the self-disclosure of the divine. God cannot have spoken with equal finality to men through Moses, through Christ, and through Mohammed, for their witness does not agree; if God has spoken with finality through one of these messengers, then the claims of the faiths which treat the messages of the other two as the full self-disclosure of God must be surrendered. And what makes a man an adherent of the religion of Moses, Mohammed, or

Christ is precisely the consideration that through this one channel God has spoken finally, as through no other, and that to identify the self-disclosure of God with the general features in which several competing faiths are alike to the exclusion of all that is specific to any one of them, would be to rob that "revelation" of what is richest in it.

We can readily understand, then, why, when reflective men who profess one of the universal religions come to discover that societies not demonstrably inferior to their own in intelligence and virtue, possibly in some respects even superior, profess another, a distinction comes to be made between convictions in which several such religions are found to agree and those specific to each; why the former, inasmuch as they are seen to be independent of any one particular historical "revelation", should be assumed to be capable of demonstration by "natural reason", but the latter to be knowable only in virtue of special revelation; why, also, in each of the great religions it should be the latter, the specific "truths of revelation", which are regarded as of supreme importance.[1] It is equally easy to understand the reaction of the critical intelligence against this point of view. Some such reaction, indeed, might have been expected to show itself, even if history has presented us with no more than one single revelational religion, with no competitors. Even in such

[1] Cf. C. C. J. Webb, *Studies in the History of Natural Theology*, p. 158-9: "We shall not find in Anselm a sharp distinction . . . drawn between the spheres of Natural and Revealed Theology. Modern Roman Catholic writers, for whom the distinction established by St. Thomas Aquinas is authoritative, sometimes find themselves obliged to apologise for Anselm's inattention to it. No doubt the reason for it is to some extent historical. The intimacy of the later schoolmen with the doctrines of Aristotle least capable of reconciliation with Christian dogma . . . as also with the writings of the Mohammedan commentators, forced upon their attention the fact of the diversity of creeds, and the consequent question whether there was not a common stock of knowledge concerning things divine independent of this diversity." [I should suspect the study of Maimonides had most to do with calling the attention of St. Thomas to the point.]

a case it would seem inevitable that the religion
should be lived and practised before it could be reflected upon, and an attempt made to say precisely what
are the "doctrines" about the unseen implied by this
life and practice. And the first attempts to answer the
question would be bound to take account of what was
most obvious. In course of time the answers would
need reconsideration, in view of constantly emerging
divergences of speculation and practice within the
growing religious community, of new situations calling
for fresh adaptations, of collisions between the earliest
formulations of the community's belief and subsequently discovered facts of the temporal and secular
order. The necessity of taking account of competing
theologies only accentuates this process a little more
acutely; even apart from that necessity, theology, the
intellectual formulation of the implications of a religion, is clearly largely tentative and progressive,
and this is enough to raise the problem whether the
religion itself may also be considered, in the end, to be
wholly provisional and tentative—a view which would
make real revelation superfluous.

If we consider the problem, as I hold that Lord
Gifford's instructions compel us to do—in its complete
generality, without any suggestion of an *apologia* for
the claims of a particular world-religion to be *the*
revelation of God to man—I believe we may fairly
summarise the main arguments against the reality of
"special" revelation as follows:

(1) A revelation, if not impossible, is at least antecedently highly improbable.[1] For either the statements

---

[1] I am of Professor Eddington's opinion that it is a much more damaging
objection to a thesis to call it "highly improbable" than to call it "impossible".
The "impossible" commonly only means that which an opponent has ruled out of
consideration by an *arbitrary* initial postulate. (*Nature of the Physical World*, pp.
74-7.) It is a trivial objection against the causal efficacy of human volitions that

alleged to be revealed are in conflict with truths ascertained by the "natural use of reason",[1] or they are not. In the second case, they are attainable in due time by the unaided patient employment of human intelligence, and so a revelation of them is, at best, superfluous; in the first, they are not even genuine truths, and therefore, *a fortiori*, not revelations.

(2) If God discloses Himself to us at all, it should be in a way intelligible and convincing to men in all times, and at all places; otherwise there can be no finality about the disclosure. But from the nature of the case, *such* disclosure is impossible.[2] A revelation made through a particular person, to particular persons, in particular circumstances, will not be intelligible—much less convincing—unless it is adapted to the "mentality"—*sit venia verbo*—of the man through whom it comes and the men to whom it comes. All truths, to be received and understood, must be thus adapted to the whole state of mind of the specific recipients, as a spoken message, to be apprehended, must be conveyed in a determinate idiom. You cannot speak without speaking some particular language—Latin, French, English, or some other—and if you are to be understood by speakers of English, you must speak not only

---

it is an "impossibility" (*i.e.* will not fit into the wholly arbitrary "determinist" metaphysical scheme); it is a grave—I should say an insuperable—objection to all theories of "parallelism" that, as James Ward urges, invariable concomitance *without* causal connection is infinitely improbable.

[1] I mean, of course, by "use of reason", the employment of reason upon data supplied to it by perception. I am not suggesting that reason can function *in vacuo*. I fully concede that, if reference to data is excluded, "reason" condemns nothing but violation of the formal "laws of thought".

[2] I must not be charged with inconsistency on the ground that I am now urging "impossibility" as a grave objection to revelation, in spite of what has been said in n. 1 to p. 47. The reasoning given here is not my own, but that of certain σοφοί whose view I am stating for purposes of examination. Cf. d'Holbach's question "s'il (viz. God) a parlé, pourquoi l'univers n'est-il pas convaincu?" and Shelley's employment of the passage in the note to *Queen Mab*, vii. 13. I am trying to make the best argumentative case I can for d'Holbach and Shelley; their own exposition contains much more bad rhetoric than tolerable reasoning.

English, but the English of a definite period, the English of the contemporaries of Cynewulf, or Chaucer, or Milton, or Tennyson, as the case may be. Now the mental outfit of men varies with place and time, like their speech, being moulded in much the same fashion by the traditions of their historical past. The very thoughts which were true and significant to a Galilean of two thousand years ago have lost their truth and significance for us, to whom they are as foreign as the Aramaic vocables in which they were originally uttered. What is the highest and most vital truth for us may similarly be unmeaning for men of the fortieth century, whose whole intellectual outlook on the world will presumably be as unlike ours as their speech. There are, in fact, no "truths for all time"; every truth, to be genuine truth, must be the truth for *its* time.[1] Revelation, then, as it has been conceived by the world-religions is not merely superfluous, but actually impossible.

(3) If we consider what has been the really valuable element in the various world-religions, we shall be led to the same conclusion. They have been of value just so far as they have been an elevating influence in life, and they have made for the elevation of life in proportion as they have taught and enforced a high standard of moral conduct, and no further. In a society which has reached a sufficiently high level of reflective moral civilisation, a variety of religions may be professed, but the recognised rules of conduct are much the same for the adherents of all, as we see, in our own society; the serious-minded men, whether they are Christians, or Jews, or stand outside all the great historical religious communities, have much the same ideal of good conduct, and conform to it about equally

---

[1] Remember, once more, that οὐκ ἐμὸς ὁ μῦθος.

well. It is reasonable, then, to look for the final and divine element in the various religions in a moral ideal and rule of life, just the characteristic in respect of which they tend to merge into one another; unreasonable to attach significance to the features which discriminate them. Thus the element of true and abiding religion in all the religions is a purely moral one, independent of revelations alleged to be made to particular persons and at particular times. At most, we might perhaps include in it, along with the moral ideal and rule themselves, whatever implications about the unseen order a genuine morality demands. But these implications will constitute only a "natural" or "philosophical" theology, "within the limits of mere reason".

(4) It might be added that there is not one of these revelational religions which has not included, as an integral part of its professedly divine revelation, assertions of fact about the course of nature and of human history. But it is difficult to believe that, in a rational universe, any man's attainment or non-attainment of his final good can be contingent on the accident of his acquaintance with events of which he may never have had the opportunity to hear. Moreover, in the case of every such religion, the assertions of fact about nature and human history which have been made on the strength of revelation have included some which have proved to be false.

This, I believe, is the main substance of such a case as a fair-minded man might make out against admitting the possibility of recognising divine self-disclosures, made at specific times and places, as a real source of knowledge about God and about man's beatitude. With more special polemical objections against the genuineness of a particular revelation, the Christian or another, we are not now concerned. I propose to offer some reflections on the cogency of such a destructive *Kritik aller Theologie, die als Offenbarung auftreten will.*

It has, no doubt, to be admitted that there is point in much of what has been urged, and that the discredit into which the notion of revelation has fallen with, perhaps, a majority of reflective men has, in large measure, been due to the fault of the representatives of revelational religion themselves. Even when, as in the case of the Christian Church, they have professedly limited the sphere of revelation to faith and morals, they have been apt to bring a great many assertions of natural and historical fact under this rubric, on the plea that they are indirectly necessary for religion and morality, and have often shown a levity in advancing this claim which has recoiled on themselves, as the assertions in question have been more and more completely shown to be mistaken. They have failed signally to distinguish, as they should have done, between the content of the primary revelation upon which they rest, the actual self-disclosures of God made through their founders and prophets, and the whole contents of the sacred writings which profess to record the circumstances of those self-disclosures, or to comment upon and expound their significance. It is a more serious matter that they have often revolted the sensitive conscience, as some of them still continue to revolt it, by making the eternal welfare of men depend on the historical accident of acquaintance with, and appreciation of, their own special revelation. Ignorance, even when wholly unavoidable, has been put, in this respect, on a level with deliberate and obstinate rejection of the truth. Thus the traditional Moslem belief has been, and presumably still is, that "idolaters", Jews, Christians, all go to "the fire", even those who have

never heard of the Prophet and his "perspicuous book";
and Christians, on their side, have only too often maintained the same thing of all the millions of the human
race who have never known of the Gospel and its contents. The claim to the exclusive possession of the final
revelation has naturally and directly led to the dictum
extra ecclesiam nulla salus, and it is instructive to note
the devices to which the sensitive and thoughtful have
been driven, in order to reconcile themselves to such a
principle. Thus we have in the Middle Ages the examples of the attempts of men like Roger Bacon and
St. Thomas to exempt the great Gentiles from the
sentence, either by forced exegeses which discover the
special doctrines of the Church's theology in the text of
Plato and Aristotle,[1] or, more modestly, by falling back,
with St. Thomas,[2] on the double possibility that the

[1] This view commended itself to Roger Bacon, from its coherence with his
"illuminationist" conception of philosophy as originating in a revelation to the
patriarchs. Cf. what is said of Aristotle in c. 1 of Bacon's "edition" of the *Secretum Secretorum* (*Opera inedita,* fasc. v. p. 36): "erat vir magni consilii et sani et
literature magne, penetrabilis intellectus, vigilans in legalibus studiis, in gratuitis
moribus et spiritualibus scienciis, contemplativus, caritativus, discretus, humilis,
amator justicie, relator veritatis. Et propter hoc multi philosophorum reputabant
ipsum de numero prophetarum. Invenitur etiam in antiquis codicibus Grecorum
quod Deus excelsus suum angelum destinavit ad eum dicens: Pocius nominabo te
angelum quam hominem . . . de morte sua diverse sunt opiniones. Quedam enim
secta que dicitur peripathetica asserit ipsum ascendisse ad empeireum celum in
columpna ignis." Bacon's own comment on these statements of his (Arabic)
author is (p. 37) that the philosophers had certain "preludia fidei, set quod suffici-
entem fidem habuerunt non debemus ponere, nec tamen debemus affirmare damp-
nacionem aliquorum dignissimorum virorum, quia nescimus quid fecerit eis Deus."
[2] *S. Th.* ii.ª ii.ᵃᵉ q. 2, art. 7 ad tertium. "Multis Gentilium facta fuit revelatio de
Christo, ut patet per ea quae praedixerunt. . . . Si qui tamen salvati fuerunt quibus
revelatio non fuit facta, non fuerunt salvati absque fide Mediatoris: quia etsi non
habuerunt fidem explicitam, habuerunt tamen fidem implicitam in divina provi-
dentia, credentes Deum esse liberatorem hominum secundum modos sibi placitos."
The case under consideration is that of the Gentiles of pre-Christian time. It is
not clear to a non-specialist whether Thomas would extend the principle to meet
the case of Gentiles in Christian times, living remote from Christendom. Possibly
they might get the benefit of the doctrine of the "baptism of desire", which Dante
introduces to explain the presence of Rhipeus in Paradise (*Par.* xx. 127-8).
Dante's own treatment of the problem *seems* singular. The great Gentiles in general
are placed in a Limbo which is technically in Hell, but where there is no *poena
sensus.* It should seem to follow that they are excluded from Paradise neither
by mortal, nor by venial, sin, but solely by the *peccatum originis,* like unbaptized

righteous man, living remote from the society which possesses the saving revelation, may either receive a strictly personal revelation, or, at any rate, may attain to an "implicit" faith in a redemption which God will effect by ways known to Himself.

With all this, however, we are not specially concerned now. Whatever may be the best solution of the question of God's dealings with those who, from no fault of their own, have been beyond the reach of an historical revelation, it is irrelevant to make difficulties of this kind a ground for denying *in limine* the possibility, or the worth, of such a revelation. If the possibility of a real specific self-disclosure of the divine be granted, the problem raised by the fact that it is not bestowed equally on men in all times and at all places becomes, in principle, identical with the more general problem, why men everywhere and at all times are not equally favoured with other good gifts; why one man has endowments and opportunities which are denied to another. That problem admits of no solution, except that of Uncle Toby[1]—and St. Paul—that God in His wisdom has disposed it so. The alleged moral difficulty only arises when we go on needlessly to complicate the problem by the assumption that a God of infinite wisdom and goodness penalises His creatures for not possessing what He has not seen fit to bestow on them; and this assumption, we may fairly say, is

---

infants. And this seems to be actually implied in the case of Virgil, of whom we are told that only Baptism is wanting to him (*Inferno*, iv. 39). Yet Dante can hardly have supposed that the most excellent Gentiles were wholly free from venial sins, and his Limbo contains persons like Julius Caesar, whom he cannot have thought clear of some mortal sins.

[1] Sterne, *Tristram Shandy*, iii. 41: "There is no cause but one, replied my Uncle Toby, why one man's nose is longer than another's, but because that God pleases to have it so. . . . That is Grangousier's solution, said my father. 'Tis he, continued my Uncle Toby . . . who makes us all, and frames and puts us together in such forms and proportions, and for such ends, as is agreeable to his infinite wisdom."

obsolete in any form of historical religion which is a "live option" for educated Europeans to-day.[1]

The other three considerations demand less summary treatment, and it may be convenient to deal with them in the reverse order from that in which we stated them. Is revelation shown to be superfluous, and therefore not reasonably to be reckoned with, as a source of knowledge of the divine by the contention that knowledge of our moral duties is sufficient for us, and on them there is agreement? For one thing, I am not myself clear that the agreement is as complete as the argument assumes. What is meant seems to be that the precepts of such a code as the Ten Commandments are, in the main, accepted and followed equally by Christians, Jews, Moslems, persons without any special religious "profession". In our own society a decent man who is theoretically a complete "Agnostic", or even an avowed Atheist, is usually about as "moral", in the way of paying his debts, abstaining from violence and fraud, and leading a wholesome family life, as the man who is a regular Church-goer. So much, no doubt, is happily true: we have long ago discovered that the man who professes no religion at all is not, as a rule, the more likely to cut our throats, corrupt our daughters, or cheat us of our property; he is not neces-

---

[1] The Anglican Church formally anathematises, in its 18th Article, those who "presume to say, that every man shall be saved by the law or sect which he professeth, so that he be diligent to frame his life according to that law, and the light of nature", on the ground that "holy Scripture doth set out to us only the name of Jesus Christ, whereby men must be saved". But nothing is said, or implied here, as to the destiny of the non-Christian. All that is denied is that the "virtuous unbeliever" will be saved by his unbelief. That no "virtuous unbeliever" will, in fact, be saved, has never, so far as I know, been the teaching of the Anglican Church, and is certainly not the belief of any responsible Anglican teacher to-day. I am surprised that a philosopher of the distinction of James Ward should have gone wrong on so simple a point. (*The Realm of Ends*, p.424, "There is one doctrine of the theology now in vogue which gives special point to the objection we have considered—the doctrine that those who die outside the pale of Christianity are "lost eternally". I do not know where this theology is "in vogue"; certainly not in any Christian community with which I am acquainted.)

sarily a would-be criminal only restrained by fear of the police, as eighteenth-century apologists were too ready to contend, forgetful perhaps of the vehement assertions of thinkers of the so-called "ages of faith" about the inferiority of the moral practice of their contemporary Christians to that of classical Paganism in its flourishing days. But when it is further assumed, on the strength of this general uniformity of moral standard and practice within our own community, that religion, as an inspiration to practical good living, is independent of all historical revelation, certain relevant facts seem to be overlooked. It is forgotten, that whatever may be the theological tenets of the individual among us, the morality by which he lives is one which he has learned from the tradition of his community, and that this tradition has been formed under the direct influence of a great revelational religion. Even where a rule of conduct has not been directly inspired by the specifically Christian tradition, the interpretation put on the rule, often a far more important thing than the formula itself, has come direct from that tradition.

It might, no doubt, be said that when once the interpretation has been reached, its reasonableness, and the unreasonableness of any other, can be discerned without reference to its origin, and, in principle, I would not dispute this. But, as Aristotle should have convinced us long ago, in moral matters there are no postulates which are self-evident *ex vi terminorum*; it is only the man who has begun by accepting the postulates by an act of faith, and thus acquired "moral insight" *pari passu* with the acquisition of virtuous habit, who comes in the end to see that the ἀρχαί of "practical philosophy" *are* true and rational. Thus the fact that men of to-day who have been trained in doing good to those who hate them and persecute them pronounce the principle of meeting hatred by love rational, even though they may no longer accept the Gospel as "revelation", is not sufficient proof either that such action would ever have come to be recognised as "conformable to right reason" without the Gospel, nor that it will continue to be regarded as reasonable in a society which has been emancipated from the influences of Christian theology long enough to be able to treat the Gospels as a mere interesting historical monument.[1]

The point can perhaps be made still clearer if we consider the most famous modern attempt to construct an exceptionally high and austere morality in complete independence of history and revelation—the attempt of Kant. There is no principle upon which Kant is more anxious to insist than the strict "autonomy" of ethics. According to him all that is valuable in religions is their *enforcement* of a right rule of conduct on the "heart" and the imagination; the rule itself is discoverable by metaphysical analysis, without any reference to historical social tradition, much more without any reference to revelation; we discover it by *analysing* the implications of the concept "reasonable action". Ethics must thus be built up from the first without any reference to God, either as the *source* of obligation or the object *towards* which we have obligations. It is only by subsequent reflection on the ultimate presuppositions of an

---

[1] The argument becomes much stronger when we compare the moral standard of persons, whether "believers" or not, who have been brought up under the influence of the Christian tradition, with that of those who have been untouched by it. Christian morality, for example, and Moslem morality, both forbid adultery. But the Moslem tradition, with its permission of polygamy, concubinage, and divorce, recognises as morally unobjectionable a great deal of conduct which, by Christian standards, is deliberate and persistent adultery. The individual Moslem, as we know, may often conform in practice to the demands of the Christian standard in this matter, but the fact remains that behaviour which to the Christian is obligatory, on pain of mortal sin, is to the Moslem a "counsel of perfection".

already constituted and recognised true morality that
we discover justification for believing in God as the
monarch of the "kingdom of ends". For ethics itself it
has to be kept an open question whether the commonwealth of ends may not be a pure democracy. It is
consequently vital to Kant's unqualified "rationalism"
to maintain, as he notoriously does, that the "Categorical Imperative" which enjoins reasonableness, and
forbids unreason in our every action, has a twofold
character. It is not only merely a general formula
under which all specific right action can be brought, as
the *dictum de omni et nullo* is a general formula under
which all valid syllogisms can be represented; it is also
an infallible direct *criterion* of the rightness or wrongness of any specific act proposed to be done.[1] We can
guarantee ourselves against the commission of moral
wrong-doing if we will only take care to ensure that
there is no latent contradiction in the principle of the
act we are proposing to perform, and that the act is, in
consequence, formally reasonable. (In Kant's theory
there can be no question of a *material* wrongness
which would be compatible with merely *formal* rightness. If the act is formally right, it is right *simpliciter*,
and the worst you can say of it is that it has had
"unwelcome" consequences, an extra-ethical consideration.) Kant thus holds out to anyone who will apply
the proposed criticism to his contemplated acts a moral
inerrancy, which may remind us of the intellectual
inerrancy promised by Descartes to those who will
suspend their judgement whenever their ideas are not
"clear and distinct".

Now it is notorious that the chief difficulty found
by later critics in Kant's doctrine arises, not from his
treatment of the Categorical Imperative as a correct

---

[1] *Werke* (Hartenstein[2]), iv. 251.

general formula for right action, but from this insistence on its further applicability as an immediate
practical criterion. As is often said, it is a defect of the
criterion that the only results Kant can get from it are
purely negative. At best, it only stamps acts of certain
kinds, like the deliberate making of fraudulent promises,
as wrong. It gives no positive guidance whatever, as
Kant might have seen if he had asked himself how the
test is to be applied to a really difficult moral problem,
like, for example, the choice a young man may have
to make between the career which will immediately
qualify him to contribute most efficiently to the support
of his mother and sisters and that in which he can
make the most valuable contribution to art or science;
or the problem whether a specific man, in specific circumstances, would do right to make a specific offer
of marriage, or, again, to break off an engagement to
marry. Kant's criterion, that the unreasonable course
is the morally wrong course, will only apply in such
cases if one has already discovered, in some unexplained way, what is the *reasonable* course. If that
is still uncertain, the application of the test leaves the
uncertainty where it was.

What is worse, but even more illuminating, the
failure of the criterion is not confined to these cases
of special decisions in highly complex situations,
where no sane moralist would expect to be able to
lay down any rule of general applicability. The test
equally fails in cases where moralists in general would
agree that there is a recognisable rule. For example,
it obviously rules out adultery, since adultery—breach
of bed-vow—is only possible where marriage, as a
status with definite rights and duties, exists, and thus
he who wills to permit himself an act of adultery is
willing at once that there shall and shall not be respect

for the rule of marriage. But the advocate, or practiser, of complete sexual promiscuity would come out unscathed from the application of the test. *His* "maxim" is simply that the sexual side of human life should be, like many other sides of it, left unregulated to the "inclination" of the parties concerned, and there is no more *logical* absurdity in such a maxim than there is in the proposal to leave men to please themselves at which end they will break their breakfast-eggs, or whether they will starch their collars. Yet we may feel fairly sure that Kant would have agreed with the common verdict that, though adultery is morally bad, universal promiscuous "free love" would be worse.[1] How, then, comes he never to have reflected that his highly extolled criterion of right and wrong cannot well be sound, since it fails in so obvious a case? The only answer I can find is that Kant all along tacitly assumes that he *already* knows what sort of acts are right, before he resorts to his criterion. He takes it unconsciously for granted that the traditional moral rules recognised by educated German Protestants of his own time are known to be the right rules, and may therefore—since his analysis has yielded the equation *right* = *rational*—be presumed to be rational. If you

---

[1] Cf. the singular argument by which Kant attempts to prove in the *Metaphysik der Sitten* (*Werke*, Hartenstein[2], vi. 76 ff.) the immorality of all sexual relations outside the limits of lifelong monogamous marriage. Strict fidelity to monogamy is demanded on the ground that an act of sexual intercourse is one in which a human being "converts himself into a thing, conduct which conflicts with the right of humanity in its own person". This, says Kant, can only be legitimated if *each* party to the act adopts the same attitude; each must "convert its personality into thinghood", *i.e.* each must assume the position of *instrument* to the pleasures of the other. This really seems to amount to no more than a certain well-known sentiment of Ovid. If Kant's description of the sexual relation were truly an adequate one, it should surely follow that it conflicts with the rights and duties of personality in a way not to be made good, and is therefore simply vicious. And, at any rate, if the conflict is removed by reciprocity, it should follow that simple fornication to which both parties are freely consenting is as unobjectionable as marriage. The artificial reasoning by which Kant tries to evade this consequence, if valid, would seem equally to prove that morality is outraged by a cricketer who employs different "professionals" to bowl to him on different occasions.

grant this, it is not very hard for him to prove plausibly that various ways of acting, which conflict with this tradition, being in conflict with what is *ex hypothesi* rational, must be irrational, and therefore wrong.

But to justify his own claims for his criterion, Kant ought to have done something very different. He ought to have shown that by applying it we can work out an unambiguous moral legislation *in vacuo* for a community of human beings[1] destitute of all tradition. If we recognise that *this* task is insoluble in principle, and that consequently pure "rationalism" in the strict Cartesian sense, rigid deduction of conclusions, through a chain of "clear and distinct ideas", from principles "evident by the natural light", is as impossible in ethics as in other fields of thought, we must admit that it is a matter of moment for morality itself what the unproved "synthetic" postulates of a moral tradition are. In point of fact, these postulates which give a moral tradition its distinctive individual quality are not found, in the history of civilisation, existing apart from the religious tradition of the community; they are part and parcel of it. Christian religious tradition is not, indeed, the only source of the moral ideal current in our own country and our own age; we have also to take into account the influence of racial and national temperament, of our inheritance from the classical moral civilisation of Greece and Rome, and, no doubt, of other factors not so easy to trace. But the influence of the specifically religious Christian tradition is *all*-pervasive in our accepted scheme of values. Even when some particular feature in our moral scheme seems at first sight most obviously due to the historical in-

---

[1] I say "*human* beings" because in their case only we may presume empirical acquaintance with the great fundamental "inclinations" common to the kind, and this empirical knowledge is necessary for "applied" ethics.

fluence of Greece or Rome, the lesson *we* learn from
classical antiquity is, commonly, profoundly modified
for us by the Christian medium through which we have
received it;[1] it is just this which makes it difficult for the
historically minded student of morals to understand
the ethical thought of a Socrates or an Aristotle,
"objectively", without unconsciously Christianising it
in all sorts of more or less subtle ways. We have, I
submit, no right to say that our moral tradition of
conduct could have come to us in any way except that
in which such tradition has historically come to every
society with whose moral tradition we are acquainted,
that is, as connected by relations of reciprocal inter-
dependence with a religious tradition.

It might be possible to admit the fact of this complication of the morality characteristic of a world-
religion with its specifically religious element, and yet
to dispute the importance of the fact. For, it might be
said, though, in fact, we never find the religious and
the ethical isolated from one another in an historical
tradition, we may isolate them for ourselves by a
Denkexperiment. Noetic analysis will enable us to
get each loose from the other, though in actual fact
they are regularly presented together. In fact, that is,
they are always "conjoined", not, in any real sense,
"connected"; why then should we make the conjunction any reason for doubting that the one may be the
precious ore, the other merely so much dross? I should

---

[1] To give a single illustration out of many which might be adduced: In one of
the most impressive of recent books on Plato, I read that "conscience" is a characteristically "religious" and "Christian" concept which is meaningless from the
moral standpoint of Plato (Stenzel, *Platon der Erzieher*, p. 278). To my own mind
such a statement makes nonsense of the *Apology*, the *Crito*, the *Gorgias*, and I
can only account for its presence in a valuable book by the reflection that whereas
I see Plato through a tradition shaped by Augustine, Cudworth, Butler, Richard
Price, the German author views him through a different medium, just as inevitably as an Englishman sees the great Attic tragedians in the light, so to say,
of Shakespeare, a Frenchman, presumably, in that of Racine.

reply that, if we take that line, we lay ourselves directly
open to a rejoinder which I find unanswerable. Each
of the great world-religions has been, for good or for
evil, a most potent force in transforming the whole
scheme of moral "valuations"; each has produced a
moral *reform*—not necessarily a salutary one—on the
grand scale, and it would be hard to point to any other
influence in history which has had the same effect on
such a scale. But it is equally true that no great historical religion has ever aimed, first and foremost, at a
moral reform as its main objective. Each has always
rested its claim on mankind primarily not on the improved morality it enjoins, but on the new light it throws
on God and man's relation to God. Mohammed is
credited with improving the morals of the Arabs of the
"ignorance" in various ways, notably by the prohibi-
tion of infanticide. Islam has also been called the
greatest of all "temperance societies". But the main
business of Mohammed, as declared by himself, was
not to prohibit infanticide, to limit polygamy, or to
abolish intoxication; it was to proclaim the unity of
God. No one, I imagine, doubts that St. Paul improved
the morals of his converts (though it is to be observed
that he seems usually to assume that what was wrong
with them in their unregenerate days was not theoretical
ignorance of the moral law, but practical disregard of
it; he does not claim to be the prophet of a "new"
morality of any kind). But his immediate concern was
not the improvement of manners and morals; it was
the preaching of "Jesus and resurrection".[1] The all-
important thing with him is that men should accept
his message about God and what God has done for
them; moral improvement follows, or ought to follow,

---

[1] *Acts* xvii. 18 οἱ δὲ (ἔλεγον). Ξένων δαιμονίων δοκεῖ καταγγελεὺς εἶναι· ὅτι τὸν
Ἰησοῦν καὶ τὴν ἀνάστασιν εὐηγγελίζετο.

as a matter of course from the consciousness of a new relation to God.

I think we may say two things about all the great religions which have proved their power, in varying degree, to mould the life of men as men, not as men of this or that stock or speech: all owe their origin to individual founders, and in no case has the founder conceived himself, or been conceived by his followers, in the first instance, as a moral reformer. A religion of this kind is the most potent of all forces in transforming moral ideals and practice, but it owes it potency to the very fact that it is something other than a project of moral reformation. Indeed, it is often urged by un-favourable critics in depreciation of the founders of such religions, as it has been urged against Our Lord, that they are wanting in ethical originality; their pre-cepts, it is said, are not found, on careful scrutiny, to contain anything which had not been said, more or less explicitly, before them. The criticism would be largely just, but for the fact that the founders of religions do not announce themselves as moral reformers, except incidentally and in the second place.

The consideration I would urge, then, is this. Even from the standpoint of those who, like Kant, judge religions by their value as instruments of moral reform, it would be a bad mistake to suppose that we can estimate the worth of a religion by artificially isolating the expressly ethical deliverances of its founder or its prophets. The real moral effects of a religion depend primarily on its new and characteristic declarations about God, and the relations into which it brings the worshipper with God. Moral improvements effected by a religion are consequences, and very largely indirect and half-unconscious consequences, of the changed attitude towards God into which the convert believes himself to have been brought. We should be misconceiving the facts if we thought of the founders of the great religions simply as men of remarkable moral insight, and consequently conceded that their directly ethical precepts, being reached by an immediate intuition of the morally right which is beyond the range of more ordinary men, may properly be regarded as a "revelation" or self-disclosure of the supreme moral personality, God, but persisted in confining the concession to these merely ethical utterances, as Kant would like us to do.[1] From the standpoint of the Kantian philosophy of religion, it would be justifiable to find a revelation from God in such sayings as "Love your enemies", "Resist not evil"; but such utterances as "No man knoweth the Father but the Son", or "Hereafter ye shall see the Son of Man coming on the right hand of the Power", would have to be dismissed as the pardonable excesses of an exuberant imagination. But in point of fact, so far as Christianity has been really operative to moral renewal, it has been so precisely through these not directly ethical utterances, with the new vistas they open on the strictly transcendent and eternal. It is they, much more than any specific moral precepts of the Gospel, which are at the roots of the Christian conception of the practical life itself, and furnish it with its "dynamic". Either the claim of Our Lord to special direct intuitive apprehension of the divine must be surrendered, or it is to these "otherworldly" utterances that we must look for the evidence of a first-hand disclosure from the supernatural. So, even from the point of view which measures the worth and estimates the truth of religions exclusively by their influence on morals, it is reasonable to attach weight

---

[1] Cf. Kant, *Werke* (Hartenstein[2]), vi. 209, on the *oberstes Kriterium aller Schriftauslegung*.

not merely to the ethical precepts of the *Religions-stifter*, but to their intuitions concerning God and the eternal world. They too will have weight, just so far as we are justified in regarding them as genuine disclosures of a reality which is there in its own right, not creations of human fantasy. And we must certainly add that it seems a bad mistake to regard religion in this fashion, as merely a useful instrument of morality, as Kant, for example, wished to do.

No doubt, we should be justified in saying that a religion which did nothing to make the standard of morality at once more elevated and more inward, still more a religion which actually debased the moral standard, must be a false, as well as a bad, religion. The indignant eloquence of Adimantus in the *Republic*,[1] when he denounces the moral corruption chargeable on the Orphic pardon-mongers and vendors of "sacraments", rightly carries us away with it, as we read. Nor should we, I conceive, feel inclined to dispute the verdict of the aged Plato, that the worst kind of "infidel" is the hypocritical trafficker for private ends in the credulity of mankind.[2] But this is no more than might also be said, with the same sort of truth, about science, or art. It may be the case that, in particular instances, this man or that man has suffered morally from his interest in science or in art, that he would have been a morally better man, in some important respects, if he had not been so good an artist, or man of science. There are undeniably men whose devotion to scientific research has made them, in some respects, inhumane, and others whose absorption in art has led them to neglect their duties to wife and children. But I think we should all deny that devotion to art or science, as such, has any inherent tendency to make men cruel,

[1] Plato, *Republic*, 363.   [2] Plato, *Laws*, 908 B ff.

or indifferent to family affections; we should be ready to admit that if, in particular societies, the practice of art, or the following of science as a vocation, has really tended generally to deprave the moral standard, the art and science in question have been debased art and false science. I believe we should go further, and might fairly say that, in the main, devotion to the highest art and to rightly conceived science tend, on the whole, to the *all-round* elevation of moral character. There are bad men among artists and men of science, and some of them rise to eminence in their vocations; but among the very greatest, in science and in art, the greatly good do not seem, to say the least of it, to be more uncommon than in any other walk of life. If we hear more of the moral frailties of famous artists than we do of the shortcomings of shopkeepers, or attorneys, or labourers, the reason is, perhaps, partly that our curiosity about the artist leads to the collection of gossip about him which is not forthcoming for the shopkeeper; partly that most of us are more like the shopkeeper than we are like the artist, and are prone to indulge the "all-too-human" habit of confining our reprobation to the vices to which we are personally least addicted.

The very unity of human personality would seem to make it impossible that courage, sincerity, self-denial, loyalty to the best one can conceive, untiring reaching out from the good to the better, should be regularly characteristic of a man in one great part of his activity, and merely wanting in another. And, on the other side, if a man is generally slack, indolent, readily satisfied with the second-best, fitful, backbone-less, in the conduct of his life, we should hardly expect to find these qualities regularly replaced by their opposites in his vocational work. Since a man is, after all, one man and not several, he will probably put the same sort of personality into what we call his vocational work as into the rest of his doings, if only we knew how to look for it there. And yet it is certain that the sole justification, or the chief justification, of science and art is not to be found in their immediate effect on moral character, and the direct aim of art and science is never moralistic. Both deteriorate at once, as soon as they are made consciously subservient to a purely moral purpose. Art and science both do us good, but the good they do is not, in the first instance, to improve our discharge of our duties to our families, our customers, or our clients. Art does us good directly by teaching us to detect and revel in beauty, science by teaching us to care for truth.

Just so it is with religion. Like science and art, and more markedly, it has its repercussions on our daily moral practice, but, like them, it is primarily something quite different from a moral rule of life. As art has its source in the intuition of the beautiful, and science its source in the vision of the true, so religion arises directly from, and is the creature's response to, the dim and vague, but intensely vivid, perception of the presence of the uncreated and adorable. The characteristic attitude of the religious soul is that of worship, and worship springs from assurance that the uncreated and complete good is no mere *Sollen*, but is given as intimately present here and now, as the overpowering reality. Now this sense of the actual presence of the divine, though, when accepted as such, it can infuse a new quality of life into all our practice, is in itself something transcending the merely moral. The furthest that moral practice, and philosophical theory based on reflection upon practice, will take us is to the inferential conclusion which Kant reaches, that *if* moral obligation is more than a mere generous illusion or *bellum somnium*, the uncreated good must be a reality too. But to draw this conclusion as a philosophical inference is not the same thing as to live in the conscious presence of the divine as *given*. Morality, at its best, and the "practice of the presence of God" are two and not one; it is because they are two, not one, that the Kantian moral autonomy, obedience to a self-imposed law of conduct, is not the same thing as what our fathers called "Gospel liberty", but only a second-best. So long as we are living only at the level of Kantian autonomy, we have not really anchored our life on the "Rock of Ages", and it is a consequence of this that the note of joy, so characteristic of religion, is so entirely absent from Kant's philosophy of life. Once more, we must say that the direct vision which gives a great religion its supreme and unique value is not an affair of commands and precepts, a vision of what we *ought* to do, but a vision of what that from which we come, and to which we return, actually *is*, and what *it* is doing and will do, in and for us. The regenerating moral effect of our religion on our conduct is most genuine and profound when the direct object of our attention is not the self and its tasks, but God; and, for this reason, the supremely important thing in any religion is its "revelation" of God. Either we must deny that religion has any relation but one of accidental conjunction with moral practice, or, if the facts of life and history are too strong for us, we must, as it seems to me, frankly admit, for all the great religions which have really elevated humanity, the presence of a genuine element of direct self-disclosure of the divine, and so of "revelation", immediately given knowledge of God.

If so much is conceded, we may attempt an answer to the argument which maintains that there can be no finality about revelation because its content must be conditioned by the antecedents of the recipients; that there can be no "truth for all time", just because every truth, to be true at all, must be a truth for its own particular time. In a sense, I grant, the fact is so, and has to be frankly admitted. It is true that, as the schoolman's phrase ran, *quidquid recipitur, recipitur ad modum recipientis,* or, in more familiar words, "not all can receive this saying, but those to whom it is given". And this is a principle with an applicability not confined to the domain of religion and theology. Art, science, philosophy, to be significant at all, must speak the language of a particular community and a particular age. There is no work of art which is neither a work of Greek art, nor of Flemish, nor of Japanese, nor of Italian, nor of any other age or place, but just a work of art *überhaupt.* A great tragedy, like *Agamemnon,* or *Othello,* is not simply *a* tragedy; it is a tragedy instinct with the spirit of a definite people, the Attic or the English, and a definite age, the age of Cimon, or the age of Elizabeth and James, and we do not properly understand the tragedy until we can recreate in ourselves something of the spirit of the place and the time to which it belongs. *Othello,* a characteristic product of the London of the reign of James I., is necessarily more or less of a sealed book to any man who can only feel and think like a man, perhaps not even like a Londoner, of our day. Even a great philosophy is always, in some sense, the product of its place and age, and is never fully understood, if it has to be studied in isolation from the whole concrete life of the society to which it belongs. If one has spent years in trying to understand a great thinker, such as Plato, and to help others to understand him, one knows well from one's own experience how dependent one is for success on the double process of purgation and enrichment of one's own mind. One has constantly to be resolute to forget so much that one knows, or supposes one's self to know, about the world, because it was unthought of in the Athens of Socrates and Plato; on the other side, one must constantly be awake to the possibility that ignorance of apparently irrelevant facts about the life of their age may have the gravest consequences for one's work of interpretation.[1] And the double process is one which can never be brought to completion. After years of purgation by the resolute effort to think historically, one can never be certain that one's interpretations are not still vitiated by undetected elements of the unhistorical; again, our documentation is so imperfect that, when every extant scrap of historical and antiquarian evidence has been utilised, our knowledge of a long-vanished age is bound to be schematic, abstract, and full of ugly gaps, and we can never be confident that the filling up of the gaps, the clothing of the skeleton with flesh, might not gravely affect our understanding of the thought of the age.

It is true everywhere that the determinable is never found actually existing, except as modified by specific determinants. Truth, to be spoken to any age, must be spoken in the age's own dialect, and the dialect of different ages is never quite the same. Nor could we escape the problem by reducing it to one of mere verbal expression, as is done by those who have said, for example, that the "language of the Christian creeds is Greek, but their meaning universal". Meaning and its expression are not related as my body and my clothes,

---

[1] How often, for example, it is forgotten that Socrates was a man of the Periclean age, that Plato came of a family in which "democratic" politics were traditional, that Aristotle had no personal experience of the life of the "citizen", and that we are bound to misunderstand all three if we neglect these facts. Even Descartes is often misrepresented and unjustly accused of insincerities from mere disregard of the fact that he was a seventeenth-century French Roman Catholic, not a concealed "free-thinker".

but rather as my body and its skin. I may disguise myself in garments of a score of different fashions, retaining the same body unchanged; to be fitted to a different skin, I should need to have a differently built body. So the transference of knowledge or thought from one society to another is no mere affair of adaptation to a new vocabulary; it is a matter of adaptation to a different set of habits of mind.

If all this has to be admitted, as it surely must be, it should be plain that it applies just as much to thought which may have originated in a specific disclosure of the divine as to any other thought. We have this treasure in earthen vessels, and the excellence of the wine makes no difference to the fact that the vessels are earthen, and that many of them may be earth of very common quality, not superfine porcelain clay. Yet, when the fullest allowance has been made for such considerations, the question still remains with us whether, because every truth communicable to man must be a truth for its own time, every truth must also be one *only* for its own time. The conclusion is congenial to a certain type of philosophy, not un-fashionable in some quarters, the philosophy of pure becoming or sheer impermanence. It is fashionable to-day in these quarters to say that "nothing is, everything becomes", just as it was fashionable to say the same kind of thing in the Athens of Socrates. The favourite modern way of saying it is, as we should expect, epistemological rather than ontological. Truth, we are told, is itself a mental fashion, and fashions are pro-verbially changeful. A philosophy, a theology, a scientific doctrine, must perish, and rightly so, by mere lapse of time, not because the answers it gives to its problems have been found to be false, but because, with the change in intellectual fashions, the problems themselves have lost their significance. No truth can be the "truth of God", valid for all time and all places, for the same reason that no costume can be the wear for all mankind, always and everywhere. This way of thinking has more than one name, and shows itself in more than one quarter. It may appear now as "pragmatism", now as "humanism", now, perhaps, as the *filosofia dello spirito*, but all these would seem to be variations on one theme, the doctrine that permanence is an illusion. Without us, there is no law in nature; within, there are no fixed principles of truth; without or within, there is nothing but "motions", the more slowly or more rapidly passing whims of *la mode*. In the language of the Heraclitean aphorism so often quoted by Nietzsche, "Time is a child playing draughts; the kingdom is a child's".[1]

When we try to meet and counter theories of universal impermanence with special reference to what concerns us most for our present purpose, their epistemological side, our most natural first thought is to look for some definite isolated body of truths which may plausibly be said to be truths for all time, because they are manifestly not clothed in a linguistic garb peculiar to any one time, and consequently do permit of transcription from any one idiom into any other without loss or increment of significance. Then we inevitably tend to think, with Plato, Descartes, and Spinoza, of the system of the propositions of pure mathematics as the great outstanding example establishing the existence of truth which is permanent, just because it is truth at the extreme limit of depersonalisation. We to-day, were we arguing for mere persuasive effect, might make an impressive point by simply exhibiting the three massive volumes of a work like the *Principia Mathematica* of Whitehead and Russell, where the

[1] Heraclitus, Fr. 79 (Bywater), αἰὼν παῖς ἐστι παίζων πεσσεύων·παιδὸς ἡ βασιληίη.

"timeless validity" of the body of pure mathematical propositions seems to have been demonstrated in act by the rendering of them all into a stereotyped language which has never been, and never will be, the living idiom of anyone anywhere, but, in compensation, can be equally apprehended by individuals of the most various idioms. The mere fact that the propositions of mathematics have been so successfully translated into a language which, being still-born, cannot grow or change might seem to have met the epistemologists of impermanence as Diogenes is fabled to have met the deniers of motion. But such a defence would be inadequate to our purpose, for a double reason.

For one thing, even in *Principia Mathematica*, the stereotyping of thought is not, and could not have been, complete. There are intrinsic limits to the capabilities of a "universal symbolism". Its not innumerous symbols for primary "indefinables" have to be accurately apprehended before their combinations can be understood, and thus presuppose preliminary explanation in an idiom which is not dead and impersonal, but personal and living. Here is, at the outset, an opening for what may prove to be serious misunderstandings. And again, in every such symbolic system, there must be some supreme principle or principles, governing all its inferences, and these obviously cannot be expressed in the symbolism itself. Thus, every symbolically expressed demonstration in *Principia Mathematica* depends on the principle that "what is implied by true premisses" is itself true", but neither this proposition nor the meaning of the terms "implication" and "truth" can be expressed in the symbolism of the authors, or any other.[1] Explanations on such

---

[1] Cf. L. Couturat, *Les Principes des mathématiques*, p. 11: "il est remarquable que ce principe ne peut pas s'exprimer symboliquement. Comme le remarque

points have to be given in ordinary language, and this makes it possible that the explanations may, from the first, have been confused or ambiguous, and again that they may cease to convey the sense intended, as the words employed shift their meaning "in use". Thus, the most rigorous system of symbolically expressed mathematical truths would not wholly escape the criticism of a resolute denier of permanence.

It is a more important consideration, for our purposes, that even if it were possible to put the *whole* body of pure mathematics, including the primitive indefinables and primary principles of inference, into a stereotyped symbolism, as a guarantee against change of significance, all we should have achieved by this would be the construction of a purely abstract and formal pattern, inadequate to the description of the simplest piece of concrete fact. The "world" with which the physicist professionally concerns himself is a sufficiently poverty-stricken abstract from the world of individual events and purposes in which we all, including the physicist, have to live as men and women, but even the physicist's "world" itself defies all attempts to build it up out of mathematical formulae. Even in physics, the formulae function as describing the structure of an elusive something which slips through their meshes; a fact, however empty of content we try to make it, is not to be manufactured out of formulae, there is an *haecceitas* about it which is proof against our analyses. It is *this* fact, and there can be no "symbol" for *this*.

If, then, we are looking for examples of permanent truths, with an interest for life which persists through

M. Russell [cf. *Principles of Mathematics*, i. p. 34], ce principe marque la limite du symbolisme. Il n'y a rien d'étonnant, d'ailleurs, à ce que le symbolisme ne réussisse pas à traduire tous les principes, car il faut évidemment définir verbalement les premiers symboles et les premières formules."

all the ages, it is not to pure mathematics, with its formulae from which the vitality has been carefully drained, that we should turn. We may perhaps derive a more helpful suggestion from consideration of the analogous case of the works of art and imagination which are found to retain abundant life and significance for generation after generation. We could all name some of the great outstanding works, in literature and the arts, which most successfully defy all vicissitudes of time, all differences in customs, manners, morals, institutions, to make them antiquated. Now a curious thing about these works which are never "out of date" is that the fact of their universal appeal to the human mind, in all times and places, seems to be connected with the other fact that they are so deeply rooted in the life of the society from which they spring. They seem to be "for all time", not *though*, but *because*, they are so very definitely of their own time. The creations of genius which remain perfect after the lapse of centuries, and the rise and fall of commonwealths, are not works which reflect the life and thought of no particular age or place, and might, so far as can be seen, have been equally well produced almost anywhere, or at any time, but those which are so full of a rich and complex life that they could only have come to birth in the soil from which they did, in fact, spring.

The play of *Hamlet* may serve as an example. In a way, *Hamlet* is a specimen of a kind of composition which has made its appearance at more than one period in the history of European imaginative literature, the tragedy of revenge.[1] Tragedies of revenge may be, and I suppose have been, composed in most societies which have any drama at all. But what makes

[1] We can trace the "family tree", so to say, of the play *Hamlet* back through Kyd and the *Spanish Tragedy* to Seneca and his *Thyestes*, and through Seneca back to the older Greek tragedies which dealt with the same and similar themes.

Hamlet unlike most other works of the type, a perennial
delight, what gives it its interest for men whose intellectual and moral convictions may be very different
indeed from those of the English of the year A.D. 1600,
is precisely its saturation with the qualities which
stamp it as the product of the whole social life of a particular community, acting as a stimulus to an individual man of genius. A tragedy of revenge, of some
sort, might be composed by almost anyone in Europe
at any time. *Hamlet* could only have been the work
of an Elizabethan Englishman, and only of just the
one Elizabethan Englishman who did, in fact, write
Hamlet. (If any of you doubt this last statement, I
recommend a careful perusal of the other contemporary
dramas of the same type.) The paradox is that it is
just this which gives the play what is called, in the
hackneyed journalistic phrase, its "universal human
appeal" to a world in which only a few students have
ever heard of the *Spanish Tragedy*, *The Duchess of
Malfi*, *Titus Andronicus*, *The Revenger's Tragedy*, or
Women beware Women. And we must note that this
does not mean that *Hamlet*, or any other work of the
same immortality, has, for mankind at large, an interest
which is primarily historical or antiquarian. *Hamlet*
is saturated with the spirit of Elizabethan England,
but the reason why it retains its hold on us is not that
it gratifies our natural historical curiosity to observe
the obsolete and unfamiliar outlook of Englishmen of
a remarkable age, now some ten generations behind us,
on the world and life. This *is* very largely why the
minority of students find some of the other contemporary tragedies of revenge which we have just mentioned interesting. But *Hamlet* "grips" us of to-day,
and not only those of us who are English by birth or
education, because it is full of an attitude towards life

and its problems which we still feel to be *our* attitude. The often-lauded universality of Shakespeare does not mean that in his vision of life he misses out what is characteristic of his own people and his own time; it means that his vision penetrates to the depths.

What is true of the great poet's vision is, I should say, equally true of the thought of the great philosopher contemplating life concretely. I meet in my reading the repeated allegation that the great constructive philosophies of antiquity, or of the Middle Ages, have lost their value for us, not by being refuted and shown to be false, but by a change in the temper and spirit of the age, which has made the problems of the past and the solutions given them equally unmeaning. I doubt whether even the able writers who say this kind of thing most glibly really feel altogether as they profess to feel, at least when they are actually opening their minds to the influence of the great teachers of the past. If they do, how comes it that they can still be aware of the greatness of that which, according to their professions, no longer means anything to them? For my own part, when I try to enter, for example, into the thought of Plato, I know well enough that there are *nuances* which must be lost on me, because I am unavoidably ignorant of so much of the mental life of the Athens of the fourth century before Christ. But I do not find that I am in an intellectual fog where I have lost my bearings, as I might be if I could listen to the conversation of a group of "Martians". The great problems man's life suggests to Plato seem to be recognisably the same with which our own society still has to reckon; the precise form in which they are stated may often not be that which would occur most readily to ourselves, but, after all, we can translate the Platonic problem significantly into terms of our own intellectual currency. If at times we feel that the rendering cannot be made a perfect equivalent, that is no more than the common difficulty which besets us whenever we try to turn a page of French, or German, or Italian into English. It does not mean that the understanding of Plato's thought is in any way analogous with the attempt to decipher an inscription in a tongue which has vanished and left no traces behind it. There is no ancient philosophy which is undecipherable in the same sense as the picture-writing of Easter Island.

It should be clear, then, that the mere fact that any truth less abstract and superficial than the propositions of pure mathematics must be the truth of a specific age need not mean that such a truth must be the nonsense or falsehood of other ages. Those who think thus seem to forget that, after all, our precursors, ourselves, and our distant successors—if we leave any—in the course of history are alike in being *men*: we all have the same ground-pattern, are all variations on one theme. A philosophy which ignores the reality of "universal human nature" as at least an *universale* IN *re* is a philosophy which does not look "under the skin". If these considerations apply to all human thought, they apply, of course, independently of any question of the historical origination of the thought. Thus, the fact that whatever is "received" is received only "after the measure of the recipient" is not in itself a valid objection against the reality of revelations made through specific channels and at specific times. Unless it is nonsense to speak of any utterance of man to man as having abiding significance, there is no reason why utterances prompted by such self-disclosures should not possess that abiding significance and, in that sense, be final.

But we shall also do well to remember certain things which advocates of the claims of a particular historical "revelation" to finality are sometimes inclined to forget. We have to remember that the conditioning of the disclosures received by the limitations of the recipient must be twofold. If we may judge by the historical records about those who have claimed to be recipients of such illuminations, the thing revealed is nearly always descried dimly and with much confusion; it can never be expressed in speech in a way which is wholly adequate. This is no peculiarity of the revelations of the world-religions; it is true of all that any man feels to be at once supremely significant and eminently personal to himself. Our deepest thoughts, as Shelley said to Trelawny, are "unintelligible even to ourselves"; they are what a greater than Shelley has called "thoughts beyond the reaches of our souls". Even in Christianity, which asserts a relation of unique intimacy between the human mind of its Founder and the mind of God—"the Son knoweth whatsoever the Father doeth"—this problem is not absent, as may be seen by the way in which Christian theologians have been exercised by the question of the human knowledge of Christ and its limitations.[1] Curiously enough, the philosophical theologian who has gone nearest towards denying the existence of this problem in the case of Christ is one who stood all his life outside the Christian community. "To Moses", says Spinoza, "God spoke face to face, but to Christ He spoke mind to mind."[2] That

---

[1] A problem forced on the most conservative mind by the express statement of the Gospel that Ἰησοῦς προέκοπτεν σοφίᾳ καὶ ἡλικίᾳ καὶ χάριτι παρὰ θεῷ καὶ ἀνθρώποις (Luke ii. 52).

[2] Tractatus Theologico-Politicus, i. 23-4. "non credo ullum alium ad tantam perfectionem supra alios pervenisse praeter Christum, cui Dei placita, quae homines ad salutem ducunt, sine verbis aut visionibus, sed immediate revelata sunt; adeo ut Deus per mentem Christi sese apostolis manifestaverit, ut olim Mosi mediante voce aerea . . . si Moses cum Deo de facie ad faciem . . . loquebatur, Christus quidem de mente ad mentem communicavit."

may be so, but it is surely equally clear that, even to Christ, God did not speak by the communication of the only thing which deserves the name of adequate knowledge on Spinoza's principles, an exactly articulated system of propositions about the relations of "clear and distinct ideas". No one, orthodox or unorthodox, I conceive, will maintain that Our Lord was either speculative metaphysician or speculative theologian. His revelation of the Father was not a speculative system, it was the whole of his own concrete personality and life; and such propositions as are ascribed to him are expressions, wholly unsystematic, and mostly, as von Hügel has somewhere said, "exoteric", of an immediate perception.

And, apart from this, a revelation on which a religion is to be built is not a perception to be kept to the immediate recipient; it has to be imparted to the community. Even if it has been received by the immediate recipient, "mind to mind", as Spinoza phrases it, it has to be conveyed to others in the language they understand, and thus adapted to their limitations, and this creates a second problem. If the conservative Christian theologian, for example, is unwilling to admit that Our Lord himself had, in his conception of past history, his expectations for the future, his outlook on the world of nature, in many respects the mind of a Galilean of his century, the only alternative is to assume that, in communicating his teaching to his disciples, whose limitations no one denies, the Lord must have translated what, as conceived in his own mind, was simple *Wahrheit* into a *Wahrheit* sufficiently leavened with *Dichtung* to be appreciated by them and fruitful in them. If he did not himself expect to reappear in the immediate future in the clouds before the eyes of his enemies, at least he must have used language which

the first generation of his followers could only understand in that sense, or the New Testament would not
be permeated, as it is, by the conviction of the imminent
nearness of the Lord's return and the "end of history".
The reality of a revelation, however assured, cannot
dispense from the duty of repeated scrutiny and careful
distinction between that in it which is the permanent
substance and that which belongs not to the substance,
but to its adaptation to the measure of the recipients;
and this should make the theologian more scrupulous
than he has frequently been to avoid the assumption
that the separation has already been accomplished, and
that what he has now on his hands is pure and unmixed
"substance of faith".

Yet, on the other side, it is unjustified dogmatism to
assume that because we cannot be certain that what
we have left after our winnowing is pure and unmixed
substance, there is really no substance at all. This is
that "emptying out of the child with the bath" of which
the proverb warns us. What *is* substance, I take it, we
only learn in what might fairly be called an empirical
way. *A priori* we are hardly entitled to say more than
this. A religion is true religion just in so far as it
achieves the purpose, on which we dwelt so long in our
former series, of thoroughly remoulding the self, so as
to make God, the supernatural good, and eternity the
very centre of a man's thought and will. Whatever, in
the life and practice of an actual religious community,
is an obstacle to this inward renewing of life is plainly
incompatible with true religion, and whatever, in the
alleged revelation possessed by the community, en-
courages and perpetuates the obstacle cannot be of the
substance of revelation. But also, what cannot be dismissed without impoverishing spiritual life, and hinder-
ing the remaking of the self into eternity at its source,

clearly is of the substance. If we would judge how the test is to be applied, I do not see that we have any sure course but to study the types of life and character actually promoted by given affirmations and denials. If we find that a high level of the right kind of spirituality and other-worldliness is regularly attained in dependence on certain convictions which have their origin in acceptance of a given "revelation", but regularly missed when these convictions are ignored or denied, we shall, if we are prudent, be very slow to treat these particular affirmations as temporary and unessential; we shall feel fairly persuaded that they at least *contain* something which is sterling substance, and that they must not be met by bare denials. It may be that the affirmation is not thus proved to be all substance without alloy; the future may yet show that there may be qualifications of the affirmation which can coexist with, or even be favourable to, the richest spirituality. But the test, if it has been fairly applied, may, for all this, entirely dispose of an unqualified denial.

We may consider a simple illustration of this point. We probably all remember Kant's violent opposition to prayer, an opposition directly due to his determination to see nothing *sui generis* in the religious, as distinguished from the moral, life. A man, being autonomous, ought, Kant holds, to do his duty in his own strength by the unaided exercise of the morally good will; to pray for "grace" to live aright is therefore no better than unethical superstition,[1] if the prayer is more than the expression of a hope that we may persevere in our virtuous resolution. We know, too, how widely even anti-materialistic philosophers in the second half of the nineteenth century were infected by the coarse

---

[1] Kant, *Werke* (Hartenstein²), vi, 294 ff.

deterministic prejudice that prayer, if it means anything
more than meditation, is an absurdity, because to pray
implies the belief that the "laws of the physical world"
can be modified or suspended by the will of God. One
might debate the Pelagianism of Kant's argument, or
discuss the ambiguity and arbitrariness of the "determinist" scheme to the end of time and "find no end, in
wand'ring mazes lost", so far as any decisive theoretical
result is concerned. In practice the question whether
prayerless life is not also wholly worldly life admits of
a much readier solution. It is not to dialectic we need
to turn to discover that a prayerless good will, reliant
on its own strength, does not remain permanently at
any high level of inward goodness, or that, even in
respect of the "external good things" of life, a man's
moral always suffers, if his theories forbid him to ask
for the provision for his needs, and to give thanks
when he receives it. There are many methods of prayer,
not all equally compatible with a true spirituality, but
it should be plain from experience of "fruits" that, whatever elements of superstition may disfigure the practice
of some forms of prayer, a philosophy of religion
which has no place at all for "prayer and supplica-
tion" is a false philosophy.

Some suspicion of this may be detected in the language of philosophers who, after proscribing prayer
proper, concede that "meditation", at any rate, may be
a real need of the religious life. The pity of it is that
those who speak thus too often abstain from specifying
the *object* of the meditation they are willing to permit.
Whether meditation is to do us good or harm must
surely depend on the nature of that on which we meditate. It will not be all one to our characters whether
the object of our habitual meditation is a Father who
knows how to give good things to those that ask him,

or a Stoic εἱμαρμένη, or a purely non-moral "law of necessity". Spinoza, to be sure, fancied that by meditation on the "absolute necessity" of all events we might be led to the *summa mentis acquiescentia* of the saint.[1] In actual life, if the meditator has not, like Spinoza, a predisposition to saintliness, such "morose contemplation" is more likely, I take it, to lead to the defiant vapourings of Mr. Russell's "free man",[2] or W. E. Henley's brags against the "bludgeonings of Fate," and oftener still to something even worse than vapouring or bluster, that listless apathy which the Middle Ages reckoned a deadly sin, and called by the name of *acedia*. Even meditation on my own autonomy as giver of the moral law to myself is more likely to end in a Stoic self-idolatry than in anything noble, and meditation on the Absolute of the more optimistically coloured nature-pantheisms in spiritual voluptuousness. The meditation which can be counted on as a source of strength and sweetness of spirit is meditation on a God to whom one can and must *spontaneously* pray. Clough,

---

[1] *Ethica* v. 5-8, 11, 26, 27.

[2] "When, without the bitterness of impotent rebellion, we have learnt both to resign ourselves to the outward rule of Fate and to recognise that the non-human world is unworthy of our worship, it becomes possible at last (? why) so to transform and refashion the unconscious universe, so to transmute it in the crucible of imagination, that a new image of shining gold replaces the old idol of clay" (B. Russell, *Philosophical Essays*, p. 66). (Exactly: the "free man" of Mr. Russell, like Nebuchadnezzar, only "worships" an image of gold, the "work of his own hands". Spinoza knew better than this.) "Brief and powerless is man's life; on him and all his race, the slow, sure doom falls pitiless and dark. Blind to good and evil, reckless of destruction, omnipotent matter rolls on its relentless way; for Man . . . it remains only to cherish, ere yet the blow falls, the lofty thoughts that ennoble his little day; disdaining the coward terrors of the slave of Fate, to worship at the shrine that his own hands have built", etc., etc. (*ib.* p. 70). But *what* does the "free man" worship at this "shrine"? On Mr. Russell's own showing, something which is a pure product of his own imagination, and known by himself to be nothing more. And what is the quality of the "worship"? Is not the plain prose of the situation—Mr. Russell, as the rhythms of his sentences show, is "dropping into poetry", of a kind—that the "free man" is sheltering himself in "make-believe" from a merely disgusting reality? Might it not be more advisable to ask the question whether Mr. Russell's bugbear, "omnipotent matter", is anything but an *alias* for "old Noboddady"?

for example, in a well-known stanza, seems to be explicitly surrendering prayer; yet the attitude of his "prayerless heart" to the object of its meditations can be described in such words as these:

> Man's inmost soul, before Thee inly brought,
>   Thy presence owns, ineffable, divine;
> Chastised each rebel self-encentred thought,
>   My will adoreth Thine.[1]

That is a meditation on the living God which is itself already a prayer.

We have still to consider the allegation that revelation, the direct disclosure of the divine, is in principle either impossible, or at least superfluous, since a revelation, even if possible, must coincide in its content with what we can independently discover about God by the "natural light". The allegation of *impossibility* may be very lightly dismissed, as the mere prejudice of a mind which has not learned to think historically. An unhistorical age is usually sceptical, at once and for the same reason, of revelation and of genius in its various manifestations. For like revelation, genius, whether it be that of the poet, the dramatist, the musician, the painter, the mathematician, the mechanician, is always a *disturbing* factor in things for the type of mind which finds its satisfaction in clarity, definition and the conscious orderly arrangement of thoughts, rather than in their depth and "grip" on reality. For it is notorious that the genius, like the poets examined by Socrates, cannot, as a rule, tell anyone whence his "inspirations" come, nor analyse their content, or reduce it to a neat and transparent structural pattern. His insights come to him, as perceptions come, direct, with the appearance of being unsought disclosures of a reality given to him, not constructed by himself; they *impose* them-

---

[1] *Qui laborat, orat.*

selves, violently and intrusively, as "impressions of sense" do, and again, as with "impressions of sense" there is a wealth of confused concreteness about them which resists analysis. This rich, but confused and intrusive content is offensive to all the intellectual habits of an age of "enlightenment" and "good sense", which, accordingly, tends to deny the fact of genius, just as it tends to deny the fact of revelation. As such an age is prone to reduce the claimant to revelation to the status of a conscious moral and social reformer, who conceals his purpose under a cloud of mystifications and pretences, with a view to impressing the imagination of the "vulgar", so it reduces the great poet to the status of a craftsman deftly insinuating moral and political "lessons" by artificial "fiction" and allegory. As it sees in the prophet only the reformer, so it sees in the poet only the teacher.[1] Both are supposed to make, in their own minds, a clear distinction between the matter they are presenting and the adventitious and artificial form in which they clothe it, and the form is regarded as a mere instrument, deliberately adopted for the conveyance of the matter. It is not, I think, a mere accident that it is also characteristic of the philosophy of such ages of "good sense" to lay great stress on the "subjectivity" of sensible qualities, to treat the inexhaustible wealth of colour, tone, fragrance, and the like, as merely superposed by "the mind" on a reality consisting only of fully analysed and articulated interconnections between monotonously simple elements, and then, finally, to suspect these very elements, just because they have been so denuded of everything obviously intrusive and qualitatively given, of being

---

[1] The eighteenth-century critic of Shakespeare tended, for example, to ask about every play what was its "moral", and even to make the value of a work like *Macbeth* dependent primarily on its supposed usefulness in teaching us that it is commonly "bad business" to murder a king and usurp his crown.

themselves "mental fictions". In the process of being divested of its mystery and refractoriness, reality is, in fact, evaporated.

Now, as regards both the sensible world and the world of art, this whole mental attitude may, I trust, be considered hopelessly discredited. I do not think we are likely to hear much more from the really competent of the mere illusoriness and "subjectivity" of the amazing wealth disclosed to us by the senses. As Mr. Meyerson somewhere puts it, the working physicist is at heart an obstinate realist, convinced that he is confronted in his work with a world which he does not *make* out of nothing by some process of mental synthesis, but *finds* given to him. If he could ever succeed in analysing the course of events without remainder into an elaborate logical construction, transparent to the intellect, he would instinctively feel that its reality had slipped through his fingers; the real, to him, *is* that which defies such complete analysis. (This explains why a coherent thinker like Dr. Whitehead will hear nothing of the "subjectivity" of the sensible. "Qualities" were pronounced to be "subjective", precisely because they are ultimates for analysis: that is, because they have just the character which should be proof of their reality.)

Again, with all its crudities, the age of romanticism has at least taught us that the genius of poet and artist is something wholly different from deft artifice; it is something which controls the artist, and is not controlled by him.[1] Homer, Dante, Shakespeare, are something very much more intriguing than men coolly devising a "fable" as a convenient vehicle for the conveyance of instruction. All of them, presumably, do

---

[1] On the philosophical significance of the "romantic" reaction against "good sense" see *inter alia* Whitehead, *Science and the Modern World*, v. pp. 109 ff.

this kind of thing incidentally, as we all do, but it is not the doing of it that stamps them as supreme poets. The *Iliad*, the *Divine Comedy*, *King Lear*, full as they may be of conscious artifice, are in *kind* very different from the frigid allegories of an Addison. Each has its source in a direct and eminently intrusive vision of a life which is overpoweringly real and inexhaustibly complex, and full of surprises—something disclosed to the poet, not fashioned by him, nor completely understood by him.[1] The form of his work is not simply selected as a well-chosen device for expounding a matter alien to itself, which might, but for assignable reasons, have been conveyed by a different vehicle; the matter itself dictates the form. The hard and fast distinction between end and means, effect and instrument, a distinction in fact borrowed from the realm of industry, if taken over-seriously, is as pernicious in the theory of art as it is in the theory of morals.

All this, to be sure, is commonplace by now, but I have a motive for reminding you of the *locus communis*. It is not in the region of religion only that we meet with the startling and apparently unaccountable, sudden self-disclosure to particular persons and at special times on the part of a reality which does not equally obtrude itself on the notice of all men every-

---

[1] I do not forget the famous *Letter to Can Grande* in which Dante himself apparently treats his *Commedia* as though it were a mere contrivance for the preaching of an elaborate "lesson". But I think it safe to say that the whole four-fold lesson described in that letter might have been perfectly set forth in a work which would have had no *poetical* value whatsoever, and further that the account is itself an obvious "rationalisation" of the real facts, based on the assumption, traditional in Dante's time, that a great poem has to be justified by showing it to be didactic. It is not a transcript of the poet's real personal experience. In fact, the letter only shows that the greatest of modern poets would have been unable to stand examination by Socrates on the question "what he meant by his poem". One can be sure that Shakespeare's sense of humour would have forbidden him to "explain" *Lear* as intended to prove that professions of affection do not always mean all they say, or that it is not always wise to anticipate one's death by a *donatio inter vivos*.

where and always; we meet it wherever we have to recognise the presence of that which has been called genius. Genius is not, as it has been called, infinite capacity for taking pains; that would rather be a defini- tion of superb and conscious craftsmanship. But we might say, perhaps, that genius is capacity for being arrested by and sensitively responsive to characters of reality which elude the average man's notice; that it is rare and unique *receptiveness*. We might then add that, apart from supernatural revelation, which has God for its object, there is *natural* revelation, and that the men of genius are its depositaries. Indeed, I should like to go further, and say that, below the level of disclosure we call genius, *sense* itself is a kind of natural revela- tion. Even the man who, without any title to be con- sidered a genius, has an exceptionally fine sensibility to delicate variations of tint and tone which the rest of us allow to pass unnoticed, might be said to be the recipient of a revelation of real riches,[1] which only reaches us through him, so far as we learn, under his tui- tion and by starting from an act of faith in his utter- ances, to see with his eyes and hear with his ears. It is a familiar fact that this can be done; we can actually learn from the work of a great painter, interpreted by a true critic, to see the visible world itself with new eyes. But the lesson is never learned without a meek docility. The work of painter and artist will be thrown away on

---

[1] Cf. what a poet of our own day has written of "the body":

> "Thy senses close
> With the world's pleas. The random odours reach
> Their sweetness in the place of thy repose,
>   Upon thy tongue the peach,
> And in thy nostrils breathes the breathing rose. . . .
>
>   "Music, all dumb, hath trod
> Into thine ear her one effectual way;
> And fire and cold approach to gain thy nod,
>   Where thou call'st up the day,
> Where thou awaitest the appeal of God."

us, if we persist in the prejudice that what we cannot see for ourselves, "with our own pair of eyes", is not there to be seen, and so must be an illusion super-added to the given and real. What is real, in the realm of colour *is* what is given, but it is not given to all in the same measure and with the same immediacy.

We may say the same thing of the vision of human life which inspires the great poet. He does not embroider the reality of life with trappings of pure illusion, or, if he does so, he is falling below the level of his own genius. What he sees is there to be seen, though the rest of us must go to school to him, if we are to learn to see it; this is why poetry could be called a "criticism of life".

If then, the very world of nature and everyday human life would largely be closed to us, but for our readiness to trust disclosures which come, in the first instance, to the exceptional few, it is unreasonable to deny the probability that the same thing may hold true of God, the transcendent reality. We should rather expect that the analogy would hold good here also; that there would be exceptional persons to whom this reality, too, is immediately disclosed in a special manner, and that here, as elsewhere, the best of what is to be discerned will be lost on us, if we refuse to learn to see through their eyes. So much, indeed, is actually admitted when it is proposed, as it often is proposed, to recognise the reality of what is called "religious genius". Unfortunately, there is a widely diffused notion that we somehow get rid of the recognition of *revelation*, actual self-disclosure on the part of a real divine, by using this phraseology. It is fancied that the "religious genius" somehow *creates* the content of what he himself regards as the "revelation"; it is magnificent, but we must not suppose

that it has "objective validity", or is strictly entitled
to be called *truth*. As against all such loose ways
of thinking and speaking, we need to be clear that
to speak of "religious genius" is not to *explain* a fact,
but merely to give the fact a new label. To explain
revelation by calling it genius is merely to explain one
mystery by another. And if we have been right in maintaining that genius, in its various forms, is special
receptiveness, and its so-called "intuitions", as the very
name implies, apprehensions of a reality actually there
and given, we have not done even so much as to replace
one mystery by another by introducing "genius" into
the argument. We have only admitted the fact that
there are special apprehensions of a self-disclosing God,
which are not bestowed equally on all of us. We have
admitted not only the possibility, but the actuality of
revelation, however we may please to boggle at that
old-fashioned name for the fact.

These same considerations should dispose of the contention that, at any rate, revelation, if actual, can only
disclose, a little sooner in point of time, what might be
made out sufficiently without it by patient unaided
"natural reason", and is therefore superfluous, though
convenient. One might as well say, in the same fashion,
that by my own account of genius, the great painter or
poet only sees in nature or human life what is there to be
seen, and that the rest of us, in time, learn to see from
him. After all, then, the painter or poet only sees what,
in a sense, the rest of us may come to see for ourselves,
"with our own eyes". Is the painter, or the poet, then,
not also a superfluity?

We all know well enough the answer to such a suggestion. What we come to see with our own eyes, by
learning the lesson of poet or painter, we only come to
see because we have first, as we say, learned from him

to look through *his* eyes. If he had not seen first, and seen distinctly, we should not have learned to see at all. And, besides this, if the artist who teaches us is a sufficiently great artist, the time never comes when we say: "I have now learned to read nature, or life, from him so thoroughly that he has no more to teach me about them. Henceforth, I can dispense with his hitherto valuable, indeed indispensable, help, and look at the object unaided." When does any of us reach the stage at which he has learned *all* that Dante, or Shakespeare, can tell him about human nature, or all that is to be learned from the great painters about the natural world as a kingdom of colour? It comes—never. It is not merely that while we are beginning to know human nature, Shakespeare's vision of it may guide us, and his knowledge furnish us with "opinions" which will be a temporary surrogate for first-hand knowledge of our own. To the end, for any man who is not a second and greater Shakespeare, there will be truths about human nature which he has not verified by his own personal vision, and knows, if he knows them at all, by trusting to Shakespeare's vision where his own fails him.

"He is most natural", says Sir W. Raleigh of Shakespeare, "when he upsets all rational forecasts. We are accustomed to anticipate how others will behave in the matters that most nearly concern us; we seem to know what we shall say to them, and to be able to forecast what they will say in answer. We are accustomed, too, to find that our anticipation is wrong; what really happened gives the lie to the little stilted drama that we imagined, and we recognise at once how poor and false our fancy was, how much truer and more surprising the thing that happens is than the thing we invented. So it is with Shakespeare. His surprises have the same convincing quality. . . . We are watching the events of real life; from our hidden vantage-ground we see into the mystery of things, as if we were God's spies."[1] This is finely said, and as truly as finely. But in principle it applies as much to revelation of the divine as to the revelation of human nature, and may supply a justification to the theologian for his belief in the possibility of "truths of revelation" about God, transcending the range of "natural reason".

God, as all who believe in Him acknowledge, must have a being infinitely richer than our own. If there is so much about human nature which would be dark to us but for the intuitions of Shakespeare and his fellows, there must be much more that is true of God which would be completely hidden but for the flashes of intense and direct insight which are granted to a privileged few. Here, too, when the recipient of the disclosure has conveyed it to us, we may recognise its "convincing quality", may discover "how poor and false our fancy was, how much *truer*[2] and more surprising" the reality than "the thing we had invented". The relation between a knowledge of God through a genuine revelation and "natural" knowledge of God, such as we may reach by analysis of the presuppositions of the moral or physical order, has an analogical counterpart in the relation between truth about human nature disclosed to us by the "intuitions" of a Shakespeare and truth about human nature reached by our own reflections on our everyday experience. If we found that Shakespeare's "surprises" were in contradiction with what we know for ourselves about human motive and purpose, we should not pronounce them "convincing", or turn to Shakespeare for

---

[1] *Shakespeare* (E.M.L.), 143-4.
[2] Italics, of course, mine, not the author's.

insight. This is exactly what we do find about the "surprises" of too many dramatists,[1] and we reject their claims to be "true to nature" in consequence. So if we find that God, as pourtrayed in what claims to be a revelation, has a character flatly contradicting that which "natural reason" is forced to ascribe to the author of physical and moral order, we may safely pronounce that we are dealing with a product of misguided imagination, not with the self-disclosure of the transcendent reality. It is because we find Shakespeare's "surprises" at once so surprising, and yet so true to the human nature of which we independently know something, that we accept them, even when they surprise us most utterly, as divinations into a reality, not as fanciful distortions of it. In the same way, if there is a doctrine of God, claiming to rest upon genuine revelation, which provides us with surprises, but surprises recognisable *après coup*, though not antecedently, as inevitable, as of one piece with, though not discoverable from, that which a strictly natural theology can tell us of the divine character, there should be no rational objection against the acceptance of such a doctrine as a further and fuller disclosure of the divine nature, and the recognition of divine self-manifestation as its source.

In historical fact, apologists for the several revelational religions have made an unnecessary complication for themselves, and weakened the defence of revelation as a source of knowledge about God, by yielding too much to the polemical desire of representing their own religion as the only one possessing such knowledge, and its rivals as mere pretenders to a wholly unreal revela-

---

[1] And about some of the surprises in Shakespeare's own lighter and cruder work. Who "believes" in the sudden conversion of Sir Proteus or Duke Frederick, or the sudden reformation of Oliver de Boys?

tion. Thus the apologist for one particular historical religion provides the rejector of all with an argument, by
using against his rivals weapons it is easy to turn upon
himself. But it is not really necessary to defend the
reality of revelation as a source of truth in one historical
religion by refusing to admit its presence in every other.
Since the historical religions do not simply contradict,
but also, on many points, confirm one another, it is
more natural, as well as more charitable, to recognise
that they cannot be summarily dichotomised into one
true religion and several false, but that truth, in different measures may be found in all of them. Since this is
so, there is no sufficient reason to deny the presence,
again in different degrees, of a genuine revelational element in them all. Thus, for example, since Christianity
and Mohammedanism are in conflict on fundamental
points, if one of them is the truth, the other cannot be.
But this does not justify a Christian controversialist in
simply dismissing Mohammed as the "false prophet",
and his religion as an "imposture". That religion, like
Christianity, testifies emphatically to the divine unity,
and the reality of providence. I can see no sufficient
ground for assuming that we have not here an element
of Mohammedanism which came as a direct disclosure
of the divine to the Arabian prophet, though, from the
Christian point of view, it would be important to distinguish carefully between, for example, the truth of
the divine unity and distortions of the conception of God
in Islam by reckless and one-sided insistence on unity.
The real antithesis is not between one religion which is
true and a plurality of others which are simply false, but
between a religion—if there is one—which is the whole
truth, *ad modum recipientis*, about man's relations with
God, and others which are partial and infected with
error, because they do not, in the poet's phrase, look at

the Lord "all at once".[1] From this point of view, while it would be possible to find an element of the revelational in all the great religions, it would remain an open question for speculation whether or not any of them is *the* true religion, the final self-disclosure of God to man. It would be conceivable that there are only more or less imperfect religions, but not a true and final religion; but it would be equally conceivable that there should be, or actually is, an historical religion which is also final, and can properly be called *the* true religion, because it integrates harmoniously, in one fuller and deeper vision of God, the different "broken lights" of the others, thus incorporating the truths of all, without the one-sidedness of any.

Whether any actual religion can advance this claim is not a question for this place. If it is made, it requires, or so it seems to me, to be substantiated by the successful application of a double test. No religion under which a genuine spiritual life has flourished can be *simply* false, and the religion which would establish its claim to be the one true faith must therefore stand the test of showing that it actually provides full recognition for all the elements of abiding truth in all the others, and does so by integrating their various insights into a real unity. It must also stand the test of being able to sustain the spiritual life of men as men, irrespective of circumscribing conditions of time, locality, race, or manners. A religion cannot be *the* true religion if, for example, it can become part and parcel of the life of the European and American West, but cannot truly naturalise itself elsewhere, and so remains something exotic for the Jew, the Hindu, the Chinese, or the Arab. The visible and

---

[1] R. Browning, *The Heretic's Tragedy*:

"The Lord we look to once for all
Is the Lord we should look at all at once."

outward sign of the true religion would be its success as a universal *missionary* religion, not in the superficial sense of ability to make proselytes all over the world at the cost of denationalising them, and on the condition that they are dependent for their life as a community on control, supervision, and stimulation from outside, but in the sense of power to make itself, in its entirety without mutilation, deformation, or contamination, part and parcel of a life which is not a borrowed one. Such a test of the claims of Mohammedanism would be, for example, its ability to produce British or French Moslems who remained British or French to the core; of the claims of Christianity, its power to produce Indian or Chinese Christians who should be not, as too many "converts" have been, inferior imitations of Europeans, but at once Christians, and Indians or Chinese, as the case may be, "in their bones".

These last remarks are by the way, and merely "illustrative". But they may conceivably serve to suggest the right way of dealing with a real difficulty. How can the mind hold together two lines of thought apparently antithetic and yet both necessary to any genuine belief in revelation? A revelation with God as its source clearly must be, in some quite real sense, "final", and yet theology, the systematised intellectual elaboration of the content of revelation, never is final, but always *in fieri*. If we feel any doubt of the fact, we may readily allay the doubt by studying the history of the theology with which we are ourselves most familiar, *Christliche Dogmengeschichte*. Every considerable Christian society has sincerely professed to regard its Christianity as something in a real sense given once and for all, a "deposit" to be transmitted unchanged down the generations. The controversy between the most unyielding of the conservative-orthodox and the most venturesome of modernists has never really been as to the existence of an unchanging "substance of the faith", but always as to its content. The modernist, admitting that there is such a "deposit", merely adds that his conservative opponent confuses that priceless deposit with accretions which have grown up round it and disfigure it. And yet, it may fairly be urged, does not history seem to show that *every* affirmation which has been regarded as part of the "deposit" has repeatedly changed its meaning? Is it so certain, for example, that the same Trinitarian formula really bears the *same* meaning in Boethius and in St. Thomas? The doctrine of "original sin" is regarded as indispensable to Christianity by St. Augustine, St. Thomas, and Kant; but do not these three eminent men mean three different things by the formula which all of them employ? It might be said, with a considerable show of justification, that the more resolutely a religious society tries to live up to the motto *semper eadem*, the more impossible it finds the task, unless it is prepared to translate the Latin audaciously into a living vernacular as *eppur si muove*. The "Liberal Protestant" of 1927 would, no doubt, have been disowned as a mere "deist" by the "Liberal Protestants" of 1727, as our friends in the Roman fold like to remind us; but may we not equally suspect that an "orthodox" Roman of our own time, a Leo XIII., for example, would have found it hard to talk theology with the Angelic Doctor, without discovering that, for good or bad, the man of the thirteenth and the man of the nineteenth century meant different things by the same phraseology?

There is a way of meeting the difficulty which is popular and tempting, but to my own mind profoundly unsatisfactory, by the drawing of a hard-and-fast distinction between the "faith" which abides, and its

intellectual expression in doctrine and dogma which is
merely mutable and subject to the law of indefinite
modifiability. I do not myself understand how so
many philosophers have been content to acquiesce in
this depreciation of "dogma" which is part of the current superior journalism of our times. The only consistent logical position for the rigid separatist of "faith"
from all intellectual formulation, I take it, is the extreme position which simply identifies religion with
some kind of emotion, and the mere identification of
any fundamental activity of the human spirit with emotion, cut loose from a *specific* object, is the degradation
and, in the end, the paralysis of the emotion itself.
Emotions of all kinds so manifestly derive their value
for human life from the character of the object on which
they are directed. Emotion inappropriate or dispropor-
tionate to the objective situation by which it is evoked
is the bane of life. We can all see this clearly enough in
moral theory when the question is raised of the worth
of this or that emotion as a "motive" to action. It is, or
should be, the stalest of ethical commonplaces that
emotions cannot be classified into the morally good
and the morally evil, and that if "motive" is taken to
mean what Mill took it to mean, the "feeling" which
"makes a man act" by breaking down a kind of mental
and moral inertia, the view that the worth either of our
acts or of our character is a function of our "motives"
would be the ruin of coherent thinking about conduct.

There would, for example, be no sense in saying that
pity is a good motive, but resentment a bad one. The
worth of either depends on the question who it is that
is pitied, what it is that is resented. Pity for the wrong
persons, or even ill-regulated pity for the right persons,
has repeatedly led to the most dreadfully wrong moral
action; anger, if it is righteous anger against oppression

or meddling, is one of the most precious ingredients in the character of the moral "hero". The moral worth of wonder or curiosity, again, depends wholly on its object. To wonder about the right things, as Plato knew, is to be on the way to become a master in knowledge; to "wonder with a foolish face of praise" at the wrong things is to be for life a *curioso impertinente*.

Nor would the edge of this criticism be turned by appealing to the now familiar distinction between belief in a statement and belief, or faith, in a person. That distinction is real, and we may have to revert to it, but it will not serve this turn. Faith in a person will not be a quickening and regenerative influence, if it is faith in the *wrong* person; nothing will wreck the moral life more utterly than an unquestioning faith in an unworthy person. The important thing is that our faith should be reposed in a person who is really adequate to sustain it, and thus it makes all the difference in the world to the spiritual fruits of such faith what we take the person we believe in to be, and whether he really is what we take him for. This surely disposes once and for all of the proposal to find the real value of religious faith in mere intense emotion, divorced altogether from any element of intellectual conviction. We may, no doubt, acquiesce intellectually in any number of propositions about a person without being moved by the acquiescence to any practical surrender of the direction of our will and conduct by our "convictions", as the devil has been imagined to accept the whole of Christian theology without being even faintly stirred to conformity of will to God. But such assent remains a merely "dead" faith, if we are to call it faith at all. It would be mere unreason to infer that since "living" faith is *more* than such intellectual assent to a number of propositions, it involves no such assent. To "believe in" a man is, indeed, always more than to believe certain statements *about* him, but it is no less true that I cannot "believe in" a man without believing something "about" him, even if that something is no more than that "this is the best and wisest man I have hitherto met", and what one believes thus is always capable of being stated in an intelligible, though commonly very incomplete, form.

A faith which was *mere* emotion—if there really can be, as I gravely doubt whether there can be, any such thing as a *mere* emotion—would be a faith devoid of anything deserving to be called conviction. Genuine faith, because it reposes on conviction, cannot be other than a *fides quaerens intellectum.* For that reason, I should say, we owe a real debt of gratitude to the much decried "dogmatists", whose concern has always been to make explicit the implicit convictions which justify faith in a person. Being, like the rest of us, human, and incident to the common intellectual and moral weaknesses of humanity, the dogmatists may execute this task very imperfectly, but it is a task which rational beings cannot decline. Thus I suspect that the secret reason why so many of us to-day incline to resent all attempts to put our convictions about God into clear doctrinal form is an uneasy suspicion that, if we were quite honest with ourselves, we should find that we have no real convictions to support our emotionalism, and are naturally unwilling to be driven into making this discovery. I should suspect the same thing of a man who professed unqualified faith in his teacher, or his country, if he resented all questions about the precise achievements of either which elicit and demand his faith.

Thus Fr. G. Tyrrell's epigrammatic declaration, "I share the faith of Simon Peter, not his dogmatic

theology", seems to me to come perilously near converting a needful distinction into a dangerous false
antithesis. I do not see how we can have a faith in
common with Simon Peter, unless there are also *some* intellectual convictions which we share with him. It may
be impossible to isolate just that element of common
intellectual conviction completely from other elements
which are not common, as it is, I presume, impossible
in practice to isolate one chemical element absolutely
from all others, and yet, in both cases, it may be a proper,
even a necessary, exercise to make our approximate
analysis as thorough as we can.

The problem is, of course, one which meets us in
every sphere of human intellectual activity. Thus the
"external world" of the ordinary practical man and
that of the physicist "physicising", especially if he is a
physicist of the latest type, may seem to have as little
in common as the simple unspeculative faith of Simon
Peter, the fisherman of Bethsaida, and the systematic
theology of the *Summa* of Thomas, or the *Institutes*
of Calvin. Yet the attempt sometimes made by the
physicist to set the two "worlds" of common experience and physical theory in absolute antithesis to one
another leads nowhere, and cannot, I should say, represent the real belief of the philosophical physicist himself. It is not many months since I had the privilege of
listening to a brilliant statement of the antithesis from
the lips of Professor Eddington.[1] If we took the professor at his word, there seemed to be so complete a
severance between the common man's world and the
physicist's world that the mere reference of an object
to the one would be enough to exclude it from the
other. The table upon which Professor Eddington, as
a man speaking to men and women, rested his manu-

[1] *Nature of the Physical World*, c. I.

script or his crayon, and the table which, as a physicist, he regarded as an object for investigation and description, were made to seem so wholly disparate that any statement which must be made about one of them would be simply false if asserted of the other. There was not even justification left for so much as calling the "physicist's table" a ghost or shadow of the "real table". And yet I am sure that the speaker never meant seriously to suggest that the physicist is only amusing himself with capricious inventions of his own unregulated fancy, or that "verification" by reference to the common man's "sensible objects" and their behaviour is not the standing test of the physicist's hypotheses. He did not really believe himself as a professor of astronomy to be concerned with an "intelligible sun" and "intelligible stars" to which the eccentricities of the sun and stars we can see have no sort of relevance. For he proceeded in subsequent lectures[1] to draw all sorts of conclusions about the probable past and future history of the sun and stars, and, of course, the sun which has had a history in the past and will have a history in the future is the sun which we all see and whose warmth we all feel. There was no serious question of forgetting that all the problems of the physicist are set for him by the sense-experience which he shares with the rest of us, and that the supreme test of his success in solving them must be found in his ability to anticipate other experiences of the same kind, or that the only kind of scientific hypothesis which can be dismissed once and for all as "illegitimate" is an hypothesis which, from its nature, is capable of possible disproof by confrontation with "facts in the sensible world". Whatever Professor Eddington might permit himself to say for the purpose

---

[1] *Op. cit.* c. 4.

of impressing his audience with the abstract and schematic character of physical science, it was clear that he knew—no one better—that the physicist means all the time to be talking of the world which "is the home of all of us", and that his genial attempts to "make our flesh creep" by telling us, for example, that the human body consists almost entirely of "empty space",[1] would have had no point if this were not so. For if the physicist really means when he talks of *my* body to be speaking only of something which has even less connection with what I, as an ordinary man, mean by my body than my shadow has, why should I feel perturbed, or even mildly interested, by anything the physicist may please to say about it?[2]

Now, a physicist like Professor Eddington really stands to you and me, in his utterances about human bodies, tables, suns, stars, precisely as the scientific theologian stands to the simple believer, Simon the fisherman, or another. The physicist is the systematic theologian of the natural world, that θεὸς εὐδαίμων of Plato's *Timaeus*. The *viri Galilaei* and their lived religion set the Christian theologian his problems, as the sense-experiences of the common man normally equipped with eyes, ears, nostrils, tongue, skin, set the physicist his. There is no legitimate physical speculation which has not its point of departure in common pre-scientific sense-experience, and there is similarly, I take it, no legitimate theological problem which has

[1] *Op. cit.* pp. 1-2.
[2] Cf. Professor Eddington's own observations in another volume: "Science is not the describing a world invented to save trouble; it is following up a problem which took definite shape the first time two human beings compared notes of their experiences; and it follows it up according to the original rules. . . . I simply do not contemplate the awful contingency that the external world of physics, after all our care in arriving at it, might be disqualified by failing to 'exist'. . . . It is sufficient that it is the world which confronts our common experience and that therefore we are interested in knowing all we can about it." ("The Domain of Physical Science" in *Science, Religion, and Reality*, pp. 196-7.)

not its point of departure in the actual life of contact
with God. In this sense, the whole of legitimate theology is implicit and given once for all in the life of the
man practising his religion, as the whole of physical
science is implicit and, in a way, given once for all, in
the actuality of the sensible.

Now, to say thus that the "dogmas" of a true physics
are, in a real sense, given once for all in our everyday
apprehension of the sensible means, to be sure, that
there must be an element of intellectual conviction
common to the physicist with the ordinary man. Their
respective certainties are not, after all, of wholly disparate orders. The physicist does not live in one world
with his intellect, as a physicist, and in a "wholly
other" world, that of human life, with his emotions
and reactions to stimulus. He takes the "world" of
common life with him into his laboratory, when the disclosures of the senses set him a problem for investigation, and he recurs to that "world" when he tests his
solution by comparing his theoretical results with the
record of another set of immediate disclosures of sense.
Thus there are convictions, as well as emotions and
motor responses, in common to him with the plain
man, though it is true that he could not set out these
common convictions in exact and abstract logical form
completely and unambiguously. For he must speak
either the language of common life itself, or the technical "jargon" of his special science. The one is always
pregnant with masses of unanalysed and imprecise
suggestion, which make it hopelessly ambiguous;[1] the
other has been devised specifically to deal with the
physicist's abstractions *as such*, and the more adequate

[1] Cf. Plato, *Ep.* vii. 342 E πρὸς γὰρ τούτοις ταῦτα οὐχ ἧττον ἐπιχειρεῖ τὸ ποῖόν τι
περὶ ἕκαστον δηλοῦν ἢ τὸ ὂν ἑκάστου διὰ τὸ τῶν λόγων ἀσθενές· ὧν ἕνεκα νοῦν
ἔχων οὐδεὶς τολμήσει ποτὲ εἰς αὐτὸ τιθέναι τὰ νενοημένα ὑπ' αὐτοῦ, καὶ ταῦτα εἰς
ἀμετακίνητον.

it proves for this purpose, the less is it fitted to express convictions which are not peculiar to the physicist as such, but shared by him with the rest of mankind. Yet these convictions are none the less present and all-persuasive, that we have no idiom in which to give them well-defined expression.

In the same way, I suggest, we should conceive of the all-pervasive presence in theology of intellectual convictions which are common to the theologian and the simple unspeculative believer, but defy precise formulation, whether in the rich but systematically ambiguous language of direct and vivid faith, or in the highly specialised and artificial technical vocabulary of theology itself. We may reasonably expect that the difficulty of formulation will be even more formidable for the theologian than for the physicist, since all our apprehension of God, the supreme reality of realities, is necessarily so much dimmer and more inadequate than our apprehension of everyday sensible body. And theology may surely learn a much-needed lesson from the procedure of the physicist. The once-for-all-ness and finality of the sense-experience through which the bodily world is given makes itself felt in physics in the recognition that a theory which demands consequences to which our senses definitely give the lie is thereby discredited. This, I take it, is the only finality known to physics. May we not say that there is only one way in which a theological doctrine is finally discredited? It is discredited if its truth would require that the religious growth of the soul should be fostered by conditions which, in fact, impede it, or hindered by conditions which, in fact, promote it. A refutation of this kind may be hard to obtain, but sometimes it is obtained, and then it is indeed final. Where it cannot be obtained, it seems premature and dangerous to con-

vert our best attempts to find formulae for the intellectual expression of the convictions by which we live into
"articles of a standing or a falling Church".

But the rival attempt to dispense altogether with
intellectual formulation is itself equally dangerous to
real spiritual life in a different way. Faith may die,
often has died, of internal ossification, when it is not
allowed to stir except under the weight of a cast-iron
panoply of ready-made doctrinal formulae; it may die,
no less surely, by a sort of liquefaction, when suffered
to evaporate in vague emotionalism. And of the rival
dangers, there cannot be much doubt that the second
is the more imminent for the average member of the
"educated" society of our own country at the present
day. Most of *us* are in no very great danger, as we
might have been in some former ages, of spoiling our
religion, our morality, our politics, or our art, by excess of rigid intellectual conviction. Our danger is
rather that living, as we do, at the end of a "romantic"
age which ran riot in the glorification of emotion for its
own sake, we may try to make out, in religion, morals
and politics, art alike, with a superficial scepticism,
feebly coloured with thin sentimentality. In an age
in which scepticism—a languid scepticism—about the
"certainties" of science, not so long ago apparently
the most assured of all "certainties", has become the
favourite intellectual attitude of the "educated public",
our most crying intellectual need, perhaps, is the need
of men who will, by their robust assertions, arouse us,
not from our "dogmatic", but from our lazily anti-
dogmatic, "slumbers". There was something heroic
about the temper of the "Mid-Victorian" time, with
its cry of

> It fortifies my soul to know
> That though I perish, truth is so.

There is nothing heroic about "keeping the mind open" on all questions, simply because we are too indolent to give ourselves the trouble of shutting a door. Nor is it well to leave all doors indiscriminately open, for, though the open door often provides an avenue for the entrance of much that is welcome, it also, as we too often forget, affords an exit through which what we can least afford to lose may disappear. The important thing is to judge rightly which doors should be left open and which should be shut.

III

RELIGION AND THE HISTORICAL

Ist es der *Sinn*, der alles wirkt und schafft?
Es sollte stehn: Im Anfang war die *Kraft*!
Doch auch in dem ich dieses niederschreibe,
Schon warnt mich was, dass ich dabei nicht bleibe.
Mir hilft der Geist! Auf einmal seh' ich Rat
Und schreibe getrost: Im Anfang war die *Tat*.

GOETHE.

THE object of our last lecture has been to urge that
there is nothing inherently unreasonable in the recognition of specific "revelation" as a source of knowledge
of God and the eternal. But it would be possible to concede all for which we have so far pleaded, and yet to
object that we have not so much as touched the real
problem created by the claims of the great positive
revelational religions of the world. At most, we have
only vindicated the reasonableness of recognising the
possibility that significant truth about God may be
made known to, or through, particular persons at a
particular place and time. We have left it an open possibility that the truths thus historically disclosed—if such
a disclosure has indeed taken place—might be one and
all of a supra-temporal order, concerned entirely with
the eternal and timeless, like, for example, the Christian
doctrine of the triune nature of God, or the great Jewish doctrine of the divine Unity. Even if we adopt the
view that the proposition "the Lord our God is One"
is at once vital to religion and incapable of rational
proof, so that it can only be received, where it is re-

ceived, on the strength of faith in an immediate historical revelation—to Moses or to another—still, the
doctrine itself, however we have come by it, is not a
statement about the historical course of events; it is a
statement about the supra-historical reality, God. But
when we examine the *credenda* propounded for acceptance by any of the great positive religions, we find that
in every case there are included among them some propositions which are themselves statements about events
of the historical order, allegations that certain transactions have taken place in the past, or will take place
in the future. The creed of each of these religions is
found to contain specific assertions about the course of
history in the past, and specific anticipations or prophecies of the course which events are to follow in the
future. In the creed of orthodox Christianity we see
this presence of an historical element in its most pronounced form. Side by side with propositions concerning the eternal divine nature, it contains a number of
distinct statements of fact about the life of Jesus Christ,
and one definite prophecy of an historical event to
occur in the future, a "coming" of Christ to bring the
temporal history of humanity to a close.

Now here, it may be said, and not in the mere concept
of revelation, lies the real *crux* for a philosophy of
religion. The revelational religions regularly treat the
whole of their *credenda* as alike "saving truth", no
portion of which can be denied without the "loss of the
soul". But how is it possible for the philosophic mind
to attach this kind of value to any statement of historical
fact? As for serious error about the divine nature, since
such error means acceptance of an unreal and unworthy
object for the soul's unqualified worship, we can understand that it must lead to impairment of the soul's life.
For we inevitably grow ourselves into the likeness of

that which we contemplate with adoration and self-surrender. There is thus, in principle, no mystery about the dependence of our attainment of eternal life upon the worthiness and truth of our real convictions about God. But how can there be any such connection between spiritual vitality and a man's convictions about the events of the past? How, to take an extreme example, can a man be the better or worse according as he believes or doubts that the Roman procurator who gave the order for our Lord's death was named Pontius Pilate?[1] How would the truth of the Christian religion as a revelation of God be affected, even if it should be discovered that the Gospel tradition had made a mistake of a few years, and ascribed to Pilate an act which really belonged to his precursor's or his successor's tenure of office?[2] Must it not be false in principle to assert that our beliefs about such historical points have any bearing upon the spiritual life? And is it not also a sin against intelligence to demand of any man that he shall affirm propositions of this kind on any ground but that of the goodness of the historical testimony for them? Must we not say that in dealing with assertions about historical events there can be no appeal from the standards of historical evidence, as in dealing with assertions about the physical there can be no appeal from accurately recorded and registered scientific observation? The philosopher, indeed, might conceivably be justified in accepting as true all the statements about

---

[1] The example is actually given by Abelard—whom I name at second-hand from Wicksteed, *Reactions between Dogma and Philosophy*, p. 115—as proof that the text of Holy Scripture alone does not contain all things necessary to be believed. (Either Abelard's memory must have played him false, or he used a bad text of the Vulgate, since the *nomen* Pontius occurs at least thrice in the New Testament, *Luke* iii. 1, *Acts* iv. 27, 1 *Timothy* vi. 13.)

[2] And *a fortiori*, how could our religion be affected by the discovery that the *nomen* of the procurator is inaccurately given in the two passages just cited, and consequently in the Creeds? (The Gospel narrative uniformly uses only the *cognomen*, Pilate.)

historical events contained in the "creed" of a given religion, but he would only be justified if he had independently convinced himself that these statements satisfy the ordinary tests applicable to all allegations about facts in the past, and assent of this kind is something quite different from religious faith, and may, in fact, exist without being accompanied by such faith. It would be easy, for instance, to name writers who have combined rejection of the Christian *faith* with assent to the mere historical truth of such articles of the Christian creed as "born of the Virgin Mary", "the third day he rose from the dead", and such assent is not what any orthodox Christian has ever meant by the faith which saves.

One might go on to support the main position thus outlined in more detail by appealing to the indisputable fact that the great historical religions have, one and all, been convicted of putting forward among their *credenda* assertions about historical fact which have undergone definite disproof, and, in the end, been abandoned, not without grave sacrifice of dignity. We have only to think of the widespread and complete surrender of "orthodox" Christianity, within the last half-century, to "critical" research in the matter of Old Testament history.[1] There is the further problem created by the fact that so many of the events included among the *credenda* of the historical religions are of a kind unparalleled in the "ordinary course" of nature. All these religions have their "miracles", and a "miracle" creates a very real difficulty for a mind in earnest with the conviction on which all philosophy is based, the conviction

---

[1] It may be objected to me that the Roman Church, at any rate, seems not to have made the surrender. It is not for an outsider to pretend knowledge of the official attitude of any Church, but *if* the Roman Church really has committed itself to some sort of "Fundamentalism" on this issue, I can only remark that, in my own opinion, that is so much the worse for the Roman Church.

that the world is an intelligible unity. Here, then, is a special problem of which the significance cannot well be exaggerated. How "actual" it is we can see for ourselves by studying, for example, the recent series of works by Dr. Gore, who may fairly be taken as representative of the position of the educated "conservative" in these matters of history, at its best. Dr. Gore is resolute in his insistence that there are certain statements of matter of historical fact which are so vital to the Christian religion that no compromise about them, no permission to take the words of the "articles" which affirm them in anything but their "plain, literal" sense, can be allowed to anyone who claims to adhere fully to the faith of the Church. Yet it is manifest that all along the line Dr. Gore is standing on the defensive in a fashion very different from the buoyant, occasionally truculent, aggressiveness of the apologists of two or three generations ago. Again, one is struck by the fact that Dr. Gore reduces his list of positions which must be defended at all costs to a minimum. What is really instructive is that a High Anglican Bishop and former Principal of Pusey House should be satisfied to draw his line round two or three propositions expressly enunciated in the so-called *Apostolicum*, where Dr. Pusey would have stood out, and did stand out, for the whole body of Scripture narrative. Even within the four corners of the *Apostolicum* Dr. Gore finds himself driven to make a distinction. There is to be no "latitude of interpretation" of the clause *natus ex Maria virgine*, but a generous latitude enough when we come to *ascendit ad caelos, inde venturus est*. In fact, the policy of "no surrender" is apparently not to be insisted on in its full rigour for more than perhaps two clauses of three or four words apiece, and this looks much as though Dr. Gore himself were conscious of being the conductor of a "forlorn hope".[1] One is naturally tempted to ask whether the foreseeable end must not be the general abandonment of all insistence on the religious value of assertions about the historical. May not Tyrrell have been a true prophet when he wrote that all that will survive permanently of Christianity is "mysticism and charity", with the possible addition of the Eucharist, reduced to its simplest form, as an impressive symbol in act of the spirit of mysticism and charity? And may not the method of "allegorical interpretation", so dear to the earliest Fathers, come once more to be adopted as the only "way out" for a great religion which has entangled itself in a web of dubious assertions about history?

We all know men of deeply religious spirit and fine intelligence who have already reached a position like Tyrrell's, or are certainly on the direct road thither, and we should all be able to understand both the strength of the temptation to secure one's religion once for all from the historical critic at a stroke, and the cruelty of the practical problem created for such men by the conflict between their conviction that one cannot cut one's self loose from the life of communal worship without grievous impoverishment of spiritual personality and the demand, still formally made by the Churches, that the participant in the common worship shall profess a belief which includes a great deal in the way of statements about history. There is, at the very least, ample excuse for those who hold that the future of the Churches depends on their willingness to rise to the opportunity of ridding their teaching about

[1] For a defence of the position in question, of which I wish to speak with the deep respect due to all the pronouncements of the author, and with which I find it hard not to feel real sympathy, I would refer to Dr. Gore's summary of his doctrine in the volume *Can We Then Believe ?* (1926). I sincerely hope that I have succeeded in describing the general attitude taken up throughout the volume without unconscious misrepresentation.

God of what has been the source of so many burnings of heart and so much disloyalty to truth. Others than "ultramontanes" might well be pardoned for feeling that they would heartily thank God to be "done with history."[1]

Still, the real question is not whether this attitude of mind is intelligible and pardonable, as it assuredly is, but whether it is justifiable. To myself the unqualified Modernist solution of this particular difficulty, like most simple solutions of serious problems, seems too simple to be trusted. It would be at least a singular paradox that one and the same age should find it necessary to save its physics, after the fashion urged by Dr. Whitehead—by reconstructing traditional doctrines in the light of biology, as a remedy for the incurably unhistorical character of the "classical" mechanics—and also to save its theology by the elimination of all historical reference. If "misplaced concreteness" has really been the curse of nineteenth-century physics, it should presumably be an equally objectionable thing in divinity. And what it would really mean to "have done with history" we may perhaps gather, if we will make a simple *Denkexperiment*. Let us suppose the elimination of the historical to have been successfully "carried to the limit". To make the illustration the more telling, we will suppose this to have happened with the religion in which we have been ourselves brought up, and whose influence is written large in the life of our own society at its best. We will suppose, then,

[1] Cf. Inge, *Philosophy of Plotinus*,[1] ii. 227: "Neo-Platonism differs from popular Christianity in that it offers us a religion the truth of which is not contingent on any particular events, whether past or future. It is dependent on no miracles, on no unique revelation through any historical person, on no narratives about the beginning of the world, on no prophecies of its end. There is a Christian philosophy of which the same might be said. . . . Christianity . . . can only exert its true influence in the world . . . when it stands on its own foundations, without those extraneous supports which begin by strengthening a religion and end by strangling it."

that the theory which denies the very existence of the founder and central figure of Christianity as a historical person should cease to be the private fad of a few amateurs of little judgement who have wandered into history from other fields, and become the accepted and unchallenged teaching of historians at large, and thus pass as a standing assumption into the "general mind". That is, we will suppose that all but the entirely un-educated, devout and undevout alike, have acquired a habit of mind to which it is as unquestioned a "truth" that the life of Christ is pure fable or allegory as it is now an "unquestioned truth" that existing animal species have "evolved" within a measurable period of time. We will imagine a society which will regard the dwindling minority among those who have passed through its schools who still cling to the belief that Jesus Christ was a real man much as our own society regards minorities who deny that "the earth is round", or that the dog and the jackal are descendants of a common ancestor. If it were true that the spiritual value of a religion is *wholly* independent of beliefs about matters of historical fact, it should follow that the Christian life would flourish just as well in these sup-posed conditions as in any others, and possibly better. It should be as easy in principle for the Christian religion and worship to make terms with the resolu-tion of Christ into an astronomical or moral symbol as it has been for it to adjust itself to the view that the story of Adam, Eve, and the serpent has only sym-bolic value. The only difference should be that the unreasoned sentimental prejudice against reducing the Cross to the status of a mere symbol might be expected to be deeper rooted, and to require a longer time for its evaporation than a similar prejudice in favour of the botanical reality of the tree of the knowledge of good and evil. The spiritual power of the "word of the Cross" for the regeneration of human life should remain un-affected. But I venture to think that we have only to envisage the suggested situation clearly to be con-vinced that this is preposterously false. The whole "power of the Gospel" to remake human personality is intimately bound up with the conviction that the story of the passion and exaltation of Christ is neither symbol nor allegory, but a story of what *has been done* for man by a real man, who was also something more than a real man, a story of a real *transaction* at once divine and human. You cannot cut the motivation conveyed by such words as "*if* God so loved us, we ought . . ." out of the practical Christian life without destroying *that* specific kind of life at its root.

Similarly, if the triumph of a human "Lord of life" over death is no more than an allegorical way of con-veying some philosopheme about the "conservation of values", the story surely loses all its power to inspire us with the hope which

creates
From its own wreck the thing it contemplates.

The *whole* point of the Christian story is that it claims to be a story of an *opus operatum*, an act which has, in fact and not in fiction, been achieved by God through man and for man. The point is that love and goodness have, in perfectly plain and downright fact, "power as they have manifest authority", and that in the face of all the apparently overwhelming testimony of history to the superior *power* of evil, and the apparent com-plete failure of nature to disclose an "All-great" who is also an "All-loving". If the story is not fact, and has no permanent value but that of a symbol, it loses all its depth, for it is a symbol of what may be dreadfully *un*-fact. If we ask ourselves seriously what it is in Christianity which is the element of supreme value to Christians, that is to men who are actually trying to live the Christian life, what it is *they* find in Christianity and nowhere else, I do not think there can be any doubt about the answer; it is, as Soloviev has said,[1] the person of Christ himself, taken as the completest revelation of God. But a religion without any historical *credenda* would be a religion without the *person* of Christ, and thus, even if it retained a host of *theologumena* expressed in Christian terminology and a mass of traditional Christian devotional practices, it would no longer be Christianity. It would be—to adopt Huxley's mordant definition of the Comtist "religion of humanity" —Catholicism (or Protestantism, as the case might be) "*minus* Christianity".

Now I can understand and respect a man who says that, whether we like it or not, this is all that loyalty to truth can leave standing in the way of a religion for mankind in the future. Perhaps we all of us sometimes feel a misgiving that it may be so. What I cannot understand is that any thoughtful man should maintain either that this is the substance of Christianity, and that the evaporation of the historical would still leave the Christian religion potent to produce the types of character we see in the Christian saints and heroes, an Augustine, a Xavier, a George Herbert, a Bunyan, or that, though it may be true that the world must never expect to see that type of man again, the world, and religion itself too, will be none the worse for the loss. And unless one is prepared to say one or the other of these things, one must admit that Christianity, at any rate, could not be simply relieved of its historical

[1] See the brilliant and suggestive dialogue "The End of History", in *War, Progress, and the End of History* (E. tr., p. 213).

credenda without being transformed into something of radically different character.[1]

It might, no doubt, be suggested that this is an accident of one particular historical religion, and I can conceive that this might actually be made a ground for depreciating Christianity by comparison with some of its rivals for world-wide allegiance. The person of Christ, so I can imagine some non-Christian but devout student to reason, is certainly central in the religion of Christians, and the obscure and perplexing "doctrine of the person of Christ" consequently central in their theology; so much the worse for it and them. By deifying their Founder (for I may fairly assume that the imagined critic will regard the Christian worship of Christ as simply a striking instance of the *post-mortem* deification of a great man by the love and admiration of his followers), Christians fatally committed themselves from the outset to a hopeless conflict with history, which knows nothing of *praesentes divi* and has the duty to reduce their figures to the proportions of flesh and blood; naturally, such a religion must not hope to survive the exposure of its initial mistake. But other historical religions have not committed the error of what the Mohammedan doctors call "association" (*shirk*), the giving of a partner to their Deity. They have kept their founders and prophets on the strictly human level, and there is thus not the same reason why the fate of their traditions of their great men should affect their value as "religious knowledge". Judaism and Islam are faiths whose message to mankind has, as its content, simply a doctrine about God ; the worst

---

[1] Here rather than in the "Copernican revolution", to which Dr. Inge attaches so much significance, I should find the secret of the now acute *crise du christianisme*. The supposed theological consequences of the deposition of our planet from its unique status appear to be in process of dissipation by the return of astronomers themselves to the old belief that the status of the Earth is unique, or at least, most exceptional. Cf. Eddington, *Nature of the Physical World*, pp. 169 ff.

that destructive criticism of their historical traditions could do would only be to disprove the supposed fact that this doctrine was integrally proclaimed at a given place by Moses the Levite, or Mohammed, son of Abdallah, a fact which obviously has no relevance to the truth and importance of the doctrine itself. It is wholly illegitimate to mistake for a universal character of revelational religion what is, in truth, an incidental weakness of one special religion.

The contention at least sounds plausible, and we should be careful not to underestimate its force. Yet, when all is said, I feel the greatest misgivings about it. Is it so obvious, after all, that Mohammedanism or Judaism is in substance nothing more than a "philosophical" Theism, or Deism, with the relatively unimportant characteristic of having been, according to tradition, first promulgated by a particular person on a particular occasion? Does common experience show that the Jew or Moslem who jettisons his historical *credenda* fares so much better than the Christian who is in the same case? Take the case of the Jew who eliminates what is, after all, the central *motif* of Old Testament religion, and a *motif* of distinctively historical kind, the "covenant" once made by the one God with the Israelite Fathers. Does he usually find that what is left him of his Judaism still serves equally well to sustain a life of active faith in eternal realities, or does he not more commonly tend to lapse into a mere agnostic worldliness? And what happens to the "young Turk" who has simply thrown overboard the great historical *credendum* of his inherited beliefs, the Day of Judgement, and everything in the traditions of his fathers which stands or falls with the Day of Judgement? These are questions which we cannot well avoid raising, and serious consideration of them may possibly suggest that it is by no accident that our own religion is as closely bound up with convictions about the significance of an historical personality as we find it to be. It may rather be that Christianity shows itself to be the most true to type of all the great universal religions, precisely by exhibiting in that intensest form a character which is present in all, though in the others its presence is less obtrusive and more easy to overlook.[1]

This, in fact, is no more than one might expect, if we have been right in holding that the great function of religion in human life is the transformation of personality by the substitution of the abiding and eternal for the merely temporary and transient, as the centre of man's interests. We should expect that in proportion as a religion succeeds in effecting this transformation, it will show a quickened and keener sense of the reality of both terms of the opposition. Unless our whole conception of the relation between "nature" and "grace", "this" world and the "other", as we tried to develop it in our former series, was false in its principle, it might have been foreseen that the religion which grapples most successfully with the practical task of reorganising life with an eternal good as its centre will be the religion which brings its God down most intimately into contact with the temporal historical process, not one of those which simply set Him outside and beyond it, and consequently that it will find its historical connecting link between God and man in a personality standing in a much closer relation to God than that of the prophet, the mere bearer of a "message from the other side" which might equally well have been put

---

[1] St. Paul's attitude, as we gather it from his epistles, seems to me very instructive. The covenant under Moses appears to have lost its main significance for him, and to be reduced to the status of a decidedly secondary episode. But his depreciation of the Law only throws into stronger relief his unwavering faith in the earlier covenant with "Abraham and his seed" as a central fact in the history of mankind.

into the mouth of another. We should naturally expect in such a religion what we actually find in Christianity, that its historical revelation of God consists primarily neither in a body of propositions about God, nor in a code of precepts from God, but in the whole of a concrete divine personality and life; that, in fact, the "revealer" would be the content of his own revelation. And for the same reason we might, as I think, anticipate *a priori* that the intellectual elaboration of such a self-disclosure of the divine through the detail of a concrete human life, its abstentions and silences, no less than its acts and utterances, would inevitably involve, as the theology of a religion which still leaves its God more or less remote need not involve, a doctrine of the person of an historical "Christ". To a religion which leaves God more or less aloof in the beyond, to be known only by the instructions and commands which come to us from Him, the teaching or the commandment is the primary thing, and the only importance which the bearer of them need have for us is that he is the conduit through which the communication has reached us. So long as we accept the message he transmits, it is really irrelevant what we believe or do not believe about his personality. But if a religion actually brings God down into the heart of temporality, as working through it, not from outside it only, then it will be the person and life in which the complete interpenetration of the eternal and the temporal has been actualised which is itself the revelation, and to believe will be primarily not to assent to the utterances of a messenger, but to recognise the person in whom the interpenetration of the two "worlds" has been achieved for what he is. In a religion which still leaves God and man, the eternal and the temporal, in their relative aloofness, the intermediary between them will be honoured for the message which he brings; when the aloofness has been abolished "by unity of person", the sayings and precepts of the intermediary will be honoured because they are *his*.[1]

If what we have tried to say in earlier lectures about the relation between eternity and temporality is at bottom sound, we can thus see that the prominence of *credenda* of an historical character in our own religion, all of them connected with the conviction that the complete interpenetration of Creator and creature has been realised in fact in an individual life, is evidence of strength rather than of weakness. It could not be otherwise with a religion which is to do justice to the given reality of human life, as the region where the eternal and the temporal are bound up with one another as the antithetic poles of a single tension. So, and only so, is eternal life, in fact, brought down within the reach of mortal men. The ultimate justification of the refusal to make religion wholly "philosophical" by the reduction of the whole element of historical *credenda* to mere edifying allegory or symbolism is to be found, then, in the character of specifically human life itself, as a life which can be, and ought to be, one of "participated eternity", one in which successiveness is increasingly penetrated by permanence and abidingness, but where, because we are and must remain men, not gods, the successiveness which marks us as "creatures" never wholly vanishes. Its complete disappearance would mean that each of us had himself become an independent *ens realissimum*, self-contained and self-supporting. If that were *our* nature and *our* destiny, it would

---

[1] Cf. Soloviev, *op. cit.*, p. 173: "Until you show me the goodness of your lord in his own deeds and not in verbal precepts to his employees, I shall stick to my opinion that your distant lord, demanding good from others but doing no good himself, imposing duties but showing no love, never appearing before your eyes but living *incognito* somewhere abroad, is no one else but *the god of this age*."

be as true as it is, in fact, revoltingly false to say of that finest of all creaturely virtues, which Christians have called the one virtue which is wholly supernatural, what Spinoza unhappily said of it, *humilitas virtus non est, ex ratione non oritur*.[1] It would follow, in the same way, that the ultimate aim of the religious life is to supersede itself, to conduct us to a heaven where, if it could ever be reached, each of the beatified would have ceased to have anything to worship, being simply "shut up in measureless content" with himself. And I conceive we might draw the further corollary that even now, while we are still *in statu viatoris* towards such a consummation, prayer of all kinds would be a hindrance, not a help to the life of the spirit, since the very point of prayer is that it is the expression of a sense of utter dependence. These are, I think, all inevitable consequences of permitting ourselves to forget that we are, and must always remain, historical beings, just because we are dependent beings, creatures and not our own creators.

"The historical", says an eminent philosopher recently taken from us, "is what we *understand* least and what concerns us most. How far below us, how far above, the historical extends, we cannot tell. But above it there can be only God, as the living unity of all, and below it, no longer things, but only the connecting, conserving acts of the one supreme."[2] By way of comment I would subjoin two reflections. Below the historical, I should say, and I think I should be in accord with the trend of the contemporary philosophy of the physical sciences in saying so, there could be nothing actual, but only the *materia prima* or *informis* of the Aristotelians, that ghost of just nothing at all which Dr.

---

[1] *Ethica*, iv. 53.
[2] Ward, *Naturalism and Agnosticism*[1], ii. 280 (after Lotze).

Whitehead is wrestling so hard to lay. And when God is said to be above the historical, this does not mean, and I take it that the philosopher I have quoted did not suppose it to mean, that God, being eternal, cannot intimately inform and work through the temporal and historical. Time, indeed, cannot be made, by stretching at both ends, so to say, to envelop eternity, but eternity can and does envelop time, and penetrate it through and through at its every point. This, as we thought we saw long ago, is the open secret of the moral and spiritual life of man, depending, as it does, all through on the delicate balancing of right attachment to and noble detachment from temporal good, and sustained, as well as initiated, by an outgoing spontaneous movement from the eternal, God, to the temporal, humanity. Carried to its extreme limit, such a self-disclosure of the eternal in and through its own creation, the temporal, would be an actual individual temporal life, subject in each of its details to the contingency inseparable from creatureliness, and so the life of a creature with its own *apparently* accidental place in the "kingdom of nature", as just the historical creature it is, when and where it is, and yet also, in every detail, the complete and adequate vehicle of the eternal. Such a life, plainly, would not be that of a creature which had somehow *achieved* beatitude, like a Buddhist *arahat*, by victory over its own initial vices and defects, nor yet the life of a creature which, though uniquely faultless, was still a *mere* creature. So long as we have the strictly eternal on the one side, and the merely creaturely, however faultless, or the other, the actual interpenetration and enfolding of the temporal by the eternal remains incomplete. If the full resolution of the ultimate dissonance is to be achieved, what is necessary is a life which is at once everywhere creaturely and yet also everywhere more than creaturely, because its limitations, circumscriptions, and infirmities, whatever they may be, interpose no obstacle to the divine and eternal purpose which controls and shines through it, but are themselves vehicles of that purpose. That there has been one human life of which this is a true description, and that the life of the Founder of Christianity, is the undemonstrated and indemonstrable conviction which gives the Christian religion its specific character.

It would be inconsistent with my duty, as defined by Lord Gifford, to assert or deny the truth of this conviction. Here it is in place only to make two observations: that the conviction, if true, though lying outside the limits of a strictly "natural" or "philosophic" theology, is in full harmony with such conceptions of the divine nature and the divine way with men as a sound philosophy leads us to entertain; and, again, that the surrender to such a conviction is definitely an act of walking by "faith", and not by "sight". That the Word has been "made flesh", and made flesh in just the specific person whom a Christian calls Lord, is a proposition which admits of no establishment by the empirical appeal to certified fact.

Some apologists for the Christian faith need, I think, to recognise this more unreservedly than they are apt to do. It is, I submit, a mistake to suppose that the unique cosmical significance Christianity ascribes to its Founder and Master can be sustained by a simple induction from the recorded events of his earthly life. In the first place, the Gospel narratives, like all records of human doings, permit of very different interpretations. Even the moral perfection of our Lord's character cannot be established beyond all possible question by the appeal to the record. Even of him, Kant's observation holds true, that, since we cannot read the secrets of men's hearts, we can never be sure as a matter of ascertained fact of the moral purity of the motives behind any act of any man.[1] The current anti-Christian attacks on various recorded acts of Jesus as indicating moral imperfections are, for the most part, malignant and stupid enough, and reflect grave discredit on those who can stoop to them; yet there really is no means of *proving* beyond cavil that all such unfavourable interpretations are false. The actual record, as it stands, *might* without logical absurdity be read as the story of a well-meaning and gracious, but self-deluded, sentimental "idealist" gradually embittered by contact with disagreeable realities; or again, even as that of an ambitious, or patriotic, "nationalist" insurgent against the political supremacy of Rome. Even apart from such crudely hostile interpretations, we have only to contrast the "liberal Protestant" reading of the story with that of the apocalyptists who find the key to Christ's conduct and teaching not in the *Sermon on the Mount*, but in eschatology, to appreciate the extreme difficulty of constructing an unambiguous and convincing portrait of "the historical Jesus".

Again, we must remember that on the most favourable estimate of our biographical material, it is painfully scanty. Even if the record permitted no alternative interpretations, it remains the fact that apart from the narrative of the week between the entry into Jerusalem and the return of the frightened women from the empty tomb, it consists only of a few anecdotes and a handful of discourses. Of the Lord's life as a whole we know hardly anything, and this of itself seems to vitiate all attempts to justify the Christian conception

---

[1] *Werke* (Hartenstein[2]), iv. 256.

of the significance of that life by appealing to the testimony of plain fact. And finally, we are bound to take into account the results of careful and unbiassed scrutiny into the sources of our narratives and the stages through which they have passed, as seriously affecting our right to regard them as trustworthy in their details. We are bound in honesty, I think, even from the standpoint of the most judiciously conservative criticism, to admit that we really know much less about the Master's life than might be supposed at first sight, or than we could wish. It is not too much to say that there never has been, and never will be, a trustworthy *Life of Jesus Christ*; we have no materials for such a work outside the Gospels, and the purpose of the Evangelists was not that of a biographer.

Similarly, if the chief emphasis is laid not so much on the Gospel narrative as upon the asserted incontestable perfection of the Gospel rule of life, it might be objected that it is not evident that the Gospels contain anything which can properly be called a *rule* of life; that what they do contain is rather a number of particular decisions on special moral issues; that it has always been a disputed question among Christians themselves what body of consistent moral principles, if any, can be extracted from these incidental decisions; and that they afford no unambiguous guidance in many of the most important moral problems of societies living in conditions very different from those of the Galilee or Judaea of the first Christian century. All this, so far as I can see, has to be conceded, and it would seem to follow that the utmost we can expect to do by appeal to the records is no more than to show that it is possible and permissible to interpret the recorded acts and teaching of Our Lord in a way which does not conflict with the claims Christian theology makes for his person.

Hostile criticism can be shown not to have made out its case; it seems doubtful whether empirical methods can show more than this. The specifically Christian "faith" in the person of Christ can be defended against attacks based on unfriendly interpretation of the records of his life and teaching, but not adequately substantiated by examination of those records.

It is clear, in fact, that the first believers were led to their belief neither by inference from the observed moral perfection of their Master, nor by reflection on the excellence of his moral precepts. What weighed with them, as we see clearly enough from the synoptic story and the *Acts of the Apostles*, was, first and foremost, the direct and immediate impression made by his whole personality of the presence in him of something "numinous", not to be understood in terms of the categories of ordinary human life, and next, the confirmation of this impression by the transcendent events of the resurrection on the third day and the wonderful manifestations of the day of Pentecost. And it seems that when the message of the Gospel was to be conveyed to a world at large which had known nothing of the Master before his death, the only facts of his career to which importance was attached were just the facts that he had been crucified "for our sins", "declared to be the Son of God by the resurrection from the dead", and was now actively "sending the Spirit" on believers. Thus it is notorious, though the fact is an awkward one for some "liberal" reconstructions of early Christianity, that St. Paul records only one incident of the life of Christ antecedent to the passion on Calvary,[1] and that an eminently "numinous" and

---

[1] 1 Cor. xi. 23. St. Paul's insistence on the point that he had "received" the narrative seems to me to demand the interpretation that it had been *officially* communicated to him by St. Peter and other eye-witnesses of the scene, and thus to be evidence for the Christianity of the date of his own conversion.

"other-world" act, the declaration that the bread and wine of the Last Supper are "my body on your behalf" and "the new covenant in my blood".

One might, I believe, go a step further and say truly that the first Christians primarily read even these facts wholly in the light of the Pentecostal "outpouring of the Spirit". If they were persuaded that their Master's death was something more than, what the world has seen so often, the murder of a wise and good man by the blinded and wicked, and his reappearance on the third day more than a signal vindication of the truth that the righteous man is not finally abandoned by his Maker, that, as they said, "Christ died *for our sins* and rose *for our justification*", they were so persuaded because they were first convinced that they had in themselves the actual experience of a new kind of life with God as its centre, and that this life had begun with the Pentecostal "giving of the Spirit".[1] They did not infer the transcendent significance of Christ from an antecedent belief in the moral perfection of his character, or the ethical elevation of his recorded sayings: rather they inferred these—though it is singular how little appeal any of the New Testament writings outside the Synoptic Gospels make to ethical precepts of Jesus—from their antecedent belief in the transcendent significance of Christ as the "glorified" sender of the Spirit. And one may fairly doubt whether, in later days, any man has ever really been converted to the Christian faith simply by the impression made on him either by the story of Christ's life or by the reports of his moral teaching. It is perhaps noteworthy that Christianity has never developed any counterpart to the enormous Mohammedan collections of Aḥādīth,

---

[1] Cf. the valuable chapter on "The Christ of History" in E. G. Selwyn's *Approach to Christianity* (1925).

traditions of the sayings of the Prophet, genuine or apocryphal, relative to the discharge of duty in all the conceivable situations in which the good Moslem may find himself. Something of this kind is indispensable in a religion whose Prophet has no significance for life beyond that of being a preacher and a moral exemplar, but Christianity has never felt the need of such a literature. Apocryphal Gospels were at one time freely invented, either to recommend specific *theologumena* like the *Gospel of Peter*, or to satisfy a craving for the marvellous, like the *Protevangelium of James* and the *Gospel of the Infancy*, but not to meet a demand for sayings of the Lord regulating in detail the moral duties of the Christian life. That need was met not by falling back on parables and precepts of Jesus, but by reliance on the guidance of the present and living Spirit.

This is not to say that there is not an appeal to history by the success or failure of which Christianity, or any other faith, may fairly be judged. But that appeal has very little to do with what are known as the "historical evidences" of a religion; it is the application to religion of the Gospel maxim "by their fruits ye shall know them". The vital question is not how much or little of the chronicled detail of the Founder's life can be authenticated in a way which will satisfy the exacting historical critic, or how far his certainly genuine utterances can be made into a code of "categorical imperatives"; it is whether he has brought, and continues to bring, a new quality of spiritual life into humanity, or not. This *is* an issue which can only be tried, so far as it can be tried at all, at the bar of history. But the historian who is to sit as judge must, of course, himself have the gift of genuine spiritual vision, if he is to discern the fact, just as he must have the dower of imaginative vision before he can pronounce on the question whether a given poet has or has not enriched our reading of nature with a new quality. (No one who understands the issues would, for example, accept the superficialities of Macaulay as the verdict of history on Loyola, or Bunyan, or George Fox; of St. Teresa, Macaulay fortunately had no occasion to say much.)

No doubt, this means that there must always be an element of the "subjective" and personal about such verdicts. Erudition, critical acumen, and honesty will not of themselves ensure the justice of any man's answer to the question whether Christ has brought us a new and true revelation of God, any more than the same gifts, by themselves, will ensure the justice of his answer to the question whether Wordsworth has brought us a new and authentic revelation of nature, or Beethoven dowered us with new thoughts and a new language. Yet true as this is, it does not leave us at the mercy of merely "subjective" impressions dictated by the prepossessions of the individual historian. The same problem arises, in a less accentuated form, whenever history is conceived as more than the construction of a register of births, accessions, and deaths, battles, treaties, and Acts of Parliament. Erudition and acumen alone will not suffice to answer the modest questions whether a statesman has, or has not, breathed the breath of life into the programme of his party, or a statute or tariff moulded the destiny of a society. Yet these questions are precisely those we ask our historians to answer for us, and the study of history would not long retain its high place as a chief instrument in liberal education if we seriously thought the historian could present us with nothing more satisfactory as an answer than a series of brilliant but wilful and contradictory "personal impressions". This may be magnificent journalism, but it is not history, and I think it would not be hard to name more than one eminent *littérateur* among us whose reputation has been already shattered by the discovery that the work by which he dazzled our fathers was, in spirit, brilliant journalism and nothing more.

For a time, no doubt, it may seem as though the historian of the religious life and thought of mankind had nothing more than his "personal impressions" to offer us. The strictly "orthodox" historian of a religion will tend always to assume as beyond question that the faith he professes does for its followers something wholly different in kind from that which any other faith can do for its own adherents; the historian of a religion in which he does not himself personally believe will equally tend to assume, again as known and certain, that it does nothing of the sort. Among ourselves, even at the present day, we have still the type of "historian" who can see nothing in the still living non-Christian faiths which even prepares the way for the light of the Gospel, and the other type who obstinately persists in seeing nothing in the provision made by Christianity for man's spiritual needs but what was equally provided by the host of more or less obscure "mystery cults" of late antiquity. It should be possible for the opposing subjectivities of the two types to cancel out against one another. The questions whether there is something unique and imperishable in the spiritual life which has its historical origin in Christ and his little band of followers, and what that something is, however complex, ought not to be in principle insoluble.

Indeed, I think it may fairly be said that so far as the presence of something entirely unique in the spiritual life historically traceable to that actual historical personality is concerned the verdict of sober history is

already clear. The attempt to retain the secret of the
specifically Christian life, when the figure of Christ and
the events of the Gospel narrative have been resolved
into symbolism, is not, after all, an experiment of recent
years. We call this tendency to dispense with the historical element in religion "Modernism", but there is
really nothing peculiarly modern about it, or, as we
might prefer to put it, our own age is not the first
which has felt itself "modern" by contrast with those
which have gone before it. George Tyrrell and his
friends called themselves modern, mainly with the great
scholastics of the thirteenth century in their minds
as the "ancients" from whose domination they were
determined to free themselves. But these very ancients,
who fashioned the Christianised Aristotelianism which
Tyrrell and the rest wished to replace by a philosophy
of the "pragmatist" or "activist" type, spoke of themselves, as St. Thomas does, as *moderni*, by way of opposition to *their* antiquity, the Platonic-Augustinian
tradition. Nor is the particular kind of modernism
which resolves historical *credenda* into symbol a new
thing in the history of the Christian Church. It is as
old as the beginnings of speculative theology itself. The
very first "heresy" with which the Church was confronted, even before the later of the New Testament
writings, such as the *First Epistle of John*, had been
composed, was Docetism,[1] the doctrine which resolved
the human personality and recorded life of Christ on
earth into a long-continued symbolic illusion. It is to

---

[1] See the useful article "DOCETISM", by Adrian Fortescue, in *E.R.E.* iv. 532 ff.
And with what follows in the next paragraph cf. E. Bevan, *Hellenism and Christianity*, p. 100 ff. "What strikes one in this Gnostic account of the descent and re-
ascension of the Redeemer is that it is just a *reduplication of the Hellenistic story
of the soul*. But in these fragments which we have of Hellenistic theology, un-
modified by the influence of Christian faith in a human Person, there is no
Redeemer. . . . Salvation by such *gnosis* and salvation by Christ present the
appearance of two alternative schemes which have been imperfectly joined together."

combat this doctrine, as we know, that the Johannine epistle insists on the denial that "Jesus Christ has come in the flesh" as the distinguishing mark of an "anti-christ", and it is apparently for the same reason that the Johannine Gospel gives a curious prominence to points of detail which illustrate the reality of the Lord's physical life, his weariness as he sat by the well in Samaria, his tears at the grave of Lazarus, his suffer-ings from thirst on the Cross, the water and blood which flowed from his side. Docetism, in that early age of the Church, seems to have spread like wild-fire among the educated, and to have been as hard to extinguish. It was the common basis of the whole be-wildering growth of half-Christian speculations known as Gnosticism, in which a symbolic theosophic figure is substituted for the historical human "Son of the Carpenter". In the end the Church succeeded in cast-ing out Gnosticism, but the success was only won by a hard struggle, to which the presence of statements of historical fact, or what was meant to be taken as such, in the traditional baptismal Confession of Faith still bears witness.

In some respects, we are sometimes inclined to think, the Church suffered in the conflict, as a man commonly suffers from wounds or maiming in a life-and-death struggle with a formidable opponent. But the known facts of the development of Gnosticism seem to have convinced serious historians that the Church did well in setting its face stubbornly against it, even at the cost of arresting philosophical speculation and losing for long enough a firm grip on the distinction between what is and what is not sufficiently attested fact. For the alternative was that Gnosticism, with its substitution of a symbolic figure for a real historical person, would kill the spiritual life of the community, and the essential thing was to preserve that life, even if it could only be preserved as a wounded life. The choice was between religion and faith, things tremendously alive, and theosophy, a lifeless thing which stands to living faith as the "bloodless ballet of impalpable categories" of Hegel's *Logic* to the breathing life and the movement of the world of sense. One cannot have a religion without something or someone whom one can trust, and to whom one can pray; but no one can trust in a category, or address heart-prayer to a symbol. Worship of a category (or a law, or a tendency) would be the most tragic of all forms of the "fallacy of misplaced concreteness".

It seems to me, then, that the actual history of Gnosticism is a sufficient warning against repetitions of the attempt to divorce the spiritual life, which we know in fact only as mediated by religions with roots in historical facts and happenings, wholly from its historical attachments. At bottom it is an attempt to manufacture God, the most tremendous of all realities, out of universals, and if there is any result that can be taken as final in philosophy, we may say that it has been finally established, beyond possibility of dispute, that the real, though pervaded everywhere by universals, cannot be constructed out of them. The metaphysician trying to make a fact out of categories is only repeating the task of twisting ropes out of sand imposed by Michael Scot on his fiends. However cunningly you complicate category with category, the process always leaves you with something which *may* be, or *should* be, or *ought* to be, and, as Baron von Hügel was fond of saying, "No amount of Ought-ness can be made to take the place of one Is-ness". As we have been trying to urge all through our argument, the great and unbridgeable gulf between a morality which

remains morality and any religion which is religion is
that morality remains an affair of the *ought*, religion
is concerned with something which overpoweringly *is*.

If we once let the mere *ought* usurp the place of the
is, however unconsciously, we may indeed try to retain,
as some of the Roman Catholic ultra-modernists of
twenty years ago tried to retain, all the wealth of devotional life which has been called into being by the felt
need of feeding the soul's life on contact with a supreme
"Is-ness", but whether we know it or not, we shall
really have reduced religion to the status of a mere
instrumental adjunct to an independent morality, and
history is there to bear witness that this reduction of
religion to a position of mere subservience to morals
regularly has two effects. The religion so treated soon
ceases to be genuine worship, and it is not long before
it also ceases to be an effective stimulus to earnest moral
action. In the hands of the Gnostics, worship became
theosophy, and a morality with no better sanction than
theosophy then ceased to be a vigorous and elevated
morality. We see the same thing illustrated by the subsequent history of some of the "modernists" censured
by the Roman *curia*. One cannot but feel deep sympathy with men who, as I suppose most of us think,
were so largely right in their opposition to traditional
intellectual idleness and stagnation, and were met by
angry and largely stupid official violence on the part
of authorities who should have mingled encouragement with admonition and caution. Probably it is just
those among us who feel most respect for the great
Church of the West who are most vehemently stirred
to indignation when we see her authorities engaged in
"putting back the clock". Yet the fact does remain that
too many of the Continental leaders of the movement,
after their breach with the representatives of official

tradition, rapidly sank into contented secularism.[1] Unintelligent as the authorities at the Vatican showed themselves in their attitude alike to critical scholarship and to genuinely personal philosophical thinking, we must do them the justice to add that they do not seem to have been wrong in their conviction that the detachment of extreme "modernism" from all vestiges of historical tradition is as incompatible with the deepest spiritual inwardness as it is with the practical necessity that a religion which is to be available for all must be one and the same for the subtle and the simple, the critical and the uncritical.

I feel sure, then, that it is not from any defect or temporary accident that there is, in all the great world-religions, more or less of insistence on an element of historical fact which cannot simply be dismissed or denied without striking a formidable blow at the substance of the religion itself. But it does not follow that it is ever possible to say with finality just how much of what has been handed down as historical fact in the tradition of the community really has this character, or that the last word can ever be said for all time by men of one age upon any single historical *credendum*. At most, we can only safely formulate very general principles; the application of them to particular cases is always a matter of infinite difficulty. One can, no doubt, see that in the case of any actual positive religion there are some *credenda* of an historical kind which cannot be denied without challenging the value of that religion as a genuine disclosure of the divine character and purpose, and that there are others which at least have not the same manifest spiritual value. Thus, merely for

---

[1] For evidence on this point I may be content to refer to the volume of *Selected Letters* of von Hügel (1927) and the accompanying *Memoir* by Mr. Bernard Holland.

purposes of ready illustration, we may consider the assertions about the historical facts of our Lord's life which figure in the great Christian confessions of belief. As I have said, Docetism, which cuts away all these assertions by denying the reality of the Lord's actual historical existence *in toto*, would clearly destroy the specific character of Christianity itself. Again, a denial, for example, of the article *tertia die resurrexit a mortuis*, if taken to mean that our Lord's personal existence ceased when he breathed his last on the Cross, and that the band of followers who believed him to be still living and directing and inspiring their activities, and shaping the whole course of history, were simply deluded, would be almost as directly fatal to Christianity as Docetism itself. Whatever religion might survive general acceptance of the thesis that from the first until now Christians have been worshipping a dead man and mistaking their reminiscences of him for experiences of direct contact with God, it would not be a religion with any right to the name of Christianity.

We can only blind ourselves to this manifest truth by committing the common confusion between the theological formulae in which men give an account of what they suppose themselves to believe and the faith by which they, mainly subconsciously or unconsciously, shape their lives. A man, in fact, often really believes so much more than he is himself aware that he believes. He says and thinks, perhaps, that he believes Christ to be no more than a good man who has been wholly non-existent for nineteen centuries. But in his life he acts on a very different assumption. He professes to think that Christ belongs to the dead past; he acts as though Christ belonged to and dominated the living present. But to be convinced that Christ is an abiding living personality, and that our own destinies are in his hands, is not exactly the same thing as to regard the New Testament narratives of his "resurrection appearances" as one and all beyond historical criticism, or to have any particular theory about the nature of those appearances. One may intelligibly hold that the belief in the real continued personal activity and the supremacy of Christ, and in the reality of the contacts between the still living Christ and his disciples, out of which Christianity arose is what is essential in the historical *credendum*, and everything else matter for criticism and speculation, not affecting the true substance of the Christian faith.

For, we may say, that Christian conception of the relation of Christ to God and to man which would be ruined by the view that Christ has been non-existent for nineteen hundred years is no more affected by an uncertainty whether he did or did not eat honey-comb or fish with his friends after his Passion than by a difference of opinion on the point whether St. Paul, on his day of Damascus, actually *saw* a vision of the features of Christ, or only *heard* the memorable words which St. Luke records in the *Acts*; or again by the possibly unmeaning question whether this hearing itself should be called an "external" or an "interior" audition. From the most completely traditionalist point of view possible to a rational man it has to be admitted that the events in question are, *ex hypothesi*, so remote from the familiar order that they can hardly be described in language devised to serve familiar daily purposes without obscurity; and again, that the descriptions we possess, like all *bona fide* independent narratives of real and striking events, are not completely consistent: and even these elementary admissions have far-reaching implications. Consensus as to the historical character of the central incidents in such narratives should be recog-

nised to be compatible with wide divergences in estimation of details.

So much seems to be conceded, even by the con-
servatives of Christian theology, at least so far as concerns some of the *credenda* of an historical kind specified in the classical Christian confessions. Dr. Gore,[1]
for example, with all his anxiety to fence round some of
these *credenda*, frankly puts a symbolic sense on the
phrase *ascendit ad coelos*, with the qualification that
the symbol must be understood as representing a real
transaction of an order indescribable in ordinary
language, and he is here, no doubt, speaking the sense
of the majority of strictly "orthodox" educated
Christians of the present day. None of them, if confronted with the question, would be likely to assert
that by "ascension into heaven" they mean physical
displacement in a direction perpendicular to the horizon
of Jerusalem. (And in respect of this particular article
it is, of course, easy to claim, as Dr. Gore does, the
authority of learned Fathers such as Gregory Nyssen
and Jerome for the "symbolical" interpretation.)
What I myself find it a little difficult to understand in a
position like Dr. Gore's—which I desire to treat with
all the respect rightly due to its author—is the hard and
fast line which is drawn between *credenda* thus admitted to contain symbolic elements and others which
are taken to be bare records of happenings with no such
intermixture.

It is not that I deny all validity to this distinction, so
long as it is regarded as one of degree; of course, I am
aware that, when we use words in a popular fashion,
we can say that the statement that Christ "ascended"
or that he "sits on the right hand of the Father" is

---

[1] *Can We Then Believe?* p. 206 ff. Cf. J. H. Bernard, art. "Assumption and
Ascension", in *E.R.E.* ii.

symbolic in a way in which the statements that he was crucified and buried are not. What I dispute is the right of any man, or body of men, to claim once and for all to limit the right to recognise the presence of the symbolic element to the case of certain specified articles and to exclude irrevocably from participation in the ministry of the Christian community those who do not make the same precise restriction. I do not understand on what *principle* the line of delimitation between the two classes of historical *credenda* is to be drawn, and—a still more fundamental difficulty—I think it actually impossible to describe *any* real event in language wholly non-symbolic.[1] No language, if I may be pardoned the merely apparent "bull", is even approximately free from the symbolic, except the artificial language of "symbolic" logic,[2] and that idiom is impotent to describe the simplest and most familiar event. I gather that Dr. Gore's own view is that the principle of distinction is itself an historical one—certain *credenda* have long been understood (but by whom?) to be expressed in symbolic language, others not so, and the line must continue to be drawn always just where it was drawn in the past (in the fourth century?). I own that I feel some doubt about the fact. I cannot help thinking that one would only have to go sufficiently far back in the history of the Church to find a time when a Council of Dr. Gore's episcopal

---

[1] Let me illustrate by an example. Dr. Gore notoriously would include the article *natus ex Maria virgine* among those which must be understood "literally". But how much is to be meant by this? We know the interpretation put on this *credendum* by St. Thomas and in the *Catechism* of Trent. Ought we, then, to insist on the whole of it, or only on some part, and if not on the whole, how shall we justify ourselves against the criticism, which might be brought against us from the Tridentine point of view, of not really accepting the article without diminution? (I learn from Dr. Gore that he insists only on the virginity of Our Lady *ante partum*. But to restrict the sense of the article in this way is the "eleventh error" with respect to it condemned by St. Thomas in the *de Articulis Fidei*.)

[2] And even this exception seems apparent rather than real.

predecessors would either have condemned his "symbolic" Ascension, or have left it uncondemned only because a distinction so clear to his mind would have been unintelligible to theirs.

The real difficulty, however, arises chiefly in connection with traditional historical *credenda* which appear to stand in no discoverable connection with the great central *credendum* of any religion, its doctrine of God and of God's ways with men. Such propositions, it is often said, have no "spiritual value"; a man's personal walk with God is in no way affected by his opinion about them: they are mere assertions about incidents of past history irrelevant to the spiritual life, and therefore *religiously* insignificant. These at least, then, should be expunged, should they not, from a confession of faith, before a rational man can be asked to accept it? But here again there are several considerations which ought to be carefully pondered.

In the first place, it is not always apparent on inspection what allegations of historical matter of fact have, and what have not, a spiritual value such that the rejection of them would seriously impair the personal religious life of the rejector. There may be such a connection in cases where it is not so patent as in those which I began by alleging. And it should be remembered that the very presence of a statement in a great communal profession of faith at least affords some presumption that it was originally placed there to rule out some opposing position which had been found practically mischievous to the religious life of the community, and may be mischievous again, if it is suffered to revive. It may, of course, not be so; the *credendum* in question may owe its place to the contentious ingenuity of theologians dogmatising for dogmatism's sake (though this motive does not appear historically to have been very prominent in the great creed-making age of the Christian Church). But the initial presumption, at least, is the other way, and modesty suggests that before we declare an "article" to have "no spiritual value", we should go to history to learn why and how it obtained its place. We may find that there has been an excellent reason for this, as in the case of certain biographical statements about Our Lord in the Christian confessions. At first sight the inclusion in these confessions of the chrono-logical detail that the Crucifixion took place in the procuratorship of Pilate might seem to be pure irrelevance. But the clause acquires a different significance when we learn from history that the purpose of in-sisting on such details was to make it clear, once and for all, that the Saviour confessed by Christians is a real man of flesh and blood, not a phantom or a theo-sophical symbol. Docetism—as we may see from the fantastical revival of it by the faddists who deny the "historicity of Jesus" in our own day—is an ever pos-sible perversion of a religion of incarnational type which is fatal to its spirit, and a philosopher cannot quarrel with Christians for their determination to keep Docetism out of their religion.[1]

Of course, it may be said that, even after the appeal to history has been made, the case is not equally clear with all *credenda* of this kind. Even when we have been at pains to discover why they were originally adopted, we may be left unable to see, in the case of some of them, that they are denials of anything which would injure religion by impairing a soul's intercourse with its God; or such mischief as might have been done in

[1] It seems to me important, in view of current controversies which I need not specify, to remember that the original purpose of all the statements made in the Creeds about the earthly life of Jesus was to insist on the reality of his *humanity*. They are directed against Docetism, not against "humanitarianism", which was not a theory of the creed-making ages.

this way in a past age may be dependent on modes of thought and feeling peculiar to that age, and no longer formidable. Hence it is a real possibility that there may be no close or clear agreement between thoughtful and sincerely religious men about the presence of a real spiritual significance in such *credenda*, and it might plausibly be argued that what cannot be seen to be thus directly connected with a true belief in God, being at best superfluous, must be actually injurious to personal religion; that whatever is more than the *unum necessarium* is, for that very reason, harmful. Here, again, I suppose we may say that private judgement needs to be tempered with humility. Even if I cannot myself see any connection between acceptance of a certain *credendum* and the quality of a man's belief in God, yet, if it also appears to be widely true that persons and societies which cherish that *credendum* enjoy a rich and vigorous spiritual life, while those who reject it do not, it is wise to suspect that there really is a connection between the belief in question and "growth in grace" which a more penetrating scrutiny would make manifest, though possibly it would also reveal hitherto unsuspected points of distinction between the substance of the *credendum* and temporary accidents of the form in which it has traditionally been held. It is not the part of the true wisdom, which is always humble, to pronounce too confidently that there is "nothing in" any conviction which has fed the spirituality of generations.

It may, no doubt, be urged by way of objection to this appeal to the *consensus* of the great multitude of the spiritually minded that, as Dr. Bevan has said,[1] fine spirituality and sound historical insight are not *in pari materia*. It is reasonable to defer to the judgement of the spiritually minded against my own when the

---

[1] *Hellenism and Christianity*, p. 245 ff.

question is one of the tendency of some practice to promote or check spirituality of mind, but what reason is there to suppose that the exceptionally spiritually minded man is an exceptionally trustworthy authority about historical fact? It is, after all, only in his own "art" that the "artist" may fairly claim to be listened to. I own that the argument would be final but for one consideration. When such an appeal is made, the point on which one is appealing to the judgement of the spiritually minded man is *not* a point of naked fact. We do not ask him whether or not there is good documentary evidence to establish the asserted fact; what we are really asking him is whether denial of it would involve deterioration in our conception of God and God's dealings with ourselves. The question itself is, in the end, one of "spiritual value", and therefore the verdict of the "spiritually minded", if it is clear and accordant, as it seems to me, does count, exactly as an accordant verdict of musicians on the question of historical fact, "Did Mozart, or Beethoven, write this piece of music?" or the accordant verdict of great men of letters on the question, "Had Shakespeare a hand in *The Two Noble Kinsmen*?" really counts, even though none of those who accord in giving it should have been specially trained in the critical investigation of documentary evidence. It seems to me, therefore, not unreasonable to allow real weight to the intuition of the spiritually minded, where they are clearly in agreement, even on the question whether acceptance of certain statements as to matters of historical fact is of the substance of religion.

But I would also add that the very ground I have just urged in favour of genuine deference to this kind of intuition is also equally a ground for recognising that the rights of such intuition are rather closely circumscribed. The whole argument rests on two broad general presuppositions: (1) that, as is implied in the assertion of the existence of God, the disjunction between "value" and "fact" is not absolute, the supreme "value", God, being also the ultimate source of the whole course of historical "fact"; (2) that the religion to which it is essential that a certain assertion about historical fact should substantially be true is a religion which conceives God rightly, so that the conviction "here is something which is significant *fact*" is equivalent to the conviction "if this is not fact, then God, the source of all facts, is something less than God". In the application of the principle to a specific case it is also presupposed that what leads the spiritually minded man to insist on the "historicity" of a certain event really is a perception that denial of the fact would involve surrendering a more for a less adequate conception of God.

If the true motive for the insistence is different, if it is no more than intellectual inertia, *a fortiori* if it is only the reluctance of officials with a prestige to maintain to admit their own liability to error—and none of us are so spiritual that these motives can be wholly excluded —the apparent consensus may lose much, or all, of its significance. In fact, I think we may say we know that a good deal of conservative traditionalism in "matters of religion" has often been inspired by little more than the intellectual apathy of good men, or the fear on the part of official men that their prestige is in danger. Even when motives of this order are not dominant, there is always the possibility to be reckoned with that they are present, and that, under their influence, a great deal which has really a very different origin may masquerade as the genuine intuition of spiritual minds. Even when we can be sure that we are dealing with real spiritual intuition, we still have to remember that the affirmations based on such intuition have regularly been elicited by specific denials; their legitimate object has been to safeguard something felt to be vital to the spiritual life which has been challenged by these specific denials, not, in the interests of "pure thought", to settle once for all the question exactly how much in the received assertions of historical fact constitutes the significant "substance". The formulation of a *credendum* cannot reasonably be regarded as intended to solve in advance problems which have never been present to the minds of the promoters. The highest regard for the intuitions of the spiritually minded need not blind us to the patent fact that such intuitions, like the immediate judgements of men of high conscience and moral insight on practical problems of conduct, are regularly evoked by concrete situations and as responses to these situations; intuition does not function *in vacuo*.

If these considerations were only borne in mind as they should be, we might anticipate not only greater humility on the part of the individual "historical critic", when he finds himself confronted by a genuine deliverance of the body of the spiritually minded, but an answering greater humility on the part of those who claim officially to speak in the name of religion. The individual critic of the traditional would have to admit that a living religion, because its God is a God of an historical world, does imply *credenda* of an historical kind among its foundations. He would have to abandon the claim, sometimes advanced by the negative critic of tradition in our own day, to be doing high service to the spirit of a religion by merely destroying its body. I would add that he would be less prone than he sometimes is to confuse the very different assertions, "This cannot be shown to be matter of fact by testimony which will satisfy the religiously indifferent, or the anti-religious", and "There is nothing in this but illusion". But equally the guardians of a religious tradition would have to admit that, in the last resort, their own claim to be "guided by the Spirit" can only be justified in so far as they really embody neither the mental indolence of the unthinking, nor the lust of officialdom for prestige and power, but the genuine insight of "holy and humble men of heart"; and, again, that however decisive the pronouncements of intuition upon the concrete situation which has elicited them, they cannot by anticipation foreclose issues which have never been presented *in concreto*.

If these limitations are remembered, it is not necessary that there should be any irreconcilable conflict between the demand of a living religion for an indispensable basis in genuine historical fact and the right of critical historical investigation to deal with all "evidences" freely and fearlessly, by its own methods and without interference. Most of our acutest trouble in this kind seems to be due to the proneness of theologians and historical critics alike to an unconscious assumption of their own infallibility in metaphysics. The theologian tends to assume too hastily that religion demands not merely that God should have disclosed Himself through the past, but that we should already know in all detail what the pattern of the past through which God has disclosed Himself is. The historical critic too often assumes, with equal rashness, that we know that certain patterns never were, and never will be, exhibited by any fact. Each is trying in his own way, with equal unreason, to canalise the same living current, which the one might call the "march of events", the other the "great river of the grace of God".

IV

THE SUPERNATURAL AND THE MIRACULOUS

τὴν θατέρου φύσιν δύσμεικτον οὖσαν εἰς ταὐτὸν συναρμόττων βίᾳ.—PLATO.

I CAN conceive that it may be felt that the considerations we have so far advanced, even when all possible weight has been allowed to them, do not remove the main difficulty presented to a philosophical mind by the historical religions. It may be conceded that if there is a God who discloses Himself to man, it is only reasonable to expect that the disclosure will have a wealth of character harmonising with, but going far beyond, anything we could discover by mere general analysis of the implications of the bare reality of a natural or a moral order, and that this is enough to justify the great positive religions in attaching importance to some *credenda* of an historical kind. The trouble, it will be said, is that, in point of fact, they are found to insist upon historical *credenda* of a very special and questionable sort. They propound for our belief assertions about alleged facts which are avowedly *miraculous*, events which are surprising, and all the more surprising to us the more fully we become acquainted with the general pattern of experienced fact. A miracle is, *ex vi termini*, a break in the order of "customary experience", even if it is not, as it is sometimes called, a violation of a "uniform law of nature", or an event without a "natural" cause; such an event is perhaps intrinsically

150

impossible, and it is, at any rate, a kind of event which we learn to think steadily more improbable, as we learn more and more from science and history of the actual course of nature and human behaviour, and of the psychological conditions which explain the rise of ungrounded beliefs in such events. But the positive religions are so bound up with this belief in miracles that it cannot be eliminated from them without fundamentally altering their character. A God who does not reveal Himself by miracles is not the God of any of these religions. There is therefore an element of falsehood in them all, against which philosophy is bound in honour to take up an attitude of permanent protest. A religion for the truth-loving man must be a religion without miracles, and it is only by disingenuous sophistry that any of the great historical religions can be identified with non-miraculous religion. The philosopher must, therefore, in loyalty to truth, reject them all on principle.

This familiar objection to what is loosely called the miraculous element in the positive religions may take any one of three distinct forms. (1) There is the old "high *priori*" contention, now for the most part relegated to the polemics of the uneducated or half-educated, that a miracle is intrinsically impossible because its occurrence would be a violation of the principle on which all distinction between truth and falsehood rests, the principle that the world is intelligible. (2) There is the contention, familiar to the readers of Matthew Arnold and Huxley, that though the question of the *possibility* of miracles is merely idle, increasing acquaintance with the facts of natural science has shown, as Arnold puts it, that miracles *do* not happen, or, as Huxley suggests, that the testimony to any miracle in which the followers of a religion have believed proves, on

examination, to be insufficient as testimony.[1] (3) Finally,
there is what is probably felt by our contemporaries to
be the gravest objection of all, that which Dr. Bevan
has called the *anthropological* objection.[2] This has been
pithily condensed into a single sentence by Sir R.
Burton, who remarks that Hume disbelieved in miracles
because he had never come across one, but if he had
lived in the East, he would have come across so many
that he would have been even more incredulous.[3] Or,
to adopt the less epigrammatic but more careful statement of Dr. Bevan, the anthropologist finds himself
constantly dealing in his work with miraculous stories
which have a marked *prima facie* resemblance to those
found in the traditions of the great positive religions.
He sets them all aside, because his particular studies
have made it so plain to him that they arise from an
ignorance and an illusion characteristic of mankind all
over the globe at a certain level of intellectual development. Why should an exception be made for the particular stories which have been attached to the names
of the great figures of the world-religions? If the Christian dismisses a thousand stories of a virginal birth,
why should he deal differently with the thousand and
first because it is told of Christ, or the Jew discriminate
between two such similar stories as that of the disappearance of Romulus in the thunderstorm and that
of the translation of Elijah in the tempest?

This, as I should agree with Burton and Dr. Bevan,
is the one and the very formidable line of argument
which impresses us all at the present day. Whatever
our agreements or disagreements with Kant, there is
one lesson which we have all learned from the *Critique*

---

[1] *Hume* (E.M.L.), c. 7.   [2] *Hellenism and Christianity*, p. 233 ff.
[3] The remark is taken from Burton's version of the *Thousand and One Nights*
(Night 236).

of Pure Reason, that logic, functioning *in vacuo*, can tell us nothing of the course of events. No assertion about the actual course of events can be shown to be unreasonable, apart from an appeal to specific experiences, unless it is found on analysis to be internally self-contradictory, and then only, if we accept the Law of Contradiction, as a real Irrationalist in metaphysics would not, as an ontological truth. Even the more moderate-sounding assertions of Arnold and Huxley are of a kind which produces no confident conviction. It is not quite clear what Arnold meant by his dictum that miracles "do not happen". If he meant only that they do not commonly happen, the remark is true, indeed truistic, but irrelevant; we should not call an event of a kind we see occurring every day a "miracle". If he meant that they *never happen in our own age*, this is a statement of fact which would be traversed by a greater number of intelligent persons than is often supposed, and ought not to be made without some attempt at justification. If he meant, as he may have done, that our knowledge of physical science, though not our knowledge of metaphysics, enables us to exclude certain types of event confidently and finally from the pattern of the real world, the argument has already lost its force as we have become increasingly alive to the abstractive and artificial character of all physical hypotheses.[1] But if he only meant that European societies in the sixties and seventies of the last century were generally incredulous of the miraculous, he was actually alleging the mere prevalence of a habit of mind as its own justification. Probably the most charit-

---

[1] Cf. E. W. Hobson, *Survey of the Domain of Natural Science*, p. 490, and the whole of the essay by Prof. Eddington in *Science, Religion, and Reality*, pp. 189-218 (references which I owe to Dr. Gore, *Can We Then Believe?* p. 52). See also the singularly able essay by H. D. Roelofs on "The Experimental Method and Religious Beliefs" in MIND, N.S. 150.

able interpretation would be that he really intended to be stating the anthropological objection in untechnical language. Similarly, when Huxley[1] insinuates that though on good and sufficient testimony we ought to be ready to believe the most astounding statements about the course of events, there never has actually been good and sufficient testimony to any of the events which the theologians of the various faiths have claimed as miracles, he seems to fall into a manifest confusion of thought. If credibility is wholly a matter of external testimony, as it should be if the rest of Huxley's theory is sound, there is better testimony for some "miracles" than there is for many non-miraculous events which are commonly accepted as historical. There is, *e.g.*, better testimony for the appearance of Our Lord alive after his crucifixion than there is for the death of St. Paul at Rome, better evidence for the stigmatisation of St. Francis than for the murder of the "princes in the Tower". It should seem that what Huxley intends to suggest is precisely what he professes not to be suggesting, that the testimony which would be sufficient for more customary events is insufficient to establish the particular *sort* of event meant by the word "miracle". Hence I should suppose that he also has the anthropological objection at the back of his mind.

If I had either the right or the desire to make my remarks on this problem into an *apologia* for the miracles of a particular religion—as, speaking in this place, I am not likely to do—I think I could offer some grounds for holding that the analogies alleged by the sceptical anthropologist between the unusual incidents in the stories of the heroes of savage folk-lore and those which figure among the *credenda* of great positive religions professed by communities of civilised men are

[1] *Hume* (E.M.L.), pp. 133-9.

not altogether as impressive as they are sometimes made to appear. There are similarities, it is true, but there are also dissimilarities which are equally significant. (The Nativity narratives in the Gospels, for example, do not strike me as being particularly like any of the folk-lore stories of virginal births I have read in the works of anthropologists, though they do remind me of Old Testament stories of a very different kind, like those of the births of Samson and Samuel, in which a virgin plays no part.) My actual purpose, however, is not, and ought not to be, that which is the legitimate business of the Christian apologist. The issue with which I am concerned is the more general one, what kind of view of the relation of the world to God is implied in the conception of the "miraculous" as a constituent of real becoming, and is there any incompatibility between acceptance of such a conception and loyalty to philosophical principle. I am not asking whether a truly philosophic mind ought to believe in this or that particular miracle, or indeed in any specific miracle in which men have ever been called on to believe, but with what antecedent convictions the problem should be approached. Is it our duty as lovers of truth to come to it with minds made up against the admission of the miraculous, in any intelligible sense of the word, into our scheme of things? Since our choice between participation in the devotional life of the actual religious societies around us and individualistic detachment cannot well fail to be influenced, and may, for some of us, be decided, by our answer to this question, the issue is a live one enough, and one which, if philosophy indeed has any function in the direction of life, the philosopher has no right to evade.

If we are to think with any approach to clarity, we must begin the discussion of the problem by drawing a distinction of the first importance which is too often obscured by loose and careless language—the distinction between the supernatural and the miraculous. Nothing but disaster can come, for our thinking about religion, from the common confusion of the two, illustrated, for example, in the last century by the title of a too-famous anonymous work on *Supernatural Religion* which was nothing more than a polemic against "miracles". We need to understand clearly that the *supernatural* is the generic term, the *miraculous* only a subordinate species of the genus, and even more clearly that the vital and primary interest of religion is in the supernatural; for religion, the miraculous is, at best, secondary and derivative. Religion is only concerned with the miraculous if, and so far as, the miraculous can be taken as an indication of the reality of the supernatural. Religion exists whenever, and only when, there is the conscious domination of life by aspiration towards an absolute and abiding good which is recognised as being also the supreme reality upon which the aspirant is utterly dependent. Where we have as the fundamental motive of life "love towards an infinite and eternal thing", there we have living religion; where we have not this motive, at least implicitly, we have not religion. Religion itself is thus consciousness of the strictly supernatural, the transcendent something which is above all mutability, passage, and history, or it is nothing. When a man really loses, if anyone ever loses, all belief in the reality of that which is ultra-temporal, and therefore strictly supernatural, at a level *above* that of the "complex event we call nature", he *ipso facto* loses religion; where, if anywhere, men have not yet attained to at least a virtual recognition of the entirely abiding as the supremely real and the true centre of interest in life, there may be cults propitiatory of non-human powers, hostile or friendly, but there is nothing we can class with Christianity or Judaism; if we are to call such cults religious, we can only do so "equivocally".

This seems to me the sure and certain kernel of Otto's now famous conception of the *numinous*, however much there may be to criticise or correct in Otto's own elaboration of his thought. But it should be clear that though religion, in our sense of the word, *is* the active recognition of the supernatural, and nothing else, this recognition of the supernatural *need* not carry with it any recognition of the miraculous, in the sense of abnormalities and singularities in the historic sequence of events, as specially revelatory of the supernatural. There is no more entirely irreligious conception of the world than that of Epicurean philosophy, the ancient theory which, more than any other, by its doctrine of the incalculable *clinamen principiorum*, insisted on the reality of the singular and abnormal. On the other hand, there is no room for the miraculous in a philosophy like that of the Stoics, or their modern counterpart, Spinoza, nor again in that of Plotinus; but a man would have to be very blind not to see the genuine spirit of religion in the hymn of Cleanthes, in many a discourse of Epictetus, or "moral epistle" of Seneca, in almost any essay of the *Enneads*, in the "fifth part" of Spinoza's *Ethics*. A Christian may, and will, hold that there are more adequate expressions of spiritual religion than any of these, but he cannot deny that in their measure they do express it, and sometimes with great beauty and nobility. That there is religion genuine and undeniable in the Stoics, in Plotinus, in Spinoza, is of itself complete proof that though there can be no religion without the supernatural, there can be religion, and profound religion, without miracle.

Prima facie, then, it might be suggested that the complication of religion with miracle which meets us in the great positive religions is purely accidental, a mere consequence of the fact that these religions had their beginnings in ages of widespread ignorance of the facts of the natural order, and that by a wholly beneficent process of development they may be expected to get clear of their miraculous accretions, as of so many unhappy encumbrances, though still retaining to the full their assured conviction of the reality of the supernatural. They will end by ceasing to look to any special events as evidence of the supernatural, because they have learned to see its presence everywhere.

> God is law, say the wise: O soul, and let us rejoice,
> For if He thunder by law, the thunder is yet His voice.

This is, as we cannot deny, an attractive and plausible, as well as a very widely held position; to many of you I may seem to be wilfully surrendering to unreason in suggesting that it is possibly not the last word on the matter, as it appeared to be to the generation for whom Tennyson wrote the verses I have quoted, and that "natural law in the spiritual world" may not prove to be the great secret of God's way with mankind. The question, to my mind, is whether the position is not *too* plausible on the surface to be quite above suspicion.

With theories, as with men, one does well not to trust the exceedingly plausible without very careful consideration. And there is at least one reflection which seems to have some pertinency at this point. The savage and the primitive man are often said by the more popular of our anthropologists to be simple-minded creatures who have not yet learned to distinguish between fancy and fact; they are held to be in the habit of treating the visions of dreams, delirium, and artificially induced hallucination as all on the same level with the perceptions of waking life, to have no conception of causality, or of the existence of a regular routine in the sequences of nature. With them, we are told, casual association is the one sufficient ground of belief, "primitive credulity" is unbounded, and here we have the simple and sufficient explanation of the origin of belief in the "miraculous". Now even if this is an accurate account of the workings of the savage mind—and I have a suspicion, encouraged by much that I have read of the work of recent and careful anthropological students such as Malinowski, that it errs seriously by over-simplification[1]—it is at least pertinent to remember that the great positive religions have all had their beginnings in historical times and among "civilised peoples" : none of them is really a simple unbroken development from the days in which the ancestors of Jews, Christians, Moslems may have been "savages" with the habits of life and thought of Australian aboriginals.[2]

As it happens, the only cases in which we have contemporary evidence about the mental life of the persons with whom a great positive religion originated are those of Christianity and, perhaps we should add, Islam,[3] the two youngest members of the group. And however different the mental habits of the first Christian disciples may have been from those of a modern European Bachelor of Science, it is at least certain that the apostles and their converts were not "primitive savages" who could not distinguish between waking

---

[1] *E.g.* "savages" appear from the evidence, in many cases, to see no causal connection between the commerce of the sexes and the birth of children. But this does not mean that they do not assign a cause of some kind for conception. They have their own rival theory of the cause, which they can defend with some ingenuity, as readers of Malinowski, or Spencer and Gillen, are aware.

[2] This becomes all the more evident if those critics are right who regard Judaism as originating in "post-exilic" times.

[3] See for a strong statement of the paucity of the evidence in this case Professor Margoliouth's article "MUHAMMAD", in *E.R.E.* viii.

life and dreams, or had never bethought themselves that a resurrection from the dead is a startling departure from the "familiar routine". It was precisely because men like St. Peter and St. Paul were as familiar as we are with the distinction between "customary experience" and "miracle" that they saw the hand of God so conspicuous in the miracle which they put in the forefront of their message to the world. If St. Paul, under bondage to "primitive credulity", had thought it just as likely that the "next best" man would rise from his tomb on the third day as that he would not, plainly he could not have found in the resurrection of Christ any proof that Christ had been declared to be the Son of God "with power". No doubt, the routine of "customary experience" as conceived by St. Paul and his contemporaries included sequences which it does not embrace for us, but this should not blind us to the more important fact that they were as much alive as ourselves to the existence of such a routine. If they appealed to a miracle as evidence of the presence of God behind the routine, this was not because they had never learned to discriminate between the familiar and the marvellous, or miraculous, but precisely because they did habitually make the discrimination.

It is a true remark of some nineteenth-century writer—I believe of F. W. H. Myers [1]—that though we should be led into misconceptions if we thought of the apostles, as eighteenth-century apologists sometimes seem to do, as men with the minds of average British jurymen, we should be led much more seriously astray if we thought of them as men with the minds of hypo-

---

[1] I have now found the precise reference: "The apostles were not so much like a British jury as Paley imagined them. But they were more like a British jury than like a parcel of hysterical monomaniacs". (*Essays Classical and Modern*, p. 448.)

thetical "primitive savages", or even of actual Hotten-
tots or Central Australians. After all, they were members, though most of them humble members, of a
society which had possessed a high civilisation for centuries, and the mental traditions shaped by the superior
intellects of a high civilisation work down to and stamp
themselves on every section of the community, and
must do so in virtue of their incorporation in its very
vocabulary. It is nonsense to assert that the society
which saw the rise of Christianity acquiesced in the
marvellous elements of the Christian story simply because it was its habit to believe any marvel related of
any one and by any one without discrimination. What
is really illustrated by the comparative ease with which
the miracles of the New Testament won credence and
have retained it to this day, except in the relatively
small circle of scientific and historical critics and those
who have come under their influence, is not inability to
distinguish between what is customary in experience
and what is not, but the persistent tendency of the
human mind, *after* it has learned to draw this distinction, to expect that the abnormal and exceptional
will attend the doings of the men through whom
God makes a special disclosure of Himself, that the
"prophet" will be accredited by a "sign".

The same tendency is interestingly illustrated by the
rise of Islam. Mohammed, as is well known, expressly,
and prudently, disclaimed all appeal to miracle in support of his own revelation. His "sign" was to be, apparently, the inimitable intrinsic divinity of the verses,
or sentences, of his Koran, and inquirers were to expect
no other. This did not prevent his followers from developing a tradition of evidential "miracles", some of
them on a cosmic scale. Now, of course, all that is
proved by the history of these two faiths is the vitality

of the tendency of the human mind to connect the performance of wonderful works with the possession of a special message from God and about God; the mere existence of the tendency is not its own sufficient justification. As Arnold said too flippantly, it would be no proof that my statements in my writings are true that I could turn my pen into a pen-wiper, though, if I could do so, men in general would be ready to believe anything I might assert. Still the very persistency of the tendency here acknowledged might tempt a cautious thinker who shares Aristotle's conviction that a view held strongly and quasi-instinctively by the "many" is not usually a pure delusion to wonder whether the popular association of the true prophet with "signs and portents" is quite so irrational a prejudice as it is made to appear by Arnold's caricature. Possibly even in the Jew's "seeking after a sign", as well as in the Greek's demand for metaphysical "wisdom", there may be exaggeration of a thought which is not in itself unreasonable.

To myself it seems that this really is so. If we grant the reality of the distinction, necessary to any religious view of life, between the temporal order of natural succession and a transcendent unseen order which pervades and dominates the sensible and natural, we still have, as it seems to me, a choice between two ways of conceiving this pervasion of the sensible by the supra-sensible, neither, on the face of it, irrational. We might think of the dominance of the supra-sensible as always strictly pervasive, but never obtrusive. The divine purpose might underlie and control the course of the familiar sensible order without anywhere disturbing it, as the conscious intelligent purpose of an artisan who is a master of his craft controls the running of adequate machinery employed on a material thoroughly pliable to the ends of the craftsman, with a mastery which is all-present, but presents no shocks or surprises.[1]

This is the way of thinking most congenial to the temper of my own generation, with its historically explicable prejudice in favour of finding gradual growth and slow and continuous "evolution" everywhere. Even the most strictly orthodox divines of that generation habitually think of the establishment of the kingdom of God itself by preference in terms of the parables of the unseen growth of the grain of mustard-seed and the slow working of the leaven hidden in the mass of dough; they allow the comparison of the revelation of the Son of Man with the sudden flash of lightning which lays the heavens bare[2] to fall into the background.

But if we believe in the reality of the transcendent, it is equally possible to think of the sensible order, with its system of "customary experiences" articulated in the process of adapting ourselves to our immediate bodily environment, as being always something of a "misfit" for a reality so much richer than this extract which has been shaped from it under the pressure of urgent physical need. If we think along these lines, we may be led to expect that there will be occasions when the "misfit" will make itself specially manifest. There will be something catastrophic, violently irruptive, at moments of critical importance in the relation between the transcendent reality and its sensible temporal disguise, and at such times anticipations based on "customary experiences" will be liable to be suddenly

---

[1] This is, in fact, the way of conceiving the divine control of the course of nature which is adopted in Plato's reply to the deniers of providence and the moral government of the world in *Laws* x., and explains why the Platonist makes the recognisable order and "uniformity" of the celestial revolutions a principal argument for Theism.

[2] *Luke* xvii. 24.

and startlingly shattered. I cannot myself see that ante-cedently either of these ways of conceiving the relation of the two orders is more rational than the other. Such analogies as we can employ, and they are necessarily very imperfect analogies, are not wholly on either side. The nearest of such analogies, that based on the rela-tions between purpose and routine in the life of an eminently wise and good man, for example, cuts both ways. Intellectual and moral dominance of one's envi-ronment and the material from which one has to fashion one's life is not the same thing as wild and unaccount-able eccentricity. Neither the saint nor the genius is an "eccentric", and the man whose behaviour is one suc-cession of astounding "adventures" does not rank high ın the scale of either greatness or goodness. Most of the good man's life exhibits a routine of its own; he is, as we say, a man of "regular" habits, one on whom we can "count". And so also with the great man; in the main, his greatness is not shown by attempting things it would never have come into the head of another to imagine, but by doing the obvious things, the things another could not well avoid attempting in his place, but doing them in a perfect way. He does what a score of his inferiors may be trying to do; the difference between him and them is that they, not being masters of their opportunities, try and fail; he, being the master of his situation, does the thing he attempts, and does it last-ingly. It is this, so largely sound, thought that is exaggerated into falsehood when genius is said to be "capacity for taking pains".

And yet the thought is not wholly sound. In a sense, indeed, the eminently good man does not "surprise" us; in a sense, we always can "count" on him. But this is only true in the sense that we can always count on him to act like a good man. It is not true that there is never anything surprising to us in his behaviour when he has to make a critical choice, or that we can always tell beforehand what he would do in a given emergency. We may be startled by the act, when it comes; it may be a reversal of all the expectations we had based on knowledge of the agent's "habits". It is *après coup*, when the choice has been made, that we discover its rightness and reasonableness. And, as I have long ago urged in another connection, the same is true of the man of genius. If, after study of some of Beethoven's symphonies or Napoleon's battles, we went on to make a study of a fresh symphony or battle, and found that it presented us with nothing we could not have anticipated on the basis of our previous study, I think this very absence of "surprises" would itself be felt in a rather painful surprise. It would be said that the master was "repeating himself", and there would be conjectures that, for some reason, he was "not quite himself" when he composed the music or fought the engagement. (In fact, Wellington, as quoted by the historians, seems to have been surprised that Napoleon had no surprises to spring at Waterloo. "Napoleon", he wrote, "did not manœuvre at all: He just moved forward in the old style, in columns, and was driven off in the old style." [1]) It is neither the absence of surprises, nor the perpetual recurrence of surprises of every conceivable sort, that reveals intelligence behind a career or a work of art; it is the presence of the right kind of surprise at the right place. There is a real element of the "irruptive" and incalculable about the relation of human purpose and intelligence to the "routine" of events, and by analogy, we might expect the divine purpose behind history, if it really exists, to display the same quality. If the course of events is indeed subdued to a supreme

---

[1] Quoted from York Powell and Tout, *History of England* (1900), p. 866.

divine purpose, it should neither be chaotic, nor yet a mere routine; it too, as a whole, should present shocks and surprises of the right kind, and in the right places.

It might further be urged, with some force, in favour of the view which is prepared to meet with the abrupt and irruptive invasion of the familiar order by the transcendent, that the expulsion of the element of surprise, marvel, and the wholly incalculable from nature and human life cannot be consistently carried out, except at a price which intellectual honesty itself forbids us to pay. However we may try to disguise the fact, the presence of something uncomfortably like "miracle" obstinately confronts us whenever we try to look at any section of the concrete becoming of things steadily, and this is no more than we may expect if we are careful to remember how much richer is the concrete reality than any of the systems of categories by which we try to stabilise it. This is the plain lesson of the now patent failure of the many and patient attempts to reduce physics to mere kinematics, biology to mere physics, psychology to mere biology, history to psychology. "Rationalisation" of this Cartesian kind is a stubborn attempt to get rid of the abrupt, startling, discontinuous, and an attempt which is being perpetually renewed, and always fails. To an intellect determined to work with the apparently transparent and self-justificatory concepts of pure kinematics, physical and chemical quality presents an intractable mystery: to one which confines itself to the concepts of physics and chemistry there is the same appearance of abruptness and sheer miracle about the entrance of organic life on the scene of becoming: the reality of consciousness is equally a pure "irrationality" to the mind resolved on explaining everything in terms of biological processes, and the reality of intelligent plan and purpose to one which will see in conduct nothing but the elaboration of highly complex patterns of sense-reflexes. The mind may, for a time, disguise the difficulty, after the fashion of the fabled ostrich, by simply pretending that what will not fit into its own picture of the world is not really there. Then one gets such doctrines as those of the "subjectivity" of sensible qualities, the purely "mechanical" character of vital processes, the epiphenomenalist version of the relation between body and mind. All these theories may now be said to have been fairly "tried out" over their respective fields and found incoherent, as, in fact, all are condemned in principle by the consideration that no feature of the historical world is really got rid of by the verbal trick of calling it an "illusion". When you have made all possible play with that disparaging "name", it still remains that what is there *is* there.

The recently prevalent fashion of talking freely about "emergent" evolution, as though the adjective could take the place of an explanatory theory, is a glaring illustration in point. The epithet is tantamount to an open confession that there is something really present in historical processes which ought not to be there if the substantive really means what it says. Something has "come out of" an alleged set of antecedent conditions which was never in the conditions, and therefore is not rationally accounted for by specifying them, though we are still to pretend, by the use of an adjective, that it has been accounted for.[1] In all such cases we have, in fact, been trying to exhaust the whole content of the individual and historical by analysing

---

[1] I need hardly say that I am not attacking the phrase "emergent evolution" as a useful *description* of certain historical processes; my comments only apply when the words are treated as conveying an *explanation*.

it without remainder into a combination of a few "universals", and so to reduce the unique and surprising to routine, and in all we have failed for the simple reason that the individual is not to be built up out of universals; being individual, it always contains the possibility of surprise for the abstractive understanding.

One might add that there appears to be a point at which the most resolute enemies of the "miraculous" are ready to abandon the undertaking of eliminating it. Even those who scruple most at admitting the occurrence of a physical "nature-miracle", an appearance of the wholly unforseeable and genuinely individual, in the course of strictly physical process, usually make no difficulty of the same kind about what we may call the human "nature-miracle" of genius, or the "miracle of grace". Yet when all is said, familiar routine is not more intrusively broken by the surprising events recorded, for example, in the Gospels than by the abrupt appearance of high poetical genius in the youthful Shelley with his antecedent record of commonplace ancestry and particularly worthless adolescent verses, or the youthful Keats, or, again, by the extraordinary reversals of character and habit, often instantaneous and singularly complete, illustrated by some of the "conversions" known to history. These are facts which the serious student of human life cannot deny or deprive of their individual and incalculable strangeness. And I would ask you to note that we cannot, without doing violence to historical testimony, confine these abrupt manifestations of an individuality not to be reduced to formula within a closed system of the psychical. For example, if there is any fact about the historical career of Christ which may be said to be thoroughly guaranteed by testimony beyond possibility of suspicion, it is the fact that he attracted attention on a large scale primarily as a worker of extraordinary acts of healing, and that his teaching was listened to on this ground. This is so manifest that hardly anyone who has seriously occupied himself with the records thinks of a simple denial of the fact, though there are numerous students who are willing to accept the record in so far as it concerns only such acts of healing as they personally think not *too* startling, and no further. We then disguise our real breach with the principle that the abrupt and intrusive is not to be reckoned with as fact by loose talk about the influence of the mind on bodily condition, conveniently forgetting that this very influence itself, as the history of psycho-physical hypotheses sufficiently shows, is just one of the outstanding "mysteries" which defy reduction to routine.

Partly, I suppose, this tendency to restrict the abrupt and really novel to the domain of mind is a mere survival of the obsolete prejudice that only the bodily is strictly real and historical, the mental being a superimposed "illusion"; partly, perhaps, it springs from the opposite equally unjustifiable prejudice that only the mental has any true individuality, whereas the physical may be treated as a mere complex of universals. But it should surely be plain that both prejudices are alike unreasonable. It is strictly absurd to treat the mental as "illusion", for the obvious Cartesian reason that illusion is only possible on the condition that there really are minds to be imposed upon; it is equally absurd to deny the individuality of non-mental things such as the Koh-i-nūr, or the planet Mercury. There are not really two water-tight compartments of the historical process, a "physical" sphere and a "mental" sphere; there is the one concrete given process with its mental and physical elements interrelated and interacting. Thus the attempt to make a clean cut between one sphere of the historical, in which room may be found for the abruptness and surprises of individuality, and a second sphere, where there is to be nothing but routine, capable in principle of complete reduction to general formula, is thoroughly arbitrary and indefensible. This means, I take it, that it is quite unjustifiable to approach the study of the actual historical process with the antecedent assumption that, however the supernatural may make its presence recognisable, it *cannot* take the form of sudden and startling intrusiveness into the course of physical happening, reversal of the routine of "customary experience"; whether it does, in fact, take this form can only be known from acquaintance with the course of the historical in its historical concreteness. It is wrong in principle to assert that testimony to the occurrence of alleged fact may ever be dismissed on the plea that the facts alleged are miraculous, after the fashion suggested by Hume in his curiously incoherent onslaught.[1] The mere consideration that a proposed interpretation of God's dealings with the world involves the recognition of the surprises we call miracles does not stamp that interpretation as unphilosophical.

To admit this is not to say that reality is ultimately irrational, nor to blink the fact that, on any theory, the great majority of narratives of alleged miracles are thoroughly untrustworthy. When we say that the world of the historical is rational and that its rationality is a postulate of sane philosophy, all that we have a right to mean is that this world has a definite pattern which connects its parts in a thoroughgoing unity. We have no right to say, in advance of historically-minded examination of detail, what that pattern is, nor pre-

---

[1] *Enquiry Concerning Human Understanding*, section x. For an examination of Hume's reasoning I may perhaps refer to my own brochure, *David Hume and the Miraculous* (Cambridge, 1927).

cisely how it dominates its constituent sub-patterns, nor to assume that our understanding of any of these sub-patterns and the mode of "ingression" of the dominant pattern into them is, or ever will be, complete and final. The proposition that the historical, that is, the actual, is rational, or intelligible, is, rightly conceived, an *imperative* of the *practical* reason. It is a command to ourselves never to stop short in the business of looking for a higher and more dominant pattern in the course of the historical than any we have yet found, not an assertion that the task has been achieved.[1] The world

[1] The perfect typical example of the process is the evaluation of a "surd" numerical value defined by a series. However far we go in the evaluation, we have never expressed the *exact* value of our "surd" (π or e or what not). But we can, in this ideal case, assign limits within which the error of our estimate falls, and by carrying the evaluation far enough we can make the interval between these limits as small as we please. In this case, of course, we do, in a way, know precisely what the "dominant pattern of the whole" is. Our "sub-patterns" are the successive approximations to the "value" of our "surd"; the dominant pattern is the, precisely-known, form of the series by which the "surd" which is its "limit" is defined; this is "ingredient in" the sub-patterns, because each departs from it by an excess or defect which the known form of the series enables us to restrict within a determined "standard". The formulae which we employ as our "laws" of physical process do not, of course, represent anything like so complete a "rationalisation" of the concrete observed facts.

For suppose, to take a very simple example, we wish to determine the fraction of its own length by which an iron rod expands when heated as a function of the increase of temperature. Our formula has, in the first instance, to be determined by measurements made when the rod has been heated to certain definitely known points, but it must also hold good when the increase of temperature is intermediate between two of those from which we start, or is less than the least or more than the greatest of them. Hence a formula which fits any series of observed results may be shown by further experimentation to demand modification if it is to fit "intermediate values" of our "independent variable", or values lying beyond either of the originally examined extremes. This is the problem of "interpolation" and "extrapolation". And, again, the general character of the formula itself is conditioned from the first by the consideration that the "law" to be discovered must be a series of a type which we can readily submit to mathematical operations (must be readily integrable); and, again, for practical reasons, must be such that a consideration of two or three initial terms of the infinite series will give a sufficiently close approximation to the "limit" of its sum. Thus, in the case just supposed, practical considerations lead us to *assume* that if x represent the fraction of its own length through which the rod expands when it receives the increment of temperature θ, the law connecting the two will be of the form $x = a\theta + b\theta^2 + c\theta^3 + \ldots$ where $a, b, c \ldots$ are arbitrary coefficients, which must now be chosen in such a way that, for all practical purposes, $a\theta + b\theta^2 + c\theta^3$ may be taken as a sufficiently exact equivalent for the value of the "sum to infinity" of the whole series. This explains why such laws are always open to revision as our knowledge of facts grows in a

is there as a problem; we have to "rationalise" it, but, in fact, we never succeed fully in carrying out the work, and, for that reason, no science which is not avowedly one of pure abstractions can dispense with a sane empiricism in its methods.

To put the point in a terminology made familiar to us by Hume, our duty as thinkers is never to be satisfied with bare "conjunctions" between events, to insist on looking behind the conjunctions for necessary *connections*. When Hume declared that the *connections* are simply "feigned", that is to say invented, by the scientific man who is looking for them, and unconsciously imported into the objective world without any real warrant, he was—as he himself very well knew—denying the very possibility of science. If that is what is meant by one who says that "the understanding makes nature", that statement is simply false. But Hume would have been absolutely right if he had been content to say that, however far we carry our process of search, we never actually reach a stage at which we have converted conjunction into connection without remainder. There always are, and always will be, loose ends, "bare" conjunctions not understood, in all our actual natural knowledge, just because it all starts from and refers to the historical and individual, which analysis cannot exhaust. To say the same thing again in different language, it is never a *conclusive* argument against the reality of a *fact* to say that it cannot be harmonised with a known "law of nature", since the law, if asserted as having objective reference, only embodies our partial divination of a pattern which we never grasp in its concrete entirety. Though our formu-

---

way in which purely mathematical "approximations" to limiting values are not. (Throughout the whole of the present paragraph my indebtedness to the brilliant work of É. Meyerson, *L'Explication dans les sciences*, will be obvious.)

lated "laws" are never merely "subjective", yet, as the history of natural science proves only too abundantly, they always contain a subjective constituent which affects them to a not precisely definable extent. Hence the fact we find so stubbornly recalcitrant *may* provide the very suggestion we need for introducing an illuminating correction into our "law".

Again, and this has a special bearing on the anthropological argument of which we have been speaking, the reality of "miracles" as a feature of the historical process is not in any way disproved by the true contention that the vast majority of narratives of alleged miraculous events are untrustworthy. The same thing is equally true of the so-called "miracles of genius". The reality of genius is not disproved by the true observation that most of what, in any age, is acclaimed as the expression of genius is a very sorry imitation. To recur to our old illustration of the "surprises" of Shakespeare, it is no disparagement of their inevitableness and truth to life to say that what are intended by the inferior dramatist to be "strong" situations, or subtly divined characterisations, are mostly hollow, theatrical, and fantastic. The "Machiavellian" villain of the ordinary Elizabethan stage, a Barabas, a Bosola, a De Flores, may be unreal and mechanical enough; it does not follow that Iago is a mere puppet of the theatre. So, I think, we may say it is with the drama of the historical process. The play as we re-shape it in our own imagination may be as unlike the work of the divine artist as *The Spanish Tragedy*, or *The Unnatural Father*, is unlike *Hamlet*; it does not follow that the divine artist's play is without its astonishing incidents, and, if we may reverently call them so, its sensational situations.

It seems to me, then, that there is nothing inherently irrational or unworthy in the conception that the relation between nature and supernature may be compatible with, or even require, that element of special abrupt and intrusive surprise which we mean to indicate when we speak of "miracles". To expect such surprises in the course of events is no proof of inferior, to deny them no proof of superior, intelligence. It is therefore, so far as I can discern, no sufficient philosophic objection to a positive religion that it involves the belief that such surprises have actually occurred, or do still actually occur. The objection would only become valid if the *kind* of surprise asserted to occur were one which, if genuine, would involve a false conception of the divine nature itself. Indeed, for my own part, though I give this, of course, as a purely personal confession, I find a scheme which allows for the occurrence of what is popularly called "miracle" apparently *more* reasonable than one which excludes it altogether. For since we cannot deny the presence in the historical world-process of the intrusive, abrupt, and discontinuous, in the form of what we call a "miracle" of genius, or a "moral" miracle, or a "miracle of grace", to confine it to these spheres seems to me to amount to one of those "bifurcations" which are in principle forbidden by the supreme postulate of a sound philosophy.

I venture, then, to make the following suggestions, in the hope of doing a little to diminish the mass of ambiguities and confusions which seem to beset current thinking on this issue of "miracles". (Beyond this initial work of clarifying the issues, I doubt whether philosophy, as such, can legitimately concern itself with the problem; I am sure it is idle to look to metaphysics either for proof that "miracles" occur, or for proof that they cannot.)

(*a*) In the first place, since the whole issue in dispute

is concerned with "nature-miracles", it is necessary to note that, when a natural event[1] is called a "miracle", two distinct assertions are being made about it. It is part of the understood meaning of the word that the event itself is in a high degree startling and unusual; it is a sequence of a kind not familiar in "customary experience", a breach of the normal routine. The miracle is a τέρας or *prodigium*, a *wonderful* event. If it were an event of a kind which we know to be common and frequent, it might still, like so many everyday events, baffle our powers of explanation, or even seem to be incompatible with recognised physical theories, but we should not on that account call it a miracle; we should only say that it presented a difficulty in the present condition of our scientific knowledge of nature. The most resolute enemy of the miraculous, if he is not a singularly ill-informed man, is aware that in all departments of science there are such stubborn facts, in apparent conflict with duly established "laws", but it never occurs to him to urge that we should extricate ourselves from the difficulties they present by a bold "denial of the fact". But, secondly, a miracle is also something more than a mere astonishing "freak" or "oddity", however extreme, in the course of events. It is also, in New Testament phrase, a σημεῖον or *sign*, an event which, in an exceptional way, reveals something of a transcendent purpose, assumed to underlie the whole course of history, but not usually transparently present.[2]

---

[1] By "natural" event I mean here, of course, simply an event belonging to the sensible order, whether it conforms to, or departs from, "customary routine".

[2] Cf. St. Thomas, *S.T.* ii.ᵃ ii.ᵃᵉ q. 178, art. 1 ad tert. "in miraculis duo possunt attendi: unum quidem est id quod fit, quod quidem est aliquid excedens facultatem naturae, et secundum hoc miracula dicuntur *virtutes*. Aliud est id propter quod miracula fiunt, scilicet ad manifestandum aliquid supernaturale: et secundum hoc communiter dicuntur *signa*." As here given, the definition of *virtus* is obviously open to the criticism that we cannot say in advance of *any* event that it

To put the point in very simple language, a miracle is, in the first place, as I once heard an Anglican divine remark, "something which makes me say *Oh!*" To be sure, when one reflects, no event ever is completely explicable; there is always about every sequence of effect or cause something which we cannot reduce to "connection", but have to accept as bare given "conjunction". At bottom, then, there is something wonderful in all events; *omnia abeunt in mysterium*. But usually we are not alive to this; it is only the unfamiliar and exceptionally surprising which "makes us say *Oh!*" We may add that, in the customary use of the word, it seems further to be implied that a surprise which is called a miracle, except when the name is employed by a conscious *catachresis*, is always an event of the *sensible* order, something which gives a shock to our senses, a reversal of the "customary routine of our *perceptions*". There are many true propositions in the pure mathematics, and, again, in the accounts physicists give us of their imperceptibles, which cause an intellectual surprise when we first make their acquaintance, but we commonly do not speak of "miracle" in connection with them. Thus the Epicurean *clinamen* of the atom, or the sudden jump ascribed in Bohr's recently famous, but as I am given to understand, now antiquated theory, by an electron from one orbit and velocity to another, are as surprising as any ecclesiastical marvel, but they are not called miraculous, because, being imperceptible, they could administer no shock to our senses. Similarly, as I am informed—I can speak only at

excedit facultatem naturae, since we do not know what the *facultates naturae* may prove to be. In this same *quaestio* Thomas says that the frogs and serpents produced by the magicians of Pharaoh (*Exod.* vii. 12, viii. 7) were real frogs and serpents, but their production was not a true miracle, since it was due to "natural causes". One wonders how Pharaoh was expected to know that this was not the case with Aaron's serpent, or Moses' frogs.

second-hand—it has been questioned whether the transubstantiation of the sacramental elements in the Eucharist taught by the Roman Church can properly be called miraculous or not; those who deny that it can basing their denial on the fact that the "sensible accidents", shape, colour, taste, and the rest, undergo no change. And though we speak of miracles of intellect, or moral miracles, we are always conscious that, however permissibly, we are here extending the primary significance of a word, by metaphor, or analogy.

(b) But it is not every startling event of the sensible order that we call miraculous. The sudden occurrence of a gigantic earthquake would probably startle most of us much more than the quiet rising of a palsied man from his couch at the word of an apostle; yet we should certainly be at least disposed to regard the curing of the disease by a word as miraculous, and the earthquake, however startling, as a purely "natural occurrence". The miracle not merely makes us "say *Oh!*" it makes us aware of the immediate presence and operation of God. Hence the frequent appearance in theological definitions of the *differentia* that a miracle is an event in which the supreme cause acts directly, and not, as commonly, through second, or intermediate causes.[1]

(c) The two characteristics may consequently be disjoined. There are startling events which are not "signs", and, I take it, there are events which are "signs", but

---

[1] *E.g.* St. Thomas, *S.C.G.* iii. 101 "hoc sonat nomen miraculi, ut scilicet sit de se admiratione plenum, non quoad hunc vel quoad illum tantum. Causa autem simpliciter occulta omni homini est Deus. . . Illa igitur simpliciter miracula dicenda sunt quae divinitus fiunt praeter ordinem communiter servatum in rebus." Cf. *De potentia*, q. 6, art. 2 "illa quae sola virtute divina fiunt in rebus illis in quibus est naturalis ordo ad contrarium effectum, vel ad contrarium modum faciendi, dicuntur proprie miracula." *S.T.* i.ª q. 105, art. 7 resp. "miraculum autem dicitur quasi admiratione plenum, quod scilicet habet causam simplicem et omnibus occultam. Haec autem est Deus. Unde illa quae a Deo fiunt praeter causas nobis notas miracula dicuntur."

are not unique and startling enough to be spoken of as miracles. Thus, to recur to our example, a great earthquake would presumably not be called a miracle by a divine, even though he saw in it a "sign" of the Creator's power. The "proximate causes" of earthquakes are, in part at least, ascertainable, and this would probably be held to remove earthquakes from the class of the miraculous. For the same reason, if our scientific knowledge of nature should ever lead to such practical control of events that we succeeded in our laboratories in converting water into wine, or even in restoring the indubitably dead to life,[1] no one, I conceive, would speak of such achievements, effected by laboratory methods, as miracles. If we could effect them for ourselves, they would, when so brought about, cease to be signs of the immediate special presence of the divine; they would, in the supposed conditions, only be signs of our human mastery over nature. The "miracle" in the strict sense of the word, must combine the two characteristics of being a superhuman "wonder" and being a "sign".

(d) But the special interest of religion in the miraculous event is due wholly to its interpretation as a "sign" of the direct operation of God. If it were not such a sign, however astonishingly wonderful it might appear, the event would not have the special religious significance the theologian attributes to it. Hence, provided that this character is indubitably present, the element of mere surprise and unfamiliarity, though it must not be absent, may be reduced to a minimum. So we find St. Thomas, for example, arranging *miracula* in three classes, one of which includes such cases as

[1] If we should ever discover how to effect such results in the laboratory, we might still continue to regard their analogues in the Gospel narratives as "miraculous", but the "miracle" would then be taken to be constituted by the absence, in these instances, of the "laboratory process".

recovery *virtute divina* from an ordinary malady which might have been successfully treated by a physician,[1] and Dante even giving the name miracle to the legendary opportune cackling of the Capitoline geese when the Gauls were making their nocturnal assault.[2]

(*e*) It follows from the combination of the two characteristics that in dealing with the credibility of narratives of alleged miracles it is always necessary to distinguish between two questions which are too often confounded—the *quaestio facti*, whether the events narrated actually occurred as narrated, and the *quaestio iuris*,[3] as we may call it, whether, if they occurred, they have the religious significance of "miracle", whether they are *signs*. The opponents of the miraculous, I think, are specially prone to forget this distinction. What they really want to discredit is commonly the value of the alleged miracle as "evidence" of the truth of a certain religion. They wish to argue that the event is not to be rightly taken for a sign accrediting a given doctrine as a revelation from God, or a given person as a messenger of God. But they frequently assume that it is further necessary to their case to prove that the alleged event was not even a "portent"; that it either did not happen, or, if it did, was a commonplace event of a familiar kind. Their antagonists, again, are only

---

[1] *S.C.G. loc. cit.* "Summum gradum inter miracula tenent ea in quibus aliquid fit a Deo quod natura nunquam facere potest . . . secundum autem gradum in miraculis tenent illa in quibus Deus aliquid facit quod natura facere potest, sed non per illum ordinem . . . tertius autem gradus miraculorum est cum Deus facit quod consuetum est fieri operatione naturae, tamen absque naturae principiis operantibus." The examples given of (1) are occupation of the same place by two bodies at once, the standing still or going back of the sun, the opening of the sea to provide a passage; of (2) the restoration of the dead to life, of the blind to sight, of the halt to the use of their feet; of (3) the healing of a naturally curable "fever", or the production of rain *virtute divina*. Cf. the shorter statement, *S.T.* i.ª q. 105, art. 8 resp.

[2] *Monarchia*, ii. 4.

[3] More accurately, we might borrow a distinction from the technical language of ancient rhetoric and distinguish between the question of the *quid* and that of the *quale*.

too prone to suppose that they need only establish the
fact that the surprising event occurred to put its
"evidential" character as a sign beyond all question. It
is this standing confusion of two distinct issues which
gives most of the literature of the controversy about
miracles its unsatisfying and unedifying character. To
me it seems clear that the fullest vindication of marvellous narratives as accounts of facts which have
actually happened would leave the question whether
the facts have the quality which makes them of
moment for religion still undecided, in point of rigorous logic.

Thus, to take the most crucial example which presents
itself, I can conceive it possible, though not probable,
that it might be established beyond all reasonable possibility of doubt that Our Lord actually died, was
actually buried, and actually seen alive again "on the
third day". But to establish these facts, I should say,
would not bring one any nearer proving the reality
of what Christians mean by the "miracle" of the Resurrection. It would still be possible for men satisfied of the
facts to dispute their significance. There would be no
formal absurdity in the position—I do not say that it is
one ever likely to be widely adopted—that it has been
proved by a well-certified historical instance that, under
conditions not yet accurately ascertained and perhaps
not accurately ascertainable, the transition of a human
organism from life to death is reversible, and yet to
deny that this is anything more than a curious and
puzzling scientific fact; to deny, that is, that its occurrence is any reason for believing that the person to
whom it happened was one standing in any unique
relation to God, or having any special significance for
the history of humanity. Presumably this was the
actual position of Seeley, who appears to have regarded

the fact as historically certain, and also to have definitely rejected the Christian conception of the relation of man to God.[1]

For my own part, I do not see how anyone who had once taken up such a position could be driven from it by argumentation. You might, I take it, establish the historical character of the most unprecedented events, provided only that the testimony to them were sufficiently good. Hume's attempt[2] to draw a distinction between two different classes of events, both equally at variance with "customary experience", but of which one type may be accepted if there is sufficient testimony, while the other ought to be rejected without so much as a scrutiny of the testimony, appears to me, as I suspect it must have done to Hume himself, arbitrary and logically worthless. But when the fact has been established, when, if ever, for example, the resurrection of Christ has been made "as certain as the assassination of Julius Caesar", the question of our right to interpret the fact as Christianity interprets it still remains an open one, and cannot be closed by any appeal to "testimony". To compare the two questions is like comparing the question of the authorship of a given work with that of its scientific or literary worth. Thus, whenever some startling and arresting event is accepted not merely as a singular event, but as a miracle with a significance for religion, as disclosing the divine character or purpose, one is, I should say, in the presence of an act of "faith". This particular act of faith would cease to be possible if the believer were to be

---

[1] Cf. Bevan, *Hellenism and Christianity*, p. 234 (commenting on Seeley's words in *Ecce Homo*, c. 2, "the evidence by which these facts are supported cannot be tolerably accounted for by any hypothesis except that of their being true").

[2] *Enquiry Concerning Human Understanding*, x. pt. 2, pp. 127-8 (ed. Selby-Bigge).

convinced that the alleged fact had never occurred, but the completest *probatio facti* would not compel the further act of faith in its significance, as demonstration compels assent to its conclusions when you have assented to its premises. The act of "faith" which converts mere belief in a *marvel* into belief in a *miracle* is, in its very nature, one of *free*, not constrained, assent.[1]

Thus belief in a miracle, like belief in God itself where it is genuinely religious belief, always involves free assent to something which cannot be proved; as the scholastic theologians rightly held, it involves a specific attitude of *will*,[2] and is thus a reaction not merely of the "intellect", but of a man's whole personality to influences from without. This is why the scholastics regard it as "meritorious", and why we are bound to recognise that a man's *faith*, what he *believes*, unlike his "opinions", makes a profound difference to his character. From a psychological point of view we may say of any act of assent of this kind that in the recognition of an event as a "sign" we have an immediate divination, comparable not so much with the drawing of an inference from premises in which the conclusion is already fully implicit, as with our direct recognition of beauty, or aesthetic significance, in a product of nature or art, and our direct recognition of rightness, or moral significance, in a human act.

(*f*) These reflections suggest to me a further question which is not, so far as I know, often raised. Is there any meaning in speaking of an alleged event as simply, or

---

[1] Assent to a demonstrated conclusion is certainly a determination of the will, as Descartes, in adherence to the scholastic tradition, maintained in the fourth *Meditation*, but there is no freedom about it. Free assent is always assent to what has not been completely proved.

[2] *E.g.* St. Thomas, *S. T.* ii.ª ii.ae q. 4, art. 1 resp. "actus autem fidei et credere ... qui actus est intellectus determinati ad unum ex imperio voluntatis. Sic ergo actus fidei habet ordinem et ad objectum voluntatis, quod est bonum et finis, et ad objectum intellectus, quod est verum."

absolutely, miraculous?[1] Is not "miraculous" a *relative* term, like "probable"? (It is only by a pardonable inaccuracy that we allow ourselves to talk of estimating *the* probability of a given event, as though the same event could only have one probability.) What we actually estimate is always probability *relative* to some set of data which constitute our assumed frame of reference.[2] ("The probability of *x*", like log *x*, is a many-valued function of *x*, though in both cases, for practical purposes, we may confine our attention to one specially important value; as for these purposes we take no notice of the infinitely numerous "complex values" of log *x*, so in dealing with the "probability of *x*" we take no account of its probability relative to "freak" sets of data.) I mean that if it is part of what we understand by a miraculous event that it is one which astounds and perplexes, it would seem that we cannot properly call any event miraculous without a reference to the mental habits and expectations of an experient of the event, as a frame of reference. Thus it might be quite reasonable to say that events rightly called miracles by one age may be rightly regarded as non-miraculous in another age which has grasped more of the general pattern of natural process, or that to an intelligence with a grasp of that pattern transcending the human, for example to an angel, as conceived in the scholastic philosophies, much that will always astound, and so be rightly called miraculous, *quoad nos homines*, might very possibly appear to be "just what might be expected", and therefore *not* miracu-

---

[1] In the passages already quoted from St. Thomas it will be seen that a genuine miracle is discriminated from events which are only *mira* to some men (*e.g.* to the unlearned, or the rustic); the *miraculum* must be *mirum* OMNI *homini*. But this leaves it still a question whether what is *mirum omni* HOMINI need be *mirum* to a higher "angelic" intelligence or not, as will be remarked below.

[2] Cf. J. M. Keynes, *Treatise on Probability*, pp. 6-7.

lous. In the same way, if we allow the existence of a whole hierarchy of intelligences, what would be miraculous to an angel of lower rank might be non-miraculous to one of higher, though it would still remain the case, seeing that complete knowledge of God *per essentiam suam* can only be possessed by God Himself, that there are works of God which are profoundly astounding, and therefore miraculous, for the highest of created intelligences. If this is so, we might still agree with men of an age and society less familiar than our own with the regular natural order that certain events which they called miraculous really happened, and really were "signs" of the power, the justice, or the mercy of God, as they had rightly discerned; but to us these events have become "natural" signs, part of the *cursus ordinarius.*

It is true that such a view would be inconsistent with the traditional hard-and-fast distinction between events traceable to God as working through the instrumentality of "second causes", and events for which there is no second cause, *res immediate a Deo productae*; but it seems in any case impossible to attach much real value to this traditional distinction. It could never be safely used as a *criterion*, for the simple reason that we could never "constate" the absence of a second cause in a given case.[1] At the most we could only say that the "second" cause, or causes, of the event cannot be discovered in the present state of our general knowledge.

---

[1] Thus on a previous page we have seen St. Thomas pronouncing that the restoration of sight to the blind is entirely beyond the power of the system of "second causes" we call nature. It is most improbable that St. Thomas would be confident on the point if he were living in our own day. According to Leibniz there is a mechanism of "second causes" everywhere; the miracles of the faith have their "second causes" which go back to the creation, when the system of nature was constructed expressly to produce these unique events at just the moments when they were called for by the divine purpose. Whatever we may think of this view, I do not see that it in any way hazards the interests of religious faith. (*Théodicée*, pt. i. § 54).

The thought presumably at the bottom of the distinction seems to me to be obscured by the scholastic expression of it. What is really meant, I suppose, is that the ultimate reason why the event which is said to have God for its immediate cause happens is that just it, and nothing else, is demanded at just this juncture by the purpose of God in His dealings with His creature, man. If anything else happened at this juncture, the "counsel of God" would be brought to nothing. God, so to say, has no alternative course of action open to Him, if His end is not to be frustrated. Consequently, so long as we leave this necessity for the realisation of a divine purpose out of account, it is useless to try to discover antecedent conditions for the event which would permit us to say "whenever these conditions are fulfilled, this kind of event must follow". For the one supremely relevant consideration, the necessitation of the event in view of a divine purpose, belongs to the order of finality, and can never figure among constateable "antecedent conditions". (Just so when the poet

> takes his pen and writes
> The inevitable word.

What makes the word inevitable is its unique aesthetic fitness for its present context; this is seen by the "amazed" poet in a moment of inspiration. It would be idle to find the explanation of the inevitableness anywhere else, *e.g.* in the "laws of the association of ideas".[1]) The thought, as I say, seems to me a perfectly sound one, but the expression given to it is unfortunate, since it suggests the possibility of deciding whether an event is a "divine miracle" by *first* ascertaining that it has no "natural cause".

To put the whole matter once more in yet another

---

[1] Cf. Stout, *Analytic Psychology*, bk. ii. c. 6, § 4.

way, a miracle, if there is such a thing, is an event
which is recognised as having what Otto has taught us
to call a *numinous* character. No amount of criticism,
however justified in other respects, will really seriously
shake Otto's central position that it is this immediate recognition of the numinous, the wholly other and transcendent, in persons, things, events, which is at the root
of worship, and so of religion. It does not follow that
there is no such thing as misrecognition of the numinous. It may be wrongly taken to be where it is not,
exactly as beauty, moral goodness, or professed truth
have been, and often are, supposed to be where they are
not. It is *conceivable* that the majority of the objects
men suppose to be beautiful are not beautiful; that most
of the acts human societies have thought morally noble
have only been thought so because our current moral
notions are perverted by false sentimentalism, that
most of the statements which have been acclaimed as
profound truths are only plausible errors; it is *certain*
that spurious beauty, sham virtue, flashy half-truths do
often impose on mankind. But just as the fact that
bad pictures and bad music are often admired, and
spurious heroism often belauded, is no proof that there
is no true beauty or moral heroism, so the aberrations of silly, lewd, or cruel worships are no proof that
there are not events, things, persons, really endued
with the numinous quality. If there are, then we may
expect the task of distinguishing the true numinous
from the counterfeit, or the more fully from the imperfectly numinous, to prove at least as difficult as that
of discriminating true beauty from false. The education
of mankind in recognition of the numinous should, by
all analogy, be as slow and hard a business as their
training in the discernment of beauty, and we might
anticipate that, in both cases, the training would only

advance *pari passu* with, and in close dependence on, the general mental development of man. The unity of human personality does not, indeed, guarantee that there shall be any precise correspondence between intellectual, moral, and aesthetic accomplishment. The age which is most sensitively responsive to beauty is not necessarily also that which is most eminent in the sciences, or most distinguished by lofty moral practice. But it is at least true that intellectual and moral childishness, or deep-rooted perversity, is commonly reflected also in the aesthetic life of a people, or an age. The art of a savage group may be in advance of its morality, or what we may, by courtesy, call its science, but, for all that, it remains the art of savages, childish, crude, or grotesque. And the same thing is true of the savages' worship and religion, and it is a part of Otto's own theory that this is so, though his more unfriendly critics seem to forget the point.

This is all that I have to say in principle on the philosophical issues raised by the miraculous. I do not pretend that the recognition of possibilities of the abrupt, invasive manifestation of the supernatural in special events of the natural order has no disturbing consequences. Any view of the relation between the eternal and the temporal which finds room for the miraculous must be disturbing to our *penchant* for what W. James used to call a neat and tidy universe. If there are such things as miraculous events, the actual historical order must be less visibly orderly, less regimented, I might say, than we like to suppose it. A world where such things happen, however rarely, must be one which is "uncanny", a place where we are not, and cannot be, quite at home. And we all tend to resent the uneasy suspicion that we are not wholly at home with our surroundings, and so cannot implicitly count on them, for the same reason that we should dislike to be living where an earthquake may at any moment shake the solid foundations of our houses. Also, of course, on such a view of the world, the ascertainment of historical truth becomes harder, the very unfamiliar cannot simply be brushed aside, with the ease permitted by a philosophy which refuses to have anything to do with real "breaches in the customary routine of experience". If there are miracles, the task of distinguishing the true from the false is likely to be hard. Hence one can readily understand why the philosopher, more than most men, should have a special bias against miracle, because he feels more acutely than others the need for a coherent representation of the world.

Yet, as has been already said, it is at least certain that whatever the central purpose which makes the historical into a unity may be, it is not the purpose of gratifying our natural indolence by making thinking easy. Even apart from miracles, the historical world as we know it is disconcerting, untidy, and, on a surface view, wildly disorderly, and the advance of science has, in fact, only increased the appearance of disorder. How much more disorderly and untidy, on a first view, is our present astronomical scheme than the system of Eudoxus with its twenty-five or twenty-six concentric rotations and their absolutely uniform velocities; or, again, our present perplexed attempts to construct an intelligible account of the behaviour of the electron than the truly childish simplicity of the Epicurean scheme of atoms falling—apart from the rare moments of παρέγκλισις— steadily in a single direction with a single constant velocity. And the world of human life and human relations, again! Does a week pass without something to remind us that its safe and settled ways and regular habits, even in the societies where these things count for most, are very much on the surface? In dealing with one's fellows, one never knows when the ground may not fail under one's feet and reveal the crude, violent, and bloody reality of elemental human passions. We who have seen the thing happen to the human race at large during the past fifteen years must surely be aware that it may happen to our little personal "world" any day. Real life is eminently disorderly and dangerous, with a disorder which is not sensibly increased by the admission of an occasional "miracle" into the pattern, and it would not be surprising if the old-fashioned "rationalist's" vision of the physical order as one where "miracles do not happen" is as wide of the mark as the "Sunday-school-book" vision of the moral world as a realm in which there are no worse crimes than an occasional over-indulgence in liquor, or a stray act of poaching. If rationality really meant, as it is sometimes mistakenly supposed to mean, monotony, it would be true to say that every step taken towards fuller comprehension of the historical structure of the world is a step away from rationality. Thus the mere consideration that to let the miraculous into the course of events makes their pattern less easy to pack into a formula affords no ground for regarding the miraculous as irrational in any sense in which the irrational must be disavowed by a sane philosophy.

Indeed, the very notion of miracle should be possible only to a conscious or unconscious rationalist. If there were really no connection, no unity of plan, in the march of events, it would be meaningless to distinguish between what is miraculous and what is not. In a world where all that happens happens without plan and purpose, any event would be just as much or as little miraculous as any other; there would be no basis for the distinction between what may reasonably be expected

and what may not. Were the world what Hume professed to think it when he said that events are "conjoined but never connected", we could, of course, note
the fact that some sequences occur frequently, others
rarely, and, if we only allowed ourselves to forget that
the observer's mind is assumed to be part of the world
to which this dictum applies, we could go on, with
Hume, to offer a psychological *explanation* of the fact
that men expect the course of events to run on familiar
lines and are incredulous of the wholly unfamiliar.
But we could do nothing to *justify* this habit of expecting the familiar, give no reason for thinking that it
yields more "intelligent" anticipations of the course of
events than expectation of the most fantastic occurrences.
This seems to be the explanation of the apparently perverse conclusion of Hume's famous essay on *Miracles*,[1]
where a page devoted to the suggestion that Christianity requires us to accept stories which are on a par
in improbability with the fairy tales of the nursery is followed by the declaration that there is nothing in what
has been said to disturb the orthodox theologian; it is
true that he believes what is irrational; but why should
he not, seeing that he is conscious of a standing miracle
in himself? His assent to the unfamiliar is itself as much
a miracle as any of the events narrated in the scriptures to which he assents; thus he actually has in his
own personal experience the certainty that miracles do
occur.

If we leave out of account the touch of satire in this
language, we see at once that the conclusion drawn is
no more than must necessarily follow from the principles Hume adopts as the basis of his own professed
theory of the world. If it is true, as Hume maintains,
that there is no intrinsic reason why any one event may

[1] *Enquiry Concerning Human Understanding*, sect. x.

not be followed by another, it is also true that there is
no reason why our expectation that an event of given
kind will be followed by the kind of event with which it
has been "customarily" conjoined in the past should not
be disappointed at any moment. Our psychologically
explicable prejudice in favour of the customary is no
guide to the real pattern of the historical process. Hence
the fact that a single miracle has been believed in by
anyone *proves* that "customary experience", though a
common source, is not the only source of conviction,
and proves nothing further as to the wisdom or un-
wisdom of holding convictions due to some different
causes. There are persons, as is proved by the mere existence of Hume's more orthodox friends and antagonists, who in fact hold, and hold with strong conviction,
some beliefs which are not due to customary experience.
That they actually hold these beliefs is that consciousness of a miracle within themselves of which Hume
speaks. On the question of the truth or falsehood,
reasonableness or unreasonableness, of these beliefs the
argument has no bearing; that question cannot even be
asked without absurdity by an irrationalist who regards
belief itself as nothing more than an unaccountable
"propensity" to view things in a certain light.[1] The
ordinary divine and the ordinary "free-thinker" can
only discuss the question and disagree in their answer
to it, because both, whether they know it or not, mean
to be rationalists in their metaphysics. Both hold, or
should hold, that there is a real, objective, coherent
pattern in the historical course of events; their dis-

---

[1] Strictly speaking, the only conclusion to which Hume is entitled by the argumentation of part i. of his essay, where "customary experience is treated as the
only cause of belief, would be that no one ever *has* believed in a miracle, since there
has been *no* "custom" to cause the belief. But this conclusion is so glaringly false
that, to avoid it, he has to correct his original assumption into the form that
customary experience is only the most usual cause of belief.

agreement is only about the precise character of the pattern.

It is even more clear that the specifically religious question about startling events, whether they are "signs", is only in place if we accept a rationalist metaphysic. On genuinely irrationalist principles, as I said, we could distinguish between rare and frequent sequences, and take note that some suggested sequences are not known ever to have occurred, though we should have no right to say that a rare, or even an unprecedented, sequence is less likely to occur at any moment than any other. But if the unprecedented sequence presented itself, we could not ask whether it might not be a "sign", a significant clue to the ultimate pattern underlying all events, since the whole point of metaphysical irrationalism is that there *is* no such pattern. Events awaken various mental expectations in us, and what expectations they will awaken depends on our personal history, but no event is a "sign" of anything, for the reason that all events are merely loose and separate; "all our distinct perceptions are distinct existences", and "the mind never perceives any real connection among distinct existences".[1]

(*g*) It is further in this double character of the miracles of the great religions that we may perhaps find the possibility of an answer to the "anthropological" difficulty. The kind of "miracle" which is only too common in the folk-lore studied by the anthropologist is one which is merely a portent without being a sign, a surprise, but an insignificant surprise. There is a real and relevant difference between such mere surprises and surprises which, if they are real, are significant disclosures of a self-coherent supernatural source of the temporal process. There is accordingly rational justifi-

[1] Hume, *Treatise of Human Nature*, Appendix (Selby-Bigge, p. 636).

cation for the refusal to treat surprises of such different
kinds as though they stood on the same level of rationality. If eminent anthropologists of the type of Sir James
Frazer are curiously blind, as I think they sometimes
are, to the relevance of the distinction, the reason of
their blindness is presumably that they start with the
uncriticised assumption of a sheer metaphysical irrationalism. They are at heart persuaded that history has
no meaning. Discussion of the miraculous, or of any
other subsidiary issue, is mere waste of time, unless the
parties to it are antecedently agreed on this most fundamental of all metaphysical issues, the question whether
"becoming", the course of history as a whole, has a
meaning or has none, or, in plainer words, whether
God exists or does not exist.

However we answer that question we shall, of course,
have to admit that, in view of the limitations consequent on our situation, that of beings who only become
very gradually aware of a small part of the indefinitely
extended historical process of becoming, we must
expect violent surprises, events which upset all calcu-
lations built on *our* customary experience, to present
themselves from time to time. But acceptance or rejection of belief in God, and, for the matter of that,
acceptance or rejection of the specific conception of God
conveyed by a great positive religion, will necessarily
affect our view as to the character of the surprises
which may reasonably be expected, and their distri-
bution through space and time. As I have put the point
elsewhere, "in an atheistic or neutral metaphysical
scheme there would be no reason to expect the surprises
to wear any special character, or to be distributed in
any special way over space and time. We should expect
them to make their appearance as simple *freaks*. If our
philosophical world-scheme is definitely theistic, the

case is altered completely. For we shall then conceive of the pattern of events not merely as providing a connection between them, but as providing a connection which is intelligible, in the sense that, like the structure of a symphony, or a well-lived life, it exhibits the realisation of an end of absolute value. We should thus antecedently look for the 'irregularities' in nature and history to exhibit a special kind of concentration, exactly as the surprises in the construction of a great piece of music, or the conduct of a life of wise originality, exhibit the same concentration. . . . Thus the difference in ultimate metaphysical outlook between a theist and a non-theistic philosopher would make a difference between the two sets of initial premisses relatively to which each estimates the probability of certain events. It is not unreasonable in a convinced theist to be satisfied with evidence for the resurrection of Jesus Christ which would not satisfy him of the resurrection of a next-door neighbour, since he may well ascribe to the resurrection of Christ a unique spiritual value . . . which he could not ascribe to the resurrection of his neighbour."[1]

It may be said, I fear, that there is, in the words just quoted, a confusion of two distinct problems which have no bearing on one another—the problem of fact and the problem of value—that the "spiritual value" attaching to an alleged event, supposing it actually to have occurred, has nothing to do with the reasonableness of judging it to have occurred; *that* is dependent solely on the amount and quality of the available "testimony". But I would rejoin that, so far as I can see, though the problems are distinguishable, they are not discon-

---

[1] *David Hume and the Miraculous*, pp. 46-8. Of course I am assuming that the theist spoken of does not base his theism itself upon belief in the fact of Our Lord's resurrection, since his reasoning would then be circular.

nected; the question of value has a real bearing on the question of fact. We all recognise this in practice, when, for example, we take into account what we call "evidence to character". We do regard evidence of facts which would be treated as altogether insufficient to convict one man of a charge—*e.g.* of "loitering with intent"—as ample in the case of another. If I am a "suspicious character", I am reasonably regarded as not having cleared myself of an allegation by evidence which would be more than enough to clear the man who is "above suspicion". Of course, though the principle is sound, there is always a good deal of danger in the application of it, and in human society, which, being human, is never quite free from snobbery, it often works out cruelly or absurdly, but I do not see that this affects its soundness as a principle. As such it is just a form of the refusal which, as I hold, sound metaphysics must make, to divorce reality from value. In the last resort, I should say, the *raison d'être* of any fact must be a "value".

However that may be, I would at least end this discussion by repeating once more that the credibility of miracles, in the theological sense of the term, can never be regarded as independent of the central issue of all religion, the reality of God. For the frame of reference by which an intelligent man estimates credibilities will itself be different according as he believes in God or disbelieves. For that very reason it seems to me impossible to appeal, as some of the old-fashioned apologists for Christianity used to do, but as philosophers of the calibre of St. Thomas were careful not to do, to the assumed actuality of miracles as a ground for the belief in God itself. Except as interpreted in the light of antecedent belief in God, no marvel, however stupendous, however well authenticated, and however marked its

results on the life of mankind, would be more than a
rare and curious fact. As Francis Bacon said long ago,
no miracle was ever wrought to convince an atheist.[1]
If a man does not see God in the *cursus ordinarius* of
nature and human life, "neither will he believe, though
one rose from the dead". Or at least, we should perhaps
say, he may in fact be converted by the rising of one
from the dead, but he will owe the fact of that conversion to the weakness of his logic; his conversion will
prove that, whatever his good points, he is no *esprit
juste*.

[1] *Advancement of Learning*, bk. ii. (E. and S. iii. 345): "There was never
miracle wrought by God to convert an atheist, because the light of nature might
have led him to confess a God: but miracles have been wrought to convert
idolaters and the superstitious, because no light of nature extendeth to declare
the will and true worship of God".

V

THE MEANING AND PLACE OF AUTHORITY

A prophet? Prophet wherefore he
Of all in Israel('s ?) tribes?
He teacheth with authority,
And not as do the Scribes.—CLOUGH.

Nulli ergo dubium est gemino pondere nos impelli ad discendum, auctoritatis atque rationis. Mihi autem certum est nusquam prorsus a Christi auctoritate discedere: non enim reperio valentiorem.—AUGUSTINE.

I CAN readily believe that an auditor of our foregoing discussions might be willing to allow the force of all we have said, and yet might contend, with a great show of reason, that we have carefully avoided facing the real problem. In the last resort, he might argue, there is an inevitable and ineradicable opposition between the very spirit of rational philosophy and the spirit common to all positive and revelational religions: philosophy is committed to the principle of "private judgement"; it is a state and habit of mind rather than a set of dogmas; it has no value unless it is the fruit of a free personal effort to understand, and it is even more important for the philosopher that his convictions should have been reached by such strenuous personal effort than that they should be true. But all the positive religions, avowedly or implicitly, are no less deeply committed to the recognition of an absolute authority before which private judgement may properly be bidden to submit itself without reserve. In a word, philosophy is, in its very nature, "Protestant", positive religion "Catholic";

the one would have us hold our convictions because we are personally persuaded of their truth, the other because of the *auctoritas*, or dignity, of the source from which we have learned them, and no man can loyally adopt both these attitudes at once. I have heard an amusing anecdote, true or false, which puts this point very neatly. It relates that a Roman Catholic theologian was in conversation with an outsider, who remarked that there seemed to be no real difference between the position of Rome and that of a well-known and widely respected "Anglo-Catholic". "Pardon me", replied the theologian, "we are at the opposite pole from *X*. He holds every doctrine that we hold, but holds them all for the entirely irrelevant reason that he thinks them true." You see at once the point of this epigrammatic criticism. By the critic's own admission, what *X* holds in theology is the truth, and the whole truth, so far as the whole truth is accessible to man; the trouble is that *X* takes it to be the truth for a wrong reason. He should take it for truth because it comes to him on the authority of the Church, but in fact only takes it as true because it commends itself to his personal judgement, and is thus, formally, though not materially, a "Protestant heretic". If a particular dogma happened not to recommend itself to his personal judgement, he would not assent to it, whereas he ought, in fact, to believe the dogma without so much as raising the question whether it approves itself to his judgement or not, on the sole ground that God, speaking through the officials of the Church, has declared it; when God speaks, we believe, not because what God says can be seen or shown to be correct, but because the speaker is God.

Though the Roman Church has given this conception of authority as the one real and sufficient basis of faith in "revealed truth" its most elaborate expression, the position is not, of course, peculiar to that Church; indeed, it may fairly be argued that it is common in principle to all the positive religions. One may reject the authority of the Church in favour of that of an infallible written Scripture, as the original Reformers did, or one may reject the authority of the body of Scripture as a whole, as some of the successors of the Reformers do, in favour of that of those utterances which, as it is held, can safely be taken to have come from the actual lips of the supreme revealer of God, the authenticated sayings of Christ, relieved of everything which can plausibly be regarded as later exegesis or amplification. But differences of this kind are only secondary disagreements about the precise channel through which infallible authority speaks; they do not affect the principle that there is somewhere an authority which is that of God Himself, and that when this authority has spoken, the question whether its deliverances recommend themselves to a man's personal judgement becomes irrelevant. If God has never spoken in this way, is there not an end of all the claims of any positive religion on the universal allegiance of mankind? If He has so spoken, *causa finita est*. The *foi du charbonnier* would thus appear to be an indispensable constituent in every positive religion.

But, it may be said, the one thing which a rational philosophy cannot tolerate on any terms is just this *foi du charbonnier*. For, as Ferrier has maintained,[1] it is even more important that a philosophy should be reasoned than that it should be true. That a man, in that resolute effort to think things out which is philosophy, should come to erroneous conclusions is a com-

[1] *Institutes of Metaphysics*, p. 2: "Philosophy, therefore, in its ideal perfection, is a body of reasoned truth . . . it is more proper that philosophy should be reasoned than that it should be true; because, while truth may perhaps be unattainable by man, to reason is certainly his province, and within his power".

paratively trivial matter. If his conclusions are erroneous, the patient following of the method of "thinking things out" will of itself, in time, lead to their correction; patient thinking can always be trusted, in the end, to repair its own mistakes. But if we once allow an assent which is more than consciously tentative and provisional to be given to that which has not been thought out by a personal effort, but taken on trust without question or criticism—and this is the kind of assent a positive religion necessarily demands when its God has spoken—the central conviction which lies at the heart of all rational philosophy—the conviction that reality has a structure which is intelligible—has been surrendered. We may call such dutiful submission to authority asserted to be divine assent to the declaration of the supreme source of truth, but it is, in plain fact, no more than a "strong propension" to view things in a certain light, dignified by a name to which it has no right.

The point, it may be said, is made abundantly clear by the history of apologetics. The philosophically minded apologist may start, like Anselm, with unbounded belief in the possibility of justifying his faith at the bar of intellect by showing that when you "think things out" you are always led to the very convictions you had begun by taking on trust. But even Anselm, when he speaks of *fides quaerens intellectum*, does not mean, as the modern Agnostic does when he takes as his motto *"we seek for truth"*, that the search is begun in the dark. It never occurs to him to doubt the indispensability of beginning with absolute and unqualified assent to the whole received content of *fides*, or to suspect that the thinking out of things might possibly lead to substantive modification of the "deposit" of faith. It is *itself*, not the "manifold of science", or

the "great mystery" that his *fides* is seeking to understand. If he had found himself completely unable to
urge anything in answer to Gaunilo's apology for the
"fool" who says in his heart that there is no God, his
faith in the Christian creed would no more have
wavered than Gaunilo's own wavered when he constructed his pamphlet. At bottom Anselm's conviction
that he is already in possession of a truth which merely
needs to be cast into a logically articulated form to
become evident amounts to an assumption that metaphysics is, to parody a *mot* of Bradley, "the finding of
good reasons for what we believe on instinct".[1] But, we
may ask, is not that which we "believe on instinct"
usually any set of ideas, true or false, which has the
advantage of being deeply interwoven with the whole
social fabric of our particular place and time? *Fides
quaerens intellectum* will be led to a Western Christianity in the atmosphere of eleventh-century Paris
or Canterbury, to Islam at the court of Bagdad or
Cordova.

Nor is the case visibly mended much by drawing a
distinction between natural theology, that part of the
contents of a positive creed for which we can succeed
in finding good and sufficient probative grounds, and
the revealed truths for which the most close and patient
thought can do no more than to show that the reasons
urged against them are inconclusive, and where, therefore, the last word must be with authority. St. Thomas'
words, indeed, read well: "To argue from authority is
supremely proper to this study, because the principles
of the study are had from revelation, and it is therefore
right that there should be belief in the authority of
those to whom the revelation has been made. Nor does

---

[1] The word "instinct", indeed, is perhaps not the best that could be chosen to
convey Anselm's thought. But neither does it really convey Bradley's meaning.

this derogate from the dignity of this study; for though the appeal to authority founded upon human reason is exceeding weak, the appeal to authority founded upon divine revelation is exceeding efficacious."[1] This may be true enough, but you have first to identify your divine revelation before you make your appeal to its authoritativeness, and thus there would seem to be only two alternatives, either to take as the accredited divine revelation whatever happens to enjoy the prestige of a revelation in your own community, or else to judge of the credentials of professed revelations by the exercise of your own intelligence, though when once the credentials have been found satisfactory, you propose for the future to ascribe your assent to reverence for divine authority.

In either case, it might be said, the whole of your faith really rests in the end on the *locus ab auctoritate quae fundatur super humana ratione*, which is *infirmissimus*. If it is a poor reason for accepting a revelation as truly divine that it seems to be so "to the best of my personal knowledge and belief", it is a worse reason still that *on dit* "this is a divine revelation". "And so", to borrow the words of Hobbes, "we are reduced to the Independency of the Primitive Christians, to follow Paul, or Cephas, or Apollos, every man as he liketh best . . . because it is unreasonable in them who teach that there is such danger in every little Errour, to require of a man endued with Reason of his own, to follow the Reason of any other man, or of the most voices of many other men; which is little better

---

[1] *S.T.* i.ª q. 1, art 8 ad sec. "argumentum ex auctoritate est maxime proprium huius doctrinae, eo quod principia huius doctrinae per revelationem habentur. Et sic oportet quod credatur auctoritati eorum quibus revelatio facta est. Nec hoc derogat dignitati huius doctrinae: nam licet locus ab auctoritate quae fundatur super ratione humana sit infirmissimus, locus tamen ab auctoritate quae fundatur super revelatione divina est efficacissimus."

than to venture his Salvation at crosse and pile."[1] The
only divine authority left with a right to demand
absolute submission thus proves, after all, to be the
authority of the "God within", the reason and conscience of the individual. But the cause of a positive
religion seems to be inseparably bound up with the
recognition of a supra-individual supreme authority,
that of a "God without", by which the aberrations of
individual judgement may be magisterially corrected
and controlled. If we are in earnest with the demand
that each man shall be left to follow "Paul, or Cephas,
or Apollos, as he thinketh best", we cannot in consistency draw the line there; a man must also be left free,
"if he thinketh best", to follow none of the three, but
to strike out his own line, to be of a school in which
there is "no man doctor" and no man disciple, except
himself, and however we may seek to disguise the fact,
there will thus really be as many religions as there are
individuals—a state of things far removed from the
"independency" of the primitive *Christians*.

To Hobbes this does not very much matter, but the
reason why it does not matter is that he really cares
nothing about religion and wholly disbelieves in its
worth as a knowledge and worship of God. Knowledge
of God, according to his philosophy, is impossible,
because God is "ingenerable", and knowledge is all of
motions, generations, and their effects;[2] conformity to
the established worship has nothing to do with convictions; it is "not philosophy, but law",[3] merely an
indication that, as good citizens, we do not propose

---

[1] *Leviathan*, c. 47.

[2] *De Corpore*, c. i. 8 "excludit a se Philosophia Theologiam, doctrinam dico de
natura et attributis Dei, aeterni, ingenerabilis, incomprehensibilis, et in qua
nulla compositio, nulla divisio institui, nulla generatio intelligi potest."

[3] *Seven Philosophical Problems*, Epistle Dedicatory (English Works, ed.
Molesworth, vii. 5): "But what had I to do to meddle with matters of that nature,
seeing religion is not philosophy, but law?"

to disturb the King's peace for any metaphysical quillets of our own. From the individualistic premisses of the sectary we thus reach the conclusions of pure indifferentism.

This seems, at first sight, a paradox, but reflection may possibly show that it is no paradox, but an inevitable consequence of consistency in individualism. For the thoroughgoing individualist begins by making a double assumption, both parts of that assumption being equally necessary to him. My religion is strictly a purely personal affair, a concern between myself and my God to which there is no third party; it is primarily a matter of the salvation of my own soul, and nothing else. ("Nothing", says a hymn I have heard sung in my boyhood, "is worth a thought beneath, But how *I* may escape the death That never, never dies".) It is because the whole transaction is so strictly individual that it appears so reasonable to hold that the only authoritative guide for me in the transaction is the interior voice of God, recognised as such by my own judgement and conscience. One only succeeds in combining such a view, as it has historically been combined, with the further conviction that there is a religion which is true and obligatory for mankind by the further tacit assumption, regularly made by enthusiasts for all creeds, that every other man's personal judgement and conscience will agree in its deliverances with my own, if only he shows good faith in consulting them. This proposition of fact is just what the cool-headed student of men and manners, with no strong personal enthusiasms, finds it impossible to grant. "No honest man", said Johnson, "could be a deist, for no man could be so after a fair examination of the proofs of Christianity."[1] At the present day—*experto credite*—an edu-

---

[1] Johnson to Boswell, February 1766.

cated layman who ventures to write in the most modest
way on the side of Christian, or even theistic, belief may
expect to receive communications from "infidels" who
are entire strangers to him, informing him in unambiguous language that he must be a dishonest person,
because no one who has considered the refutations of
Christianity (or of Theism) with attention can possibly
retain any belief. To a dispassionate mind it is meanwhile patent that there are very honest Papists and
equally honest Protestants, sincere Christians and Jews,
and also sincere atheists, at all levels of general education and intelligence. The reason and judgement of all
the individuals cannot be trusted even to lead in the
same general direction, on the single condition that it
shall be loyally followed. If there is no other authority,
it seems natural to draw one of two conclusions: either
there is no truth to be reached in matters about which
equally intelligent and sincere persons draw such divergent conclusions from the same data, or if there should
be any truth which will ultimately emerge from the
endless welter of inquiry and controversy, truth so hard
to find cannot be of much moment for the practical
conduct of life and the attainment of the "good for
man". And this is Indifferentism.

But a positive religion can flourish only when it is
recognised that the direction of life by its light is the
supreme and very practical concern of mankind; no
such religion can tolerate reduction to the status of
an interesting speculation which may prove to be not
entirely unfounded, but has no pressing importance for
the ordering of conduct and life. We can thus readily
understand why it is that, in actual fact, even those
religious bodies which theoretically push the rejection
of "external authority" to an extreme almost always,
in practice, prove to retain some authority to which

they expect private judgement, in the last resort, to submit itself; and, again, why every movement which effects much for the quickening and deepening of the personal spiritual life seems regularly to be accompanied by a revival of insistence on the authoritativeness of something which is not "private judgement", whether the something is the organised Church, the letter of a Scripture, a particular interpretation of a Scripture, or some new revelation, attested by physical or moral wonders.

Thus, to illustrate the point by the history of a particular religious community, it is manifest fact that the gravely enfeebled spirituality of the English Church of two hundred years ago has been wakened into new vitality chiefly by three great movements—the Methodist, the Evangelical, the "Anglo-Catholic". The broad fact remains certain, however badly any man may think of some of the incidental characteristics of some or all of these movements. (I can understand that to some minds the ardent Methodist, the eager Evangelical, and the earnest Anglo-Catholic may all be distressing, but I should not understand the denial of the proposition that all three are alive, if sometimes disconcertingly alive, while the decorous Latitudinarians of George I.'s time were dead, or moribund.) Each of the three movements was, in its own way, a somewhat violent revolt against the domination of individual judgement and "good sense" in matters of religion, towards some form of "non-rational" authoritarianism. Wesley, Toplady, Newman are, in various ways, unlike enough, but they all agree in seeing the enemy in what Newman called "Liberalism"; all, like the priest in Blake's poem,[1] or, for the matter of that, Blake himself, regard it as the supreme blasphemy to

[1] "A Little Boy Lost", in *Songs of Experience*.

Set up reason for the judge
Of our most holy mystery.

We see the same thing, in a highly grotesque form, in the curious contemporary American movement which calls itself Fundamentalism. That the Fundamentalists, being for the most part extremely ill-educated, should be violently obscurantist in their attitude to natural and historical science is only what might be expected, though I doubt whether their *caeca fides* is really more obscurantist at heart than the equally blind confidence of the aggressive "rationalist" in the competence of scientific methods, of which he most commonly knows next to nothing, to answer all questions "in the earth, or out of it". But it is, I should say, a mere mistake to see nothing in the Fundamentalist movement but its hostility to Darwin and Huxley and the "higher critics" of Biblical documents. What is really at the back of the movement, and supplies it with its driving force, is the conviction that any attempt to eliminate absolute supernatural "authority" from Christianity, or any other great positive religion, is destructive of its character as religion. Such attempts convert "the faith" into a philosophy, and by consequence, since there can be no such thing as an authoritarian philosophy, into a mere body of tentative "personal opinions", a collection of *Privatmeinungen*. And a man for whom his religion has become an affair of *Privatmeinungen* has ceased to have a religion.

The real issue is not whether the opening chapters of *Genesis* are "fundamental", but whether there is anywhere a genuine *fundamentum*, a "sure cornerstone", on which positive religion can build. It is felt that such a corner-stone cannot be found in any purely rational theology or metaphysic, since the God of such a system is a God whom we have succeeded in understanding, a God who is not a *deus absconditus*, and does not "move in a mysterious way". We accept His disclosure of Himself through theology or metaphysic because, so far as one can see, it contains no mistakes, not because *haec dicit Dominus Deus*. But such a God divested of mystery, a God whom we understand, as we understand the properties of integers or triangles, would be a God who "has no more in Him", or, indeed, "has less in Him", than the mind which can thus understand and dispose of Him, a mere *dieu des savans et des philosophes*, and therefore not a being whom we can adore, and so not a true God at all, in the sense in which "heart-religion" demands a God. Worship, indeed, is not mere abjection and abasement before something which baffles our intelligence, but without the element of the baffling there is no worship. If, then, such a God has ever declared Himself to mankind, the communication cannot owe the claim of its content to acceptance to the transparent intrinsic reasonableness and good sense which pervades it; there must be something in it which has to be accepted, not because, with the expenditure of sufficient industry and acumen, we can see it to be "what could not be otherwise", but because God has spoken it, and it rests on *His* word for it.

> State contenti, umana gente, al *quia*;
> chè se possuto aveste veder tutto,
> mestier non era parturir Maria.[1]

Now, I own that it is just this recognition of the principle of absolute authority, in one form or another, which is, in the end, the *scandalum* offered by all positive and historical religions to the philosophical mind, honestly bent on the understanding of things. The mysterious always presents a problem to intelligence,

[1] Dante, *Purgatorio*, iii. 37.

and the intellect would be playing the traitor to itself
if it merely sat down idly in the presence of the problem
without any serious effort to grapple with it. Yet, on the
other side, it seems impossible to remove the scandal by
denying that there is any ultimate mystery at the heart
of things. When we consider how utterly the attempt
to locate absolute authority in a definitely circumscribed
seat, and to codify its deliverances, has always broken
down, we may, indeed, be strongly tempted to cut the
knot in this fashion. To consider only the solutions of
the problem of the seat of authority which have been
propounded within the limits of Christianity itself, it
seems impossible, without great feats of sophistry, to
place it in the official declarations of Popes or Councils,
or of both together, for some of them seem to contradict others openly, and some to be in disagreement with
independently ascertained truth. The same and similar
difficulties attend the appeal to the written text of the
Bible; the text appealed to is sometimes corrupt, sometimes speaks with an ambiguous voice, sometimes asserts what we know to be historical or scientific error.
Moreover, before we can so much as know what Bible
it is to which we are appealing, since the Bible itself
never enumerates its own component parts, we have to
go to an extra-biblical authority to learn what "books"
are part of the infallible Bible, and what are not. (So
far the "Fundamentalists" apparently have shirked the
question what is the authority which fixes the canon of
Scripture, but it is a question which they must be prepared to face—with curious consequences for Fundamentalism.)

If we fall back from the Biblical writings as a whole
on the recorded personal utterances of Our Lord, there
is the desperate problem of ascertaining how far these
utterances have been accurately transferred from the

idiom in which they were primarily spoken to another, and then transmitted to us without mutilation, addition, or deformation.[1] (If careful and unbiassed criticism is steadily delivering us, as it seems to be, from the more extravagant speculations which once threatened to dissolve the whole Gospel story into a tissue of "tendencious" misrepresentations of fact in the interests of early quarrelsome theological controversialists, it is no less steadily making it plain how very little we know of the actual words and deeds of the Lord with anything like certainty.) And the various ingenious devices by which the theories of the infallibility of Popes, of Councils, of Scripture as a whole, of the reports of the sayings of Christ, is kept intact under difficulties, what a lame affair they all are! The Pope infallible? Yes, of course; but somehow one can always make out a case for holding that *this* Pope, making *this* pronouncement, has omitted to comply with some condition necessary to make his utterance one of the infallible ones. General Councils liable to err? Why, no; but it may always be possible to discover that *this* Council had some defect which made it not really oecumenical, or that its Acts are interpolated, or have been misunderstood. The words of Scripture are inerrant, but we may disagree about the canon, or allow for unlimited corruption in transcription, or may take strange liberties of interpretation. The actual words of

---

[1] The problem has its very practical bearings. *E.g. if* we are to take the *ipsissima verba* of Christ as they fell from His lips as our absolute authority and our only absolute authority, how is a Christian Church to deal with the problems of divorce? Everything will turn on the questions—(1) Did Christ actually utter the words "apart from a case of fornication", which appear in *Matt.* v. but not in *Mk.* x.? (2) What is the precise signification of the word "fornication" in this clause? (3) In view of the actual institutions of Galilee in the first century, does the presence or absence of the clause make any difference? It seems impossible to hold that all three questions can be answered with certainty. I am not asking, be it understood, whether divorce in case of fornication is Christian or unchristian, but whether anything could be determined either way by simple appeal to the *litera scripta*.

the Lord are beyond question, but He may be credited with a double meaning, or a recorded utterance may be shown to have suffered from imperfect rendering out of Aramaic into Greek, or to have been misunderstood from unfamiliarity with Galilean tradition, or to have undergone "development", whenever it suits our convenience. All transparent subterfuges by which our absolute authority is nominally respected, while in fact we trim its deliverances to suit our changing fancy. It is an old story over which the world has made merry until it is ashamed of its own jest.

And yet when all has been said, it is as hard to conceive of an adequate religion without mystery, and consequently without the note of authority, as it is easy to smile at the shifts to which the theorist is driven when he attempts to provide authority with its clearly defined seat and to compile a register of its declarations. It remains true that "God comprehended" would be no God, but a mere artificial construction of our own minds. *Christianity not Mysterious* is no proper title for a work on the Christian religion by a writer who seriously believes that religion to be something more than an invention of ingenious moralists and statesmen. Butler's famous *Analogy*, it has been said, cuts both ways, for it seems to make "revealed religion" superfluous by demonstrating that it leaves the course of the world as mysterious as it finds it.[1] But the criticism is surely much more smart than sound. It is true, after all, though it is an unwelcome truth, that in the Aristotelian phrase so often repeated by the great schoolmen,[2]

[1] Leslie Stephen, *English Thought in the Eighteenth Century*, c. 5.

[2] *Met.* a 993 b 9 ὥσπερ γὰρ τὰ τῶν νυκτερίδων ὄμματα πρὸς τὸ φέγγος ἔχει τὸ μεθ' ἡμέραν, οὕτω καὶ τῆς ἡμετέρας ψυχῆς ὁ νοῦς πρὸς τὰ τῇ φύσει φανερώτατα. In the *vetus Latina of the Metaphysics*, the νυκτερίς is replaced by the *noctua*. Is there some chance reproduction of the original image in Blake's words,

"The Bat that flits at close of Eve
Has left the Brain that won't believe"?

the eye of man's mind for truth is like the eye of the owl for daylight. A theology which finds mystery it cannot explain away at the centre of things may not be true, but it is certain that a theology which professes to have cleared away all the mystery out of the world must be false. In any true account of the concrete and individual reality one must somewhere come upon something of which it can only be said, "Why this thing should be so, or even just what it is, is more than I can tell, but at all costs it must be recognised that here the thing is". If this is all we mean by "irrationality", we may safely say that historical individuality is the great supreme irrational from which thought can never succeed in getting free. If by the "rational" we mean that which is wholly transparent, that which *va de soi* for the logical mind, the one ubiquitous irrationality is the very fact that there should be anything more than the "bloodless ballet of impalpable categories", the fact that something exists. For the something that exists is always individual, and this means, in the first place, that it is not constructed by, but *given* to, our thinking, and in the second, that it is inexhaustible by analysis, an implicit and dimly apprehended "infinite". The actual function of thought is neither to create its own data, nor yet to fit data otherwise given in a number of clear-cut simple apprehensions into an alien pattern, or relational scheme, of "universals", independently given by a second kind of simple apprehension, but to analyse and articulate the present experience, which is our one, always confused, real datum; to transmute apprehension, if I may so express myself, into recognition.[1] It is of the essence of the situation that this transmutation is never complete; there is

---

[1] This, I should say, is the real meaning and the permanent truth of the Platonic doctrine that all knowledge is ἀνάμνησις.

always in the confused, concrete, given fact a remainder of the perplexing, the not yet recognised, which intrigues us, and yet cannot be ignored without killing the experienced fact. A mere "laboratory" fact, from which this element has been artificially subtracted, is no longer the living fact.

So far as I can see, the function of authority is just to insist upon the reality and omnipresence in religion, as in all our contact with the objectively real, of this element of refractoriness to complete intellectual analysis which is the stamp of objectivity, this never wholly removable misfit between the real and the categories in which we try to confine it. "A God comprehended is no God"; also, a "nature" completely comprehended would not be the real natural world. But the misfit is so much more patent when it is God who is the object of our thinking, because of the incomparable wealth of intrinsic reality in the object. In dealing with a God who does not simply stand aloof "on the other side", but has entered into the historical and become truly immanent in it, though never merely immanent, authority provides us with the way of escape from the agnosticism which is the despair of the intellect. For *ignorabimus* it substitutes the happier watchward, *console-toi, tu ne me chercherais pas, si tu ne m'avais trouvé*.[1] The possession is in the puzzling form of dim and vague contact, but it is a genuine fact, which guarantees us that the *au delà*, where we can detect no clear and definite outlines, is not, after all, a mere *terra incognita* which may prove, like the unexplored regions in mediaeval maps, to be filled by fantastic man-destroying monsters. Or, to put it rather differently, what I would suggest is that authority and experience do not stand over against one another in sharp and irreconcilable

[1] Pascal, *Pensées*, 553 (Brunschvig) (*Mystère de Jésus*).

opposition; authority is the self-assertion of the reality of an experience which contains more than any individual experient has succeeded in analysing out and extricating for himself. It is indispensable for us as finite historical beings who need a safeguard against our inveterate tendency to supplement the statement "this is what I can make of this situation" by the perilous addition, "and this is all there is in it".

It is instructive, I think, to consider the analogy of what we often call the "authority" of sense-perception, and the part it plays in our knowledge of the natural world. As has been remarked before, we may safely say, following in the steps of Mr. Meyerson, that it is just the impossibility of resolving the course of physical becoming without remainder into a complex of universal connections, in accord with exactly formulable laws, that forbids us to regard the whole of physical nature as no more than a coherent dream of the physicist. If the physicist could ever succeed in getting rid altogether of the element of intrusive and perturbing brute fact which will not square wholly with his scheme of formulae, he would probably feel, as I think Mr. Meyerson has said, that the real world had evaporated before his eyes into a mere collection of logical or mathematical symbols. Now, of course, the brute facts which thus save the natural world from being sublimated away into a system of differential equations are, in the end, facts about our *sensations*, and what they disclose. The natural world is obstinately real because, however far we have carried the reduction of its processes to "law", we have always still to take account of experiences in the way of sensation for which we can give no justification beyond the fact that they are there. Sense furnishes a standard of appeal which seems to be external to thinking, and by which the results of thinking have to be corrected. In the end, if there are undeniable facts recorded on the testimony of sense which refuse to square with the apparently best assured analyses and deductions of the intellect, it is the intellect, with its deductions and analyses, which has to submit.[1] This is as annoying to the typical "thinker" as the theologian's demand that "reason" should give way before "authority"; the same repugnance to admit the control of thought by anything beyond itself which gives rise, in one sphere, to the contemptuous rejection of all "authority" produces, in another, the types of philosophy which, in various ways, attempt to deny that sense as sense makes any contribution to the fabric of natural knowledge. In the one case, as in the other, theories which try to deny or conceal the fact that in all our thinking, whether about physical becoming or about God, the eternal Being, thought is working on an object which it has neither created nor "postulated", but finds there, given in a contact which is not mere thinking, seem doomed to failure, as all unqualified *a-priorism* must be, by the consideration that the thinker is himself an historical being, and that nothing has significance for him except in so far as it affects him by historical contacts.

In the case of the sensible experiences[2] which give us

---

[1] This explains what Democritus meant when he made the senses say to the intellect τάλαινα φρήν, παρ' ἡμέων λαβοῦσα τὰς πίστεις ἡμέας καταβάλλεις; πτῶμά τοι τὸ κατάβλημα (fr. 125 Diels). Cf. the observations of É. Gilson with reference to the ultra-rationalism of Descartes: "à un phénomène réel qu'il ne pourrait pas s'expliquer s'il le connaissait Descartes préfère de beaucoup un phénomène qui n'existe peut-être pas mais qu'il peut expliquer pour le cas où ce phénomène existerait. Tels ces escadrons de fantômes qui combattent en l'air.... Les scolastiques croient au phénomène et renoncent à l'expliquer. [They ascribe it to the agency of God, or of good, or bad, angels.] Descartes n'y croit guère, mais il indique cependant les causes qui lui semblent capables de le produire" (*Études de philosophie médiévale*, p. 285).

[2] If I am asked exactly what I mean by *sensible*, I do not know that I can do better than quote the definition of Augustine: "iam video sic esse definiendum, ut sensus sit passio corporis *per se ipsum* non latens animam" (*de quant. animae*,

our historical contacts with nature there are several
points which call for remark. In the first place, it is
obvious that there is no possible *proof* that all present
sensation may not be mere illusion, as some of the
ancient philosophies seem to have taught that it is.
Descartes may make his immediate inference to an
objective reality, the *sum*, from a single *cogito*, the
fact, for example, that he is aware of colour or warmth,
but that he *is* aware, that he *cogitat*, is not even an
immediate illation.[1] If it is denied, the denial cannot be
met by the production of grounds, but must be swept
aside by a mere reiteration of the original assertion. In
the second place, though the whole edifice of philosophy
and science is built, in the end, on a basis of direct simple
apprehension, of which no further account can be given,
this does not mean that one could ever isolate the simply
apprehended content from the context of interpretation and "construction" with which it is complicated.
Sense and thought, direct apprehension and the interpretation of what is given to it, may both be involved
in any articulate perception, but we can never sort them
out, so as to be in a position to say *"this*, and no more,
is the element in my present perception which is *given*,
simply apprehended as present; *that* is the result of
recognition, analysis, comparison, and so is not given,
but *made"*.

Kant, indeed, seems to undertake such a separation
in his doctrine of the forms of intuition, but Kant, as I
imagine we should all agree now, did not probe deep
enough. Apparently, he would be content to assign to

23, 41). See the exposition of É. Gilson (*Introduction à l'étude de saint Augustin,*
72), from whom I borrow the reference.

[1] We must be careful to avoid the mistake of Huxley in his essay on Descartes,
who argues that the premiss of the inference should be stated in the hypothetical
form, *si quis cogitat, est*. The absence of existential import in such a premiss would
make it incapable of yielding the existential conclusion Descartes needs. *His*
premiss is really *ille homo qui est Renatus Descartes hic et nunc aliquid cogitat.*

the side of construction everything in the perception
recorded in a simple perceptive judgement which has to
do with the spatial or temporal shape, size, position of
what is perceived; but supposes that when you get down
to the purely qualitative, when, for example, your perception constates no more than could be adequately
conveyed by the monosyllable "green", or "sour",
you have reached the merely given. In that case, the
element of construction would only come in with that
which the exclamation "green!" may imply, but does
not convey—the implication "just here and just now".
Yet it seems plain on reflection that merely to say
"green" with significance is to perform an act of comparison and recognition; interpretation has already
begun, before we proceed to the implication "here, not
there; now, not then". If there ever was a time, as we
may fairly doubt, in our own past history when we were
purely receptive, the time must have passed before we
could so much as name things, and to recapture the
condition must be beyond the power of "articulate-
speaking men".[1]

The analytic psychologist may produce reasons, and
possibly good reasons, to show that there must be such
a thing as "pure" sensation, but it is abundantly clear
that no such thing as a sensation pure of all elements
of interpretation can enter as such into the fabric of
our perception of the natural world, or be produced
for the inspection of the psychologist who is reflecting
on the problem of perception. In any bit of what we
call our sense-experience, however elementary, which
can be detached for examination, we find the given,

---

[1] Plato shows more insight, when he subjoins to an account of the intellectual
activity implied in the grasping of a geometrical truth the words ταὐτὸν δὴ περί τε
εὐθέος ἅμα καὶ περιφεροῦς σχήματος καὶ χρόας, περί τε ἀγαθοῦ καὶ καλοῦ καὶ δικαίου,
καὶ περὶ σώματος ἅπαντος σκευαστοῦ τε καὶ κατὰ φύσιν γεγονότος, πυρὸς ὕδατός τε καὶ
τῶν τοιούτων πάντων, καὶ ζῴου σύμπαντ οσπέρι καὶ ἐν ψυχαῖς ἤθους, καὶ περὶ ποιήματα
καὶ παθήματα σύμπαντα (*Ep.* vii. 342 D).

or received, and the interpretative work of mind on this datum already inextricably complicated, a fact too readily ignored by the many promising young philosophers who treat the theory of knowledge simply as an affair of theorising about "sensa" and the relations between them.

In the third place, there is an important consequence which follows from this impossibility of making a quasi-chemical separation between a definite, exactly describable *given*, in respect of which we are simply receptive, and an equally definite and describable construction performed upon it, in respect of which we are active, and, it may be, wrongly active. The so-called authoritativeness, or infallibility, of sense is based wholly on the presence in it of the given and simply received. It will not cover anything which must be assigned to interpretation of the given, or construction on the basis of the given. And since we can never, as a fact, make an unambiguous separation, by reflective analysis, between one element in an experience which is all givenness, and a second which is all construction, the so-called "infallibility" of sense in respect of its proper sensible is never a sufficient guarantee that a specific experience involving sense is simply veridical. We *may* be mistaken when we appeal to any particular "sense-experience", for none of the experiences we call by the name is pure unalloyed receptivity of a *given*. In part, all are manufactured, and we can never say certainly and exactly *what* part has been manufactured.

It is true, as Locke used to say, that there is a difference between real life and a dream, between actually burning my hand and only dreaming that it is burned. But there is no certain criterion by which, in *a given* case, we can distinguish waking from dreaming, actual perception from imagination. A careful psychologist may accumulate a number of distinctions which commonly stand us in good stead, for example, the superior vividness of actual waking perception, its steadiness, its coherency. Yet, in a given case, we know that any, or all, may fail us. In general, "images" may have less vividness than the corresponding percepts; they may be incoherent, or may flicker in a way in which the percepts do not. Yet there is always a real difficulty in discriminating a distant and faintly heard noise, or a colour seen by a dim and flickering light, from a sound or colour which we have only imagined; again, it seems undeniable that a "pure hallucination" *sometimes* has all the intensity, the fullness of detail, the steadiness and persistency which are, as a rule, marks of a true perception of the physically real. It is always hazardous to tell a man that he has not really observed, but only imagined, what he claims to have observed, because his observation, if genuine, would upset an important and apparently well-accredited theory. If we allow awkward observations to be disposed of in this fashion, we are plainly taking a dangerous step towards the arrest of all progress in natural knowledge. Yet there are cases where the procedure would be justified, and we can lay down no rule for their detection. There is a meaning, and an important meaning, in the assertion that sensation is authoritative, and even, if you prefer the more emphatic word, in a way infallible, and yet it is also true that no "observation" can be guaranteed as beyond criticism and correction.

I do not mean only that an observation may prove to have been made with defective instruments, or in neglect of some condition which might conceivably have been relevant to the result observed. I mean, further, that when all possible precautions have been taken to exclude error arising from such causes, error, that is, due to definitely identifiable special misinterpretation, there is still a more insidious source of error. We talk of "reading off" a record made by our "instruments of precision", but in actual fact all "reading off" is itself inextricably mingled with interpretation because the very construction of the "instrument" itself involves and embodies interpretative theory; we never can be sure that we have successfully made ourselves the purely passive and recipient registers of "external fact". The use of a measuring-rod presupposes the previous selection of a whole system of geometrical postulates; the appeal to a chronometer involves a theory of the "flow of time". "Omnes perceptiones, *tam sensus quam mentis*, sunt ex analogia hominis, non ex analogia universi. Estque intellectus humanus instar speculi inaequalis ad radios rerum, qui suam naturam naturae rei immiscet."[1] Thus, though there could be no real knowledge of physical nature if we had not in sense, with its core of receptive passivity, an authoritative "control" of active speculation, we can never treat the particular "observation" as though it were all pure receptivity, and therefore absolutely infallible. It is not our *thinking* only that *recipit infusionem a voluntate et affectibus*.[2]

We may reasonably expect to meet with similar difficulties when we turn to examine our human knowledge of God, just because the *subiectum* which owns both kinds of knowledge is the historical human individual. Here also, if knowledge is to be more than personal

---

[1] *Novum Organum*, i. 40.

[2] *Ib.* i. 49. One might almost say that the "theory of Relativity" is no more than an illuminating comment on these two aphorisms. As an illustration of the source of difficulty I have here in mind, the reader may ask himself, carefully comparing Einstein, *Theory of Relativity* (E. tr.), pp. 53-4, with Eddington, *Nature of the Physical World*, p. 11, whether or not the "FitzGerald contraction" is a fact, and just what he means by his answer to that question. And cf. the whole of Eddington's essay "The Domain of Physical Science", in *Science, Religion, and Reality*, particularly pp. 209-18.

opinion (δόξα), there must be control of our personal
intellectual constructions by something which is not
constructed but *received*. Not only must we begin as
little children, if we would *enter* either the *regnum
hominis super naturam* or the kingdom of God, but
we must retain the submissiveness and docility of the
childlike mind all through our subsequent progress.
A true humility of soul in the presence of the given is as
much a condition of advance in natural knowledge as
it is of "growth in grace". The problem in both cases is
how to combine rightly two characters, both of which
are distinctive of gracious and unspoiled childhood,
humility and the spirit of fresh and fearless adventure,
τὸ πρᾷον and τὸ θυμοειδές, to speak with Plato; we
should, like the best and most attractive kind of boy, be
at once receptive and eager—receptive without servility
and eager without presumption and waywardness. The
combination will only be effected if we remember always
that there is, in the case of our knowledge of God also,
that which is simply received, not invented by ourselves, and is therefore, in its nature, simply authoritative, a genuine control on the wilfulness of our
individualism. It is not by "searching" that we find
out God. And it is clear what this control must be. It
must be the experience of rich, but confused, contact
with the supernatural which plays, in our knowledge of
God, the same part that immediate contact through
sense with a confused "other" does in our knowledge
of nature. The difference between the two cases is partly
that the contacts with the supernatural are at once
dimmer and richer than our contacts through sense
with the natural, partly that whereas contact with the
natural, being a necessity of physical existence, is
common to us all, and exhibits only moderate variations, except when there is definite bodily disease or

malformation, *impressive* and frequent contacts with the supernatural are given to the few, and there is a much wider range of variation in sensibility to them. It is not hard to find the human individual of "good normal" acuteness of sense-perception, and the divergences between the reports of such "normal" individuals on the same situation can be made negligible, or nearly so. In respect of natural eyesight, most men in health and the prime of vigour are beings with fairly "normal" delicacy of vision; the myopic or markedly astigmatic are a minority, sufferers from serious ophthalmic disease a smaller, and the downright blind a still smaller, minority. But in the matter of spiritual vision not a few of us are perhaps the born blind, the vast majority are myopic; the clear-sighted are the very few. Clear-eyed spiritual vision seems to be at least as rare as penetrating mathematical insight or exquisite musical sensibility.

Hence, while we rightly take as the authority to which we must, in the end, defer in questions of natural fact the perceptions of the "normal" man, exercised under carefully prearranged conditions of observation, in questions about facts of the supernatural order we cannot similarly make our authority the "common", or "average" man. It is as though the great majority of a certain population were markedly short-sighted, or colour-blind, and were therefore forced to take as authoritative the visual perceptions of the few who stood out as exceptionally free from those defects—a case which would presumably actually occur if there were a group of human beings who had become, by past "adaptation" to a special environment, generally colour-blind, or myopic.[1] In such a kingdom of the

---

[1] Cf. the famous parable of the cave-dwellers at the opening of the 7th book of Plato's *Republic*, 514 A ff.

blind, the one-eyed would actually be king. And, in fact, we do act on this principle in the closely analogous case of aesthetic perception. We do begin by trusting the authority of the few of exceptionally keen perceptivity, *e.g.* in music, on the question whether a composition has beauties to be found in it, and what those beauties are, and it is only by our initial submissiveness to their authority that we come, if we do come, to acquire ability to perceive for ourselves. Even so, none but the few among us ever come to perceive for ourselves independently more than a part—in my own case, alas, how small a part!—of what the more favoured few perceive, though we are content to believe that much which we shall never learn to discern is really there, because the few agree in assuring us that it is so. We have found that we perceive the more clearly for having believed them, and therefore we continue to believe their assurances, even where we never expect to be able to see directly for ourselves. In the same way, it is reasonable to recognise that if a great religious tradition has ennobled and purified human life, over a wide range of space and time and circumstance, by bringing the supernatural down into it, and is actually, so far as we have been able to assimilate its content, doing the same thing for our own lives, what has been intensely perceived and lived by the chosen spirits who have shaped the tradition, even where we have not been personally able to assimilate it and build it into the substance of our own lives, is no mere "subjective" illusion, but embodies real apprehension of a real supernatural.

But the point on which I am personally most concerned to insist is a different one. It is that in immediate apprehension of the supernatural, as in immediate apprehension of the natural, we are dealing with concrete, individual, historical, experiences which resist complete intellectual analysis, at the same time that they demand it. In both cases, no man can communicate what he sees in its totality and individuality. Any attempt at communication involves rationalisation and analysis, at least in an unconscious form, and communication, in consequence, brings with it loss and gain together. In the effort to say what one sees there is always an intellectual concentration which makes it clearer to the beholder himself what certain central features of the *chose vue* are. This is why a prudent man distrusts "impressions" of which he cannot "give clear account" to another; and, again, why it is a good rule never to be satisfied with one's own proof of a proposition unless one can "set it down in black and white on paper". But the central features of the *chose vue* are always in fact given in a setting of *penumbra* or marginal vision, and this setting falls more or less completely outside the range of that which can be imparted by communication. No one can answer the simple question, "What do you see at this moment?" in a way which will convey "the truth, the whole truth, and nothing but the truth". The thing simply cannot be done, even if the statement is being made to a second person with vision as perfect as the speaker's;[1] much less, if the second person is lamentably colour-blind. It follows that it is with perception of the supernatural as it is with perception of the natural; it is impossible to make an unambiguous presentation of the actually given and the reflective interpretation of the given in separation from one another. In every attempt to communicate the content of the experience there is inevitably an accompaniment of interpretation, and therefore of construction, even if the construction amounts to no more than the negative

---

[1] At least the answer would have to be "much what you **see** yourself", and this is an evasion of the difficulty.

omission of the "marginal", and it is never possible to say with precision *how much* is construction. (Even if the construction is no more than a leaving out of the "marginal", you cannot say just what and how much you have left out; if this could be done, the "marginal" would have ceased to be marginal.) And, as in the case of sensation, so in the case of contact with the supernatural, the reality and authoritativeness of the given as given does not guarantee the infallibility of the individual declarations based upon immediate contact.

It seems to me, then, that the rightful demand of the intellect for individual freedom to think sincerely and fearlessly, and the equally rightful demand of religion for objectivity and protection against the vagaries of pure subjectivity, can only be harmonised in one way, through the cultivation, by all parties who are concerned that human life shall be the prey neither of worldliness nor of superstition, of the two complementary qualities of docility and adventurousness. In the past untold mischief has been wrought by their separation. The *ecclesia docens,* the official body of teachers in the religious community, has often shown a high degree of adventurousness in its bold formulations of articles of faith, or other propositions claiming to embody the content of what is authoritative; from the rest of the community it has demanded unqualified submissiveness. Or, in the reaction against this demand, individual thinkers have denied the right of authority, reposed in any external body, to exercise any control over, or receive any deference from, the solitary mental adventurer. Indeed, not so long ago, there seemed to be, at least in Western Europe, a still more complete inversion of the parts played for so many centuries by the *ecclesia docens* and the individual. We have witnessed something hardly to be distinguished from a

claim on the part of self-constituted representatives of
the secular sciences to be the sovereign authority which
dictates but does not obey, while official theologians
have, in large numbers, been almost comically anxious
to show their docility by accepting almost any speculation put before the British Association by a Professor,
or a Fellow of the Royal Society, or communicated to
the newspapers by a medical man of any notoriety,
as the latest deliverance of an infallible authority, to
which religion must at once conform itself, at its peril.
Neither the ends of pure religion, nor the purposes of
sound science are well served by these attempts to make
authoritarian dictation the duty, or privilege, of one
set of men and teachable humility that of another. No
man will be either a true saint or a man of the right
scientific temper who does not know how to be at once
docile and adventurous in his own personal thinking.

This fairly obvious truth has very important bearings on the duties of those whose office it is to be, for
their time, the representatives of authority in the religious community. It is inevitable that, for the necessary purpose of avoiding pure anarchy in thought and
consequent anarchy in practice, there should be somewhere in the community a body thus charged with the
duty of safeguarding the foundations of its life. The
whole *raison d'être* of the religious community as such
depends upon its possession of a genuine disclosure
of the supernatural, too precious for human life to be
surrendered at any man's bidding. But where there is
not a true and deep docility of spirit in these official
custodians of the "deposit", there is certain to be, along
with rightful jealousy for the real spiritual treasure of
the community, a great deal of unreasonable jealousy
of surrendering, or even modifying, much in the existing tradition which is mere temporary incrustation upon

the true jewel. The motives for this conservatism in authorities need not always be, and most often, perhaps, are not chiefly the more discreditable ones of lust of dominion, or professional *esprit de corps*, though a "man in authority" does well to be vigilantly on his guard against the unsuspected presence of both in himself. But the excellence of the motives in no case removes the mischievousness of their effects. If one age, from the worthiest motives, persists in defending the indefensible, the next is likely to see a panic surrender of the indispensable.

Now the danger to the spirit of religion itself from an improper exercise of authority is not sufficiently guarded against by merely drawing such distinctions and marking such limitations as have already been recognised by even rigidly authoritarian religious communities. It is true that even when the claims of an infallible authority—Pope, Councils, Bible—have been most insisted upon, it has been customary, in theory at least, to admit a whole mass of such limitations. Thus there has always been some sort of recognised distinction made between the primary and indefeasible authority of the official person, or persons, as custodians of the truth and a second and temporary authority of a purely executive or administrative kind to determine what, in view of existing conditions, may be taught or practised with the consent of the community, and I suppose it would be pretty generally conceded that actual repositaries of authority have not infrequently misused their position by confusing the two different kinds of authority. If, for example, in the too famous case of Galileo, it had simply been decided that, at the existing juncture, the Church must not be distracted by the teaching of Copernicanism as a definitely established truth, there would, I take it, have been no serious

reason to complain of the decision; the scandal arose
from the presumptuous declaration of the Cardinals
Inquisitors that Copernicanism is *false*.[1] So, again,
it has generally been held by the supporters of an
infallible authority that the range of its infallibility is
circumscribed; authority is only infallible in matters of
"faith and morals". And, once more, even within this
domain itself, a distinction has been taken between the
express words of an authoritative deliverance itself and
the explanations given of them, or the inferences drawn
from them, by individual theologians, which are said
to be authoritative only in the sense that they deserve
a respect based on the eminence of the expositor in his
own speciality. Unfortunately, in practice Popes and
Councils determine for themselves what questions are
questions of faith and morals. Where the authority
recognised is the text of a written Scripture, either the
determination of this point is left with some group of
divines who happen to be prominent and influential, or,
as in societies of "Fundamentalist" views, the text of
Scripture is taken indiscriminately as equally authoritative in all spheres whatsoever. What is really needed,
if there is to be no faltering of specifically religious life
and thought, as well as no dictation by theologians,
acting in the supposed interests of religion, to natural
and historical inquiries, is, I suggest, the making of a
distinction between authority and inerrancy, and the
recognition on all sides that the claim to rightful authority is not a claim to inerrancy.[2]

[1] Of course there was a further issue, viz. how far any decisions of the Inquisition are binding outside the Pope's dominions. Were the Universities of France
in any way bound to respect such a decision? But this is a wholly secondary
matter.

[2] Cf. the distinction always felt by the Romans, from whom we have borrowed
the very word *authority*, between the *imperium* of the consul, or praetor, and
the *auctoritas* of the senate. As W. G. de Burgh says (*Legacy of the Ancient
World*, p. 191 n. 1), "*auctoritas* means 'moral influence'; the English word 'authority' in the sense of executive power would be expressed in Latin by *imperium*

The justification of this distinction has already been provided by what we have said of the impossibility of making any intelligible statement, whether about the natural or the supernatural, which shall have as its content the simply objective and given, with no element whatever of the subjective and constructed. It is worth while to reflect that even the unique authority ascribed by orthodox Christianity to Our Lord, as the man in whom humanity and deity, nature and supernature, the temporal and the eternal, are in perfect interpenetration, does not seem to affect the application of this distinction to the authoritatively enunciated doctrines of the Christian religion. From the Christian conception of the person of Christ it follows, no doubt, that the spiritual vision of the one man Jesus Christ, unlike that of any other of our race, must be thought of as adequate, never obscured by wilfulness, self-centredness, consciousness of alienation from the divine. But we have also to remember that equally, according to the conception of orthodox Christianity, Christ is no *Mischwesen*, not something more than human but less than divine, like the daemons and heroes of Hellenic fancy, but at once truly divine, and no less truly and utterly human. Both the soul and body of Christ are held to be, in the fullest sense of the word, "creatures"; the historical, human experience of Christ is thus a creaturely experience, though an absolutely unique creaturely experience, of the divine; hence the strictest traditional orthodoxy has found itself confronted with the problem of the limitation of the human knowledge of the incarnate Christ, a problem raised from the first by the simple statement of an Evangelist that, as he advanced from childhood to manhood, he "grew in wisdom and

or *potestas*". What some of us find amiss in the attitude of "authoritarian" divines is precisely that they seem to us to confuse *auctoritas* with *imperium*.

grace with God and man",[1] by the record of his frank
admission of ignorance of the day and hour of the final
triumph of the divine purpose,[2] and still more impressively by the narrative of his devastating experience
of sheer dereliction at the crisis of his history, the
prayer of passionate prostration in the garden, and the
dying quotation from the most heart-broken of the
Psalms. It is only the creaturely that can pray, and when
a Christian speaks of the adequacy of the Lord's
human experience of the supernatural, he must not, I
take it, forget that the adequacy meant is still relative
to the conditions of creatureliness inseparable from
genuine humanity. The human experience even of a
humanity "personally united with the Word", being
human, is still temporal experience of the supra-temporal, and of it, too, it must hold true that *quidquid
recipitur, recipitur ad modum recipientis*. If it were not
so, Christian theology would have had no obstinate
Christological problem to wrestle with.

It is hardly necessary to recur again in this connection to the point already dealt with earlier, that in dealing with the recorded utterances of the historical Christ,
even if we could be sure of their actual words, we have
to allow for qualification of the received by the very real
limitations of the recipients to whom the utterances were
addressed, and of those for whose immediate benefit
they repeated them. But we must add, finally, that before
a doctrine, however derived, becomes a defined *dogma*,
a formula approved by the community or its representatives, there is still a further stage of more conscious reflection, regularly attended by prolonged, and
often prejudiced and inflamed, discussion and debate;
there are also always, or nearly always, the dissentients
who, at most, silently acquiesce in the formula finally

---

[1] *Luke* ii. 52.   [2] *Matthew* xxiv. 36; *Mark* xiii. 32.

adopted for the sake of peace because adoption is the alternative which "divides least", and even among those whose acceptance means more than this acquiescence to avoid strife, verbal agreement often covers a wide divergence of interpretation. On all these grounds it seems a dangerous confusion to treat a rightful claim to authority as if it could ensure the formal infallibility of a dogmatic formula. The permanence of truth, I hold, is perfectly compatible with the transience of the precise formulae in which we try to give truth its expression.

We are all, I hope, alive to the reality of this distinction in the realm of natural knowledge. There we rightly revere the authority of the great names: we regard the Galileos and Newtons as having really made imperishable additions to our stock of apprehended objective truth, additions which will never have to be simply removed or dismissed as subjective fancies, but we do not dream of declaring that the formulae in which they gave expression to their truth are lifted once and for all above all possibility of modification. There seems to be no sufficient reason why the same distinction between authority and inerrancy should not be quite frankly recognised in connection with the theologian's attempts to formulate human knowledge about God. If it were recognised, we might look for a double advantage. We might fairly expect the candid lovers of science to lose their natural, but unfortunate, prejudice against theology, as they came to realise that the kind of authority claimed for himself by the theologian is, in principle, the same sort of authority with which they are familiar, and to which they properly attach weight, in their own sphere. With the clear distinction between authority and inerrancy once before them, it would become increasingly apparent that what the theologian is really asserting as the foundation of his claims is simply the reality and autonomy of experiences of contact with God as a genuine feature of human life, and the legitimacy of co-ordinating the contents of such experiences into a coherent system by trusting the testimony of those in whom it is richest and most pronounced. There are many signs in the present attitude of outstanding leaders in natural knowledge to the great religions that a claim of this kind would be understood and respected, if it were not supposed to carry with it the further claim of some specific man, or body of men, to decree the truth of anything they please, without condescending to any account of the why and wherefore. If the official custodians of religion would but cultivate the virtue of wise docility, the gain would not be only to their own characters and reputation. Theology itself, I believe, would once more win a more general recognition as a true science, and we should be delivered, to our great spiritual and moral profit, from the ruinous compromise which makes over the whole field of real knowledge to the various branches of secular study, and reduces religion to a mere affair of elegant but meaningless emotionalism, our latest method of honouring God with our lips while our hearts are far from Him. Unfeigned docility in the representatives of theological authority would have as one consequence a salutary advance, on the part of philosophers and men of science, from religiosity to religion.

And, moreover, such an advance would carry with it also an increased inward respect, from the scientific side, for the positive doctrines and even the dogmatic formulae of the great religions. When the claim to authority had been put on its true basis, appeal to a spiritual insight and experience which have proved their power to sustain a definite and unique type of life of supreme value, it would no longer be possible to

regard the agelong systematic reflection on the principles underlying and regulating that life embodied in
the dogmas of great theologies, and the expositions of
them by great theologians, as mere intellectual curi-
osities which stand in no vital connection with the
realities of spiritual experience, and may, without loss
to our personality, be relegated to a museum of obsolete
fashions. It would be increasingly understood that
where there is a genuine *given* for the intellect to work
on, the fruits of generations of continuous elaboration
of the *given* by those whose aptitudes make them specially at home in the field are never to be lightly set aside
as having exhausted their significance.

We know how, a century ago, this sort of treatment
was meted out to the great constructive philosophies
of the past; the thought of Plato, of Aristotle, of Descartes, was treated as a curious, but mainly wrong-
headed, divagation of the human intellect with no significance for the direction of the modern mind, which
would, in fact, best prepare itself for its own conquer-
ing advance by freeing itself once and for all of all this
antiquated lumber. We all know, also, how within less
than a century, the quickening of interest in the great
philosophical systems has not only made the history of
philosophy and science a living subject, but has also
helped to provide some of the most modern and "progressive" of our scientific and philosophical thinkers
with significant "direction-cosines" for their own work
and their own specific problems. Even in my own
youthful days, most of my teachers would have said
that at any rate the physical speculations of Plato,
Aristotle, Descartes, were things simply dead, mere
monuments of perverse and wasted mental ingenuity.
To-day we see Professor Whitehead, in one work,[1]

[1] *The Concept of Nature.*

consciously and avowedly going back to the *Timaeus*; and in another,[1] less consciously perhaps, but none the less really, to the *Physics* of Aristotle for the foundations of a singularly fresh and living and eminently "modern" doctrine of the principles of natural knowledge; and Mr. Meyerson[2] throwing a new and brilliant light on the tendency and the logic of the "theory of relativity" by exhibiting it as the unforeseen outcome of the conception laid down in its great outlines in Descartes' *Principia*, as, in fact, the fulfilment, in an unexpected form, of the Cartesian demand for the geometrising of physics. If, to our own grave intellectual detriment, we have so long missed the light we might have drawn from thought wrongly supposed to have lost its vitality, one cause which excuses, though it does not justify, our error has been, as we all know, the way in which earlier generations had converted the authority attaching to the doctrines of great men into something like a formal inerrancy of their dicta. Now that, as we may hope, this reaction has fairly spent itself, it is not too much to say that the *authority* of great thinkers, like those I have named, has once more become real to us, just because we no longer confound it with this formal inerrancy. Because we do not treat their utterances, still less the official pronouncements of members of their "schools", or the explanations of their commentators, as verbally infallible, we do not need to understand their teaching in a forced and unnatural sense, or to explain it away into truisms, in order to safeguard their words against all modification. This sets us free to look for their real meaning with a reasonable conviction that even when their express statements can be seen to require most modification, they

---

[1] *Science and the Modern World.*
[2] In *La Déduction relativiste*, pp. 135 ff., 267 ff.

mean something which has real and permanent significance. We appreciate their authority better because
we do not mistake it for a mechanical inerrancy. When
there is no longer danger that the same mistake will be
made about "authority" in the theological sphere, we
may look to see the real significance and authority of
the great theologies regain the same kind of general
recognition.

It will, no doubt, be said that the suggested analogy
between authority in the domain of theology and
authority in philosophy or science is misleading, since
the claim made by every theology of revelation is that
it has behind it the *absolute* authority of God, whereas
the authorities in other fields are avowedly no more
than human. But I do not think that this historically
famous distinction can really be maintained as ultimate.
So far as it exists, it is a difference in degree rather than
in kind. On the one side, we must remember what has
been already said about the way in which both actual
contact with the supernatural and the communication
to others of the disclosures made in such contacts
are conditioned by the inherent creatureliness of the
recipients. On the other, when we speak of the purely
"human" character of philosophical and scientific
authority, we must not forget that, according to the
authors of the very distinction we are discussing, supernature and nature have the same source. It is the same
God who discloses Himself, at different levels, through
the order of nature, through prophets charged with a
special message, through a Son who is the "express
image" of His person. In all three cases we have a
contact with the supreme source of actuality and value,
mediated by a contact with something or someone
historical and temporal. The mediation may be more
or less remote, and the type of life it sustains correspond-

ingly poorer or richer, merely natural, simply human
and ethical, or vividly supernatural. The content of the
disclosures may be as loosely connected with the occasion by which it is afforded as a scientific law with the
particular incidents which set its discoverer on the track
of his discovery,[1] or as closely bound up with it as the
doctrine of the great prophets with the special spiritual
experience through which it has been won and without
which it would lose the best part of its meaning. But in
all cases alike, in different ways, the same fundamental
type of situation recurs. There is an element of the
wholly given and trans-subjective which is *absolutely*
authoritative, has unquestionable right to control our
thinking or acting, just because it is so utterly given
to us, not made by us; also in any communicable expression of the experience, there is the other element of
construction, always relative to the mental habits, or
rather to the whole physical and mental condition, of
the experient at the specific moment of experience, and
so always, to an unknown extent, infected with "subjectivity". It is the presence, in however subordinate
a form, of this second factor which seems to make it
impossible to equate authority with inerrancy. Whenever, in nature or supernature, we are face to face with
objectivity not to be explained away, God is speaking,
but whether God speaks through the processes of
nature, through a specific message brought by a specific
messenger, or through a unique human life as a whole,[2]
the communications, of very different worth and depth,

---

[1] Cf. the disputes on the question whether an incident of the year 1665 connected with an apple had or had not anything to do with the genesis of Newton's
planetary theory.

[2] "The work of our redemption was an intire work, and all that Christ said,
or did, or suffered, concurred to our salvation, as well his mothers swathing him
in little clouts, as Josephs shrowding him in a funerall sheete; as well his cold lying
in the Manger, as his cold dying upon the Crosse" (Donne, *Sermon for Christmas
Day*, 1625). It would be relevant to meditate upon the implications of this.

coming to us in these different ways, all come through a channel which is creaturely, and none of them ever wholly loses all marks of the creaturehood of the channel.

Perhaps the reality and worth of an authority which, for all its reality, is not the same thing as a formal inerrancy, is most readily illustrated from the sphere of the moral life, a life which is more than merely natural and yet not fully and consciously supernatural. How impossible to maintain the inerrancy of a man's conscience, and yet how necessary to any serious morality to insist upon its authority, and even its absolute authority! Kant, it is true, if he is to be tied down to the letter of his teaching, appears to confound the authority of conscience with a formal inerrancy. In his anxiety not to weaken the sense of obligation in man he actually maintains that an honestly mistaken judgement on the morality of an act I am contemplating is impossible; "an erring conscience is a *Chimaera*"[1] an imaginary danger not to be met with in the real world. But Kant only takes himself in by this pronouncement because he has first made a false simplification of the typical situation in which we "consult conscience" about a course of action. The only "conscientious difficulty" he contemplates is that of the man who knows quite well that what he is proposing to do is a violation of positive moral law, but is looking for some plausible "colour" for the transgression. Had he considered the kind of decision which is really critical, choice between alternative lines of conduct where there is no traditional rule to afford any guidance, and the whole responsibility of deciding right or wrong thus actually falls on the individual conscience, the decision, for

---

[1] *Werke* (Hartenstein[2]), iv. 251, vii. 204 (where an erring conscience is expressly called an *Unding*, the word rendered in our text *Chimaera*).

example, to accept or refuse an offered post, to make or
not to make a proposal of marriage, he must have seen
the extravagance of maintaining either that in every
such case we pronounce one alternative right and the
other wrong, or that when we do with difficulty arrive
at such a pronouncement, its honesty is sufficient guarantee of its correctness. Yet when the pronouncement
has been arrived at, in any case, it is authoritative, and
even absolutely authoritative, for the person who has
reached it. I know that my conscience is not inerrant,
but the knowledge does not excuse disobedience. When
we are once clearly awake to the relative extreme in-
frequency in our actual moral life of uncertainties of
the kind Kant selects for sole consideration, uncertainties whether we are morally at liberty to break a
generally sound moral rule, we may perhaps be tempted
to say that an erring conscience, so far from being an
imaginary "bogey", is an ever-potent source of moral
mistake. When we have to make up our minds to a
really critical choice, is not our *maximum* of conviction
represented by language like that of the Prince in
R. L. Stevenson's story, when he throws the Rajah's
diamond into the river, "God forgive me if I am
doing wrong, but this is what I mean to do?"

Most moralists, after all, have admitted that an
erring conscience is only too common in actual life,
but have not held that the possibility that my conscience may be in error diminishes my obligation to
follow it. St. Thomas, for example, is as convinced
that an erroneous conscience absolutely obliges as he is
that it does not relieve from responsibility.[1] Hutcheson
is teaching the same doctrine of an authority which
is absolute, though not formally inerrant, when he
distinguishes between the *material* goodness of the act

[1] *S.T.* i.ª ii.ᵃᵉ q. 19, art. 5, 6; cf. *ib.* q. 76, art. 3.

which is in fact demanded by the situation and the *formal* goodness of the act which the agent honestly believes to be demanded;[1] so is Henry Sidgwick,[2] in different language, when he says that conscientiousness, though not a sufficient, is always a necessary, condition of virtuous action. The *opinio melior* among moralists is unmistakably that conscience may, and sometimes does, err, but that this want of complete inerrancy does not affect its authority. The light it gives is not always that of the sun at noonday, and may at times be as fitful as that of a taper in a dark night, but it *is* light, and is all the light I have. I could wish always to have the sun, but if the brightest light I can get is that of the taper, I must guide myself by it. In other words, conscience, when it speaks, is authoritative and, if you like, absolutely authoritative, but its authority is not inerrancy. Even Butler, the great classical moralist of the doctrine of the unqualified authoritativeness of conscience, never, so far as I can remember, credits the "principle of reflex approbation" with simple inerrancy.[3]

Next observe that the drawing of this formal distinction between the *authority* of conscience and inerrancy does not imply that all consciences are equally liable to err in all matters. How far my conscience can in practice be treated as secure against the danger of error will depend on many things: on the questions, for example, whether I am a callow youth, with all the inability of the young to see the full bearings of a confused and complex moral situation and to fix on those

---

[1] Though, to be strictly accurate, Hutcheson expresses himself rather differently about formal goodness; an act is formally good "when it flows from good affection in a just proportion" (*System of Moral Philosophy*, i. 252).

[2] *Methods of Ethics*, bk. iii. c. 1.

[3] Though he does regard its possible "aberrations" as confined within a narrow range (*Sermon* ii. par. 2, iii. pars. 5, 6).

which are most truly relevant, or a man made clear-sighted by experience of life; whether I have made it my practice to reflect on moral issues and to wait for the determination of conscience before committing myself, or have habitually allowed myself to act on headlong first impressions; whether the issue on which I have now to pronounce is, in its general character, of a type which experience of the situations presented by life has made familiar to me, or is, to me, unprecedented; whether I am facing a choice to be made by myself, or trying to give sound advice to another, and the like. Yet our moral experience may fairly be said to show that the surest way to get a more clearly illuminated conscience is to be steadily loyal to the light one already has, partly within one's self, partly in the practice and the counsel of those whom one discerns, by the light one possesses, to be better and wiser than one's self. A caterpillar, says James Ward,[1] eats to fill its skin, but in doing so it gets a better skin to fill. Even so, by loyalty to the conscience one has—if we carefully remember that amenability to the admonition of those whom that conscience reveals as one's betters is a point of this very loyalty—one gets a better conscience to be loyal to. The one *certain* way to miss getting a better conscience is to treat the conscience one has as less than absolutely authoritative, by living at random, or by handing over the direction of one's conduct blindly to another. The more loyally one thus follows conscience, the more assured and delicate do one's own personal discriminations between right and wrong become, and the more surely does one also learn who are the "others" who really stand out, in virtue of their moral insight, as guides whose help may be most safely relied on. There is thus nothing very paradoxical in a remark, made somewhere by Bosan-

[1] *Psychological Principles*, p. 268.

quet, that a man of habitual loyalty to conscience may, with sufficient experience of the situations of life, reach something not very different from infallibility of moral judgement, *for himself and his own personal choices*.

If, further, we find that, throughout a great historical civilisation in which our own life forms an integral part, and which has the prospect of indefinite further extension from age to age, and race to race, the deliverances of conscience, as interpreted by those who are most delicately sensitive to them and listen most loyally for them, steadily tend to integrate themselves into a coherent system, covering the whole sphere of human action and pervaded by definite principles, we may fairly say that in such a moral tradition we have, not indeed as yet fully given, but as in process of being given, a truly objective morality which is not only of obligation and authoritative for man as man, but guaranteed in all its essentials against error, a morality which is an adequate basis for an ethical *science* at least as assured and certain as the most indubitably scientific of physical sciences. I do not myself see why we might not entertain the same hopes for the future of theology as a genuine, assured, and yet progressive *science* of God, if once the claim for authority could be disassociated from the very different claim of formal inerrancy for the precise words of statements made in the past, or to be made in the future, under certain strictly defined "standard" conditions. "Dead" authority and "living" experience are sometimes talked of as if they formed a natural and irresoluble antithesis, but the two are only antithetic when the authority is conceived of as dead and sterotyped.

"I should not believe in the Gospel", says Augustine, *nisi me catholicae ecclesiae commoveret auctoritas*, "were

I not constrained by the authority of the Church universal".[1] Had Augustine meant by the *auctoritas ecclesiae catholicae*, as has sometimes been meant by the words, a formal order issued by ecclesiastical officials, it might be said that he is committing the circle of crediting the inerrancy of officials on the strength of passages in the very Gospel which he professes to receive only because it is vouched for by the inerrant officials. But the thought permits of a very different interpretation. The *auctoritas* of the Church universal is not dead and canalised, but intensely alive. It is the weight attaching to the undeniable reality of a new and vivid experience which transforms life. In the life actually lived by the members of the Christian community there is a unique dominant quality, and it is historical fact that the source of this new life is, by the consenting utterances of all generations of the community in which it is manifested, a new relation to the supernatural, mediated through the human personality of which the Gospel narrative is the record. Understood so, the "catholic" appeal to the authority of the Church as a ground for belief is not opposed to the familiar "evangelical" appeal to the personal experiences of the individual. Both are forms of the appeal to a direct and personal experience, but when the experiences thus appealed to are those of the whole community throughout its existence, the impressiveness of the argument is immeasurably increased. The testimony of one man to the source of his own changed life, if it stood alone, might easily be discredited. He may be thought to have wrongly found the genuine

---

[1] *Contra Epist. Manichaei*, v. 6. The context is to this effect. How is the claim of Mani to be an apostle of Jesus Christ to be defended against one who denies it? It is suggested that the Manichaeans may appeal to passages in the text of the Gospels. Augustine replies, "I only accept the Gospel because it comes to me with the *auctoritas* of the Church behind it. But it is the same Church which denies the apostolic mission of Mani. Its *auctoritas* is valid to substantiate both positions or neither."

source of the change in someone or something only
incidentally connected with it. Or that which has really
been mediated to him through one channel may be
equally capable of being mediated with the same success to a second man through another, just as some
other work than Chapman's Homer may do for another youth of poetic genius what Chapman's book did
for Keats. The concurrent testimony of generations of
a community with members from every "people and
nation and kindred and tongue" is a different matter.
It is not in the nature of things that the whole of such
a community should be under a standing collective
hallucination, either as to the reality of the special
quality of its life, or as to its source.

You cannot explain away the entrance of a new
spiritual life into the world through Christ as a consequence of " Jewish apocalyptic" ferment in the Pales-
tine of the first century, for the *ecclesia catholica* embraces Greek and Scythian as well as Jew, and its history covers many generations; yet you find it bringing
the same specific new quality into men's lives, where-
ever and whenever it comes into contact with them.
So, again, you cannot account for "conversion" to the
life of the *ecclesia catholica* as a psychological accompaniment of the attainment of puberty, a by-product of
sexual development, for the "converted" are not all
adolescents: some are children, some men and women
in the prime of life, some in advanced age, and it is the
same new quality which the "conversion" brings into
the lives of them all. The "catholicity" of the community is precisely that which gives the driving force to
the appeal to its authority, for what it means is that since
the community does not belong to one sex, or one period
of life, or one special age, or place, or national or social
tradition, there can be no explaining away of its experi-

ence as illusory, unless one is prepared to believe in the recurrence of the same identical illusion, with the same identical *dominus Christus* as its centre, in all places, at all times, and in spite of all variations in individual and social endowment and tradition. The wider one spreads one's net the more "universal" the *ecclesia* which exhibits the common experience, the more incredible that it should be under an illusion about the genuineness of this experience, or the source of it. A scepticism which sees "collective illusion" here cannot well see anything else in any conviction of humanity, and if all our convictions may be an illusion, the very meaning of the distinction between truth and illusion is lost. That, I take it, is what is really meant by the *auctoritas* of the Church universal, and there could be no better illustration of an authority wholly independent of the claim of any set of officials to a formal inerrancy. And this is precisely why, with all respect for the "great church" of the West, I cannot but think that the attempt to locate the "seat of authority" in a specific official, or group of officials, is on a level with the attempts of some political theorists to localise "sovereignty" in the same fashion within the body politic and of some psycho-physicists to localise "the mind" in some delimited region of the nervous system.

VI

INSTITUTIONALISM

πάντα δὲ εὐσχημόνως καὶ κατὰ τάξιν γινέσθω.—I Cor. xiv. 40.

To the type of man who is bent, before all things, on doing his thinking for himself, the great stumbling-block in the historical religions is, no doubt, that authoritarianism of which we have been speaking. Such a man, as Newman says of himself, can no more think to order than he can see with another's eyes, or breathe with another's lungs. But most men probably do not seriously resent authority in matters of belief as such; they are only too ready to have their thinking done for them in advance by others. If they reject the dictates of one "authority", it is usually only to surrender themselves to another. The mentally indolent—and we are all mentally indolent in many things—must have a pillow for their heads; if they throw away St. Paul or Calvin, it is only to repose on Karl Marx or Bernard Shaw. Less deep, but more widely diffused, is the resentment aroused by the tendency, shown by all the great historical religions, to evolve an elaborate system of ritual and ceremonial words and acts, and more particularly to develop *mysteries*, or *sacraments*, in which material objects and external acts terminating on them are treated as channels through which a specially rich and direct contact is made with a supernatural spiritual reality. The history of any great positive religion abundantly illustrates both the universality and depth of this tendency to ceremonialism and the persistency of the opposition it evokes.

Thus it would be hard to imagine anything much simpler, more spontaneous, less formal than the worship of the early Christian congregations, as known to us from the New Testament, the Apostolic Fathers, and the first apologists, or more complex, conventionalised, and artificial than the systems which have grown out of those beginnings and still regulate the practice of the great majority of Christians. In the former the element of freedom and spontaneity of approach to the divine is at a *maximum*, that of artifice at a *minimum*; within a framework of the simplest, all detail is left to free improvisation. In the latter there is a fixed rule for almost everything—the words to be said, the tones in which they are to be uttered, the gestures to be made, the postures and garments of the officiants, the precise fashion of all sorts of accessories. Simplicity seems to have given place everywhere to rather cumbrous complexity, nature to artifice, spontaneity to rigid traditional formula. And the curious thing is that, after every reaction towards simplification, the same development seems regularly to begin again. The "reform" which started as a "return to nature" commonly ends in the adoption of a new conventional ceremonial, often less complex and usually less aesthetically rich than the old, but equally rigid and as little spontaneous. Thus, among ourselves, I suppose, we should expect to find spontaneity and freedom from fixed ceremonial form in the Salvation Army, if it is to be found anywhere. Yet I well remember being present years ago at a great "rally" of that body and receiving a very strong impression that in the "knee-drill", "volley-firing", and handkerchief-waving executed to order, I was witnessing the initial stages in the growth of a new ritual, cruder and noisier than those with a longer history, but no less truly artificial and conventional. (Whether the growth has resulted in further development to-day, I regret that I cannot state.)

It is a mistake to confuse this tendency of the historical religions to conventional ceremonial and ritual with a mere movement towards display, pomp, or materialistic splendour. Ritual, as such, is neither beautiful, nor pompous, nor glowing; it may be bald, ugly, drab, without ceasing to be ritual. There is nothing glowing or pompous about the Gregorian "modes"; the bands and Geneva gown of a Presbyterian minister, the garb of a Captain in the Salvation Army, are just as much ritualistic or ceremonial vestments, in the proper sense of the word, as alb or chasuble, since all are alike the conventional "uniform" appropriated to persons set apart to discharge specific functions. Ritualism, reduced to its simplest elements, is just the tendency to confine the expression of a specific human activity to one artificial form prescribed by convention; the antithesis to it is not simplicity, or baldness, but free spontaneity, permission granted to the activity of the moment to find its expression for itself unhampered by precedent, convention, or custom.

Both the tendency to ceremonial, or ritual, and the revolt against it are universal features of human life, present in many spheres besides that of worship. The difficulty, indeed, would be to find any human activity in connection with which both tendencies do not make themselves felt. Every human social activity inevitably tends to develop its own conventions, and so to create a ritual for itself. There is a recognised ritual of the breakfast-table, the dinner-table, the drawing-room, embodied in the rules which we speak of sometimes as those of etiquette, sometimes as those of civilised manners. Whenever we have intercourse of any kind with our fellows, there are always ways in which things are done and other ways in which they are not done, rules of mannerly behaviour to be adhered to, whether we are personally disposed to follow them or not. We all know that careless infraction of the rules, disregard of all the "conventions", is commonly the beginning of that neglect of the "decencies of civilised life" which, surrendered to, means relapse into "barbarism", loss, in great measure, of the rational man's command over himself and his moods. We can understand well enough what Mr. Belloc means when, in one of his stories,[1] he speaks of a man assailed by mortal illness as preserved from the complete collapse of his manhood by "habit, or ritual, the mistress of men sane". Nor do we hesitate to condemn, as at least an early symptom of what may grow by neglect to be a serious moral disorder, needless or wilful departure, when there is no adequate reason, from the conventionally fixed way of conducting ourselves, even though we may be able to give no further ground for conformity than that the established way is established.

That the members of a family, for example, should ask after one another's health, or greet one another with a kiss when they reassemble daily in the breakfast-room is, in itself, only a piece of conventionalism, a bit of ritual. But we know that disregard of the convention only too readily leads to a real preoccupation with self and a dulling of one's concern for the other members of the family group. The habit of answering letters when possible, within twenty-four hours of their arrival, is a ritual which it is often a little "costing" to practice, and of no great moment to neglect, but—I speak with shame as an offender in this matter—refusal

---

[1] *Emmanuel Burden,* c. 12.

to have some rule of the kind, and to keep to it always, means that our "unconventionality" will, sooner or later, cause serious detriment to our own, or our correspondents', interests. A rule of conversation, like that which forbids a well-bred man to gesticulate, or raise his voice, in the drawing-room when he feels justifiably excited or aggrieved, is never more necessary than at the moments when observance of it is hardest. We need an artificial barrier as a protection against the very real moral danger of "letting ourselves go", and the impulsive man whose natural tendency is always to the unrestrained expression of all his moods in bawling, strong language, sharp contradiction, table-banging, needs the safeguard of the convention more than any of us.

Mr. Chesterton,[1] indeed, has glorified freedom from all these conventional restraints as the essence of true masculine *camaraderie*, but I should suppose that even he would find the respect of some conventions necessary in one whom he could regard as *bon camarade*; he would not like to be hugged and slobbered over, or even perpetually thumped on the back, or prodded in the ribs, by his "comrade", and still less to have the comrade performing all necessary natural functions in his presence. Without some foundation of respect for my whole personality, body as well as soul, a man, or even a dog, cannot be a "comrade" to me, and what lies at the bottom of ritual and convention is just this respect, which involves recognition of barriers which must not be broken down. The two most intimate associations of human life are, I take it, the "dear love of comrades" and the *consortium totius vitae* which is marriage;

---

[1] *What's Wrong with the World*, p. 96. Mr. Chesterton was ill-advised when he took the social behaviour of Johnson as his classic example of "unconventionality". The "Club" was something different from a boozing-ken, and the records of Johnson's actual conversation are marked by a degree of regard for "conventions" which strikes us to-day as exaggerated.

neither can exist without respect and the sense of inviolable privacies, and where these are there must always be some element of convention which finds its embodiment in ritual.

Of course, like all things which are of good use in life, convention and ritual have their obvious abuses. In all relations of life there must be certain barriers and self-repressions, and it is natural that mankind, once alive to the fact, should go to excess in setting up barriers and multiplying forms beyond what is needed; convention, the sustainer of wholesome human relations, then passes into a conventionalism which withers them. The proper respect for the bodily presence of another which is modesty, a thing no less salutary than beautiful, whatever Blake and his idolaters may have said falsely to the contrary, passes into the false modesty, or prudery, which affects to ignore the very fact of the body and its functions. The respect for parents which is the foundation of human relations between the young and the old is no less easily converted into an affected self-abasement which makes mutual confidence, true affection, and right guidance of the young by the old impossible. The different, but equally necessary, courtesy of equal towards equal, without which there could be no honourable friendship, is as readily overlaid by the forms of a ceremonialism which makes real friendship impossible. And thus, while convention is indispensable to sustain all the relations which give civilised life its superiority over savagery, the sense of the value of convention needs always to be kept in due restraint by wholesome impatience of the multiplication of superfluous rules of ceremony, etiquette, ritual. We can take our pattern of civilised life neither from a *Roi soleil* or a Castilian *grande*, nor from a *sansculotte* zealot for "fraternity", or an Elijah Pogram. Civilised existence is "art", not undressed "nature"; but art must not be allowed to ossify into artificiality. Here, as in all the problems of life, our business is to find a "right mean", and the finding of the "mean" is never easy. We only find it at all on the condition that the two antithetic tendencies, to fixed form and to free spontaneity, compensate one another.

I have dwelt so long on what may appear obvious for a simple reason. If we are to appreciate the true strength and weakness, in the religious sphere or any other, of both the antithetic tendencies which we may conveniently call the ritualistic and the anti-ritualistic, it is important not to confuse the essence of either with some of its accidents; a confusion which is made only too often, especially in connection with the manifestation of the ritualistic tendency in the institutionalising and conventionalising of a community's religious practice. In popular controversy among ourselves, it is common to hear ceremonial, or ritual, spoken of by those who sympathise with it as "imposing", or "magnificent", and equally common to find it confused by those who dislike it with such things as a taste for millinery and fancy-dress. In much the same spirit William James has somewhere, a little complacently, contrasted the European demand that rulers should exhibit themselves, on public occasions, in uniform with the gratification which, as he avers, the "democratic" sentiment of Americans derives from seeing a President discharge his public duties in a badly fitting morning coat.

Talk of this kind seems to me to betray complete misapprehension of the source of the opposing tendencies. What is really at the bottom of the demand for ceremonial is not the desire to be "splendid", or "imposing", but to be *formal*. The object of a fixed ritual is not to *impose*, but to *impress* in a certain specific way, and the impression may be, and often is, produced even more effectively by unusual austerity and artificial simplicity than by gorgeous show. There is, for example, a great deal of pomp and splendour about the ceremonial of a *Missa Pontificalis*, with its brilliant and varied vestments, its wealth of music, lights, and incense. A "plain celebration", correctly conducted, dispenses with nearly all this show, and is sensibly austere and bare; the traditional worship of Good Friday, with its open and empty "sanctuary", stripped altar, unkindled lights, and sombre black vestments, is artificially simplified to the extreme of austerity. But attention to the correctness of the worship is equally "ritualistic" in all three cases, and, to some temperaments at least, the austerest ceremony is much the most impressive.

Similarly it would be pure misunderstanding to suppose that the leaders in what is often called the "ritualistic" movement within the Anglican Church in the last century took any very profound interest in millinery and perfumes as such; indeed, the gentle satire of humorists like Thackeray, who saw the beginnings of the movement, is as often directed against its austerity in some respects as against its magnificence in others. The "Tractarian" of Thackeray's satire makes it one part of his pose to affect an unusual simplicity in the cut of his surplice and the hang of his stole; like the early Methodist preachers, he crops his hair close and brushes it straight; in general, he makes a point of sacrificing the personal adornments of the older type of fashionable clergyman and even of cultivating an artificial monotony of delivery in his sermons, by way of protest against the meretriciousness of rhetoric and elocution.[1] If he also wanted vestments and ceremonies,

---

[1] See the amusing account in *The Newcomes* of the effects of "Puseyism" on the Rev. Charles Honeyman.

he wanted them not because they were rich, or artistic, but because they were traditional, charged with a certain conventional significance as symbols. To be sure, there were persons who attached themselves to the "movement" for different reasons; because, for example, their slightly barbaric aesthetic cravings found satisfaction in a riot of colour, light, and fragrance. It is conceivable even that there may have been a few foolish young curates here and there who did really at heart simply want to dazzle milkmaids and servant-girls by a showy costume. But it would be childish calumny to confuse such weaklings with the men who bore the brunt of the prosecutions and imprisonments for "ritual offences".

On the other side, also, I can hardly believe that the typical American of whom James speaks is really much concerned that the coat worn by his President on public occasions shall be a misfit. His feeling, I take it, is one of protest against the principle of "uniform",[1] not a preference for ill-made and badly sitting clothes. The real issue is directly between convention and spontaneity. What the supporter of "forms" and "ceremonies" feels, often unconsciously, is that without regulation by convention there is no guarantee that expression, in word or act, will be adequate and appropriate to the thing to be expressed. The spirit which should dominate an occasion will not do so, as it should, if it gets a wrong embodiment, and without guidance by regulations carefully conformed to, it will constantly be getting an embodiment which is, more or less, a

---

[1] A "uniform", I take it, displeases him because he regards it as a kind of livery, a badge of the "menial", who is not a really "free" citizen. His livery is the outward and visible sign that he is not *dominus sui*, his own master. The zeal of Puritan reformers against vestments had a different source. The traditional vestments were objected to not because they were uniform, and uniform is *in se* objectionable, but because they were the *Pope's* uniform, "rags of Rome", as the urbane phrase went. James's American possibly also has a touch of more special animosity against a "militaristic" uniform.

wrong one. What the enemy of "set forms" feels no less strongly is that the conventionalised embodiment of a spiritual activity is always in danger of becoming a *dead* body. If he sometimes talks as though he were positively attracted by slovenliness, crudity, and disorder, he only does so because he thinks, rightly or wrongly, that those things are inseparable from life; life itself is an untidy, disorderly, crude affair.

The whole controversy is, in the end, only one form of the wider disagreement between the votary of significant form and the enthusiast for a rude vitality which cannot be confined within any bounds of form, precisely because it never knows fully what it would be at. We find a precisely similar clash in letters between the worshippers of "style" and the worshippers of rough force, and in philosophy between the "intellectualist" and the partisan of the *élan vital*. To ignore this is to be unjust to both parties. And if we are to be discriminatingly just, we must be careful, in discussing the issue thus raised, to take it at a sufficiently universal level. We are not principally concerned with the worth of a certain kind or amount of ceremony, as against more or less ceremony, or the relative worth of the various "uses" of different communities; these are not questions for philosophy. Whenever it is maintained that certain activities, to flourish at all, must get special expression at special times and places, and in special ways, what is being asserted is the necessity of ritual, in the wide sense, for life. Complete denial of the principle, involving the position that set times, places, forms, are matters of indifference, or are even dangerous to the spiritual life, means unqualified adoption of a strictly individualistic "quietism".[1]

---

[1] I use the word, perhaps not quite conventionally, to mean any kind of "waiting for the spirit to move" one, and letting the expression take care of itself.

Now we have, I think, only to conceive of "quietism" as systematically applied to the whole range of human activities to see that its results would pretty certainly be the very reverse of those at which the advocates of unfettered spontaneity aim. Consider, for example, what would be the probable effect of the unqualified suppression of form and conventional ritual on the most intimate of our personal affections. What would happen if the ritual of family life were entirely abolished? It would follow, in the first place, that we should recognise no special occasions on which family affections manifest themselves in some way consecrated by tradition. The keeping of birthdays within the family, with its traditional accompaniment of special salutations, letters, dinners, presents, the manifestation of the sense of loss after bereavements by the observance of a season of mourning, and the wearing of the garb of mourning, would have to be discontinued; though marriages, in view of their legal consequences, would still require to be celebrated with some sort of official formality, the formality would be reduced to the indispensable minimum; one must suppose that a wedding would cease to be a scene of festivity, and that the married would cease to mark the annual return of the wedding-day by any of the little customary observances.

Nor would this be all. Strict carrying out of the principle would even forbid the use within a family circle of such formal conventional gestures as the kiss of welcome and good will at morning and evening, at return from and departure on a journey. These are all pieces of customary ritual, and against all it may be argued that those who are most careful in observing the conventional form are by no means always the persons who feel most deeply and steadily the affection the form is meant to

symbolise; and, again, that the truly loving father or
brother does not really feel more love on the anniver-
sary of a birthday than on other days of the year, or
that those who display their grief in bereavement by
the punctilious donning of mourning garb often seem to
lay the memory of their lost friends and kinsmen aside
with their sables. All this is true enough; one can easily
understand the feeling which has often prompted
sincere and warm-hearted persons to make a point of
defying the conventions by disregard of these rituals.
We can appreciate, even if we do not unreservedly
approve, the contention that when a man's heart is full
of sorrow, or of family affection, he has no need to put
on mourning or to celebrate birthdays.

Yet it is no less certain that, since men are very forgetful creatures, if they do not assist nature with art by
providing themselves with occasions for contemplating
the object of their affection and giving outward expression to the emotions aroused by the contemplation,
remembrance and emotion must tend to fade. "Out of
sight" really is "out of mind". And if there is one point
which has fairly been established in the psychology of
the emotions, it is the falsity of the popular notion that
emotion is deepened by inhibition, when the inhibition is
more than temporary. James was at least right in saying
that our real object in training children to suppress facile
displays of emotion is not to make them feel more, but
to make them *think* more and feel *less*.[1] One may safely
say, justified by one's personal experience of life and
the known practice of universal humanity, that if a man
means to keep his own deepest personal affections alive,
there is only a choice for him between two alternatives.
Either he must fall back on the opportunities for recollection, and the expression of emotion in act, provided

[1] *Principles of Psychology*, ii. 466.

by social convention, or if he finds the provision for any reason unsuitable, he must devise a fresh ritual for himself, as a surrogate for that in general practice. If one will do neither, the "world", the βιωτικαὶ μέριμναι, always "too much with us", will infallibly choke the fountains of the inner life. For, without such an outlet,

> Each day brings its little dust
> Our petty souls to fill;
> And we forget because we must,
> And not because we will.

Further, even the most private ritual of occasions and opportunities never becomes completely individual. The little family circle, narrow as it is, is, after all, a circle, a community; it is indispensable to the wholesomeness of life that its affections shall be communal, and that the special occasions and opportunities which sustain them shall be opportunities and occasions for the whole group. For example, the keeping of a child's birthday is such a special opportunity not merely to remember and display the father's, and again the mother's, affection for the child, but also for the parents to remember and display their affection for one another, and their *common* participation in affection for the child, and also for brothers and sisters to remember and display *their* love, not only for the child whose birthday is being kept, but for each other and for their parents. A true birthday celebration, like an annual reunion of the household, is a feast of the family and of family affection. It comprises a whole complex of finely discriminated and graded affections, and demands a ritual which gives comely and appropriate expression to them all. It may fail of its purpose if it strikes too loudly, or not loudly enough, any one of the notes which it ought to sound. And this means that, to be utilised to the full, it must contain features which are less spontaneously prompted

by the special mood of some of its celebrants than by
those of others. The parents would not spontaneously
exhibit their parental affection for their child in precisely the behaviour which is most appropriate and
spontaneous in his small brothers and sisters; yet the
birthday feast must not fall apart into two concurrent
but distinct festivals, a festival of parental, and another
of fraternal, love; that would be destructive of its whole
significance as a manifestation of the spirit of the family.
This, of itself, implies that the observance will necessarily embrace features which some of the parties concerned will feel to be definitely conventional and artificial so far as they in particular are concerned, features
which the general spirit of the occasion would not have
dictated to *them*, if they had stood alone, or even features they might definitely wish to be away, if they were
the only parties to be considered. Even within the close
family group, the individualist temper which refuses
to take its part in any detail of the conventional observances not directly fraught with meaning to itself
would shatter the unity of the group, if it were allowed
unfettered free play. Even here in practice life requires
a certain amount of give-and-take, such as is called for
on a larger scale by all institutionalism.

Nor have we, even now, exhausted the significance of
art and convention for the life of the family circle. So
far we have spoken chiefly of the value of comparatively rare special occasions for contemplation and the
exercise of the emotions which attend it. In point of fact
convention has a subtler part to play in the daily routine. We need recollection daily, not only once or twice
in the year. If we are to meet the demands made on us
by personal intimacies adequately, we shall have to
show ourselves loving and sympathetic, to give appropriate expression to what we have at heart, not only on

special occasions but daily, and we cannot trust to the moment always to provide the best response to situations. Some of us are by nature reticent and awkward; we do not find it easy to meet a situation properly, if it calls for the expression of what is deepest in us; our habitual tendency is to very inadequate expression. We shall seem careless and cold when we are not really so, unless we are at some pains to make ourselves speak and act as the situation demands. Others are naturally prone to the expression of surface moods, and so are constantly making a wrong impression. We seem, for instance, to be irritated when we are really not so. And all of us are careless, thoughtless, and preoccupied. From some or all of these causes we may only too easily spoil the most precious intimacies of life, and there is no better way to guard ourselves against this ever-present danger than to protect ourselves by the habit of little observances which are "conventional" in the sense that we should often not practise them if we left ourselves to the suggestion of the moment, and that it costs some effort to keep them in being.

The point to be made, then, is that a certain element of art, even of artifice, is indispensable everywhere in life, if the activities which give it its highest value are to be permanently sustained at an adequate level. Nowhere can we afford to be wholly "free-and-easy". Least of all is it possible to be simply free-and-easy in the expression of activities aroused by the objects of our highest reverence, or even respect. If reverent devotion is to be kept at the level necessary for its rightful place in human life, there must be set occasions and opportunities for its special manifestation, and the forms in which it is manifested must not be left to improvisation, or they will inevitably be largely incongruous and jarring. We see this in connection with the

maintenance of a national patriotism, a profound and
ennobling sense of the worth of our national ideals and
history and our gratitude to our national past. It would
be impossible to keep a true patriotism alive without
particular occasions for commemoration of the great
achievements and deliverances of the past, and worthy
celebration of the memory of those whom, under God,
we have to thank for them. We should not be better
Frenchmen, Englishmen, or Scots, nor even better
Europeans, but worse, if we refused to honour the recurrent anniversaries of our deliverance from oppression or danger, if we forgot the memory of St. Joan
of Arc, or Nelson, or Wallace. We cannot be always
dwelling on these things in the routine of daily life, and
it is well that we should not do so too often, or too
obtrusively; but if daily life is to be unconsciously
leavened through by the right kind of love of country,
it is needful that there should be regular provided
occasions when we may dwell very specially with
the recollections which specially evoke the feeling of
patriotic devotion.

Again, because the very function of such commemo-
rations is to raise us, for the time, out of the atmosphere
of every day, it is specially important that the forms
taken by our "patriotic exercises" should be, in a high
degree, conventional and, in no bad sense, artificial.
If a whole community is to be lifted above its common
level into a mood of worthy patriotic thought and
emotion, we cannot trust for that effect to the inspirations of a haphazard spontaneity. Even a minor inadequacy in expression will, for example, pervert what
might have been a stimulus to the finest type of
national public spirit into a degrading exhibition of
vulgar complacent or truculent "flag-flapping". In any
really appropriate public expression of true patriotism,

the form taken by the expression will be consciously
"conventional", or "ceremonial"; it will be felt, to some
degree, as an imposed restraint, just because it is so
difficult to keep any mood, at its best, clean of the
degradation which attends any lapse from the highest
standard.

What Kant says of reverence for the moral law is
true, in some measure, of all respect for an object of the
mind's contemplation. The attitude is hard to keep up;
it is one of conscious constraint, and so "painfully
tinged", as Kant puts it, because of the inhibition of the
commonplace and less worthy which it involves.[1] It is
the function of proper ceremony, or ritual, to maintain
this inhibition at the same time that it gives expression
to the exalted mood. We ought, therefore, to understand that there is real justification for the common
feeling of mankind that the solemn public acts of
national functionaries should be marked as having a
public significance by an external dignity and decorum
which stamps them as having a character out of the
ordinary. There is something reasonable in making the
inauguration of magistrates, the holding of courts of
justice, the assembling of the legislature, notable by
an etiquette of costume, gesture, utterance, which impresses the imagination, inhibits commonplace associations, and makes the spectator or auditor aware that he
is being taken, for the time, out of the sphere of the
merely domestic and private. There ought, for instance,
to be a suggestion of the extraordinary and "other-
worldly" about such a transaction as the administration of criminal justice. It would not be well that we
should not be reminded by the surroundings that judge,
jury, prisoner are engaged in a business which is not
their private and personal affair; the "tonality" appro-

[1] *Werke* (Hartenstein[2]), v. 82.

priate to the office or the market would be out of place *here*. If we are among the audience when a convicted murderer receives sentence of death, we need to have it brought home to us that the speaker who pronounces the sentence is not Jones or Smith signifying his personal pleasure; he "bears *our* person" and announces a purpose to which *we* are consenting parties; the responsibility for the doom pronounced rests on each of us. The real judge in the cause is "Everyman", and this is why the execution of the murderer is not simply a second and premeditated murder. This is what the often thoughtlessly decried ceremonial of the courts of justice is meant to keep us from forgetting.[1]

Similarly there is just one department of life in connection with which even the type of American described sympathetically by William James seems to feel as the rest of us do. So far as I know, even he does not carry his hostility to ritual and ceremonial to the point of objecting to uniform in the Army and Navy. I do not believe that the explanation of this inconsistency is completely given by the utilitarian consideration that the very distinctive dress of combatants is a convenience to the combatants themselves and a protection both to them and to non-combatants. True as this is, it will not explain the universality of regulations requiring the wearing of uniform on public occasions in times of peace, or the strength of the sentiment that is outraged by the use of "colourable" imitations of the national uniform for purposes of advertisement, and by the exhibition of it in ludicrous circumstances on the comic stage. The truth, I believe, is that the national uniform is felt to be the symbol of a life dedicated to

---

[1] Something of the same effect is produced in our own country even by the use of the old Norman-French formula in signifying the royal assent to an Act of Parliament. There is a feeling which is satisfied by the formula *Le roy le veult*; it would be dissatisfied by "very well", and outraged by "Yep".

specially arduous devotion to the public service. We expect the sight of it to sustain noble public feeling at a high level. It marks out the soldier of the country to the rest of us for recognition and honour, and it should keep him from forgetting that he is under a special obligation of honour not to fall in his daily conduct below the standards demanded by his position as a dedicated man. I cannot help wondering, therefore, whether the anti-ritualism regarded by James as so typically American may not be connected with a certain failure in the population of the United States at large to take statesmanship and the administration of justice quite seriously. (There can be no harm in alluding to this failure, since American writers themselves have been among the first to proclaim and deplore it.) If the mass of any people are contented to see in political life, or in the administration of justice, only a set of artifices by which professional rogues compass their personal ends, it is quite intelligible that they should feel no need to invest the acts of the legislator and the judge with any special impressiveness. When the conviction has really come home to them that these acts are public and representative, and that the society as a whole, and its several members in particular, have a genuine responsibility in connection with them, I should think it most likely that the sentiment in question may be profoundly modified.

We may now apply what we have said to the special problem of the right place of the element of institution, ceremony, ritual, in the communal religious life. In principle, indeed, there seems nothing left to be said beyond what has been said already. But I think we can see why the conflict between the tendency to fixed forms and institutions and the complementary tendency to unregulated spontaneity should be exceptionally acute

in this particular field. On the one side, it is in the acts
which give expression to the religious life of the community that its members are lifted most completely
into an atmosphere remote from that of all their everyday this-world transactions. In their communal worship they are conscious of being brought, as they are
brought nowhere else, into direct relation with the
wholly transcendent, supernatural, and "other". Here,
more than anywhere else, the sense of being in the
presence of something entitled to absolute and unqualified reverence will be paramount, and it will carry
with it the completest inhibition of all incongruous
lower activities. The state of soul in which a man is
wholly taken out of himself and filled with an adoring
sense of the immediate presence of God is therefore exceptionally hard to maintain. At best it can be maintained by most of us in its intensity and purity for only
a short time; the concentration and withdrawal demanded are eminently hard and exhausting, and we feel
the need that they should be supported and encouraged
by all the suggestions of an environment differentiated
in subtle ways from that of our more everyday and
worldly hours.

Again, as all experience proves, the very depth and
intensity of the emotional mood of worship is itself a
source of grave dangers. The danger—it is one which
besets all deep and intense moments of feeling—is that
other and incongruous emotions, which in the ordinary
affairs of life only figure on a reduced scale, may intrude
themselves. If one merely shuts out, for the time, the
commonplace outer world and its surface interests, and
does nothing more, there is the risk that the house of
the soul, which has been swept and garnished for the
coming of the supreme guest, may be occupied by
"unclean" spirits. The "tumults" of the soul may usurp

upon its "depths"; excitement, and that of a very evil kind, may take the place of intense interior stillness and the "waiting" spirit. I need not particularise to make it obvious why importance should be attached to the fostering of the true temper of worship by devices which aim at shutting out both the commonplace and the unworthy, and so erecting an environment which makes it easier to maintain in the worshipping assembly the right, not a wrong, mood of unworldliness. No doubt, if we could make the soul entirely independent of "environment", we should have no need of these devices, but if we could do that we should have ceased to be what, in fact, we are, and must remain, "creatures". It is part of the humility of the "creature" to recognise that there is for it no absolute escape from "environment". This, as it seems to me, explains and largely justifies the tendency of all worships to take on a traditionally conventionalised form.

On the other side, there is no attitude in life which is so intensely *personal* as the attitude of the worshipper in the felt presence of his God. Unless adoration has occupied the inmost citadel of my personality, I am not really worshipping; I am merely complying with an external form. Religion is not, as the quietist holds it to be, merely a personal affair between myself and my Maker, but it is at least that, however much more it may be; when the intimate personal relation is absent, nothing can replace it. This is why we rightly feel that the *cultus* of a Greek city-state of the classical times is something quite different from what we mean by religion; it is *cultus* and it is nothing more. The philosophy of a man like Plato *is* profoundly saturated with religion, and for that very reason it treats the *cultus* with irony, or open hostility. Now there is always sure to be much in the conventional *cultus* of my group which does not stand in any felt relation to my own personality, much which to me individually is a matter of mere form imposed from outside, and perhaps felt to be more or less repugnant.[1] We can understand, therefore, why in this department of life, more than in any other, the institutional and conventional should provoke the individual's resentment. I want that in my worship of my God, so far as possible, there should be an utter breaking down of every barrier between my personality and His; that the two should come into a contact "closer than breathing"; that He should flow in upon me without let or hindrance. And the whole apparatus of conventional forms may readily appear to me no better than an artificial multiplication of hindrances and barriers, the banishing of God to an inaccessible distance. Hence it is often the most deeply religious men who feel the keenest resentment against the whole of the institutional and ceremonial element in the religion of their own communities. The very depth and sincerity of a man's devotion to his God will make him impatient of the suggestion that there is not a way of access to God which stands open to the human soul at all times, in all places, and independently of all prescribed formal avenues of approach. It is in this spirit that we find Plotinus refusing to take any part in the revived Hellenic worship which carried some of his friends off their feet. He refused to visit the temples on the ground that "it is for the gods to come to me, not for me to go to them".[2] That is, the true temple of God is a soul made fit for His habitation. When a man has done all that is in him to make his own mind fit for the heavenly visitation, it must be left for Deity to

---

[1] Is there any deeply religious Christian of any Christian church, I wonder who does not find *some* features in the worship sanctioned by his church decidedly repellent?

[2] Porphyry, *Vit. Plot.* 10, ἐκείνους δεῖ πρὸς ἐμὲ ἔρχεσθαι, οὐκ ἐμὲ πρὸς ἐκείνους.

choose when and how He will come to His temple; it is not for us to control His movements. It is the same spirit which inspires the vehement protests of the greatest Old Testament prophets against the cere-monialism of a people who draw near to their God through sacrifice and ritual, while there is no real con-tact of their personality with His: "Their hearts are far from Him".

(In modern times these protests have often been ex-aggerated to the pitch of maintaining an absolute anti-thesis between two incompatible types of religion, a "priestly", which is *ex hypothesi* false in principle, and a "prophetic", which is true; but this is something of a caricature of the facts. It has not unreasonably been retorted that the two prophets who did most for the creation of the Jewish Church out of which Christianity has directly arisen, Jeremiah and Ezekiel, were them-selves priests,[1] and that "prophetic" religion is so far from being the same thing as *true* religion that the majority of prophets appear to have been *false* pro-phets. Indeed, it might perhaps be said that what Jeremiah, the greatest of all the prophets, foresees in the famous anticipation which has meant so much to the Christian Church is not the disappearance of in-stitutionalism, but the supersession of the special func-tion of the prophet: "In that day a man shall not *teach* his neighbour . . . for they shall all know me".[2] And according to the same prophet, in the Messianic days, "Neither shall the priests the Levites want a man before me to offer burnt offerings, and to burn oblations, and to do sacrifice continually".[3] But it is true to say that

---

[1] The force of the retort would not be affected even if the recent theory that *Ezekiel* is a pseudonymous work of the Greek period should come to be generally accepted. In any case it is a "priestly" work.

[2] *Jer.* xxxi. 34.

[3] *Ib.* xxxiii. 18.

in the great Israelite prophets we see the tension between institutionalism and spontaneity at its acutest.)

The actual attacks upon institutionalism characteristic of certain quarters in our own times seem to me,
indeed, to be very largely on a lower level. To some
extent, to be sure, they are prompted by the impatience
of an intense spirituality with things which are felt as
hindrances in the way of free access of the individual
human spirit to God. But largely, also, they appear, at
least, to be inspired by different and inferior motives.
Thus there is a widespread tendency to decry everything in the nature of institution, not so much on the
ground that it is found to interfere with personal spirituality of temper, as on the ground that it is "childish"
or "unreasonable". Why, it is said, should I trouble, for
example, to go to a church on set days and at set hours,
to find God, when I am just as near Him every moment
at home or in the fields? Why should I even have any
special times of the day for private prayer, when God
can be addressed by the human spirit at any moment?
It would not, I believe, be unfair to say that most of the
anti-institutionalists who urge these considerations are
not persons of exceptionally high and ardent spirituality; more often, probably, they are worldly and indifferent. When a man declines to pray with the "congre-
gation", he does not most commonly decline with a view
to making his prayer more intense and heart-felt; it is
rather that he does not really feel any great need or
desire to pray.[1]

There is also a position intermediate between that
of the indifferentist and the passionately religious man
of markedly individualist type. The one real function of

---

[1] That God is as truly present in the fields as in the church is an argument
not unknown on the lips of the sort of man who really means that he prefers "joy-
riding" to worship.

religion, it is often said, is to promote the leading of a morally good life. The whole institutional side of a religion is valuable so far as it conduces to this end, but no further. And there is no close intrinsic connection between any part of it and the leading of a good life. Such connection as does actually exist is extrinsic and accidental, and it is chiefly those whose intelligence and reason are least developed who are "helped" in living a good life by institutional religion. It, with its apparatus of set times and places, prescribed forms and rites, may be temporarily allowed as a concession to the weak, but the aim of a rational piety should be to make men strong enough to live as they ought without such supports; a true and robust spirituality should be independent of them.

In large part this alleged irrationality and unspirituality of the specifically institutional in the historical religions may fairly be regarded as disposed of by the general considerations on which we have been dwelling. But some further points suggested by the particular anti-institutional arguments just rehearsed seem to call for separate brief examination. In particular there are two widespread and mischievous mistakes which are between them responsible for a great deal of the present fashionable depreciation of what used to be called "religious observances"; though both these mistakes spring from misconception of the specific character of religion, they may seriously impair the inner life of naturally deeply religious souls.

(1) It is a complete mistake to find the sole value of religion for life in its instrumental services to morality. The reality of these services, and the extreme difficulty of attaining a high level of social or personal moral practice except under the influence of the "religious sanction"—by which I do *not* mean expectation of mere

personal rewards and punishments—are facts patent and undeniable. But though religion, like art, may have, and when it is good religion will have, a morally ennobling effect, the effect is something different from its cause. To be religious is not the same thing as to try to be morally good, any more than to enjoy, or practise, art is to try to be morally good, though a man's religion is not worth very much if it does not lead him to try earnestly to be virtuous. And it is a familiar fact of life that the persons who try most consciously to be morally good are by no means always those who respond most readily to "religious impressions", while, on the other side, very real sensitiveness to the supernatural, like sensibility to beauty, is often found co-existing with grave moral weakness. It is still largely true that publicans and harlots — I do not mean *ex*-publicans and *ex*-harlots—can be much nearer to the kingdom of God than morally earnest Pharisees. The secret source of what is definitely religious in life is the vivid sense of creatureliness and the felt attitude of the creature towards its Creator, the experience of worship or devotion; and to adore is not the same thing as to cultivate moral betterment. To repeat what we have said so often already, morality which remains morality and nothing more is an attitude to that which *ought* to be; adoration and religion are attitudes to that which overpoweringly and tremendously *is*. To degrade worship into a mere instrument of moral improvement would be to make the same sort of mistake as that made when art is degraded into a mere vehicle of instruction.

By consequence, much as art would be deprived of most of its power to influence character if the artist, in producing his work of art, consciously aimed at being didactic, or the contemplator of the work at learning a "moral lesson", so a religion would lose its best actual moral effects on life if its worship were consciously directed on moral reformation. A great religion produces noble moral fruit only because it is aiming, first and foremost, at something else. It aims at making a vision of God a real and dominant presence in life; moral ennoblement follows spontaneously on the vision. It is not myself and my "moral being", but God and God's being which occupy the centre of my attention in proportion as I have a really religious experience of reality.

(2) It follows, further, that a man's religion, to be worth anything, must be something more than a purely personal and private transaction between himself and his God. Religion is degraded from its rightful place in life not only when it is conceived as a mere support of moral endeavour, but also when it is thought of, as it so often is, as primarily concerned with the personal "salvation", however conceived, of the individual's soul. God, not the self and its private destiny, is the true centre of genuine religious interest, and the supreme religious motive to action is the "glory of God", not the safeguarding of a man's personal interests. For this very reason that my private selfhood is not the true centre of religious interest, religion, though an intensely personal thing, is emphatically not a *private* concern. The saint's interest in God, and worship of a God felt to be present, are no more the private affair of the saint than the scientific man's interest in truth and its discovery is his private affair, or the artist's interest in the making and contemplation of things of beauty his. In all these cases there is an experience of vision, or contemplation, and the experient, who is one term in the experience, has, of course, his own private, and in its concreteness incommunicable, personality. But the other term in the experience, the object

contemplated, Truth, Beauty, the God of the spirits of all flesh, is above these privacies, and it is the object which gives the experience its significance. The experience, in all these cases, is one with a core of direct cognitive apprehension, and *therefore* an experience of being possessed, "informed by", "assimilated to" the apprehended object, an *adaequatio cognoscentis cum re*, which takes the experient out of his private solitude without impairing his individuality. Worship, like the pursuit of truth, or the fashioning and enjoyment of beautiful things, is essentially a community-function, not because the individual person is something less real than the community, but for a different and deeper reason, because of the *supereminence* of the "form" to which the experient is "assimilated". An adequate human worship of God cannot be the attitude of one single human soul, for the same reason that the whole of truth cannot be the knowledge of one mind, nor the whole of beauty the intuition of one artist. From these theoretical considerations there follow two consequences of a practical character.

(1) It may be true, indeed I would admit that it is very largely true, that many of the forms of an institutional religion have no direct connection, nor even such an indirect connection as could be detected by analysis, with any particular moral improvement. But, however true this may be, it affords no reason to pronounce observation of the occasions and opportunities provided by institutional religion irrational, nor even for denying that neglect of them is likely to be attended by specifically moral loss, since, as we said, the characteristic function of religion is not moral improvement, and its real, though indirect, influence on character is exerted, like that of the pursuit of truth or beauty, in infinitely subtle and obscure ways. It is similarly true

that I shall, unless I am a very abnormal creature, be morally the better because I feed my mind on the greatest art, but in this case also it would be futile to undertake to show the precise moral benefit I derive from this and the other work of art. I cannot say precisely what particular moral profit I get from the contemplation of *Othello* or the *Third Symphony*; yet there is no denying that morally, as well as in other ways, I am the better for the contact of my mind with Shakespeare's or Beethoven's. True, a man may be morally excellent and yet unable to appreciate great art, and, as we know only too well, a man may be at once a true artist and a vicious man. But the question is whether the second man, in most cases, without his sensibility to art would not have been more vicious than he is with it. Some other man may be more virtuous than, for example, the art-loving man of strongly carnal appetites, and yet be without his sensitivity to art. But the comparison which is really relevant is not that of the sensual and art-loving man with the man who is neither sensual nor responsive to art; it is the comparison of the art-loving sensualist with *himself* as *he* would be without his love of art.

(2) Again, if worship itself is more than a merely private activity, it is not reasonable, but eminently unreasonable, to expect that the community's institutional provision for it shall contain nothing which I do not find clearly beneficial to myself in particular. That which means little to me, or is even repugnant to me, may to another be a very real occasion for the lifting up of the heart. To forget this is as unreasonable as it would be to wish to banish from the world's store of poems and pictures all works which leave me personally cold, or possibly actually annoy me. I have, in such a case, to remember two things. One is that I myself, like every-

one else, have my personal limitations of defective sympathy. There is true and genuine beauty, it may be of a high quality, to which I do not personally yield a quick and spontaneous response; a second man, who does respond to it, may have his difficulties in appreciating some of the particular beauties which speak most directly to me. It is good for both of us that each should have the opportunity of learning to correct his own defects and limitations by going humbly to school to the other. Each may learn from the other in a way which really enriches his own capacity for personal appreciation. Even when this is not the case, we have to remember that all members of the community are not on the same level of appreciativeness. The poem or the picture which really is only a poor or mediocre achievement, and is correctly seen by me to be so, may also, if it has any beauty at all, be a real avenue to appreciation of beauty for my neighbour, whose perceptions have been less cultivated. There is thus a double reason why a society anxious, for example, to provide its members with opportunities for the appreciative enjoyment of pictorial art would be acting unwisely and irrationally if it admitted to its public galleries no paintings except those which satisfied the tastes of a small body of experts and *connoisseurs*. The smaller the group of these experts, the more serious the probability that some works really of the highest value would be excluded; there would also always be the still graver danger that a collection exactly to the taste of even a considerable body of experts would be "over the heads" of the great bulk of the public for whose benefit it is designed.

These considerations apply with undiminished force to the provision of opportunities for the cultivation of the spirit of religious adoration. There, too, we have to

guard against the ever-present danger of the spiritual
sin of priggishness. Religion, like art, is for everyone;
we cannot afford to leave any part of the community,
whatever its crudity or hebetude of perception, untouched by either. Genuine religion and genuine art
are both profoundly "catholic" in the sense that neither
can tolerate appropriation by a small intelligentsia of
superior persons, and in both there is a very real
necessity, in particular for those of us who are occupied
with some department of the "academic life", to protect
ourselves against the danger of degenerating into
"superior persons". The grace of a true humility is just
the grace we need more than any other, and we cannot
afford to disregard the opportunities for growth in it.
We ought to be alive to the truth that in literature and
art we lose much, if we do not take pains to keep alive
in ourselves the capacity for appreciating the simple
and perhaps second-rate, or third-rate, poetry and
painting which makes its direct appeal to the "common
people". The superfine person who cannot, in his reading, condescend to be interested in anything less subtle
and unobvious than the verse of Donne or the prose of
Henry James is not the sort of person we ought to wish
to be. Similarly, if we would keep the spirit of worship
alive in us, we cannot afford to neglect the opportunities
for contact, it may be at the cost of overcoming some
personal repugnances, with the forms of *cultus* which are
most potent in evoking worship and the sense of being
in the presence of God in the mass of simple folk.

The same thing is true of the cultivation of the sense
of national loyalty and love of country. The appeal of
such things as the national anthem, or the flag, to the
"common people" may be a crude one; it may cost us
the overcoming of an intelligible repugnance to sympathise with these things, knowing as we do how often

they are traded on to provoke ignorant and prejudiced explosions of feeling on wrong occasions. If we
know something of the detailed facts of history, we may,
and often do, feel the same kind of annoyance with the
"patriotic" rhetoric which converts very faulty "national
heroes" of the past into figures without spot or reproach.
No one can fairly expect me, for example, to see nothing in Oliver Cromwell but sheer devotion to the
good of "God's people", or in Bruce nothing but
Scottish patriotism, to imagine that the actual issue of
the fight at Naseby or Bannockburn was just national
freedom on the one side or "chains and slavery" on the
other. Yet it is also certain that a man does not really
promote intelligent love of his country by punctiliously
refusing to honour its flag, or national anthem, or to
join in the commemoration of its national achievements
and its national heroes. A good Englishman or good
Scot will not lie about facts for the greater glory of
Nelson or Bruce, but he will take his share, along with
his neighbours, in commemorating thankfully the deliverance of Trafalgar or Bannockburn, and will be
all the better for doing so, even while he may be
amused, or possibly annoyed, by some of the *naïvetés*
of the commemoration. He feeds on what is wholesome
in these things, and what is less wholesome does him
no more harm than the inevitable "impurities" of the
articles on which physical life is nourished. Neither for
the soul nor for the body does a wise man expect to find
a diet which can be assimilated wholly without remainder; he knows that if he refuses everything which
contains the least trace of an "impurity" he will merely
die of inanition. And so, I take it, philosophers have
had other motives besides that of self-protection for their
traditional recommendation that a man should worship
God νόμῳ πόλεως.

It ought to be added that in practice the great institutional religions, in proportion to their inwardness, actually allow more scope for spontaneity in worship than
might appear from much that is said in the popular
controversies on the topic. In some of them, indeed,
we seem to find a complete, or all but complete, conventionalising of the forms of public corporate worship.
But every great religion recognises and insists upon
the reality of a personal and intimate worship of its
God in the temple of the worshipper's own heart. There
are such things as private prayer and secret meditation
in the presence of Him who sees in secret, and no considerable historical religion has forgotten to dwell on
them as privileges and duties. None seeks to take the
spontaneity out of them. None, so far as I know, absolutely prescribes all words, postures, times for this private
worship, though most, reasonably enough, as a matter
of guidance, recommend fixed times as a protection
against forgetfulness, or definite words and postures as
most appropriate. Even when this recommendation is
most emphatic and most systematised, it still leaves
room for a very real spontaneity. When a religion has,
for example, enjoined the observance of set offices for
the "hours" of the day, it has never meant that the
access of the worshipper to God is confined to these
times and these prescribed forms. It is not meant that
there is to be no lifting up of the heart to God except
at the canonical hours, or that there are any prescribed
and conventionalised forms for this secret personal
devotion. Indeed, it is worthy of notice that among
Christians the very Church which has gone furthest
in developing a minutely systematised public worship,
in which every utterance, gesture, and posture is subjected to precise regulation, has also the richest literature dealing with all the many ways in which the soul

of the individual Christian may directly approach God in personal prayer, and lays most stress on the importance of the adaptation of the type of prayer to be employed to the special needs of the individual soul.

Nor is the same element really forgotten even under all the elaborate systematising of the visible acts and audible utterances of public communal worship. To take the most obvious instance, the principle of institutional ceremonial regulation could not well be carried further than it is carried in the rubrics of the *Missale Romanum* for the celebration of the Mass. Rules are laid down there for all the minute particulars of accessories, dress, posture, gesture, vocal inflection, on the part of the officiants. And yet one has to remember that, with all this stereotyping of the visible and audible, there is another and inner side to the public act of worship which is not stereotyped. Behind all that can be seen, or heard, there is the "intention" with which the celebrant is "offering the sacrifice", a matter between him and his Maker. And, again, each of the silent worshippers is also "offering the sacrifice", and each again with an "intention" of his own. One may be seeking guidance in perplexity; a second, strength to overcome or avoid some special temptation; a third, patience under bereavement; and so forth. Each worshipper may thus have his particular "intention"; what it is depends on his individual situation, and is a secret between himself and God. Thus, under all the apparent outward conventionality and fixity of such an act of worship, there may be intense and spontaneous prayer *in secreto* on the part of each of hundreds of worshippers. Each, if he is following the instructions of his Church and making *his* sacrifice really "acceptable", is *solus cum solo*, though he is also one in a crowd. When all is said, the prayer of each is a spontaneous utterance of his own need.

The same thing is apparently to be seen even in Mohammedanism, a religion generally held not to be very favourable to the cultivation of inwardness of spirit. There, too, the hours of prayer and the words, tones, and gestures of the worshipper are exactly prescribed. But it appears that the Moslem's prayer is actually invalid without the direction of it to a particular "intention", as is humorously illustrated by Mr. E. W. Lane's story of the man who was overheard in the mosque prefacing his recitation of the evening prayer with the declaration, "I purpose to steal this excellent pair of shoes". The doctrine of the direction of intention is, of course, liable to be abused, and it is commonly in connection with real or supposed abuses that it is referred to in our own literature. But in its main principle it merely enforces the true perception that the purpose of the institutional in religion is not to replace, but to sustain, the spontaneous movement of the personal spirit. That a worship may be spiritual, it must be intensely personal; it is not necessary, and the history of Montanism, or again of the Anabaptist ferment of the sixteenth century, fairly proves it undesirable, that it should be anarchical.

When all has been said, it no doubt remains true that a due balance, both in the public and the private practice of devotion, between prescribed and hallowed form and free initiative is a "costing" thing, not easy to reach or to maintain. And it seems to be the fact that no one balance is equally adapted to the needs of all souls. What will be the right adjustment, even in private prayer, between the broken, perhaps wordless, aspiration of the individual creature to its Creator and the rethinking and reuttering for one's self of time-honoured petitions, must be largely a matter of personal temperament and interior state. And so also in acts of public and communal worship, I cannot doubt that while, for practical purposes, we have to be content with such an adjustment as experience over a long period and a wide area shows to be beneficial to a great majority of average men, there will always be the difficulty that a degree of fixed form and ceremonial which positively helps some souls to realise the presence of God is a real hindrance to others; and, again, that the very absence of these things which is felt by some as setting the soul free to mount up to God on her own wings is to others what the exhaustion of the atmosphere would be to a bird. If it were my business here, as of course it is not, to make practical suggestions to those in authority over me, I would say, with great deference, that it seems to me desirable for this reason that any worshipping society should have the benefit of a plurality of alternative "uses", leaving different degrees of external freedom in these matters; and, again, that individual congregations should not be allowed to become slaves to any single "use". I conceive that congregations accustomed to a high degree of fixity in forms of prayer and an elaborate ritual of worship, and finding such a system on the whole most beneficial to them, would be the gainers if, at times at any rate, they varied their practice by reverting to something simpler and barer. A Church, for example, which has "high Masses", celebrated with abundance of ritual, cannot well be too simple and unadorned in its "low" or "plain" celebrations. Again, I should say that a Church accustomed to the use of fixed forms of prayer, couched in words of chosen beauty and solemnity, would also do well to make provision for homely public utterance of "extemporary" prayers somewhere in its devotions.

And I think, on the other side, that a Church whose public worship is for the most part devoid of ceremony and fluid in form, would be wise if it actually enjoined the occasional use of these things. It is desirable not to let even our most serviceable habits get too complete mastery over us. The best of them, too seriously followed, will impoverish our experiences. But to follow up this line of thought would be quite alien to my purpose in these lectures; indeed, I should hardly have ventured to forget myself so far as to express the *Privatmeinungen* of the present paragraph at all had I been speaking in any place other than the familiar and beloved city of St. Andrews, and to any audience but one of old friends.

VII

SACRAMENTALISM

φαντάσματα θεῖα καὶ σκιαὶ τῶν ὄντων.—PLATO.

IT is not uncommon to find all that we have so far said about the institutional and ceremonial element in the historical religions of the world admitted by many who yet hold that these considerations do little or nothing to remove the real scandal these religions present to the rational philosopher. His trouble, it may be said, arises not from the bare fact that these religions are institutional, but from the peculiar character of the institutions which are fundamental in them. Full recognition of the value which ceremonial has for religion, as for other human activities, is no justification of *sacraments*, and sacraments, under one name or another, are prominent and central in positive religions all the world over. The sacraments of the various religions are alike, under all their differences, in possessing a character which distinguishes them sharply from mere ceremonial practices which are found effective as means of aiding the created spirit to realise the presence of the Creator, or as simple external symbols of devout states of mind. According to the claims regularly made for them, sacraments are physical acts, concerned with sensible objects, through which the Creator conveys a spiritual benefit, exercises a spiritual effect within the spiritual life of a rational creature.[1] Here we have the feature

[1] A few typical statements may be given here for reference. *Catechismus ex decreto Concilii Tridentini*, ii. 1: "definitio a divo Augustino tradita quam deinde

which distinguishes sacraments from rites in general. In a rite we may have nothing more than an action on the part of the human agents who take part in its performance; in a sacrament "God offers something to man". What makes a rite into a sacrament is that the ritual act is taken to be neither a device by which men induce a certain frame of mind in themselves, nor a mere symbolic declaration of their conviction that a certain state has been, or is being, induced in them by the action of God; the sacramental rite is itself an actual "channel" of grace, an "efficacious sign", or "instrumental cause" by the intermediation whereof the Creator affects the created spirit".[1]

I think that, in the light of all we know from the comparative study of religions, we must confess recognition of sacraments and sacramental acts, in this sense, to be so widely diffused a characteristic of actual religions that it must be regarded as typical; and, again, that it can hardly be eliminated from our own religion, by general admission at least the most adequate example of the type *historical religion*, without most gravely

---

omnes doctores scholastici secuti sunt. Sacramentum, inquit ille, est signum rei sacrae: vel, ut aliis verbis, in eandem tamen sententiam, dictum est: Sacramentum est invisibilis gratiae visibile signum ad nostram iustificationem institutum." (The passages meant seem to be Aug. *De civ. Dei*, x. 5: "sacrificium ergo visibile invisibilis sacrificii sacramentum, id est, sacrum signum est." Bernard, *In cena Domini*: "sacramentum dicitur sacrum signum sive sacrum secretum".) *Articles of Religion*, xxv.: "Sacraments ordained of Christ be not only badges or tokens of Christian men's profession, but rather they be certain sure witnesses, and effectual signs of grace, and God's goodwill towards us, by the which he doth work invisibly in us. . . ." *Anglican Catechism*: "Q. What meanest thou by this word *Sacrament?* A. I mean an outward and visible sign of an inward and spiritual grace given unto us, ordained by Christ himself, as a means whereby we receive the same, and a pledge to assure us thereof." *Shorter Catechism*, q. 91: "A sacrament is an holy ordinance instituted by Christ; wherein, by sensible signs, Christ and the benefits of the new covenant are represented, sealed, and applied to believers."

[1] These various expressions are, perhaps, not all exactly equivalent, but the distinctions between them, if there are any, are not easy to make out, and at least it is clear that the Roman, Anglican, and "Reformed" statements cited above are all in substance agreed in rejecting any reduction of sacraments to the level of declaratory symbolism.

modifying its character. A "non-sacramental Christianity" might, or might not, be an improvement on what
has been known for nineteen centuries as Christianity;
it ought to be impossible, in the face of a chain of witnesses from St. Paul's day to our own, to pretend that
it is the same thing.

Now here, it may fairly be said, is the real *crux*. It
is an affront to reason and intelligence to ask men to
believe that an act resoluble by analysis into a contact, or series of contacts, between my own body and
others can effect a change in my spiritual state. Such
a belief has often been called, not merely in the heat
of sectarian recrimination, a discreditable survival
or artificial resuscitation of pre-civilised superstitions
about the efficacy of "material magic", a throwback to
the cult of the "fetish". Some of our contemporaries
notoriously make the sacramentalism of historical
Christianity a reason for pronouncing it no religion for
a rational man; others find themselves driven to escape
that conclusion only by the desperate expedient of
declaring that a sacramentalism already found full-
fledged in St. Paul's *Epistles to the Corinthians* and
the Fourth Gospel is no part of "historic" Christianity.
My own purpose, in this place, is neither to make an
apologia for Christian sacramentalism, nor to discuss
a problem of ecclesiastical history. What concerns me
is the broad philosophical issue whether the conceptions on which all sacramentalism, Christian or non-
Christian, rests are in their intrinsic character irrational
superstitions or not, and, as a student of philosophy,
I am interested in this issue because of its bearing on
the still more general question, raised at the beginning
of this course, of the relation between positive religion
and a purely philosophical, or natural, religion. The
question I have before me for treatment to-day is still

the very general one whether what a positive religion professes to disclose of God, whenever it goes beyond what we are warranted in asserting by a metaphysic of nature and of morals, must be regarded as, at best, temporary illusion, or not. Hence the only issue with which I shall be concerned, in what I have to say of the sacraments of historical religions, is the broad one whether belief in physical objects and bodily acts connected with them as "means of grace", instruments through which a special contact of the created spirit with its Creator is effected, involves thinking of God and of the divine activity in a fashion incompatible with a sound and reasonable metaphysic. Any references I shall make to the sacraments of Christianity, or the sacramental doctrines of Christian Churches, in particular will be meant to be illustrative of general principles, and my illustrations will be taken from this quarter rather than another for the double reason that the Christian sacraments are those with which we are all most familiar, from our education in a Christian society, and that they have been made the object of the reflective study of theologians and philosophers in an exceptional degree, and throughout an extended period of time. Many other religions possess sacraments of some kind; none possesses the same kind of conscious sacramental theory.

When we look at sacramental practice and theory from this point of view, we can at least see without much trouble that controversial language about "materialistic magic", like most controversial rhetoric, merely confuses the issue. Whatever the sacraments of Christianity, or its precursor Judaism, may be, they are not a survival or recrudescence of "primitive" magic. In saying this I do not mean to imply that some practices of a sacramental kind found in the historic faiths of the

world may not prove to be little more than the continuation of the nature-magic of savages into a more
civilised age. That is a question for the anthropologist
and the historian of "civilised origins". I may have
doubts whether even they know very much about the
matter, and I am quite sure that I do not. The ritual
drinking of *soma* among the early Aryans, or of wine
in some of the Hellenic mysteries, certainly has the
character of a sacramental act as we have defined it,
and at the same time *may* be continuous with, or a
throwback to, practices which may fairly be called
savage and magical, devices for the induction of an
abnormal state of exaltation valued for itself merely as
abnormal, independently of any thought of a special
contact with deity. (As I say, I doubt whether anyone
knows whether this statement is true, but I see no
reason why it should not be true.) Circumcision, the
great sacrament of the "older law", presumably had
its origin in something very savage and superstitious,
though the anthropologists seem at present as much
in the dark as anyone else as to what that something
may have been.[1] The same thing may be true of the
ritual application of water to the body which has been
adopted by Christianity from pre-existing practice as
its sacrament of initiation. Nor do I wish to deny that
investigation might reveal strange origins for a whole
number of the secondary accessory details which, to
this day, accompany the celebration of sacraments in
the most spiritual and philosophical of the historical
religions. The point I want to make is, that whatever
may have been the far-away origin of specific ritual
acts which in these religions are sacramental, the acts
do not become sacramental in the sense in which our
own religion, for example, possesses sacraments, until

[1] See art. "Circumcision" in *E.R.E.*

they have received a specification and sanction which take them wholly out of the class of the magical.

This ought to be suggested, in the first place, by a simple historical reflection which forces itself on us the moment we make a serious study of the facts about the sacraments of the "old" and the "new" law. Both Judaism and Christianity are religions which have been historically preceded by a conscious breach with the nature-cults we loosely call "primitive" because no one can say how they arose. Whenever and however the practices of circumcision and of ritual reception of bread and wine originated, the conviction of the believing member of the Jewish synagogue who circumcises his son, or the faithful Christian who approaches the Lord's Table, is that *for him* the act receives its significance and obligation from an historical divine institution, in virtue of which it procures him or his a definite divine gift. Many other nations might practise circumcision for known or unknown reasons; it *may* be that the Hebrew of the days of the monarchy himself practised it merely as a custom of which he could give no explanation. But the Jewish Church founded on "the Law" practised it (and it is irrelevant to my point whether the Jewish Church had an existence before the Exile or not) because it had been instituted by a divine command to Abraham, and made by that command the title-deed to a share in the divine promises to Abraham and his descendants. There might be, indeed, we know that there were, ritual meals in various cults of the first century A.D., but the Christian came to "the Lord's Supper" because the command to do so had been given on an historical occasion—"in the night when he was given up"—by his divine Master, and the Master had promised "eternal life" to those who fulfilled it.

For our purpose the important point is not so much

whether these beliefs were strictly accurate in point of fact, but that they were accepted as accurate, and that it was these beliefs which gave the acts their character as sacraments. There have been many divergent modern speculations about the origin of the widely diffused practice of circumcision. It has been pronounced to be a hygienic precaution of a purely utilitarian kind, or a prophylactic against imaginary dangers attending on entrance on the active exercise of sexual functions, or a symbolic consecration of the whole person to a deity, and these are only some of the conflicting hypotheses. But an orthodox and pious Jew, when he circumcises his child, may be presumed to be thinking neither of hygiene nor of protection against vaguely imagined dangers besetting the performance of sexual acts, but of the promise of God to Abraham, and it makes no difference in principle whether this promise to Abraham is an incident of authentic history or not. If it could be demonstrated that every detail of every act which is regarded as sacramental in a sacramental religion had pre-existed as a piece of so-called nature-magic for ages before the religion adopted it, this would not alter the fact, which is of primary importance for us, that the reason why the adherents of that religion practise these acts has nothing to do with the known or unknown reasons for its earlier performance. The reason why the act continues to be practised, and is regarded as sacramental, is that it is believed to be historically of divine institution, and to have specific effects attached to it in virtue of its character of being divinely appointed. This character would not be affected by the fullest proof that the same act had been performed by others without divine institution, and with no reference to consequences attached to it by an historical divine promise. The Biblical record of the covenant with Abraham, for example, does not pretend to be a narrative of the *origin* of the custom of circumcision; it is a narrative of its appointment to be a sacrament to Abraham and his descendants. We cannot really suppose intelligent Jews not to have known the notorious fact that the same rite was general with such a nation as the Egyptians, nor need we suppose them to have fancied that the Egyptians had borrowed the practice from themselves. But they did not regard the Egyptians as qualified by their circumcision to inherit the blessing. The rite was not, in their case, a sacrament.[1]

· These reflections suggest at once the true *differentia* which distinguishes sacraments from "materialistic magic". A magical act, if we use the words with any precision, means an act which, provided it is correctly performed, produces its supposed consequences automatically. Magic, like early science, is a matter of technique. It may, and does, exist where there is little or no belief in the control of events by any kind of divine will or agency; in fact, in developed systems of magic, the performance of the prescribed acts, or the recitation of the prescribed spell, is thought of as actually compelling divinities, whether they will or not, to the execution of the magician's will.[2] At bottom, therefore, magic and religion, in the sense in which we have used that word throughout our discussion, are directly opposed in principle. The second draws all its signifi-

---

[1] It might be said that circumcision lacks the character of a sacrament, inasmuch as it is only a "token", or *declaratory*, not an *efficacious* sign. But such a view hardly does justice to the demand of *Gen.* xvii., that the "uncircumcised manchild" shall be "cut off" because "he hath broken my covenant". The implication here surely is that the Israelite enters personally into the "covenant" relation by being circumcised. If he neglects the rite, he has wilfully cut himself off from the covenant.

[2] Naturally, I cannot justify this view of the *essentia* of magic at length here. For a useful summary of the sort of evidence on which I am basing it, and a conspectus of the various anthropological theories, I may conveniently refer to the elaborate composite article "Magic" in *E.R.E.*

cance from the tension between this world of the temporal and the other world of the eternal, which so mys-
teriously encloses and interpenetrates this: the first is a
purely this-world affair, as much so as sanitary engin-
eering or electric lighting. In fact, it is not the priest,
but the technician, who knows how to turn physical
science to an utilitarian account, who is the real counterpart in our society of the wizards and sorcerers of
darker ages. In the "temporal world" as conceived by
Hume and his later disciples, that is to say, as conceived by the leading representatives of the *Natur-
philosophie* of half a century ago, there is really no
difference between the functions of science and the functions of magic. Science, on the Humian view, consists
in discovering formulae which "sum up the routine of
our sense-perception", and may therefore be used as
practical receipts for the production of desired effects.
Since, on the theory, all that the formulae record is
conjunctions of events which stand in no sort of rational
connection, the scientific laws which supply the modern
inventor with his rules for procedure have exactly the
same arbitrary character as the spells and incantations
of magic. And the one justification admitted by a philosophy of this kind for its belief in its "laws of nature",
the plea that, in some inexplicable way, they are found
to "work" when applied to practice, is precisely the
kind of justification a savage might allege for his belief
in spells and charms. Without any desire to prejudge
a case by rhetorical exaggeration, I must confess that
I can see in principle no difference between physical
science *as conceived by Mach or K. Pearson*, and the
magic of an African medicine-man, except that the
spells of the European man of science prove themselves
in fact so much more trustworthy and potent; they are
uncommonly "big" medicine.

The fact that *our* "customary experience" leads us to disbelieve in the particular conjunctions on which the magician of savage or semi-savage societies relies must not blind us to the much more important fact that it is purely "this-world" conjunctions which are the foundation of his procedure. It is true that "this world", as he conceives it, may contain constituents not recognised by the European secularist, ghosts of the dead, powerful spirits and demons, and the like, though those things are not indispensable to magic. Magic can flourish wherever there is belief in the potency within the sensible world of inexplicable and unintelligible "conjunction". And spirits and demons, as such, are just as much of the temporal and secular world as electrons or "wavicles"; it is only with the contrast of the eternal and the temporal that we reach the conception of the genuinely "other", and absolutely unsecular. When the superstitious revive the old magical practices in an age of high secular civilisation, it is true that they commonly attempt to give them a laughable dignity by calling them *occult* science. But, in principle, the conjunction in which the modern patrons of sorcery are interested are no more "occult" than any other conjunction which has to be accepted as a bare unexplained conjunction, that is, according to an empiricist metaphysic of nature, than any of the conjunctions summed up in our scientific laws.

For according to a consistently empiricist metaphysic, there is no real difference in respect of arbitrariness between the conjunction of administration of a dose of prussic acid and death and the conjunction between the same effect and the decapitation of the deceased's portrait by an enemy: the first is certainly the more familiar, but is every whit as unintelligible as the second. And if the proceedings of the medicine-man are occult in the different sense that the knowledge of the receipt for them is confined to a few experts, the same thing is equally true of the proceedings of the modern "wizard" of electrical science. Very few of us know how to make the "grand projection", or to "tie the knot"; very few also know how to construct a "wireless" set.

Thus, if we are to look for a modern equivalent for magical operations, we shall find it much more truly in the triumphs of applied science than in the sacraments of religion. In magic, as in "science," there is a complete absence of that which lies at the root of every sacrament, the free outward-moving activity of the divine. When "gods" are brought into connection with magic, they are degraded from their position as gods; their part in the magical act is not to be the sources of "grace", the bestowers of a gift, but to be passive instruments in the hands of the magician; the activity comes, in the end, from him. Hence the very fact that *ex hypothesi* a sacrament is a channel through which free and unconstrained divine activity expresses itself, an act in which "God gives something to man", as is indicated in religions like Christianity and Judaism by the stress laid on historical divine institution of the rite, definitely takes sacraments once and for all out of the domain of the magical.[1]

And as there is no "magic" in them, there is, for the same reason, no materialism. The sacramental act is, indeed, performed by contact with bodily objects, but it is never held that the bodies employed have any intrinsic efficacy to produce the effect of the sacrament. No theologian, to my knowledge, has ever held that

---

[1] The so-called *messe noire* of the "Satanists", if it really exists, on the other hand, is a deliberate attempt to convert a divine sacrament into a magical act, to "put a spell" on the Creator, to use His power for ends which are not His; hence its essentially blasphemous character.

wheaten flour and wine have in themselves any intrinsic
efficacy in conferring on him who partakes of them
"remission of sins and all other benefits of the Passion";
they are not analogous to the ambrosia and nectar of
classical fables.[1] It has always been held that if their
reception is instrumental to these effects, it is so simply
by virtue of divine appointment, and that God might,
had He pleased, have conjoined the same benefits
with different instruments, or produced them without
any physical instrument at all. *Ex post facto* theological reflection has discerned a symbolic appropriateness
of the instruments appointed to the effects, but this is a
very different thing from ascribing to them an intrinsic
efficacy of their own. The whole of the instrumental
efficacy actually ascribed to them is assumed to be freely
conferred on them by the divine volition. References
to "materialistic magic" thus misrepresent the true
character of the objection they are intended to convey,
and should be dismissed from serious self-respecting
argument.[2]

The objection really intended gains in point and seriousness by being freed from these vulgar irrelevancies.
The thought, at bottom, is that any action of the
Creator on the created spirit should be direct and without physical instrumentality; it is conceiving unspiritually of God to imagine that the Spirit of all spirits
needs, or employs, any bodily intermediary in His
action on the spirits He has created. He is intimately
present to them all; "to Him every heart is open and
every volition speaks"; can we suppose that His re-

---

[1] Cf. the prayer in the Roman Office, "quod ore sumpsimus, Domine, pura
mente capiamus: et de munere temporali fiat nobis remedium sempiternum" (said
by the celebrant immediately after reception).

[2] Of course I do not mean to deny that popular superstitions connected with
the Christian sacraments have sometimes degraded them into instruments of
"magic", but such superstitions misrepresent the Christian conception.

sponse to our needs requires to be conveyed, or can be conveyed, through objects and acts in the physical world? This line of thought is further reinforced by the consideration that no religion of high ethical quality can conceive of graces of character as conferred on a man by the mere performance of a bodily act, independently of all internal state of soul. We need no witness beyond our common experience of men to see that the carnal, worldly, and proud do not derive spiritual life from mere bodily participation in the ordinances of any religion.

> Sumunt boni, sumunt mali,
> sorte tamen inaequali,
> vitae, vel interitus.

We can thus readily understand the wide diffusion of a strong prejudice against the belief that bodily acts and objects can be "instruments" and "efficacious signs" of spiritual benefits, even among those who would probably be shocked to discover that their prejudice, if carried to its logical consequences, would be fatal to rites and sacraments which they themselves prize and reverence. To take a trivial illustration, I have found a professedly Anglican writer denouncing, not merely as childish, but as actually blasphemous, the practice of blessing medals, crosses, and the like, on the ground that it is impious to ask the Holy Spirit to bless "purely *material* things". Yet I have little doubt that the writer makes no scruple about asking God, several times in the day, to "bless" his meat and drink, or that he is sincerely attached to the English *Communion Office*, with its formal and visible blessing of the bread and the cup, a prayer actually described in the rubric which accompanies it as one of "consecration". Clearly, if the principle is sound that God cannot without impiety

be asked to bless anything which is material, we must
be prepared to be consistent with it. If it forbids us to
recognise sacraments as *means* of grace, it must equally
prohibit the irrationality and impiety of praying that
a leg of mutton or an apple-pie may be "blessed to our
use". In neither case is the blessing on the physical
object really disjoined from the blessing on the user.
In the central sacrament of Christianity, for example,
the oblation of bread and wine is blessed, or consecrated, "that it may become *to us*", *ut nobis fiat*, the
Body and Blood of the Lord, or, as another rite says,
"to the end that all who shall receive the same may
be sanctified and preserved to eternal life", exactly as
the meat on our tables is blessed that it may become
to the partakers sustenance for the temporal life of
soul and body. In both cases, improper reception is
expected to effect disease, and not health; in neither
is the beneficial effect conceived to follow in any
purely mechanical way from the performance of an
external act.

Thus the real question at issue is whether it is incompatible with a rational conception of God to hold
that certain specific physical things and acts may be,
not from an intrinsic necessity grounded in their character as these particular physical things and acts, but
by free divine appointment, channels, or vehicles of
a specific contact between the divine spirit and the
created. It is important to remember that in Christianity, at any rate, it has never seriously been held that
these specific contacts can only be effected by this
specific mediation. It is a general position, accepted
by the theologians of the most highly "sacramental"
Christian societies, that "God has not *bound* His power
by the sacraments", *i.e.* that though the things and
acts in question have been appointed as the usual and

regular channels for the reception of these specific gifts
or graces, the effects can be and are produced directly,
without the intervention of the physical things and acts
when these are not to be had. This is what is meant, for
example, by the well-known phrase of the *English
Catechism* that the two great distinctive "sacraments
of the new law" are "generally" necessary to salvation.
The meaning is not that they are *universally* indispensable, as De Morgan asserts in a passage of his
Formal Logic.[1] The framers of the sentence were too
familiar with Aristotelian terminology to make a careless
confusion between the καθόλου and the ὡς ἐπὶ τὸ πολύ, and
too acute to miss the point that, if the meaning had been
what De Morgan takes it to be, they would be asserting that the penitent thief was lost after all, in spite of
the formal promise, "This day shalt thou be with me in
Paradise".[2] The meaning of the proposition, a meaning
admitted by the extremist sacramentalists, is that the
sacramental acts are "as a rule", when they can be had,
the vehicles of certain spiritual gifts; when they cannot
be had, this impossibility is no bar to the bestowal of the
gifts without them. This explains a whole series of
positions, familiar in the literature of the sacraments,
which would otherwise be unintelligible. It accounts,
for example, for the *Crede et manducasti* of Augustine,
an utterance not meant to excuse neglect of the sacraments, but to comfort the Christian who is physically
cut off from them by no fault of his own with the
assurance that he is not cut off from their Giver, or their
benefits. It explains also the doctrine of the "baptism

---

[1] *Formal Logic*, p. 272.

[2] For, even if the penitent thief had been baptized, it is certain that he was
not one of the company gathered a few hours before in the upper room. De
Morgan also forgot that one Anglican rubric forbids the admission of children
of tender years to the Communion, while a second pronounces that "baptized
infants dying in infancy are certainly saved".

of desire" as replacing baptism with water, in the case of necessity,[1] and the still more famous doctrine that "desire" in its extreme form, that of martyrdom, "supplies the lack" of all sacraments.[2] Unless we are careful to bear in mind both the qualifications, that sacraments are held to owe their efficacy wholly to divine appointment and in no way to the intrinsic properties of their matter or their form, and also that "God has not bound His power by the sacraments," we shall be discussing a falsified issue.

It is, no doubt, true that one can find examples in various religions of *quasi*-sacramental rites which are thought of without these important qualifications, as producing their effects in virtue of a kind of natural necessity,[3] and therefore independently of any interior disposition on the part of the community [4] who receive

---

[1] St.Bernard (to Hugh of St.Victor, *Ep*. 77) "cum his (*sc*. Ambrose and Augustine), inquam, me aut errari aut sapere fateor, credens et ipse sola fide hominem posse salvari, cum desiderio percipiendi sacramentum, si tamen pio adimplendo desiderio mors anticipans seu alia quaecunque vis invincibilis obviarit. Vide etiam ne forte ob hoc Salvator cum diceret *qui crediderit et baptizatus fuerit, salvus erit,* caute et vigilanter non repetierit *qui vero baptizatus non fuerit,* sed tantum *qui vero,* inquit, *non crediderit, condemnabitur.*" Cf. St. Thomas (*S.Th*. iii.ᵃ q. 66, art. 11 resp.), "eadem ratione aliquis per virtutem Spiritus Sancti consequitur effectum baptismi, non solum sine baptismo aquae, sed etiam sine baptismo sanguinis, in quantum scilicet alicuius cor per Spiritum Sanctum movetur ad credendum, et diligendum Deum, et poenitendum de peccatis." iii.ᵃ q. 68, art. 2, resp. "potest sacramentum baptismi alicui deesse, re, sed non voto . . . et talis sine baptismo actuali salutem consequi potest propter desiderium baptismi, quod procedit ex fide per dilectionem operante per quam Deus interius hominem sanctificat, cuius potentia sacramentis visibilibus non alligatur."

[2] *S.Th*. iii.ᵃ q. 68, art. 2 ad secund. "dicendum quod nullus pervenit ad vitam aeternam, nisi absolutus ab omni culpa et reatu poenae: quae quidem universalis absolutio fit in perceptione baptismi, et in martyrio: propter quod dicitur quod in martyrio omnia sacramenta baptismi complentur, scilicet quantum ad plenam liberationem a culpa et poena."

[3] The point is illustrated by the doctrine of Christian theologians on the necessity of an "intentio ministri" to make a sacrament valid. On this see, *e.g.*, St. Thomas (*S.Th*. iiiᵃ q. 64, arts. 8 and 10). His doctrine is that there must be an intention of the "minister" to administer a valid sacrament, or there is no celebration of the sacrament; an intention to celebrate a valid sacrament for an ulterior nefarious purpose (*e.g.* to consecrate a Host for purposes of sorcery) is a grave sin on the part of the ministrant, but does not annul the *veritas sacramenti*.

[4] A difficulty might be felt here in connection with the baptism of infants. It is raised by St. Thomas (*S.Th*. iii.ᵃ art. 68, q. 9, where it is objected against the

them; and, again, as, for the same reason, absolutely indispensable for the effect. But this only means that in such religions the notion of a sacramental has not yet been duly discriminated from that of a magical act. Our concern here is with the sacramental concept when it has been clearly formulated, and it is irrelevant to consider stages of thought and practice at which the important logical distinction between the sacramental and the magical has not yet been drawn.

Now that we have got our issue properly formulated, we should, I think, see at once that the prejudice against the sacramental in historical religions is only one of the many forms assumed by a more universal prejudice against the physical itself, the standing prejudice of that false spirituality which does so much mischief to the thinking and moral practice of many circles in our own society. There can be no sound logical foundation for *a priori* rejection of the possibility that certain specific spiritual benefits may normally be conveyed through special physical channels, apart from the allegation that it is, in general, irrational to hold that the physical can act upon the spiritual. If our physical state can, and does, in general make a specific difference to our spiritual state, there is no good philosophical reason for dismissing as "superstitious" the assertion that sacraments, in particular, are instrumental in specific ways to the spiritual life. And if we look at the world of experience as a whole, without preconceived bias, nothing seems more certain than that, speaking generally, the rule is that the physical is everywhere instrumental to the psychical. If we take the word *sacrament* in a wide sense to mean any physical occa-

practice that infants can have neither intention nor faith). St. Thomas's reply is in substance taken from St. Augustine: the faith and intention are there, on the part of the Church which is receiving the child into its fold.

sion which normally ministers as an instrument to the soul's life, we may clearly say that these are natural, as well as supernatural, sacraments, and that the physical world is everywhere pervaded by the sacramental principle.

It is the notorious fact, for instance, that the effect of the regular reception of proper food at the proper hours is instrumental to mental as well as to physical health; that we suffer in intellect and character, as well as in body, if we cannot get our proper sleep; that proper change of air and bodily occupation reinvigorate a man's moral being as well as his physique; on the other side, the explanation of bad intellectual and artistic work, and, again, of bad moral conduct, is often very largely to be found in unwholesome physical surroundings. You can seriously affect a man's thinking and his conduct for the better by seeing that he is fed as he ought to be, gets due sleep and exercise, and fresh and untainted air.

Here, again, it holds good that the connection between the instrument and the effect is found to hold *generally*, not universally, and that the benefit of the "natural sacraments", like that of the sacraments of religion, depends on co-operation in the recipient. A man may do work of the highest excellence, or lead a life of singular moral nobility, in spite of bad, or insufficient food, or air, or sleep; unfavourable surroundings may throw him back the more on his own inner resources, and impel him to make a specially vigorous assertion of his superiority to circumstance; bodily infirmity, as philosophers have noted, seems sometimes to provoke an exceptional activity of mind. But these qualifications do not destroy the truth of the general rule that vigorous and healthy intellectual and moral life needs the instrumental ministration of the physical;

the *mens sana* is not ensured by the possession of the *corpus sanum* and it may be found coexistent with a *corpus morbidum*, but it would be the height of presumption to count on retaining the *mens sana*, if I neglect to take the ordinary and available means of keeping my body in health. The possibility of a nature-miracle gives me no right to expect that the miracle will be forthcoming to counteract the consequences of my own negligence.

Further, over and above this general dependence of intellectual, artistic, and moral activity on physical environment, specific achievement in all these kinds is also, ὡς ἐπὶ τὸ πολύ, dependent on specific features of the physical environment. The "miracle of genius", it is true, occurs, from time to time, in the most unpromising surroundings. But, speaking generally, it is the rule that a man's specific intellectual, or moral, or artistic, accomplishment is conditioned by the way in which his interest has been awakened by his natural and social environment. A man is not likely, in spite of the dubious and exaggerated stories of the childhood of Pascal, to become a great mathematician if, in the most receptive period of life, he has never seen a mathematical book or diagram, nor to become a great painter, if he is brought up where there are neither paintings nor drawings to be seen, nor a great musician, if he has heard no music. He is not likely to develop a burning love of justice if he is born and brought up in the *zenana* of an Oriental Sultan, or of purity of thought, word, and act if his boyhood has been passed in a society permeated by the worship of the *lingam*.

We recognise this, when we speak, as we so often do, of the defects which may mar the whole work of even a rarely gifted artist for want of early opportunity to study good models, or the imperfections in the work of a scientific man caused by unavoidable ignorance of what has been done in his own subject before him. Opportunity to study the best models at the right time, to take the most obvious illustration, is, in the last resort, one provided by the physical order. It is a physical fact that a given northern artist had no access to any works of the great Italian masters, or a given poet to those of Sophocles or Shakespeare, until an advanced period of life, but it is a physical fact which may mar the artistic quality of his whole life-work. We may fairly say that, when all allowance has been made for the mystery of "genius", it is the normal thing that genius should get its inspiration and direction from specific occasions, furnished, in the end, by its natural surroundings. The same opportunities are not utilised in the same way without the genius, but without the right kind of opportunity the genius will be imperfectly developed, or developed on false lines. It may be a sentimental exaggeration to fancy that a common village churchyard holds a group of "mute, inglorious Miltons". A Milton is not likely to go through the world "mute", in any case. But it is at least true that if Milton had been condemned by circumstances to be all his life the thatcher or hedger of a country village, he would hardly have uttered himself in *Paradise Lost* or *Samson*.[1]

Indeed, one does not see how the rule could well be otherwise, in view of the elementary fact that a man is an embodied, not a discarnate, intelligence, and that the more we get to know of the whole life of man, the closer and more intimate we find the connection between the intelligence and the embodiment to be. The logical outcome of the tendency to deny or minimise the

---

[1] And if Blake had not been condemned by circumstances to lifelong semi-illiteracy, we may safely say that we should have had something from him very different from the fitfully splendid nightmares commonly called his "prophecies".

dependence of mental life on suggestions and opportunities presented by the physical would be the extravagant modern Docetism called, very improperly, "Christian Science", which, if I am rightly informed, declares that we really have no bodies, but dupe ourselves into fancying that we have them. This is a doctrine not merely intellectually fantastic, but morally dangerous, from its tendency to encourage unconscious hypocrisy in its professors. If one may judge them by their actions, many of them seem habitually to take exceptional care to surround themselves with a plentiful provision of theoretically non-existing comforts and luxuries for their theoretically non-existent bodies. They may persuade themselves in speculation that they have no bodies; in practice they seem commonly to behave as if they had, and as if the comfort of the body were a much greater good, and its discomfort or suffering a much worse evil, than most religions or philosophies admit. If we agree, not with their verbal profession, but with the operative beliefs revealed by their practice, we shall expect that the regular rule of life will prove to be that moral, intellectual, and aesthetic good is mediated to its human recipients through definite physical channels. "Spirituality" will mean to us not behaving as though we had no bodies, and were not set in a framework of bodily happening, but utilising the transactions between our own body and others to the full as opportunities for the discernment of truth, the practice of virtue, the creation or enjoyment of beauty. We need no proof of the falsity of the kind of "spirituality" which consists in pretending that the body is not there, beyond the moral havoc which it makes of the whole life of sex, marriage, and parenthood. Our true business with it is not to ignore it, but to keep it "in its proper place".

We should expect, then, in the light of analogies supplied by normal intellectual and moral life, that if there
is a still further level of the life of the spirit concerned
with conscious relation to the divine, at this level also
the fact that such a life has to be lived by embodied
creatures would be pertinent. We should no more expect
the body, with the occasions and opportunities it provides, to play no part in ministering to such a "supernatural" life than we should expect the same thing in
connection with life at other levels: thus we should anticipate as more probable than not that the highest gifts
God has in store for us would, as a general rule, come
to us in connection with, and dependence on, physical
things and bodily acts as their channels, or instruments. In a world where nature is so full of sacraments,
it would be strange that "grace" should not have its
sacraments too. Nor would this anticipation mean that
we look on divine agency as tied down to, and only able
to exert itself through, these particular special channels,
since their *raison d'être* lies not in the nature of God,
but in the nature He has given *us* as *embodied* creatures.
If there are wholly disembodied intelligences who are
"separate" from "matter", like angels in the Thomistic
philosophy,[1] we cannot well suppose that their intercourse with the Creator, however it may be conditioned,
is mediated by the channel of "sacraments"; but we at
least are not such angels, and nothing has ever come of

---

[1] But it is well not to be sure that there are. Even the most convinced Thomist
will not deny that the higher "intelligences" communicate with, and have social
relations with, one another. And he is forbidden by his own philosophy to credit
any created intelligence with the power directly to read the thoughts of another:
that, as Donne says, is held to be "beyond an angel's art". It would seem to follow
that every such intelligence must have some such instrument and vehicle of communication with its fellows as is provided for us by our "weight of body and
limb", though it may be well to avoid occasion for error by not calling that
vehicle a "body". Only it would serve the same function as is now served by
our familiar organism, that of being a standing instrument of intercommunication. But this is purely speculative, and by the way.

the attempts of men to forget that they are not angels except deadly evil; ignoring the body commonly ends in sinking below the level of the beasts that perish. Since, when all is said, at our highest we are and remain *men*, we should naturally expect our most direct contacts with the divine to be contacts under conditions which take account of our embodiment.

No doubt, it might be urged in reply to reasoning of this kind that there is a real difference between the part played by bodily channels and instruments in ministering to our moral and mental life generally and the part sacramental religions ascribe to their sacramental objects and acts. In the first case, the instrumentality is part of the *cursus ordinarius* of nature; in the second, it is, in a sense, arbitrary. This difference, however, ought not to create a difficulty for a philosopher who has already accepted the Theism without which there can be no rational religion. From the theistic point of view, the *cursus ordinarius* of nature itself ultimately depends on divine appointment; *la nature* is not a name for an independent agency, but for the instrumentality through which the Creator commonly acts; the one real difference between the two cases is that the instrumentality, for example, of food, sleep, and air in ministering to mental and moral health does not depend, as it is held that the efficacy of sacraments in ministering to the soul's "eternal welfare" does, upon specific divine institution at a definite time and place inside human history. And this difference itself does not seem to hold good for all the acts which can fairly be called sacraments of grace. It seems impossible to deny that we have in matrimony an institution which falls short of its full purpose, if its effect is merely to promote temporal happiness and prosperity; a marriage which deserves to be called a "marriage of true minds" is definitely productive of fine spiritual graces in the parties, and thus, as it seems to me, since the *dona matrimonii* transcend the secular, we do not think worthily of the institution unless we regard it as a sacrament of grace.[1]

Yet it is notorious that theologians have been hard put to it to answer the question precisely where and when the "sacrament" was instituted. Thus we are told in the supplement added to the *Summa Theologica* of St. Thomas[2] that "matrimony, in so far as it is ordained for the procreation of offspring", was instituted at the creation of Eve; "so far as it is a remedy against sin", it was instituted after the Fall, "in the time of the law of Nature"; so far as it involves restriction and specification of the persons, it was instituted "in the law of Moses"; so far as it represents "the mystery of the union of Christ and the Church", it was instituted "in the new law"; but so far as it promotes friendship and mutual *obsequium* between the parties to it, it is an institution of the civil—*i.e.* the Roman —laws. The first and last of these "institutions", however, do not concern marriage in its character as a sacrament.

In the light of our present historical knowledge, such an answer would amount to saying that the one definite historical occasion to which we can point as that of the institution of matrimony, "as far as it is a sacrament", is the occasion when Christ was asked a casuistical question about the legitimacy of divorce by opponents, who perhaps wished to involve him in trouble with

---

[1] The Anglican Church seems officially to "hedge" on this point. In the 25th Article Matrimony is said not to have "like nature of a Sacrament" with Baptism and the Lord's Supper, on the ground that it has no "visible sign or ceremony ordained of God". This might mean either that it is not a sacrament, or only that it is not on the same level as the two great "generally necessary" sacraments of the Gospel. The second interpretation *seems* most consonant with the language of the *Catechism* about sacraments, and with the assertion of the *Office* for Matrimony that "it is an honourable estate instituted of God".

[2] Q. 42, art. 2.

Herod Antipas. I confess that to me it seems fanciful to make a reply to such a question amount to a formal act of institution; I doubt, again, whether all theologians would be willing to make the status of Baptism as a principal "sacrament of the new law" stand or fall with the strict historicity of the words of the command, "make disciples of all nations, baptizing them", etc. It is interesting to read that the hard-and-fast limitation of sacraments conferring grace to the afterwards traditional seven did not, apparently, make its appearance until the twelfth century, and that in the thirteenth Bonaventura expressly ascribed the institution of two of the seven, Confirmation and Unction, to the *apostles*, while his master, Alexander of Hales, had actually traced the origin of Confirmation as a sacrament to a ninth-century Council. The effect on the Western Church of the hard-and-fast dogmatising of the divines of Trent, and the Reformers alike, about the number of the sacraments of grace and their immediate institution by Christ seems to me to have been wholly unfortunate.[1]

It would perhaps be a better taken point to attack on principle the validity of the analogy we have presupposed between the action of God as the source of the order of nature and His action as the source of "supernatural" grace. It might be said that we must look for no such analogy, since the bestowal of grace is *ex hypothesi* a strictly *supernatural* transaction between the Creator and the creature. Since the gift bestowed, then, does not belong to the order of nature, the divine action by which it is bestowed should itself be wholly independent of nature and of opportunities afforded by nature, as its channel. It should strike straight, without

---

[1] Cf. for the whole subject the articles "Sacraments" (Christian, Western), "Sacraments" (Christian, Lutheran), and "Sacraments" (Christian, Reformed) in *E.R.E.*

any "means" at all, from the depths of the Creator to the depths of the creature. Where there is a recognisable instrumentality, it might be said, its very presence is an indication that we are dealing with an effect which belongs to the natural order. This, I suppose, is the thought in the mind of an anti-sacramentalist critic when he says, as such critics have done, that he cannot see why any Christian should expect or receive any particular grace from participation in the sacrament of the Lord's Supper. (It is meant, in fact, that this rite, or "ordinance", is not really a sacrament, in the sense in which the word has been historically employed in the theology of the Christian religion.)

I confess that this line of argument seems to me not unplausible, though it appears to lead to consequences which are probably not before the minds of those who employ it. That the grace of God needs no physical channels is a favourite controversial argument in the mouths of those who give the supreme place in devotion and worship to the "ministry of the word", as against opponents who attach importance as great, or greater, to sacraments. Yet, after all, the "word" itself is ministered in dependence on physical occasions; its reception involves hearing or reading, and hearing and reading are as much physical acts as eating and drinking, or any others which are performed sacramentally in any religion. Again, the hearing or reading is just as liable as any other activity to become divorced from appropriate preparation and interior disposition, and to become merely external and mechanical. It is as easy to hear or read unspiritually as it is to receive a sacrament unspiritually.

It is quite impossible, with the best will in the world, to construct a worship for men which will be really independent of contacts with the physical. Thus the objection to sacraments on the ground of their physical character, carried to its logical conclusion, should issue in an extreme quietism hostile to all use of "means", though common sense really forbids the conclusion to be drawn. If it is not drawn, if marks apprehended through the eye, and sounds apprehended through the ear, are once recognised as a regular and ordinary "mean" by which the spirit of man may be awakened to consciousness of the presence of God, and may draw "grace to help" from that presence, there is no obvious reason why other physical experiences also should not be normal and appointed vehicles for the same contact with the divine.

But the truth, I take it, is that the whole question is one we cannot settle by appeal to *a priori* anticipations. It is irrational to attempt to decide on the strength of general metaphysical theory how God must act in bestowing good gifts on His creatures. The one question we can ask with sanity about such a matter is the *historical* question how in fact God is found to deal with us. Repugnance to give recognition to the sacramental element in historical religions as having abiding value seems to be, in the last resort, only one more form of the persistent reluctance shown by the numerous philosophers who, consciously or unconsciously, regard mathematics as the one type of what knowledge should be, to do justice to the reality of the historical. Far too many of our contemporaries—not all of them "idealists" —are still beset by the ambition to contemplate human life in all its detail under a supposed "form of eternity" which actually means the dismissal of time and history as illusions. Yet the whole poignancy of human life arises from the fact that it is an unsolved tension between the temporal and the eternal, in which the eternal, though steadily gaining on and subduing the temporal to its purposes, never absorbs it. To suppose that I can understand my own life without recognising the temporal everywhere in it is to repeat the old error of Lucifer, who mistook himself for God.

At the cost of some reiteration of the already said, I cannot escape recurring once more to what I regard as the true and important thought that it is just this presence of a never completely resolved strain of temporality in human life as we know it which makes the presence of uneliminated mystery and the stubbornly factual so characteristic of it. If we could compass a vision of life from which the last vestige of bare succession and contingency had vanished, all mystery would have disappeared with them. The work which God works from the beginning would stand revealed to us as something transparent and self-evident to the understanding; we should comprehend the ways of God finally and completely. But then also all opposition between the comprehender and the comprehended would have vanished; the world, thus completely comprehended, would present no single feature which stood over against the understanding as irreducibly foreign and given "from the outside"; it would be to each of us what a work of art might be to the artist who had constructed it with complete and conscious mastery, never for an instant uncertain as to his own meaning, never carried "out of himself" by an "inspiration" which mastered *him*, and never hampered by the intractability of a medium less than absolutely plastic to his purpose.

In fact no work of a human artist is ever of this kind. Every human artist is at times uncertain of the effect he means to produce, at times in the grip of an invasive inspiration which carries him to unforeseen effects, at times condemned to wrestle with difficulties due to the obstinate intractability of the medium in which he works.

And in our attempts as philosophical thinkers to understand a world which we have in no sense created, we are
not even in the position of the human artist towards
his product, but at best in that of the audience before
whom a great drama or symphony is being rendered
for the first time. We cannot say, before the curtain goes
up on a scene, what the dramatist has in store for us.
At the most we may hope so far to catch something
of the spirit of the whole piece that the scene, when we
have witnessed it, will be found to be in keeping with
the none too clearly discerned purport of the whole.
What that purport is we can only divine from the scenes
which have already been enacted before us; we see the
play only once, we have to leave the theatre before the
performance is ended, and we are not allowed to bring
a "book of the words" to the representation.

To complicate the situation still further, we are not
merely an audience, we are also ourselves part of the
cast for some of the scenes, and we are not furnished in
advance with the text of our own part. The drama of
history, as we sometimes call it, is like a play in which
each actor is provided with some general knowledge of
what has been said and done before he comes on the
stage, and is perhaps aided by some whispered hints
from an unseen prompter, but otherwise has to fashion
and conduct his part for himself, as best he can. There
is no going behind the scenes to secure a book of the
play in advance, and the book of the play is what philosophers who set themselves to "geometrise" history
falsely imagine themselves to possess. If they really had
it, faith and proof would alike be swallowed up for them
in vision.

It is wrong in principle, then, I should say, to attempt an *a priori* answer to the question whether belief
in sacramental "means of grace" is rational or irra-

tional, for the simple reason that the geometrising of the historical is wrong in principle. However strongly the philosopher may be convinced that history has the unity of a dominant pattern, he is bound to be equally assured that he can bring no knowledge of the pattern with him in advance to his study of history. Such light as he may gain on the character of the pattern will only come to him fitfully and tentatively, as the historical dance unfolds itself to his gaze. And the historical includes not only the interplay between man and man, but all the contacts there may be, in the depths of the soul itself, between man and his super-historical Maker. If He is beyond and above history, we are always immersed in it, and since *quidquid recipitur recipitur ad modum recipientis*, He can only reach us by an activity striking down into the temporal and historical. His dealings with us cannot be what they might be if we were non-temporal beings.

The real question we have to answer, then, is this. Granting that there is a quality or level of life which is specifically religious, not merely scientific, or aesthetic, or ethical, do we find, when the appeal is made to history, that life with this quality is normally and customarily exhibited at its rarest and best in connection with definite practice of sacramental acts, or in detachment from them? Is it, on the whole, true that religions lose or gain in the clearness and concentration with which they bring God and eternity as dominant realities into the lives of their followers, in proportion as the sacramental element is absent from them, or present in them? If the testimony of history is that such sacramental acts are normally most prominent in those religions, or in those periods of the history of a given religion, in which there is the most sensitive and abiding appreciation of the eternal values, this would be, not indeed mathematical demonstration, but historical proof that normally God does utilise the physical things and acts we call sacramental as genuine instruments for the conveyance of His best gifts. If the verdict of impartial history is found to be that the real appreciation of the eternal values and the control of life by that appreciation is equally well, or even better, sustained by the types of religion which rely least on sacraments, this would be fair historical proof that the sacramentarianism of some existing historical religions is a temporary accident, and possibly an unfortunate accident, which religion may be expected to outgrow as it reaches a clearer understanding of its own significance. This, as it seems to me, is the only form of the question whether sacramentalism is rational or irrational which admits of a determinate solution.

Naturally, it is no part of my business to answer the question for anyone else. But it may be in place to make some observations in defence of an over-hasty answer in either sense. The appeal, to be of real worth, must be made to history, not simply to the mere personal experience of a single individual. If we base our judgement only on our convictions about our personal experience, it is liable to be affected both by our own imperfect intellectual interpretation of our experience, and by mistaking our personal "temperamental" bias for something typically and universally human. The case is not sufficiently made out for sacramentalism by merely urging, however vehemently, that I believe my own spiritual life to have benefited from devotion to the sacraments of my Church. I may even be mistaken about the fact. I may take for personal growth in grace what is really something very different.[1] Or supposing

---

[1] *E.g.* advance in mere "refinement", or even that subsidence of carnal passion which is effected by growing physically older.

the fact to be indubitable, I may be committing the common fallacy of ascribing a real effect to a wrong cause. Finally, if I am right both about the fact and about its explanation, I may be wrong in arguing that a practice thus necessary and beneficial to me must have the same worth for everyone else, in spite of all individual variations of temperament. (This is actually recognised by ardent sacramentalists among Christians when they say, as they often do, that there can be no single rule equally valid for everyone, *e.g.* in the matter of frequency of Communions.)

On the other side, the anti-sacramentalist would not establish his case by merely asserting, however sincerely, that in himself a genuine spirituality exists in conjunction with abstention from sacramental observances. He, again, may be mistaken about the alleged fact; he may take for spirituality in himself what is only fastidiousness, as I believe is not uncommonly done.[1] If he is not mistaken about the fact, he may always be met by the suggestion that he would have received the gift of a still higher spirituality if he had not neglected "the means", or that he is possibly neglecting to allow for the special peculiarities of his own idiosyncrasy, and forgetting that the whole question is not one of what is possible in exceptional cases, but of what is the general rule. To avoid all these sources of mistake it is necessary that the appeal be made to a super-individual experience, over a sufficiently wide range of space and time. And for the same reasons, I should say, it would be improper, in a thoroughly philosophical treatment of the question, to confine attention to the history of a single religion, with its specific hallowed traditions, since it

---

[1] As, *e.g.*, when the vegetarian plumes himself, as he sometimes does, on his superiority in spirituality to the flesh-eater. All that is true is that the vegetarian has the daintier palate, but there is no special connection between daintiness and spirituality.

does not seem possible to maintain the *simpliste* view that there are no genuine contacts with God outside the boundaries of some one historical religious community. In that sense, at any rate, *extra ecclesiam nulla salus* would be a palpable untruth.

It would thus not be dealing with the question on a sufficiently wide scale, for example, to study and compare the types of spiritual life provided, within the limits of the Christian religious tradition, by a highly sacramentarian community, like the Roman Catholic Church, and a non-sacramental body, like the Society of Friends. If one relied simply on that comparison, there would, I think, be serious risk of overestimating the spirituality compatible with rejection of the sacramental, for a reason which has been more than once dwelt on by von Hügel. One needs to remember that the Society of Friends sprang up and has continued to flourish in the midst of a wider Christian community which *is* sacramental in its practice, and that the type of religion which the Society seeks to cultivate was from the first conditioned and prescribed by the existing and powerful tradition, and has ever since been more or less fed by the great devotional literature, of this wider community. As von Hügel observes,[1] though George Fox turned his back on the sacramental system and believed himself to have received a new and special illumination directly from God, the actual content of the illumination is determined throughout by the Johannine Gospel, the high sacramentarian writing, *par excellence*, of the New Testament. And, of course, the Society at the present day, does not dream of trying to screen the life of its members from the influence of the great devotional literature of Christendom at large. Hence, though Fox and the Society he founded may not

---

[1] *Essays and Addresses on the Philosophy of Religion*, pp. 231, 293.

practise the Christian sacraments, his life and theirs could not be what they were and are but for the living influence of the sacramental tradition of the Church at large. When one is, so to say, within the "sphere of influence", even if one is outside the "occupied terri- tory" of the organised historic Christian Church, one is never really far away from the operation of the Christian sacraments.[1]

For this reason an historical inquiry would not be complete if confined to a study of the types of spiritual life fostered by various Christian communities. One should further attempt a comparison between the spiritual fruits of a religion like Christianity, which, in its most significant historical forms, is intensely sacra- mental, and a religion like Islam, which is overwhelm- ingly non-sacramental. Of course, in such a survey, it would be indispensable to avoid the besetting unfair- ness of the controversialist. One would be scrupulously careful not to make the comparison one between Christianity, as it shows itself in the lives of its saints, and Mohammedanism, as shown in the lives of its average men. In fact, one would have to make a double comparison, between the saints of both religions, and, again, between the average sinners of both. One would require to know whether the average, faulty, largely worldly minded Christian reveals himself to be, at any rate, more sensitive to non-secular influences than the average Moslem, or not, and also whether in the highest and best of the saints of Islam, there may not be some- thing lacking which we find in the saints and heroes of Christianity, and which, so far as we can see, is secured

[1] One might fairly say that the graces manifested, often strikingly enough, in the lives of members of the Society of Friends are mediated by the reception of the Christian sacraments, though not by their own personal reception. The reception by the Christian community at large plays the same part here that the "faith of the Church" does in the baptism of infants.

for them, directly or indirectly, by the Christian sacra-mental tradition.

To be really fruitful, the inquiry would need to be conducted with anxiety to avoid a further insidious source of misapprehension. If the judgement finally reached is to be worth anything, the effects on which it is based must be themselves quite definitely fruits of the religious life. The question is not at all whether societies honouring and practising sacraments will be found, on appeal to history, to enjoy marked social and economic prosperity, to make striking contributions to art and science, or to acquire and retain political eminence. Macaulay's well-known attempt to decide whether Calvinism or Romanism is the better religion by con-trasting the post-Reformation history of Scotland with that of Spain[1] is an obvious example of a bad *ignoratio elenchi*. One cannot simply take advance in wealth, comfort, political prestige, and the industrial arts as unfailing indications of special nearness to God.

But we need equally to remember that a similar, though less obvious, *ignoratio elenchi* would be com-mitted if judgement were based upon "*moral* statistics", unless the word "moral" is to be understood in a sense which would make it impossible to prefix it as an epi-thet to the noun "statistics". Two societies may exhibit much the same degree of respect for the commonly recognised moral duties of regard for life and property, female honour, and the spoken word, and yet stand on different levels in apprehension of God and the eternal. The commonly recognised and easily constated obli-gations are of a kind which men find forced upon them as conditions of a tolerable secular civilisation. Their importance may be clearly perceived, and a high aver-age standard in the practice of them attained, by a

[1] In the Essay on Ranke's *History of the Popes*.

society intelligently bent on the pursuit of a worldly and second-rate aim in life, and grossly indifferent to the eternal and transcendent. Even men who are content to aim at nothing more than stable, comfortable existence, if they are clear-sighted, will discover the necessity of being, in the main, honest and humane, faithful husbands, decent parents, loyal observers of their promises, though their whole conception of good may remain thoroughly worldly.

There are, it is true, virtues for which a completely this-world scheme makes no provision, such as the humility which expresses our sense of our creatureliness. But a virtue like humility does not manifest itself in a recognisable distinct group of performances; it is rather an attendant disposition of soul by which all the performances connected with the various "departmental" virtues gain an added beauty. It shows itself not so much in what is done as in the manner of the doing, and thus the sort of moral statistics which may be instructive about the standing of a society in regard, for example, of respect for human life, or for the bond of legal wedlock, will throw no light on the degree of humility present in it. And speaking more generally, the real differences between a highly religious man or society and a man or society with a morality of a worldly minded type will mostly escape the notice of the collector of moral statistics. Both types of society may, for example, respect the bond of marriage; the difference between the two lies not so much in their respect for that bond as in their conceptions of the principal good to be promoted by regard for it. The divergence between the man to whom marriage has a sacramental significance and one in whose eyes it is merely an important social institution of the civil law means that the first will not be satisfied with himself as a husband, if he has succeeded in being what the second understands by a model husband; it need not show itself in the records of the percentages of divorces, or in any similar form recognisable by the moral statistician.

In general, the kind of information provided by such statistics would be inconclusive for the purposes of the sort of inquiry I have in mind for a double reason. All that these statistics can tell us is whether grave transgressions of overt act are relatively many or few in a community. This throws some light on the moral condition of the average man in the community, though not all the light we could desire. But it leaves it quite uncertain whether in a society in which the average moral practice is high, and there are not many who fall below it, there are, or are not, those who rise above it.

It is conceivable that the same society which is shown by statistics to be fertile in gross offenders may also be unusually fertile in great saints. The gross sinners affect the statistics; since the saint cannot be detected by externals, the great saints do not. Again, the sins which will show up in the statistical record—sins of carnality and violence—though grosser, are not so fatal to the soul's life as the highly respectable sins of self-sufficiency, cold egoism, and spiritual pride. But these, not being transgressions of the civil code, do not appear in the records. One society may be more disfigured than a second with offences springing from appetite and anger, and yet more fruitful in examples of spontaneous self-forgetting, kind offices, and little heroisms which go unchronicled, and these are the things which really reveal life of supernatural quality. But they do not stand out visible to the human observer, except where we find them displayed on an exceptional scale in the life of the saint. This is why, as it seems to me, in instituting the appeal to history of which I have spoken, it is imperative to take into account not only the comparative level of average goodness exhibited in two societies, but the comparative fertility of the two societies in the highest types of heroism and sainthood.

THE ULTIMATE TENSION: TIME AND THE HISTORICAL

Nulla tempora tibi coaeterna sunt, quia tu permanes; et illa si permanerent, non essent tempora. . . . Quid est ergo tempus? si nemo ex me quaerat, scio; si quaerenti explicare velim, nescio.—AUGUSTINE.

τυπωθέντα ἀπ' αὐτῶν τρόπον τινὰ δύσφραστον καὶ θαυμαστόν, ὃν εἰς αὖθις μέτιμεν —PLATO.

WE have now, only too inadequately, passed under review some of the outstanding characteristics of the great positive religions which might seem, at least on a surface view, least conciliable with the spirit of rational metaphysics, and may, I believe, say that such opposition as we have detected has, under all its varied forms, a single root. The intellectual discomfort of the metaphysician confronted with positive institutional religion is not due to any merely accidental features of the different great faiths and worships of the world; it has a deeper source in the way in which all these faiths apprehend God, the central object of religion. It is not that there is any ultimate *conflict* between the Theism of the great religions and a strictly philosophical Theism, based on a sound metaphysic. We have not to make our choice between a *dieu des savants et des philosophes* and a *dieu des pauvres et des humbles*, as Elijah bade the people make their choice between Baal and the Lord. The "god of the poor and lowly" is no other than the eternal source of all being demanded by the intellect of the metaphysician; neither the "head" nor the "heart" can be contented with less. Historically Christianity, the faith of the *pauperes et humiles*, has proved to be also the religion which has been most successful in assimilating the natural theology of the great philosophical thinkers. The actual tension between natural and revealed religion arises in a different way. Because they are historical, and in proportion as they are historical, all the great positive religions conceive the relation between man and God as itself involving an irreducible element of the historical; hence their insistence on the permanent significance of individual historical persons, incidents with a date and place, membership of definite historical societies, participation in acts and practices which belong to the web of physical becoming. The tendency of the metaphysical mind, on the other hand, is to find in God simply an answer to a problem about the *rationale*, it may be of nature, or of the moral, or of the specifically religious life, but, in any case, an answer to a problem which deals with *universal* features of the realm of becoming, prescinding from reference to the individual quality of this or that becoming. The problem being posed in this non-historical way, the answer given to it inevitably ignores history.

To reduce the element of permanent truth about God contained in actual religions and theologies simply to the contents of a rational "natural theology" involves committing ourselves to the view that though the metaphysical analysis of becoming, as such, may reveal the presence of God as its super-historical ground, the particular *what* of an individual piece of becoming can never disclose anything not already revealed by this general analysis. Hence acceptance of a positive historical religion requires us to ascribe a significance to time and temporal events and processes which is denied to them by that large body of metaphysicians, old and new, who regard temporality as a sort of illusion which must be overcome before we can reach truth. If time is only a dream, it is reasonable to hold that we shall attain truth about God, or indeed about anything else, only in proportion as we avoid attaching significance to the concrete detail of the historical. Our theologians *par excellence* should be metaphysicians as indifferent to history as Spinoza or Schopenhauer, and our chosen watchword should be *Alles vergängliche ist nur ein Gleichnis*, with a particular emphasis on the *nur*. If time is more than an illusion, the irrationality would be precisely in this indifference to the significance of the concrete historical person, or event, as revelatory of the character of the supra-historical source of all real becoming. At the end of our review we are once more thrown back on the same problem of the status of time of which we spoke, almost at the beginning of our discussions, as the most insistent and perplexing of all the questions of metaphysics.

We may illustrate the insistency of the problem, as well as its importance for theology, by a reference to the marked tendency of definitely Christian thinkers of our own day, under the influence of contemporary philosophical speculation, to revolt from the type of doctrine about God so common in the more philosophical of the Fathers, and, I suppose, universal in the great schoolmen, whose minds had been moulded on the study of Plato and Aristotle. Patristic and scholastic divinity is emphatic in its insistence on the kindred thoughts of the absolute unchangeableness and consequent utter "impassibility" of God. To admit becoming, still more to admit suffering of any kind into the divine nature itself is, from the point of view of this theology, on, if not over, the verge of formal blasphemy. Indeed, if we would be rigidly orthodox scholastics, we

must not even admit the reality of any reciprocal relation between God and His creatures. When we speak
of them as made by Him, as the objects of His love, or
of His displeasure, we are at best using language which
tells us something about the creatures, viz. that they
depend in various ways on God, but nothing about God
Himself. There is no "real" relation of God to anything *ab extra*.

As we know, this line of thought led, in the early
centuries of the formation of dogma, to grave difficulties even about the reality of the redemptive sufferings
of the God-Man. That Christ suffered in reality, not in
mere semblance, in the Garden and on the Cross, could
not be denied without plain and direct contradiction
of the emphatic and repeated declarations of the New
Testament Scriptures, and complete surrender to the
Docetism which, almost from the first, threatened to
evaporate the Gospel into a theosophical fairy-tale.
But how difficult the Graeco-Roman mind found it to
reconcile its conception of Deity with the conviction
that the Passion of Christ is genuine historical fact is
proved by the paradoxical phraseology, ἀπαθῶς ἔπαθεν
and the like, in which the more metaphysically minded
of the Fathers strove to express the thought. Nor are
such phrases a mere antiquarian curiosity. Until well
on in the last century they continued to flourish in the
current language of Christian devotion among ourselves. I can myself well remember a hymn—I do not
know whether it may not still be in use—in which it was
said of the crucified Christ, in the very terminology of
St. Gregory Nyssen, "impassive, he suffers, immortal,
he dies".

When we remember the marked contrast between
Greek metaphysical speculation and the radically
unmetaphysical, frankly anthropomorphic, tone of

Hebrew prophecy, in which the language of human action and passion is unreservedly used about God, it should not be surprising that the last generation has seen a violent reaction, conducted in the name of Christianity itself, against this whole body of conceptions. Whether or not it is good divinity and metaphysics to look for process, suffering, defeat, in the very heart of the divine life itself, there is no doubt that language which implies the real presence of mutability and suffering in the life of God is constantly heard to-day from Christian pulpits—from those of the Roman Church, with all its tenacity of established theological formula, as well as from others—and that everywhere, outside the Roman Church at least, there is a marked tendency on the part of theological writers themselves to attempt an intellectual justification of such language. The late Dr. Fairbairn wrote years ago that "Patripassianism is only half a heresy"; more recent divines of more Churches than one seem ready to go further, and to maintain that Patripassianism is the true Christian orthodoxy, working itself clear at last of entanglement with the errors of Stoicism,[1] that most unhistorical of the major philosophies of antiquity. The late Baron von Hügel has included in his second series of *Essays and Addresses* what to myself seems a wise and timely warning against the dangers of this excessively "Christocentric" theology. But to me the most significant thing about his admirable essay on *Suffering and God* is that the warning should have been felt by the author to be so imperatively needed. It could only be necessary in an age which ascribes to process and temporality a significance very different from that given to them in any Hellenic philosophy. For good or bad, the growth of the sense

---

[1] I may refer for an account of this tendency in contemporary divinity to the careful study of J. K. Mozley, *The Impassibility of God* (Cambridge, 1926).

of the historical has made what our American friends
call the metaphysical "status" of Time the most urgent
of our philosophical problems.

It may be instructive to remind ourselves, at this
point, that according to a view which has a great deal
to say for itself, the permeation of Graeco-Roman
civilisation by a great positive religion is actually the
cause to which we owe it that European thought, unlike Indian, for example, has become, as a whole, thoroughly historical. The κόσμος of pre-Christian Greek
thought only became a really historical world under the
influence of Christianity and its ancestor, Judaism. The
point is excellently put by a very recent writer on the
history of philosophy in a passage which summarises
the position of M. Laberthonnière—a position not accepted by the historian himself—in a few admirable
sentences. " The κόσμος of the Greeks is, as we might
say, a world without a history, an eternal order in which
time counts for nothing, whether because it leaves that
order always self-identical, or because it produces a
series of events which always reverts to the same point
through an indefinite repetition of cyclical changes. Is
not even the history of mankind, according to Aristotle, a perpetual recurrence of the same civilisation?
The antithetic thought that there really are radical
changes, absolute beginnings, genuine discoveries, in
a word, history and progress in the wide sense—such
a thought was impossible until Christianity had swept
away the Greek κόσμος. A world created from nothing,
a destiny which man does not receive from without, but
shapes for himself by his own obedience, or disobedience, to the divine law, a new and unforeseeable divine
intervention to save man from sin, redemption purchased by the sufferings of the God-Man—in all this we
have a dramatic picture of the universe . . . in which

nature is effaced, and everything depends on the intimate spiritual history of man and his relations with God.
Man sees before him a possible future of which he may
be the author; he is delivered for the first time from
Lucretius' melancholy *eadem sunt omnia semper*, from
the Fate of Stoicism, from the eternal geometrical
scheme in which Plato and Aristotle imprisoned the
real. This was the outstanding peculiarity which impressed the first pagans who took the Christians seriously. What is the reproach brought against them by
Celsus? . . . That they worship a God who is not *immutable*, since He takes initiatives and decisions to meet circumstances, nor yet *impassible*, since He is touched by
pity; that they believe in a kind of myth, that of the
Christ, which 'will not permit an allegorical explanation'; in other words, it is presented as genuine history,
and cannot be made into a symbol of physical law."

In reproducing Laberthonnière's thought,[1] M. Bréhier
rightly warns the reader against the danger of making
the antitheses too rigid, but the caution, though necessary if justice is to be done, for example, to the
Platonic conception of the relation of Becoming to
Being, leaves the substantial truth of the contrast un-
affected. It is, in the main, true that all Greek philosophy
au fond teaches the doctrine *plus ça change, plus c'est
la même chose*, exactly as the same thing is taught, with
some small variations in the manner of the instruction,
by the most illustrious of the modern philosophers who
have been markedly in revolt against the traditions
of historical Christianity, Spinoza, Schopenhauer,
Nietzsche; that the moral consequence of brooding on
such doctrines of self-sameness, or of eternal recurrence, has always been *taedium vitae*; that without
new beginnings and non-reversible changes there is no

---

[1] E. Bréhier, *Histoire de la philosophie*, i. 489-90.

genuine history, but only a surface illusion of history; that, in point of fact, the conception of history as a whole with a real significance, and consequently, the idea of a "philosophy of history", makes its first appearance in the great literature of the world with Augustine's *De civitate Dei*, and that its source must be found in the Jewish and Christian Scriptures, with their doctrine of the redemptive purpose of God as the key to history.

These are facts which cannot well be gainsaid, and they have no real counterpart in the pre-Christian Hellenic world, not even in the philosophy which, of all the Hellenic doctrines, comes by far the nearest to a worthy appreciation of the historical, that of Plato. Plato and others might speak of human life as a divine puppet-play,[1] in which God is at once the sole spectator and the manipulator of the marionettes; Thucydides might set himself to compose an accurate narrative of the doings and motives of the two great warring powers, the Athenian "empire" and the Peloponnesian confederacy,[2] as a lesson in statesmanship for future generations, and might incidentally show himself to students who know how to read with understanding the noblest and austerest moralist who has ever written history.[3] But even the "divine" Plato has not yet the clear conviction that the play is working out to an end in which its author-spectator takes a supreme interest, nor does Thucydides see the struggle of which he is the historian as an act in a drama which has significance as a whole, a stage in the "education of humanity". To see things thus, you must understand what is meant by

[1] *Laws*, 803 C φύσει δὲ εἶναι θεὸν μὲν πάσης μακαρίου σπουδῆς ἄξιον, ἄνθρωπον δέ, ὅπερ εἴπομεν ἔμπροσθεν, θεοῦ τι παίγνιον εἶναι μεμηχανημένον, καὶ ὄντως τοῦτο αὐτοῦ τὸ βέλτιστον γεγονέναι.

[2] Thuc. i. 22, 4.

[3] Though he has been strangely mistaken for a Machiavellian by Nietzsche, who does not know how to appreciate the great men of the fifth century B.C. historically.

sic Deus dilexit mundum, and that thought is only very faintly adumbrated when Plato makes his Timaeus speak of the delight the Creator took in the perfection of his handiwork.[1]

The modern historian of civilisation, though often enough he may not know it, is what he is because he cannot get away from the influence of convictions born of the belief that human history has a significance which only became transparent in the concrete individual happening of certain events which began with the call of Abraham out of Harran, reached their climax in the procuratorship of one Pontius Pilate, and the opening of their fifth act on the day of Pentecost. It is in the end the Jew, to whom the "oracles" were entrusted, from whom the Christian community, and through them the modern Western world, has learned to think historically, just because Judaism and Christianity are absolutely bound up with convictions about certain historical events as no system of philosophy is. We owe the "historical sense", on which we sometimes pride ourselves, to the very peculiarity of the "Christian myth" which disconcerted Celsus, the impossibility of sublimating it into a symbol of "physical law", its incorrigible and unabashed concreteness.

I believe we may trace a more subtle effect of the same influence of Christian theology in the fundamental distinction which separates our own most abstract "scientific world-view" from that of all Greek philosophers. If there is one thought rather than another about the physical order itself which is specially characteristic of the Hellenic natural philosophers, it is their conviction that all physical processes are reversible;

---

[1] *Tim.* 37 C ὡς δὲ κινηθὲν αὐτὸ καὶ ζῶν ἐνόησεν . . . ὁ γεννήσας πατήρ, ἠγάσθη. This is an exact counterpart of "God saw his work that it was good"; but even Plato does not know that God loves sinners.

whatever has taken the "way up" may always be expected, in time, to take the "way down" again, and
vice versa. If vapour condenses into water, and water
into earth, earth is once more rarefied into water, and
water into vapour. If atoms once come together in an
eddy and so form a "world", they must scatter again, and
the scattering will unmake the world;[1] but the *débris* will
again come together a second time after the scattering,
and a "world" will be made over again. So in Aristotle's
universe, though it never was made and never is unmade,
there is one, and only one, set of motions which are
irreversible, the revolutions of the celestial "spheres",
and the reason of the irreversibility is precisely that these
motions and no others have a direct *supra-mundane*
source. In Plato's *Timaeus* we are told, indeed, that the
making of the world will not, in fact, be followed hereafter by an antithetic unmaking; but here again the
reason for the irreversibility is a theological and supra-
mundane one, the will of its Creator. "Ye are indeed
not wholly immortal, nor indissoluble", says the
Creator in that dialogue to the "created gods", who are,
in fact, the stars, "yet ye shall have no dissolution, nor
taste of death, since ye have in my will a greater and
stronger bond than those with which ye were com-
pacted in your making".[2]

---

[1] Cf. Lucretius, v. 243:

quapropter maxima mundi
cum videam membra ac partis consumpta regigni,
scire licet caeli quoque item terraeque fuisse
principiale aliquod tempus clademque futuram;

ii. 1144:

sic igitur magni quoque circum moenia mundi
expugnata dabunt labem putrisque ruinas:
omnia debet enim cibus integrare novando
et fulcire cibus, etc.

The Christians agreed with Lucretius in expecting an "end" of the "world",
but they looked forward to this end as the entrance on a better and abiding
world, not as a recurrence to the beginning of an old and tedious story.

[2] *Tim.* 41 B.

Our thought about nature, on the other hand, is dominated by the so-called principle of Carnot, the law of the "dissipation" of energy, which, by forbidding us to believe in the complete reversibility of any temporal processes, profoundly modifies our conception of time itself. For us the "world's great age" does not and cannot "begin anew"; the images of the phoenix renewing its youth in its own funeral pyre,[1] or the snake casting its senility with its skin, have lost their cosmic significance. What has happened once does not, and cannot, happen again, and thus the historical event has won for us an absolute and unique individuality which it could not have for any ancient thinker. To us it is not irreversibility but reversibility which would be the *miraculum*, demanding an immediate cause *extra rerum naturam*.

The reluctance of many men of science to accept Carnot's principle as valid for natural processes at large without restriction, their readiness to make heavy draughts on imagination of what may be contained in inaccessible regions of space and time to upset it,[2] are still with us to testify to the difficulty with which physical science accommodates itself to a strictly historical way of conceiving becoming. If, in spite of these protests, the mass of our scientific men look askance at ingenious devices for getting rid of the second law of Thermodynamics, the reason seems to be that they are antecedently prepossessed in favour of irreversibility by the distinctly modern "sense for the historical", itself so largely a creation of Christian theology. It is from the history of human life that they have drawn the conviction that the past does *not* recur, and when they make its non-recurrence into a corner-stone of

---

[1] The phoenix has its meaning as a Christian symbol too, as when Crashaw writes "the phoenix builds the phoenix' nest," but it does not mean the κόσμος.

[2] Cf. É. Meyerson, *L'Explication dans les sciences*, i. 206, ii. 405-6.

their physics, they are definitely breaking through the old classical Platonic tradition of a purely geometrical natural world. We see exactly the same tendency to make physical science historical, in a way in which it could not be historical under the classical tradition, from Plato to Newton, in the anxiety of Dr. Whitehead to save natural philosophy from becoming flatly "incredible" by making the eminently historical concept of "organism" its foundation.[1] Must we not say, in the light of such considerations, that the peculiarity which Celsus alleged as a reproach against the spirit of Christianity, its insistence on a μῦθος which cannot be allegorised, is in fact its glory? What the complaint really means is that with Christianity there came, for the first time, into the Graeco-Roman world, a really adequate appreciation of individuality.[2] We are still far from having done full justice in our philosophy and science to all the implications of this heightened sense of the reality of the individual, but we are on our way to do so. The historicising, if I may call it so, of the physical sciences, now apparently in process, is but one further step along the same road which has led, in our moral, social, and religious thinking, to the conquest of the great conception, so imperfectly grasped in ancient philosophy, of personality in God and man.

The particular point to which I would ask attention at present, then, is this. All the various tendencies, so familiar to us in the intellectual life of our age, which are most hostile to the recognition of the historical as an indispensable element in religion, the disparagement as merely temporary and accidental of everything in the positive religions which resists reduction to positions

---

[1] Cf. *Science and the Modern World*, cc. 5, 6.

[2] I suppose the nearest Greek equivalent to "individual" is the Aristotelian τόδε τι. But the equivalence is most imperfect. The most commonplace John Smith is something a great deal more than ἄνθρωπός τις.

of general metaphysics, the hardly concealed desire of some even among our theologians to obliterate the distinctions between a faith like Christianity and the kind of religion possible to a Neo-Platonic philosopher, the anxiety of metaphysicians of various schools to interpret the affirmations of all the positive religions as no more than figurative expressions of some vague principle of "conservation of values", all are, if we come to reflect, only forms of the old protest against the "myth which refuses to be allegorised". And this means that they spring from inability to adjust one's mind to the characteristically modern habit of thinking historically, as one sees, in fact, quite plainly in the efforts of the small minority who "follow the argument wherever it leads" to discard even the bare fact of the actual historical existence of a personal founder of Christianity.

It should be easy to see that the position of these extremists is at variance with sane judgement and common sense, and one takes no great risk in prophesying that their thesis, in its cruder forms, will soon be laughed out of the world. Men who can believe that Christ and the apostles are astral symbols, or Semitic nature-deities, or the creations of pious romancers, deserve to end by believing that Francis Bacon was the heir to the crown of England and the creator of Falstaff, or that the date of the Millennium is built into the Great Pyramid. But it is not so easy, in view of the tardiness with which the full implications of the significance of individuality are making their way from the human into the physical sciences, to guard our own thinking from infection by subtler forms of the same prejudice. We are all still too much, in a great part of our thinking, under the spell of the ancient conception of the unhistorical, purely geometrical, world. If we were not, it would surely strike us as something of a paradox that philosophers should be trying to make religion truer by the elimination of the historical in the same age in which they are trying to make physical science truer by its introduction. If the geometrising of nature, thoroughly carried out, leads to the incredible,[1] is it likely that the geometrising of God will have any other result?

Perhaps I can best illustrate what I mean by the characteristic difference between the ancient geometrical and the modern historical conceptions of time and the temporal, if I start from a well-known and eloquent passage of Plato's *Timaeus*, and consider how the description of time given there differs from that to which our own modern physical science appears to be finding its way. This may look like going a long way back for the purposes of the contrast, but it will, I think, be seen as we proceed that the ideas of Timaeus are in principle those which dominate the seventeenth-century classical mechanics from Galileo and Descartes to Newton. In the passage to which I refer, time is being described as a uniform "measure" of becoming, becoming having already been set in the strongest possible contrast with the stable and selfsame *being* of eternity. We have already been told in a general way that the world which *becomes*, the historical world, was fashioned by its Maker in the likeness of a model which does not *become*, but *is*, the αὐτὸ ὃ ἔστι ζῷον, or intelligible pattern of a supreme living organism embracing all other organisms. The narrative proceeds, "And when the Father who had begotten it beheld it, a created image of the eternal things,[2] moving and quick, he was well-

---

[1] Whitehead, *Science and the Modern World*, p. 80: "It"—*i.e.* the Newtonian scheme taken as an account of the real world—"is fully worthy of the genius of the century which produced it. . . . It is not only reigning, but it is without a rival. And yet—it is quite unbelievable."

[2] *Tim.* 37 C. The MSS. read τῶν ἀιδίων θεῶν "of the eternal *gods*", but θεῶν is pretty certainly an old corruption.

pleased, and rejoicing devised how to make it yet more like its model. Since, then, that model is, of a truth, a thing living and eternal, he essayed to make this All also such, so far as he might. Now the nature of that living thing was in truth eternal, and this it was impossible to bestow wholly on a creature. But he contrived the making of a moving likeness of eternity; so in his ordering of the heavens, he fashioned an everlasting likeness, proceeding by number, of eternity that abides in unity, even that we have named time."[1]

There are several points in this passage deserving notice. In the first place, time is conceived, as it was to be in the classic mechanics of later days, as something in its nature independent of extension, or volume, and adventitious to it. We have already heard of "becoming", and also of corporeality and its three dimensions as characteristic of "the creature", before it is mentioned that it was endowed with temporality, as an added perfection. Timaeus clearly does not think of "that we have named time" as logically complicated with that which we name *volume*; to him it is manifestly conceivable that there might be volumes, and even movements, without time, though a world of this kind would be less "like its eternal model", and therefore a worse world, than the one which is actual. This means that, like Dr. Whitehead, Timaeus distinguishes between "passage", transitoriness, as a universal character of the physical world throughout its parts, and the *measure* of that passage which we call "time". It is also implied that there is just *one* such measure of passage, one time which, in the well-known phrase of Newton, "flows equably". We may, indeed, use the periodic movements of any of the heavenly bodies we please as our timepiece, and Timaeus is careful, in a

[1] *Tim.* 37 C-D.

later passage,[1] to censure the dullness of mankind in general, who speak of the periods of sun and moon as "time", but do not see that the name is equally applicable to those of any other "planets". But all that he means by this is that the period of any one of these bodies may always be computed in terms of the period of any other, so that if you reckon by periods of Mars, for example, you will speak of a lapse of five such periods where another man, reckoning in the more customary way, would talk of a lapse of ten years. He really means only to complain of the general neglect to determine the periods of all the planets with proper precision.[2] This complaint does not affect his fundamental assumption that any lapse or interval in the universe has an unambiguous measure; in the sense there is a single "universal" or "absolute" time, in which events may be unambiguously located, though we may use different unit-intervals for its computation, just as we may measure a single unambiguous interval of length either by the foot or by the metre.

The "time" of Timaeus is thus precisely the "true, absolute, or mathematical time" of Newton's *Principia*. This explains what is perhaps the most striking feature of the description I have quoted. The *temporality* of "becoming", because it has been thus carefully distinguished from its mere transitoriness, or successiveness, is dwelt upon not as the character which distinguishes what "becomes" from what "is", but as the point of closest resemblance. The world is given the form of time, not to differentiate it from its "intelligible" model, but to make it as like that model as the case will

---

[1] *Tim.* 39 C.

[2] In fact, his point seems to be simply that mankind at large do not understand that the revolutions of all the planets—the word means literally the "tramps" of the sky—are as much embodiments of "natural law" as those of the sun and moon upon which man depends for his knowledge of times and seasons. The "tramps" are not really vagabonds.

permit. The thought is that by receiving its unambiguous location in the universal time-order, a given piece of becoming is de-individualised; it is taken out of the immediate concrete "flow" of things, and receives a kind of quasi-eternalisation by being made thus abstract. This is why time is said to be not merely an εἴδωλον or ἄγαλμα, an image, but an εἰκών, a true *likeness* of eternity.[1]

If we put all this together, may we not fairly state its implications thus? The temporal as we directly experience it, in all the concreteness of actually lived life, is at the furthest remove from the reality of things; "perceptual time", *durée réelle* as Bergson calls it, with its indefinitely varied pulsations, is mostly according to the estimate suggested by the language of the *Timaeus*, illusion. It is the "abstract" and "conceptional" duration of the Newtonian scheme, divorced from all setting in a framework of individual experience, "clock-time", as fixed by reference to a single flawless ideal time-keeper for the universe at large, and sharply contrasted with the personal and "local" time of a particular observer, which is the *real* time, so far as the epithet "real" is applicable to the temporal. The nearer we get to the locating of events in such a cosmic chronological scheme, the nearer we are getting to the "truth about the facts". The further we are from it, the further from reality. When we speak of the "glorious hour of crowded life" as brief, and the hours of monotonous pain or boredom as intolerably long, we are nearest to concrete experience, but furthest from reality and truth. What is most vivid in the actual experience is also most delusive. If by "rationalisation" of the individual we mean

---

[1] It is also why "time", like the exact geometrical structure of the corpuscles of Timaeus, is expressly said to be contributed to the physical world by νοῦς or God, the intelligent and purposive "cause", not by ἀνάγκη.

what rationalists in philosophy have only too often meant, the reduction of it to a featureless uniformity of pattern, succession is all but completely rationalised in Newton's account of "true, mathematical" time, or, what comes to much the same, Kant's account of time as a pure "form of intuition"; the only element of the unrationalised "given" left is that provided by the bald fact that, as Timaeus says, the likeness is not the same thing as the model, that succession itself is irreducibly there, that there *is* "temporal location". All that makes the *tempo* of one succession so recognisably different from that of another has been eliminated, exactly as, to use an arresting phrase of Dr. Whitehead, "the shapiness of shapes"[1] is eliminated from pure geometry. In being thus reduced to uniformity succession has lost its significance for life and become unhistorical, just in proportion as it has lost its character of being mysterious and baffling. Time, thus standardised, becomes what it has been pronounced to be by an eminent philosopher recently lost to us, a form which reveals very little of the true nature of reality.[2]

Let me turn for a moment, by way of contrast, to very different conceptions which have been made widely current in our own day, first by the brilliant polemic of Bergson, and then by the rise among the physicists of the ideas to which we owe the "theory of Relativity", in its various forms. I am speaking, of course, as an utter

[1] *Science and the Modern World*, p. 38: "This fact, that the general conditions transcend any one set of particular entities, is the ground for the entry into mathematics, and into mathematical knowledge, of the notion of the 'variable'. It is by the employment of this notion that general conditions are investigated without any specification of particular entities. This irrelevance of the particular entities has not been generally understood; for example, the shapiness of shapes, *e.g.* circularity and sphericity and cubicality as in actual experience, do not enter into the geometrical reasoning."

[2] Bosanquet, *Logic*[2], i. 258: "Time is real as a condition of the experience of sensitive subjects, but it is not a form which profoundly exhibits the unity of things".

outsider in all matters of physical science, and I am not suggesting that either Bergson or any later *Natur- philosoph* has actually succeeded in working out a final and consistent metaphysic of time. We are, I take it, only at the beginning of a philosophical reinterpretation of nature which will need to be developed further, by men of the highest originality and acumen, before its deepest implications become fully clear to us. Yet both in Bergson and in the later theorists of Relativity we may note certain definite advances in the direction of a sound metaphysic of temporal process, which are bound to affect future "philosophy of history" very deeply.

To begin with Bergson. The permanently valuable feature of his treatment of succession appears to me to be simply his insistence on the real and profound difference between *durée réelle* and the artificial "mathematical" or "clock" time of our scientific manuals. That point, as I venture to think, Bergson made plain once for all in unusually impressive fashion in the three chapters of *Les données immédiates de la conscience*, though his own account of the process by which the second comes to be so easily confused with the first has always seemed to me unsatisfactory, since, so far as I can see, it both involves error of fact and also manifestly never gets to the heart of the problem. It is confusing and mischievous to see in intellect itself, as Bergson professes to do, a faculty inherently deceptive.[1] Reasoned philosophy cannot credit intellect with this inherent deceptiveness without committing suicide. It is not, I should say, true that the intellect is what Bergson seems to think it, essentially a *geometrising* faculty, if by this is

[1] Cf. Whitehead, *Science and the Modern World*, p. 74: "I agree with Bergson in his protest; but I do not agree that such distortion is a vice necessary to the intellectual apprehension of nature."

meant, as Bergson shows by the development of his argument that he means, a *measuring* faculty. If it were true that the fundamental operation of the understanding is to measure, surely metrical geometry ought not to be, as it appears in fact to be, a complex doctrine resting on the application of special metrical axioms and conventions to the simpler system of pure descriptive geometry; it should itself be the whole of the science, and descriptive non-metrical geometry ought to have no existence.[1] And, again, there ought to be no sciences but those of measurement and calculation; there should be no such things as the historical sciences, whose task is not to measure, calculate, and compute, but to interpret; and, again, no branches even of the mathematical sciences in which the fundamental conception is neither magnitude, nor number, but order. Indeed, if the intellect were really limited in its procedure in the way Bergson assumes, it is hard to understand how it could ever have discovered and proclaimed its own defect.

Again, the evolutionary explanation of the alleged limitation offered us, by the suggestion that intelligence has been fashioned under the stress of the practical necessity of finding our way about among the bodies around us, and is therefore naturally only competent for that task, seems to be naught. Even if we accept this speculation about the "origins" of intellect without misgivings, as we are not all prepared to do, it is a dangerous assumption that a power "evolved" to meet a particular practical need, can, when it has been evolved, do nothing but meet that particular need. Consider, for example, our capacity to appreciate beauty. Either this appreciation has come into exist-

---

[1] On the relation of metrical to projective and descriptive geometry see Russell, *Principles of Mathematics*, cc. xlvii., xlviii.; Couturat, *Les Principes des mathématiques*, pp. 190 ff.

ence by being "evolved" to meet a practical need, or it
has not. If it has not, there seems no reason to assume
that our capacity of understanding must have its origin
in the pressure of practical needs. If it has, then it is at
least clear that a "faculty" originally called into existence to meet a practical need continues, in this case, to
serve wholly different purposes, and why may not the
same thing be true about the "intellectual powers"?
Finally, if we agree to leave these questions unraised,
even on the double assumption that intelligence has
"originated" entirely under the pressure of specific
practical needs, and can do nothing, now that it is in
existence, but meet those particular needs, it is pertinent, is it not, to remember that ever since living creatures have existed, it has been as much a practical
problem for them to understand one another and establish a *modus vivendi* among themselves as to pick their
way among their inanimate surroundings. So that, even
on Bergson's own assumptions about the way in which
intelligence has been developed, there seems to be no
particular reason why its capacities should have the
limitations he supposes.

Moreover, it seems a subordinate falsification of the
facts to say, as Bergson apparently does,[1] that the whole
"distortion" effected by the intellect in its attempts to
deal with time arises from the dependence of all measurement on the primary measurement of segments of
straight lines. All measurement is not measurement
of lengths on a straight line; there is a second most important measurement of intervals, independent of such
measurement of lengths, the estimation of angles, or,
what comes to the same thing, of the ratios of arcs of

---

[1] At least this seems to be assumed throughout the argument (*op. cit.* c. 2)
offered to show that time "as a homogeneous medium" is reducible to space.
(E. Tr. *Time and Free Will*, p. 98.) It seems to be forgotten that "spatial" measurement itself has its own problems.

circles to the whole circumferences. In point of fact, it is by angular measurement that we habitually estimate temporal intervals, whenever we appeal to a watch or a clock, and in the prehistoric past, the first rough estimates of intervals within the natural day must presumably have been made, independently of measurement of lengths, by this same method, with the sky for clock-face. Measurement of temporal intervals is thus primarily angular measurement, and angular measurement is, in its origin, independent of measurement of straight lines.

It is true, of course, that when we come to the construction of a complete metrical theory, we find ourselves driven to establish a correlation between these two, originally independent, systems of measurement. For in practice I can only assure myself that two angular measurements are equal by reference to the circle, the one plane curve of constant curvature, and I satisfy myself that my curve of reference is a circle by ascertaining the equality of length of its diameters, and this is done by the rotation of a measuring-rod. This consideration suggests two observations. One is that the problem which has attracted Bergson's special attention is not rightly conceived when it is spoken of as the translation of temporal into spatial magnitude, or the imposing of spatial form on the non-spatial. It is only one case of the more general problem of the "rectification of a circular arc", which, of course, meets us in metrical geometry itself, independently of any application to the estimation of temporal intervals. The only inevitable "deformation" which arises in connection with measurement, so far as I can see, is the element of approximation and error introduced when we attempt to find an expression for the *length* of an arc of a curve, and *this* "deformation", as I say, has no necessary correlation with time. The difference between *durée réelle* and "mathematical" time must therefore be due to some other cause than the alleged artificial establishment of a correlation between temporal intervals and intervals on a straight line. It must come in already in the first attempt to apply *angular* measurement to temporal lapses, if it comes at all.

It should be further observed that the estimation of linear intervals themselves, apparently assumed by Bergson to be the special function of the intellect, and therefore to involve no difficulty or mystery, presents a real problem on its own account. Measurements made with different straight lines as axes can only be compared if we presuppose that the rotation of a measuring-stick, or its transference from one point of application to another, either makes no difference to its length, or affects it in a way which we can precisely determine. If our measuring-rods can change their length as they are turned through an angle, or carried from one place to another, and that to an unknown extent, there is an end of all comparison between segments of different straight lines. We have to postulate that our measuring-stick either remains of constant length during the process of transference from one position to another, or, at any rate, that if it changes its length during the process, it does so in accord with some knowable law of functional dependence. For this reason, some reference to *time* would appear to be involved in any set of postulates of spatial measurement. The complication of space with time is thus more intimate than it would be on Bergson's assumption that measurements primarily form an exclusively spatial framework into which duration is subsequently and, in fact, accidentally inserted, with a good deal of deformation, by the misguided "surface" intellect. This is what I had in mind in saying above that Bergson's doctrine seems to me, after all, not to get to the heart of the real problem.

It is just here, as I think, that the broad philosophical implications of the theory of Relativity come to our aid, and would still be forced upon us as metaphysicians, even if there were not well-known specific difficulties in the details of physical science, which seem to be most readily disposed of by the theory. The general implications of which I am thinking are, so far as I can see, independent of the divergences between the versions of "Relativity" advocated by individual physicists; their value, as I think, is that they enable us to formulate the problem to which Bergson has the eminent merit of making the first approach in a clear and definite way, and to escape what I should call the impossible dualism to which Bergson's own proposed solution commits him. So long as you think, as Bergson does, on the one hand, of an actual experience which is sheer qualitative flux and variety, and on the other, of a geometrical ready-made framework of sheer non-qualitative abidingness, there seems to be no possible answer to the question how *such* a "matter" comes to be forced into the strait-waistcoat of so inappropriate a "form", except to lay the blame on some wilful *culpa originalis* of the intellect. But if the intellect suffers from a *culpa originis, all* philosophical or rational thinking, including Bergson's own theorising about the purely qualitative nature of "real duration", is vitiated at its source. If the intellect is so radically corrupted, philosophy or science ought to be as impossible without supernatural revelation as morality must be, if the human will had been *totally* "depraved by the fall of Adam". Yet Bergson puts forward his own philosophy as the product of ordinary rational reflection, not of special supernatural illumination. Moreover, as I have said already, his speculation loses its attractiveness when we reflect that it must always have been as much an intellectual necessity for our ancestors to find a *modus vivendi* among themselves as to explore the topography of their *habitat*. The "social environment" is as old and as insistent a condition of life as the geographical. Hence, even if we feel no difficulty in bisecting our experience into two mutually exclusive domains, an "outer" acquaintance with the bodily environment, and an "inner" experience of social and moral environment—though meditation on Kant's *Refutation of Idealism*[1] ought surely to suggest serious difficulty— it is hard to see what features of the second, if Bergson has described it correctly, can have suggested the systematic deformation of it by the imposition of a radically alien type of structure. We should rather expect to find the whole *given* falling apart into two separate and disjunct fields, the intrinsically geometrical field of an "outer world", devoid of temporal form, and an intrinsically durational "inner world", ungeometrisable, and therefore wholly non-metrical. For it is obvious that not every "matter" is susceptible indifferently of every "form"; the "matter" which is to exhibit, on being subjected to certain operations, the metrical "form" must at least have *dispositionem quandam ad formam*.

I believe we escape this difficulty when we put ourselves at the point of view from which the various formulations of the theory of Relativity agree in taking their departure. In the recognition that the true source of the problem to which Bergson has called attention lies deeper than he supposed, in the impossibility of *locating* an experience temporally without reference to space, or spatially without reference to time, we

---

[1] *KdrV*.[2] 274 [*Werke*, iii. 197]. Cf. N. Kemp Smith, *Commentary on Critique of Pure Reason*, 298 ff.

reach a standpoint which no longer presupposes the primitive bisection of experience into "outer" and "inner" against which the Kantian refutation of "idealism" protested, and therefore no longer requires us to believe in the transference of metrical structure from one domain, where it is supposed to be wholly adequate, to another, where it is merely inappropriate. We do justice to the patent fact that in life as it is lived the "inner" and the "outer" are given to us inseparably conjoined in every pulse of experience, and that every constituent of the "given" thus has intrinsically, for each experient, its own orientation in an individual "space" and dating in an equally individual personal "time", and the two are given together.

Every one of my concrete "experiences" has its own intrinsic *when* and its own intrinsic *where* in the "fourfold continuum" of my life of personal interaction with my "environment". Our difficulties, the very difficulties which lead in the end to the formulation of the theory of Relativity, arise in the process of "transsubjective" intercourse between persons, because such communication imposes on us the necessity to devise a supra-personal system of reference by which experients at different *wheres* may adjust their statements about the *when* of an event, and experients at different *whens* their statements about its *where*. Thus it becomes necessary to construct a scheme of location in space without reference to "local time", and of location in time without reference to the experient's momentary *where*. This process, described by Bergson as the forcing of an alien geometrical form upon experiences of pure duration, is really something different; it is a process of cutting location in time and location in space, originally given in actual experience together, loose from one another, and the motive for the artificial separation now becomes obvious. It arises from the need of mutual understanding between a plurality of experients. The separation of space and time is thus seen to be no freak of the intellect presuming beyond its proper limits, but an inevitable and justified moment in the execution of its rightful business. We are thus delivered from the view, really fatal to serious thinking, that we can get nearer to understanding reality by merely setting ourselves to undo the results of intelligent reflection, and reverting to a primitive intuition which is only another name for crude apprehension of the unanalysed and *not* understood. At the same time, the discovery that all metrical comparison of spatial magnitudes involves reference to time and date, and all comparison of durational magnitudes reference to place, makes it clear that, necessary as the separation is, it can never be carried completely through.[1]

If there is to be intercommunication, the intercommunication must have a common "timeless space", and a common "spaceless time", which may be used indifferently as frameworks of reference by experients located in different *whens* and *wheres*, but it is inherently impossible to construct a single timeless space, or spaceless time, which could serve as schemes of reference indifferently for *all* experients whatsoever. Thus the most "spaceless" temporal scheme we can construct for the purpose of unambiguous dating is, after all, weighted with an inherent reference to our *ubi*;

---

[1] The process is necessary, because it is part of that "rationalisation" of experience without which communication between persons would be impossible, and the communication of experience is necessary for the understanding of it. It can never be fully carried through, because no experience is completely communicable in its concreteness. Plato understood this better, perhaps, than any philosopher before or since. *Ep.* vii. 343 E ἡ δὲ διὰ πάντων αὐτῶν (*sc.* names, λόγοι, δόξαι, etc. ᾿διαγωγή, ἄνω καὶ κάτω μεταβαίνουσα ἐφ᾿ ἕκαστον, μόγις ἐπιστήμην ἐνέτεκεν εὖ πεφυκότος εὖ πεφυκότι, and yet none of the indispensable means of communicating ἐπιστήμη can ever communicate it whole and unambiguous. *Ib.* 343 B μυρίος δὲ λόγος αὖ περὶ ἑκάστου τῶν τεττάρων, ὡς ἀσαφές.

it is a "local" time, though independent of the particular *ubi* of the individual experient who uses it, exactly
as "Greenwich time" provides a common scheme for
unambiguous dating, but a scheme only common to
experients who are related by the condition that their
particular *wheres* are all on the surface of our planet, and
that they thus all partake in the motions of the planet
relative to other bodies. There can be no one unambiguous scheme of location in either space or time valid for
all experients, independently of *every* restricting condition. And the restricting condition of a common supra-
individual scheme of spatial location will always involve
reference to time, that of a common impersonal scheme
for dating reference to space.[1] The presence of these
restricting conditions plainly means that every supra-
personal space or time system of reference is artificial, or
"conventional", and, to that extent, arbitrary. But the
arbitrariness is not the same thing as wilful caprice.

The difference is this. As the exponents of the theory
put it, all such schemes involve the making of a "cut"
between separation in time and separation in space, and
the precise way in which the "cut" is to be made depends on the position of the experient making it in
the fourfold "space-time" continuum. This position is
arbitrary, in the sense that it is not dictated by the intrinsic character of the continuum itself that *A* should
have his position in it here and now, *B* there and then.
But it is not capricious; *A* does not assign himself his
position "at his own sweet will". That his position is
what it is is given fact from which *A* cannot get away.
It is thus, to take a simple example, arbitrary that the
"common time" of a plurality of human observers
should be Greenwich time, or Paris time. But it is not

[1] Cf. Whitehead, *Principles of Natural Knowledge*, cc. 9-12; *Theory of Relativity*, c. 2; Eddington, *Nature of the Physical World*, lecture 3.

a matter of caprice, of "postulation" in what *seems* to be
the Pragmatist sense of the word,[1] that the "common
time" of human astronomers and cartographers should
be based on the selection of a meridian of the earth for
reference; this condition is dictated, not indeed by the
intrinsic character of temporal reckoning, but by the
given fact that these *savants* are human beings, and
that the habitat of man is just this particular planet.

The impossibility of working out a single unambiguous scheme which shall make the "cut" between the
spatial and the temporal in precisely the same way for
all experients, without any cross-reference to their
when in the one case, or their *where* in the other, once
more illustrates the principle on which we have repeatedly insisted, that though "rationalisation" of the
given is the rightful and sole function of human intellect,
the rationalisation, from the very nature of the problem,
can never be carried out to the point of resolving the
whole content of the given into completely analysed
connections. However far the process may be carried,
we are always still left with an unexhausted residue of
the simply given and unexplained. In the words of
our homely proverb, there are always more fish in the
sea than have ever come out of it, and this is why we
need never fear that the successive triumphs of intellect will ever have the melancholy consequence that
experience will cease to furnish men with mysteries
which provoke their curiosity, and so supply the intellect itself with its necessary stimulus.

My point, then, is that Bergson was right in asserting that duration as lived through has a rich individual
content, and that when the immediate experience is,

---

[1] I say "seems", because I have never been able to discover with certainty
whether the leading professed "Pragmatists" really mean what their insistence
on the "personal factor" ought to imply, or something much more moderate, to
which I, for one, should have no objection, or both at once.

for perfectly legitimate purposes, replaced by the concept of monotonous uniform clock-time, this actual content of experienced duration has been artificially eliminated. He is right, again, in holding that it is this wealth of unanalysed content which makes duration as experienced historical and individual, and the elimination of it which explains why chronology is so different from, and inferior to, history. But in his further speculation I should contend that he is doubly wrong: wrong in supposing, as he seems to suppose, that there is not a difference of exactly the same kind between real volume and the qualityless, purely "mathematical" volume of the geometer,[1] and wrong, also, in treating the process of "abstraction" by which we form the concept of clock-time as a sort of wanton blunder of the intellect, which the philosopher is called on simply to undo. The abstractive process, indispensable if the given is to be understood, is as salutary as it is necessary; the only pure error which calls for mere reversal is the error, which there is no logical necessity to commit, of supposing that the result of abstractive analysis has preserved the whole content of the concrete experience, of forgetting the presence of the unexplored remainders, of taking the function of analysis, which is to discriminate features within an unexhausted whole, to be the substitution for the whole of something else. If we are clear on these points, we shall not be tempted to imagine that scientific analysis and persistent thinking are no more than an elaborate process of misunderstanding, or to believe that the way to understand an inexhaustible reality is to stop thinking about it, and surrender ourselves to an undirected impressionism.

The defect of Bergson's method in philosophy has

---

[1] I am thinking of Prof. Whitehead's happy references to the mathematician's complete neglect of the "shapiness of shapes" already quoted.

always seemed to me to be that, however sound his impressions may be, as they clearly were in his intense appreciation of the variety of *durée réelle*, by his depreciation of logical thinking he deprives himself of all means of convincing us that they are sound. This, I imagine, is why, in spite of what seems to be the ultra-Monism of his metaphysic, he could be so eagerly welcomed as a philosophical Messiah by a professed radical pluralist like William James. It really looks to me as though James was more anxious that a philosophy should be *un*reasoned than that it should be true. Whatever else the philosophical exponents of the "theory of Relativity" have done, or failed to do, they have at least succeeded in showing that the distinction between real "becoming" and the de-individualised events of an abstract kinematical scheme can be reached as surely (and more intelligently) by exceptionally resolute hard thinking as by surrender to first impressions.

The main point for which I am contending, then, is this. We have at last learned to think of the simplest processes of "becoming", or "happening", as historical in a sense to which none of the familiar classical philosophies of ancient or modern times does justice, unless we are to make an exception in favour of Leibniz. We can think of all such processes as individual to the core, as intrinsically irreducible to any mere kinematical scheme. None of them, it seems, can any longer be thought of as no more than a mere translation through a temporal interval of an object which is what it is, and all that it is, "at a mathematical instant", so that the time through which the object "lasts" is external to its specific nature.

I may illustrate the point from an analogous difference remarked upon by M. Meyerson,[1] between our

---

[1] É. Meyerson, *L'Explication dans les sciences*, i. 273 ff.

view of the spatial character of events and that which reigned until yesterday. M. Meyerson observes that we find a difficulty to-day in conceiving the adventures of Gulliver in Lilliput and Brobdingnag which could not have been felt by a reader of the eighteenth century. To the men of that, and indeed of the greater part of the nineteenth century, there was no inherent incredibility in the fiction that there are somewhere on our planet creatures precisely like human beings in every respect but their "absolute size", English and French, like the English and French we know, except for the single fact that they are constructed on a much smaller or larger physical scale.[1] For such a supposition was in keeping with the standing assumption of the science of the period that the only difference between the "molar" and the "molecular", or "sub-molecular" worlds is one of scale, groups of molecules or atoms, for example, behaving exactly after the fashion of reduced solar systems. Even after the rise of modern chemistry, as we know, the physics of the early nineteenth century was still dominated by this analogy; physicists and physical chemists were looking everywhere for explanations of natural processes based on the transference of the Newtonian conceptions of attraction and the law of the "inverse square" to molecules or atoms. To-day Swift's fiction is incredible to us for a much more serious reason than the absence of Lilliput and Brobdingnag from the map. We are satisfied that size is not a purely external and accidental character; molecules do not simply behave after the fashion of big visible lumps of stuff, nor atoms or electrons after the fashion of molecules. The molecular world is not a

[1] Johnson, who was prejudiced against Swift, it may be remembered, denied that his fiction showed any real invention. "When once you have thought of big men and little men", he said at the Club on Friday, March 24, 1775, "it is very easy to do all the rest."

reduced replica of the molar, nor the sub-molecular of the molecular.

No one, it appears, has so far succeeded in devising a wholly satisfactory account of the behaviour of the electrons which constitute an atom, but one thing, at least, seems clear, that they behave in ways to which the deportment of members of a solar system offers no analogy. Thus, our conviction is that, in some unexplained way, there is an intrinsic connection between the scale on which a thing is built and its qualitative behaviour. In the same way I should anticipate that the philosophy and science of the future will probably come to recognise an intrinsic connection between the quality of real "happenings" and their temporal scale. (Indeed, I presume it follows from the mutual implication of space and time by each other that the connection cannot show itself in the one without showing itself in the other as well.) We may, I think, take it that a piece of real becoming regularly has its own distinctive *tempo*, intrinsic to it in the same way in which the *tempo* of a musical "movement" may be said to be intrinsic. If one changes the *tempo* of a funeral march, what one gets is not a funeral march with the pace of a polka, but something which is not a funeral march at all. So, I feel confident, if we could cut down the duration of the rhythmic cycle of our daily physical existence from twenty-four hours to twelve, we should not have left the quality of the life standing. A being who got through two of his periods to our one would not be a man living twice as fast as the rest of us, but a creature with a new type and quality of life.

Now this, if it is true, means that every different type of "continuant" involved in the cosmic "becoming" has quite literally its own "biography": the translation of the historical succession of its phases into events in an abstract scientific "absolute time" demands the same sort, though not necessarily the same degree, of artificial reconstruction and schematisation as does the transcription of a piece of living human experience, in which, as lived, time has now raced, now ambled, now crawled, into a succession of chronological dates. The differences between the *tempi* of various "becomings" in the infra-conscious world will not, of course, reveal themselves to the continuants involved as such differences disclose themselves in our human sense of the contrast between "swift-footed" and "slow-pacing" time, but, for all that, they will show themselves in the qualitative character of the contribution made by each continuant to the whole "becoming" of the world. And this should make a very real difference to a philosophy of history. The more thoroughly we are convinced that the course of events is a complex of patterns of which the ingredients are individual "lives", or, if the suggestions of that word are thought unduly biological, individual "adventures", with a bewildering maze of *tempi*, the more completely shall we be emancipated from the tendency to look on history as a mere transcription into temporal succession of some general "law", capable of being formulated in advance of the facts, just as we are the more emancipated from the confusion of history with such disciplines as economics, the more vividly we apprehend the truth that human history is not made by "economic forces", but by countless individual men and women, not one of whom is an "economic man". To be aware that history, the course of the actual, is made by individual creatures, and therefore by agents saturated with contingency, is to be delivered from that *a-priorism* which has beset philosophies of history in the past just because the philosophers who have constructed them have not sufficiently understood the difference between the historical and the merely chronological.

I do not, of course, mean that, like too many who have fallen under the spell of Bergson's admirable rhetoric, we should see in history nothing but sheer contingency, confused and meaningless flux, any more than we are condemned to see nothing but meaningless flux in the succession of the themes of a symphony, or the scenes of a drama, though both are typical examples of a *durée réelle* very different from the "time" of text-books of kinematics. The symphony, or the drama, can exhibit a wide range of different *tempi*, but the differences and their order are prescribed by the unitary purpose of the composer or dramatist, present to all, transcending all, and *freely* expressing itself through all. I mean that the artist's purpose is at once really in control of the "flux", and itself—apart from incidental conditions which hamper it, such as the need to make a living by pleasing the fancy of a particular patron or audience—subject to no overriding "law". One cannot presume, for example, to say that the supremely significant passages which most definitely disclose the artist's purpose, and have to be taken as the clues for our understanding of his work as a whole, *must* be looked for in such and such a place (at the beginning, let us say, or in the middle, or near the end), nor exactly what contrasts we may expect to find in his work, and where we may expect to find them. These things are the artist's "secret"; they may come to us quite unexpectedly as daring surprises, though, when we have read the whole in the light of them, we may end by finding them as much "in place" as they are surprising. If we found that we had a formula which would, of itself, tell us where we must anticipate the peculiarly revelatory passages of a man's work, or just what contrasts it had in store for us, we should judge at once that our artist was not at his best, that his mind had been working, as we say, "mechanically". It is the capable tradesman in the arts, not the great artist, who works with a formula.

Similarly it is the second-rate critic who comes to the study of a genius like Shakespeare with a philosophical formula out of Aristotle or Hegel which determines for him in advance what a great tragedy must be like, and proceeds to estimate works like *Macbeth* or *Othello* by their conformity to the formula. The truly intelligent method in criticism, as I take it, is inductive and tentative. It is to discover what the tragedian, for example, can do and should do for us by attentive study of what the supreme tragedies actually have done. Of course, such a method is hard to apply, because the fruitful application of it presupposes the soundness of our initial immediate aesthetic response to the work of art. If our "taste" is initially wrong, so that we begin, for instance, by founding our induction on Seneca's plays rather than Shakespeare's, this initial want of perception will vitiate our whole consequent theory. To say this is only to say, with Aristotle, that where there is absence of some form of $\alpha \ddot{\iota} \sigma \theta \eta \sigma \iota \varsigma$, direct apprehension of an aspect of the immediately given, there must also be corresponding absence of the "science", the reflective analysis, which presupposes *that* aspect of the given as its foundation.

All this applies to the philosophy of History as much as to Aesthetics. The conviction that history is a drama with a meaning, and with a divine author of the play, does not mean that we can hope to invent any general formula on the strength of which we could anticipate the actual march of events, or tell just where to look for the particular episodes in which the purport of the drama is most plainly unveiled. History would be much more mechanical than it is, if we could say, for example, that it is dominated by a definite law of progression (or retrogression) on such and such specific lines. This is, in fact, what writers like Spencer and Comte, and, to a minor degree, Hegel, have tried to do, with the result that though their influence has often supplied a potent stimulus to interest in historical studies, adherence to their dogmas has generally ended in the distortion of historical actuality to make it fit some preconceived scheme, usually one which flatters our own vanity. It is manifestly preposterous, for instance, to maintain that Proclus or Damascius, rather than Plato or Aristotle, *must* be the "high-water mark" of Greek philosophical development, merely because the fifth and sixth centuries of our era are so much later than the fourth century before Christ, or that, for a similar reason, "industrialism" *must* be a sounder basis for the organisation of society than "militarism". The facts may be as alleged, but the point has to be established by examination of them on their merits, not by appeal to an assumed law of the order of historical development. Reliance on such laws is only possible for us, if we lose sight of the all-important consideration that the rhythm of history is a very complex one, built up out of a multitude of intensely individual processes, each with its own characteristic rhythm. A truly historically minded philosophy of history has, for this reason, to recognise contingency, the possibility of "being otherwise", as something much more deeply ingrained in the character of all historical fact than most philosophies of history hitherto attempted have been willing to allow.

As for the old bold programme of contemplating the world of fact not as *suggestive* of that which transcends time, but as *itself* transcendent of time, "under a form of eternity", is it not really a proposal to contemplate that which is in grain historical as unhistorical; in plainer words, to contemplate it as though it were just what it is not? Along those lines there seems to be only one goal for thought, the Indian denial that finite individuality is more than an illusion, and, I suppose, an illusion which deceives the very finite individual who is declared not to be there. We might, indeed, have reached these conclusions independently of the particular reflections which have occupied the greater part of this discourse, but it was necessary to my purpose to take the route we have taken, since it seems to be conscious or unconscious preoccupation with the de-individualised spatial framework, or system of reference, mistakenly assumed to be given reality, which commonly does more than anything else to create the prejudice against finite individuality, at least in our Western world.

Spinoza's *Deus sive natura*, for instance, is plainly simply "Euclidean space", assumed to be conscious of itself and of all its possible geometrical configurations. The *intellectus* of this "god", for that reason, consists of awarenesses of all these configurations in their various interrelations, in Spinoza's own phraseology, of "ideas" corresponding one to one with all the "modes" of the attribute "extension". The "finitude" of *my* mind means the fact that my mind has as its correlate only one small selection out of this system of geometrical determinations, the successive configurations of *my* body (my body being conceived simply as so much figured extension). Since, in such a purely geometrical world of uniform spatial relations, there are no real boundaries between one region and adjacent regions, my individuality is, *of course*, an illusion. But so also, though Spinoza seems not aware of this, is the individuality of "God". An infinite "Euclidean" space is not a

whole, nor a unity, and a mind which is by definition
simply awareness of the possible determinations of such
a space is not a unity either. So far as I can see, the only
way in which personal individuality can get recognition as even an apparent fact, in such a system, is
through consideration of the body. The finite body may
perhaps be regarded as at least *quasi*-individual, on the
ground that it is capable of being displaced relatively
to other finite bodies, while retaining unchanged the
geometrical relations between its sub-regions; *i.e.* it
moves as a whole. But to urge this, as the explanation of
the fact that I seem to myself to have an individuality,
is to make the unity and individuality of my body
depend on its character as a continuant through an
interval of time, and time thus becomes an ultimate of
the system, an "attribute of God" on exactly the same
footing as space. The proposition that *deus est res
extensa*[1] ought to apply to extension through time exactly as it does to extension over space; duration should
belong to God in the same way in which volume does.

"Adequate" knowledge, therefore, ought to involve
knowledge of a "mode" under an "attribute" of duration, exactly as it does knowledge of it under an
"attribute" of extension. Or, alternatively, if reference
to duration is, as Spinoza maintains,[2] characteristic of
*imaginatio, in*adequate thinking, the same thing must
be true of reference to extension. But this is just what
Spinoza will not admit. He wants us to think of volume
as real in some sense in which temporal continuance
is not real. At the end of his short life, indeed, he seems
to have become aware of the immense difficulty of his
position, as we see from his significant admission to
Tschirnhaus that "Descartes was wrong in defining
matter by extension, whereas it must and ought to be

---

[1] *Ethics*, ii. 2.   [2] *Ib.* ii. 30, 31, 44, cor. 2

explained by an attribute which expresses an infinite and eternal essence".[1] Now this is precisely what extension does "express", according to the *Ethics*.[2]

Apparently, then, if Spinoza had lived to the normal term of man's life, he would have reconstructed his doctrine on lines which require the disappearance of "extension" from the divine "attributes". Such a reconstruction from the foundations might or might not have led him to an agnosticism as complete as that in which Parmenides in Plato tries to entangle the youthful Socrates;[3] in either case it would have been completely destructive of the "double-aspect" metaphysic of mind and body which recommends Spinoza to so many of our contemporaries. In view of the thoroughly unhistorical character of Spinoza's ideal of knowledge, complete agnosticism would seem to be the reconstruction requiring the minimum amount of transformation in the system, since it would follow naturally from the combination of two positions—the elementary one that kinematics can no more dispense with the notion of duration than with that of configuration, and the familiar Spinozistic rejection of duration from "adequate cognition". This would bring us back to the doctrine, with which Greek philosophy ended in the hands of Damascius, that the historical "phenomenal world" is throughout dependent upon a supra-historical principle, but a principle which is strictly "ineffable", since we have, and can have, not even so much as an "analogical" knowledge of its nature. Metaphysics would have uttered its last word in formulating the doctrine of absolute nescience. This is, in fact, the goal which has been historically reached by all those theologies, within and without Christendom, which, starting from the

---

[1] *Ep.* 73 (V.V.L.).   [2] I. 15 Schol., ii. 2.
[3] Plato, *Parm.* 133 A ff.

sharp and absolute antithesis between the eternal and
the temporal, foreclose all avenues to knowledge of
God except that of the *via remotionis*, the rejection on
principle of all propositions which characterise the
divine by definite predicates.

How we are to escape from such a conclusion has, I
think, been already indicated. If we look a little closely,
we may see that, as I have suggested, what all philosophers of the Spinozistic type really resent in their experience of life is not so much its successiveness as its
individuality. It is individuality they are trying to strip
from the real when they bid us conceive it under what
they call a "form of eternity"; they would like to get
the *hoc aliquid* with no *haecceitas* about it. But in fact,
to preserve reality as real, without its individuality as
the given and *this*, is as impossible as it is to divest a
man of his skin without killing him. The supra-historical, if sought along these lines, turns out to be nothing
but the mere abstract forms of Newtonian uniform
space and time themselves. Whatever is "in" them has
a history and individuality of its own, and must therefore be relegated to the level of the merely contingent,
the "passing" show. When we are in earnest with this
way of thinking, we readily find that nothing is left of
which we can say that it is not "in" time and space,
beyond the time and space of the Newtonian kinematics themselves; they, and only they, are left standing as the "eternal" reality. And of them, as distinct
from configurations and patterns within them, there is
really nothing significant to be said; they are the merely
formless, and consequently ineffable.[1]

It is this, I suppose, which explains the lifelong

---

[1] Cf. Plato, *Tim*. 50 E πάντων ἐκτὸς εἰδῶν εἶναι χρεὼν τὸ τὰ πάντα ἐκδεξόμενον
ἐν αὑτῷ γένη, 51 A ἀνόρατον εἰδός τι καὶ ἄμορφον, πανδεχές, μεταλαμβάνον δὲ ἀπορώ-
τατά πῃ τοῦ νοητοῦ καὶ δυσαλωτότατον.

furious crusade of that half-educated man of genius, William Blake, against the work and name of Newton, a hatred springing from Blake's intensely vivid sense of individual historical reality, the "minute particular", as he repeatedly calls it. Like William Morris after him, Blake "looked on science as the enemy"—you may remember that his chosen name for the Aristotelian logic which he supposed to be its characteristic method was "the mills of Satan"[1]—because to him also science seemed to aim on principle at depriving things of the individual character which gives them their interest for the artist. It is suggestive, in this connection, to take note of the support Blake has incidentally received at the moment at which I am writing these words from a recent public utterance of one of our most distinguished mathematicians, who certainly intended no reflection on the fame or genius of Newton. In his address to the mathematical section of the British Association, delivered in the summer of 1927, Professor E. T. Whittaker contrasts the attitude of the "modern" physicist to geometry with that of the classical physicists of the seventeenth century, and, in doing so, makes striking use of a simile we have ourselves employed in an earlier passage. Geometry, he says, was formerly imagined to set the stage for the play in which the physicist's atoms and molecules are the *dramatis personae*; now we have come to think of the characters of the play as making their own stage, as they move about. That is, I take it, we think of our protons and electrons historically, as genuine individuals, with real characters of their own, which determine the situations in

---

[1] When Blake asks

> "And was Jerusalem builded here
> Among these dark Satanic Mills?"

he must not be supposed to be making a prophetic attack on factories and "industrialism".

which they find themselves, much as the personalities of men and women determine the situations to which they are called on to respond; on the older, classical view, the physicist's atom could hardly be said to have an intrinsic character of its own; its adventures were prescribed for it by a situation it did nothing to make, and this was why it could be called a "manufactured article".

It is true, indeed, that the simplest and minutest corpuscles with which the classical physicist could actually work were supposed to have at least one intrinsic endowment which contributed to determine their adventures, their *mass*, and that the masses of the atoms of different chemical elements had to be taken as differing. But in theory the hope was persistently cherished that the chemist's atoms might still some day be resolved into complexes of still more primitive "prime atoms", all indistinguishably alike even in mass. To-day, I understand, we are told that even the mass of the atom is not strictly invariable, but undergoes modification in the course of its adventures. To say that for the physicist of the future the personages of the play will be envisaged as creating their own stage is definitely to say that they must henceforth be thought of as genuine historical individuals, whose adventures will at once determine and be determined by their intrinsic characters, not be prescribed for them by the restrictions imposed by an external framework. Geometry will, in fact, apparently stand to physics much as "sociology", if there really is such a study, stands to history.

If this is really so, we seem to be on the verge of a new and fruitful conception of the relation between the eternal and the temporal. Everywhere in the world which science appears to be opening to us we are dealing with the adventures and reactions on one another

of genuinely historical individuals. Nowhere do we
come on anything which has no more individuality
than that of being located *here* and *now*, rather than
there and *then*, in an external framework. It looks as
though the conception of a "matter" which is no more
than a name for the *here* and *now* as a sufficient
"principle of individuation" had received a death-blow.
But within the world of historic individuals there are
indefinitely numerous conceivable degrees of wealth of
individual character. A man has a richer individuality
of his own than a terrier, and a terrier than a cabbage.
And below the level of the animate there may well be a
whole complicated hierarchy of types of individual, all
lower than the cabbage, yet all graded among themselves. If so, the richer the type of an individual's individuality, the more will his adventures on his course
through history be seen to be determined by his own
intrinsic character and his relations with individuals of
his own or a higher type; the less will they appear to be
prescribed for him by anything which can be plausibly
mistaken for an indifferent and homogeneous framework. One might suggest (and I presume this is the
significance for metaphysics of Professor Whittaker's
statement that in future the starting-point for the
physicist's construction of space will be the Rieman-
nian geometry of infinitesimal regions) that what
wears the look of such an indifferent framework, in
reference to the adventures of creatures among their
equals and superiors, is in truth itself a complex of
adventures of individuals of poorer types among *their*
equals.

Thus, to make my meaning clear by an example,
since a man has a richer type of individuality than a
beast, or a lifeless thing, it is the man's relations with
his fellowmen, much more than his relations with the

brutes, or with inanimate nature, that determine his course through life; for they, in the main, make his *personality* what it is, and personality counts increasingly as shaping a man's destiny, as we advance from the life of the savage "child of nature" to that of the civilised man who has an organised and conscious "personal" code of duties and rights. Similarly, among the beasts themselves, it is just those which have been admitted to some degree of intimate fellowship with men, such as our household dogs, among whom we most readily detect something analogous to an individual, not a merely specific, character as a determinant of the course of the creature's life.

In practice the inanimate and the merely animate world are here for us as something to be increasingly overcome and moulded to our own characteristic human purposes, not as a source of fixed and final checks and limitations. Man, as we read in *Genesis*, was placed among the beasts "to have *domination* over the fish of the sea, and the fowls of heaven, and all living creatures which move on the earth". Even the apparent indifference of inanimate nature to human purposes, the apparent ruthlessness which caused searchings of heart to Tennyson and his contemporaries, may most truly be read as an indication that this nature is there to be subdued increasingly to the real dominant interest of a fully human life, the establishment of right relations between a man and his fellows, or his God. Our main business in life is not that of the electron, to come to an understanding, if I may so express myself, with an environment of electrons; it is to "follow God", and to be *Mensch mit Menschen*. It is the electron, not the man, for which the principal thing is to steer its way in the whirl of electrons. And yet this very complex of individuals of poorer content, which for us wears the *prima facie* appearance of an external framework of limitation to human individuality, is itself seen on closer inspection to be a complex of individuals with their own histories of adventure. Neither do we seem to come upon a reality which is, like the space and time of the classical kinematics, wholly de-individualised; that is a useful fiction constructed by selective abstraction, and nothing more.

It should follow that, with a strictly historical interpretation of individuality, we are forced to recognise that the ideal type of individuality, perfect and complete personality, can only be actual in an individual whose own inner character is not only the dominant and principal, but the complete and sole, determinant of the individual life, and such an individual could be no other than the *ens realissimum*, God. Here, with the complete disappearance of "outside", or background, we should at last have transcended the historical, and risen from "becoming" or "process" to a life which is all activity of self-expression. And this, I believe, is the right way in which to understand the antithesis between the temporal and the eternal. When we say of God that He, and He only, is strictly and fully the eternal being who knows "no change, nor shadow of turning", but is *immotus in se permanens*, we do not mean that there is nothing in this life in any way answering to what we experience as movement and process; we mean that the experience is there, but that in Him it is not, as it is in varying degree with all His creatures, one of being, more or less, "at the mercy" of circumstance; there is nothing in Him like what we experience as movement to an unknown or half-known, goal. He cannot say, as all of us have to say, "we know not what to-morrow will bring forth", "we know not yet what we shall be". For Him there is neither "*unborn* to-morrow," nor "*dead* yesterday". We are temporal, not because there is a foreign element in our being which does not come from God, but because what there is in us is not the whole plenitude of the riches of God's being. That is withheld from us, not because "deity is jealous", or is subjected in its generosity to some external limitation, but because full and perfect personality is unique in its very nature. And *for us* the meaning of this is that God always has in reserve more to give than we can either "deserve or desire".

The bearing of all this on the problem to which we find ourselves once more recurring, of the relation of time as experienced, *durée réelle*, to eternity, would be briefly this. "Becoming" and time, as we know them by actual acquaintance, should be thought of not as the logical "contraries" of being and eternity, but as depotentialised, imperfectly communicated, being and eternity. Even at the lowest level of individuality to be met with in the actual world, what I have called the "adventures" of the humblest individual are not *mere* "becoming", mere *absolutes Werden*, incessant "turning into something else", such as Plato has in mind when he speaks of a γιγνόμενον ἀεί, ὂν δὲ οὐδέποτε. A real becoming is rather what the *Philebus* calls a γένεσις εἰς οὐσίαν, change, or process, tending to the establishment of self-maintaining activity of self-expression,

> Still as while Saturn whirls, his luminous shade
> Sleeps on his steadfast ring.

In the degree to which there is such self-expression on the part of the individual, its formal character is, *so far*, abidingness, not successiveness, eternity, not time; it does not become, but is. In the case of individuality which has reached the level of conscious personality in proportion as personality is realised, it is always possible to say

> relation stands,
> And what I was, I am,

and this is to possess a communicated and imperfect, but still a conscious, "form of eternity". In our moral life, the word *moral* being taken in its widest sense to cover the whole of specifically human endeavour, our one omnipresent task is to convert mere γένεσις, transition, into γένεσις εἰς οὐσίαν, transition into abiding being, a task only completed as, in theological language, grace, the supernatural, comes to and crowns the achievement of effort, the natural. In so far as what has been said in our earlier discussion of eternity and temporality may seem, for expository purposes, to have treated the conversion of succession into abidingness almost as though it *began*, without any "natural" preparation, with a sudden passage from nature to supernature—though I doubt whether anything we said really implied so much—it calls for rectification in the light of this subsequent reconsideration, and in virtue of the sound and familiar principle that the work of grace is not to undo nature, but to complete it.

Now this has a direct bearing, both on the claims of institutional religion, with all its apparent contingency and externality, on our allegiance, and on the more speculative difficulties connected with the conception of divine immobility and impassivity. If abiding being is not the mere contrary opposite of becoming, but the end to which all real becoming strives, and which all, in varying degrees of fullness, achieves, we shall not be acting advisedly in trying to attain the "form of eternity" within our own souls by simply cutting ourselves off from participation in and profit by the ordinances of an institutional religion, on the ground that they are full of contingency as to their origin and suffer strange vicissitudes in their historical development. It will be an entirely invalid reason for denying that these ordinances may be for us eminently precious ways of access to God to urge that their worth could never have been discovered *ante eventum* by speculative metaphysics or "philosophy of religion", that they are possibly historically continuous with practices which had at first no such spiritual value, or that their significance has undergone traceable modifications within historical times. For they, also, are γενέσεις, but γενέσεις εἰς οὐσίαν, and the question which really concerns us in practice is not how they began, or what transitions they have passed through, but what they succeed in being. If eternity does not simply stand outside time and opposed to it, but permeates it, contingency of origins and fortunes is compatible with abiding significance and value, and there is an end at once of two great prejudices which have done much to impoverish the spiritual life of serious aspirants after the eternal in all ages; the prejudice which is perpetually trying to create a fatal divorce between the "intellectual"—a phrase only too often virtually equivalent to the "conceited and half-educated"—and the "common people" in matters of religion (as though there were some special route to Heaven for the graduates of Universities), and the rival prejudice which sets up the real or supposed practice of some one age, the age of the Councils, or of the apostles, or of the little Galilean community of the years or months before the "giving of the Spirit", as a stereotyped model for the spiritual worship of all mankind in all times, and at all places.

It ought, indeed, to be evident that the presence of contingency throughout the historical domain makes the establishment of such a fixed model once for all impossible. We know so little of what the future may hold for us, that we cannot say, for example, that Europe will hereafter continue to be, as it has been for so many centuries, the main home of the Christian tradition of worship. If it should ever happen, and we do not know that it may not, that the living centre of the Christian religion should be in India or China— or even in the younger of the United States—we may safely predict that the effects of such a change may be even more marked than the known past effects of the transplantation of that centre from Jerusalem to Rome.

Let us suppose, merely for the sake of illustration, that the existing dissipation of Christians into a plurality of conflicting Churches and sects should end in a general submission to the Papal See, with a full acknowledgement of the claims advanced for the Roman Pontiff. Even were that to happen, it is at least fairly certain that a Catholicism in which Popes and Cardinals were regularly Chinese, or Indian, or even Western Americans, steeped in the general national traditions of China, India, or, if the suggestion is thought too fantastic, even of the Pacific States, would be something very different in all sorts of unpredictable ways from a Catholicism such as we see to-day, with its long established traditions of exclusively Italian Popes and a preponderantly Italian Cardinalate. The "deposit" might be retained substantially intact through the transmigration, but the experience of the transmigration would certainly entail interesting discoveries about the precise nature and limits of this unchanging deposit.

And, again, with reference to the speculative problems of the meaning of divine immutability and impassivity, and the difficulties these conceptions suggest about the attitude of God to human folly, perversity, and wickedness. If we conceive the relation of time to eternity rightly, it will hardly be possible for us to interpret immutability and impassivity as though they meant that there is nothing at all in the divine life corresponding to the experiences we know as sorrow, disappointment, distress due to the disloyalty of those who profess to love us, and the ingratitude of those for whom we have done much, honest indignation at wrong. We shall hardly be satisfied to explain away the strongly anthropomorphic language of the Old Testament prophets on all these topics, after a fashion too prevalent among some older divines, as though it all meant nothing very much in particular, or to think of our Maker as a martinet schoolmaster, who makes a hollow pretence of prefacing his flagellations with the formula, never seriously believed by the victims, that "it hurts me more than it hurts you". Nor, again, shall we be likely to take the "easy way out" adopted by many, really ditheistic, pietists of our own early days, who transferred all the real feeling to the human Christ, and at heart thought of the Father as looking on at the Passion from the outside, much as Edward III. is said to have looked on at the Black Prince's struggle at Crécy from his safe observation-post in the windmill. If we have once understood that eternity is the characteristic form not of inaction, but of activity of self-expression, we shall hardly be likely to retain the prejudice that emotion has no place in a strictly eternal life, or the fancy that any such phrase as Aristotle's "thinking upon thinking" can be adequate as a description of the abiding self-expression of Deity. There will be as good reason for believing that emotion has its place in the divine life as for holding the same thing of intellectual apprehension.

In neither case, indeed, can we possibly think of the

divine activity as merely identical with the poor human counterpart we know in ourselves. Emotion in God *must* be of a different tonality from emotion in ourselves, since there it cannot have the special characters which tinge even our richest emotional life, derived as it is from the experiences of aspiration to an unattained self-expression, of baffled endeavour, endurance of final impoverishment or defeat. But we may learn something from those richest of emotional experiences which in us accompany patient conflict with opposition and acceptance of wounds, when there is also serene and confident faith in the victory which is to crown the conflict. These experiences we should rightly refuse to describe by the superficial name of pleasures, but we should hardly hesitate to say that they are experiences of a joy which is all the richer for its costliness.

Imagine the experience Shelley has in mind when he tells us

> To love and bear; to hope till Hope creates
> From its own wreck the thing it contemplates;
> Neither to change, nor falter, nor repent,

as it would be if vision took the place of hope. Would not that be to "enter into the joy of the Lord"? It is along such lines, I should say, that we must try to find a real meaning in the traditional language about the "impassivity" of the Supreme. Nor is it really harder to conceive of an emotional life which transcends our own in this fashion, in virtue of its freedom from *transition*, whether from a less to a more perfect, or from a more perfect to a less perfect, activity, than it is to conceive of an intellectual life free from our human need of crawling, hardly and slowly, from truth to truth by groping and inference. Neither in our own experience of knowing nor in our own experience of feeling do we ever reach the point at which there is actual achieved and complete saturation of subject by object, full and final possession of object by subject. Yet we may be sure that this point is always reached and rested in in God's perfect possession of His own being. Our joy, and our self-apprehension, at their highest, can only be distant analogues of such an experience; but it is as true that the analogy is real as it is that it is distant.

FAITH AND KNOWLEDGE. REVIEW AND CONCLUSION

*Ex divinorum et humanorum malesana admistione non solum educitur philosophia phantastica, sed etiam religio haeretica. Itaque salutare admodum est, si mente sobria fidei tantum dentur quae fidei sunt.—*F. Bacon.

We have now, very rapidly and imperfectly, tried to consider some of the outstanding characteristics which distinguish an historical, or revelational religion from a purely philosophical. We must finally attempt to deal directly with the issue which has been long enough in my own mind, as I do not doubt that it has been in yours. Have we anywhere, by anything we have said, compromised the rightful claims of either living religion or reasoned science and philosophy to independence and freedom from alien interference, each within its own sphere ? In particular, have we advanced anything which can prejudice the demand of a rational philosophy to pursue its own problems, by its own methods, in a strictly disinterested spirit, without apprehension of being arbitrarily arrested by dictation from the priest, or the dogmatic theologian? Or have we, in all good faith, anywhere played into the hand of the "obscurantist" who, in the famous image of St. Peter Damiani,[1] would confine the critical intellect to the

[1] *De divin. omnipotent.* v. (Migne, *Patrolog. Latin.* cxlv. 603), "quae tamen artis humanae peritia, si quando tractandis sacris eloquiis adhibetur, non debet ius magisterii sibimet arroganter arripere, sed velut ancilla dominae quodam famulatus obsequio subservire." On this conception of the strictly "ancillary" functions of human knowledge see É. Gilson, *Études de philosophie médiévale,*

functions of an *ancilla*, a handmaid, and in fact a slave, to a purely authoritarian and supra-rational theology? A sense can be put on the familiar formula, "philosophy the handmaid of divinity", in which its adoption would be a formal treason against rationality in God or man, and a surrender to the intellectual indolence which is itself a capital spiritual sin. To such a sin I trust I may plead not guilty with a good confidence. Yet it may be that this same metaphor of the mistress and the servant, rightly interpreted, may yield a valuable lesson. This is the point on which I could wish, in conclusion, to be a little explicit. I must therefore crave your indulgence if I raise, quite briefly, by way of conclusion, the general question what sort of autonomy or independence may, and what sort may not, be legitimately demanded for any intelligent activity of the human mind.

When does the reasonable demand for freedom pass, as it so easily may do, into the unreasonable and arrogant claim to play the dictator? Universal history has taught us how light-heartedly the transition is made in practical mundane affairs; how imperceptibly, for instance, the "patriot", with his passion for national independence, becomes the aggressive "imperialist", proudly conscious of a mission *parcere subiectis et debellare superbos*. There is also an imperialism of the speculative intellect against which we need no less to be on our guard. Nor is it only the theologian who requires the warning; metaphysicians, physicists, biologists are all only too apt, in the hour of their dominance, to assert the same right *regere imperio populos*

---

essay ii., "La servante de la théologie". Presumably the image is connected by some obscure link of derivation with the *mot* attributed in antiquity to Aristippus that those who give themselves to the ἐγκύκλια παιδεύματα, but neglect philosophy, are like the suitors in the *Odyssey* who consoled themselves for their ill-success with Penelope in the embraces of the "handmaids" (Diog. Laert. ii. 79) (or is the allusion simply to the domestic arrangements of Abraham and Jacob?).

pacisque imponere morem. There was only too much
truth in the complaint once made by a brilliant living
writer against the science of thirty years ago, that
"science appears to be developing the vices of theology
without any of its virtues—the dogmatism, the 'index
expurgatorius', and the whole machinery for suppress-
ing speculation, without any of the capacity to impose
upon the conscience a clear and well-defined scheme of
life".[1] And though our most eminent professed metaphysicians of the same period were conspicuously
modest men, and expressed themselves more decor-
ously, I think it would be true to say that they were not
without some touch of the same temper. They often
tended to assume that a general metaphysic, and that
a metaphysic which is at bottom an epistemology, can
prescribe in advance the ground-plan of a rational universe so completely that the epistemologist is in a position to say definitely just what is the permanent truth
embodied in the great religions, and that everything
in their divinity or their devotions which cannot be
covered by his formulae is no more than imaginative
fable, often actually, and always potentially, mischievous.

Towards natural science the attitude of these metaphysicians was often formally deferential; yet it was
made politely clear that knowledge of nature was not
rated very high as a possible source of valuable contribution to the philosophical interpretation of the
world. Since epistemology, either alone or, at most, in
conjunction with ethics, was widely supposed to be able
to indicate the ground-plan of a rational world, there
was a tendency to assume that, in all essentials, the
work of philosophical interpretation had already been
done by Aristotle, and might, indeed, have been equally

[1] G. Lowes Dickinson, *The Meaning of Good*, p. 193.

well done by the Milesians in the sixth century, if they had only possessed Aristotle's capacity for logical analysis, in spite of their inevitable ignorance of the detail of natural processes. Perhaps no other view could have been expected from philosophers who derived so much of their inspiration from Kant. For Kant seriously believed himself to have drawn the ground-plan of a rational world once and for all in the *Critique of Pure Reason*, in a way admitting of no serious modification or improvement; his successors were to do no more than build up the fabric of positive knowledge on the foundations so well and surely laid in 1781.[1] It is in making this assumption that Kant gives the supreme proof of the radically unhistorical character of his thinking. The world in which a philosophy of this type moves, just because it is, in principle, a completely comprehended world, is a dead world. If our philosophical thought is to keep its contact with the living world of the historical, it will have to reckon everywhere with the contingent and surprising, and will have therefore to be empirical, in a sense in which the best thought of the last century was not empirical, even when it was loudest in its repudiation of *a-priorism*. And this unavoidable empiricism will be reflected in our interpretation of the claims of the various activities of the mind to autonomy.

True empiricism cannot mean, as has sometimes been supposed, that it is the business of the philosophical interpreter of nature to jump at the first impressions conveyed by the observation of sequences in nature, make sweeping generalisations from them by "simple induction", and canonise the results as dogmas. A metaphysic of first impressions would be no better than an intellectual house of cards. But to be truly and sanely

---

[1] *KdrV.*[2] xxiii-xxiv. (*Werke*[2], iii. 21).

empirical, which is the same thing as to think historically, must mean that we are to be in earnest with the
conviction that in our metaphysic, our science, our art,
our divinity alike, we are "moving about in worlds not
realised". It must mean that the conviction of the
rationality of the world, on which all pursuit of truth
is founded, is strictly a postulate of the "practical"
reason. An historical world is not rational in the sense
that it ever has been, or ever will be, actually rationalised, made self-explanatory and self-justifying, by the
labours of philosophers, even to the extent of successfully mapping out its ground-plan with finality. It is our
unending task to divine the supreme pattern of the real,
and so to rationalise it, to the best of our power, knowing well that the element of the disconcerting and perplexing will never be eliminated.[1]

For our intelligence, which is not "intuitive", but
works by painfully piecing fragments of reality together, a world in which time and contingency are more
than illusions must always remain in large part unfamiliar and "uncanny". Since this is so, one thing at
least seems certain; whatever the ultimate structure of
the real may be, it cannot be discovered by any mere
consideration of an abstract scheme of logical categories. Epistemology, *Kategorienlehre*, analysis of the
methods of the sciences, taken by themselves, cannot
furnish the sole and complete clue to the character of
the historical reality in which our thought and action
are embedded, for the obvious reason that we are not
related to the real as spectators to a picture. The world,

---

[1] Cf. Jeans, *The Universe Around Us*, p. 330: "There is no need to worry
overmuch about apparent contradictions. The higher unity of ultimate reality
must no doubt reconcile them all, although it remains to be seen whether this
higher unity is within our comprehension or not. In the meantime a contradiction
worries us about as much as an unexplained fact, but hardly more; it may or may
not disappear in the progress of science."

indeed, sets us questions and provokes our curiosity. If it did no more than this, it would be conceivable that in constructing a critical theory of knowledge we should *eo ipso* arrive at a true metaphysic. The reason why this is not so is that we are not in the position of the spectator before the picture; our "picture" is a *tableau vivant* in which we are ourselves actors.

So much has often been said before with an eloquence which I cannot aspire to rival. I do not know whether the inference I would draw has always been made as explicitly as I would make it. It seems to follow that it is a grave mistake to assume, as I think must be assumed by anyone who accepts the full claims made by Kant for criticism, or by Hegel for his logic, that a theory of knowledge is, by itself, a sufficient basis for a metaphysical philosophy. For is it not perfectly possible that epistemology may only present us with an account of reality which is systematically ambiguous? With what right can we assume that unhistorical analysis, such as is the business of the logician and the critical student of scientific method, must conduct us to a single and determinate conception of the pattern of a historical reality? Might it not prove that these inquiries, pursued with the utmost vigour and subtlety, end by offering us a scheme in which there are ambiguities, just as the attempt to solve a numerical problem in which there are more unknowns than known independent relations between them leads to a system of indeterminate equations?

There might prove to be alternative metaphysical interpretations of the given historical reality, all equally consistent with the only condition which the epistemologist can legitimately insist on, the condition that, on any interpretation, the real world must be capable of being progressively known as intelligence is steadily brought to bear upon it. I do not see that a critical theory of knowledge entitles us to presuppose more about the character of the real world than that it must be such that an intelligible question about it is capable of receiving an intelligent answer, if investigation is patiently pursued far enough, though that answer may sometimes be only that data such as would lead to a determinate solution of the problem are not available. If this is so, it is obvious that the last word about the structure of reality cannot be uttered by the epistemologist. Where the critical theory of knowledge has left open alternatives, it will be permissible to ask whether other than purely speculative considerations may not properly have weight as closing some of the apparently open alternatives, and to admit such a claim will involve no disloyalty to reason. It would be disloyalty to reason to deny that the real world is one in which the prosecution of science is possible; it is not disloyalty to hold that the world is something other and more than a mere field for the elaboration of science.

As we all know, Kant himself definitely held that there are alternative interpretations of the pattern of reality, equally providing for all the legitimate claims of the sciences, and the choice between them has to be made on other than purely speculative grounds. So far as the sciences are concerned, the real world might equally well be an assemblage of mindless and purposeless automata, or a commonwealth of free and purposive agents under the moral government of God; only the extra-scientific consideration that if the first account is the true one genuine moral responsibility must be an illusion justifies our acceptance of the second, and the justification has no force except for the man who accepts the fact of moral responsibility, and accepts it, not because there would be a demonstrable absurdity in denying it, but because he is personally a

man of high inward morality, whose *life* would become
purposeless if morality were dismissed as an illusion.
So far, as it seems to me, Kant's procedure is thoroughly
sound, and his philosophy, whatever other defects it
may have, is sounder in principle than that of Spinoza
or Hegel, precisely because it is not a *panlogism*; it does
not try to stand on logic alone; but if it has one foot
planted, so to say, on logic, it has the other securely
planted on life. But Kant, I would submit, is not sufficiently alive to the full possibilities of what I have called
the systematic ambiguity of epistemology. The places
left open in the metaphysical interpretation of reality,
when epistemology has "done her do", are, according
to him, very few; we know exactly where to find them,
and the possible alternatives left open are, in each case,
just two and no more. Since he only finds room for this
limited amount of ambiguity, it is possible for him to
hold, as he does, that what ambiguities there are are
completely removed by the appeal to ethics.

If the possibilities of such ambiguity are greater than
Kant was willing to allow, it may be in principle impossible to say exhaustively beforehand just where we
shall find them, or how many alternative readings of
the facts they permit, and, again, it will be premature to
assume that it is only to ethics that we may look for
guidance in these cases. It may be, for example, that
the specifically religious life has the same right to un-
prejudiced consideration by the metaphysician as the
specifically moral life. There may be alternatives which
ethics leaves still open, and, if so, some may be closed
when we take into account experiences which are
neither those of the man of science, nor of the morally
virtuous man as such, but belong specifically to the personally religious man, and to no one else. If this should
prove to be the case, religion will have its claims to a

real autonomy, no less than science or morality, and we have no right to determine in advance of examination that it is not the case.

There is at least a fair *prima facie* reason for thinking that the state of matters I have just described as possible is actually the fact. I would adapt here to my own purpose a line of argument which has been forcibly employed by Dr. E. R. Bevan against the type of "rationalist" who regards reason as identical with secularistic natural science, and religion as a mere widespread popular delusion. As Dr. Bevan has urged,[1] the "appearances" are very strongly against this kind of rationalist, much more decidedly than they are, for example, against the average, more or less orthodox, Christian. For it is no part of the orthodox Christian's case that the articles of his creed are all capable of being shown by demonstration, or by probable reasoning, to be either certainly true, or, at least, possessed of a high degree of probability. Such a claim is excluded by his belief in an actual historical revelation, and his acceptance, in some form, of the principle of authority. He does not assume that, with sufficient native intelligence and adequate education, every man must necessarily come into his own convictions, since they are admittedly inspired by a "faith" which, unlike the assurance won by proof, involves a "free assent" of the will. On his own theory it is no paradox that there should be men of the highest intelligence and the best education who reject his convictions as false. But it is part of the militant "rationalist's" case that the orthodox Christian belief can be proved to be false, or unfounded, to anyone of high intelligence and good education. It ought therefore to be a serious paradox to him, as it is not to

[1] See the acute essay " Christianity in the Modern World " in *Hellenism and Christianity*, pp. 249 ff.

his orthodox opponent, that in actual fact the line of division between the orthodox and the "infidel" is not lateral, but vertical, so that, at all levels of intelligence and education, from the lowest to the highest, we find the believer and the "unbeliever" side by side. Among the most ignorant and least intelligent you will find both the devoutly orthodox and the scornfully anti-religious, and you will meet the same situation at the very top of the pyramid, or at any intervening level. This of itself is good reason for holding that, whether orthodoxy is true or not, it is at least not a mere product of dullness or ignorance.

The same line of argument may fairly be used to vindicate the autonomy of religion as a specific apprehension of features of reality, against attempts, like those of Kant in his work on *Religion within the Limits of Mere Reason*, to deny the serious value of everything in the historical religions which is not strictly ethical. If it were really true that everything in a great religion which is not directly ethical—in other words, the great body of its theology and cultus—is no more than super-fluous "survival", to be explained by the conservatism of human emotion, but not to be justified, we might fairly expect to find that the influences which make for such survival are regularly most potent where intelligence and education are at their lowest level; they should be weakest at the top of the pyramid. It ought to be the rule that, though I may attach value to these elements in the tradition in which I have been brought up, and persons of feebler intelligence and fewer "educational advantages" than myself may value them more highly still, when I look upwards to those whom I recognise to be more acute and better informed than myself, I should see them sitting more loosely to all these things than I do, and more generally agreed than myself and my intellectual equals in a "religion of all men of sense" which amounts to little more than the "morality touched with emotion" of Matthew Arnold's unhappy definition.

Whether this state of things is what we do in fact see, each of us must judge for himself. For my own part, I have to confess, that I do not see the facts so, though I might have been predisposed in that direction by some of the educational influences to which I have been subject in earlier manhood. Among the dull or ill-informed I do, indeed, often see vehement confessional and theological attachments which I cannot share, but I often also see among them marked confessional and theological indifferentism which I cannot share either. And when I consider those whom I am constrained to regard as my superiors in mental acumen, or solid education, or both, in some of these again I find indifferentism, but in others very marked attachments with which I do not always personally sympathise. Consequently, for my own part, I discover no connection between intellectual eminence and any one particular attitude to Christian or other "orthodoxy", certainly no connection between such eminence and agnosticism or scepticism about the possibility of knowledge concerning God.[1]

There is, indeed, one particular mental attitude which, so far as my observation goes, is commonly an accompaniment of recognisable intellectual inferiority of some kind, the contemptuous and rancorous self-satisfaction which springs from inability either to see

---

[1] And, in the same way, among those whom I cannot but recognise as morally better than myself I find a similar disagreement. Some of them are devoted adherents of a Church and a creed, some are indifferent in the matter, some decidedly "anti-confessional". Moral purity and elevation of character thus seem to be no adequate guarantee for agreement in "religion" any more than for agreement in aesthetic appreciation.

any difficulties in one's own position, or any advantages
in that of one's opponents; but this moral defect seems
to show itself among inferior adherents of all the possible
points of view. There are rancorous militants of all
varieties of possible belief, contemptuous and angry
deniers of everything, even bitter and scornful indiffer-
entists. The men of unmistakable mental distinction,
again, are to be found alike among believers in a positive theology, convinced disbelievers, sceptics. Only
they, in whichever of these classes they are found,
regularly combine the power to hold their own position
with confidence with the ability to appreciate the difficulties it involves; they know the "weak side" of their
own case better than most of their opponents do, just
as in political life a man of real statesmanlike insight
usually knows better than any critic from outside the
vulnerable spots in the programme of his own party.
We must all have learned long ago that it is a delusion
to imagine that the "infidel"—the man who denies the
convictions which make up our own "faith", whatever
it is—*must* be "wicked"; it is an equal delusion to fancy
that the "orthodox" of an orthodoxy which is not our
own must be stupid, or insincere. Behind the orthodoxy
of a really great historical religion—and this is peculiarly true of our own religion—there is safe to be a
great philosophy. It is not the only philosophy tenable
as an interpretation of the actualities so far disclosed
by everyday practical life and the prosecution of the
natural sciences—this is what I meant by speaking of
the systematic ambiguity of a metaphysic based on mere
epistemology, or on a mere combination of ethics with
epistemology—and, like all philosophies, it is sure to
have its difficulties: there are sure to be some "appearances" which are intractable to it, but it is a great philosophy, not to be spoken of except with respect, and no

man is entitled to presume lightly that it may not prove to be the true philosophy. To understand this is the first condition of approaching the problem in the right spirit.

The case, then, as it seems to me, stands thus. Theologies arise, in the first instance, not from the indulgence of an idle curiosity, but from the attempt to take as a clue to the interpretation of the historical world certain experiences, or phases of experience, which, to those who are sensitive to them, come stamped with a significance that marks them as authoritative self-disclosures of the supreme reality, and, moreover, are not self-contained, but at least appear to throw light on the whole pattern of historical reality. As we have said before, the claim that these experiences have this significance is not refuted by the objection that, in their full intensity, they are confined to the few. For, as we remarked, the same thing may be said of the appeal of art to those who are sensitive to it. Thus, to take a definite example, and one which I choose with a great deal of trepidation, to a very large number of men Beethoven's *Third Symphony* probably conveys no impression whatever beyond that of being a vast volume of pleasing or unpleasing sounds. Many more, I suppose, find such a work vaguely suggestive of something which impresses them as fine and great, but would be incapable, if left to themselves, to give any more precise account of the impression made on them. But there are some hearers to whom the composition has a much more precise significance. Rightly or wrongly, they find in it a "meaning" which is of importance for the appreciation of the whole of human life, and perhaps of something more. It suggests to them a specific attitude of the human soul to the vicissitudes of human fortunes, or even to the entire rhythm of the cosmic process. I suppose it would not be exaggerating to say that to such hearers the *Eroica* is something of a "revelation" of the meaning of life and death, though not a revelation which can be digested into propositional form.[1]

Now a philosopher who is also a wise man, if he happens to be one of the many to whom the work says nothing of all this, will not argue that what he cannot find for himself was never meant to be found, and in fact is not there to be discovered. Nor, again, if he is truly wise, would he take the line of admitting that there is "something" there, but denying that the "something" can be what the more "suggestible" auditor supposes it to be, on the ground that, if this is so, there must be something in the world of which his own analyses have taken no account. He would not, for instance, argue that it *must* be a delusion to find there a disclosure of the meaning of life and death, because there can be no truth except truth capable of expression in the form of propositions. He will rather reckon with the fact that there are those who agree in finding some such disclosure there, and note the fact as suggesting a possibility that there may be "truth", apprehension of reality, which is not "propositional",[2] however difficult he may find it to make a place for such "truth" in his metaphysical scheme. He may find himself incapable of making the necessary reconstruction of his scheme, and have to be content with recording an outstanding and unexplained fact which he does not know how to rationalise. But, if

[1] Cf. the words of Romain Rolland, *Vie de Beethoven*[15], p. 75: "il est bien davantage que le premier des musiciens. Il est la force la plus héroïque de l'art moderne . . . et quand la fatigue nous prend de l'éternel combat inutilement livré contre la médiocrité des vices et des vertus, c'est un bien indicible de se retremper dans cet océan de volonté et de foi." Romanticism perhaps; but, then, Beethoven *was* a "romantic", and the greatest of them, and we are not likely to understand him as he meant to be understood if we forget the fact.

[2] On this whole much-neglected subject of "non-propositional truth" see the instructive and too brief chapter 9 of L. A. Reid's *Knowledge and Truth*.

he does so, he will recognise that the inability shows that his own intellectual scheme is an inadequate instrument of rationalisation and calls for amendment, though he may be quite unable to say what precise form the amendment should take. He will note not only the presence of an outstanding and perplexing fact, but the presence of a definite problem raised by that fact for the philosophy of the future. He will avoid, if he is wise, both the temptation to pretend that there is no problem to be solved, and the temptation to produce a premature solution.

It is this second temptation to which philosophers appear to be peculiarly ready to succumb. They are too ready to assume that to say that an intelligent question must be capable of receiving an intelligible answer is equivalent to saying that it must be capable of being answered in terms of the "categories" with which their own thought habitually works. They forget that in speculation, as in practice, the obviousness and reasonableness of a solution to a problem is often apparent only *après coup*. The rationalising of the given, we must remember, is an "inverse" problem; the solution of it is comparable not with differentiation, where we have a simple universal rule for procedure, but with integration, a procedure just as "rational",[1] for which no general rule can be given, and where success depends on the combination of original "divination" with a well-stored memory of the devices which have proved serviceable in the past.

---

[1] "Just as rational." I mean that though the integration may only be achieved by a stroke of ingenuity for which no rule can be given, when it has been obtained, we can reverse the process. One can differentiate the integral now found, and so recover the expression from which one started as the datum to be "integrated", and for this "verificatory" procedure there is a precise and definite rule. Similarly there is no rule for the solution of an equation of a higher degree than the fourth, but if one has, by some ingenious manipulation, hit upon the roots of a particular "higher equation", one can verify one's result by reconstructing the original equation from the roots, and for this there is a simple rule.

I trust I am not dwelling with too wearisome an iteration on a type of illustration of which I have already made some considerable use. My special reason for reintroducing it at the present moment is this. If great music, or great art of any kind, is something more than a clever sporting with geometrical or quasi-geometrical patterns—and the great artists, I think, have regularly believed that it is something much more than this—it seems undeniable that it makes a real contribution to the understanding of the world, and has a profound metaphysical signification. At the same time, this signification cannot make its appearance anywhere among the categories of a logic, or the principles of an epistemology; we cannot call it irrational, but it is certainly extra-logical. When it has been grasped by those to whom immediate apprehension of it has been granted it can be reasoned upon, and attempts can be made, as they so often are made, to transcribe it into a language created by the analytical understanding. But such transcriptions are notoriously unsatisfactory, and, what is more, they are only intelligible to those who already possess in some measure the immediate apprehension itself.

We all, perhaps, remember the famous declaration of Hegel,[1] that the categories of his logic describe "God as He is in His eternal being before the creation of nature or any finite spirit". I would not deny that there is an intelligible meaning in Hegel's boast. No "true worshipper", of course, can concede that a system of logical categories describes the "eternal being of God", but there is something which the system should elucidate, the "intelligible" ground-plan of the historical world, and if Hegel's own *Wissenschaft der Logik* does not fully realise this ideal, it might be fairly said that

---

[1] *Logik*, Einl. (*Werke*[1], iii. 36).

it is, at any rate, the ideal which a perfect logic would embody. But my point is that Beethoven would have had the same right to make the claim for his symphonies. They too declare to us something about the ground-plan of the historical world, and it is something which could not be disclosed by any system of logical categories, the most flawless that could be devised. It might be asked, indeed, how we know that the claim is substantiated. But the answer would be simple. It would be, in the first place, that the witness of those who are sensitive to the disclosure is concordant; they are in a story together, to a degree which makes it incredible that their story should be fiction, and, further, that many of us who do not belong to their number can at least learn, with their story before us, to see for ourselves that they are telling us of no wholly strange country, but of one of which we have ourselves had our more perplexed and uncertain glimpses. And the case, as I have argued at some length before, appears to be typical.

My purpose in recurring to all this is to urge that, if it be true, we shall be led to recognise a genuine autonomy, for both religion and its intellectual elaboration in the form of theology, against all over-confident metaphysical short-cuts to a final "synthetic" interpretation of the world. For it will follow that no metaphysical system, working, as all such systems must, with the implements of the analytical understanding, can give a final account of that ground-plan of the real which the metaphysician is seeking to formulate. An intelligence before which the whole plan lay bare would be the intelligence not of a metaphysician, but of God. Philosophy, as Diotima is made to teach in Plato's *Symposium*, is not the fruition of such a vision, but the always unfinished and partly baffled aspiration to it.[1] If we think thus of the functions of philosophy, we shall be careful not to make the mistake of requiring the theologian, any more than we require the interpreter of literature or art, to work under the control of a body of "categories" prescribed to him from without, whether they are "categories" dictated by reflection upon the natural, or by reflection upon the moral sciences. What we have a right to demand of the theologian, as of the workers with whom I have compared him, is that the matter upon which his thought works shall be something genuinely *given*, and that in his reflective elaboration of it he shall be true to *it*. I do not see that we have a right to demand more.

We have no more right to expect that the theologian as such shall be himself a super-metaphysician than we have to expect the same qualifications in the interpreter of art, the moralist, or the scientific specialist. I may find it beyond my powers to fit in the convictions of any of the four with the scheme which guides my own thinking in metaphysics, but this difficulty need not require me to censure any of them. What would be fatal to the claims of any of the four is not that *I* should not see where he is going, but that he should have no definite goal before him. His reality need be none the less real, nor his own account of it any the less true, that *I* do not know what to make of it. He, presumably, in such a case, will say with equal justice that he does not know what to make of me and my metaphysic. All that is necessarily proved by our misunderstanding is that neither of us has done what no man ever will do, rationalised the whole of "possible experience". Neither of us, so far as I can see, has any right to dismiss the other as "under an illusion", because he himself does not see just what to make of the other's work. If either of us did adopt this attitude to the other, he might profitably be admonished to attend more to the beam in his own eye than to a mote—or even a beam—in his brother's eye.

The claim, too often advanced by eager metaphysicians, to prescribe with finality to all the rest of the world what "categories" may be employed in the attempt to understand experiences of specific type is, after all, only a form of the dangerous spiritual sin of pride, the very fault justly charged by the metaphysicians of to-day upon so many of the constructive theologians of the past. A contemporary divine may fairly retort, as Plato is fabled to have retorted on Diogenes, when he set his muddy feet on the carpet with the brag, "Thus I trample the pride of Plato", *Yes, with an equal pride of your own.*[1] There is a sense in which there can be no metaphysic which is final, even relatively. If the last word could ever be said even on the world of man —itself no more than a fragment of the whole world— the speaker who should utter it would need to be furnished with the experiences of all men as his matter, to be, in his own person, at once St. Paul and Newton, Caesar and Columbus and Keats (and how many more besides!), and also to be Plato, or Aristotle, or Hegel into the bargain, and "there is no such man". He who lives one life intensely cannot live all. It is just conceivable that it might lie in a man's choice, for example, to be St. Paul, to be Caesar, or to be Newton. But in choosing to be St. Paul he would be cutting himself off from effective possibility of being either of the others.

Again, those whose mental vision is most habitually

---

[1] Diog. Laert. vi. 26 οἱ δέ φασι τὸν Διογένην εἰπεῖν, "πατῶ τὸν Πλάτωνος τῦφον"· τὸν δὲ φάναι, "ἑτέρῳ γε τύφῳ, Διόγενες."

limpid do not commonly live any life with the richest intensity; like Browning's *Grammarian*, they determine "not to be, but know", and the quality of the knowing itself is affected by the choice. Systematic allround clarity is hardly possible except for a vision content to remain on the surface. The system-maker in metaphysics—and it is the system-makers who prescribe dogmatically for the human mind—is a man who has made it his special business to see what he does see with exceptional clearness, but he commonly does not see so deep as some other men. It is not to the great systematisers who supply us with admirable "bird's-eye views" of the *omne scibile* that we naturally turn, if we want to sound the depths of a specific sphere of human experiences, if, for instance, we would know the heart of the lover, the adventurer, the sinner. When a man is, like Plato, a great metaphysician, and also has, like Plato, an eye for the depths, he refuses, as Plato did,[1] to make a system. But I think it is the common experience that, when all is said that there is to say in the way of a *sed contra*, we get the most penetrating and convincing glimpses of a tremendous reality less often from the most illustrious of the great systematisers, an Aristotle, a St. Thomas, a Hegel, than from the intense unsystematic thinkers, the Pascals and the Schopenhauers.

I would seriously urge, then, that the systematic, methodical metaphysician is going outside his province

---

[1] *Ep.* vii. 341 C τοσόνδε γε μὴν περὶ πάντων ἔχω φράζειν τῶν γεγραφότων καὶ γραψόντων, ὅσοι φασὶν εἰδέναι περὶ ὧν ἐγὼ σπουδάζω . . . τούτους οὐκ ἔστιν κατά γε τὴν ἐμὴν δόξαν περὶ τοῦ πράγματος ἐπαΐειν οὐδέν. οὔκουν ἐμόν γε περὶ αὐτῶν ἔστι σύγγραμμα οὐδὲ μήποτε γένηται. This is clearly meant as Plato's refusal to put the substance of his famous discourse on "the Good" into writing, and I believe we may add that it is also meant to dissociate himself from responsibility for the versions of the discourse which we know to have been circulated by some of those who heard it. It was one of his grievances against Dionysius II. that he had composed, or at least circulated, such a professed exposition of "Platonism".

if he undertakes to prescribe to religion, to morality, to art, limits beyond which they must not expatiate, on pain of losing contact with reality. It is not for him to declare with authority what religion, or art, or morality must be if they are to be capable of a rational justification. Their legitimate bounds are set to them, not from without, but from within, by the character of the specific living experiences which are their matter, and by nothing else. The "irrationality" which would be fatal to any one of them is not some failure of adjustment to a preconceived epistemological scheme, but absence of internal unifying principle. And what is true of morality, religion, art, as ways of life will hold good equally for the intellectual reflective interpretation of them in the disciplines of ethics, theology, "aesthetics". It would be fatal to the claims of an ethical or theological body of doctrine if it were found to contradict itself, or if, again, there were an unremoved and unremovable conflict between the ethical or theological interpretation and those very facts of the moral or religious life which it professes to interpret. But mere inability to see how the presuppositions of the religious life can be harmoniously adjusted to those of the moral, or both, again, to the presuppositions of our natural knowledge, seems no valid reason for disputing the rights of ethics or theology to be genuine knowledge of a genuine reality, or to deal autonomously and independently with its own specific "matter", any more than the acknowledged difficulty of adjusting biology with physics is a reason for disputing the character of biology as a genuine field of knowledge, with a right to its own presuppositions and methods.

When we bear in mind that all our knowledge is always *in fieri*, in the process of making, not finally made, it is manifest that this lack of complete adjustment is no more than a consequence of the fact that everywhere "we know in part and we prophesy in part".

It is our business to do all we can to effect a completer adjustment and to wait patiently for its arrival, not arbitrarily to suppress one part of a necessarily imperfect apprehension of an infinitely rich whole, because we are puzzled about its precise links of contact with other apprehensions which are equally partial. Indeed, I think we may fairly say that an apparently flawless synthesis, for example, of natural knowledge and theology must be a *false* synthesis, since its very faultlessness—when we remember how fragmentary and confused is our knowledge of nature, and much more our knowledge of God—would be proof that it had been obtained by the mutilation of one, and probably of both constituents. (Just as the once fashionable "reconciliations" of physics with the opening chapters of *Genesis* ought to have been seen to be condemned as vain in principle by the single consideration that a complete agreement between *Genesis* and the physical text-books of the current year must inevitably lead to contradiction between *Genesis* and the text-books of twenty years later—unless, indeed, the interpretations of the supposedly infallible narrative of *Genesis* should prove to be just as much perpetually *in fieri* as the doctrines of the physical text-books, in which case each successive conciliator's labour is once more in vain.)[1]

It seems to me, then, that in the matter of the claim to autonomy, theology, ethics, and natural knowledge stand all on one footing. All have a right to exist, and each has the right to deal with its own problems without

[1] Thus I have read works of the last generation in which "religion" was reconciled with "science" by a proof that Scripture teaches the doctrines of Herbert Spencer's *First Principles*. If this could really be proved, where would Scripture be to-day?

dictation from either of the others. We have a right, and
a duty, to be satisfied, in the case of each, that we are
being presented with real problems, not with senseless
conundrums excogitated by our own vanity, and, so
far as theology is concerned, the whole of what we have
said throughout these discussions, may be regarded as
a continued attempt to plead that its problems are real
problems, forced on us by life, whether we will or no.
We have also the right to demand everywhere that the
problems thus forced upon us shall be met by strenuous
thinking, that there shall be none of the idle mystifica-
tion which, in fact, has, in different ages, infected men's
attitude towards all the problems set us by life, no substitution of acquiescence in an accepted formula for
honest thinking, whether in natural science, in moral
science, or in divinity. But if, as we have urged is the
case, theology itself has inevitably arisen in the honest
attempt to think out the implications of genuine experiences, which are other than, or at least more than, the
experiences intellectually elaborated by the natural and
moral sciences, it is as vain to dismiss theology as illegitimate on the strength of the acknowledged difficulty
of fitting its presuppositions into a metaphysical scheme
based on the assumption that the course of physical
nature and the history of our social relations with our
fellowmen, between them, disclose all the reality there
is to be known, as it would be to deny some adequately
established position in natural science for the like reason
that it is hard to adjust it to a metaphysical scheme
inspired by exclusive attention to experiences of a distinctively religious kind.

We may all of us probably remember Pascal's inci-
sive comment on the attempt to subject natural science
to theological dictation: "The Jesuits have procured a
decree from Rome that the earth does not revolve, but,

if it really revolves, no decrees can alter the fact".[1] In
our own day we more commonly, perhaps, see the process reversed: we see the invoking of something like a
"decree" from the Royal Society in condemnation of
the doctrines of theology. But here also we may comment, in the spirit of Pascal, that if the life of which
theology attempts to give us the theory is real fact, no
decree of anyone can make it unreal. If, for example,
sin and the remission of sins are real facts of life—and
the physicist or biologist assuredly cannot pretend to
settle *that* question by his physics or biology—it is idle
to dismiss the theologian's doctrines of sin and grace
on the plea that the biologist, for the purposes of his
biology, can dispense with the notions. Both theologian
and biologist are dealing with a restricted selection from
our experiences of a rich and bewildering reality; it is
preposterous to dispute the worth of the special view
into that reality disclosed by either on the plea that we
are at a loss how to combine the two views into one.

In principle the difficulty is the same, though in degree it may be less, when we try to understand how the
living organism can be at once what the pure physicist
says it is and what the biologist declares it must be. It
is not the least of Prof. Whitehead's services to clear
thinking that he has made it so apparent that the "conflict of theology with science", so much talked of in the
nineteenth century, has its counterpart, on a smaller
scale, in a similar conflict between the biology of the
century and its physics. It may be that the remoulding
of scientific concepts which is so busily prosecuted from

---

[1] *Lettres écrites à un provincial*, xviii: "Ce fut aussi en vain que vous obtîntes
contre Galilée un décret de Rome, qui condamnoit son opinion touchant le
mouvement de la terre. Ce ne sera pas cela qui prouvera qu'elle demeure en
repos; et si l'on avoit des observations constantes qui prouvassent que c'est elle
qui tourne, tous les hommes ensemble ne l'empêcheroient pas de tourner, et ne
s'empêcheroient pas de tourner aussi avec elle."

within at the present moment may bring us, in the
course of a generation or two, to a fairly complete solution of this lesser problem. It would be too much to
hope for any final solution of the graver problem, but
at least we may learn the lesson that difficulties of this
kind are not to be removed by the facile device of refusing to see those features of the reality on which we
live which conflict with our natural preference for a
simplified and unified view of the world.

It is our duty as rational beings to aim at the unified
view, but it is surely an illusion to imagine that the
unified view will ever be within the grasp of finite intelligences, condemned by their finitude to get at truth
piecemeal. Any account of the real which is to do justice to all the features it presents to us is bound to be
untidy in places, to be scored with seams and ridges.
What we can do is to note where the gaps are found and
to try our best, with hope, but also with patience and
a fixed resolve to avoid premature syntheses, towards
filling them up. So we shall best make our own contribution to the only true *philosophia perennis*, a philosophy which is, as Francis Bacon said,[1] the work, not
of some single superman, but of Time, and of which,
just because it is always in the making, we might use
the phrase of Tennyson, that it is

> never built at all,
> And therefore built for ever.

Of course, to defend the claim of theology, or any
other discipline, to autonomy on these lines is, at the
same time, to recognise that the right to autonomy is
never merely unilateral. Theology, we have urged, is

---

[1] *N.O.* i. 84 "summae pusillanimitatis est authoribus infinita tribuere, authori
autem authorum atque adeo omnis authoritatis, Tempori, ius suum denegare
Recte enim Veritas Temporis filia dicitur."

entitled to deal with its own very real problems without suffering either its procedure or its conclusions to be clipped and curtailed to the pattern presupposed in the natural sciences, and no less entitled to refuse to let itself be made into a mere instrument of morality. For the very same reasons there must be no well-meant edificatory interfering with the unfettered and single-minded investigation of natural fact in the supposed interests of a sound social morality, nor any shirking or wresting of the results of either natural or moral science for the convenience of the divine. If we would be intellectually honest, as it is no easy task to be, it must be our rule, whether our particular work is done in the field of natural science, of ethics, or of theology, to "follow the argument wherever it leads". To force the "argument" to a conclusion dictated in advance, to cut it arbitrarily short in its progress, when the goal to which it is tending is an unwelcome one, to avoid so much as entering on a legitimate investigation because we are afraid of the conclusions to which it might conduct, all these devices, so often illustrated by the history of both divinity and science, are but so many ways of "offering to the God of truth the unclean sacrifice of a lie". In the realm of thought, as in the sphere of political relations, independence is something very different from a right to domineer over a neighbour who has an equal right to an independence of his own, though it is the lamentable fact that sciences, like nations, are always apt to overstep the boundary which divides independence within one's own borders from domineering outside them.

At the same time, it needs equally to be said that, however fully natural science, moral science, divinity, are justified in asserting their several rights to pursue their own tasks without interference, no one of the

three can be indifferent to the conclusions asserted by
the others. The conclusions of natural science cannot be
wholly irrelevant to those of moral science, nor the conclusions of either to divinity, since all alike deal with
elements in the same *given*. Life and the world are, in
the end, one and not many, and therefore any version
of the doctrine of the "double truth" must, in the long
run, be destructive of the ideal of truth itself. Hence
it is only as a rule of method that we can unreservedly
accept the principle of what has been called "ethical
neutrality", and the analogous principle of "theological
neutrality". It is perfectly true that in pursuing any
line of inquiry we have a duty, as well as a right, to
refuse to be diverted by considerations which, however important, are strictly irrelevant to the question
what conclusions are indicated by the evidence before
us. To urge that, as may perfectly well be the case, the
moral practice, or the devotion of a given community
is likely to suffer from the general admission of certain
inferences in natural science or in history is strictly
irrelevant to the question whether the available evidence
justifies or supports those inferences. So far[1] it is our
business, in pursuing any special branch of knowledge,
to be consistently "neutral" towards all considerations
which fall outside the purview of that branch of knowledge itself. What cannot be true is that there should
be one "truth" of physical science, another of moral
science, and possibly a third of divinity, all incompatible with one another and irrelevant to one another.

[1] But no further. If, for example, biological investigations should provide evidence that it is possible, by various artifices, to control the fertility of marriages,
or the sex of the resulting offspring, the moralist may not deny the possibility
because he thinks that the practice of the artifices is morally deleterious. So far
he is bound to be "ethically neutral", and the obligation is itself a moral one. But
if the biologist goes on to advocate the practice of these artifices, he has himself
ventured into the field of morals, and the moralist is not *free*, but actually bound,
to judge the recommendation from the moral point of view. Here he has no right
to be "neutral".

The moralist cannot afford to be indifferent to an alleged scientific account of the world which would make it a system with no place for genuine effort, real freedom and causality, true responsibility and desert, or the divine to a scientific or ethical reading of life which leaves no room for God. In view of the ultimately practical character of our concern as individuals with the ordering of our lives, this may at least explain, though it does not follow that it justifies, the attempts which have been made at various times to arrest the advance of scientific and historical inquiry in the real or supposed interests of morality and religion.

Without subscribing to Newman's unqualified assertion of the inherent right of ecclesiastical authority to prohibit further pursuit of investigations in every department at its discretion, we may at least be able to understand that such interference has not necessarily always been prompted simply by arrogance and meddlesomeness, or by the criminal and impious concern of a powerful order for its own prestige. Human nature being what it is, it is not surprising that these unworthy motives have played only too prominent a part in history, but it would be the blindness of the mere partisan to deny that behind the "obscurantism" of ecclesiastical authority there has often been a genuine, I do not say an unadulterated, concern to safeguard the interests of practical good living, and that the quality of the practical morality advocated by the so-called "advanced scientific thinkers" of the past and the present has often shown this concern to be well founded. Some part, at least, of the "domineering" of the divine and moralist has been provoked by a correct perception that the autonomy of religion and morality has been challenged from the other side and needs to be defended.[1] The pity is that so often the defence has been conducted on the wrong lines.

By way of illustration we need only remind ourselves of the attitude taken up, often for quite honourable reasons, by moralists as well as divines, in the last century towards Darwin's researches into the origin of species. The legitimate procedure for a divine or moralist who anticipated, correctly enough, that the actual consequences of general acceptance of the doctrine of our physical kinship with the brutes might be, in various ways, injurious to morality, would have been twofold. It should have been argued that the scrutiny of the available evidence and the full interpretation of it must necessarily be the work of years; what *precise* conclusions would in the end emerge under patient examination could not have been said at the time, and, I suppose, cannot be said even now, except in a very general way, and with a good deal of reserve on all points of detail. And, further, and this is, of course, the important point, it should have been persistently repeated that even if the facts on which Darwin's speculations were based were absolutely certain, and known to be the whole of the relevant facts, they could not be, and still less could his, or any man's, speculative inferences from them be, more certain than the certainties on which morality and religion are based, the certainty of absolute moral obligation, of human responsibility and

---

[1] Cf. the remarks of Lord Acton on the suppression of the Albigenses: "There was a practice which the clergy desired to restrain, and which they attempted to organise. We see by their writings that they believed in many horrible imputations. As time went on, it appeared that much of this was fable. But it also became known that it was not all fabulous, and that the Albigensian creed culminated in what was known as the Endura, which was in reality suicide. It was the object of the Inquisition that such people should not indeed be spared, but should not perish without a trial and without opportunity of resipiscence, so that they might save their souls if not their lives. Its founders could claim to act from motives both of mercy and of justice against members of a Satanic association" (*Lectures on Modern History*, p. 111). The words are the more weighty from the writer's notorious hatred of "persecution".

freedom of choice, and of the reality of the saint's "life in God, and union there". The facts in this order are as certainly facts as those of the breeder of plants and animals, or the palaeontologist, and inferences about what men are which are really guaranteed by them are at least as trustworthy as inferences about what their remote ancestors once were which are guaranteed by the others. We may therefore rest assured of one thing, and it is the only thing which matters very much, that whatever the newly discovered facts of the natural order really prove, they cannot prove anything incompatible with what is really proved by the already familiar fundamental facts of the moral and religious order. They may seem for a time to do so, and we may not at present see how this apparent contradiction is to be avoided, but we may also be assured that it cannot be more than apparent, and may therefore be content to confess our perplexity, without concealment, but also without dismay. There should really have been none of the unedifying eagerness which was shown, and not by professed theologians only, to get rid of inconvenient facts by hasty denials, or to disguise the conclusions to which they, *pro tanto*, pointed, by ingenious special pleading and forced interpretations. The appeal to certainties of one order should have been met by a counter-appeal to equal certainties of a different order, not by disingenuous or irrelevant rhetoric, nor by the superfluous invocation of official custodians of faith and morals to cut investigation short by the *fiat* of authority.

I should not, however, like to maintain that there are not circumstances in which this last procedure may be justified as a temporary and purely *administrative* act, since the prosecution of scientific research is neither the only interest of mankind, nor necessarily the principal interest of all human societies in all cir-

cumstances. We can all think of researches in course of
eager prosecution at the present time which it might be
for the immense gain of humanity to arrest, if the thing
could be done, on precisely the grounds on which, by
general consent, it is also desirable, if we can, to "call
a halt all round" to naval construction, and I have
sometimes been inclined to wonder whether, in the
absence of some authority capable of enforcing such
a general arrest, civilisation is not in some danger of
being destroyed by its own men of science. It does
not seem quite impossible that "divine philosophy" may
yet fulfil Tennyson's mournful prophecy,[1] and become "procuress to the Lords of Hell" in a fashion
undreamed of by sober, decent "mid - Victorians",
who had never heard of "poison-gas", "death-rays",
"rejuvenation", or artificial birth-control. Indeed the
possibility is, I fear, something more than a bare possibility, unless the world can be won to take the
poet's warning to "hold the *good*" in a degree of earnest
of which, at present, it shows no sufficient signs. It may
even be that society will only, in fact, save itself at the
eleventh hour by desperately reverting to an iron
authoritarianism more rigorous than any claimed by a
Hildebrand, or a Boniface VIII. But if that should
prove to be the price of holding fast the good, it will
only be a mutilated good which will have been preserved from the general wreck; for an unforeseeable
time, philosophy and science will once more have
retired, like Astraea, from the earth, as once long ago
in the midnight between the age of Justinian and that
of Charlemagne, and the recovery from the new "dark

---

[1] *In Memoriam* liii.:
> "Hold thou the good: define it well:
>   For fear divine Philosophy
>   Should push beyond her mark, and be
> Procuress to the Lords of Hell."

age" may be more painful and slower than the recovery from the old. One must at least hope that mankind will find a more excellent way while there is still time, and the Avar and Vandal are not as yet actually within the gates.

If we are to find that more excellent way, we must, I should say, safeguard ourselves in all our thinking, alike as theologians, as metaphysicians, as workers in the various sciences, by a real and frank confession of a sane agnosticism, unwelcome to the temper of a self-confident age. We inheritors of such an age—for I cannot, of course, speak for a younger generation—are all too prone to exaggerate the amount of our certain knowledge. Theologians have often been specifically derided, as by Matthew Arnold, for their alleged tendency to take it for granted that they know all about God, and with respect to all but the greatest theologians there is too much truth in the charge. But metaphysicians are no less apt to assume that they know so well what "ultimate reality" is as to be able to say with some confidence what can happen and what cannot possibly have happened; men of science, at least when they are addressing the public at large, frequently speak with a great deal of assurance about the lines on which "nature" has been laid down. It is true that, as a matter of form, all these classes are ready enough to make a "general confession". In words, the men of science will readily admit that "nature" is, after all, in the main a still unexplored field, and the metaphysician that "the absolute" is very much of a mystery; the theologians even adopt it as a truth of their science that though we know *that* God is, in this life, at least, we do not know, except in the most distant fashion, *what* God is. Yet when we come to the application of the admission in practice, we only too often find that each party uses it mainly to keep his rivals in their place. If you are an average divine, you dwell on the limitations of human knowledge chiefly by way of rebuke to the over-confident assertions of metaphysicians, or men of science, who do not accept your theology; if you are a metaphysician, you labour the same theme to confute the rashness of the divine, or the scientific specialist; if you are yourself a scientific specialist, you apply the whip to repress the self-confidence of everyone who has not cultivated your own particular specialism.

A genuine agnosticism, which is neither that of indolent indifference nor that of despair, means something different. It means the repression not of another man's self-confidence, but of my own. Nor does repression of my own self-confidence mean treating my most assured convictions as quite probably mere illusions. It means taking care to avoid the assumption that "what *I* don't know isn't knowledge"; in other words, scrupulous conscientiousness in distinguishing what is really forced upon me by the given from what may be personal and arbitrary in my interpretation of the given, and capable of being shown to be so by comparison with the attempts of others to say what they find given to them. We need always to remember that there is a double source of fallibility in our personal interpretation of the common given. Our personal intellectual interpretation of our most familiar experiences may be vitiated by want of thoroughness, or by reliance on un-criticised categories of thought; and, again, not all of us are equally responsive to every element in the common given. On both grounds we can only hope for approximation to a true understanding of the "common" in which our life is set on the condition that we are willing to learn the lessons of an experience which is not our own, in a spirit of docility. None of us can escape from

intellectual disaster, unless he is ready to walk somewhere in life by the faith which comes by hearing;
no man's soul can successfully walk by its own private
light alone.

The particular danger against which such a sane
and hopeful agnosticism is most needed as a prophylactic in our own day does not seem to me to be undue confidence in dogmatic theologies or metaphysical
systems. These have been dangers in the past, but our
present peril is rather that of being too confident in
science, or what we take for science. We commonly do
not realise as fully as we need to do that there is so much
in life, so much, too, which is of the first moment to us,
which is not knowledge, and yet must imperatively be
acted on, and that very much which is knowledge is not
science. Science is not the whole of life; it is not even the
whole of knowledge, but one rather curious and restricted department of knowledge. Life would be a poor
affair if there were not many things which each of us
knew with much more certainty than the scientific man
knows any of the theorems of his own science. And,
again, as our philosophically-minded scientific men
seem almost unnecessarily eager to convince us at the
present moment, the more scientific we make our
science, the nearer we bring its conclusions to being demonstrations, the more remote they appear to be from
all contact with actuality, and the more completely do
they take on the character of hypothetical inference
from assumed postulates, which are themselves declared
to be no more than hypothetical. If the day has gone
by for ever when science could be treated, in the fashion
of some of the older apologists, as a short cut to the
establishment of a particular theology, no less has the
day gone by, though this is not always equally recognised, when theology could be treated as though it had

been rendered absurd or superfluous by the existence of natural science. The very fact of our own existence and the existence of our world sets us problems, and thereby imposes on us the moral obligation of dealing with problems, not all of which can be treated by the special methods of natural science, nor yet all by the special methods of theology, and thus justifies the existence of both studies, while the necessarily tentative character of all our human thinking makes it impossible that either should ever be simply absorbed into metaphysics. That consummation would only be possible if the actual could be completely rationalised without ceasing to be a *given* actual. And if we were in possession of a completely rationalised actual, we should no longer have either science or theology; both would have given place to something better than either—vision.

"ἀλλ' οὔτ' ἀπολέσθαι τὰ κακὰ δυνατόν, ὦ Θεόδωρε· ὑπεναντίον γάρ τι τῷ ἀγαθῷ ἀεὶ εἶναι ἀνάγκη· οὔτ' ἐν θεοῖς αὐτὰ ἱδρῦσθαι, τὴν δὲ θνητὴν φύσιν καὶ τόνδε τὸν τόπον περιπολεῖ ἐξ ἀνάγκης. διὸ καὶ πειρᾶσθαι χρὴ ἐνθένδε ἐκεῖσε φεύγειν ὅτι τάχιστα. φυγὴ δὲ ὁμοίωσις θεῷ κατὰ τὸ δυνατόν...."[1]

---

[1] Plato, *Theaetetus*, 176 A, B.

APPENDIX

IT may be advisable to add here one or two observations on certain important topics which present themselves at more than one stage in the argument of these lectures, and could not therefore be disposed of in footnotes. I select, in particular, three such topics, because I think it possible I may be thought to have treated them, in different places, in inconsistent ways. I do not believe there has been serious real inconsistency, and I would ask the reader who suspects it at least to suspend his judgement until he has weighed the remarks now to be made.

A. *The Rationality of the Universe*

In some places I have spoken of the conviction that reality is a rational whole as the fundamental postulate alike of true science, true philosophy, and true religion; in other places I have spoken of the "rationalisation" of the universe as a task which, from the nature of the case, can never be finally achieved. The apparent consequence might be stated epigrammatically by saying that I maintain, in effect, that there are "irrationalities" which are not unreasonable. If this sounds like paradox, the paradox, I believe, is only apparent and arises from what Plato calls[1] τὸ τῶν λόγων ἀσθενές, the inadequacy of language to convey the whole of a speaker's meaning and nothing beyond that meaning.

[1] *Ep.* vii. 343 A.

By the "irrational" we may mean (1) that which is in conflict with the first principles of coherent thinking, the inherently *unreasonable*, as I should prefer to call it. It would be irrational in *this* sense to maintain that there are integers which are at once odd and even, are not, and yet also are, divisible by 2 without a remainder. To say that the real, or the universe, may be irrational in this sense would be to say that it is not only a riddle, but a riddle to which there can be no answer, because it is a question with no genuine meaning. A riddle which has no answer is not even a riddle. If reality were a pseudo-enigma of this sort, manifestly science, philosophy, religion would be alike worthless; all would be vain attempts to solve a conundrum which, *ex hypothesi*, has no solution, to translate "gibberish" into sense. But "gibberish" which could be rendered into sense would not be "gibberish".

But we also speak of the "irrational" in a very different sense to mean (2) that to which we can find an approximate answer, or even a series of ever more closely approximate answers, but not a complete answer. "Irrationality" in this sense means only that we are dealing with a problem which we are always on the way to solving, but never *have* solved and never *shall have* solved. This is what we mean when we speak, in the language of the discipline from which the very word "irrational" has been borrowed, of an "irrational" magnitude or number. When we say that $\sqrt{2}$ is an "irrational", we do not mean that the question "What number, multiplied by itself, will give the product 2?" is insoluble in the sense in which Lewis Carroll's conundrum "Why is a raven like a writing-desk?" is presumably insoluble. For, as we know, we can readily find an unending series of fractions such that the product of any term of the series by itself is more nearly equal to 2 than that of any of its precursors by itself. We have a simple rule for constructing this series, and by travelling far enough along it, we can find a number of which the product by itself differs from 2 by a fraction smaller than any we please to assign. What we cannot do is to get to the end of this unending series, or, again, when we "extract the square root of 2" by the more rough-and-ready familiar arithmetical method, to come to a last "decimal figure", or a group of recurring "decimal figures". That is, we cannot answer our question "What number, when multiplied by itself, gives the product 2", by producing a fraction which has finite integers for its numerator and denominator. If $x^2/y^2 = 2$, x has not to y the λόγος or *ratio* of an integer to an integer, and this is why $\sqrt{2}$ has been called an ἄλογον, or "irrational". But there is nothing *unreasonable* in the statement that some integers have "irrational square roots"; the unreasonableness would lie in denying this. For by denying it we should be asserting one or other of two propositions, (*a*) that there are actually pairs of integers which satisfy such equations as $x^2 = 2y^2$, $x^2 = 5y^2$, or (*b*) that if we consider the pairs of values of x and y yielded by the integral solutions of the equations $x^2 = 2y^2 \pm 1$, $x^2 = 5y^2 \pm 1$, though the "absolute difference" between 2 or 5 and the fraction x^2/y^2 steadily diminishes as we consider higher and higher values of x and y, it always remains greater than some assignable rational fraction σ. And both these propositions are at variance with the foundations of coherent thinking. The example will explain what I mean by a reasonable irrationality.

I hold, then, that because our intellect is not creative of the universe, but receptive of a reality which it has to understand but does not freely create, our problem of interpreting that reality by theory is in principle like the evaluation of a "surd". We may, and should, make persistent efforts to carry our valuation a "place" further than any we have actually reached, but we can never expect to write down the "last decimal figure", or the "last convergent", if I may so express myself. This is what the rationalist *pur sang*, whether he is confessionally as orthodox as Descartes at least meant to be, or as fanatically anti-orthodox as the contributors to the "Rationalist Press", assumes that we can do, and this is why rationalism of that kind is inherently unreasonable. On that point, at least, I may claim to be loyal to the central thought of Kant. I would add that, so far as I can see, the case would be the same with a "separated intelligence", supposing that intelligence not to be itself the Creator of the world. Even for the angels, the "works of the six days" remain the *"unbegreiflich hohen Werke"*.

B. *Freedom and Contingency*

To prevent misunderstandings I should like to state briefly what I take to be the essentials of such a doctrine of "choice and avoidance" as seems to me indispensable if our moral accountability for our voluntary actions is to be regarded as more than illusory.

(1) It is a fact that we, sometimes at least, really choose between alternative courses of action. It is not true that when we think we are choosing, the real fact is *always* that we are discovering that there is no choice open to us. (Whether there are *some* occasions when we fancy ourselves to be choosing, but are mistaken, I am not called upon to decide, but I am not concerned to deny that it may be so. My only concern is to maintain that sometimes at least all of us really do choose, and that the fact must not be explained away. *All* our choices are not "Hobson's choice".)

(2) Again deliberation is a real process, not a mere illusion. Sometimes, at any rate, we really weigh the goodness whether of alternative acts, *A* and *B* themselves, or of their consequences, before making our choice, and the weighing, sometimes at least, affects the choice. Deliberation is neither, as Hobbes thought it was, a mere oscillation between conflicting "appetites"[1] nor yet a pretence of looking for reasons for an act which we are already "determined" to do. It is genuine "practical" *thinking*.

(3) Further, there is no reason to doubt that we can, and sometimes do, come to this process of practical thinking with minds not already prejudiced for or against either of the alternatives under examination, just as we sometimes consider the evidence for or against a statement of alleged matter of fact without secret prepossession either way. A man may come to the estimation of evidence with an "open mind", devoid of any antecedent bias other than a desire to reach the truth about the matter under examination.[2] Similarly he may weigh the alternative courses of action *A* and *B* with no prepossession beyond the intention to adopt the course which shall, on examination, approve itself to him as the "right", or the "better". If many men mistakenly suppose themselves to be impartial in deliberation when they are not really so, men also often suppose themselves to be weighing testimony or arguments with an open mind, when this is not actually the fact. Yet a man can be, and ought to be, candid and open with himself

[1] *Elements of Law*, pt. i. c. 12: "This alternate succession of appetite and fear during all the time the action is in our power to do, or not to do, is that we call DELIBERATION". *Leviathan*, c. 6: "When in the mind of man, Appetites and Aversions, Hopes and Fears, concerning one and the same thing, arise alternately ... the whole summe of Desires, Aversions, Hopes and Feares, continued till the thing be either done, or thought impossible, is that we call DELIBERATION".

[2] *E.g.* Did Virgil write (*Ecl.* iv. 62) "*qui* non risere *parenti*," or "*quoi* non risere *parentes*"? Surely it is ludicrous to suggest that I cannot consider the question without a secret antecedent bias.

in deliberation, as he can be, and ought to be, candid and open in the balancing of testimonies, or the scrutiny of arguments.

(4) When the conditions thus laid down are fulfilled, it is strictly true to say that during the process of deliberating a man is "indetermined" *ad utrumque* : in fact, it is the deliberation itself which puts an end to this "freedom", and "determines" him to one of the alternatives. Until he has deliberated he is "free" to take either course, to do a proposed act, say *A*, or not to do it.

(5) Such "freedom" does not mean that a man is ever "free" to take just any course he pleases. The alternatives between which I am effectively "free" to choose in a given case will always be limited in number, partly by my present situation, partly by my "past". I am not "free", at the moment of writing these lines, to choose whether I will go on with my writing in Edinburgh or spend the evening with a friend in Westminster, since I cannot transport myself forthwith to Westminster. Nor am I "free" to lay down my writing and read the Chinese classics; I have not in the past learned the Chinese language and so could not read a Chinese book, even if I had one at command. But I *can* choose either of the alternatives to go on with my writing or not to go on with it. If I could not, it would be equally futile to express moral approbation of my conduct if I stick to my work, in spite of the temptation to lay it aside for a diverting romance, and to express disapproval if I abandon my work for the story. Life would not be an education into morally stable character for us if it did not present situations in which we are confronted with the real alternative of doing the act *A* or not doing it, both courses being really open to us until one of them is blocked by our deliberation itself. Genuine morality would be impossible if it were true that when we take

a decision, or suppose ourselves to do so, we are in a position like that of an engine-driver at the point of divergence of two sets of tracks, one of which is already closed against him by an invisible pointsman. I am my own pointsman, as well as the driver of my own engine.

(6) It follows that when I really deliberate and decide, my decision and the ensuing act, though largely *conditioned* by the past, which restricts the range of effective alternatives open to me (as in the supposed example, it excluded the dropping of my work to read a Chinese classic, though not the dropping of it ἁπλῶς), are not wholly *determined* by it. And therefore, when we prescind from the question of the range of effective alternatives, and consider simply the choice "to do *A* or not", the "past" leaves the issue truly undetermined. To put the point in quasi-mathematical language, if my act is to be considered as a *function* of my "past", it must be regarded as a *many*-valued, not as a *one*-valued, function of it. This, not the mere difficulty of obtaining sufficiently minute information about the events of another man's past history, is the reason why it must always be impossible to calculate a man's future unambiguously from knowledge of his past, and why there could never be such a science as the "ethology" contemplated by J. S. Mill (*Logic*, bk. vi. c. 5).

(7) It does not follow from these positions that it must always be open to a "free" rational agent who is not the Creator to make a morally *evil* choice (so that we should have to say that if men, or angels, are free agents, any man, or any angel, may at any moment commit any conceivable sin). For the discipline of the past closes many paths, though it may not close all. Our choice is not always between a morally right and a morally wrong, not necessarily always between a good

and a better; it may perfectly well sometimes be between two courses equally good, but different.[1] There is thus no inconsistency between such "freedom" as is implied in moral responsibility and the attainment of a stable character from which the discipline of the past has eliminated all possibility of effectively preferring the morally evil, or even the morally less good, alternative. It would even be possible, humanly speaking, that God Himself should always have open "alternatives", though, if He has, they cannot differ as a morally better and a morally less good. But it is not *necessary* to make this assertion about God, since always to see the absolute best and to follow it because it is best is to enjoy a "freedom" far transcending our human "freedom of choice" between a bad and a good, a best and a less good. A man who loves his wife is not the less free because his *love* forecloses any effective possibility of deserting her.[2]

I think it will be apparent that these positions do not involve any unreasonable version of Indeterminism, and that they are fully consistent with the acceptance of the Socratic and Platonic *dictum* that to be in assured and unclouded apprehension of the "best" would always entail following it. And, so far as I can see, such "freedom of the will" as I am here maintaining is equally in harmony with the teaching, *e.g.*, of St. Thomas

---

[1] As, for example, when a man considers whether he will spend his holiday in the Scottish Highlands, seeing lochs and mountains, or in Italy, seeing cities and pictures. It may be that, for a given man, either course is as good as the other, though the two goods are different. Or one might have to choose between two different careers without being able to say that one could serve God or man better in the one than in the other.

[2] Thus *God's* freedom should probably not be called "freedom of *choice*". (Kant, it will be remembered, denies that we can properly speak of *Triebfeder* in connection with the divine activity.) "We must not conceive God to be the *freest* agent, because he can doe and prescribe what he pleaseth, and so set up an Absolute will which shall make both Law and Reason, as some imagine. For as God cannot *know* himself to be any other than what indeed he is; so neither can he *will* himself to be anything else than what he is. For this were to make God free to dethrone himself" (John Smith, *Of the Existence and Nature of God.* c. ii. § 6).

Aquinas. If a man likes to say that he means something more than this by "freedom", and therefore regards Plato and St. Thomas as "determinists", I can, of course, have no objection to his saying the same of myself. But the doctrine here laid down is so different from anything which was taught by the inventors of the word "determinism", or the scientific men who have adopted it as a badge of their profession, that I believe nothing but confusion can come of such a careless use of terminology. I may add a remark or two about "contingency" to make the position adopted still clearer.

C. *Contingency in Nature?*

There are writers for whom I have a deep respect who would, I believe, on consideration, accept all, or most, of the foregoing seven propositions, but would, at the same time, reject the whole conception of any real "contingency" in the course of events.[1] As will have been visible from more than one passage in these volumes, I am compelled to take a different view, and to agree with James Ward that any interpretation of the world which is to make room for real history, real morality, real religion, must "let contingency into the heart of things".[2] Accordingly, though I do not appeal to the return of so many eminent physicists at the moment to the assertion of a "principle of Indeterminacy" in the physical at large as an *argument* for our moral freedom, I believe it to be an important step in the direction of a sounder metaphysic and cosmology. The opposing

---

[1] I am thinking particularly of the avowed "determinism" of such moralists as Dr. Rashdall and Dr. McTaggart, and, again, of the position taken by the Rev. C. J. Shebbeare in his recent *Problems of Providence.* To judge from the incidental remarks on the subject in *Five Types of Ethical Theory*, Dr. Broad would probably agree still more closely with the general view I have tried to set forth.

[2] *Naturalism and Agnosticism*, ii. 280.

view, which regards contingency as an illusion begotten
of our ignorance of the details of becoming, seems to me
to rest in the end upon a misunderstanding of the meaning of the "contingent". It is taken to mean the capricious occurrence of events which have no sufficient "why
and wherefore" in the plan of reality, and might "just
as well never have occurred at all"; such meaningless
"random" occurrences are then truly said to be incompatible with a genuine theistic faith in the divine
government of the world. Or it is also said that they are
excluded by the divine *omniscience*; "if God eternally
knows the whole course of history, how can any of the
events so known be contingent?" And yet an intelligence which does not know the whole course of history
cannot be the God demanded by religious men, for of
it it could not be said without reserve, "Trust in the
Lord with *all* thy heart, and lean not to thine own
understanding".

Now here there is, I believe, a bad confusion of
thought. It is antecedently most unlikely that such philosophers as Plato and St. Thomas—if I do not add
Aristotle, my reason is that the famous αὐτὸν ἄρα νοεῖ
seems intended to exclude the course of *events* from
God's knowledge—should have believed with equal
conviction in divine omniscience and divine government of the world, and also in contingency (the πλανωμένη
αἰτία of the *Timaeus*), without seeing the glaring contradiction, if it really does "glare". And I think it not
hard to satisfy one's self that the contradiction is no
more than apparent. As St. Thomas is careful to explain,[1] a *contingent* event does not mean an event which

---

[1] Cf. *S.C.G.* i. 85 "requirit autem ordo universalis aliquas causas esse variabiles,
cum corpora sint de perfectione universi, quae non movent nisi mota . . . unde
videmus quamvis causa remota sit necessaria, si tamen causa proxima sit contin-
gens, effectum contingentem esse." *S. Th.* i.ᵃ q. 19, art. 8 resp. "cum igitur voluntas
divina sit efficacissima, non solum sequitur quod fiant ea quae Deus vult fieri, sed

has no cause, or is not "determined" relatively to the
supreme (in the older terminology the "superessential")[1] cause, the divine purpose, but one which is not
unambiguously determined by its more "proximate"
causes. (Thus, to take the standing example, it was held
that the motions of the heavenly bodies are "necessary"
causes of certain effects, *e.g.* of the alternation of day
and night. But among the effects of the motion of these
bodies we have also to include the growth and ripening
of crops on earth. Now in this particular case the effect
of a "necessary" cause is a *contingent* event, because
there may be some *debilitas* in the seed which has been
sown, and in that case the effect, the ripening of the
harvest, does not follow. In fact, in this case, the revolutions in the heavens are not the proximate,but a remote
(though not the ultimate and "superessential") cause
of the result considered, and it is therefore not fully
"determined" by them.)

It would, no doubt, be hard to defend this doctrine of
contingency to-day in the precise form in which it was
used by the great schoolmen, who inherited Aristotle's
unfortunate and perverse crotchet of a radical distinction between terrestrial and celestial "matter" and
their respective dynamics.[2] We tend at once to meet the
Thomist example of the harvest which is "contingent"

---

et quod eo modo fiant quo Deus ea fieri vult. Vult autem quaedam fieri Deus
necessario, quaedam contingenter, ut sit ordo in rebus ad complementum universi." Professed Thomists, I observe, commonly speak of *three* kinds of effects—
"necessary, contingent, and *free*". But I presume that "free effects" are not
meant to be "contra-divided against" the other two as a third species, but to be
understood as a sub-class of the contingent, "contra-divided against" the contingent but unfree.

[1] Thus R. Bacon in his Commentary on Aristotle, *Physics*, i.-iv. (Oxford, 1928,
p. 249), speaking of the succession of the seasons, distinguishes (1) the *superessential* cause, the divine *dispositio* of the universe; (2) the remoter cause (*causa
longinqua*), the revolution of the *primum mobile*; (3) the *proximate* cause, "the
movement of the sun in his proper circle", viz. that of the Ecliptic.

[2] It cannot be too carefully remembered that the distinction was *introduced*
into cosmology by Aristotle, and that it is, in particular, anti-Platonic.

because it is sometimes abundant and sometimes fails, by saying that the presence or absence of a *debilitas* in the seed is itself a part of the whole cause of the effect— so far, of course, the scholastic could concur—and that it is a neither more nor less "necessary" cause than the *motus solis*; if the scholastic thinks otherwise on this last point, that, we say, is because by a cause he means an *agent*, and he mistakenly supposes the "seed" *not* to be an agent in its own growth, but to be simply and purely passive, a view made impossible to us by our conception of reciprocal interaction in physics. And, as already said, he is also unfortunately imbued with the Aristotelian fancy of the contrast between the immutability of the "heavens" and the mutability of the sublunary region of the universe. If we are to retain the distinction between necessary and contingent causation, we shall be driven to say that the "superessential" cause, God, is the *only* cause which causes with complete necessity, *all* other causes, remote or proximate, "celestial" or "terrene", being infected with contingency.

If we make this modification, the doctrine seems to me to be perfectly intelligible. It means, in effect, that while everything that happens in cosmic history happens as God ordains or permits, no event is a perfectly determinate "one-valued function" of other specific events, and that when we say that the occurrence of X may certainly be inferred from the occurrence of A, B, C, . . . there is always an understood *Deo volente*. It may be that the ultimate "pattern of the whole" demands a divergence from the most uniformly exhibited "routine of sequence", and if it does, the sequence will not occur; the sun will, at need, "stand still upon Gibeon". But whether the sun stands still or "hastes to go down", it is certain that there is a "pattern of the whole" and that *it* will not be violated. No "innovation" will be a capricious departure from it. But it is impossible in principle to calculate from data already in our possession whether and when an "innovation" will take place, because the "pattern of the whole" is not and cannot be a *datum*. (Or, to take an illustration from human action, it would be manifestly fallacious to argue that a phrase found in the published work of a writer must be an "error of the press" because the same writer has published many thousands of lines, but has nowhere else used that particular phrase. If it is the specially right and appropriate expression of the thought in his mind at the moment of writing he may use it, though he never used it before and will never use it again. A man's habits of speech have a great deal of influence on his choice of phraseology, but they never absolutely dictate it.)

It would thus be wholly consistent with theistic belief in the government of the world by God to recognise a genuine element of contingency in all historical events. You may in a sense resolve this contingency into defect of knowledge on our part, but only if you mean that we are not fully acquainted with the divine *purpose*. The defect could not be removed by any extension of our acquaintance with the details of past cosmic history, since the fullest acquaintance with them would not put us in possession of the "whole counsel of God." There is thus, so far, no reason to take up *a priori* an attitude of opposition to physicists who tell us they are led by their own special studies to admit a "principle of Indeterminacy" pervading the whole physical order. They may be right, or they may be wrong, but they are not saying anything which conflicts either with the inherent reasonableness of the universe, or with theistic faith. Professor Eddington, for example, is not maintaining that Δῖνος βασιλεύει, τὸν Δί' ἐξεληλακώς.

Nor do I see that the admission of contingency conflicts with belief in the divine *omniscience*, as is often
supposed. It would do so, if we impiously thought of
God as inferring our future from our past much as an
astronomer calculates the future positions of a planet
from a record of positions it has occupied in the past.
But no theologian, I take it, ever thought of God's
knowledge in this fashion. To quote James Ward, "How
God knows, or even what knowledge means when attributed to the Supreme Being, few of us will pretend to
understand".[1] But, as Ward is arguing in the context
of the remark, at least it will not be imagined that He
calculates the course of events, like a "Laplacean
demon", from a multitude of differential equations.
Whatever omniscience is, it is not this.[2]

These observations leave it still an open question
whether it is *requisite* for human freedom of choice that
there should be "contingency" in nature at large. May
we not accept all the seven theses we began our discussion
of choice by formulating, and at the same time deny
that any natural event really is contingent ? (Perhaps
nature, at all events, really is bound "fast in fate"?)
Clearly, of course, the denial of contingency, if it is to
leave human moral freedom unaffected, must not be
extended to those physical events which are the expressions of our responsible choices, the *actus imperati* which
carry the *actus elicitus* which is my decision over into
the physical order. If it is true that the movement of my

---

[1] *Naturalism and Agnosticism*[1], i. 42.
[2] Cf. the remark of St. Thomas (*S.Th.* ii.ae ii.ae, art. 171, q. 6 ad. sec.) that
"divina praescientia respicit futura secundum duo: scilicet secundum quod sunt in
seipsis, in quantum scilicet ipsa praesentialiter intuetur; et secundum quod sunt
in suis causis, in quantum scilicet videt ordinem causarum ad effectus. Et quamvis contingentia futura, *prout sunt in seipsis*, sint determinata ad unum, tamen
prout sunt in suis causis, non sunt determinata quin possint aliter evenire." That
is, it is eternally part of the divine providential plan that a certain event shall
happen: also, it is not the case that this event is what I have called a "one-valued
function" of preceding events. *Both* these truths are known to the divine Mind.

hand is ever the result of my choice, then *that* movement cannot be a determinate one-valued function of previous events of the physical order; these events must leave it an open issue whether my hand is to move or not. Consequently, the same consideration must apply to all events of the physical order which depend causally, no matter at how many removes, on the choice of a moral agent. And of how many actual events, if of any, could we say that no actual choice by *any* moral agent is conceivably to be found among their causal antecedents? Theoretically, however, we might, I conceive, say that events of the physical order which have no acts of choice by moral agents among their causal antecedents, *if there are any such events*, might be regarded as wholly non-contingent without any compromise of the positions upon which the reality of man's moral freedom depends. Even *if* God be needlessly assumed to have bound "nature" fast in fate, *our* moral freedom may be none the less real, provided that by "nature" we only mean whatever in the actual physical order is entirely independent of causation by the choice of a moral agent, if anything is so independent. To assert moral freedom, one *need* not assume the omnipresence of an element of "indeterminacy" in physical processes as *such*. There are apparently good grounds for this assumption, but they are of a different order. (I should perhaps add that I should regard it as very rash to assume that there is a single physical event which is wholly independent of the causality of *some* moral agent, since I see no reason to suppose that men are the only such beings in the universe. And in this context, when I speak of "moral agents", I am, of course, intending *created* moral agents, whether human or otherwise.)

I suspect that the reason why some excellent writers who seem to assert freedom of choice in express terms yet describe themselves as "determinists" is that they assume that Libertarianism is *necessarily* committed to this admission of contingency as a *cosmic* principle; and that they regard such a conception as "unscientific". I would urge on any reader of my own who takes this point of view, two considerations: (1) In point of fact there is apparently reason to believe that contingency is actually making its way back into scientific thinking on strictly theoretical grounds, as forced upon us in the interpretation of experimental results[1]; (2) in any case, this is not the issue really at stake between Libertarian moralists and the "scientific determinists". It is not contingency in "nature", but *choice* which the determinists of the nineteenth century were anxious to explode as a superstition, and they have left their representatives behind them. If anyone doubts this, I recommend to his notice an address on "The Nature of Life", delivered by Professor L. Hogben to the British Association at Cape Town on July 25, 1929. Mr. Hogben, at least, makes no attempt to disguise his conviction that all human moral purpose is an illusion; the whole social and moral life of man consists of "conditioned reflexes" which have no purpose, and a "new school of psychologists", with whom the speaker clearly sympathises, "has come into being with the express object of . . . relieving Man, the celestial pilgrim, of his burden of soul".[2] It is surely

---

[1] On this see, *e.g.*, Eddington, *Nature of the Physical World*, pp. 220 ff.; Whitehead, *Process and Reality*, p. 30.

[2] "The modern mechanist", says Mr. Hogben in the next paragraph of his discourse, "does not say that thought and love and heroism do not exist; he says, show me behaviour to which you apply the adjectives thoughtful or loving or heroic, and we will, one fine day, endeavour to arrive at predictable conclusions with reference to it by following the only method of enquiry which we have learned by experience to trust". But if the "endeavour" is to be successful, if we are, "one fine day", to discover that all the acts we call thoughtful, loving, heroic, can be predicted without taking the existence of thought, love, heroism, into account (and not one of the three can be discovered as a "laboratory" fact), how does the position Mr. Hogben accepts on behalf of his "mechanist" differ from the position he disclaims? What is meant by saying that "love exists", but

a pity that moralists who would regard this reduction of the spiritual life to "conditioned reflexes" as the death of all morality should mark their dissent, where it exists, from those of us who believe in contingency in "nature" at large, by adopting a label which confounds them with the "scientific" enemies of responsibility and practical reason.

It is hardly necessary to add that the "Libertarian" is left by his theory perfectly free to recognise that the full character of human "free" action is only to be found in acts of conscious deliberate choice. How far impulsive acts can be said to be done with freedom, and, again, how far my choice is free when my own past misconduct or negligence has closed alternatives which would otherwise remain open, is another question.

D. *Free Will of Indifference*

A reader of the preceding paragraphs may conceivably ask whether I mean to assert or to deny the reality of what has been called "free will of indifference". Do I, or do I not, mean that we can, and sometimes do, choose between alternatives without a "motive" for our preference? I should reply (1) that if there are such "unmotived" choices, they must surely have no significance for our moral life, since they do not express the *character* of the agent supposed to be making the choice. It is just the choices which are rooted in our personal moral *quality* and give expression to it with which the moralist is concerned. If "motiveless choice" occurs at

---

that there are acts which *cannot* be predicted without knowing that the agent *loves* someone, or something? And does Mr. Hogben never count on the good behaviour of his banker, or his servants? If, like other men, he sometimes does so, will he say he has studied banker or servant "by the only method of enquiry" he has "learned by experience to trust?" (My references are to the report of the discussion published by the *Cape Times* as "revised by the authors".)

all, it may fairly be taken to occur only in connection with the kind of insignificant movements regularly treated by the schoolmen as their standing examples in discussing the possibility of morally indifferent acts (*barbam vellere, festucam de terra tollere*, and the like). Or, to put the point differently, "motiveless choice", if really possible at all, would be a grave abuse of our liberty in any matter of the slightest moment, because it would mean refusing to deliberate in a case where we ought to deliberate.

Further, it is not clear that there is, even in these apparently trivial cases, anything we can properly call *unmotived* preference. This becomes clear, I think, if we define our terms with a little care. A *motive*, we must remember, is not the same thing as a mere impulse which releases, or discharges, an act. To act with a motive is not merely to be impelled to act in a certain way, but also to regard one's act as *justified* by a certain consideration. When I say that I act thus and with this motive, I mean both that the considerations I allege are truly those which impel me to act as I do, and also that they make my acting as I do the right and reasonable thing for me to do. A motive is always something which, at the time of acting, the agent regards as a *reasonable* incentive. It is a "reason" in the double sense that it explains why the agent does what he does, and that, so long as he does not repent, it is held by him to justify his behaviour. It follows that a man's "motives" are rarely, if ever, present to his own mind at the moment of action in "clear and distinct" apprehension; they are usually very largely "subconscious", or "habitual". But this does not detract from their rationality. A driver who has learned the British rule of the road "drives to the left", because he has learned that this is the established rule, and that it is dangerous to

disregard it. He does not actually recall these considerations—if he has really "learned how to drive"—as he
steers himself through the traffic. If he is at all practised, he regulates himself "automatically" by the rule.
But it is a *rule*, and it is because he has *knowledge* of the
rule so deeply ingrained in him that his "secondary
automatic responses" are what they are. His whole conduct is an example of *rational* choice; it does not issue
from what some writers are fond of calling the *passional*
nature, but from intelligence. In the vast majority of
those voluntary acts which are not preceded and conditioned by explicit deliberation, scrutiny will, I believe,
reveal "motives" as rational as the driver's preference
for the recognised rule of the road. In most cases there
is intelligent "justification" for the course adopted, and
the agent would not have taken that course if he had
not been acquainted with that justification, though he
was not actually thinking about it at the moment of
acting. (I do not, of course, mean that the "justification" will always bear strict investigation; in the case of
our morally wrong acts it will not. I mean that there
are considerations which the agent regards as justification, and to which he will sincerely appeal, if the morality of his act is disputed. The man who has taken a
human life will at once plead, if his act is impugned,
that "it was his life or mine", and this is meant, and is
felt by the homicide to be a rational justification of the
fatal shot or blow, though it is another question whether
the plea will satisfy the "impartial spectator".[1])

[1] Or, to take a standing example from St. Thomas, fornication is *malum in se*,
and therefore has no real justification. But it is true that the fornicator—unless
he is actually deliberately sinning "in contempt of God"—is taking the means to
a *delectatio carnalis* which is, considered simply as such a delectation, *bonum
quoddam temporale*. He is not wrong in thinking that this *bonum* is a *bonum* so far
as it goes; but there is a superior *bonum* with which it is incompatible. The
sinner is not alive to the superiority of this other *bonum*, and hence, from his
point of view, his conduct *appears* to be rationally justified. (This is, of course,
why Aristotle says that it συμβαίνει πως ὑπὸ λόγου ἀκρατεύεσθαι.)

I believe this analysis applicable to almost all the normal acts of human beings, when free from external constraint. There are grounds which, in the opinion of the agent at the time of acting, make his act the reasonable one to be done. Those grounds are not commonly *before* his mind, since most of his acts are done without explicit deliberation between alternatives. But they are *in* his mind, as is shown by the readiness with which they are produced in reply to any suggestion that his conduct has been unreasonable. I am, therefore, convinced that it is a mistake to attack the standing doctrine of Greek moralists, that the sinner does wrong because he is misled by a false judgement of good, on the ground that it over-rationalises human action. If unmotived, or unreasonable, choice occurs at all, it only occurs, I would submit, in connection with alternatives which are taken to be morally indifferent. It might be alleged that it occurs *here*. "Where you can take either of two courses, A_1 or A_2", it may be urged, "and there is no reason for regarding either as in any way more or less good than the other, clearly the fact that you take the course A_1 shows that you are making a choice, and yet, *ex hypothesi*, you know of no reason why A_1 should be chosen rather than A_2. Here, then, there must be unmotived choice".

But will the argument really stand examination? A typical example would be that of a man who is about to play a game of chess and is "offered his choice" of taking the white pieces (and attacking) or the black (and defending). In discussing such a case we need to draw distinctions. It may be that the player to whom the option is given knows himself to be stronger and more practised in attack than in defence, or *vice versa*, and chooses accordingly. He may do this with clear and full consciousness of the reason for his choice. Or he may not be consciously thinking about the matter, and yet it may be what really decides his option, as is shown by his reply, when asked, *e.g.*, why he chose white, that "I am more accustomed to the white pieces and more at home with them".[1] In neither case can it fairly be said that there is not a rational motive for his choice, though it may be a "subconscious" one.

But what of the case of the man who is *equally* expert in the attack and the defence, and knows this? He also may be offered his option, and he must make it, or there will be no game. Is not this a clear case of making a choice which *must* be unmotived? It does not seem to me that it is so. The man in question has, indeed, no motive for choosing White rather than Black, or Black rather than White. But he *has* a motive for making either option rather than declining to opt, since if both players are equally expert, and both know it, and therefore refuse to make any option, the game, which is what both desire to have, will never begin. I think, therefore, that what really happens in such a case is that the player who is "offered his choice" makes a real choice which has a motive, and a sound one, the choice to foreclose one of the alternatives, but does not *really* choose as between White and Black. He simply says the word which happens to "come to the tip of his tongue". In practice we commonly avoid this situation of having to make what appears to be a choice between equally desirable alternatives by enacting a rule that the point shall be decided by "tossing up". That is, we voluntarily remove the particular decision from the sphere of the voluntary. So again, when I, who am not much interested in such things, am offered a choice between two

---

[1] Or, as might be the case, "I am more accustomed to Black, and so wish to take this opportunity of practice in handling White". Greater familiarity with the pieces of one colour may lead to either choice, according as the chooser cares more about winning on this particular occasion, or about "improving his game".

dishes or two wines, I feel sure that I often make no real option; I say the word which "comes handiest", merely because I want to get the point decided one way or the other. This is making a real and rational choice between settling the question and leaving it open, but not, as it seems to me, a real choice for one alternative as against the other.

On these grounds I feel very doubtful whether any genuine choice is really without a rational motive, *i.e.* without what the chooser, at the moment of choosing, regards as a reasonable ground for preference. Even when, to take the old example of the schools, I pick up a straw from the ground, I should probably not do so consciously unless I disliked the look of "litter", or wanted to exercise a group of muscles, or something of the kind, and these are rational grounds for choice. The nearest approach we make in actual life to "indifferent" choice, I should say, is made in the cases when we rationally will to eliminate one of two alternatives, but do not care which is eliminated. This is not a typical case of morally significant "free choice", but rather, in the words of Descartes,[1] *infimus gradus libertatis*. It is not in our "indifference" in such a case that we show our freedom, but in our resolution to bring the indifference to an end.

A final word may perhaps find its place here, as a *Rechtfertigung* against the charge, urged more than once in private correspondence against the present writer by Dr. Rashdall, of clinging to an "unintelligible" Libertarianism. If I have no desire to find the source of responsible moral freedom in a liberty of caprice, why am I not content to treat moral freedom,

---

[1] *Meditat.* iv. "indifferentia autem illa quam experior cum nulla me ratio in unam partem magis quam in alteram impellit, est infimus gradus libertatis, et nullam in ea perfectionem, sed tantummodo defectum sive negationem quandam in cognitione testatur".

after the fashion of Leibniz, as spontaneity *along with the consciousness of spontaneity*?[1] Why do I hold that a free man is not adequately described as *automaton spirituale*? I would reply by reminding my reader of a striking passage in Kant's second *Critique*.[2] Kant is there admitting the existence of moral "incurables", on whom *all* education and discipline is wasted. They manifest utter moral depravity in early childhood, and grow only the more depraved as they grow older. But we are justified, he says, in treating them morally and juristically as no less responsible and accountable than others, and they themselves admit the justice of this attitude, "in spite of the desperate native mental constitution thus imputed to them". This, Kant pleads, is an argument for his rigid distinction between temporal appearance and eternal reality. The depravity displayed through life by the "incurables" is itself merely the consequence of the "free causality" of their morally evil wills.

What does this amount to, if we have once rejected Kant's identification of the temporal with mere appearance, but to the doctrine that the "incurable" is *created* incurable, and then held accountable by his "dark Maker" for the flaw in the *Naturbeschaffenheit seines Gemüths*? It is the horrible Augustinian notion of the *massa perditionis* reduced to its simplest terms. The "incurable" is imagined to be sent into the world already "damned", with a will already and unalterably "wholly averse from God". And we are expected to acquiesce in the justice of this situation. (I do not dwell on the difficulty of the *quaestio facti* whether there *are* such "incurables". If our failure to strike the right note

---

[1] Though possibly this is an unduly minimising interpretation of Leibniz's own phrase, "spontaneity along with intelligence" (spontanéité qui devient liberté dans les substances intelligentes), *Discours de métaphysique* xxxii.

[2] *KdprV*. I. Th. i. B. iii. *Hptst. (Werke*, v. 104).

with some transgressors could be taken as evidence of their incurability, I am afraid, when I consider how helpless candid self-scrutiny seems to prove us all to be against some of our weaknesses, that we may fairly suspect ourselves and all mankind of belonging to the *massa*.) If we seriously believe in the theory, can our moral theology be anything better than a dishonest attempt to curry favour with a malevolent Maker by flatteries we know to be undeserved? If there were no Creator, or an evil Creator, the difficulty would not arise. But since there is a Creator, and a righteous and merciful Creator, we cannot reconcile determinism with an ethical Theism by assuming that some men have been created already "damned". And we must not shirk the issue, as Kant tries to do, by saying that the "incurable" is not created "damned", but damns himself once and for all by a primal free act of wrong choice which is not "in time".[1] *This* is a rank "unintelligibility". For a "first act" of the series of my transgressions must have a place in the temporal series to which the rest of my transgressions belong, and thus, on Kant's own theory, it should be part of the "pheno-

---

[1] I put the matter as Kant himself puts it in *Religion innerhalb d. Grenzen d. blossen Vernunft*. In the *KdprV*. (*Werke*, v. 106-7) he speaks less pictorially. We are there told that if space and time were more than "appearances", it would follow that the moral responsibility for the conduct of creatures rests with their Creator, and not with themselves. But a Creator creates only realities, and space and time are merely phenomenal. God is therefore the cause of my existence as a free agent in the intelligible world, but not of my actions in time and space. Surely we must say that *this* way of relieving my Creator from responsibility for my sins reduces the whole moral life to an illusion. Kant apparently wants to reproduce the scholastic reasoning which argues that God is not the author of my misdeeds, since God created me free, and I freely choose to do wrong. But he ruins the force of the argument by trying to make it turn on the "ideality" of time and space. If that were part of the argument, it should also follow that God is not the cause of any of the observed events of the natural order. The "argument from design" must not only cease to be probative; it must also lose all that right to our respect which Kant himself claimed for it. And it then becomes very hard to understand how Kant's virtuous man can be entitled to a rational faith that the natural order is controlled by God in the interests of a moral end,—the crowning of virtue with happiness.

menal series" of consequences, not the "intelligible" cause of the whole series. If Kant's language is to have a tolerable meaning, the primal free wrong choice should be taken merely as an imaginative *symbol* of the character exhibited by all our temporal wrong choices, and in becoming such a symbol it ceases to be an explanation. If it is more than such a symbol, our actual moral life is deprived of the significance Kant in particular is anxious to ascribe to it as a discipline into goodness of will; in the case of the "incurables", the discipline and struggle must be no more than illusion, and none of us can be sure that he is not himself one of their number.

I see no way out but to strike at the root of the whole conception by insisting on the utter "creatureliness" of all finite agents. Nowhere in them is there any element of character which is unmade, an eternal and unalterable datum. Their being is always a γένεσις εἰς οὐσίαν, never simply οὐσία. And the admission destroys in principle the foundation of all determinism, "hard" or "soft". The real "unintelligibility" seems to me to be with the determinist who is, consciously or unconsciously, transferring to the creature, or to some ingredient in its composition, the "once-for-allness" incommunicably proper to the Creator. And for that reason I cannot feel certain that there are actually any "incurables"; the notion may have its uses, as a check on moral presumption, but it may be only a "limiting concept".

INDEX OF PROPER NAMES

Printed in Great Britain by R. & R. CLARK, LIMITED, *Edinburgh.*

By Prof. A. E. TAYLOR

THE PROBLEM OF CONDUCT: A STUDY IN THE PHENOMENOLOGY OF ETHICS. 8vo. 12s. 6d. net.

PHILOSOPHICAL STUDIES. 8vo. 15s. net.

WORKS ON PHILOSOPHY

NATURE, MAN AND GOD: GIFFORD LECTURES, 1932-1933 AND 1933-1934. By Dr. WILLIAM TEMPLE, Archbishop of York. 8vo. 18s. net.

THE BUDDHA AND THE CHRIST: AN EXPLORATION OF THE MEANING OF THE UNIVERSE AND OF THE PURPOSE OF HUMAN LIFE. By Dr. BURNETT H. STREETER. 8vo. 7s. 6d. net.

STUDIES IN CHRISTIAN PHILOSOPHY: BEING THE BOYLE LECTURES, 1920. By Rev. Prof. W. R. MATTHEWS, D.D. Second Edition (1928). Extra crown 8vo. 6s. net.

A CREED FOR SCEPTICS. By C. A. STRONG, LL.D. 8vo. 6s. net.

HOLISM AND EVOLUTION. By General the Right Hon. J. C. SMUTS. Third Edition (1936). 8vo. 12s. 6d. net.

SPACE, TIME, AND DEITY: GIFFORD LECTURES, 1916-1918. By Prof. S. ALEXANDER, O.M., LL.D. 2 Vols. 8vo. 25s. net.

BEAUTY AND OTHER FORMS OF VALUE. By Prof. S. ALEXANDER, O.M., LL.D. 8vo. 10s. 6d. net.

MACMILLAN AND CO. LTD., LONDON

WORKS ON PHILOSOPHY

BY PROF. HENRI BERGSON

CREATIVE EVOLUTION. Translated by ARTHUR MITCHELL, Ph.D. 8vo. 12s. 6d. net.

THE TWO SOURCES OF MORALITY AND RELIGION. Translated by R. A. AUDRA, C. BRERETON, and W. H. CARTER. 8vo. 10s. net.

LAUGHTER: AN ESSAY ON THE MEANING OF THE COMIC. Translated by CLOUDESLEY BRERETON, M.A., and FRED. ROTHWELL, B.A. Fcap. 8vo. 3s. 6d. net.

MIND-ENERGY: LECTURES AND ESSAYS. Translated by Prof. H. WILDON CARR. 8vo. 7s. 6d. net.

BY PROF. NORMAN KEMP SMITH

A COMMENTARY TO KANT'S "CRITIQUE OF PURE REASON." Second Edition (1923). 8vo. 25s. net.

PROLEGOMENA TO AN IDEALIST THEORY OF KNOWLEDGE. 8vo. 10s. 6d. net.

KANT'S CRITIQUE OF PURE REASON. Translated. 8vo. 25s. net.

KANT'S CRITIQUE OF PURE REASON. Translated. Abridged Edition. 8vo. 10s. 6d. net.

BY DR. JOHN S. MACKENZIE

OUTLINES OF METAPHYSICS. Third Edition (1929). Crown 8vo. 5s.

COSMIC PROBLEMS: AN ESSAY ON SPECULATIVE PHILOSOPHY. 8vo. 6s. net.

MACMILLAN AND CO. LTD., LONDON